SECURING DEMOCRACIES

Securing Democracies examines the attacks on voting processes and the broader informational environment in which elections take place. The volume's global cadre of scholars and practitioners highlight the interconnections among efforts to target vulnerable democratic systems and identify ways to prevent, defend against, and mitigate their effects on both the technical and the informational aspects of cybersecurity. The work takes a wider view of defending democracy by recognizing that both techniques – attacking infrastructure and using misinformation and disinformation – are means to undermine trust and confidence in democratic institutions. As such, the book proposes a wide range of policy responses to tackle these cyber-enabled threats focusing on the geopolitical front lines, namely Eastern Europe, the Middle East, and East Asia. This title is also available as open access on Cambridge Core.

Scott J. Shackelford is Provost Professor of Business Law and Ethics at the Indiana University Kelley School of Business. He serves as Executive Director of the Ostrom Workshop and the Center for Applied Cybersecurity Research. Shackelford has written more than 100 articles, book chapters, essays, and op-eds for diverse publications.

Frédérick Douzet is Professor of Geopolitics at the University of Paris 8. She serves as Director of the French Institute of Geopolitics research team (IFG Lab) and Director of the Center Geopolitics of the Datasphere (GEODE). In January 2020 she was appointed as member of the French Defense Ethics Committee.

Christopher Ankersen is Clinical Professor of Global Affairs and Faculty Lead, Global Risk Specialization at New York University's Center for Global Affairs. He has previously worked for the United Nations and the Canadian Armed Forces. He is coeditor (with W. P. S. Sidhu) of *The Future of Global Affairs: Managing Discontinuity, Disruption and Destruction* (2021).

Securing Democracies

DEFENDING AGAINST CYBER ATTACKS AND DISINFORMATION IN THE DIGITAL AGE

Edited by

SCOTT J. SHACKELFORD
Indiana University

FRÉDÉRICK DOUZET
University of Paris 8

CHRISTOPHER ANKERSEN
New York University

CAMBRIDGE
UNIVERSITY PRESS

CAMBRIDGE
UNIVERSITY PRESS

Shaftesbury Road, Cambridge CB2 8EA, United Kingdom

One Liberty Plaza, 20th Floor, New York, NY 10006, USA

477 Williamstown Road, Port Melbourne, VIC 3207, Australia

314–321, 3rd Floor, Plot 3, Splendor Forum, Jasola District Centre, New Delhi – 110025, India

103 Penang Road, #05–06/07, Visioncrest Commercial, Singapore 238467

Cambridge University Press is part of Cambridge University Press & Assessment, a department of the University of Cambridge.

We share the University's mission to contribute to society through the pursuit of education, learning and research at the highest international levels of excellence.

www.cambridge.org
Information on this title: www.cambridge.org/9781009574136

DOI: 10.1017/9781009574105

When citing this work, please include a reference to the DOI 10.1017/9781009574105

First published 2026

A catalogue record for this publication is available from the British Library

Library of Congress Cataloging-in-Publication Data
NAMES: Shackelford, Scott J., editor. | Douzet, Frédérick, editor. | Ankersen, Christopher, editor.
TITLE: Securing democracies : defending against cyber attacks and disinformation in the digital age / edited by Scott J. Shackelford, Indiana University, Bloomington; Frédérick Douzet, Paris 8 University; Christopher Ankersen, New York University.
DESCRIPTION: Cambridge, United Kingdom ; New York, NY : Cambridge University Press, 2025. | Includes bibliographical references and index.
IDENTIFIERS: LCCN 2024048026 (print) | LCCN 2024048027 (ebook) | ISBN 9781009574136 (hardback) | ISBN 9781009574129 (paperback) | ISBN 9781009574105 (epub)
SUBJECTS: LCSH: Cyberterrorism–Law and legislation | Cyberterrorism–Prevention–Technological innovations. | Disinformation–Technological innovations. | Information warfare (International law)
CLASSIFICATION: LCC KZ7225.C93 S43 2025 (print) | LCC KZ7225.C93 (ebook) | DDC 344.05/325–dc23/eng/20241010
LC record available at https://lccn.loc.gov/2024048026
LC ebook record available at https://lccn.loc.gov/2024048027

ISBN 978-1-009-57413-6 Hardback

This volume is dedicated to our families for their ongoing support and encouragement, as well as to all those working for peace, both online and offline.

Contents

Figures

Tables

Contributors

Barbara Allen is James Woodward Strong Professor of the Liberal Arts and Professor of Political Science and former chair of the Department of Political Science and Director of Women's and Gender Studies, Carleton College, Minnesota. She was named the first senior research fellow of the Vincent and Elinor Ostrom Workshop in Political Theory and Policy Analysis in 2012, a position she continues to hold at Indiana University. She also teaches as a visiting professor at the University of Luxembourg. With coauthor Daniel Stevens, she has recently published a book on this research, *Truth in Advertising? Verbal, Visual, and Aural Lies in Political Advertising and How They Affect the Electorate*, which won the 2019 Richard E. Neustadt Book Award.

David Amsellem holds a PhD from the French Institute of Geopolitics (University of Paris 8) and specializes in gas issues in the Eastern Mediterranean and their impact on Israel's energy sector. As part of his professional activities within the consultancy firm CASSINI, which he founded, he focuses on state influence and communication strategies, particularly in online media and social networks.

Christopher Ankersen is a clinical professor at New York University's (NYU) Center for Global Affairs, where he coordinates their Global Risk specialization. His research and teaching focus is in the fields of international security and civil–military relations. Prior to joining NYU, he worked for the United Nations in the Department of Safety and Security. His most recent publication is a coedited volume (with Waheguru Pal Singh Sidhu) entitled *The Future of Global Affairs: Managing Discontinuity, Disruption and Destruction* (2021).

Gabrielle Dora Beacken received her MSc from the London School of Economics and Political Science, and is currently a PhD student in Journalism and Media at the University of Texas at Austin. She is a graduate research assistant at the Center for Media Engagement's Propaganda Research Lab. Previously, she was a trading analyst in the advertising technology industry and earned a BA in Journalism from the College of New Jersey. Beacken's research investigates the creation, spread, and reception of political propaganda through emerging technologies, such as social media, encrypted messaging apps, and artificial intelligence tools.

Rachel Brooks-Bitterli is a risk intelligence professional focused on curbing digital threats to democracy. She specializes in analyzing disinformation, hate speech, and extremism. Most recently Project Manager at Microsoft's Democracy Forward initiative, Brooks-Bitterli supported the company's information integrity, journalism, and media literacy workstreams. She previously served as an intelligence analyst on Concentric's Global Intelligence team, where she authored hundreds of intelligence products assessing emerging open-source and dark web threats facing clients. She also researched foreign disinformation campaigns targeting democracies with Army Cyber Command's Virtual Student Federal Service and Rotary International's Peace Fellowship.

Jean Camp is a professor at the Luddy School of Computing, Informatics, and Engineering at Indiana University. She is a fellow of the Institute of Electrical and Electronic Engineers and a fellow of the American Association for the Advancement of Science, and has been inducted into Sigma Xi, The Scientific Research Honor Society. She joined Indiana after eight years at Harvard's Kennedy School. She began her career as an engineer at Catawba Nuclear Station and with an MSEE from the University of North Carolina at Charlotte. She has authored more than 200 publications, including more than 150 peer-reviewed publications and two books.

Frédérick Douzet is Professor of Geopolitics at the University of Paris 8, Director of the French Institute of Geopolitics research team (IFG Lab), and Director of the Center Geopolitics of the Datasphere (GEODE). She was appointed a member of the French Defense Ethics Committee in January 2020. From 2017 to 2020, she was a commissioner of the Global Commission on the Stability of Cyberspace. In 2017, she was part of the drafting committee for the French Strategic Review of Defense and National Security. Her current research deals with the geopolitics of cyberspace.

Lindsay B. Flynn is Associate Professor of Political Science at the University of Luxembourg and Deputy Director of the Master in European Governance. She is Principal Investigator of the FNR-funded PROPEL project (PROactive Policymaking for Equal Lives), which examines the links between government policy, housing markets, and inequality. This multi-method project engages in evidence-based policy analysis and creates opportunities for social policy innovation through workshops and activities. Flynn received her PhD in Government at the University of Virginia and previously taught at Wheaton College, Massachusetts, where she cochaired the committee that implemented a new undergraduate curriculum designed for the challenges of the twenty-first century.

Julia R. Fox received her PhD at Cornell University and is an associate professor in the Media School at Indiana University. Her research interests focus on the content and impact of political humor. Related publications include a synthesis of published research on learning from comedic versus serious news and a comparison of substantive election campaign coverage on *The Daily Show with Jon Stewart* and broadcast television networks, both published in the *Journal of Broadcasting & Electronic Media*, as well as an analysis of Jon Stewart's media critiques on *The Daily Show* published in *Journalism and Mass Communication Quarterly*.

Andrew Grotto is the founder and director of the Program on Geopolitics, Technology, and Governance at Stanford University, where he is a William J. Perry International Security Fellow at the Freeman Spogli Institute for International Studies. Grotto's research interests center on cybersecurity and the national security and international economic dimensions of America's global leadership in information technology innovation. He also serves as the faculty lead for the Cyber Policy and Security specialization offered through Stanford's Ford Dorsey Master's in International Policy program. Previously, Grotto served in a variety of senior roles in the US government, most recently as the Senior Director for Cyber Policy on the National Security Council at the White House.

Jaclyn A. Kerr is a Senior Research Fellow at the Center for Disruptive Technology and Future Warfare within National Defense University's Institute for National Strategic Studies. She is also a Nonresident Fellow with the Brookings Institution, an adjunct professor at Georgetown University's Center for Eurasian, Russian and East European Studies, and an affiliate with the Center for International Security and Cooperation at Stanford University. Her research, teaching, and policy advising focus on digital and emerging technologies and their impacts on international politics, national security, and democracy. Kerr has previously served as a policy advisor in the State Department's Office of the Science and Technology Advisor to the Secretary and at the US Cyber Solarium Commission. She has held research fellowships at Lawrence Livermore National Laboratory, Harvard and Stanford Universities as well as overseas in Russia, Kazakhstan, and Qatar. She holds a PhD and MA in Government from Georgetown University, and an MA in Russian, East European, and Eurasian Studies and BAS in Mathematics and Slavic Languages and Literatures from Stanford University.

Joyce Kerstens is Associate Professor of Police, Partners and Digitization and conducts research on cybercrime and trends in digitization, the use of digital technology by police and partners and, innovative forms of citizen participation on behalf of the detection of cybercrime. The associate professorship is part of the Cyber Safety Research Group at NHL Stenden University of Applied Sciences and the Police Academy. Kerstens is a sociologist with a focus on the significance of a technology-driven and data-driven environment for humans, that is, users.

Inna Kouper is Associate Scientist at the Luddy School of Informatics, Computing, and Engineering and a Data Analyst at the Center for Survey Research at Indiana University Bloomington. Her research focuses on emerging technologies, digital media, and data practices. Dr Kouper has copublished on topics related to digital technologies, including hypertext, biotechnology, big data, data curation, and social media. Her current projects explore interdisciplinarity and collaboration in science and the history of research on shared and common-pool resources. She is an active member of professional organizations including the Research Data Alliance (RDA), the Association for Information Science and Technology (ASIST), and the Association of Computing Machinery (ACM).

Sandra Kübler is Professor of Computational Linguistics in the Department of Linguistics at Indiana University. Her main research areas are syntactic parsing, with a focus on morphologically rich languages, and machine learning approaches to sentiment analysis, emotion detection, hate speech detection, and conspiracy detection, with a focus on decisions made during data collection and annotation. Dr Kübler currently serves as an associate editor for the journal *Natural Language Engineering*.

Jun Liu is an award-winning author and Associate Professor at the Center for Tracking and Society, the University of Copenhagen. His research areas cover political communication, political sociology, communication technologies, and comparative and computational social science, with publications in the fields of sociology, political science, communication, and computer science. His latest research outcome is *Shifting Dynamics of Contention in the Digital Age* (Oxford University Press, 2020).

Renée Marlin-Bennett is Professor of Political Science at Johns Hopkins University in Baltimore, Maryland, USA. Her research focuses on the nature of political power, information flows, bodies and emotions, and borders. From 2017 to 2019, Marlin-Bennett served as the founding editor-in-chief of the *Oxford Research Encyclopedia of International Studies*, a peer-reviewed, joint publication of Oxford University Press and the International Studies Association. Previously, she was the general editor (2013–2016) and co-general editor (2012–2013) of the predecessor publication, *International Studies Online* (Wiley), also known as the International Studies Compendium Project. From 1987 to 2007, she was on the faculty of International Relations at the School of International Service, American University, where she served as Division Director of International Politics and Foreign Policy.

Ashray Narayan is a program manager at the Center for International Security and Cooperation where he conducts policy-oriented research on the political, legal, and economic implications of digital innovation and global competition. Prior to Stanford, Ashray was a visiting research scholar at the University of California, Berkeley, where he assisted Professor Daniel Sargent on research pertaining to US foreign policy and transnational criminal law enforcement. Ashray has worked in the U.S. Department of State's Bureau of Economic and Business Affairs and conducted research on vaccine diplomacy with Steven Lamy, the former director of the University of Southern California School of International Relations.

Ravi Nayyar is a PhD scholar at the University of Sydney. His research concerns how critical software regulation fits into critical infrastructure regulation. He holds a BCom (Hons I) and LLB from the University of Sydney. He has worked in technology law and policy, including for the OECD. He has also written extensively on cyber law and policy.

Małgorzata Pańkowska is PhD, Full Professor of Social Science and Chair of the Department of Informatics at the University of Economics in Katowice, Poland. She received the qualification in econometrics and statistics from the University of Economics in Katowice, the PhD and the Doctor Habilitatus degree from the University of Economics in Katowice. She was visiting professor at various universities in European Union countries, as well as in Egypt, Turkey, and Colombia. She is Vice-President of the Board of Information System Audit and Control Association (ISACA) Katowice Chapter and the Coordinator of the International Week "Internet Communication Management," for Teaching Staff Exchange within Erasmus, Erasmus+, and CEEPUS programmes.

Pavlina Pavlova is a public policy advisor at the CyberPeace Institute in Geneva, Switzerland, where she designs policies to advance accountability in cyberspace and engages in multilateral negotiations to raise awareness about the impact of systemic cyber threats on people. Before joining the Institute, Pavlina served as an official at the Organization for Security and Co-operation in Europe (OSCE). In 2019, she was appointed as the OSCE Chairmanship's Liaison Officer and later coordinated programmes strengthening the human dimension of security. Pavlina's policy experience spans a decade of work in security, human rights, and political advisory roles at international organizations and national institutions. Her research is positioned at the intersection of technology and governance.

Dustin Sajoe works as a lecturer-researcher in Safety and Security Management at NHL Stenden University of Applied Sciences, Thorbecke Academy. An alumnus of the Safety and Security Management studies, he contributed to the field of digital literary through his thesis on disinformation and online research, with a particular emphasis on open-source intelligence (OSINT). As of February 2022, Dustin has been actively engaged in an international research collective dedicated to investigating war crimes regarding the Russo-Ukrainian war. He co-coordinates the minor Intelligence and Counterintelligence, a one-of-a-kind program in the Netherlands. Through this program, he has the opportunity to share his expertise in OSINT with students.

Deike Schulz currently heads the professorship in Organizations and Social Media at NHL Stenden University of Applied Sciences. Working alongside fellow academics, students, and external stakeholders, her research delves into various aspects of online communication, examining how online content, dialogue, and commitment develop and become meaningful (or meaningless) for organizations and society. Central to her research is a relentless commitment to understanding and promoting responsible leadership on both an individual and a collective level, going beyond the realms of online and offline spaces.

Scott J. Shackelford serves on the faculty of Indiana University where he is the Provost Professor of Business Law and Ethics at the Kelley School of Business along with being the Executive Director of both the Ostrom Workshop and the Center for Applied Cybersecurity Research. He is an affiliated scholar at Harvard Kennedy School's Belfer Center for Science and International Affairs and Stanford's Center for Internet and Society. Professor Shackelford's academic work and teaching have been recognized with numerous awards, including a Harvard University Research Fellowship, a Stanford University Hoover Institution National Fellowship, a Notre Dame Institute for Advanced Study Distinguished Fellowship, the 2014 Indiana University Outstanding Junior Faculty Award, and the 2015 Elinor Ostrom Award.

Maria Shardakova is an associate professor in the Department of Slavic and East European Languages and Cultures at Indiana University, where she leads the Russian Language and Russian Flagship programs, funded by the National Security Education Program under the U.S. Department of Defense. Dr Shardakova serves on of the Editorial Advisory Board for *Slavica* and *Issues in the Teaching of East European and Eurasian Languages and Cultures*. Her research focuses on cross-cultural and interlanguage pragmatics, cross-cultural humor, politeness, multilingualism, and linguistic identity construction. Dr Shardakova has published on humor in interpersonal communication, exploring its role in identity performance, the connection between humor and (im)politeness, and the comprehension of Russian humor by American speakers of Russian.

Simon Sun is an assistant professor at the National Yang Ming Chiao Tung University School of Law. Simon specializes in internet intermediary liability, privacy, cybersecurity, Artificial Intelligence (AI), blockchain governance, and space technology. His research also explores the application of Elinor Ostrom's Commons theory and polycentric governance in the digital society. He holds an SJD from Indiana University Maurer School of Law, an LLM from Duke University School of Law, and an LLB from National Chung Cheng University College of Law.

Inga Kristina Trauthig (PhD, King's College London) is the head of research of the Propaganda Research Lab at the Center for Media Engagement (CME). In her role, she conducts original research and helps lead the Lab's strategy and management. Previously, she has been a research fellow with the International Centre for the

Study of Radicalisation (ICSR) at the Department of War Studies at King's College London and received an MLitt from the University of St Andrews. She is also an associate with institutions such as the Institute of Middle Eastern Studies (IMES) at King's College London, Stanford University, and Konrad Adenauer Foundation in Berlin.

Ioana Vasiu is a full professor at the Faculty of Law, Babeş-Bolyai University. She is Coordinator of the Erasmus+ Blended Intensive Programme "Cybersecurity Strategies in the Era of Artificial Intelligence," member of the Babeş-Bolyai University's Scientific Council, and external affiliated member of the Ostrom Workshop Program on Cybersecurity and Internet Governance, Indiana University, USA. She was member of the Romanian National Council for Ethics in Scientific Research, Technological Development, and Innovation and member of the Board of Directors of the International Association of Penal Law. She worked as expert for the European Commission and the United Nations Development Programme Romania, was partner and lead researcher on several scientific projects, and Co-Chair of the Management and Delivery of Justice Group of the European Group of Public Administration.

Acknowledgments

This volume is like an iceberg: What you see reflects only a small part of the enormous efforts that lie below the surface.

The book began with a workshop on election security cohosted by Indiana University and Australia National University in Washington, DC, in 2018. The gathering brought together academics, practitioners, and policymakers from both universities, setting the stage for a follow-up engagement in 2019, this time in Canberra, Australia. From these conversations sprung a realization that more work was needed that would consider the broader set of challenges surrounding election security, including threats to election infrastructure along with managing misinformation and disinformation. The editors would like to thank all those who facilitated these early discussions, including Angie Raymond, Chris Painter, Amanda Craig Deckard, Fred Cate, and Rachel Dockery, for their support.

An additional Defending Democracy Colloquium took place in 2023, facilitated by the Ostrom Workshop. A special thanks goes out to the team that made those events possible including Emily Castle, Anna Goodman, and Kari McMullen.

The editors would like to acknowledge the contributions made by the phalanx of graduate students from Indiana University involved in copy editing the chapter drafts, including Simon Sun and Sarah Doherty.

Finally, our thanks go out to Matt Galloway, Jadyn Fauconier-Herry, and the team at Cambridge University Press for their editorial and production assistance.

Funding for this volume has been graciously provided by the Ostrom Workshop, GEODE, and the Hewlett Foundation, with open access being generously supported by a gift from the Microsoft Corporation.

1

Introduction

Scott J. Shackelford, Frédérick Douzet, and Christopher Ankersen

Rising to speak in the House of Commons in November 1947, Winston Churchill – by then no longer prime minister but still member of parliament, his party having been defeated in the general election of May 1945 – remarked that "No one pretends that democracy is perfect ... Indeed, it has been said that democracy is the worst form of Government except for all those other forms that have been tried." Churchill felt especially convinced that it was superior to those varieties of governance that relied upon "a group of super men and super-planners ... 'playing angel' ... and making the masses of the people do what they think is good for them, without any check or correction."[1] The following year, the Universal Declaration of Human Rights was signed. While the term democracy is not mentioned, its essence is enshrined in the document, signed by democracies and autocracies alike: "The will of the people shall be the basis of the authority of government; this will shall be expressed in periodic and genuine elections which shall be by universal and equal suffrage and shall be held by secret vote or by equivalent free voting procedures."[2]

Despite its fundamental recognition, democracy has never been guaranteed. Benjamin Franklin once famously quipped after being asked what sort of government the Founders had gifted the new nation of the United States of America: "a republic, if you can keep it" (Beeman, n.d.). Since that time, many threats to democracies have emerged, stemming from internal divisions fed by inequality, injustice, and racism and from foreign nations wishing to distract and destabilize democratic governments, most recently through cyber-enabled means (Zeitz, 2016).

Portions of this chapter have been previously published under Scott J. Shackelford, Angie Raymond, Abbey Stemler, & Cyanne Loyle, Defending democracy: Taking stock of the global fight against digital repression, disinformation, and election insecurity, *Washington and Lee Law Review*, 77, 1747 (2021).

[1] Winston Churchill, HC Deb, 11 November 1947, vol. 444 cc203–321, https://api.parliament.uk/historic-hansard/commons/1947/nov/11/parliament-bill.

[2] Universal Declaration of Human Rights (1948) Article 21, para. 3.

Recently, Russia has been particularly active, by one estimate interfering in twenty-seven elections since 1991, beginning with the nations of Eastern Europe that had been former members of the Cold War-era Warsaw Pact (Way & Casey, 2018). Such efforts have been extended since 2014 to Western Europe and the United States, reaching a culmination in their interference with the 2016 Brexit vote and US presidential election, made easier by the rise of internet platforms generally and social networking in particular (Way & Casey, 2018). Such efforts continued into the 2018 US midterm elections, when U.S. Cyber Command shut down a Russian troll farm on Election Day (Thomsen, 2019), and have expanded to target elections across Africa and Asia (Alba & Frenkel, 2019; Tennis, 2020), as other nations have similarly both followed and improved upon Russia's playbook.

Furthermore, today's threats to democratic institutions are both acute and expansive, extending from the protection of voting machines and media sites to related issues of critical infrastructure, 5G, and even Internet of Things (IoT) vulnerabilities (Shackelford et al., 2017). The weaponization of artificial intelligence (AI) and spread of immersive environments such as the Metaverse that make targets more receptive to emotional manipulation are reinforcing these threats (Rosenberg, 2022). Defending democracy for the next century, then, requires a range of policy responses from reigning in the rampant spread of disinformation on leading internet platforms to securing the voting process itself. Luckily, there are a number of success stories from around the world that policymakers can and should learn from what has worked elsewhere in our common quest to make democracy "harder to hack" (Shackelford et al., 2017). Consider Australia, which has long been grappling with repeated Chinese attempts to interfere with its political systems through cyber-enabled means including disinformation (Borys, 2018). Yet Australia has taken a distinct approach in how it has sought to protect its democratic institutions, including reclassifying its political parties as "critical infrastructure," a step that the US government has yet to take despite repeated breaches at both the Democratic and Republican National Committees (CNN Editorial Research, 2023).

In this edited volume, we have – for the first time – assembled a diverse cadre of scholars and practitioners to address both vulnerabilities in election infrastructure as well as the overriding problem of managing disinformation. A common thread throughout this edited volume is that democracies can and should work closely together to share both cyber threat information and best practices to build democratic resilience the world over, and that a multifaceted approach is needed that combines both targeted reforms to secure election infrastructure – such as requiring paper ballots and risk-limiting audits – with deeper structural interventions to limit the spread and impacts of disinformation that are being made that much more challenging by the rapid evolution of cyberattacks and AI technologies. We assert that it is vital to take this wider view of defending democracy against foreign nation-state-sponsored cyber-enabled threats that includes not only a focus on protecting election infrastructure but also digital repression – both are means to an end, that is,

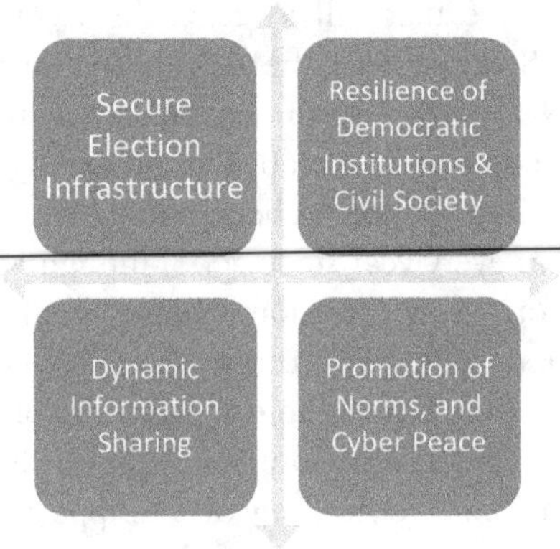

FIGURE 1.1 Defending democracy matrix.

undermining trust, and confidence, in democratic institutions. As such, defending democracy requires implementing multilevel policy responses that tackle this full range of cyber-enabled threats, which include such pressing issues as insecure voting machines and processes but also relate to the promotion and operationalization of cyber norms. This may be envisioned as the matrix illustrated in Figure 1.1.

This edited volume investigates attacks on both voting processes and on the broader informational environment within which voting takes place around the world. It highlights interconnections among such attacks across sectors and countries and identifies ways of preventing, defending against, and mitigating the effects of such attacks on both the technical and informational aspects of cybersecurity. As a case in point, the 2020 US election was among the "most secure in American history" according to the U.S. Department of Homeland Security (CISA, 2020), and yet also, in many ways, it was among the most divisive, leading to record levels of distrust that fueled the toxic political environment leading to the insurrection on the U.S. Capitol on January 6, 2021 (Pew Research Center, 2022). As such, this edited volume is both a call to action and the first draft of a game plan to operationalize needed next steps. Democracy's enemies are determined and innovative; its defenders must be likewise.

WHAT ARE DEMOCRACIES?

The word "democracy" is derived from the Greek words "demos," (people), and "kratos" (power) (Annan, n.d.). Although the ancient Greeks are often credited with establishing the first nascent democracy in the fifth century BC, earlier examples abounded; the Athenian model is noteworthy for the facts that it was direct (i.e., not representative), and who counted as the "people" was much more narrow than today given that it excluded women, along with immigrants and slaves (Annan, n.d.). The franchise has expanded throughout much of the Western world since the era of self-determination following World War II and accelerating after the end of the Cold

War. However, it is the case that still in 2023, the Economist Intelligence Unit reported that less than 8 percent of the world's population reside in a liberal democracy, whereas "nearly 40% live under authoritarian rule – a share that has been creeping up in recent years" (European Intelligence Unit, 2023). The trend toward global democratic backsliding has been noted by Freedom House, which has tracked aggregate declines every year since 2006, though 2022 did mark a dramatic improvement from previous years (Freedom House, 2023). This global retreat from democratic rule then predates the rise of social media-fueled disinformation and polarization, though these phenomena hold the promise of exacerbating the trend if left unchecked as is explored throughout the volume. Still, definitions abound, though for purposes of this work we will rely on Philippe Schmitter and Terry Karl's definition, that is: "a system of governance in which rulers are held accountable for their actions in the public realm by citizens acting indirectly through the competition and cooperation of their elected representatives" (Lynn-Jones, 1998).

WHY ARE DEMOCRACIES WORTH DEFENDING?

The year 2024 is "a remarkable milestone in human history." From Bangladesh to Venezuela, "over four billion people – more than half of the world's population across more than 40 countries" are eligible to vote (Reece, 2024). Included in this group are new, emerging, and established democracies. Where once the latter category may have appeared immune from election anxiety, this is no longer the case. US President Joe Biden has said, "Make no mistake: Democracy is on the ballot" (Milligan, 2022). Such sentiments paint a stark contrast to the remarks of former President Donald Trump, who as of this writing is facing dozens of criminal counts, including for his role in inciting the January 6 insurrection at the U.S. Capitol. Even more worryingly, Trump has claimed that if elected, he will act as a dictator on day one of his new term in office (Colvin & Barrow, 2023). Yet what can get lost in the partisan noise is the big picture of *why* democracy is so important, and worth the cost of defending both at home and abroad. The reasons are manifold, many of which are beyond the scope of this edited volume but include democratic peace theory (the notion that democracies do not attack one another), prosperity, empowerment of civil society, promotion of international peace and security, and less corruption than autocracies (Lynn-Jones, 1998). That is not to say that democracy in and of itself is a panacea for all the ills of humanity – what is after all – but it is a proven system that allows people to "choose how to live together, realizing our freedom in rational and consensual constraint … without being ruled" (Salter, 2022). We believe that is worth defending.

THEMES

This edited volume is not designed to diagnose and offer treatments for all the myriad ails afflicting democracies around the world, from disenfranchisement and gerrymandering to the impacts of structural racism and socioeconomic divides in the electorate. Rather, it is focused on exploring how cyber-enabled themes are making these problems that much tougher to solve, particularly efforts to interfere with voting itself by targeting election infrastructure or by shaping opinions through disinformation and foreign influence operations.

Foreign electoral interference is nothing new. One study found that from 1945 to 2000, the United States and Russia combined tried to influence foreign elections 117 times, using both overt and covert methods (Levin, 2016). It is not even a novelty to use cyberattacks to influence the outcome of an election. As far back as 1994, Nelson Mandela's presidential victory in South Africa was initially diluted due to an illicit computer program.[3] Russia, in particular, has been developing its disinformation capabilities for decades, long before the first packet of information was sent on a fiber-optic cable. Pre-Soviet Union, the Tsarist secret police (the Komitet Gosudarstvennoy Bezopasnosti [KGB], now Federalnaya Sluzhba Bezopasnosti [FSB], which is the predecessor of the Federal Security Service) used disinformation (Popken, 2018). Joseph Stalin created an independent agency for *dezinformatsiya* designed to undermine political opponents and mislead Soviet citizens and foreigners alike as to the USSR's intentions (Popken, 2018). During the Cold War, for example, Russian agents helped plant "hundreds of bogus headlines around the world" such as the claim that the US government created the autoimmune disease AIDS, a false claim that was first mentioned in an Indian newspaper in the 1980s after being planted by a KGB agent (Popken, 2018). That story eventually circled the world, and was even mentioned by a famous American newsperson, Dan Rather, on the *CBS Evening News* in 1987 (Popken, 2018).

Effective foreign disinformation campaigns typically have three components: (1) a state-sponsored news outlet to originate the fabrication; (2) alternative media sources willing to spread it without adequately checking the underlying facts; and (3) witting or unwitting "agents of influence" (e.g., accomplices or unknowing agents) to advance the story in other outlets (Popken, 2018). Not all covert operations follow this formulation; many, for example, do not involve news outlets at all, and others may be better considered as exercises of public diplomacy using disinformation. But the advent of cyberspace has put the disinformation process into overdrive, both speeding the viral spread of stories across national boundaries and platforms with ease, using at times deceptive practices, and causing a proliferation in the types of traditional and social media willing to run with fake stories (Alba & Satariano, 2019). One tragic example is a false story about adopted children being butchered for their organs and sold to wealthy US citizens that first appeared in Honduras in 1986, which was quickly debunked with the official who was quoted denying the episode and issuing a correction, but that did not stop Soviet newspapers from spreading it

[3] Unfortunately, the hacker who installed this program was never identified (Laing, 2010). For more on this topic, see Shackelford et al. (2017, p. 629).

around the world (Popken, 2018). But this is just one tool among many. Nations such as China and Russia also inundate internet discussion forums with so-called flooding attacks that enable distraction and disinformation. As Henry Farrell and Bruce Schneier write: "Libertarians often argue that the best antidote to bad speech is more speech. What Vladimir Putin discovered was that the best antidote to more speech was bad speech" (Schneier & Farrell, 2018).

Such actions are not confined to the physical or digital borders of illiberal regimes. Russia has been linked with "confidence attacks" aimed at destabilizing democracies (especially those in bordering countries, such as Ukraine) and undermining trust in elections (Schneier & Farrell, 2018), a practice that, as we have seen, dates back centuries but now makes use of modern technologies along with the implicit trust and openness in democratic societies. Russia, of course, is not alone in such efforts. As will be discussed further, China is increasingly emulating Russian disinformation efforts, particularly in Taiwan and Australia, as is Iran, North Korea, and an array of non-state actors including criminal organizations, terrorist groups, and hacktivists (Mak, 2018). These groups are employing a range of tactics to undermine trust in electoral processes ranging from directly or indirectly intimidating voters to compromising candidates by releasing damaging (and potentially fabricated) information (listing thirty-five ways in which the integrity of an election could be compromised by foreign actors; Janda, 2017). This points to the multifaceted phenomenon of disinformation, which needs to be thought of as a spectrum from licit to illicit actions, including more transparent and covert techniques using both true and false information and organic as well as fabricated virality. One way to analyze this nuance is in reference to the ABC Disinformation Framework offered by Camille François in which: "A is for Actors (manipulative Actors) who knowingly engage in online deception campaigns while obfuscating their identity and intentions; B is for Behaviour (deceptive Behaviour), encompassing a variety of techniques and vectors (platforms, websites, blogs) used to amplify the reach, virality and impact of the campaigns on line; C is for Content (harmful Content), the most subjective and complex criterion to define" (Francois, 2019). Understanding this continuum is key to managing these threats and then, in turn, gauging policy responses that avoid the pitfalls of potentially playing into manipulators' hands.

It is impossible to say with certainty what the long-term impacts have been of Russian, Chinese, and other state-sponsored efforts to undermine trust in democratic elections. John Sides, Michael Tesler, and Lynn Vavreck, for example, did not find a lasting measurable impact of Russia's efforts in the United States following the 2016 election (Sides, Tesler, & Vavreck, 2018, as cited in Francois, 2019), while Yochai Benker, Robert Farris, and Hal Roberts have argued "that Fox News was far more influential in the spread of false news stories than any Russian effort" (Benkler, Farris, & Roberts, 2018, as cited in Francois, 2019) Still, the fact that such efforts are spreading and that, to date, the efforts of the US government, allied nations, and internet platforms have proven insufficient to stem the flood raises questions about how best to inoculate both advanced and emerging democracies against these threats, some of which stem from authoritarian regimes as is discussed throughout this volume. It should be noted, though, that domestic political actors and groups can also use the same tools to undermine democracies from within, sometimes acting in concert with external actors that may be manipulating the ideology of existing factions.

DIGITAL REPRESSION

As Farrell and Schneier have argued, "Cybersecurity today is not only about computer systems. It's also about the ways attackers can use computer systems to manipulate and undermine public expectations about democracy" (Schneier & Farrell, 2018). This process has only accelerated after the end of the Cold War, with the vast majority of nations enjoying some degree of internet access and more than thirty nations developing offensive cyberattack capabilities (Ranger, 2017; Schneier & Farrell, 2018). Rather than being the final nail in the coffin of authoritarianism, as was hoped by early cyber libertarians such as John Perry Barlow's maxim in his *Declaration of the Independence of Cyberspace*: "Governments of the Industrial World, you weary giants of flesh and steel . . . [,] [y]ou have no sovereignty where we gather" (Shea, 2006), illiberal regimes from Damascus to Beijing have coopted the internet to entrench their power and control their populations (Morozov, 2011). The autocratic threat to democracy is therefore not confined to election interference or disinformation campaigns. There are a myriad other ways in which illiberal regimes are using digital technologies to undermine democratic values at home and abroad.

Generally conceived, digital repression is the coercive use of information and communication technologies by the state to exert control over potential and existing challenges and challengers. Digital repression includes a range of tactics through which states are able to use digital technologies to monitor and restrict the actions of their citizens that include, but are not limited to, digital surveillance, advanced biometric monitoring, disinformation campaigns, and state-based hacking (Feldstein, 2019). While digital repression does not specifically entail the use of physical sanctions against an individual or organization, it often carries with it the implicit assumption that information gathered could be used for more violent means. This often has the outcome of inflicting a chilling effect on dissent against the state without sustained violence (Feldstein, 2019, p. 42). Furthermore, as discussed earlier, these repressive activities can be directed to individuals outside the state's national borders, in some cases compelling them to organize domestic dissident groups or even compromise the election process itself (Shane, 2018).

States have always repressed (Davenport, 2007; Goldstein, 2001). Even democracies, particularly those democracies under threat (Rummel, 1995), have used surveillance and sometimes physical repression against their own citizens (Conrad,

Hill, & Moore, 2018; Davenport, 2007). Repressive tactics include the violation of physical integrity rights, such as harassment, detainment, torture (Rejali, 2007), and extrajudicial killings (Krain, 1997; Midlarsky, 2005; Valentino, 2004), as well as covert repression through monitoring and surveilling which can include wiretapping, organizational infiltration, and the use of informants and agents provocateurs (Davenport, 2005). Repression in all forms is costly for the state, and its citizens. Repression carries the physical costs of maintaining a coercive apparatus and, in more open regimes, it carries the potential audience costs of having these actions exposed to the public. States choose to incur these costs when they are under (real or perceived) threat, which may be created or reinforced through disinformation (Davenport, 2007a, p. 2).

While the repressive power and potential of the state is not a new phenomenon, digital technologies are offering a fresh platform through which governments can exercise their powers of control and self-preservation domestically. Rather than offering the liberating potential originally associated with these technologies (Diamond, 2010), many are now arguing that "social media [is] driving the spread of authoritarian practices" (Deibert, 2019). Examples of this phenomenon include the Arab Spring, as well as more recent conflicts across the Middle East, and beyond (Caywood, 2018).

Digital technologies are changing the nature of state repression in two primary ways. First, the speed and scope with which information can be collected and processed is far greater than any monitoring or surveillance techniques of the past. As Ron Deibert and Rafal Rohozinski write, "Digital information can be easily tracked and traced, and then tied to specific individuals who themselves can be mapped in space and time with a degree of sophistication that would make the greatest tyrants of days past envious" (Deibert & Rohozinski, 2010). This can be done on a much wider swath of the population than was ever previously possible. For example, states threatened by mass mobilization are able to closely monitor, in real time, crowd formations with the potential to become mass rallies allowing police to be put on standby to immediately break up a protest before it grows (Feldstein, 2019, p. 43). They can use facial recognition to identify their leaders.

Second, the nature of repressive technologies has shifted the capacity required for repression, which in turn has shifted the costs. As outlined earlier, repression is costly. It carries the physical costs associated with maintaining a repressive apparatus (e.g., training and paying soldiers and police, maintaining detention facilities, etc.). In the past, mass surveillance required an extensive network of informers. In Poland in 1981, for example, at the height of the Sluzba Bezpieczenstwa's (Security Service) work to undermine the Solidarity movement, there were an estimated 84,000 informers (Day, 2011). New technologies produce the same level of surveillance or greater from far fewer people. Such digital technologies can be expensive. The Xinjian authorities, for example, reportedly budgeted more than $1 billion in the first quarter of 2017 for the monitoring and detention of the Uyghur population there

(Chin & Bürge, 2017). Yet this is likely a low figure when compared with the amount the Chinese state would have spent to construct a comparable system without using digital technologies (Feldstein, 2019, pp. 45–46).

Steven Feldstein attributes these impacts of digital repression to the increased availability of big data from both public and private sources, enhanced machine learning and algorithmic approaches to the processing of that data, and the corresponding advances in computer processing power (Feldstein, 2019, p. 41). As Feldstein writes, "From facial-recognition technologies that cross-check real-time images against massive databases to algorithms that crawl social media for signs of opposition activity, these innovations are a game-changer for authoritarian efforts to shape discourse and crush opposition voices" (Feldstein, 2019, p. 41). In many ways, digital technologies have ushered us into a new era, what Larry Diamond calls "postmodern totalitarianism," in which we appear to be free to go about our daily lives, but governments are controlling and censoring all information flows.

Furthermore, digital technologies serve a very specific function for autocratic states. While leader removal by coups and civil war defeats are declining, it is increasingly common for leaders to be removed on the basis of internal pressure and mass public uprisings (Hollyer, Rosendorff, & Vreeland, 2015). In this way, "the gravest threats to authoritarian survival today may be coming not from insider-led rebellions, but from discontented publics on the streets or at the ballot box" (Feldstein, 2019, p. 43). Such observations might explain Vladimir Putin's response to the December 2011 protests in Russia, along with the color revolutions and Arab Spring (Crowley, 2016). These new trends in leadership removal increase the incentives for leaders to pursue repressive tactics capable of monitoring public opinion and mobilization potential.

As is discussed further in Parts II and III, the target of digital repression need not solely be a country's own citizens. Surveillance, state-sponsored hacks, election interference, and disinformation campaigns have all been documented strategies of autocratic governments' attempts at destabilizing rivals and undermining democracy globally. In several cases, those interfering governments target, or at least attempt to instrumentalize, members of their own diaspora groups (Onishi, 2023). In addition to challenging the functioning of democratic governments, there have been attempts to change the behavior of non-state actors in pursuit of a global liberal agenda, such as human rights nongovernmental organizations (NGOs).[4] Moreover, while the focus of this volume is mainly on digital influence from major powers, the nature of digital technologies is impacting which states can monitor and repress. As the financial and material costs of digital repression decrease, the capacity to influence is no longer confined to global powers. Finally, much like repression itself, digital repression is not and will not be confined to autocratic regimes.

4 See many of the reports written on this topic by Citizen Lab, for example, (Marczak et al., 2019; Scott-Railton et al., 2019).

Democracies monitor, surveille, and repress their own citizens, particularly in times of threat. We should, therefore, not only look for digital repression and interference from our autocratic rivals but acknowledge its potential even within the most stalwart democracies, including the United States. Democracies must be alert to the temptation to silence legitimate dissent, including protest activity that asserts a difference of opinion, in the name of rooting out disinformation (Nardi, 2024). All democracies have a great deal to learn from one another in partnership with the private sector, and similarly can help buttress their common defenses against common cyber-enabled threats, which is a key theme that is explored throughout this collection.

STRUCTURE

The book is structured as follows. It is broken into three main parts, each with several chapters. Part I is entitled "Challenges to Democratic Institutions" and consists of four chapters. In Chapter 2, "Hacking Elections: Contemporary Developments in Historical Perspective," Andrew Grotto and Ashray Narayan from Stanford University advance the argument that the twenty-first century challenge of safeguarding elections from cyberattacks should be understood through the lens of the U.S. Constitution's silence on an affirmative right to vote. In Chapter 3, Professor Rachel Brooks of the University of Bradford builds from this foundation in her piece, "From Free Speech to False Speech: Analyzing Foreign Online Disinformation Campaigns Targeting Democracies," in which she globalizes the issue by comparing and contrasting the roles and goals of Russia and China in undermining trust in democratic institutions. Next, in Chapter 4, Professor Renée Marlin-Bennett from Johns Hopkins University analyzes antidemocratic efforts using cyber-enabled technologies as malign soft power in her contribution entitled, "Cyber Challenges to Democracy and Soft Power's Dark Side." In Chapter 5, entitled "Cyber Disinformation Risk Perception and Control: Integration of the Extended Theory of Planned Behavior and a Structural Equation Model," Professors Małgorzata Pańkowska and Ioana Vasiu of Babeş-Bolyai University take on the global challenges presented by these technologies, arguing that individual users' behavior plays a key role in the control of the phenomenon, and aim to identify factors that impact on users' behavioral intentions and cyber hygiene behavior.

Part II builds from the global challenges to both election infrastructure and more broadly democratic integrity that were introduced in Part I by exploring a series of regional case studies. These were curated from leading academics and practitioners from around the world and focus on three primary regions that are at the frontline of geopolitical fissures pitting authoritarian and democratic regimes against one another. These include the Middle East, Eastern Europe, and Ukraine, along with Asia, in particular India, China, and Taiwan. Chapter 6, "Innovative Frontrunner or

Delayed by Political Gridlock? Israel's Attempts at Countering Disinformation," authored by Inga Kristina Trauthig and Gabrielle Dora Beacken from the University of Texas-Austin's Center for Media Engagement, kicks off the case studies by examining Israel's efforts to counter disinformation through both policy and its private industry related in particular to its controversial push to reform the judicial review powers of the Israeli Supreme Court. The next contribution, Chapter 7, similarly focuses on Israel and the broader Middle East, with a submission authored by David Amsellem entitled "Israeli Information Strategies and Maneuvers," which focuses on the extent to which Israel has been able to achieve many of its strategic objectives despite global public opinion turning against it.

Chapter 8 pivots our case study analysis away from the Middle East and toward Eastern Europe beginning with "Ukraine's Support Coalition and the Long (Info) War: Mitigating the Disinformation Threat to Democratic Collaboration" by Jaclyn A. Kerr, which examines the role of cyber-enabled information and influence in relation to transatlantic support for Ukraine as a case study of the challenge of addressing transnational coordinated strategic disinformation campaigns. Chapter 9 then follows on this broad theme and features a contribution from Professors Jean Camp, Julia R. Fox, Inna Kouper, Sandra Kübler, and Maria Shardakova entitled "Weapons of Mass Derision: Humor, War, and Democracy." In this chapter, they explore the role of humor in building resilience to authoritarianism and disinformation, especially among the younger generation of Russians. The focus then remains on Russia but shifts to Central Asia in Chapter 10, entitled "Election Cyber Threats in Central Asia: A Multistakeholder Approach to Tackling Election Interference and Increasing Resilience," by Pavlina Pavlova of the Cyber Peace Institute. This chapter analyzes regional trends in influencing elections and impacting electoral integrity by cyber means in two key areas, the informational and the technical domain, and proposes action-oriented recommendations for cross-sectoral cooperation toward securing elections and the wider digital ecosystem across Central Asia. In Chapter 11, Ravi Nayyar, a PhD candidate at the University of Sydney, brings our focus to South Asia with "Stacking Up for Resilience: Digital Public Infrastructure – The India Way." This contribution links together democratic integrity with broader issues surrounding critical infrastructure protection, focusing on India's efforts aimed at securing Digital Public Infrastructure (DPI). Finally, Chapters 12 and 13 focus on China and Taiwan respectively. Professor Jun Liu of the University of Copenhagen examines the narrative of cybersecurity in China's mass media, with a focus on the domestication of cybersecurity and its subsequent challenge to democracy in her chapter entitled, "The Domestication of Cybersecurity in Authoritarian Regime: China's Media Narrative on Cybersecurity and Its Challenge to Democracy." Simon Sun, an SJD candidate at Indiana University, next analyzes Taiwan's approach to internet governance relative to China's embrace of cyber sovereignty in his chapter entitled, "Defending Taiwan's Democracy in the Internet Commons."

Part III, "Policy Responses," applies lessons from these case studies as they relate to managing disinformation by relying on theoretical insights gleaned from the literature and frameworks associated with the Ostrom Workshop. In Chapter 14, entitled "Some Truths about Lies: Misinformation and Inequality in Policymaking and Politics," Professors Lindsay Flynn of the University of Luxembourg and Barbara Allen of Carleton College use insights gleaned from the Institutional Analysis and Development (IAD) Framework to explore how the dual trends of increased disinformation in politics and increased socioeconomic inequality contribute to an erosion of trust and confidence in democratic institutions. Finally, the volume concludes in Chapter 15 with Professors Deike Schulz, Joyce Kerstens, and Dustin Sajoe of NHL Stenden University and their contribution, "Getting a Grip on Disinformation: From Distrust to Trust within Learning Communities," which highlights an experiment with methodology to empower communities to recognize and fight disinformation.

Together, these chapters can barely scratch the surface of the myriad efforts underway around the world both in and between democracies to secure election infrastructure and build trust in democratic institutions such as by battling disinformation and deep fakes. Yet they do illustrate the common challenges that are faced by both advanced and emerging democracies, along with the important roles played by technological, regulatory, and geopolitical trends in shaping the landscape of defending democracy in the digital age. Our hope is that this is among the first, but certainly not the last, such effort, particularly given the series of consequential elections taking place around the world in 2024.

REFERENCES

Alba, D., & Frenkel, S. (2019, October 30). Russia tests new disinformation tactics in Africa to expand influence. *The New York Times*. https://thehill.com/policy/cybersecurity/431614-us-cyber-operation-blocked-internet-for-russian-troll-farm-on-election/

Alba, D., & Satariano, A. (2019, September 26). At least 70 countries have had disinformation campaigns. *The New York Times*. https://nytimes.com/2019/09/26/technology/government-disinformation-cyber-troops.html

Annan, K. (n.d.). *Compass: Manual for human rights education with young people. Democracy*. Council of Europe Portal. https://coe.int/en/web/compass/democracy

Beeman, R. R. (n.d.). *Perspectives on the Constitution: A republic, if you can keep it*. National Constitution Center. https://constitutioncenter.org/learn/educational-resources/historical-documents/perspectives-on-the-constitution-a-republic-if-you-can-keep-it

Borys, S. (2018, May 28). *China's "brazen" and "aggressive" political interference outlined in top-secret report*. ABC News Australia. https://abc.net.au/news/2018-05-29/chinas-been-interfering-in-australian-politics-for-past-decade/9810236

Caywood, C. (2018, November 21). *This is how social media is being used in the Middle East*. The National Interest. https://nationalinterest.org/blog/middle-east-watch/how-social-media-being-used-middle-east-36857

Chin, J., & Burge, C. (2017, December 19). Twelve days in Xinjiang: How China's surveillance state overwhelms daily life. *The Wall Street Journal*. https://wsj.com/articles/twelve-days-in-xinjiang-how-chinas-surveillance-state-overwhelms-daily-life-1513700355

CISA. (2020, November 12). *Joint Statement from Elections Infrastructure Government Coordinating Council & the Election Infrastructure Sector Coordinating Executive Committees*. CISA. https://cisa.gov/news-events/news/joint-statement-elections-infrastructure-government-coordinating-council-election

CNN Editorial Research. (2023, October 23). *2016 presidential campaign hacking fast facts*. CNN. https://cnn.com/2016/12/26/us/2016-presidential-campaign-hacking-fast-facts/index.html#:~:text=According%20to%20the%20report%2C%20hackers,Podesta%2C%20according%20to%20the%20report

Colvin, J., & Barrow, B. (2023, December 7). *Trump's vow to only be a dictator on "day one" follows growing worry over his authoritarian rhetoric*. AP News. https://apnews.com/article/trump-hannity-dictator-authoritarian-presidential-election-f27e7e9d7c13fabbe3ae7dd7f1235c72

Conrad, C. R., Hill, D. W., Jr., & Moore, W. H. (2018). Torture and the limits of democratic institutions. *Journal of Peace Research*, 55(1), 3–17.

Crowley, M., & Ioffe, J. (2016, July 25). Why Putin hates Hillary. *Politico*. https://politico.com/story/2016/07/clinton-putin-226153

Davenport, C. (2005). Understanding covert repressive action: The case of the U.S. government against the Republic of New Africa. *The Journal of Conflict Resolution*, 49(1), 120–140.

(2007a). *State repression and the domestic democratic peace*. Cambridge University Press. https://doi.org/10.1017/CBO9780511510021

(2007b). State repression and political order. *Annual Review of Political Science*, 10, 1–23. https://doi.org/10.1146/annurev.polisci.10.1140.143216

Day, M. (2011, October 18). Polish secret police: How and why the Poles spied on their own people. *The Telegraph*. https://telegraph.co.uk/news/worldnews/europe/poland/8831691/Polish-secret-police-how-and-why-the-Poles-spied-on-their-own-people.html

Deibert, R. J. (2019). The road to digital unfreedom: Three painful truths about social media. *Journal of Democracy*, 30(1), 25–39.

Deibert, R. J., & Rohozinski, R. (2010). Liberation vs. control: The future of cyberspace. *Journal of Democracy*, 21(4), 43–57.

Diamond, L. (2010). Liberation technology. *Journal of Democracy*, 21(3), 69–83.

European Intelligence Unit (EIU). (2023). *EIU report: Democracy index 2023*. EIU. https://eiu.com/n/campaigns/democracy-index-2023/

Feldstein, S. (2019). How artificial intelligence is reshaping repression. *Journal of Democracy*, 30(1), 40–52.

Janda, J. (2017, November 5). *A framework guide to tools for countering hostile foreign electoral inference*. European Values. https://europeanvalues.net/wp-content/uploads/2017/05/35-measures-in-15-steps-for-enhancing-the-resilience-of-the-democratic-electoral-process-1-1.pdf

Francois, C. (2019, September 20). *Actors, behaviors, content: A disinformation ABC*. Transatlantic Working Group. https://ivir.nl/publicaties/download/ABC_Framework_2019_Sept_2019.pdf

Freedom House. (2023, March). *Freedom in the world 2023*. Freedom House. https://freedomhouse.org/sites/default/files/2023-03/FIW_World_2023_DigtalPDF.pdf

Goldstein, R. J. (1978). *Political repression in modern America: From 1870 to the present*. G. K. Hall.

Hollyer, J. R., Rosendorf, P. B., & Vreeland, J. R. (2015). Transparency, protest, and autocratic instability. *The American Political Science Review*, 41(3), 764–784.

Krain, M. (1997). State-sponsored mass murder: The onset and severity of genocides and politicides. *The Journal of Conflict Resolution*, 41(3), 331–360.

Laing, A. (2010, October 24). Election won by Mandele "rigged by opposition". *The Telegraph.* https://telegraph.co.uk/news/worldnews/africaandindianocean/southafrica/8084053/Election-won-by-Mandela-rigged-by-opposition.html

Levin, D. H. (2016, February 13). When the great power gets a vote: The effects of great power electoral interventions on election results. *International Studies Quarterly*, 60(2), 189–202. https://doi.org/10.1093/isq/sqv016

Lynn-Jones, S. M. (1998, March). *Why the United States should spread democracy*. Harvard Kennedy School, Belfer Center. https://belfercenter.org/publication/why-united-states-should-spread-democracy

Mak, T. (2018, June 20). *Former U.S. diplomat warns China is emulating Russian political interference*. NPR. https://npr.org/2018/06/20/621963286/former-u-s-diplomat-warns-china-is-emulating-russian-political-interference

Marczak, B., Hulcoop, A., Maynier, E., Razzak, B. A., Crete-Nishihata, M., Scott-Railton, J., & Deibert, R. (2019, September 24). *Missing link: Tibetan groups targeted with 1-click mobile exploits*. The Citizen Lab. https://citizenlab.ca/2019/09/poison-carp-tibetan-groups-targeted-with-1-click-mobile-exploits/

Midlarsky, M. I. (2005). *The killing trap: Genocide in the twentieth century*. Cambridge University Press. https://doi.org/10.1017/CBO9780511491023

Milligan, S. (2022, November 2). *Biden: "Make no mistake: Democracy is on the ballot"*. U.S. News & World Report. https://usnews.com/news/elections/articles/2022-11-02/biden-make-no-mistake-democracy-is-on-the-ballot

Morozov, E. (2011). *The net delusion: The dark side of internet freedom*. PublicAffairs.

Nardi, C. (2024, January 24). Trudeau's use of the Emergencies Act was ruled unconstitutional. What happens now? *National Post.* https://nationalpost.com/news/politics/a-judge-ruled-trudeaus-use-of-the-emergencies-act-unconstitutional-so-what-happens-next#:~:text=OTTAWA%20%E2%80%93%20In%20a%20landmark%20ruling,Convoy%20blockades%20in%20early%202022

Onishi, N. (2023, December 14). He won election to Canada's Parliament. Did China help? *The New York Times.* https://nytimes.com/2023/12/02/world/americas/canada-elections-china.html#:~:text=Lawmakers%20are%20separately%20examining%20whether,Dong%20%E2%80%94%20has%20been%20named

Pew Research Center. (2022, January 5). *Trust in America: Do Americans trust their elections?* Pew Research Center. https://pewresearch.org/2022/01/05/trust-in-america-do-americans-trust-their-elections

Popken, B. (2018, November 5). *Factory of lies: Russia's disinformation playbook exposed*. NBC News. https://nbcnews.com/business/consumer/factory-lies-russia-s-disinformation-playbook-exposed-n910316

Ranger, S. (2017, January 5). *US intelligence: 30 countries building cyber attack capabilities*. ZDNet. https://zdnet.com/article/us-intelligence-30-countries-building-cyber-attack-capabilities/

Reece, N. (2024, January 14). *More than 4 billion people are eligible to vote in an election in 2024. Is this democracy's biggest test?* The Conversation. https://theconversation.com/more-than-4-billion-people-are-eligible-to-vote-in-an-election-in-2024-is-this-democracys-biggest-test-220837

Rejali, D. (2009). *Torture and democracy*. Princeton University Press.

Rosenberg, L. (2022, December 27). *Mind control in the Metaverse*. Medium. https://medium.com/predict/mind-control-in-the-metaverse-48dfbd88c2ae

Rummel, R. J. (1995). Democracy, power, genocide, and mass murder. *The Journal of Conflict Resolution*, 39(1), 3–26.

Salter, A. (2022, August 22). *Why American democracy is worth defending*. Imaginative Conservative. https://theimaginativeconservative.org/2022/08/american-democracy-alexander-salter.html

Schneier, B., & Farrell, H. (2018, November 19). *The most damaging election disinformation campaign came from Donald Trump, not Russia*. Vice. https://vice.com/en/article/mbyg3x/the-most-damaging-election-disinformation-campaign-came-from-donald-trump-not-russia

Scott-Railton, J., Marczak, B., Anstis, S., Razzak, B. A., Crete-Nishihata, M., & Deibert, R. (2019, March 20). *Reckless VII: Wife of journalist slain in cartel-linked killing targeted with NSO group's spyware*. The Citizen Lab. https://citizenlab.ca/2019/03/nso-spyware-slain-journalists-wife/#:~:text=Key%20Findings,Andr%C3%A9s%20Villarreal%20and%20Ismael%20Boj%C3%B3rquez

Shackelford, S., Schneier, B., Sulmeyer, M., Boustead, A., & Buchanan, B. (2017). Making democracy harder to hack. *University of Michigan Journal of Law Reform*, 50(3), 629–668. https://doi.org/10.36646/mjlr.50.3.making

Shane, S. (2018, February 18). How unwitting Americans encountered Russian operatives online. *The New York Times*. https://nytimes.com/2018/02/18/us/politics/russian-operatives-facebook-twitter.html

Shea, C. (2006, January 15). Sovereignty in cyberspace. *Boston Globe*. http://worldtradelaw.typepad.com/ielpblog/2006/01/sovereigntyjuri.html

Tennis, M. (2020, July 20). *Russia ramps up global elections interference: Lessons for the United States*. Center for Strategic & International Studies. https://csis.org/blogs/technology-policy-blog/russia-ramps-global-elections-interference-lessons-united-states

Thomsen, J. (2019, February 26). US cyber operation blocked internet for Russian troll farm on Election Day 2018: Report. *The Hill*. https://thehill.com/policy/cybersecurity/431614-us-cyber-operation-blocked-internet-for-russian-troll-farm-on-election/

Valentino, B. A. (2004). *Final solutions: Mass killing and genocide in the 20th century*. Cornell University Press.

Way, L. A., & Casey, A. (2018, January 8). Russia has been meddling in foreign elections for decades. Has it made a difference? *Washington Post*. https://washingtonpost.com/news/monkey-cage/wp/2018/01/05/russia-has-been-meddling-in-foreign-elections-for-decades-has-it-made-a-difference/

Zeitz, J. (2016, July 27). Foreign governments have been tampering with U.S. elections for decades. *Politico*. https://politico.com/magazine/story/2016/07/russia-dnc-hack-donald-trump-foreign-governments-hacking-vietnam-richard-nixon-214111

PART I

Challenges to Democratic Institutions

2

Hacking Elections

Contemporary Developments in Historical Perspective

Andrew Grotto and Ashray Narayan

Nowhere in the text of the U.S. Constitution is there an explicit reference to an affirmative right to vote. And yet, the Constitution and its amendments contain numerous provisions relating to the *integrity* of elections – what counts as a valid or legitimate electoral process. For the Framers of the Constitution, election integrity was fundamentally about ensuring that, if elections were held, only qualified persons could vote. As state legislatures and especially the Congress incrementally ruled out voting discrimination on the basis of whether a person owned land, was Black or another minority, was female, or was over eighteen years of age, those whose political fortunes were adversely affected by the expanding electorate have exploited features and bugs in the elections architecture of American democracy to uphold their own vision of election integrity – and in the process, disenfranchise eligible voters and influence election outcomes. Their tools have included poll taxes, literacy tests, identification requirements, residency conditions, disenfranchisement for certain criminal convictions, and a range of other measures.

The argument we advance in this contribution is that the twenty-first-century challenge of safeguarding elections from cyber threats must be understood as part of this history, and not solely as a niche engineering or information security problem. Especially since the 2016 presidential election, which brought cybersecurity risks to elections into the mainstream, political discourse about the magnitude of these risks and how best to mitigate them has become wrapped up in ideological conflict about who the threat actors are and what they aim to accomplish. It is against this backdrop of intensifying ideological conflict about the integrity and legitimacy of democratic procedures that efforts in 2016 and its aftermath to address cyber risks have occurred.

In information security, a hacker is someone who uses their skills and knowledge of digital systems to solve problems or achieve desired outcomes, even if it means subverting those systems by exploiting a vulnerability to undermine the confidentiality, integrity, or availability of the system or its information. Confidentiality ensures that systems and information are accessible only to authorized individuals or entities; it involves protecting systems and information from unauthorized access or disclosure. Integrity focuses on maintaining the accuracy, completeness, and trustworthiness of a system or information. It ensures that data remain unaltered, complete, and reliable. Availability ensures that systems and information are accessible and usable when needed. It involves protecting against disruptions, outages, or denial of service attacks that may render systems or data inaccessible.

Hackers may don a metaphorical white, black, or gray hat, depending on whether their actions and goals are rightful, wrongful, or somewhere in between. Rightful actions consist of compliance with legal and ethical norms concerning hacking and use of information technologies; a rightful motivation is identifying and responsibly showcasing vulnerabilities so that they can be fixed ("patched"). Wrongful actions and motivations consist of illegal or unethical conduct or goals. Gray hat hackers may employ illegal or unethical means to achieve rightful ends, or otherwise straddle a line between good and bad.

We port this concept over to election integrity and its preoccupation with hackers of a different kind: political hackers who use their skills and knowledge of law, psychology, and democratic procedures to subvert those procedures in pursuit of their political interests. Political hackers could be white, black, or gray hatted. Civil rights activists of the 1950s and 1960s like John Lewis are prototypical white hat hackers.

We begin with a review of American electoral history through 2016, with a focus on conceptions of election integrity and perceived threats to integrity. We then review developments that occurred between the 2016 and the 2020 presidential election cycles – an especially sensitive period for both election integrity generally and cybersecurity of elections specifically – with a focus on efforts to enhance the resilience of election infrastructure against cyber threats. As we shall see, the debate about the resilience of election infrastructure against cyber threats is at risk of becoming polarized along familiar themes from the history of American elections, with progressives viewing the principal threats as a combination of voter suppression by Republicans and their ideological allies and conservatives viewing voter fraud – people voting who are not eligible to vote – as the principal threat.

CONSTITUTIONAL FOUNDATIONS OF THE ELECTORAL PROCESS

Elections are abundant in American democracy and are held for certain federal, state, and local government offices. The constitution gives Congress the power to regulate how elections are held for these offices and specifies the qualifications and procedures for elections for the legislative and executive branches. It does not, however, dictate to the states which offices at the state and local levels are to be filled by elected or appointed officials.

The constitution was negotiated over four months in 1787 and ratified by the states in 1789. Among the fifty-five delegates that the states had sent to negotiate on their behalf in 1787, there was cynicism about the compatibility of universal suffrage – the idea that all free adults, which at the time usually meant free White men could vote[1] – with their vision of a constitutional order that safeguarded the individual rights of propertied White men against populist forces that could be manipulated by malign actors. Most of the Framers, as these delegates came to be known, preferred to eliminate the vulnerability by restricting voting privileges to White property owners. James Madison expressed apprehension about the potential influence of populist appeals on the less affluent classes and argued that limiting voting to the wealthy was essential for preserving Republican liberty and election integrity. Similarly, Gouverneur Morris, the author of the preamble to the constitution, voiced the belief that the ignorant and dependent could not be trusted to act in the public interest, drawing a comparison to children (Klarman, 2016).

Benjamin Franklin was among the dissenters; he argued against constitutional restrictions on the franchise based on wealth (Klarman, 2016). He highlighted the significant contributions of the commoners in the fight for American independence and pointed out that the decisions of the wealthy were susceptible to external influences as well. In the end, Franklin's view prevailed, with its rhetorical weight backed by the mathematics of ratification: Voting practices in many states had already extended suffrage beyond landowners, and expecting these voters to approve a constitution that would then strip them of their right to vote seemed wholly unrealistic. The Framers therefore left the responsibility of determining voting rights to the individual states. However, they devised a system wherein state legislators, rather than the voting public, would select US senators and the president. This was intended to serve as a safeguard against potential disruptions caused by populist elements within the electorate.

Hacking the 15th Amendment

The 15th Amendment, ratified in 1870 as the last of the Reconstruction Amendments,[2] prohibited states and the federal government from denying or limiting a citizen's right to vote "on account of race, color, or previous condition of servitude." The Reconstruction Amendments did not stop states from making it difficult or impossible for Black Americans to vote, however. The states' hack was to erect a host of barriers to voting that were keyed to vulnerabilities experienced disproportionately by Black Americans, as opposed to blatant race-based bans on voting: poll taxes that exploited the poverty of most Black Americans at the time, literacy tests to exploit the legacy of brutal repression of literacy among enslaved people and the limited educational opportunities of their progeny, and organized

[1] The New Jersey Constitution, adopted on July 2, 1776, uses the gender-neutral pronoun "they" and doesn't include racial categories in its election law.

[2] The 13th Amendment outlawed slavery and the 14th Amendment gave citizenship to all persons "born or naturalized in the United States," including formerly enslaved people, and provided all citizens with "equal protection under the laws."

violence by non-state actors (such as the Ku Klux Klan) to deter Black participation in elections, among other measures. Especially in the American South, so-called grandfather clauses restricted voting to those whose grandfathers had voted, which had the effect of disenfranchising generations of Black Americans with grandfathers who had been enslaved and ineligible to vote.

The Supreme Court ruled in 1915 that grandfather clauses were unconstitutional. The Court reasoned "the grandfather clauses in the Maryland and Oklahoma constitutions to be repugnant to the Fifteenth Amendment and therefore null and void."[3] In 1920, voters extended the right to vote to women with the 19th Amendment, which "prohibits the United States and its states from denying the right to vote to citizens of the United States on the basis of sex." This followed the establishment in 1913 of direct popular election of senators upon ratification of the 17th Amendment.

The poll tax exploited a vulnerability that was pervasive in the American South through much of the twentieth century and cut across racial lines: poverty. In 1959, 56.2 percent of Black Americans and other people of color lived below the poverty line. This proportion of persons below the poverty line eventually declined to 13 percent in 1968, but the poverty rate among Blacks and other people of color remained about three times the rate among White Americans (U.S. Department of Commerce, 1969). As of 1966, eleven states in the American South had poll taxes. Americans outlawed the practice for federal elections in 1964 with the 24th Amendment, but five states – Alabama, Arkansas, Mississippi, Texas, and Virginia – retained poll taxes for state elections (Lebetter Jr., 1995). In *Harper v. Va. Board of Elections*, the Supreme Court invalidated the practice for states, on the basis that "once the franchise is granted to the electorate, lines may not be drawn which are inconsistent with the Equal Protection Clause of the Fourteenth Amendment." The Court held that "a State violates the Equal Protection Clause of the Fourteenth Amendment whenever it makes the affluence of the voter or payment of any fee an electoral standard," because "voter qualifications have no relation to wealth nor to paying or not paying this or any other tax" and thus have no rational basis other than to discriminate against poor people.[4]

The 26th Amendment, ratified in 1971 amid social turmoil in the United States over the Vietnam war and US reliance on a conscript military, lowered the voting age to eighteen, giving Americans eligible for the military draft the right to vote in state and federal elections – and thus have a say in national policy on the deployment of US armed forces (Baum, Cea, & Cohen, 2021).

This collection of constitutional requirements and accompanying Supreme Court case law establishes the constitutional floor for voting rights in the United

[3] *Guinn v. United States*, 238 U.S. 347 (Supreme Court of the United States, June 21, 1915).

[4] *Harper v. Virginia Board of Elections*, 383 U.S. 663 (Supreme Court of the United States, March 24, 1966).

States. The constitution otherwise defers to state and federal legislators on most ballot decisions, saying that the "times, places and manner" of elections are state matters unless Congress sets nationwide standards. This entails that the selection, implementation, and oversight of elections and polling-related infrastructure (e.g., voting machines) are also left to the states, which, in turn, often leave many aspects of election administration to local (often county) governments.

Electoral Infrastructure Basics

Election infrastructure in the United States rests on this constitutional foundation and is usefully broken down into several discrete components: partisan campaign infrastructure and interest groups; voter registration; ballot casting; and ballot counting and certification of election results. Each of these components is subject to different state and federal laws, as well as having different cybersecurity and other risk attributes pertaining to the vulnerability of election infrastructure.

Partisan Campaign Infrastructure, Interest Groups, and the Media

Partisan campaign organizations generally determine how their political party nominates candidates to compete in the general election for a given office. Candidates' campaign organizations provide the management infrastructure and support for their candidates to run for office. Core campaign functions such as fundraising, advertising, and get-out-the-vote initiatives are the responsibility of what might be termed the partisan elements of election infrastructure. These partisan elements are subject to a variety of state and federal laws relating to such matters as fundraising, advertising, coordination and contact with outside interest groups engaged in electioneering activities, and voter registration drives. Interest groups, political action committees (PACs), and other nonpartisan organizations such as think tanks may seek to influence public opinion, candidates' policy preferences, and election outcomes by endorsing candidates, issuing position papers, producing policy research, advertising, and otherwise engaging in the political process; they too operate in a distinct legal context. Objective, fact-based media is essential to ensuring that voters have access to timely and accurate information about candidates, issues, election processes, and election outcomes. The First Amendment's heightened protections for political speech are a core element of the constitutional foundation for partisan campaign infrastructure and interest groups.

Voter Registration and Identity

Persons eligible to vote must register to cast a ballot and have their vote counted toward determining the winner of the election. The United States employs a decentralized voter registration system, with each state responsible for maintaining its own registration rolls. State-level agencies, such as election boards or secretaries of state, oversee the voter registration process. To register to vote in the United

States, individuals must meet certain eligibility requirements, which typically include being a US citizen, meeting the minimum age requirement of eighteen years old, and being a resident of the state or jurisdiction in which they wish to vote. Some states also require individuals to provide proof of identity or residency during the registration process. States provide various methods for citizens to register to vote, including in-person, online, and mail-in registration.

Individuals can register to vote in person at designated government offices, such as election offices, Department of Motor Vehicle (DMV) offices, or public assistance agencies. Many states also offer online voter registration systems, allowing eligible individuals to register conveniently through secure websites. Some states allow individuals to register to vote by mailing in registration forms obtained from election offices or through voter registration drives. States are also responsible for maintaining accurate voter rolls by regularly reviewing and updating voter registration records. This process includes removing ineligible or deceased voters and updating address changes.

Voter identity and pollbooks are key components of the voting process in the United States and help to ensure the integrity and accuracy of elections. Voter identity verification refers to the process of confirming the identity of individuals who show up to vote. The purpose is to prevent voter fraud and ensure that only eligible voters cast their ballots. The specific requirements and methods for verifying voter identity vary across states. Some states have implemented strict voter identification laws, while others have more lenient or no specific requirements. Voter identification laws, enacted by individual states, determine the types of identification documents that voters must present at the polling place. These laws aim to verify the identity of voters and prevent fraudulent voting. The specific requirements and accepted forms of identification differ among states. Some states require a photo ID, such as a driver's license or a state-issued ID card, while others accept non-photo IDs, utility bills, or other documents showing the voter's name and address. Pollbooks are registers or electronic databases that contain voter information, such as names, addresses, and registration status. They serve as a reference for poll workers to verify voter eligibility and ensure that individuals are registered to vote in a particular precinct or district. Pollbooks help prevent individuals from voting more than once and allow election officials to track and update voter participation (U.S. Election Assistance Commission, 2023). Around three-quarters of registered voters live in jurisdictions where pollbooks are used (Verified Voting, 2020).

Ballot Casting

Voting machines are used in the United States to facilitate the casting and counting of votes in elections. It is up to individual states to decide which machines to purchase; states are also responsible for maintaining these systems and ensuring their readiness for election day. Nine states and the District of Columbia require testing against federal standards (the Voluntary Voting System Guidelines (VVSG), discussed later), sixteen require testing by a federally accredited laboratory, and twelve require full federal certification (Verified Voting, 2021).

For most of the nation's history, voting machines were mechanical devices that a voter used to mark a ballot. In the past two decades, however, the United States has replaced a substantial percentage of wholly mechanical machines with ones incorporating digital functionalities. These include optical scan machines, direct-recording electronic (DRE) machines, and ballot marking devices (BMDs). Optical scan machines read marked paper ballots, which are manually filled out by voters. The machines scan and tabulate the votes recorded on the paper ballots. DRE machines are electronic devices that allow voters to make their selections directly on a touchscreen or through other input mechanisms. These machines store and tally the votes electronically. BMDs assist voters, including those with disabilities, in marking their ballots electronically. Voters use the device to make their selections, which are then printed on a paper ballot for tabulation.

Vote Counting and Certification of Election Results

Vote counting involves the aggregation and tabulation of individual votes to determine the outcome of an election. The specific methods and technologies used can vary by state and jurisdiction. Common vote counting methods include manual counting of paper ballots, electronic scanning of marked ballots, or the use of electronic voting machines that tally votes electronically. Election laws and procedures govern the entire vote counting process. These laws vary at the federal, state, and local levels, and they cover areas such as canvassing and certification, recounts and audits, and reporting requirements.

Canvassing refers to the official examination and verification of election results, including the validation and counting of provisional or absentee ballots. Once the canvassing process is completed, election officials certify the results, declaring the winners. Election laws often provide procedures for recounting votes in cases where the margin of victory is close or when requested by candidates. Recounts can be conducted manually or through machine recounts. Some states also require post-election audits to verify the accuracy of the voting system and ensure the integrity of the results. Election laws mandate the reporting of election results to the appropriate authorities and the public. These requirements include timelines for reporting, formats for result presentation, and mechanisms for transparency and public access to the reported data (U.S. Election Assistance Commission, 2022). A state official, often a state's secretary of state, certifies the results of elections.

News organizations track these counting processes and results so that they can report on developments and election outcomes in a timely manner. For example, the Associated Press maintains a network of stringers – thousands of local reporters with "first-hand knowledge of their territories and trusted relationships with county clerks and other local officials" – and public sources such as state and county websites for its reporting on elections (Associated Press, n.d.).

Vulnerabilities

As we shall see subsequently, hackers have exploited vulnerabilities in each component of election infrastructure for centuries, but the digitalization of this infrastructure adds an additional attack surface for threat actors to attempt to exploit. For example, campaign organizations strive to keep their internal communications confidential, but threat actors might try to breach confidentiality to collect intelligence on campaign strategy and policy preferences – as China did with its cyber intrusions into campaigns of presidential candidates Barack Obama and John McCain in 2008 (Isikoff, 2013) – or distract and embarrass the campaign by leaking information – as Russia did in 2016 when it hacked the Democratic National Committee and leaked emails (Nakashima & Harris, 2018). Voter registration purges can be performed for the legitimate purpose of ensuring that registration rolls are up to date, but the technique can be hacked by unscrupulous election officials to purge eligible voters who are likely to vote for the opposition. Hackers might also target voter registration rolls, as Russia did in 2016, and potentially alter them in ways that threaten their integrity (McFadden, Arkin, & Monahan, 2018).

These are just a few of the many ways in which hackers can identify and exploit vulnerabilities in election infrastructure. We discuss additional examples later in the chapter.

Breaking down election infrastructure into discrete components has analytic value, but it is also important to consider election infrastructure as a systemic whole, especially when overall public confidence in the integrity of an election is at stake. A threat against any one component of election infrastructure could shake confidence in the integrity of the voting process and the legitimacy of the outcome.

WHITE HATS HACK BACK

The Congress, the executive branch, and the federal courts have frequently intervened against efforts by states to curtail voting, especially when those efforts are animated by racism toward Black Americans. The Civil Rights Act of 1870 was Congress' first attempt at enforcing the 15th Amendment's ban on denying Black Americans the right to vote;[5] subsequent amendments in 1957, 1960, and 1964 further expanded federal protections for Black Americans' voting rights.[6] Congress enacted the Voting Rights Act of 1965 (VRA) to ban racial discrimination in the

[5] Specifically, the 1870 Act, referred to variously as the Enforcement Act or First Ku Klux Klan Act, made it a federal criminal offense to prevent Black Americans from voting or threatening violence or other retaliation for voting, such as loss of employment or eviction from their home.

[6] The 1957 amendment authorized the U.S. Attorney General to seek federal court injunctions to safeguard the voting rights of Black Americans. The 1960 amendment bolstered court enforcement of voting rights and mandated preservation of voting records. The 1964 amendment required desegregation of voting places, among other provisions.

administration of elections and enforce the 14th and 15th Amendments; it has amended the VRA five times since then to expand its protections (Waldman et al., 2021b).

Legislation enacted in 1984 required polling places to be accessible to people with disabilities, and the 1986 Uniformed and Overseas Citizens Absentee Voting Act (UOCAVA) permitted service men and woman and overseas US voters to register and vote by mail. In 1993, Congress legislated federal voter registration guidelines in the National Voter Registration Act of 1993, which required each state to have a designated official for overseeing election administration and streamlined the voter registration process (National Conference of State Legislatures, 2022).

Following the controversial presidential election of 2000, where "hanging chads" in Florida required Supreme Court intervention to decide the winner,[7] Congress enacted the Help America Vote Act (HAVA), which aimed to bring about significant changes in election administration. Congress has not enacted major new voting rights legislation since HAVA.[8]

Meanwhile, the Supreme Court has intervened in ways that tilt constitutional momentum away from protecting voting rights – especially among Black Americans – and toward giving states greater discretion to make changes to their election infrastructure to save money and guard against voter fraud, even when those changes foreseeably erect barriers for eligible voters, especially Black Americans, to cast their ballots.

John Lewis, White Hat Hacker

In June 1964, three voting rights activists were murdered in Mississippi for helping Black Americans register to vote.[9] The violent episode galvanized support for the Civil Rights Act, which Congress passed, and President Lyndon B. Johnson signed, one month later.[10] The Civil Rights Act outlawed segregation in public places and in businesses that serve the general public and banned discrimination on the basis of race, color, religion, sex, or national origin in employment. It also required that laws relating to voter qualification be applied equally within a jurisdiction, banned the practice of using errors in registration documents and ballots to disqualify a Black American from voting even when an error was not material to that person's eligibility

7 *Bush v. Gore*, 531 U.S. 98 (United States Supreme Court, December 11, 2000).

8 The VRA was reauthorized in 1970, 1975, and 1982, with the most recent reauthorization occurring in 2006 when President George W. Bush signed legislation to extend the VRA for an additional twenty-five years. In 2009, Congress enacted the Military and Overseas Voter Empowerment Act ("MOVE Act"), which amended UOCAVA to establish new voter registration and absentee ballot requirements for federal elections to further facilitate the ability of Americans living overseas to vote.

9 *United States v. Price*, 383 U.S. 787 (Supreme Court of the United States, March 28, 1966).

10 Civil Rights Act, Pub. L. No. 88-352, 78 Stat. 241 (1964).

to vote, and outlawed literacy tests unless all voters had to take them and certain transparency requirements about them were met.

On March 7, 1965, John Lewis, a prominent civil rights activist and future Member of Congress,[11] led a march of over 600 people across the Edmund Pettus Bridge in Selma, Alabama to protest racial discrimination in the American South. The peaceful protesters encountered violent resistance at the top of the bridge from Alabama state troopers, whose unprovoked brutality against the procession was captured by television cameras and broadcast nationwide, turning the event in Selma into a pivotal moment in civil rights history. Outrage over the local incident, known as Bloody Sunday, swept the nation and further fired up support for the civil rights movement (Klein, 2020). Congress passed the VRA five months later.

The VRA patched numerous vulnerabilities in America's election infrastructure at the time. Aimed at safeguarding the voting rights of racial minorities, it prohibits discriminatory measures in elections that hinder their ability to cast ballots, such as literacy tests and poll taxes. The VRA also introduced federal oversight of states with a history of voter suppression, requiring them to seek federal approval before changing their voting laws. This "preclearance" requirement aimed to ensure fair and equitable access to the ballot box. The immediate impact of the VRA was substantial, leading to the registration of 250,000 Black Americans by the end of the year and ensuring that by the end of 1966, only four out of the thirteen southern states had less than 50 percent of eligible Black Americans registered to vote (National Archives, 2022).

In 2013, the Supreme Court ruled 5–4 in *Shelby County v. Holder* that the VRA's preclearance requirements were unconstitutional because the coverage formula was, in the majority's view, "based on 40-year-old facts having no logical relationship to the present day."[12] The decision made it possible for state governments previously subject to preclearance requirements to move forward with a variety of measures that made it more difficult for eligible voters to cast a ballot, with the effects being disproportionately felt by Black Americans, who voted for Democratic candidates 86 percent of the time in 2022 (Alexander & Fields, 2022). These measures – which included voter registration purges, polling location closures, limitations on absentee and mail-in ballots, and restrictions on the ability of third-party groups to facilitate registration and ballot casting – were predominantly the product of Republican-led state governments, who justified them as saving money or guarding against voter fraud (Waldman et al., 2018).

In the decade since *Shelby*, the ideological composition of the Court has shifted further rightward. Senate Republicans refused to advance President Obama's

[11] John Lewis was elected to Congress in 1986, representing Georgia's fifth congressional district spanning most of Atlanta, Georgia, where he served as lawmaker until he passed away on July 17, 2020.

[12] *Shelby County v. Holder*, 570 U.S. 529 (Supreme Court of the United States, February 27, 2013).

nomination of Merrick Garland to the Court in 2016 to replace the late Justice Antonin Scalia, and so President Trump was able to replace Justice Scalia with another conservative, Neil Gorsuch. President Trump replaced the retiring Justice David Kennedy, a moderate, with the conservative Brett Kavanaugh and the late Justice Ruth Bader Ginsburg, a liberal, with the conservative Amy Coney Barrett. In a 2021 decision from the Court's six conservative justices, *Brnovich v. Democratic National Committee*, the Court upheld Arizona's policy of discarding out-of-precinct ballots and prohibiting third-party groups from returning early ballots for another individual, which had been challenged under the VRA as racially discriminatory due to the disproportionate effect the policies have on persons of color.[13]

Since 2021, lawmakers in at least nineteen states have passed thirty-three laws that make it more difficult for people to vote. In Iowa and Kansas, election officials who typically assist voters with ordinary and essential tasks in the electoral process, such as returning ballots on behalf of voters with disabilities, are now deterred from doing so by the threat of criminal charges. Similarly in Texas, election officials that attempt to regulate poll watcher conduct or encourage voting by mail can now face criminal prosecution. These laws disproportionately affect voters of color. Again in Texas, the recently enacted Senate Bill 1 (SB 1) makes it more difficult for those who face language barriers to get help to cast a ballot. The law additionally bans twenty-four-hour and drive-thru voting (Waldman et al., 2021a).

The policy objectives of protecting and expanding access to voting and preventing those who are ineligible to vote from voting are not necessarily in conflict. After all, votes cast illegally dilute the political power of eligible voters. Even so, there are trade-offs between these two objectives, which is where the ideological conflict lies. On the American left, the emphasis has long been on protecting and expanding access, with an implicit acceptance that this could in theory result in a higher incidence of voter fraud. The principal adversaries are partisan (Republican) legislators and elected officials. Voter fraud is a federal crime and an exceedingly rare one at that: In a 2007 report, the Brennan Center for Justice found incident rates of fraud between 0.0003 percent and 0.0025 percent (Levitt, 2007).

On the American right, the emphasis is on preventing fraud, even if it means that otherwise eligible voters encounter more barriers to casting their ballot. The principal adversaries are fraudsters and their partisan (Democratic) enablers. To the extent that these additional barriers are encountered primarily by the right's political opponents, it could be a feature rather than a bug of their efforts to address fraud. Following the Supreme Court's decision in *Brnovich*, Texas Governor Greg Abbott, a member of the Republican Party, approved the implementation of SB 1, a law aimed at imposing restrictions on voting methods and schedules (Wilder & Hira, 2021). The *Texas Tribune* reported that the legislation targets voting initiatives

[13] *Brnovich v. Democratic National Committee*, 594 U.S. _ (2021) (Supreme Court of the United States, July 2, 2021).

employed in Harris County, a populous and diverse county with a Democratic lean (Ura, 2021). The law prohibits overnight early voting hours and drive-thru voting, which were both well-received by voters of color in the previous year's elections.

Hanging Chads and the Help America Vote Act (HAVA)

On November 20, 2000, the State of Florida officially declared George W. Bush as the winner of its twenty-five electoral votes in the race for the U.S. Presidency. The declaration came three weeks after a tumultuous election night on November 7, with reports of significant problems plaguing Florida's administration of the election. The Florida Division of Elections reported that Governor Bush had beaten Vice President Gore by 1,784 votes, which was less than one-half of a percent of the votes cast. This triggered an automatic machine recount under Florida elections law. The machine recount showed Governor Bush still winning, but by a substantially diminished margin of just 537 votes.[14] Vice President Gore sought manual recounts in several key counties, but this would take more time; the State of Florida and Governor Bush opposed the manual recount on the grounds that there was no basis in law for extending the deadline for local county canvassing boards to submit their results to the Florida secretary of state – the official responsible for election administration in Florida. The dispute was eventually decided in a 5–4 decision by the Supreme Court in *Bush v. Gore*, which ordered a stop to the manual recount underway in Florida and effectively made Governor Bush the winner of Florida's electoral votes and, as a result, the winner of the presidential election (for a timeline of this episode, see Stanford Law School, 2021). As the Supreme Court observed in *Bush v. Gore*, "This case has shown that punchcard balloting machines can produce an unfortunate number of ballots which are not punched in a clean, complete way by the voter,"[15] resulting in ballots with paper fragments still attached – so-called hanging chads. County officials grappled with deciphering voter intent amid hanging chads and the controversial "butterfly ballot" design in Palm Beach County, which caused confusion and inadvertently affected thousands of votes.

The U.S. Commission on Civil Rights (USCCR) investigated the administration of Florida's election and issued a report in June 2001 that documented widespread problems. In the years before the election, Florida had purged from its voter registration rolls tens of thousands of individuals suspected to be ineligible to vote, but the purge snared thousands of eligible voters as well. The USCCR found that Black voters were placed on purge lists "more often and more erroneously than Hispanic or White voters" (U.S. Commission on Civil Rights, 2002). A person on the so-called exclusion list had to affirmatively prove their eligibility to be relisted in voter registration rolls – a nontrivial burden. The USCCR also found that Black

[14] *Bush v. Gore*, 531 U.S. 98 (Supreme Court of the United States, December 12, 2000).

[15] See ibid., p. 104.

voters' ballots were ten times more likely to be rejected on technical grounds, such that of the 180,000 spoiled ballots cast in Florida during the November 2000 election, over half were cast by Black Americans despite comprising around 11 percent of Florida voters (U.S. Commission on Civil Rights, 2002).

ELECTIONS GO DIGITAL AND A NEW THREAT TO ELECTION INTEGRITY EMERGES

In 2002, the Federal Election Commission (FEC) approved the Voting System Standards (VSS) on a partisan 3–2 vote, with the Republican commissioners critiquing the VSS as too burdensome on state and local governments and downplaying the problems that the 2000 presidential election had exposed (Federal Election Commission, 2002). The partisan split at the FEC helped catalyze Congress to act (Weiner, 2019), and its main answer to the problems that the 2000 election exposed in US election administration was the bipartisan HAVA of 2002 (U.S. Election Assistance Commission, 2023). HAVA is the most ambitious effort yet to modernize America's election infrastructure, and has three principal aims: "establish a program to provide funds to States to replace punch card voting systems," which produced the infamous chads; "establish the Election Assistance Commission to assist in the administration of Federal elections" and provide related support; and "establish minimum election administration standards for States and units of local government with responsibility for the administration of Federal elections."

Going chadless meant embracing digital systems, using them to replace punch card voting systems. By January 2004, states were also obligated to establish computerized statewide voter registration lists to streamline and centralize the registration of voters. These lists were to be integrated with other agency records to verify the accuracy of information provided on voter registration applications. HAVA shifted the responsibility of defining, maintaining, and administering the voter registration lists from local officials to the states themselves. The legislation also mandated regular maintenance of the statewide lists to ensure ineligible voters and duplicate names were removed.

Cybersecurity and the Help America Vote Act (HAVA)

HAVA sought to facilitate the digitalization of election infrastructure presented by creating a new federal agency, the Electoral Assistance Commission (EAC), comprising four commissioners subject to Senate confirmation and a specialized staff, and creating new election-related responsibilities for the National Institute of Standards and Technology (NIST), an existing federal agency with deep experience developing digital governance standards, guidelines, and best practices. Among other responsibilities, the EAC would test and certify voting equipment as compliant with standards that the legislation tasked NIST to develop on the security, reliability, and accessibility of voting systems as chair of a Technical Guidelines Development Committee (TGDC).

HAVA set a deadline of nine months from the appointment of the four EAC commissioners for the TGDC to provide its first set of recommendations on voting system security, reliability, and accessibility. To meet this deadline, the TGDC formed three subcommittees focused on core requirements and testing, human factors and privacy, and security and transparency, hosting a series of workshops, meetings, and teleconferences in accordance with NIST's established practice of developing standards, guidelines, and best practices through open and transparent processes. The effort produced the VVSG 2005, which the TGDC submitted to the EAC in May 2005, meeting the established timeline.

The VVSG 2005 focused on usability, accessibility, and security of election systems. The goal of the usability-related guidelines was to ensure that the system was user-friendly and intuitive, allowing voters to interact with ease. Additionally, the guidelines emphasized the need for the system to incorporate error alert mechanisms, such as notifying voters about overvoting to reduce the number of improper ballots. The accessibility guidelines detailed requirements aimed at ensuring that individuals with limited vision and other disabilities, or non-English-speaking voters, would have equal access to the voting process – including accommodations to protect their privacy.

The security section of the VVSG 2005 provided explicit guidelines regarding the distribution and validation of voting system software. These requirements were put in place to guarantee that states and localities receive the accurate and verified version of the voting system software that has undergone testing and certification. By ensuring the correct software deployment, the integrity of the voting process is safeguarded, as the software used in the voting systems aligns with the approved and validated version.

Furthermore, the security section included provisions for validating the setup of the voting systems. This involved conducting inspections of the voting system software after it has been loaded onto the voting systems, verifying that it corresponds to the tested and certified software. This additional validation step played a crucial role in enhancing the security and reliability of the voting systems, reinforcing confidence in the accuracy and integrity of the election results. By emphasizing these security measures, the VVSG 2005 aimed to mitigate potential risks and protect the integrity of the voting process (U.S. Election Assistance Commission, 2005).

To help states meet HAVA's requirements, the law authorized $3.9 billion in funding for a grants program that the EAC would administer. Congress appropriated $2.8 billion for the first phase of the grants program to help states and localities purchase new voting equipment, upgrade their voter registration systems, and make other improvements to their election infrastructure. In 2006, Congress appropriated

$1.1 billion, which was used to continue the work of phase one and fund new initiatives such as the Help America Vote College Program (HAVCP). In total, the EAC has awarded $3 billion in grants to state and local governments.

Vulnerabilities in Digital Systems Identified

The passage of HAVA in 2002 and its push for digitizing voting systems led to greater interest among security researchers in the security of voting systems. For example, Bannet and coauthors demonstrated the relative ease of injecting malicious code in DRE systems and the difficulty of detecting them. Bannet et al. (2004), and Kohno et al. (2004) demonstrated major security problems in a Diebold DRE system by studying source code that an independent researcher, Bev Harris, found online.[16] In 2006, it was expected that electronic voting would be utilized by approximately 80 percent of American voters in the upcoming midterm elections, where control of the House of Representatives was on the line (Tapper & Venkataraman, 2006). In the run-up to the election, researchers identified new problems with the security and reliability of electronic voting systems. Princeton Professor Edward Felten and graduate students Ariel Feldman and Alex Halderman acquired a Diebold AccuVote-TS machine from an undisclosed source and successfully identified methods to rapidly upload malicious programs onto the machine (Feldman, Halderman, & Felten, 2006). They discovered that malicious programs could be installed by gaining access to the machine's memory card slot and power button, which were located behind a locked door on the side of the machine. The lock could be easily picked in a mere ten seconds, enabling unauthorized access. Once inside, the installation of the malicious software took less than a minute to complete.

The researchers developed software capable of modifying all records, audit logs, and counters stored by the voting machine. They ensured that even a thorough forensic examination would not detect any tampering. These programs had the ability to change vote totals or cause machine malfunctions, which could potentially impact the outcome of an election, especially if the compromised machines were located in critical polling stations. Furthermore, the researchers discovered the possibility of spreading malicious programs to multiple machines through a computer virus. This could be achieved by piggybacking on a new software download or an election information file being transferred between machines.

These studies are part of a line of research documenting security shortcomings in election infrastructure, with a primary focus on voting systems – the machines used to record and potentially document and count votes – and how an attacker could

[16] Harris wrote a book documenting her discovery and examination of the source code, which Diebold had previously refused to make public (Harris, 2004). A Government Accountability Office (GAO) report from September 2005 reviews these and other studies documenting security problems in digital voting systems (Government Accountability Office, 2005).

subvert those systems to affect election outcomes or undermine the public's perception of the integrity of an election. For example, a study from the Brennan Center for Justice on the security of voting systems documented numerous attack scenarios on voting systems that resulted in changed votes (Lawrence, 2006). The State of Ohio's EVEREST study examined the usability, stability, and security of voting systems and found that every voting system used in Ohio had "critical security failures that render their technical controls insufficient to guarantee a trustworthy election" (McDaniel et al., 2007, p. 3). Its threat model focused on how a threat actor could exploit cyber vulnerabilities to influence election outcomes by producing incorrect vote counts or blocking eligible voters, or undermine integrity by delaying the results or violating the secrecy of the ballot (McDaniel et al., 2007, pp. 14–15). California's "Top-to-Bottom Review" in 2007 of voting systems used in California yielded similar results (Bowen, 2007) and focused on how an attacker might change election outcomes (Bishop, n.d., p. 1);[17] it also "made no assumptions about constraints on the attackers" and did not consider the likelihood of any of its attacks (Bishop, n.d., p. 2). Florida and Connecticut pursued studies of their own, with a comparable threat model and similar results about the poor cybersecurity of voting systems. In 2015, Norden and Famighetti used interviews and data from the Verified Voting Foundation to document a range of vulnerabilities across election infrastructure (Norden & Famighetti, 2014). They too emphasized the risks of altered election outcomes and soured confidence, but in ranking the severity of threats, they also incorporated such factors as feasibility and cost. Finally, in the run-up to the 2016 elections, several other researchers and research groups issued recommendations about shoring up election systems considering the growing cybersecurity threat (National Institutes of Science and Technology, 2016).

A common thread running through many of these studies is a narrow focus on how an adversary might exploit cyber vulnerabilities to affect election outcomes and undermine confidence, in isolation from other means to achieve the same outcomes. As we have seen, however, hackers have exploited vulnerabilities in electoral infrastructure for centuries to affect election outcomes and challenge confidence in the integrity of elections: Hostile, black hat measures such as poll taxes and grandfather clauses were intended to affect election outcomes in favor of a dominant White majority, while white hat actions by civil rights leaders such as John Lewis exposed legitimacy shortcomings in electoral infrastructure that led to legislative reforms. The researchers behind the studies invested time and energy to acquire voting systems or their source code, identify vulnerabilities, and develop techniques to exploit them. A malicious hacker would have to as well, and if their goal is to subvert democracy, they might reasonably conclude that there are proven and

[17] The goal of the study was "to identify and document vulnerabilities, if any, to tampering or error that could cause incorrect recording, tabulation, tallying or reporting of votes or that could alter critical election data such as election definition or system audit data."

potentially more cost-effective ways to do so than carrying out cyberattacks against voting machines: Why go to the trouble, risk, and expense of hacking a voting machine when partisan gerrymandering or selective shuttering of polling places could yield a comparable result?

This reasoning could explain why the initiative that arguably most reflected the cyber policy zeitgeist in Washington, DC for much of the period between the enactment of HAVA and the 2016 presidential election did not mention voting system security at all. The Center for Strategic and International Studies convened a commission of experts chaired by the bipartisan pair of Representatives Jim Langevin (D-RI) and Mike McCaul (R-TX) in advance of the 2008 presidential elections to provide analysis and recommendations to the new presidential administration. The commission's report emphasized "the militaries and intelligence services of other nations" as the main cyber adversaries, and highlighted American economic competitiveness and US critical infrastructure – "electricity, communications, and financial services" as being most at risk from cyberattacks (Center for Strategic and International Studies, 2008). At the time, however, the US government did not consider election infrastructure to be part of critical infrastructure – that infrastructure's designation as critical by the Department of Homeland Security (DHS) would have to wait until shortly after the 2016 election (U.S. Election Assistance Commission, 2022).

THE 2016 PRESIDENTIAL ELECTION AND ITS AFTERMATH

Russia hacked the 2016 election at Vladimir Putin's direction to damage Hillary Clinton and undermine Americans' confidence in the legitimacy of the electoral process. How much the Russians contributed to Clinton's loss to Donald Trump and the precipitous drop in the aftermath of the campaign in Americans' trust in electoral infrastructure is a matter of ongoing debate; the fact of those outcomes, however, is not.

Understandably, the events of 2016 provoked unprecedented interest in the resiliency of electoral infrastructure against digital risks – not only cyberattacks on voting systems or other infrastructure but also the use of social media platforms to spread falsehoods and lies. It also injected partisan discord into what had previously been a largely technocratic and, to some election security researchers, an often quixotic quest to shore up election infrastructure against digital hackers – the salience of the research would resonate in even-numbered years in the run-up to an election, and then taper off once the election passed. As we have seen, the impetus for HAVA and its drive toward digitizing electoral infrastructure stems from the 2000 presidential election, where a contest for the president was lost due to voting system irregularities amid bitter partisan debate over the cause and consequences of those irregularities. HAVA was supposed to fix those irregularities, but its push for digitizing elections, warned security researchers, introduced new risks: voting systems that were vulnerable to hacking. The implied threat actor in this research on the machines that record and tabulate votes was not a foreign government, but a domestic political partisan trying to boost their preferred candidate. The cyber policy community, meanwhile, was focused primarily on foreign military and intelligence services as the primary threat actor and critical infrastructure – which didn't include electoral infrastructure at the time – and American economic competitiveness as the threat actors' main targets. Therefore, 2016 caught both the technocratic cyber research and cyber policy communities off guard: As it happened, it was a foreign government that sought to subvert electoral infrastructure through digital means. And the infrastructure it targeted was not voting systems, but other components of electoral infrastructure – notably, voter registration databases and partisan campaign infrastructure.

What Happened in 2016

The story of the 2016 election and its brush with cyberattacks is documented in the Senate Select Committee on Intelligence's bipartisan opus, "Russian Active Measures Campaigns and Interference in the 2016 U.S. Election" (Senate Select Committee on Intelligence, 2020). The condensed depiction presented here is intended to further contextualize efforts to shore up electoral infrastructure in the aftermath of 2016.

The digital elements of the Russian campaign involved cyberattacks aimed at compromising the confidentiality, integrity, or availability of targeted systems and information operations aimed at denigrating Hillary Clinton, exacerbating political polarization, and undermining the public's confidence in the integrity of democratic procedures. In June 2016, a hacker posted online a trove of nonpublic documents from the Democratic National Committee (DNC). One month later, a hacker calling themselves Guccifer 2.0 claimed to have shared 20,000 nonpublic DNC emails with WikiLeaks, the notorious publisher of stolen information (Thielman, 2016). Cybersecurity researchers and the US government have concluded that the Russian government was behind these operations, though Moscow denies the allegations. The emails, consisting of 19,252 messages and 8,034 attachments, were leaked on October 7 by WikiLeaks and a pop-up sister site called DCLeaks (Krawchenko et al., 2016). The leaked correspondence revealed a bias within the DNC toward Hillary Rodham Clinton over her primary rival, Bernie Sanders, despite the DNC's earlier claims of neutrality, and contained other embarrassing vignettes about the inner workings of the DNC. The timing of the leaks was noteworthy, happening within hours of video footage airing Clinton's rival Donald J. Trump boasting about sexually assaulting various women. Later that day, a statement from Federal Bureau of Investigation (FBI) Director James Comey, DHS Secretary Jeh Johnson, and Director of National Intelligence (DNI) James Clapper warned that the US government was "confident that the Russian

Government directed the recent compromises of e-mails from U.S. persons and institutions, including from U.S. political organizations" (Department of Homeland Security & Director of National Intelligence, 2016).

Russian government hackers also systematically scanned election-related state infrastructure in likely all fifty states and breached the systems of at least two of them.[18] The hackers were able to access voter registration data, and while there is no evidence that the hackers altered data, their access would have allowed them to do so. The hackers also researched voting systems and other aspects of electoral infrastructure, though there is no evidence that any such systems were compromised in 2016.

In August 2016, DHS Secretary Johnson hosted a conference call with state election officials to "to discuss the cybersecurity of the election infrastructure" (Department of Homeland Security, 2016). He told the officials that while "DHS is not aware of any specific or credible cybersecurity threats relating to the upcoming general election systems," he offered DHS assistance in helping state officials manage risks to voting systems in each state's jurisdiction. He also mentioned the possibility of designating electoral infrastructure as critical infrastructure, which would enable DHS to prioritize the sector for support and establish protected channels for information exchange.

The reaction to such a designation from officials who spoke out during the meeting, Secretary Johnson said later, "ranged from neutral to negative," with those expressing negative views asserting that administering elections was their responsibility, not the federal government's (Department of Homeland Security, 2016; Johnson, 2017). Later in August, the FBI issued an alert about malicious activity targeting election-related state infrastructure, and in September, Congressional leaders issued a bipartisan plea to state officials to accept DHS support. Forty-nine states requested technical assistance, which DHS delivered primarily in the form of remote scans of internet-facing election-related state infrastructure (Government Accountability Office, 2020).

In December 2016, Brian Kemp, then-secretary of state for the State of Georgia, sent letters to the DHS and President-elect Trump alleging that the DHS had scanned Georgia's voter registration systems as a precursor to attacking them and asking Trump to investigate the matter upon taking office (Fulghum, 2017). Secretary Johnson's response days later explained that there was no scan, and that the traffic described in Kemp's letter was from a DHS contractor at the Federal Law Enforcement Training Center (FLETC) conducting research on "whether incoming FLETC contractors and new employees had a certain type of professional license – a service that, as I understand it, your website provides to the general public" (Fulghum, 2017). He further explained that "the technical information we have corroborated [this explanation], and indicates normal Microsoft Internet

[18] Illinois has admitted to being one of them, and Arizona is believed to be the other.

Explorer interaction by the contractor's computer with your website" (Fulghum, 2017). DHS Congressman Jason Chaffetz, Chairman of the House Committee on Oversight and Reform, followed with a letter to DHS complaining that Secretary Johnson's written response and subsequent briefings from DHS staff "did not provide adequate information to verify or validate" this explanation; he requested that relevant records be preserved and that the DHS inspector general undertake an investigation. In June 2017, the inspector general notified Congress that Kemp's allegations were "unsubstantiated" and that "the activity Georgia noted on its computer networks was the result of normal and automatic computer message exchanges generated by the Microsoft applications involved" (Department of Homeland Security, 2017).

The bitterness of the 2016 election, with the incumbent administration warning that Russia had interfered in the election in support of the opposition's candidate, Donald J. Trump, and the opposition's distrust of the incumbent administration's motives as well as baseless claims throughout the election by Trump that the election was "rigged" against him, set the stage for post-2016 efforts to address cyber threats to electoral infrastructure.

Measures Taken between 2017 and 2020

The period between 2017 and 2020 – with the Congressional midterm elections in 2018 and the 2020 presidential contest – were an especially sensitive moment for American democracy, especially debates around electoral integrity and the resilience of election-related infrastructure. The 2016 election highlighted that cynical partisans were not the only potential threat to electoral integrity: Foreign governments also had reason to intervene. That the foreign government's preferred candidate, Donald J. Trump, won the presidential contest raised the uncomfortable question of the extent to which Russia's efforts contributed to it. His own linkages to Russia – including his public invitation in the summer of 2016 for Russia to find and presumably release deleted emails from Hillary Clinton's private email server – and the Department of Justice (DOJ) inquiry into those linkages further sharpened the potential ideological stakes of whether and how to make election infrastructure more resilient against digital threats. In particular, the Trump administration, facing a series of threats to its legitimacy built in part on the vulnerability of electoral infrastructure to digital threats, could have denied or played down the existence of the vulnerability in policy. The fact that it didn't is fairly remarkable.

Ten weeks would elapse between election day on November 7, 2016 and inauguration on January 20, 2017. On December 28, 2016, President Obama signed an Executive Order (EO) 13757, "Taking Additional Steps to Address the National Emergency with Respect to Significant Malicious Cyber-Enabled Activities," to authorize economic sanctions against actors involved in "tampering with, altering, or causing a misappropriation of information with the purpose or effect of interfering with or undermining election processes or institutions" and sanctioned Russian organizations and individuals in connection with the 2016 election interference. It also expelled Russian intelligence officers operating under diplomatic cover from the United States and forced the closure of two Russian diplomatic facilities. In January 2017, Secretary Johnson designated electoral infrastructure as critical infrastructure. In addition to enabling the DHS to forge a deeper partnership with the sector on security issues, the designation also signaled to international partners and adversaries the sensitivity of electoral infrastructure from a national security perspective. For example, the United States had been engaged in diplomatic deliberations over norms of behavior in cyberspace during peacetime and was advocating inter alia for a norm that states do not interfere with critical infrastructure during peacetime.

When Trump took the oath of office on January 20, 2017, he inherited a policy trajectory from the Obama administration of trying to hold Russia accountable for its actions while deterring Russia or any other country from running a similar play as Russia in future elections. He rejected the assessment that Russia had intervened in the election to support him, however, and instead focused his attention on alleged voter fraud. The threat actor he had in mind was not a foreign government such as Russia or even a cyberthreat actor, but a person who is ineligible to vote that nevertheless casts a vote.[19] Such instances are exceedingly rare – in the 2016 election, for example, the Associated Press identified "fewer than 475 – a number that would have made no difference in the 2020 presidential election (Cassidy, 2021). In May 2017, however, he signed an EO to launch a "Presidential Advisory Commission on Election Integrity" charged with identifying and rooting out fraudulent or improper voting and voting registration (Trump White House Archives, 2017). Not surprisingly, the commission had uncovered no evidence of widespread voter fraud when it disbanded in January 2018.

Inside the bureaucracy of the Trump administration, however, agencies such as the DHS and the FBI were positioning themselves as allies of state election officials in those officials' efforts to prepare for the 2018 midterm elections and later the 2020 presidential elections. The DHS and the FBI hosted briefings with state election officials on threats to election integrity and how to build resilience against them (Department of Homeland Security, 2018), and in March 2018, the DHS announced the launch of the Elections Infrastructure Information Sharing and Analysis Center (EI-ISAC) to coordinate the sharing and exchange of cyber threat information among election officials and organizations (Center for Internet

[19] The public record about the commission, including statements from President Trump and the commission's leadership, Vice President Mike Pence and Kansas politician Kris Kobach, is devoid of any mention of cyber threats.

Security, n.d.). In addition, the designation of electoral infrastructure as critical infrastructure enabled DHS to convene a Government Coordinating Council (GCC) and a Sector Coordinating Council (SCC) to facilitate information sharing among public and nongovernmental actors engaged in election administration. In September 2018, President Trump signed EO 13848, "Imposing Certain Sanctions in the Event of Foreign Interference in a United States Election" (Trump, 2018). The EO directs the DNI to prepare a report within forty-five days of an election on whether foreign governments interfered with it; the EO also directs that DOJ and DHS prepare a report within forty-five days of the DNI's report on whether the foreign interference affected the election outcomes. The order also authorized sanctions and other measures against actors found to have interfered with a US election.

Congress, meanwhile, had debated multiple major legislative proposals[20] and three passed both houses: the consolidated appropriations acts of 2018[21] (Royce, 2018) and 2020 (U.S. Government Publishing Office, 2019) appropriated $380 million and $425 million, respectively, to the EAC to give to states to improve election technology and security, and the Coronavirus Aid, Relief, and Economic Security Act (CARES Act) included $400 million in HAVA emergency funds for the 2020 federal election cycle. The 2018 funding came too late to contribute much to the 2018 Congressional midterms, but by September 2020, states had spent nearly 94 percent of the 2018 funding, with thirty-five states spending their allocation completely and another thirteen spending above 90 percent of theirs (U.S. Election Assistance Commission, 2021). The CARES Act funding could only be used in direct connection with helping states manage elections in the context of a pandemic, though some states used the funding to purchase new enterprise IT in support of remote work, which could have some modest cybersecurity benefit as newer IT tends to be easier to secure than older IT (U.S. Election Assistance Commission, n.d.).

In October, the heads of the DHS, the DOJ, the FBI, and the Office of the DNI jointly warned of "ongoing campaigns by Russia, China and other foreign actors, including Iran," to influence elections as well as attempted intrusions into state election-related infrastructure, though in the latter instance, the heads explained, "[i]ncreased intelligence and information sharing among federal, state and local partners has improved our awareness of ongoing and persistent threats to election infrastructure" and there was no evidence of a successful breach (Office of the Director of National Intelligence, n.d.).

[20] Examples include the Secure Elections Act of 2017, the Election Security Act of 2018, the Protecting American Voting Rights Act of 2019, the Secure Elections Act of 2020, and the John Lewis Voting Rights Advancement Act of 2020.

[21] Relatedly, the legislation also appropriated $300 million to the FBI for combating Russian cyber operations against the United States.

A joint statement on November 5 from the same group took on a reassuring tone and described the government's efforts to guard against digital threats to election infrastructure as "unprecedented":

> Our agencies have been making preparations for nearly two years in advance of these elections and are closely engaged with officials on the ground to help them ensure the voting process is secure. Americans can rest assured that we will continue to stay focused on this mission long after polls have closed. (Office of the Director of National Intelligence, 2018)

The agency heads warned voters to be vigilant, especially in the face of foreign influence campaigns designed to shape "public sentiment and voter perceptions … by spreading false information about political processes and candidates, lying about their own interference activities, disseminating propaganda on social media, and through other tactics." Voters should seek ground truth about elections and election processes by contacting their local election organizations and be cautious consumers of information.

After the election, news reports surfaced that the U.S. Cyber Command had carried out cyberattacks against the Russia-based Internet Research Agency (IRA) to shut it down during the election. The IRA was a notorious "troll farm" engaged in propaganda operations, often using social media. The IRA, its leader Yvgeniy Prigozhin, and others connected with it had previously been indicted by the DOJ on criminal charges stemming from the IRA's interference in the 2016 election,[22] and in September 2018 the DOJ indicted a Russian accused of overseeing Project Lakhta, the Russian codename for a propaganda operation targeting the United States and other countries, carried out in part through the IRA. The goal of the attack, according to this reporting, was to keep the IRA out of commission from election day until election results were certified (Barnes, 2019). The attack was reportedly part of a broader campaign by US military and intelligence organizations to interfere with the ability of foreign actors, especially Russia, to interfere in the midterm elections (Barnes, 2018).

The DNI submitted the Intelligence Community (IC)'s required report under EO 13848 on foreign interference in the 2018 midterm elections to the President on December 21. DNI Coats' public statement about the classified report said that "the Intelligence Community does not have intelligence reporting that indicates any compromise of our nation's election infrastructure that would have prevented voting, changed vote counts, or disrupted the ability to tally votes." In their public comments about the required follow-on report, which was classified, the Attorney General and DHS Secretary said there was "no evidence to date that any identified activities of a foreign government or foreign agent had a material impact on the

[22] *Indictment, United States v. Internet Research Agency et al.*, 1:18-CR-32 (DLF) (D.D.C. Feb. 16, 2018).

integrity or security of election infrastructure or political/campaign infrastructure used in the 2018 midterm elections" (U.S. Department of Justice, 2019).

These efforts to enhance the resilience of electoral infrastructure and disrupt adversaries' operations continued into the 2020 election cycle, with similar results, at least as far as foreign interference goes. The DNI submitted a classified report to the president in January 2021 pursuant to EO 13848; in March, the Biden administration released a declassified version. According to that report, the USIC found "no indications that any foreign actor attempted to alter any technical aspect of the voting process in the 2020 US elections, including voter registration, casting ballots, vote tabulation, or reporting results." It also "identified some successful compromises of state and local government networks prior to Election Day – as well as a higher volume of unsuccessful attempts – that we assess were not directed at altering election processes" (Director of National Intelligence, 2021). The follow-on report from the DOJ and DHS echoed the DNI, reporting that there was "no evidence that any foreign government-affiliated actor prevented voting, changed votes, or disrupted the ability to tally votes or to transmit election results in a timely manner; altered any technical aspect of the voting process; or otherwise compromised the integrity of voter registration information of any ballots cast during 2020 federal elections" (U.S. Department of Justice, 2021, p. 2) Both reports, however, highlighted the growing range of foreign actors engaged in digitally enabled influence operations against the United States.

President Trump lost his reelection bid to former Vice President Joseph Biden in 2020. He claimed without evidence, however, that the election was stolen from him because of widespread voter fraud. He denigrated the results of the election as illegitimate and sought ways to stay in power, despite the election's outcome. In contrast, the DHS issued a joint statement from the elections infrastructure GCC and SCC nine days after the election describing it as the "most secure in American history" and said "[t]here is no evidence that any voting system deleted or lost votes, changed votes, or was in any way compromised" (Cybersecurity & Infrastructure Security Agency, 2020).

CONCLUSION

Though cybersecurity of elections is a recent concern, hacking elections is not. The relatively limited constitutional discipline on elections and the fact that the constitution distributes responsibility for administering elections to state and local governments means that the attack surface of America's election infrastructure for would-be hackers is large. Technology has added a new dimension to this attack surface in the form of digital technologies that facilitate tasks ranging from voter registration to vote casting and vote counting. Digital technologies are prevalent throughout electoral infrastructure – which technologists were quick to identify risks to voting systems in the years following enactment of HAVA in 2002 – but the mainstream cybersecurity policy community did not consider these risks a priority on par with the risks to critical infrastructure (which at the time didn't include state election-related infrastructure) and economic competitiveness posed by foreign military and intelligence services.

The digitalization of election infrastructure has lowered one of the barriers to entry for threat actors seeking to disrupt democratic processes: Before then, a hacker usually needed partisan allies to carry out an attack. Gerrymandering, poll taxes, even organized violence at polling places all require partisan allies. Hacks like these are, in a sense, inside jobs that rely on willing partners and a complacent public. The digitalization of electoral infrastructure makes it possible for outside actors to potentially hack elections: A lone wolf, criminal group, or foreign government can potentially interfere with elections on their own.

The 2016 presidential election pulled election security into the mainstream of cyber policy, with the DHS, FBI, and other federal agencies investing significant effort in building partnerships with state election officials and taking direct action against suspected threat actors with criminal indictments and economic sanctions. The partnership-building efforts with state officials after the designation in January 2017 of election systems as critical infrastructure created new information sharing channels and trust relationships that facilitated the ability of the federal government to provide security and other assistance. That these efforts in the Trump administration thrived despite President Trump's open hostility toward the notion that Russia interfered in the 2016 election to support his candidacy speaks to the ability of the agencies and their partners in state and local government to pursue their efforts as a technocratic versus political or partisan initiative. President Trump's benign neglect of his administration's efforts to protect election infrastructure from digital threats ended when he fired Chris Krebs, head of the Cybersecurity and Infrastructure Security Agency (CISA), which leads federal government cybersecurity initiatives for critical infrastructure (including election infrastructure), for claiming that the 2020 election had been the most secure in the history of the country. Trump did not quibble with claims about the cybersecurity of the election against foreign interference; his cavil with Krebs and with others who touted the cybersecurity of the election was that it conflicted with his claim that the election was stolen by the Democrats.

The hack of the DNC and breach of election-related infrastructure by Russian government-directed actors in 2016 elevated concerns regarding the cybersecurity of election infrastructure. In the immediate aftermath of the foreign interference in the 2016 election, then President Obama signed an EO authorizing economic sanctions against actors seeking to interfere with or undermine electoral processes or institutions. Shortly thereafter the DHS designated electoral infrastructure as critical infrastructure, notably signaling to allies and adversaries alike the acute sensitivity and importance of election infrastructure to national security.

Despite partisan differences, noteworthy strides have been made to counter continued attempts at undermining US elections and election infrastructure. The passage of major legislative proposals such as the Consolidated Appropriations Acts of 2018 and 2020, as well as the CARES Act, have directed funds toward further improving election technology and security.

Following the 2016 election, a noticeable shift was made toward paper ballots to increase election security. In the 2020 election, it is estimated that 93 percent, up from 82 percent in 2016, of all votes cast had a paper record. This uptick resulted from states and local jurisdictions replacing outdated and vulnerable paperless voting machines (i.e., DRE machines). Paper-based systems are better for security because they create a paper record that can be reviewed by election officials in postelection audits. Further measures such as postelection audits – a process that enables states to verify the accuracy of voting equipment and counting machines – act as additional defenses against election interference. As of 2023, forty-five states have mandated some form of postelection audit, up from thirty-five in 2016 (U.S. Election Assistance Commission, 2023).

These measures have paid off. Reports on the 2020 elections from the DOJ, DHS, and DNI noted that while an increasing number of foreign actors had engaged in influence operations against the United States, there was no evidence that these foreign actors were able to compromise the integrity of election infrastructure during the 2020 federal elections. The same is true for domestic actors: There is no evidence of successful election-related hacking in 2020 by partisans or other politically motivated actors.

As the saying goes, however, past performance does not guarantee future results: Some states still lack some form of paper trail for ballots cast and some form of postelection audit. All states should eliminate paperless voting machines and implement postelection audits. In addition, as the epidemic of ransomware attacks against municipalities and other targets shows, vulnerabilities remain. Owners and operators of election infrastructure, from local governments to candidate campaign operations, must make cybersecurity a core priority for risk management. This prioritization must come from the top: Senior leaders involved in election administration must make cybersecurity a priority, ensure that resources are devoted to it, and hold themselves and their teams accountable for managing cyber risks. Fortunately, owners and operators have resources they can turn to for guidance and support. For example, the CISA maintains a "Cybersecurity Toolkit and Resources to Protect Elections" website with guidance on best practices and free or reduced-price cybersecurity tools from leading vendors (Cybersecurity & Infrastructure Security Agency, 2024).

History teaches us further that cyber risks to election integrity, though real, cannot (perhaps yet) shine a candle to the myriad other ways that intrepid hackers have sought to subvert democracy. An all-hazards approach to election integrity is warranted.

REFERENCES

Alexander, A., & Fields, G. (2022, December 30). *Black support for GOP ticked up in this year's midterms*. AP News. https://apnews.com/article/2022-midterm-elections-brian-p-kemp-stacey-abrams-politics-us-democratic-party-53d31c9c8a87231d00784b6effa8d59e

Associated Press. (n.d.). *Counting the vote*. Associated Press. https://ap.org/about/our-role-in-elections/counting-the-vote

Bannet, J., Price, D., Rudys, A., & Singer, J. (2004, February). Hack-a-vote: Security issues with electronic voting systems. *IEEE Security and Privacy Magazine*, 2, 32–37.

Barnes, J. E. (2018, October 23). U.S. begins first cyberoperation against Russia aimed at protecting elections. *The New York Times*. https://nytimes.com/2018/10/23/us/politics/russian-hacking-usa-cyber-command.html

(2019, February 26). Cyber command operation took down Russian troll farm for midterm elections. *The New York Times*. https://nytimes.com/2019/02/26/us/politics/us-cyber-command-russia.html?searchResultPosition = 1

Baum, S., Cea, B., & Cohen, A. (2021, June 30). *The 26th amendment turns 50 amid renewed voter suppression*. Brennan Center. https://brennancenter.org/our-work/analysis-opinion/26th-amendment-turns-50-amid-renewed-voter-suppression

Bishop, M. (n.d.). *Overview of red team reports*. Voting Systems. https://votingsystems.cdn.sos.ca.gov/oversight/ttbr/red-overview.pdf

Bowen, D. (2007, August 3). *Top-to-bottom review*. California Secretary of State. https://sos.ca.gov/elections/ovsta/frequently-requested-information/top-bottom-review

Cassidy, C. A. (2021, December 14). *Far too little vote fraud to tip election to Trump, AP finds*. Associated Press. https://apnews.com/article/voter-fraud-election-2020-joe-biden-donald-trump-7fcb6f134e528fee8237c7601db3328f

Center for Internet Security. (n.d.). *Elections Infrastructure Information Sharing & Analysis Center*. Center for Internet Security. https://cisecurity.org/ei-isac

Center for Strategic and International Studies. (2008, December 8). *Commission on cybersecurity for the 44th presidency*. Center for Strategic and International Security. https://csis.org/programs/strategic-technologies-program/archives/cybersecurity-and-governance/other-projects-2

Cybersecurity & Infrastructure Security Agency. (2020). *Joint statement from Elections Infrastructure Government Coordinating Council & the Election Infrastructure Sector Coordinating Executive Committees*. Cybersecurity & Infrastructure Security Agency. https://cisa.gov/news-events/news/joint-statement-elections-infrastructure-government-coordinating-council-election

(2024). *Cybersecurity toolkit and Resources to protect elections*. Cybersecurity & Infrastructure Security Agency. https://cisa.gov/cybersecurity-toolkit-and-resources-protect-elections

Department of Homeland Security. (2016, August 15). *Readout of Secretary Johnson's call with state election officials on cybersecurity*. Department of Homeland Security. https://dhs.gov/news/2016/08/15/readout-secretary-johnsons-call-state-election-officials-cybersecurity

(2017, July 5). *Allegations of unauthorized scans of Georgia voting systems are unsubstantiated*. Office of Inspector General. https://oig.dhs.gov/sites/default/files/assets/pr/2017/oigpr-070517-allegations-unauthorized-scans-georgia-voting-systems-unsubstantiated_1.pdf

(2018, August 24). *DHS, FBI hold joint briefing for election officials with Facebook and Microsoft*. Department of Homeland Security. https://dhs.gov/news/2018/08/24/dhs-fbi-hold-joint-briefing-election-officials-facebook-and-microsoft

Department of Homeland Security & Director of National Intelligence. (2016, October 7). *Joint statement from the Department of Homeland Security and Office of the Director of National Intelligence on Election Security*. Department of Homeland Security. https://dhs.gov/news/2016/10/07/joint-statement-department-homeland-security-and-office-director-national#:~:text=The%20U.S.%20Intelligence%20Community%20 (USIC,including%20from%20US%20political%20organizations

Director of National Intelligence. (2021). *Foreign threats to the 2020 US federal elections*. Director of National Intelligence. https://dni.gov/files/ODNI/documents/assessments/ICA-declass-16MAR21.pdf

Federal Election Commission. (2002, May 15). *FEC approves new voting systems standards*. Federal Election Commission. https://fec.gov/updates/fec-approves-new-voting-systems-standards/

Feldman, A. J., Halderman, A., & Felten, E. W. (2006, September 13). *Security analysis of the Diebold AccuVote-TS voting machine*. Center for Information Technology Policy. https://citp.princeton.edu/our-work/voting/

Fulghum, C. (2017, February 28). *Correspondence between DHS and U.S. Representative Jason Chaffetz*. Department of Homeland Security. https://dhs.gov/sites/default/files/publications/Correspondence%20between%20DHS%20and%20U.S.%20Representa tive%20Jason%20Chaffetz%20%28R-UT%29.pdf

Government Accountability Office. (2005). *Federal efforts to improve security and reliability of electronic voting systems are under way, but key activities need to be completed*. GAO-05-956.

(2020, February). *DHS Plans Are Urgently Needed to Address Identified Challenges before the 2020 Elections*. U.S. Government Accountability Office. https://gao.gov/assets/710/706312.pdf

Harris, B. (2004). *Black Box Voting: Ballot Tampering in the 21st Century*. Talion Publishing.

Isikoff, M. (2013, June 7). *Chinese hacked Obama, McCain campaigns, took internal documents, officials say*. NBC News. https://nbcnews.com/id/wbna52133016#:~:text=on%20NBCNews.com.-,The%20U.S.%20secretly%20traced%20a%20massive%20cyberespionage%20operation%20against%20the,intelligence%20officials%20tell%20NBC%20News.

Johnson, J. C. (2017, June 21). *Statement of Jeh Charles Johnson before the House Permanent Select Committee on Intelligence*. Federation of American Scientists. https://irp.fas.org/congress/2017_hr/062117-johnson.pdf

Klarman, M. J. (2016). *The framers' coup: The making of the United States Constitution*. Oxford University Press.

Klein, C. (2020, July 18). *How Selma's "Bloody Sunday" became a turning point in the Civil Rights Movement*. History.com. https://history.com/news/selma-bloody-sunday-attack-civil-rights-movement

Kohno, T., Stubblefield, A., Rubin, A. D., & Wallach, D. S. (2004). Analysis of an electronic voting system. *Proceedings of the IEEE Symposium on Security and Privacy*. IEEE Explore.

Krawchenko, K., Judd, D., Cordes, N., Goldman, J., Flores, R., Shabad, R., et al. (2016, November 3). *The John Podesta emails released by WikiLeaks*. CBS News. https://cbsnews.com/news/the-john-podesta-emails-released-by-wikileaks/

Lawrence, N. (2006). *The machinery of democracy: Voting system security, accessibility, usability, and cost*. The Brennan Center for Justice. https://brennancenter.org/sites/default/files/press-releases/The%20Machinery%20of%20Democracy.pdf

Lebetter Jr., C. R. (1995). Arkansas amendment for voter registration without poll tax payment. *The Arkansas Historical Quarterly*, 54(2), 134–162.

Levitt, J. (2007, November 9). *The truth about voter fraud*. The Brennan Center for Justice. https://brennancenter.org/our-work/research-reports/truth-about-voter-fraud

McDaniel, P., et al. (2007, December 7). *Everest: Evaluation and validation of election-related equipment, standards and testing*. U.S. Election Assistance Commission. https://eac.gov/sites/default/files/eac_assets/1/28/EVEREST.pdf

McFadden, C., Arkin, W. M., & Monahan, K. (2018, February 7). *Russians penetrated U.S. voter systems, top U.S. official says*. NBC News. https://nbcnews.com/politics/elections/russians-penetrated-u-s-voter-systems-says-top-u-s-n845721

Nakashima, E., & Harris, S. (2018, July 13). How the Russians hacked the DNC and passed its emails to WikiLeaks. *The Washington Post*. https://washingtonpost.com/world/national-security/how-the-russians-hacked-the-dnc-and-passed-its-emails-to-wikileaks/2018/07/13/af19a828-86c3-11e8-8553-a3ce89036c78_story.html

National Archives. (2022, February 8). *Voting Rights Act (1965)*. National Archives. https://archives.gov/milestone-documents/voting-rights-act#:~:text=The%20Voting%20Rights%20Act%20had,African%20Americans%20registered%20to%20vote

National Conference of State Legislatures. (2022, November 1). *Election administration at state and local levels*. National Conference of State Legislatures. https://ncsl.org/elections-and-campaigns/election-administration-at-state-and-local-levels

National Institutes of Science and Technology. (2016, September). *Protecting the 2016 elections from cyber and voting machine attacks*. National Institutes of Science and Technology. https://nist.gov/speech-testimony/protecting-2016-elections-cyber-and-voting-machine-attacks

Norden, L., & Famighetti, C. (2014). *America's voting machines at risk*. The Brennan Center for Justice.

Office of the Director of National Intelligence. (2018). *Joint statement on election day preparations*. Office of the Director of National Intelligence. https://dni.gov/index.php/newsroom/press-releases/press-releases-2018/item/1921-joint-statement-on-election-day-preparations

(n.d.). *Combating foreign influence in U.S. elections*. Office of the Director of National Intelligence. https://dni.gov/index.php/newsroom/press-releases/item/1915-joint-statement-from-the-odni-doj-fbi-and-dhs-combating-foreign-influence-in-u-s-elections

Royce, E. R. (2018, March 23). *H.R.1625 – Consolidated Appropriations Act, 2018*. Congress.gov. https://congress.gov/bill/115th-congress/house-bill/1625/text

Senate Select Committee on Intelligence. (2020, November 10). *Russian active measures campaigns and interference in the 2016 U.S. elections*. Senate Select Intelligence Committee. https://intelligence.senate.gov/publications/report-select-committee-intelligence-united-states-senate-russian-active-measures

Stanford Law School. (2021, October 15). *Timeline of Florida Recount, Florida litigation, and Bush v. Gore*. Stanford Law Library. https://guides.law.stanford.edu/c.php?g=991108&p=7170216

Tapper, J., & Venkataraman, N. (2006, November 2). *Hackable democracy?* ABC News. https://abcnews.go.com/Politics/Vote2006/story?id=2623854&page=1

The Brennan Center Task Force on Voting System Security. (2006). *The machinery of democracy: Protecting elections in an electronic world*. The Brennan Center for Justice, NYU School of Law. https://brennancenter.org/sites/default/files/publications/Machinery%20of%20Democracy.pdf

Thielman, S. (2016, July 26). DNC email leak: Russian hackers Cozy Bear and Fancy Bear behind breach. *The Guardian*. https://theguardian.com/technology/2016/jul/26/dnc-email-leak-russian-hack-guccifer-2

Trump, D. J. (2018, September 12). *Executive Order 13848 – Imposing certain sanctions in the event of foreign interference in a United States election*. Authenticated U.S. Government Information. https://govinfo.gov/content/pkg/DCPD-201800593/pdf/DCPD-201800593.pdf

Trump White House Archives. (2017, July 13). *Presidential advisory commission on election integrity*. Trump White House Archives. https://trumpwhitehouse.archives.gov/articles/presidential-advisory-commission-election-integrity/#:~:text=On%20May%2011%2C%202017%2C%20President,serves%20as%20the%20vice%20chair.

U.S. Commission on Civil Rights. (2002, September). *Ten-year check-up: Have federal agencies responded to Civil Rights recommendations*. U.S. Commission on Civil Rights. https://usccr.gov/files/pubs/archives/10yr02/vol1/vol1.pdf

U.S. Department of Commerce. (1969, December 31). *Poverty in the United States: 1959 to 1968*. Census.gov. https://census.gov/library/publications/1969/demographics/p60-68.pdf

U.S. Department of Justice. (2019, February 5). *Acting Attorney General and Secretary of Homeland Security Submit Joint Report on Impact of Foreign Interference on Election and Political/Campaign Infrastructure in 2018 Elections*. U.S. Department of Justice. https://justice.gov/opa/pr/acting-attorney-general-and-secretary-homeland-security-submit-joint-report-impact-foreign

(2021). Joint report of the Department of Justice and the Department of Homeland Security on Foreign Interference Targeting Election Infrastructure or Political Organization, Campaign, or Candidate Infrastructure Related to the 2020 US Federal Elections. https://justice.gov/media/1148336/dl?inline

U.S. Election Assistance Commission. (2005). *Voluntary Voting System Guidelines Volume 1, Version 1*. U.S. Election Assistance Commission. https://eac.gov/sites/default/files/eac_assets/1/28/VVSG.1.0_Volume_1.PDF

(2021, July). *2020 grand expenditure report*. U.S. Election Assistance Commission. https://eac.gov/sites/default/files/paymentgrants/expenditures/2020_State_Grant_Expenditure_Report_FINAL.pdf

(2022, March 11). *Elections – Critical infrastructure*. United States Election Assistance Commission. https://eac.gov/election-officials/elections-critical-infrastructure

(2023, June 7). *Help America Vote Act*. United States Election Assistance Commission. https://eac.gov/about/help_america_vote_act.aspx

(n.d.). *Election assistance commission plans for use of CARES Act report to the pandemic response accountability committee*. United States Election Assistance Commission. https://eac.gov/sites/default/files/paymentgrants/cares/PRAC%20Reports/15011%20EAC %20Report%20on%20CARES%20Funding.pdf

U.S. Government Publishing Office. (2019, December 20). *Consolidated Appropriations Act, 2020*. U.S. Government Publishing Office. https://govinfo.gov/content/pkg/PLAW-116publ93/html/PLAW-116publ93.htm

Ura, A. (2021, September 7). *Gov. Greg Abbott signs Texas voting bill into law, overcoming Democratic quorum breaks*. Texas Tribune. https://texastribune.org/2021/09/01/texas-voting-bill-greg-abbott/

Verified Voting. (2020, August). *Electronic poll book use in the United States*. Verified Voting. https://verifiedvoting.org/wp-content/uploads/2020/08/Verified-Voting-Electronic-Poll-Book-Use-in-the-United-States-20200831.pdf

(2021, May). *The business of voting*. Verified Voting. https://verifiedvoting.org/wp-content/uploads/2021/05/the-business-of-voting-single-page.pdf

Waldman, M., Weiser, W. R., Moraels-Doyle, S., & Sweren-Becker, E. (2018, August 6). *The Effects of Shelby County v. Holder*. Brennan Center for Justice. https://brennancenter.org/our-work/research-reports/effects-shelby-county-v-holder

Waldman, M., Weiser, W., Morales-Doyle, S., & Sweren-Becker, E. (2021a, October 4). *Voting laws roundup*. Brennan Center for Justice. https://brennancenter.org/our-work/research-reports/voting-laws-roundup-october-2021

(2021b, October 1). *Voting Rights Act analyses, reports, and explainers*. Brennan Center for Justice. https://brennancenter.org/our-work/research-reports/voting-rights-act-analyses-reports-and-explainers

Weiner, D. I. (2019, April 30). *Fixing the FEC: An agenda for reform*. Brennan Center for Justice. https://brennancenter.org/our-work/policy-solutions/fixing-fec-agenda-reform

Wilder, W., & Hira, E. (2021, December 15). *How the Freedom to Vote Act can blunt the worst of Texas's Voter Suppression Law*. Brennan Center of Justice. https://brennancenter.org/our-work/analysis-opinion/how-freedom-vote-act-can-blunt-worst-texass-voter-suppression-law

3

From Free Speech to False Speech

Analyzing Foreign Online Disinformation Campaigns Targeting Democracies

Rachel Brooks-Bitterli

INTRODUCTION

Popular technology platforms enable users to create an account, sometimes anonymously or with minimal identity verification. Users can post and share content instantaneously to networks online. As this user-generated content is available immediately and not fact-checked first, social media is ripe for manipulation from disinformation. By the time disinformation campaigns are detected, they may have propagated rampant misinformation – unintentionally false information – as real users share untrue content they see and believe to be accurate with their networks.

Online disinformation efforts pose challenges for detection and mitigation. Technology companies, governments, and civil society struggle to promptly and adequately respond to ongoing threats to the information environment. Governments can be disinformation campaigns' culprits within their own countries; look no further than *New York Times* reports of US President Donald Trump's disinformation-perpetuating commentary on mail-in voting leading up to the 2020 election (Sanger & Kanno-Youngs, 2020; Stolberg & Weiland, 2020). However, this chapter's scope focuses on Russian and Chinese campaigns rather than within-country campaigns.

Disinformation campaigns can drive people to reinforce confirmation biases and spread fabricated information they believe is accurate. Today's vast online information environment bombards users with headlines and makes it challenging to discern trustworthiness. This information overload can benefit education and knowledge accessibility. However, it also allows actors to manipulate social media for their agendas.

This chapter investigates the extent to which Russian and Chinese online disinformation campaigns attempt to influence democracies to further their strategic aims. It is vital to first locate the challenge of disinformation within the international security landscape and today's "post-truth" world. While disinformation – intentionally false information – is not new, the internet presents unique challenges in detecting, responding to, and curbing such content.

States can exploit this environment by using social media's algorithms and capabilities to spread disinformation. Bots and other technologies offer cheap, scalable, automated ways to amplify coordinated campaigns. These efforts intentionally center on existing societal divides in the targeted countries. Such divisions include the climate crisis, racial strife, and democratic processes. The latter is this study's focus.

Research Questions and Methodology

This research discusses the extent and how Moscow and Beijing employ online disinformation campaigns to exploit the vulnerabilities of democracies and advance strategic aims. At the heart of this research is an assessment of the chief similarities and differences in tactics identified through dyads between Russia, China, and specific democracies.

The methodology employs a review of public reports, archives, and news content coupled with contextualized case studies. This approach centers on Russia and China as the primary propagators of online disinformation against democracies. We focus on well-researched, major democracies to achieve a global perspective of countries affected, although we acknowledge there are other, often less-studied examples, including democracies in developing countries. Each case study incorporates varying examples of global disinformation attacks credibly attributed to originating countries.

Limitations

Limitations stem from the difficulty of studying something inherently involving deception. The internet's ability to provide anonymity presents challenges in identifying disinformation's exact origin and extent. Aspects of social networks can obfuscate whether untrue content is ill-informed misinformation or deliberate disinformation. This work focuses on coordinated, professionalized examples of disinformation against democracies attributed to authoritarian states. Many authoritarian states' aims remain covert; thus, we look to history, current events, and scholarly experts to analyze authoritarian goals when official statements are unavailable. Another challenge to disinformation is accurately measuring reach and impact, including the outcomes of a disinformation-heavy article or tweet on voter preferences. Confounding factors influence users' views; therefore, we look to available social media data for best estimations.

DEMOCRACY AND AUTHORITARIAN THREAT

Inherent in the research is the belief democracies need to increase their resilience against foreign governments' efforts to exert influence through disinformation and acknowledgment of disinformation's complexity and international prevalence. Disinformation is not one-sided from authoritarian regimes to democracies but can also emerge within democracies, including sometimes targeting authoritarian states. We also recognize differences between stable, established democracies and emerging, vulnerable, or crisis-ridden democracies.

Russia and China present two intriguing case studies of authoritarian regimes deploying disinformation against democracies for multiple reasons. Russia's President Vladimir Putin and China's President Xi share a rapport engendering security cooperation and "remarkably frequent" engagements supporting a "growing agreement about how the world should be" (Kendall-Taylor & Shullman, 2018, p. 1). They share an understanding that eroding democracy will contribute to their mutual aims, including weakened Western power. Later sections present core similarities and differences between known Russian and Chinese disinformation campaign strategies aimed at democracies.

Many influence operations are at least partially covert, notably aided by the internet's potential for anonymity and globalization (U.S. Department of Homeland Security, 2020; Wray, 2020). A frequent tactic of influence operations is adversaries creating artificial personas and fabricated narratives to denigrate democratic institutions (Wray, 2020). Despite most disinformation's covert nature, reputable sources, such as official government documents, international institutions, and fact-checked nonpartisan media, linked examples discussed to the Russian or Chinese government. While this research focuses on governments' foreign influence campaigns, non-state actors are also responsible for initiating disinformation campaigns. Including non-state operations would become unwieldy; thus, we remain focused on efforts judged to be launched, backed, or otherwise supported by governments.

Definitions: Misinformation and Disinformation

While disinformation and misinformation are both dangerous and deepen societal divides, the critical difference is intent. This research is concerned with disinformation – sharing false information in intentional efforts to harm or deceive. Misinformation is the "spreading of unintentionally false information" (Theohary, 2018, p. 5). Misinformation can manifest as internet users sharing hoaxes or conspiracy theories they believe are authentic.

Typical examples of disinformation include doctored photos, inaccurate news articles, or tampered official documents purposely planted online. These instances occur within the information environment, which encompasses systems and actors "collect[ing], disseminat[ing], or act[ing] on information" (Theohary, 2018, p. 5). Disinformation in international relations is a pervasive challenge, especially given the internet's potential for anonymity, low entry cost, and global spread.

Analyzing Online Disinformation from Russia and China

Russia and China are two powers seeking to challenge or undermine norms they view as dominated by the West. Where publications sometimes focus on one or the other, this research analyzes their distinct aims side by side in deploying disinformation against democracies. While there is ample research on historical disinformation from the Soviet Union during the Cold War and its aftermath, renewing this study after Putin's presidency began in 2000 is helpful. Likewise, President Xi rose to power in China in 2012 and implemented bold breaches of international norms and law, including cyberattacks (White House, 2015). Coupled with China's economic and geostrategic power, these influence campaigns make valuable case studies.

Despite authoritarian similarities between Russian and Chinese disinformation targets and strategies, there are distinct contrasts. One difference is Russia's longstanding tradition of implementing international disinformation campaigns that precede the internet's advent. In comparison, China's power and participation in the global disinformation landscape have grown in recent years (Bradshaw & Howard, 2019; Wray, 2020). This chapter creates an analytical framework to map authoritarian regimes' foreign influence efforts against democracies: (1) through longer-term, ambient disinformation, (2) during transitions of political power, and (3) during social and cultural divides. This framework drives our analysis.

RUSSIAN ONLINE DISINFORMATION CAMPAIGNS TARGETING DEMOCRACIES

Russian Disinformation's Strategic Aims

Moscow's aims and global positioning as an authoritarian geostrategic power help us contextualize Russian disinformation. Because Russian disinformation provides some of the most well-known and credibly attributed examples of foreign interference, Kalathil (2020, p. 36) suggests the Russian state serves as a "model for other authoritarians' efforts." Evidence of Russian online disinformation affecting democracies across Europe, North America, and elsewhere confirms the reach of Kremlin-initiated interference campaigns.

Bernstein (2011) calls Russia a "'hybrid' authoritarian regime" under Presidents Putin and Medvedev because of the existence of some democratic institutions, including multiparty elections and competitive parties. These democratic institutions are restricted yet noteworthy. In theory, these institutions' existence should indicate that democracy's norms are accepted and a possibility – if meager under Putin's regime – of movement toward a more complete democracy.

Russia's strategy has long incorporated influence operations, with the Kremlin-supported Internet Research Agency (IRA) beginning as an effort to exert influence within Russia (Pomerantsev, 2019). Turning to Russia's foreign targets, this research concentrates on two categories: geographically close democracies and Western democracies. Russia deployed strategic efforts externally with post-Soviet "near abroad" targets of Estonia, Georgia, Latvia, Moldova, Lithuania, and especially Ukraine (Kalathil, 2020; Sukhankin, 2019). Because Russia assesses its might compared to the United States and other powers, the Kremlin also targeted Western democracies. Weakened democracy, particularly in the West, helps increase Russia's perception of its power and influence.

Kendall-Taylor and Shullman (2018) describe Russia's global strategy as "confrontational and brazen." The Kremlin's assault on democratic institutions spans foreign interference in elections, disinformation campaigns, and corruption to erode global commitment to democracy. This research focuses on the disinformation component while recognizing disinformation as one method within the broader Russian foreign influence approach. Even within disinformation, multiple strands of influence emerge. While some understand disinformation as only overt falsehoods, this work asserts that disinformation is a complex challenge for democracies, including tactics such as the Russian military intelligence (GRU) use of narrative or information laundering and boosterism, as supported by DiResta and Grossman (2019). Narrative laundering is when "a story is planted or created and then legitimized through repetition or a citation chain across other media entities," and boosterism is repetitious content "created and disseminated to reinforce the perception that a given position represents a popular point of view" (DiResta & Grossman, 2019, p. 5). These tactics rest at the heart of the Kremlin's foreign influence efforts.

The U.S. Department of State's Global Engagement Center (GEC, 2020) organizes Russia's disinformation strategy into five pillars. Those pillars are official government communications, state-funded global messaging, cyber-enabled disinformation, proxy source cultivation, and social media weaponization (GEC, 2020). These activities' explicit connection to the Russian government ranges from clear-cut, such as official government communications, to more covert strategies, such as cyber-enabled forgeries or cloned websites. By employing a combination of overt and covert tactics, the Kremlin's penetration of the information environment is multifold for increased effect.

Analytical Framework Applied to Russian Campaigns

Considering Russia's aims, this section studies Russian online foreign influence in the form of ambient disinformation campaigns, exploitation of social divides, and interference during transitions of power. Ongoing, ambient disinformation plays a critical role in this strategy for amplifying falsehoods' reach. With continuous foreign disinformation, a divided democracy can become a less powerful threat with reduced capacity to withstand further attacks, and this diffusive disinformation strategy can create optimal conditions for more targeted disinformation efforts (Beskow & Carley, 2019). The Kremlin's strategy capitalizes on these advantages by employing long-term, ambient disinformation campaigns against democracies between more targeted information attacks.

Military leaders denote the movement from isolated periods of conflict to persistent information operations from authoritarian powers in the international system.

Current warfare is not always declared but is undeniably already happening (Beskow & Carley, 2019; Gerasimov, 2016). Thus, democracies must be perpetually vigilant about widespread disinformation. The continual nature of Russian disinformation necessitates planning and foresight for successful long-term influence efforts. Researchers suggest the Kremlin organized disinformation activities on social networks far before notable moments, including elections (Kalathil, 2020; Starks, Cerulus, & Scott, 2019). The long-term preparation allows for increasingly effective targeted attacks during moments of particular vulnerabilities. While the exact extent is difficult to quantify, ongoing campaigns continually seek to decay democratic institutions and progress authoritarian vigor.

Influencing Transitions of Political Power

The Kremlin leverages disinformation to influence transitions of political power in the West and neighboring countries, such as during the 2014 Ukrainian Maidan Revolution and the 2016 US presidential election. Russia increased its influence efforts targeting its post-Soviet "near abroad" since the early 2000s, leading to escalation into the Russia–Ukraine war in 2022. This section turns to the 2014 Ukrainian Maidan Revolution to analyze Russian interference during political transitions as part of broader aims still unfolding today.

The 2014 Ukrainian Maidan Revolution

Moscow's efforts to influence nearby post-Soviet countries since the early 2000s include foreign influence campaigns during countries' political transitions. Ukraine is a geographically close democratic target with evident strategic importance to Russia. There is much to learn about the extent of Russian foreign interference across time, including the Kremlin's 2014 to 2016 interference in Ukraine and social media's ongoing role in the Russia–Ukraine conflict.

The 2014 Ukrainian Maidan Revolution was a period of civil unrest and demonstrations in Ukraine, beginning with protests in late 2013 when the Ukrainian government chose not to sign the "Association Agreement and the Deep and Comprehensive Free Trade Agreement with the European Union" (Federal Department of Foreign Affairs, 2020). This protest for greater European integration grew into the removal of Ukraine's pro-Russian President Viktor Yanukovych and unrest over ongoing corruption, human rights violations, and abuses of power (Federal Department of Foreign Affairs, 2020). In response to President Yanukovych's ousting, the Kremlin organized attempts to delegitimize Kyiv's new government and Ukraine's growing inclination to the West through disinformation, proxy war, and militaristic aggression (Sokol, 2019). Through disinformation-heavy influence campaigns, Putin painted adversaries as detesting Jews and the new government as a "fascist junta" spreading antisemitism, racism, and xenophobia (Sokol, 2019, para. 3). This disinformation tactic was significant – and effective – because of World War II's lasting impact throughout the post-Soviet arena.

The Russian disinformation effort to frame Ukraine's post-revolution leaders as racist and violent occurred at a similar time to when Russia was aiming to conquer the Crimean Peninsula. This invasion of Ukrainian territory and the Crimean annexation began as a Russian state-sponsored media campaign targeting Ukraine (Summers, 2017). Russian disinformation efforts inundated Crimeans with narratives that they were at risk from their fellow people in Kyiv (Yuhas, 2014). This disinformation led many Crimeans to welcome Russian military presence's perceived protection. Disinformation efforts worked to overwhelm the information environment and advance the Kremlin's aims by distracting from their actions and negatively framing others' activities.

A component of this and other Russian campaigns is the ability to morph actual events into a new, carefully crafted narrative removed from reality – but rooted in it and recontextualized. An example is the assertion that Jewish people felt forced to leave Ukraine. While tens of thousands left Ukraine for Israel, as reported by Israeli interior ministry statistics, the departure's motivation was reportedly the danger felt due to Russian aggression, not racism as Russia sought to contrive (Sokol, 2019). Russia maximized the opportunity to frame the exodus as Ukraine's doing and leveraged cyber-enabled attacks to create a perception of chaos and instability within Ukraine (Summers, 2017). Beyond the outside perception of Ukraine, the efforts contributed to Ukrainians' eroding faith in their government and overall unity.

Evidence of the Kremlin propagating anti-Western, pro-Russian content targeting Ukrainians across social media spans years (Chen, 2015; Summers, 2017). The strategically crafted messages from Russia across time and networks showcase the Kremlin's attempts to grow Ukrainian support for Russian interests (Chen, 2015). While it remains a democracy's responsibility to address public opinion within its citizenry, acknowledgment of Russian interference's role in shaping Ukrainians' perceptions is critical.

The 2016 US Presidential Election

The Kremlin's foreign interference attempts are not limited to nearby post-Soviet countries. A highly publicized context of Russian influence campaigns during political transitions is the 2016 US presidential election. Russian interference in the 2016 US presidential election was confirmed by official US government agency investigations, most notably an extensive bipartisan U.S. Senate Intelligence Committee report. Moscow employed a combination of disinformation and hacking intended to push the 2016 US presidential election in favor of Trump (Funke, 2020). Trump became the eventual winner, although assessing how much Russia influenced the outcome from open-source information is challenging. This chapter is less concerned with disinformation's effectiveness as it is with the extent authoritarians deploy campaigns in attempts to influence democracies.

TIME's Shuster (2020) details how Russia initiated a two-pronged attack centered on spreading online disinformation and incorporating cyberattacks to hack the

Democratic Party and election infrastructure. Compared to 2020, the 2016 US presidential election saw more invasive interference with a focus on influence through state-run media and social media disinformation (Shuster, 2020; Wray, 2020). Experts, including the Alliance for Securing Democracy's Bret Schafer, contend that Russia's interference in the 2016 election was stronger than in 2020 because social networks had yet to improve the removal of disinformation-spreading Russian bots and fake accounts (Shuster, 2020). Between 2016 and 2020, American discourse became increasingly divided and fraught with false information and conspiracies originating domestically; thus, Russian efforts in 2016 sowed lasting seeds but arguably did not need to continue amplifying the disinformation already in motion and impacting outcomes (Shuster, 2020).

The U.S. Senate Intelligence Committee shared its final report on Russian influence in the 2016 presidential election in 2020. *The Hill* Staff (2020) published that the report was similar to the findings of the investigation by special counsel Robert Mueller with "overwhelming evidence of Russia's efforts to interfere in the election through disinformation and cyber campaigns but . . . a lack of sufficient evidence that the Trump campaign conspired with the Kremlin to impact the outcome of the 2016 election." Regarding Moscow's influence in the US 2016 election and Donald Trump's involvement, *Slate*'s Stahl (2020) argues "at the very least, the Trump team was aware of and welcomed this meddling." In-country complicity in foreign disinformation is a complicating factor, as most politicians benefiting from disinformation may be disinclined to intervene or discredit it.

Russian involvement in the 2016 election appears motivated by aims to "tarnish U.S. democracy" and enable Moscow's assertions "Washington has no right telling other nations how to conduct their elections" (Kendall-Taylor & Shullman, 2018, p. 1). Such foreign influence can undermine legitimate democratic processes as people question if events are authentic or resulting from foreign influence. While it is challenging to quantify disinformation campaigns' outcomes, it is undeniable that disinformation's hundreds of millions of social media impressions had lasting effects (*Al Jazeera English*, 2018). Even in the years-later aftermath following Trump's defeat in the 2020 election, 2016's disinformation impacted US sentiments, political views, and rhetoric, including growing distrust and challenges to democratically decided outcomes.

This assessment of Ukraine's 2014 Maidan Revolution and the 2016 US presidential election analyzes Russian disinformation attempting to exploit transitions of political power. These political transitions often include social fractures, and a disillusioned citizenry is vulnerable to adversaries' efforts. The following section focuses on periods of social and cultural divides as democratic vulnerabilities offering powerful opportunities for foreign influence.

Social and Cultural Divides

Social and cultural divides provide periods of vulnerability where adversaries may strike on democracies' existing societal cleavages. These tensions include those between races, religions, political parties, or a country's people and its military (Beskow & Carley, 2019). This section analyzes efforts to capitalize on democracies' social and cultural divides through the Brexit referendum.

Brexit Referendum

An example of alleged Russian interference through disinformation is the United Kingdom European Union referendum, also known as the Brexit referendum in 2016. The UK's Intelligence and Security Committee of Parliament (ISC) investigated Russian interference targeting this social divide (Dearden, 2020). The ISC report uncovered insufficient evidence "Russia meddled to any significant extent . . . nor did Russia influence the final outcome," although it found UK intelligence neglected Russian threats (Castle, 2020, para. 6). The ISC report was complete long before its release, which was delayed until after the general election (Castle, 2020; Ellehuus & Ruy, 2020).

The disinformation-spreading *Strategic Culture Foundation* (SCF) published "editor's choice" articles, such as "The Russian Brexit Plot That Wasn't," to discredit evidence of Russian interference (Robinson, 2020, p. 1). While the extent of Russian disinformation was determined insufficient to sway results, leadership reportedly choosing not to investigate evidence of interference sooner provided a window of opportunity for Russia to bolster its campaigns. Indications of Russian interference in the British government predate the Brexit referendum, including Russian permeation in London, with Castle (2020) referring to the capital as "Londongrad." While Russian interference in the Brexit referendum likely did not alter the vote's outcome, its extent is nonetheless concerning, as is the lack of democratic safeguards from interference in Britain and elsewhere.

CHINESE ONLINE DISINFORMATION CAMPAIGNS TARGETING DEMOCRACIES

Chinese Disinformation's Strategic Aims

Despite authoritarian similarities to Russia, China's strategy maintains unique qualities, making it an attractive second case study. The Chinese Communist Party (CCP) is well-known for its propaganda, censorship, and disinformation (Blumenthal & Zhang, 2020). China's political leaders deny any chance of movement to democracy and favor authoritarian norms. However, China's authoritarian leadership maintains both soft and hard aspects along with self-branding as a "consultative democracy" (Bernstein, 2011; Kim, 2019). While China was previously content to coexist with democracies, its growing power brings a willingness to challenge democracy's broader norms.

The CCP acknowledged that China's military and economic power was insufficient to achieve its aims and turned to increased information warfare through disinformation (Cole, 2019). President Xi lionized "discourse power" to influence narratives and share China's story on the global stage (Rosenberger, 2020, para. 9). Under President Xi, China created a narrative of democracy to grant their political system more "ideological legitimacy" in mainland China, Taiwan, and Hong Kong – and among other communities watching (Kim, 2019, para. 8). There has been a marked increase in the CCP's investment in technologies and its disinformation efforts' intensity in positively branding China.

China increasingly prioritizes the global race for technological advancement. Citing security risks, the United States restricted Chinese companies Huawei and ZTE and encouraged European restriction of their reach (Bartz & Alper, 2022; Mukherjee & Soderpalm, 2020; Shepardson, 2021). Amid this technological power struggle, the CCP expanded its funding for the China Standards 2035 and Made in China 2025 initiatives, aiming to minimize reliance on the United States and promote domestic products (Sinkkonen & Lassila, 2020).

In the State Council Information Office's *White Paper on China's Political Party System*, the CCP shared "socialist democracy" branding, combining consultative and electoral democracy (Kim, 2019, para. 2; USC US-China Institute, 2007). China's vulnerability to criticism spurred leaders to create an image of a democracy differentiated by "Chinese characteristics" instead of blanketly criticizing democracy (Kim, 2019, para. 2). Still lacking specific democratic processes and values, this effort sought to protect China's domestic and international image. Beijing shifted its strategy to project China's system as legitimate and necessary for its prosperity. China's concerns about its global standing contextualize its foreign disinformation strategy.

Kendall-Taylor and Shullman (2018, p. 1) assert that China "used a subtler and more risk-averse strategy, preferring stability that is conducive to building economic ties and influence." This argument contends China's approach focuses on offering resources to weaker democracies to distance them from the West (Kendall-Taylor & Shullman, 2018). These CCP efforts would be less influential without Russian and other countries' concurrent campaigns to erode democratic fixtures.

The CCP's economic, relatively risk-averse, and opportunistic strategies align with this research's examination of Chinese online disinformation. We contend there is a combination of an insufficient public understanding of past foreign interference operations from China coupled with a marked increase in China's disinformation activity in recent years. Kalathil (2020, p. 38) notes the CCP's foreign influence operations were seen as mainly consisting of apparent, innocuous propaganda on official channels for "relatively minimalist and ineffective" outcomes. However, the CCP's approach had likely been oversimplified and underestimated. Kalathil (2020) adds that this analysis ignores China's longtime foreign influence activities to affect the international information environment in their favor.

The CCP seeks to alter broader narratives through private business and journalism, making China's strategy more complex than merely promoting its economic interests. The likely underestimation of China's foreign influence through disinformation partially stems from the deception involved. Evidence of Chinese computational propaganda existed largely within its borders through QQ, WeChat, and Weibo until 2019 (Bradshaw & Howard, 2019). The CCP can maintain power over messaging in China by employing censorship and banning social networks. Despite their ban for Chinese citizens, the CCP's interest in global platforms indicates a wider strategy. Their strategy targets norms, standards, infrastructure, governance, and technology (Kalathil, 2020).

Two central trends of the CCP's disinformation against democracies are a notable rise in disinformation campaigns in recent years and a greater investment in technology for foreign influence. The following sections analyze examples of this shift to include increasingly global platforms and audiences related to our analytical framework's themes of political transitions, societal divides, and ambient disinformation.

Analytical Framework Applied to Chinese Campaigns

Ongoing disinformation proves significant to China's aims to emit a positive reputation. Online campaigns enable China to project favorable information while also burying criticisms. Within China, the CCP can swiftly erase dissenting comments on Chinese platforms while banning other networks. Disinformation allowed China's reach across social networks to grow commensurately with its global stance (Lee Myers & Mozur, 2019). While the CCP can censor and crack down on unwanted information to curate its narrative within China, it can also deploy bots to bury unwanted information and spread pro-CCP messaging across global networks.

In addition to creating supportive press for China and unfavorable press for adversaries, some CCP disinformation aims to deflect attention from China's perceived national failings, including COVID-19's early mishandling, by inundating Chinese and global audiences with heightened campaigns to drown criticisms (Lee Myers & Mozur, 2019; Wallis et al., 2020). Given the CCP's intent to maintain positive narratives and geostrategic relationships globally, ongoing disinformation proves valuable in burying negative commentary and projecting pro-China content.

China–Australia relations provide a compelling example of this strategy. Australia's democracy experienced decades of economic benefits from its relationship with China, including Chinese tourism and student populations (Searight, 2020). However, the revelation of Chinese disinformation to impact Australian politics and discourse stirred the relationship, with some attempts to rebuild trust (Morrison, Barnet, & Martin, 2020; Wallis et al., 2020; Woo, 2023). Evidence revealed CCP-linked disinformation and political donations aspiring to influence major Australian political parties' policies on China (Searight, 2020; Wallis et al., 2020). Because China's ongoing disinformation and soft power in Australia are pervasive, this dynamic presents economic and security challenges for their relationship's future.

While these ongoing disinformation efforts targeting democracies serve as a backdrop to the international system, there are marked periods when China opportunistically exploits democratic vulnerabilities through societal divisions. This chapter next analyzes Taiwan as a case of Chinese influence during political transition before assessing the Hong Kong protests as Chinese influence during social and cultural divides.

Influencing Transitions of Political Power

China's relationship with Taiwan and Hong Kong is contested and complex; therefore, this research acknowledges China's disinformation against Taiwan and Hong Kong's pursuit of democracy as having both domestic and international aspects (Hernández & Lee Myers, 2020; Horton, 2019). With different political systems, Taiwan and Hong Kong showcase examples of China's interference in democratic institutions through disinformation.

Taiwan

Taiwan presents a timely example of China targeting its influence operations at democratization and political transitions. Themes of China's online disinformation include undermining Taiwan's ruling Democratic Progressive Party (DPP) and President Tsai Ing-wen (Steger, 2020). The CCP recognized Taiwan's democratization complicates its aims to acquire control of Taiwan (Cole, 2019). China is willing to pursue great lengths to interrupt Taiwan's democratization, including military force and information warfare (Hernández & Lee Myers, 2020).

Inaccurate information across Facebook, YouTube, and Twitter (now X) targeted Taiwan's democratic institutions, including presidential elections and DPP leadership. Wallis et al. (2020) uncovered increased Twitter accounts created by China's Ministry of Foreign Affairs diplomats, spokespeople, state media, and embassies through 2018 and 2019. Disinformation from China included homophobic rumors regarding President Tsai Ing-wen's sexuality. These disinformation attacks capitalized on the resentment some citizens felt toward her policies supporting LGBTQIA + rights (Steger, 2020). Fact-checking organizations debunked unfounded claims; however, closed messaging groups' popularity throughout Taiwan proved troublesome as users could privately forward untrue information (Steger, 2020).

Taiwan's response showcases an instructive model for fighting foreign influence from disinformation. Taiwan fined CtiTV, a primary cable network, in response to inadequate fact-checking and created its Department of Cyber Security and ministry-specific disinformation detection task forces (Halpert, 2020). Before Taiwan's 2020 presidential election, the country passed the Anti-Infiltration Act to impose potential fines and prison sentences for actors peddling disinformation, obstructing elections, or interfering with international politics (Halpert, 2020).

China's Taiwan Affairs Office spokesperson asserted the act generates "panic that everyone is treated as an enemy" and China has never engaged in "elections in the Taiwan region" (*Reuters*, 2019, para. 6). The wording of the "Taiwan region" rejects its autonomy, and the framing of this policy as hurting "everyone" offers context to inform our analysis. The "infiltration sources" Taiwan's legislation aims to protect against are understood to mean Chinese interference (*Reuters*, 2019, para. 4). Taiwanese media focuses on Chinese intelligence as a key player in discrediting Taiwan President Tsai Ing-wen and her advocacy for Taiwan's independence (Aspinwall, 2020). Taiwan's efforts to institute anti-disinformation laws in reaction to China follow examples from Finland and Estonia as recipients of Russia's foreign influence through disinformation (Aspinwall, 2020).

Taiwan's societal divides aid Chinese disinformation's effectiveness, such as disinformation against LGBTQIA+-supporting Taiwanese President Tsai Ing-wen leveraging certain citizens' homophobic sentiments. Taiwan's 2020 election depicts a period of vulnerability through the potential transition of power, which overlaps with societal divides the CCP exploited to undermine Taiwan's president. These divisions present opportunities for further analysis of Chinese influence against democratic institutions.

Social and Cultural Divides

HONG KONG PROTESTS. In recent decades, grassroots protests became increasingly menacing for authoritarian regimes. Hong Kong presents a noteworthy case of Chinese interference in democracy. There appears to be a three-pronged approach to China's online disinformation targeting Hong Kong: (1) accusations that the protesters are dangerous and violent, (2) allegations of United States and other interference being involved, and (3) demands to support the police in Hong Kong and undermine protests (Wallis et al., 2020).

The CCP's strategy shifted from efforts to contain democracy in Hong Kong to more direct control, influencing its use of disinformation to be more interventionist. Chinese responses to the Hong Kong protests were to increasingly suppress opposition, especially through technological methods, including disinformation amplification on social networks (Sinkkonen & Lassila, 2020). In 2019, China's government incorporated worldwide social media platforms to paint democracy advocates in Hong Kong as violent radicals lacking popular opinion (Bradshaw & Howard, 2019; Lee Myers & Mozur, 2019). Digital repression has not entirely eclipsed physical means of influence but offers new opportunities for attacks against adversaries (Sinkkonen & Lassila, 2020). Disinformation is a dangerous method for regimes to distort or otherwise control narratives about the extent of physical measures, popular opinion, and other forms of interference. Twitter and Facebook removed various accounts tied to the CCP's efforts to undermine the protests in Hong Kong, and Twitter announced policies to prohibit "state-controlled news media" advertisements

(Halpert, 2020; Twitter Inc., 2019). However, limited staff, scale, and other factors complicate timely response.

China shared content through social and state media to increase nationalist and anti-Western views. This strategy includes manipulating photos and videos to subvert protesters or label the protests as a dangerous gateway to terrorism (Lee Myers & Mozur, 2019). In mid-2019, Twitter, Facebook, and YouTube uncovered and suspended accounts tied to Beijing propagating Hong Kong protest disinformation (Alba & Satariano, 2019). These efforts intensified opposing views. As seen from Hong Kong, the demonstration movement was popular. However, the Chinese perspective led people to believe a violent, small group of radicals yearned to tear China apart.

As China advances its disinformation strategy, it likewise increases its expertise and ability to leverage social media's reach to networks worldwide. The CCP employs teams of citizens to "actively shape public opinions and police speech through online channels" (Bradshaw & Howard, 2019, p. 17). Networks of people and bots amplify disinformation to manipulate opinion (Alba & Satariano, 2019). China invests in professionalizing its disinformation tactics, including formal organizations with hiring plans and bonuses for performance (Alba & Satariano, 2019).

These data support the conclusion that China uses social media networks to exert influence and power worldwide, particularly regarding claims of land in Taiwan and Hong Kong as its sovereign territory. The extent of Chinese disinformation campaigns aimed at these regional territories reflects the aims and energy of the CCP to such ends until recently. These geographically close and territory-based ends are critical, but they are not the only form of influence operations as China's aims evolve with its growing geostrategic power.

ANALYSIS AND INSIGHTS

Our analytical framework is applicable across authoritarian contexts and finds certain similarities in its analysis of Russian and Chinese disinformation. Moscow and Beijing are both prominent disinformation-propagating actors in the international system, and they target robust Western democracies and neighboring states of strategic importance. However, it would be a mistake to assume the substance, aims, and contexts of these different authoritarian states' disinformation campaigns are neatly comparable. Each authoritarian state – and democratic target – has specific complexities.

While this research's analytical framework offers valuable insight broadly, there are core differences in how, to what aims, and to what extent these authoritarian states deploy their disinformation campaigns. Russia and China may share interests in diminished Western powers and antidemocracy efforts, but different ideologies and objectives drive the states' activities (Jeangène Vilmer & Charon, 2020). Each authoritarian state's disinformation campaigns against democracies requires analysis within the dyadic relationship between the authoritarian state and the target of its disinformation.

Distinguishing Aims and Leadership Profiles

While Russia and China's disinformation campaigns share similar strategic aims, they may or may not use similar strategies. Broadly speaking, Russia builds on its longstanding history of propaganda for a more direct, manipulation-driven approach, while China invested heavily in technological innovation more recently for a gradual, permeating, censorship-driven approach. The CCP prioritizes its efforts to show China's global image as respectable, uncorrupt, and morally sound and subdues content indicating otherwise (Jeangène Vilmer & Charon, 2020). Russia is less concerned with its image and appears as a "well-armed rogue state" aiming to disrupt the present international order (Dobbins, Shatz, & Wyne, 2019, para. 1). While China seeks increasing power, it is less concerned with Russia's goals to disrupt the system because it holds greater power and faces steeper reputational risks. Part of Russia's impetus for disinformation is its weakening global stance and lack of benefits from the present international order (Jeangène Vilmer & Charon, 2020). The Kremlin is thus willing to embrace risks in its disinformation strategy to disrupt the system for greater power and influence.

In contrast to Russia, China more strategically prioritized economic relationships, including investment, trade, and development assistance, to grow its influence in the international system (Dobbins, Shatz, & Wyne, 2019). China's export of products and services aids the country financially and helps develop other countries' relationships with – and dependency on – China. Chinese exports' breadth showcases Beijing's infrastructure investments to lead technologically and globally (Sinkkonen & Lassila, 2020). China's Belt and Road Initiative incorporates a Digital Silk Road component to further Chinese global advancement (Greene & Triolo, 2020). These relationships make China more risk-averse, reputation-oriented, and gradual in its disinformation than Russia.

China holds a more dominant role in the current international order and must be more careful and less overtly aggressive in its strategy. Despite their deflection and denial, Russia and China do little to hide their interference efforts because there is little need. With low costs, lack of gatekeepers, and accessible social networks, disinformation is an alluring way to further aims with relative anonymity (Garcia, 2020). While research indicates the most likely source of disinformation against a specific democracy, exact proof of culpability is challenging. The disinformation-deploying state can evade consequences by denying responsibility while inflicting ramifications on the targeted state.

If President Xi's foreign policy becomes more aggressive, these differences in Russian and Chinese aims may shrink. For the first time in July 2021, China announced sanctions against Western institutions criticizing them (Rudd, 2022). Another example is China's growing interest in near abroad territories and lack of concern for positive relations with certain democracies, particularly Taiwan. Rudd (2022, para. 3) contends "ideology drives policy more often than the other way around" under Xi's leadership, and he seeks to strengthen the Communist Party by stirring nationalism and asserting foreign policy to solidify China's power. In contrast, President Putin projects a "clever, manipulating strongman" image to protect his power as a ruler (Kovalev, 2023, para. 4). A strongman losing the appearance of might could lead to drastic action or demise. The Russia–Ukraine war, especially the Wagner Group rebellion, prompted doubts about Putin's crafted image (Kovalev, 2023; Sly, 2023). While Putin moves to preserve his leadership status, Xi appears driven by a "Marxist-inspired belief" that Chinese strength means a "more just international order" (Rudd, 2022, para. 3). These approaches centering the person versus the party lead to different strategies for authoritarianism.

While it is unlikely that China will forgo its priority of positive international relations, President Xi is likely watching the Russia–Ukraine war closely as it assesses possible territorial moves. While analysis of disinformation campaigns needs to happen within the individual dyads of the instigating state and the targeted state, it is useful to analyze the extent of partnerships between or among authoritarian states in pursuing their interests to undermine democracy. This is especially true when interests align, such as Russia in Ukraine and China in Taiwan for territorial conquests.

Power Relations and Strategic Cooperation

This inquiry requires analysis of strategic cooperation between authoritarian states to target democracies. China and Russia share a border and adversarial US relations, with Xi and Putin projecting an "intimate" friendship (Lau, 2023, para. 1). Russia and China's agendas share aims to influence the hallmarks of democracy, including free speech and public debate. Both measure their power relative to Western democracies, meaning that weakened democracy could increase their strength (Kendall-Taylor & Shullman, 2018). Both states leverage disinformation to legitimize authoritarian systems and delegitimize democratic systems. While some cooperation between Russia and China exists, this dynamic is more nuanced than simply an authoritarian alliance. Despite sharing similar adversaries, authoritarian regimes are also competing with each other.

Disinformation-propagating authoritarian regimes learned from each other's anti democracy campaigns, especially from Russia under Putin, to grow more robust disinformation strategies. With the Russian government's disinformation appearing as the most visible, it is understandable yet simplistic to apply the same motivations to China. China is unlikely to cooperate extensively with Russia and its aggressive approach for fear of losing its dominant position in the international trading system. Unless necessary, the CCP will likely tread carefully to avoid harming its economic and strategic relationships.

While priorities differ, authoritarian states' collective efforts create a "more corrosive effect on democracy than either would have single-handedly" (Kendall-Taylor

& Shullman, 2018, p. 1). Russia and China's aims are specific to their regimes, yet they operate within the same antidemocratic ecosystem. Without Russian campaigns to erode global commitment to democracy and democratic institutions, China's foreign interference efforts would likely be less powerful (Kendall-Taylor & Shullman, 2018).

Some experts designated 2020 and 2021 as "years for Russian–Chinese science cooperation with the focus on communications, AI and the Internet of Things" building off of past partnerships like 2019's "Sino-Russian Joint Innovation Investment Fund" (Sinkkonen & Lassila, 2020, p. 6). As much of this cooperation would presumably occur in private due to disinformation's deceptive nature, we lack concrete evidence of the extent the governments are strategically cooperating.

As there are moving pieces to disinformation campaigns and the states' individual aims vary, coordination may not be necessary. Russia, China, and other authoritarian states can and do act independently and amplify each other when it aligns with individual interests (Jeangène Vilmer & Charon, 2020). Given Beijing's central aim to promote pro-CCP messaging, it is unlikely Moscow would spread pro-CCP propaganda without benefiting the Kremlin or eroding adversaries' powers. Although antidemocracy disinformation serves both states' interests, applying a blanket model to authoritarian regimes' influence operations would be a disservice to countering interference.

Resilience and Democracy

Foreign interference efforts from authoritarian states have implications for democratic health and vulnerabilities, and democracies must take preemptive steps to protect themselves. There are multiple technical and governance strategies that democracies can consider to increase resiliency against targeted disinformation campaigns (RAND Corporation, 2023). Two useful methods are improved digital and media literacy among citizens and partnership-building across affected sectors and countries. Creating and promoting information literacy support for citizens can reduce vulnerabilities to disinformation. Especially in recent years, practitioners created resources for citizens to safely navigate the online information environment, including IREX's Learn 2 Discern curriculum, Stanford's Putting Civic Online Reasoning Program initiative, Google's Interland, and the News Literacy Project's Checkology curriculum (Brooks, 2020; News Literacy Project, 2023; RAND Corporation, 2023; Stanford History Education Group, 2023). Civil society education alone is insufficient against targeted online disinformation, but greater information literacy is vital for democracies to stay resilient against foreign interference (Brooks, 2020).

Another means to reduce democratic vulnerabilities to online disinformation is through partnerships. Much like disinformation-propagating outlets partnered to spread their nefarious content, collaboration among reputable outlets can reduce democratic vulnerabilities. For disinformation happening in the context of Hong Kong or Ukraine, partnerships between citizen journalists and mainstream media can strengthen the quality of information (Brooks, 2020; Huang, 2020). In places where high-risk geopolitical events or other conditions make international reporting challenging, networks of trusted citizen journalists are critical to mitigating erroneous information and reporting timely authentic news (Visram, 2020).

By combining education and partnerships, Taiwan's response showcases a whole-of-society approach to combating Chinese disinformation (Huang, 2020). The creation of laws, notably the Anti-Infiltration Act, imposed potential prison sentences and heavy fines for people spreading disinformation (Aspinwall, 2020; Halpert, 2020). Taiwan's institutional approach formed ministry-specific disinformation detection task forces and supported programs led by Taipei's digital minister. Other countries implemented other forms of regulations and protections, and democracies should continue to assess what models work best for their online and in-country contexts.

For democracies to stay healthy and competitive against targeted disinformation, they must create policies and safeguards to protect the free flow of reliable information online. Sokol (2019, p. 1) describes how successful disinformation campaigns are "based on a core of truth . . . distorted and exaggerated beyond recognition." The challenge of disinformation requires democracies to protect their institutions in mundane times and times of greatest vulnerability. So long as they support transparency, public debate, and free speech, democracies will likely remain targets of disinformation. By addressing the root of divisions within democracies, they have greater resiliency to foreign influence efforts.

CONCLUSION

Technology has become a permanent fixture in society and will continue to pose opportunities – and challenges – to the international system. As new technologies evolve, so must democracies to stay resilient against foreign adversaries' attempts to weaken democratic institutions through disinformation.

This research analyzed the extent to which and how foreign online disinformation campaigns target democracies, specifically disinformation from the Russian and Chinese governments toward specific democracies. We found Russia is a manipulation-driven, rogue state with a history of disinformation aiming to disrupt the international order as it senses its slipping power. China likewise seeks increasing power, yet is less concerned with disrupting the international system because it holds a more powerful global position and deploys a more gradual, censorship-driven approach.

Assessing authoritarian states' online disinformation campaigns through the same analytical framework proves useful; yet assuming all authoritarian states operate similarly is a mistake. Each authoritarian state's disinformation campaigns necessitate assessment within dyadic relationships between disinformation-propagating states and their targets. Examples of democracies targeted by Russia and China fit into our analytical framework of long-term, ambient disinformation, transitions of political power, and social and cultural movements. They also exposed patterns in targets primarily categorized as either Western powers or neighboring states of strategic importance.

The main distinctions between Russia and China and their various targets reflect different aims, objectives, risks, and contexts for using targeted disinformation depending on the target state. Another line of argumentation is that disinformation-propagating authoritarian regimes learned from each other's campaigns and partnered to some extent in antidemocracy efforts. While Russia and China may share interests in authoritarianism and diminished Western powers, different ideologies, objectives, and relationships drive them. Cooperation among authoritarian states appears to be out of convenience more than partnership, as they are simultaneously competing with each other.

Russia and China present two of the authoritarian powers most threatening to democracies with their strong capacities to deploy antidemocratic disinformation. Russia appears as a more immediate and brazen threat; however, China presents a long-term threat to democracies as it strategically grows its geopolitical power. China is more concerned with promoting its positive image and creating reasonable working relations with Western democracies than Russia's abrasive approach. The recent progress in China's disinformation ecosystem merits continued analysis in the coming years, coupled with lessons learned from Russia's extended disinformation ecosystem, particularly in the Russia–Ukraine war. Application of this research's analytical framework to other authoritarian regimes, including Iran and North Korea, can assess additional influence efforts.

A healthy democracy relies on trust and access to quality information. Social networks drastically changed the information environment, offering opportunities for increased online information and disinformation. We found varying authoritarian strategies to undermine faith in democratic processes through disinformation. The extent to which these efforts swayed outcomes is tangential to how these campaigns worsened societal divides and eroded trust among citizens. Even the most resilient democracies must protect themselves and their information environments against the ongoing threat of foreign interference.

REFERENCES

Al Jazeera English. (2018, February 1). *Disinformation and democracy (part I), People and power*. YouTube. https://youtube.com/watch?v=eZEz6Pc3Z24

Alba, D., & Satariano, A. (2019, September 26). At least 70 countries have had disinformation campaigns, study finds. *The New York Times*. https://nytimes.com/2019/09/26/technology/government-disinformation-cyber-troops.html

Aspinwall, N. (2020, January 10). Taiwan's war on fake news is hitting the wrong targets. *Foreign Policy*. https://foreignpolicy.com/2020/01/10/taiwan-election-tsai-disinformation-china-war-fake-news-hitting-wrong-targets/

Bartz, D., & Alper, A. (2022, November 30). *U.S. bans new Huawei, ZTE equipment sales, citing national security risk*. Reuters. https://reuters.com/business/media-telecom/us-fcc-bans-equipment-sales-imports-zte-huawei-over-national-security-risk-2022-11-25/

Bernstein, T. (2011, April 11). *Video: Varieties of authoritarianism – Comparing China and Russia*. USC US-China Institute. https://china.usc.edu/video-varieties-authoritarianism-comparing-china-and-russia

Beskow, D. M., & Carley, K. M. (2019). Social cybersecurity an emerging national security requirement. *Military Review*. March–April 2019, pp. 117–127. https://armyupress.army.mil/Portals/7/military-review/Archives/English/MA-2019/Beskow-Carley-Social-Cyber.pdf

Blumenthal, D., & Zhang, L. (2020, July 10). *China's censorship, propaganda & disinformation*. Jewish Policy Center. AEI. https://aei.org/articles/chinas-censorship-propaganda-disinformation

Bradshaw, S., & Howard, P. N. (2019). *The global disinformation order: 2019 global inventory of organised social media manipulation*. University of Oxford. Computational Propaganda Research Project. https://demtech.oii.ox.ac.uk/wp-content/uploads/sites/12/2019/09/CyberTroop-Report19.pdf

Brooks, R. (2020). *Research Plan & Weekly Updates. Research Fellowship: Digital Threats to Election Integrity*. The Carter Center Democracy Program. Unpublished research.

Castle, S. (2020, July 21). Five takeaways from the report on Russia's interference in Britain. *The New York Times*. https://nytimes.com/2020/07/21/world/europe/uk-russia-report-takeaways.html

Chen, A. (2015, June 7). The agency. *The New York Times*. https://nytimes.com/2015/06/07/magazine/the-agency.html

Cole, J. M. (2019). *Chinese disinformation in Taiwan*. Taiwan Sentinel. https://sentinel.tw/chinese-disinformation-in-taiwan

Dearden, L. (2020, July 21). *Russia report: Moscow's disinformation campaign fuelling 'political extremism' and division in UK*. The Independent. https://independent.co.uk/news/uk/home-news/russia-report-uk-national-security-brexit-terror-islam-a9630126.html

DiResta, R., & Grossman, S. (2019). *Potemkin pages & personas: Assessing GRU online operations, 2014–2019*. Stanford: Internet Observatory Cyber Policy Center. https://fsi-live.s3.us-west-1.amazonaws.com/s3fs-public/potemkin-pages-personas-sio-wp.pdf

Dobbins, J., Shatz, J., & Wyne, A. (2019). *Russia is a rogue, not a peer; China is a peer, not a rogue: Different challenges, different responses*. RAND Corporation. https://rand.org/pubs/perspectives/PE310.html

Ellehuus, R., & Ruy, D. (2020, July 21). *Did Russia influence Brexit?* Center for Strategic and International Studies (CSIS). https://csis.org/blogs/brexit-bits-bobs-and-blogs/did-russia-influence-brexit

Federal Department of Foreign Affairs. (2020). *Swiss Cooperation Programme Ukraine 2020–23*. Swiss Confederation. https://eda.admin.ch/dam/deza/en/documents/laender/cooperation-programme-ukraine_EN.pdf

Funke, D. (2020, September 25). *What we know about 2020 election interference: It's not just Russia*. Politifact: The Poynter Institute. https://politifact.com/article/2020/sep/25/what-we-know-about-2020-election-interference-its

Garcia, C. (2020, April 17). *Untangling the disinformation problem: Russia, China and the West*. The Wilson Center. https://wilsoncenter.org/blog-post/untangling-disinformation-problem-russia-china-and-west

GEC (2020). *GEC special report: August 2020 pillars of Russia's disinformation and propaganda ecosystem*. U.S. Department of State. https://state.gov/wp-content/uploads/2020/08/Pillars-of-Russia%E2%80%99s-Disinformation-and-Propaganda-Ecosystem_08-04-20.pdf

Gerasimov, V. (2016). The value of science is in the foresight: New challenges demand rethinking the forms and methods of carrying out combat operations. *Military Review*. January –February 2016 , pp. 23 –29. https://state.gov/wp-content/uploads/2020/08/Pillars-of-Russia%E2%80%99s-Disinformation-and-Propaganda-Ecosystem_08-04-20.pdf

Greene, R., & Triolo, P. (2020, May 8). *Will China control the global internet via its Digital Silk Road?* Carnegie Endowment for International Peace. https://carnegieendowment.org/2020/05/08/will-china-control-global-internet-via-its-digital-silk-road-pub-81857

Halpert, D. (2020, April 8). *Disinformation prevention and defending democracy in Taiwan*. Brown Political Review. https://brownpoliticalreview.org/2020/04/disinformation-prevention-and-defending-democracy-in-taiwan/

Hernández, J. C., & Lee Myers, S. (2020, July 1). As China strengthens grip on Hong Kong, Taiwan sees a threat. *The New York Times*. https://nytimes.com/2020/07/01/world/asia/taiwan-china-hong-kong.html

Horton, C. (2019, July 5). Hong Kong and Taiwan are bonding over China. *The Atlantic*. https://theatlantic.com/international/archive/2019/07/china-bonds-between-hong-kong-and-taiwan-are-growing/593347/

Huang, A. (2020, July). *Combatting and defeating Chinese propaganda and disinformation: A case study of Taiwan's 2020 elections*. Belfer Center for Science and International Affairs at the Harvard Kennedy School. https://belfercenter.org/sites/default/files/files/publication/Combatting%20Chinese%20Propaganda%20and%20Disinformation%20-%20Huang.pdf

Jeangène Vilmer, J.-B., & Charon, P. (2020, January 21). *Russia as a hurricane, China as climate change: Different ways of information warfare*. War on the Rocks. https://warontherocks.com/2020/01/russia-as-a-hurricane-china-as-climate-change-different-ways-of-information-warfare/

Kalathil, S. (2020). The evolution of authoritarian digital influence: Grappling with the new normal. *PRISM*, 9(1), 33 –50. https://ndupress.ndu.edu/Portals/68/Documents/prism/prism_9-1/prism_9-1_33-50_Kalathil-2.pdf?ver = DJRX5DRHKfqeXbyt6et98w%3D%3D

Kendall-Taylor, A. & Shullman, D. O. (2018, October 2). *How Russia and China undermine democracy*. Foreign Affairs. https://foreignaffairs.com/articles/china/2018-10-02/how-russia-and-china-undermine-democracy

Kim, J. (2019, December 6). Exploring China's new narrative on democracy. *The Diplomat*. https://thediplomat.com/2019/12/exploring-chinas-new-narrative-on-democracy/

Kovalev, A. (2023, June 27). *Putin's strongman image suddenly unravels for Russians*. Foreign Policy. https://foreignpolicy.com/2023/06/27/putin-prigozhin-wagner-mutiny-weakness-russians-opposition-war-ukraine/

Lau, S. (2023, March 20). Why Xi Jinping is still Vladimir Putin's best friend. *Politico*. https://politico.eu/article/xi-jinping-china-vladimir-putin-russia-best-friend-ally-war-in-ukraine/

Lee Myers, S., & Mozur, P. (2019, August 13). China is waging a disinformation war against Hong Kong protesters. *The New York Times*. https://nytimes.com/2019/08/13/world/asia/hong-kong-protests-china.html

Morrison, S., Barnet, B., & Martin, J. (2020, June 23). *China's disinformation threat is real. We need better defences against state-based cyber campaigns*. The Conversation. https://theconversation.com/chinas-disinformation-threat-is-real-we-need-better-defences-against-state-based-cyber-campaigns-141044

Mukherjee, S., & Soderpalm, H. (2020, October 20). *Sweden bans Huawei, ZTE from upcoming 5G networks*. Reuters. https://reuters.com/#:~:text=STOCKHOLM%20(Reuters)%20%2D%20Sweden%20has,Chinese%20suppliers%20on%20security%20grounds

News Literacy Project. (2023). *Checkology*. News Literacy Project. https://newslit.org/educators/checkology/

Pomerantsev, P. (2019). *This is not propaganda: Adventures in the war against reality*. PublicAffairs. https://ndupress.ndu.edu/Media/News/News-Article-View/Article/3108041/this-is-not-propaganda-adventures-in-the-war-against-reality/

RAND Corporation. (2023). *Tools that fight disinformation online*. RAND Corporation. https://rand.org/research/projects/truth-decay/fighting-disinformation/search.html

Reuters. (2019, December 10). *China says Taiwan anti-infiltration bill causes 'alarm' for investors*. Reuters. https://reuters.com/article/us-china-taiwan-idUSKBN1YF09Y

Robinson, P. (2020, November 27). *The Russian Brexit plot that wasn't*. Strategic Culture Foundation. https://strategic-culture.org/news/2020/11/27/the-russian-brexit-plot-that-wasnt/

Rosenberger, L. (2020). Disinformation disorientation. *The Journal of Democracy*, 31(1), 203 – 207.

Rudd, K. (2022, October 10). *The World According to Xi Jinping*. Foreign Affairs. https://foreignaffairs.com/china/world-according-xi-jinping-china-ideologue-kevin-rudd

Sanger, D. and Kanno-Youngs, Z. (2020, September 22). The Russian trolls have a simpler job today. Quote Trump. *The New York Times*. https://nytimes.com/2020/09/22/us/politics/russia-disinformation-election-trump.html

Searight, A. (2020, May 8). *Countering China's influence operations: Lessons from Australia*. CSIS. https://csis.org/analysis/countering-chinas-influence-operations-lessons-australia

Shepardson, D. (2021, November 11). *Biden signs legislation to tighten U.S. restrictions on Huawei, ZTE*. Reuters. https://reuters.com/technology/biden-signs-legislation-tighten-us-restrictions-huawei-zte-2021-11-11/

Shuster, S. (2020, October 7). *What U.S.-Russia talks on election meddling say about the Kremlin's shifting strategy*. TIME. https://time.com/5897310/russia-us-election-interference/

Sinkkonen, E., & Lassila, J. (2020). *Digital authoritarianism in China and Russia: Common goals and diverging standpoints in the era of great-power rivalry*. Finnish Institute of International Affairs. FIIA Briefing Paper 294. https://fiia.fi/en/publication/digital-authoritarianism-in-china-and-russia

Sly, L. (2023, June 28). Putin's standing as global strongman in jeopardy after revolt. *The Washington Post*. https://washingtonpost.com/world/2023/06/28/putin-strongman-image-damaged/

Sokol, S. (2019, August 2). *Russian disinformation distorted reality in Ukraine. Americans should take note*. Foreign Policy. https://foreignpolicy.com/2019/08/02/russian-disinformation-distorted-reality-in-ukraine-americans-should-take-note-putin-mueller-elections-antisemitism/

Stahl, J. (2020, August 18). The top five "revelations" of the Senate Intelligence Committee's Russia Report. *Slate*. https://slate.com/news-and-politics/2020/08/senate-intelligence-russia-report-mueller-comparison.html

Stanford History Education Group. (2023). *Civil online reasoning: Sorting fact from fiction on the internet*. Stanford History Education Group at Stanford University Graduate School of Education. https://online.stanford.edu/courses/gse-xshego006-civic-online-reasoning-sorting-fact-fiction-internet

Starks, T., Cerulus, L., & Scott, M. (2019, June 5). Russia's manipulation of Twitter was far vaster than believed. *Politico*. https://politico.com/story/2019/06/05/study-russia-cybersecurity-twitter-1353543

Steger, I. (2020, January 6). *Taiwan's president is battling a deluge of election-linked homophobic fake news*. Quartz. https://qz.com/1780015/taiwan-election-tsai-ing-wen-faces-homophobic-fake-news/

Stolberg, S. G., & Weiland, N. (2020, September 30). Study finds 'single largest driver' of coronavirus misinformation: Trump. *The New York Times*. https://nytimes.com/2020/09/30/us/politics/trump-coronavirus-misinformation.html

Sukhankin, S. (2019). The Western alliance in the face of the Russian (dis)information machine: Where does Canada stand? *University of Calgary: The School of Public Policy Publications*, 12(26), 1–31. https://papers.ssrn.com/sol3/papers.cfm?abstract_id = 3454249

Summers, J. (2017, October 25). *Countering disinformation: Russia's infowar in Ukraine*. The Henry M. Jackson School of International Studies at the University of Washington. https://jsis.washington.edu/news/russia-disinformation-ukraine/

The Hill Staff. (2020, August 18). Read: Final Senate Intelligence Committee report on Russian election interference. *The Hill*. https://thehill.com/policy/national-security/512493-read-final-senate-intelligence-committee-report-on-russian-election

Theohary, C. A. (2018, March 5). *Information warfare: Issues for Congress*. Congressional Research Service. https://fas.org/sgp/crs/natsec/R45142.pdf

Twitter Inc. (2019, August 19). *Updating our advertising policies on state media*. Twitter. https://blog.twitter.com/en_us/topics/company/2019/advertising_policies_on_state_media.html

U.S. Department of Homeland Security (2020). *Homeland threat assessment*. U.S. Department of Homeland Security. https://dhs.gov/sites/default/files/publications/2020_10_06_homeland-threat-assessment.pdf

USC US-China Institute. (2007, November 15). *White paper on China's political party system*. USC US-China Institute at USC Annenberg. https://china.usc.edu/white-paper-chinas-political-party-system-2007

Visram, T. (2020, June 29). *Citizen journalists are documenting COVID in the world's conflict zones to stop disinformation*. Fast Company. https://fastcompany.com/90521383/citizen-journalists-are-documenting-covid-in-the-worlds-conflict-zones-to-stop-disinformation

Wallis, J., Uren, T., Thomas, E., Zhang, A., Hoffman, S., Li, L., Pascoe, A., & Cave, D. (2020, June). *Retweeting through the great firewall: A persistent and undeterred threat actor*. Australian Strategic Policy Institute. International Cyber Policy Centre. https://s3-ap-southeast-2.amazonaws.com/ad-aspi/2020-06/Retweeting%20through%20the%20great%20firewall_0.pdf?zjVSJfAOYGRkguAbufYr8KRSQ610SfRX

White House (2015, February). *National security strategy*. Obama White House Archives. https://obamawhitehouse.archives.gov/sites/default/files/docs/2015_national_security_strategy.pdf

Woo, R. (2023, November 6). *China, Australia agree to turn the page as tensions ease*. Reuters. https://reuters.com/world/asia-pacific/australias-albanese-retraces-historic-beijing-walk-visit-mend-ties-2023-11-06/

Wray, C. (2020, September 17). *Worldwide threats to the homeland.* Federal Bureau of Investigation. Statement before the House Homeland Security Committee. Washington, D C. https://fbi.gov/news/testimony/worldwide-threats-to-the-homeland-091720

Yuhas, A. (2014, March 17). Russian propaganda over Crimea and the Ukraine: How does it work? *The Guardian.* https://theguardian.com/world/2014/mar/17/crimea-crisis-russia-propaganda-media

4

Cyber Challenges to Democracy and Soft Power's Dark Side

Renée Marlin-Bennett

Despite initial hopes that advances in information technology would spread and deepen democracy around the world, new platforms for communicating have instead provided opportunities for the weakening of democracy. Social media, website hosting, messaging apps, and related technologies provide easy and cheap ways for micro-actors such as individuals and small groups (in addition to more traditional state and non-state actors) to wield soft power for antidemocratic purposes. Of course, the probability that any one soft power action on the part of a micro-actor will have a consequential effect in the world is minuscule. Yet cyber-enabled micro-actions by micro-actors can make a difference, often one that has a negative effect on democratic institutions. QAnon, the anti-vaxx movement, and the spread of racism, antisemitism, and Islamophobia online are just a few examples of the effects of aggregated micro exercises of soft power. Spreading mis- and disinformation as well as divisiveness and hateful messages through social media is a kind of malign soft power that undermines democracy.

Although soft power is generally thought to be the "good" kind of power, since it works by attraction rather than coercion,[1] it has a dark side (Marlin-Bennett, 2022) when the motive is to harm – and I include undermining democracy as a kind of

I presented an early draft of this chapter at the 2023 International Studies Association in Montreal. My thanks to fellow panelists Christopher Ankerson and John Bonilla, as well as the audience members, including Greg Olsen, for their critical engagement and helpful observations. Scott Shackelford and Frederick Douzet provided extremely useful critique during a workshop for the present volume. I am also grateful to Nandini Dey, Thomas Risse, Richard Katz, Sebastian Schmidt, Susan T. Jackson, and Patrick Thaddeus Jackson for clarifying questions and constructive criticism on my larger project on malign soft power and information flows.

[1] The term "soft power," as the power of attraction rather than coercion, was first coined by Joseph Nye (1990a, 1990b). The term encompasses public diplomacy efforts (Hayden, 2017; Nye, 2008) as well as the efforts of other actors who are not working at the direction of states (Zaharna, 2010). This chapter only briefly mentions antidemocratic hard power. Hacking voting machines to corrupt their data files would be an example of hard power and coercion rather than soft power and attraction. In cyberspace, as in the physical world, hard power actions often happen alongside soft power ones.

harm. While adversarial state actors or other large and well-resourced non-state actors can easily deploy malign soft power, micro-actors can as well because the costs of doing so are low.[2] Exactly who is acting is often unknown, which complicates how to fight back. Furthermore, even when micro-actors are behind antidemocratic activities, such efforts may hook up with the interests of states or non-state adversaries that seek to subvert democracy and weaken democratic states. Despite the difficulties of identifying the actors who wield this power, we can observe the *wielding*[3] of it as flows of information move through social networks.

This chapter provides a framework for analyzing antidemocratic soft power that focuses on flows of antidemocratic messaging. I begin with a review of the initial hopes for information technologies' contributions to a more democratic world and why those hopes were dashed. In the second section, I explain why it is reasonable to analyze these attacks on democracy by focusing first on the information as it flows rather than on the actors who are attacking. Actors, I argue, are emergent, which is especially relevant in the context of cyber-enabled technologies. In the third section, I focus on conceptualizing soft power, including its malign form that can be used to undermine democracy. In the fourth section, I examine the wielding of antidemocratic soft power through control of information flows (content, velocity, and access). The chapter ends with brief concluding comments.

INITIAL HOPES

In 2004, the internet became truly interactive. Previously, accessing the internet meant users seeing the information that was provided to them and providing the information that was requested of them. Web 2.0, the web of social media, allowed users to post content they chose to share online and to do so in a way that allowed their posts to be visible to their friends or interested others. This was widely considered to be a very good thing. By 2006, *Time Magazine* named "You" the person of the year, because "[y]ou control the Information Age" by providing content. Lev Grossman, then a technology writer for the magazine, and also a novelist, praised internet users – "for seizing the reins of global media, for founding and framing the new digital democracy, for working for nothing and beating the

2 Nye himself notes the advent of twenty-first century information technology "means . . . that foreign policy will not be the sole province of governments. Both individuals and private organizations, here and abroad, will be empowered to play direct roles in world politics" (Nye, 2002, p. 61). The context here is that Nye foresees greater volatility in the kinds of soft power efforts that circulate via information technologies. Malign efforts are not excluded from the future as he imagines it in 2002, but his emphasis is on the positive aspects of soft power: advocacy for human rights and actions taken in the global public interest.

3 I use the gerund form, wielding, intentionally (albeit awkwardly) to indicate the action as it unfolds. Unknown actors wield power by controlling flows of information.

pros at their own game." The tribute continues with a minor caveat, but ends with what in hindsight seems to be recklessly positive spin:

> Sure, it's a mistake to romanticize all this any more than is strictly necessary. Web 2.0 harnesses the stupidity of crowds as well as its wisdom. Some of the comments on YouTube make you weep for the future of humanity just for the spelling alone, never mind the obscenity and the naked hatred.
>
> But that's what makes all this interesting. Web 2.0 is a massive social experiment, and like any experiment worth trying, it could fail. . . . This is an opportunity to build a new kind of international understanding, not politician to politician, great man to great man, but citizen to citizen, person to person. It's a chance for people to look at a computer screen and really, genuinely wonder who's out there looking back at them. Go on. Tell us you're not just a little bit curious. (Grossman, 2006, n.p.)

Many others writing in the popular media and scholarly/scientific literature echoed this optimism, sometimes downplaying the obvious caveats. Canadian commentators Don Tapscott and Anthony D. Williams argued for a positive vision of the transformative nature of information technology-enabled interaction, focusing on the possibilities for collaboration to radically alter (in a good way) business and society (Tapscott & Williams, 2006). In later work they also claimed that collaborative governance – citizens being able to weigh in on domestic and transborder policy issues – would improve the democracy of governments and open the world to democratic participation (Tapscott & Williams, 2010). In an interview in *CIO Insight*, an information technology industry trade magazine, Williams lauded the potential of "governance webs" – interactive websites for policy deliberation and sharing of information. The new capacity for interactivity online "provides a mechanism for collaboration of public agencies, the private sector, community groups and citizens." While Williams cautioned that Web 2.0 would not be a "silver bullet [delivering] world peace," he still foresaw "a new golden age of democracy" (quoted in Klein, 2008, p. 36).

Many of the early scholarly publications on Web 2.0 and its broader social consequences also made optimistic claims about the exciting democratizing potential of e-democracy, though scholarly works tended to be more moderate than publications written for a broader audience. Many scholars acknowledged that various hiccoughs, such as the possible lack of citizen interest in participating online, could limit the democratizing potential of this new technology. For example, Kalnes (2009), writing on the 2007 elections in Norway, found that Web 2.0 allowed for greater ease of participation for citizens who wished to engage, even though its effect on pluralism was limited. (See also Anttiroiko, 2010; Boikos, Moutsoulas, & Tsekeris, 2014; Breindl & Francq, 2008; Costa Sánchez & Piñeiro Otero, 2011; Parycek & Sachs, 2010; Raddaoui, 2012; Reddick & Aikins, 2012.)

Yet, other scholars provided strong warnings. In an early article on this topic, Cammaerts (2008, p. 359) notes the high hopes that analysts had for a more expansively pluralist society in which anyone could say what they wish (enabling the "radical plurality of the blogosphere"). More to the point, though, he identifies antidemocratic pressures, including those resulting from peer-to-peer intimidation leading to self-censorship, and "the existence of anti-publics, abusing the freedom of expression with the aim to weaken democracy and democratic values" (Cammaerts, 2008, p. 372).[4] (Also see concerns raised by, inter alia, Marlin-Bennett, 2011; Schradie, 2011; Van Dijck & Nieborg, 2009.) In the years that have passed since those earlier assessments, Cammaerts' and other scholars' pessimism has been validated. The failure of this massive social experiment (to use Grossman's term) has had and continues to have correspondingly negative social repercussions.

Despite prior naive expectations that social media and related forms of communication would only encourage people to embrace democracy, these cyber-enabled technologies have also opened opportunities for actors to use soft power to undermine democracy.

WHY NOT START BY FIGURING OUT WHO THE BAD GUYS ARE?

The analysis of power usually starts with an assessment of who (or what) is acting on whom. However, the nature of actors on social media and using related technologies is a moving target. All actors continue to change as a consequence of their interactions, and new and often surprising actors pop up (and often disappear). As Berenskötter (2018) suggests, actors' ontologies and their motives are constructed through their interactions. In this section, I discuss the governing logics of cyberspace and the emergence of actors to buttress my claim that it makes sense to first focus on the *flows* of information rather than on *who* is enacting the flows in the analysis of antidemocratic soft power.[5]

Libertarian and Neoliberal Logics

Cyberspace, encompassing the interactions among users of websites, social media platforms, messaging, and related technologies, has been constituted through the libertarian and neoliberal logics that generate the technical and regulatory structures

4 Cammaerts also identifies the commodification of the internet, unequal power leading to censorship by states and intimidation by employers, and the outsized ability of elites to further their own interests.

5 I do not mean to imply that efforts to demand accountability by identifying actors are worthless or counterproductive. Such efforts may be easier or more necessary in cases of hard power attacks. Governments and nongovernmental organizations do attempt to identify who is acting when malicious actions are detected (Mueller et al., 2019; The RAND Corporation, 2019). Herbert Lin (2016) discusses how to identify those who are responsible for hard power cyberattacks. He separates aspects of attribution into the machine or machines that originated the malicious action, the human who took action, and the "ultimate responsible party." Such efforts are easier, I believe, in the context of specific hard power, such as ransomware attacks. The ubiquity of malign soft power makes tracking down culprits, including the misguided people who do not understand that they are sharing misinformation, a Sisyphean task.

of internet development and policymaking. Cyberspace consequently usually permits anonymity, pseudonymity, and even spoofing.[6] Although early in the development of the internet many computer scientists and engineers held a soft socialist view that saw code as something to be shared and the internet as something of a public service, by the 1980s that had changed (in tandem with larger social shifts). Internet developers had adopted a Silicon Valley worldview: "'Technolibertarianism' became one of the central ideologies of the Internet" (Rosenzweig, 1998, p. 1550; see also Borsook, 1996). Decentralized, participatory decision-making procedures, which in the earlier period signaled equality and camaraderie, were repurposed to fit libertarian norms of limited government intervention and individualism. The emphasis on individual liberty fits with allowing the individual to hide their identity as the default setting, making anonymity and pseudonymity permitted and warranted (See Berker, 2022 on deontic and fitting categories.) Put differently, it would have been possible to engineer into internet systems a strong requirement or an expectation that users would have to identify themselves truthfully to have an online presence. That did not happen.

The move to libertarian logics included a shift toward business and profit-making, prioritizing the commodification of information and the protection of intellectual property (Marlin-Bennett, 2004), all of which overlap with neoliberal logics. The Clinton administration designed support for neoliberal logics into its formative internet policies, as evinced by the decision to open the internet to commercial activities and by the creation of the Internet Corporation for Assigned Names and Numbers (ICANN) as a private, nonprofit, multistakeholder organization that would perform internet governance functions. In doing so, the United States maintained its hegemonic position and the power of corporations in cyberspace (Taggart & Abraham, 2023).[7] To require identification by default would have added friction to the system, which was optimized for efficient, fast transactions of a market. What this meant for users' anonymity and pseudonymity was that there was no reason to change course and require that users identify themselves truly by default. Nor was there any requirement that a person (natural or legal) could have only one cyber identity. In short, the libertarian and neoliberal underpinning of the structure of the internet is constitutive of cyberspace in which users generally may keep their (multiple) identities hidden.

Actors as Emergent

Furthermore, actors and agencies are emergent (Abraham, 2022; Chatterje-Doody & Crilley, 2019; Dunn Cavelty & Jaeger, 2015; Elder-Vass, 2008), regardless of whether

6 Spoofing can be considered a form of pseudonymity.

7 Internet pioneers would have preferred privatization without the United States maintaining a good deal of control (Mueller, 1999).

the actors are identified, pseudonymous, or anonymous. As Karen Barad explains: Actors "do not preexist their interactions; rather [actors] emerge through and as part of their entangled intra-relating." Emergence continues as actors "are iteratively reconfigured through each intra-action" (Barad, 2007, p. ix). When actors' identities are reasonably stable, efforts to identify bad actors open opportunities for deterring their actions in the future. That is often the case when actors are states or recognized as institutionally coherent non-state actors, though even if they do exist in a recognizable form, they are changing.

The emergence of surprising new micro-actors whose messages undermine democracy is not a novel phenomenon of the Information Age. Henry Ford (1863–1947), well-known as the founder of Ford Motor Company, surprisingly became a leading proponent of antisemitic hate and disinformation. His hate-filled screed, *The International Jew*, was subsequently used for Nazi propaganda (Flink, 2000). The anti-Black and antisemitic Ku Klux Klan, which was created in 1865 by a group of Confederate Army veterans in Pulaski, Tennessee, is another example (Baudouin, 2011; Quarles, 1999).

However, cyber-enabled technologies, because of their affordability, make it easier for surprising new micro-actors to participate in spreading hate, divisiveness, and mis- and disinformation. The resurgence of racism, antisemitism, Islamaphobia, and other forms of intergroup hatred spread through cyber-enabled technologies, and a large proportion of people were exposed to abusive content (ADL, 2023; Vidgen, Margetts, & Harris, 2019). Cyber-enabled technologies have allowed anti-vaxx groups to share anti-vaxx misinformation and promote vaccine hesitancy and rejection, eroding trust in public health agencies and causing a drop in vaccination rates, as these groups become a "political force" in democratic societies (Piper, 2023; see also Burki, 2020; Wilson & Wiysonge, 2020). Perhaps most surprising is the pseudonymous QAnon, which first emerged on the 4chan social media site. QAnon adherents spread a bizarre conspiracy theory that combines alt-right divisiveness, disinformation about the outcome of the 2020 US presidential election, confabulation about the so-called deep state, and hatred for Jews, the LGBTQ+ community, and immigrants (*QAnon | ADL*, 2022). Many of the participants in the January 6, 2021, attack on the United States Capitol were QAnon followers (Lee et al., 2022).

In the next two sections, I focus upon conceptualizing malign soft power and exploring how it is wielded using cyber-enabled technologies.

CONCEPTUALIZING MALIGN SOFT POWER

Cyber-enabled technologies can be used to wield soft or hard power. Hard power cyberattacks, including sabotage of critical infrastructure[8] and ransomware, is only deployed in adversarial situations. Soft power, on the other hand, seems almost

[8] For example, Iranian-backed hackers attacked an Israeli-made industrial control device used by water authorities in a number of United States systems in October of 2023 (Bajak & Levy, 2023).

friendly.[9] The usual view is that soft power practices "contribute to a positive image that *endears* nations with soft power to other nations, which in turn enhances these soft power nations' influence in world politics" (Gallarotti, 2011, p. 32, stress added).[10] Those who advocate for relying on soft power over hard claim that soft power "cultivates cooperation and compliance in a much more harmonious context" than hard power does (Gallarotti, 2022, p. 384, stress removed).[11] Other scholars have questioned this positive view. Successfully wielding soft power – even of the most pleasant sort – is forceful, in the basic sense of getting others to do what they would not have otherwise done, which means that interests have been denied or manipulated (Bially Mattern, 2005; Hayden, 2012, 2017). Soft power can also have negative unintended consequences (Johnson, 2011; Siekmeier, 2014). And to the point for understanding how soft power can negatively impact democracy: Soft power can be wielded in ways that undercut democracy.

As such, antidemocratic soft power is a kind of malign soft power, as opposed to good or neutral soft power. Malign soft power is a power of attraction used for harm (Marlin-Bennett, 2022), but discerning that a particular action was motivated by a wish to do harm is difficult. Nevertheless, even when we cannot see who is acting – as is often the case with cyber-enabled technologies – we can reasonably infer the motivation behind an action by drawing upon our own practical reasoning. Members of society routinely make such judgments, and inferring motivations from actions and their consequences is a normal part of social life. While it is possible that otherwise well-meaning people accidentally do something that has a malign consequence or is misconstrued does not cancel out the quotidian way people adjudge actions. In addition, judgments of harm depend on the standpoint of whoever is making the determination,[12] and I acknowledge that my analysis comes from a pro-democracy position.[13] As I discuss in the next section, messages of divisiveness, hate,

9 A full-fledged review of the voluminous literature on soft power in International Relations and other fields of scholarship is beyond the scope of this chapter, but some additional IR works include: Gilboa (2008), Henne (2022), Wilson (2008), Goldsmith and Horiuchi (2012), Goldthau and Sitter (2015), Nye (2021), Keating and Kaczmarska (2019), and Tella (2023).

10 Nye's quote from this early article refers to "countries" rather than the more general "actors" I have substituted here. Most assessments of soft power, including works by Nye (e.g., 2019), also hold that non-state actors, such as small groups and individuals, can wield soft power. Soft power is a strategy micro-actors can use to similarly endear themselves to other actors and become influential in world politics. Soft power can be generated by using resources that are relatively cheap and accessible, a much lower bar than micro-actors would face if they wished to deploy hard power. See also Zahran and Ramos (2010) and Nimmo et al. (2019).

11 Some efforts at wielding soft power do seem quite positive in effect, and it is hard to find fault in some cultural exchanges that promote democracy (e.g., Atkinson, 2010).

12 For example, patriotic Russians who support Putin and are suspicious of too much freedom and supporters of Western liberal democracy will certainly have different views of what is harmful.

13 I also acknowledge the inescapable tension between democracy's expansive protections of freedom of speech and the dangers of hateful speech and speech that spreads lies and bullshit (Frankfurt, 2005).

and mis- and disinformation become attractive (and therefore power*ful*) when they seduce, trick, or amuse those who are exposed to them into feeling that they share the sentiments.

Ironically, in Western democracies, wielding malign soft power is often legal, which further sets this kind of power apart from hard power. Democracy's guarantee of freedom of speech makes punishing antidemocratic speech more difficult, though jurisdictions have different laws about the limits of protected speech. (European laws generally have more limits on speech than the US laws, but rights to freedom of expression still provide ample room for the lawful spread of politically divisive messages.) In some cases, state actors (e.g., Russia and China) initiate and/or amplify these messages; in other cases, they may simply be "home grown." How these messages are received is important, too. Most people who see a message of hate on X (formerly Twitter) or a bit of disinformation on TikTok will probably not be susceptible to the soft power lure of the antidemocratic content and will simply move on to the next message, one that is unlikely to be similarly problematic. However, some people *will* be affected in that they will be attracted to the underlying antidemocratic message and the normalization of antidemocratic language and images is problematic.[14]

WIELDING MALIGN SOFT POWER: CONTROLLING FLOWS OF ANTIDEMOCRATIC INFORMATION

Wielding malign soft power, the action of power*ing* the soft power, refers to the instance of controlling flows of messages that are politically divisive, hate-filled, and/or mis- or disinformation through social networks, exposing recipients, some of whom are attracted by the antidemocratic messages. The flows have the properties of *content* (the messages that are divisive, hate-filled, or mis- or disinformation), *velocity* (direction and speed of the messages), and *access* to them (by choice of the person who is exposed, by chance, or by force).[15] Focusing on these properties allows *patterns of actions* rather than *actors* to be the subjects of analysis and rule in an interactional, social sense (Szabla & Blommaert, 2020).

14 Soft power can be adversarial without being malign, though the determination depends on standpoint and context. State actors routinely use soft power actions to portray themselves as more attractive in an effort to bolster their own image and undercut adversary countries' relations with others. For example, China's Belt and Road Initiative has adversarial elements to it, but in practical terms, it seems to fall short of the threshold for being malign.

15 Common sense tells us that actors wield power through material means, through informational means, or through a combination. Examples are bullets (material), brainwashing (informational), and Foucault's panopticon (combination). This chapter focuses on wielding power with information, but it is also possible to translate the material into the informational for the purpose of analysis. The bullet informs the wounded body of injury and triggers signals of pain (Marlin-Bennett, 2013).

Content

The property of *content* refers to messages being transmitted and the emotions they convey. Message density is important as well, as the more times a particular message is received, the more it seems to be correct because it is common knowledge (Unkelbach et al., 2019). I focus here on three commonly deployed modes by which the content works: seduction, trickery, and amusement.[16] When malign soft power seduces, tricks, or amuses, it does so through a combination of semantic and emotional content of messages.

Seduction links semantic content to emotion by invoking desire in the recipient. Online, as in person, we recognize how attracting through seduction[17] (of the sexual (e.g., Faisinet, 1808) and nonsexual varieties (e.g., Bjerg, 2016)) can cause harm. Content eliciting these desires spreads online in various ways, including through social media and via niche websites. Antidemocratic seduction convinces people to feel attachments that are inconsistent with democracy, such as hatred for political opponents, rather than simple disagreement with them. The spread of White Christian nationalist identitarianism in North America and Europe, a movement that is profoundly antidemocratic (Zuquete & Marchi, 2023), is an example. Individual participants produce and reproduce seduction through identitarian practices. For example, sharing "dog whistles" that express hatred in coded language gives participants a seductive sense that they are in on the secret (Marlin-Bennett, 2022). Much of the content antisemitic feed of Stew Peters (@realstewpeters) on X (formerly Twitter) seeks to draw a White Christian audience into solidarity against Jews. Peters, who has a following on X of over 500,000 accounts (some of which may be automated) also engages in trickery about vaccines and other alt-right topics.

Trickery replaces falsehoods for facts, with claims that lies (known to be false) and/or bullshit (statements that are disconnected from the truth) (Frankfurt, 2005) are actually true. This practice is in play when disinformation is spread as misinformation by gullible users. For example, the Stew Peters Network disseminated disinformation about the COVID vaccine in a video, *Died Suddenly* (Skow & Stumphauzer, 2022), on "Rumble, a moderation-averse video-streaming platform"

[16] Other modes are possible. Modes often work in combination.

[17] I am referring here to a plain language understanding of "seduction" and "seduce" such as one finds in an English language dictionary (e.g., "Seduce, v.," 2023). For malign soft power, the *OED Online*'s second definition of seduce – "To lead (a person) astray in action, conduct, or belief; to draw (a person) away *from* the right or intended course of action *to* or *into* a wrong or misguided one; to entice or beguile (a person) *to* do something wrong, foolish, or unintended – is particularly apt and helpfully covers both sexual and nonsexual kinds of conduct. For a more complex rendering, see Felman, 2003. Baudrillard's and Freud's treatments of seduction are not useful in this context. Laura Sjoberg (2018) cautions that news accounts of women around the Islamic State frequently portray them as nonagentic and subject to being duped because of their inherent feminine characteristics. Her argument is a compelling reminder that all secondhand accounts are imperfect retellings of actual motivations, knowledge, and desires.

(Tiffany, 2023). Peters also promoted the video on X, Gab, and other social media sites. The many likes his tweets have received suggest that his falsehoods have been received by and are attractive to other users. The many reposts suggest that others spread his disinformation as misinformation.[18] Peters' seductive messaging and lies connect with similar views disseminated by other individuals, creating interconnected networks of people who share antisemitism, White Christian nationalism, and anti-vaxx views. The widespread campaign to convince people that Joe Biden stole the US 2020 presidential election works similarly, drawing on trickery and often blending with the seductiveness of White Christian nationalism. Its success can be seen in a March 2023 CNN/SSRS poll that found that 63 percent of Republicans continued to believe it (Durkee, 2023). Individuals who believe in this falsehood have been tricked by antidemocratic mis- or disinformation.

When amusement is used for antidemocratic purposes, the content links humor or other pleasures to messages that in other contexts would be transgressive. A racist joke does not seem as bad to those who find it amusing. The mode of amusement allows funny or entertaining content to seem acceptable even when it is harmful (Apel, 2009; Gaut, 1998). Topinka (2018) examines the Reddit platform and specifically the r/ImGoingToHellForThis subreddit (now banned), in which members of the subreddit used humor to express racism, misogyny, antisemitism, and extreme anti-immigrant sentiments. Topinka provides a close analysis of how the redditors treated the famous, haunting picture of Alan Kurdi, the two-year old Syrian refugee who drowned along with his mother and brother in the Mediterranean Sea while fleeing to the Greek isle of Cos. The posts remixed the image of the dead toddler on the beach into jokes that were at once racist and anti-immigrant extremist. As soft power practices, "[t]he very ostentation on which this humor relies thus functions as a cloak concealing the networks of racist sentiment that the discourse sustains" (Topinka, 2018, p. 2066). This now defunct subreddit and other similar sites simultaneously rely on the democratic principle of free speech and eschew core democratic values. More generally, humor is often used on social media platforms to catch the eye of the user who is scrolling through feeds, be they TikTok or Instagram or another app, to find a quick laugh. Amusement is antidemocratic when it works to normalize hate or convince people of the truthfulness of fallacious claims relevant to current politics. Jokes may intensify the connection between humor and hate (Askanius, 2021; Marlin-Bennett & Jackson, 2022).

Velocity and Access

Controlling velocity (direction and speed) and access to messages are the other two properties for acting on soft power. Cyber-enabled technologies afford actors at all

[18] Likes and reposts are generally indications that a message has been received with approval – in other words, that the soft power worked. However, that is not always the case. Likes and reposts can be done by bots or cyborgs. Also, people who disapprove sometimes repost in order to critique it.

scales the capacity to manipulate these, but it is not necessarily the case that any specific techniques are relevant solely for antidemocratic purposes. If the content is antidemocratic, then increasing its velocity[19] – that is, increasing the speed at which the messages move and the spread of the messaging – is a means of wielding soft power to undermine democracy. Directions can be direct (going from a source to an expectant recipient) or circuitous. Speeds of message transmission range from fast to slow, and from constant to intermittent. The metaphor of a unit of information (e.g., a meme) "going viral," means it is spreading quickly and in multiple directions. Messages can also jump from platform to platform and across technologies (DiResta, 2018).

Bots are usually designed to increase velocity. Bessi and Ferrara analyzed tweets about the 2016 presidential election during a five-week period in the fall of 2016. They found that approximately one-fifth of these tweets were generated by bots. They conclude:

> The presence of social bots in online political discussion can create three tangible issues: first, influence can be redistributed across suspicious accounts that may be operated with malicious purposes; second, the political conversation can become further polarized; third, the spreading of misinformation and unverified information can be enhanced.(Bessi & Ferrara, 2016, n.p.)

Micro-actors can also increase velocity, which they do by reposting and commenting, as well as by moving posts to new platforms (Marlin-Bennett & Jackson, 2022). Wielding malign soft power could also work by decreasing the velocity of messages that support democracy.

Controlling access to information is another means of wielding soft power. At stake is whether someone is exposed – or not exposed (denied access) – to information by choice, by chance, or by force. A choice approach means providing access to those who have requested the information, those who are already attracted to the messages. This soft power doubles down on existing attachments. Social media sites like r/ImGoingToHellForThis work this way. Users choose to subscribe and, in doing so, build community among those who are attracted to the divisiveness, hate, and mis- and disinformation. An access-by-chance approach is not targeted at any specific actor but instead involves providing access widely and anticipating that some who happen upon the messages will be swayed by them. The actors behind bot accounts uncovered by Bessi and Ferrara (2016) probably disseminated manipulated information on X using a chance strategy of sending out a

[19] Boichak et al. (2021), citing Yang and Counts (2010), capture velocity in their study of the speed, scale, and range. "[S]peed [. . .] reflects temporality of information events; scale [. . .] speaks to the visibility of a message on a platform through popularity metrics, such as 'likes'and 'retweets'; and range [. . .] denotes the depth of diffusion once the message gets propagated through user networks, reaching new audiences in the process" (Yang & Counts, 2010, pp. 356–357).

lot of content quickly and widely. The effectiveness of a chance approach depends on whether the messages find a core group of people who are receptive to it. Hindman and Barash (2018) also find more real news than fake news on X in the months before and after the 2016 election in the United States, but they remain concerned about the dense networks of followers of popular fake news accounts: "[T]he popularity of these accounts, and heavy co-followership among top accounts, means that fake news stories that reach the core (or start there) are likely to spread widely" (p. 4). (See also Grinberg et al. 2019.) The movement of antidemocratic messaging thus accelerates when it reaches a community who are disposed to be attracted to it. Forced access involves exposing a user to information in a targeted way but without prior subscription or other sort of confirmation of willingness to receive it. Algorithms that display increasingly extreme messages to users force access to antidemocratic information upon them.

An algorithm's control of the flow of antidemocratic information is an instance of deploying malign soft power even though the algorithm itself does not have motivation in the same way a human does. Algorithms that determine what appears in social media newsfeed are part of an assemblage (Bennett, 2005) determining access to information. DeCook and Forestal argue that "digital platforms not only curate and channel certain content to individual users but also facilitate a particular mode of collective thinking that [they] term *undemocratic cognition*" (2023, p. 631).[20] The practice of curating and channeling is clearly an instance of soft power in which individuals are subject to attraction. Motivations, I suggest, are written into algorithms that collect data, analyze what would attract users in a way that serves the motivations of the assemblage, and then produce a newsfeed that gives users access to certain messaging and withholds access to other messaging. (And because of the vagaries of coding, the outcomes of this process may or may not be wholly what the firm's management had expected.) While "make money!" is a compelling motivation for many social media firms, concerns have been raised about Chinese-owned social media like TikTok (*The Economist*, 2023). Kokas notes that China seeks to "manipulate messaging to key [Western] constituencies" for (implicitly) antidemocratic ends (2022, p. 95; see also Zhong, 2023). Additionally, a failure to actively protect against undermining democracy by preventing access to a biased stream of information in one's newsfeed also suggests a motivation that undervalues the protection of democracy. This is perhaps a lesser kind of maliciousness, one of omission rather commission.

Control over content, access, and velocity usually operate together. For example, information flows that flood social media quickly move a large volume of messages

[20] Some studies (e.g., Brown et al., 2022; Chen et al., 2023) have found that YouTube algorithms do not radicalize users by sending them "down the rabbit hole" but that YouTube does make extremist content available. Other studies do find that algorithms can serve to radicalize. See Whittaker et al. (2021).

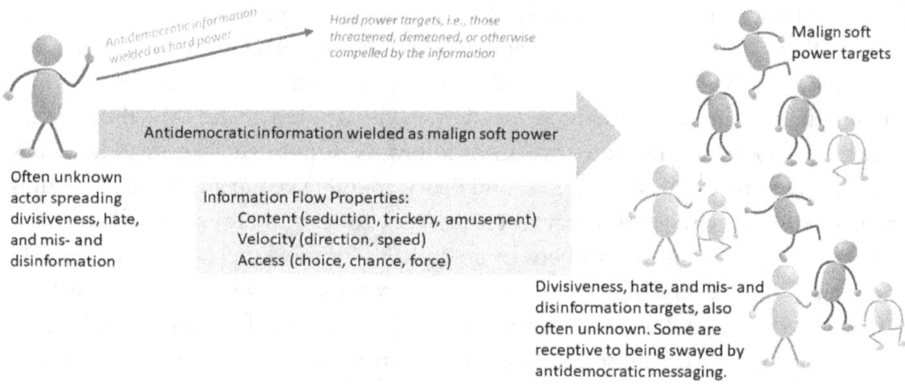

FIGURE 4.1 Wielding malign soft power.

in terms of the number of posts and/or the amount of message within posts (Cirone & Hobbs, 2023). These flows characterized by steady streams of the same untruth contribute over time to making those false claims seem true as a function of "truth by repetition" (Lewandowsky et al., 2012; Morgan & Cappella, 2023; Unkelbach et al., 2019).

As Figure 4.1 summarizes, someone or something wields malign soft power for antidemocratic motives by controlling the flows of information. In the background of this analysis are those for whom the information flow is a hard power attack. In the foreground are the targets of malign soft power, the recipients of flows of attractive hate, mis- and disinformation, and other content that undermines democratic institutions. The intended recipients are those likely to be swayed by the information presented to them.

CONCLUDING COMMENTS

This chapter makes a simple point: By carefully analyzing antidemocratic efforts using cyber-enabled technologies as malign soft power, we can see that the power of attraction is not necessarily harmless nor even less harmful than the power of coercion. The affordances of social media platforms and other participatory media make it easy for emergent actors to contribute to efforts undermining democracy. Antidemocratic content that is seductive, deceptive, or amusing flows easily and quickly throughout social networks. Some new actors further disseminate information while cognizant of the nature of the content and being willing participants in its spread. Others are seduced, distracted by the fun they are having, or simply duped. These are the unwitting actors who further spread hate and mis- and disinformation.

Who the bad actors are may or may not be easy to discern. The low cost of malign soft power resources means that both existing actors and surprising new ones can wield this kind of power. Actors are emergent: Wielding malign soft power dynamically constitutes actors' identities. Moreover, that information *flows*, that it moves over time and space, is key. Manipulating content, velocity, and access and thereby making divisiveness, hate, and mis- and disinformation more available, more quickly, more widely, and to more users is harmful. The common interest is in discovering means of preventing or, if necessary, stopping these power flows and remediating existing harms. While governance can also be harmful, especially if it limits freedom of speech, limits rights to privacy, and is targeted toward vulnerable populations, good governance methods do not single out individuals but rather look at patterns of flows. A purpose of this framework for analyzing antidemocratic soft power is to uncover possible intervention points, the points in the flow of information at which defensive mechanisms can prevent or remediate the harms of malign soft power.

Each of the properties of information flows, the content, velocity, and access, provides opportunities for countering antidemocratic challenges, but undertaking democracy-affirming efforts must be done in a manner that preserves freedom of information. I am mindful of Friedrich Nietzsche's warning:[21] "He who fights with monsters should be careful lest he thereby become a monster. And if [you] gaze long into an abyss, the abyss will also gaze into [you]" (2012, p. 83, sec. 146).

Cyber-enabled technologies have become an essential part of life in many ways and are necessary *for* democracies to function, but these technologies also afford the means to disrupt democracy. Understanding how antidemocratic soft power works and is wielded is just one tool for building resilient democracies.

REFERENCES

Abraham, K. J. (2022). Midcentury modern: The emergence of stakeholders in democratic practice. *American Political Science Review, 116*(2), 631–644. https://doi.org/10.1017/S0003055421001106

ADL. (2023, March 23). *HEAT Map*^{TM} | *ADL*. https://adl.org/resources/tools-to-track-hate/heat-map

Anttiroiko, A.-V. (2010). Innovation in democratic e-governance: Benefitting from Web 2.0 applications in the public sector. *International Journal of Electronic Government Research (IJEGR), 6*(2), 18–36. https://doi.org/10.4018/jegr.2010040102

Apel, D. (2009). Just joking? Chimps, Obama and racial stereotype. *Journal of Visual Culture, 8*(2), 134–142. https://doi.org/10.1177/1470412909008002020 3

Askanius, T. (2021). On frogs, monkeys, and execution memes: Exploring the humor-hate nexus at the intersection of Neo-Nazi and Alt-Right movements in Sweden. *Television & New Media, 22*(2), 147–165. https://doi.org/10.1177/1527476420982234

Atkinson, C. (2010). Does soft power matter? A comparative analysis of student exchange programs 1980–2006. *Foreign Policy Analysis, 6*(1), 1–22. https://doi.org/10.1111/j.1743-8594.2009.00099.x

[21] Antoinette Verhage (2009, p. 9), writing on similar conundrums of how to find the right balance between governance to limit harm and not impinging on rights, includes this quote.

Bajak, F., & Levy, M. (2023, December 2). *Breaches by Iran-affiliated hackers spanned multiple U.S. states, federal agencies say*. AP News. https://apnews.com/article/hackers-iran-israel-water-utilities-critical-infrastructure-cisa-554b2aa969c8220016ab2ef94bd7635b

Barad, K. (2007). *Meeting the universe halfway: Quantum physics and the entanglement of matter and meaning*. Duke University Press.

Baudouin, R. (Ed.). (2011). *The Ku Klux Klan: A history of racism and violence* (6th ed.). Southern Poverty Law Center. https://splcenter.org/sites/default/files/Ku-Klux-Klan-A-History-of-Racism.pdf

Bennett, J. (2005). The agency of assemblages and the North American blackout. *Public Culture*, 17(3), 445–465.

Berenskötter, F. (2018). Deep theorizing in International Relations. *European Journal of International Relations*, 24(4), 814–840. https://doi.org/10.1177/1354066117739096

Berker, S. (2022). *Fittingness: Essays in the philosophy of normativity* (pp. 23–57). Oxford University Press. https://doi.org/10.1093/oso/9780192895882.001.0001

Bessi, A., & Ferrara, E. (2016). *Social bots distort the 2016 U.S. Presidential election online discussion*. First Monday. https://doi.org/10.5210/fm.v21i11.7090

Bially Mattern, J. (2005). Why soft power isn't so soft: Representational force and the sociolinguistic construction of attraction in world politics. *Millennium-Journal of International Studies*, 33(3), 583–612. https://doi.org/10.1177/03058298050330031601

Bjerg, O. (2016). How is Bitcoin money? *Theory, Culture & Society*, 33(1), 53–72. https://doi.org/10.1177/0263276415619015

Boichak, O., Hemsley, J., Jackson, S., Tromble, R., & Tanupabrungsun, S. (2021). Not the bots you are looking for: Patterns and effects of orchestrated interventions in the U.S. and German elections. *International Journal of Communication (19328036)*, 15, 814–839. https://ijoc.org/index.php/ijoc/article/view/14866

Boikos, C., Moutsoulas, K., & Tsekeris, C. (2014). The real of the virtual: Critical reflections on Web 2.0. tripleC: Communication, capitalism & critique. *Open Access Journal for a Global Sustainable Information Society*, 12(1), 405–412. https://doi.org/10.31269/triplec.v12i1.566

Borsook, P. (1996, August). *Cyberselfish*. Mother Jones. https://motherjones.com/politics/1996/07/cyberselfish/

Breindl, Y., & Francq, P. (2008). Can Web 2.0 applications save e-democracy? A study of how new internet applications may enhance citizen participation in the political process online. *International Journal of Electronic Democracy*, 1(1), 14–31. https://doi.org/10.1504/IJED.2008.021276

Brown, M. A., Bisbee, J., Lai, A., Bonneau, R., Nagler, J., & Tucker, J. (2022). *Echo chambers, rabbit holes, and algorithmic bias: How YouTube recommends content to real users* (SSRN Scholarly Paper 4114905). https://doi.org/10.2139/ssrn.4114905

Burki, T. (2020). The online anti-vaccine movement in the age of COVID-19. *The Lancet Digital Health*, 2(10), e504–e505. https://doi.org/10.1016/S2589-7500(20)30227-2

Cammaerts, B. (2008). Critiques on the participatory potentials of Web 2.0. *Communication, Culture and Critique*, 1(4), 358–377. https://doi.org/10.1111/j.1753-9137.2008.00028.x

Chatterje-Doody, P., & Crilley, R. (2019). Populism and contemporary global media: Populist communication logics and the co-construction of transnational identities. In F. A. Stengel, D. B. MacDonald, & D. Nabers (Eds.), *Populism and world politics: Exploring inter- and transnational dimensions* (pp. 73–99). Springer International Publishing. https://doi.org/10.1007/978-3-030-04621-7_4

Chen, A. Y., Nyhan, B., Reifler, J., Robertson, R. E., & Wilson, C. (2023). Subscriptions and external links help drive resentful users to alternative and extremist YouTube channels. *Science Advances*, 9(35). https://doi.org/10.1126/sciadv.add8080

Cirone, A., & Hobbs, W. (2023). Asymmetric flooding as a tool for foreign influence on social media. *Political Science Research and Methods*, 11(1), 160–171. https://doi.org/10.1017/psrm.2022.9

Costa Sánchez, C., & Piñeiro Otero, T. (2012). Social activism in the Web 2.0. Spanish 15m movement. *Vivat Academia*, 117, 1458–1467. https://doi.org/10.15178/va.2011.117E.1458-1467

DeCook, J., & Forestal, J. (2023). Of humans, machines, and extremism: The role of platforms in facilitating undemocratic cognition. *American Behavioral Scientist*, 67(5), 629–648. https://doi.org/10.1177/00027642221103186

DiResta, R. (2018, November 8). *Of virality and viruses: The anti-vaccine movement and social media*. Nautilus Institute. https://nautilus.org/napsnet/napsnet-special-reports/of-virality-and-viruses-the-anti-vaccine-movement-and-social-media/

Dunn Cavelty, M., & Jaeger, M. (2015). (In)visible ghosts in the machine and the powers that bind: The relational securitization of anonymous. *International Political Sociology*, 9(2), 176–194. https://doi.org/10.1111/ips.12090

Durkee, A. (2023, March 14). Republicans increasingly realize there's no evidence of election fraud—but most still think 2020 election was stolen anyway, poll finds. *Forbes*. https://forbes.com/sites/alisondurkee/2023/03/14/republicans-increasingly-realize-theres-no-evidence-of-election-fraud-but-most-still-think-2020-election-was-stolen-anyway-poll-finds/

Elder-Vass, D. (2008). Searching for realism, structure and agency in actor network theory. *The British Journal of Sociology*, 59(3), 455–473. https://doi.org/10.1111/j.1468-4446.2008.00203.x

Faisinet, N. (1808). On seduction. *The Lady's monthly museum, or Polite repository of amusement and instruction: Being an assemblage of whatever can tend to please the fancy, interest the mind, or exalt the character of the British fair. / By a society of ladies, 1798–1828*, 5, 286–289.

Felman, S. (2003). *The scandal of the speaking body: Don Juan with JL Austin, or seduction in two languages*. Stanford University Press.

Flink, J. (2000). Ford, Henry (1863–1947), automobile manufacturer. In *American National Biography*. Oxford University Press. https://anb-org.proxy1.library.jhu.edu/display/10.1093/anb/9780198606697.001.0001/anb-9780198606697-e-1000578

Frankfurt, H. (2005). *On bullshit*. Princeton University Press.

Gallarotti, G. (2011). Soft power: What it is, why it's important, and the conditions for its effective use. *Journal of Political Power*, 4(1), 25–47. https://doi.org/10.1080/2158379X.2011.557886

(2022). Esteem and influence: Soft power in international politics. *Journal of Political Power*, 15(3), 383–396. https://doi.org/10.1080/2158379X.2022.2135303

Gaut, B. (1998). Just joking: The ethics and aesthetics of humor. *Philosophy and Literature*, 22(1), 51–68. https://doi.org/10.1353/phl.1998.0014

Gilboa, E. (2008). Searching for a theory of public diplomacy. *ANNALS of the American Academy of Political and Social Science*, 616(1), 55–77. https://doi.org/10.1177/0002716207312142

Goldsmith, B. E., & Horiuchi, Y. (2012). In search of soft power: Does foreign public opinion matter for US foreign policy? *World Politics*, 64(3), 555–585. https://doi.org/10.1017/S0043887112000123

Goldthau, A., & Sitter, N. (2015). Soft power with a hard edge: EU policy tools and energy security. *Review of International Political Economy*, 22(5), 941–965. https://doi.org/10.1080/09692290.2015.1008547

Grinberg, N., Joseph, K., Friedland, L., Swire-Thompson, B., & Lazer, D. (2019). Fake news on Twitter during the 2016 U.S. presidential election. *Science*, 363(6425), 374–378. https://doi.org/10.1126/science.aau2706

Grossman, L. (2006). You, yes, you, are TIME's person of the year. *TIME Magazine*, 168(26), 38–41.

Hayden, C. (2012). *The rhetoric of soft power: Public diplomacy in global contexts*. Lexington Books.

(2017). Scope, mechanism, and outcome: Arguing soft power in the context of public diplomacy. *Journal of International Relations and Development*, 20(2), 331–357. https://doi.org/10.1057/jird.2015.8

Henne, P. (2022). What we talk about when we talk about soft power. *International Studies Perspectives*, 23(1), 94–111. https://doi.org/10.1093/isp/ekab007

Hindman, M., & Barash, V. (2018, October 4). *Disinformation, "fake news" and influence campaigns on Twitter*. Knight Foundation. https://knightfoundation.org/reports/disinformation-fake-news-and-influence-campaigns-on-twitter/

Johnson, C. G. (2011). The urban precariat, neoliberalization, and the soft power of humanitarian design. *Journal of Developing Societies*, 27(3–4), 445–475.

Kalnes, O. (2009). Norwegian parties and Web 2.0. *Journal of Information Technology & Politics*, 6(3–4), 251–266. https://doi.org/10.1080/19331680903041845

Keating, V., & Kaczmarska, K. (2019). Conservative soft power: Liberal soft power bias and the 'hidden' attraction of Russia. *Journal of International Relations and Development*, 22(1), 1–27. https://doi.org/10.1057/s41268-017-0100-6

Klein, P. (2008). Web 2.0: Reinventing democracy. *CIO Insight*, 92, 30–36.

Kokas, A. (2022). *Trafficking data: How China is winning the battle for digital sovereignty*. Oxford University Press. https://doi.org/10.1093/oso/9780197620502.001.0001

Lee, C., Merizalde, J., Colautti, J., An, J., & Kwak, H. (2022). Storm the Capitol: Linking offline political speech and online Twitter extra-representational participation on QAnon and the January 6 insurrection. *Frontiers in Sociology*, 7. https://doi.org/10.3389/fsoc.2022.876070

Lewandowsky, S., Ecker, U., Seifert, C., Schwarz, N., & Cook, J. (2012). Misinformation and its correction: Continued influence and successful debiasing. *Psychological Science in the Public Interest*, 13(3), 106–131. https://doi.org/10.1177/1529100612451018

Lin, H. (2016, September 20). *Attribution of malicious cyber incidents: From soup to nuts*. Lawfare. https://lawfareblog.com/attribution-malicious-cyber-incidents-soup-nuts-0

Marlin-Bennett, R. (2004). *Knowledge power: Intellectual property, information, and privacy*. Lynne Rienner Publishers.

(2011). I hear America tweeting and other themes for a virtual polis: Rethinking democracy in the global infotech age. *Journal of Information Technology & Politics*, 8(2), 129–145. https://doi.org/10.1080/19331681.2011.53675

(2013). Embodied information, knowing bodies, and power. *Millennium: Journal of International Studies*, 41(3), 601–622. https://doi.org/10.1177/0305829813486413

(2022). Soft power's dark side. *Journal of Political Power*, 15(3), 437–455. https://doi.org/10.1080/2158379X.2022.2128278

Marlin-Bennett, R., & Jackson, S. (2022). DIY cruelty: The global political micro-practices of hateful memes. *Global Studies Quarterly*, 2(2). https://doi.org/10.1093/isagsq/ksac002.

Morgan, J., & Cappella, J. (2023). The effect of repetition on the perceived truth of tobacco-related health misinformation among U.S. adults. *Journal of Health Communication*, 28(3), 182–189. https://doi.org/10.1080/10810730.2023.2192013

Mueller, M. (1999). ICANN and Internet governance: Sorting through the debris of "self-regulation". *Info*, 1(6), 497–520. https://doi.org/10.1108/14636699910801223

Mueller, M., Grindal, K., Kuerbis, B., & Badiei, F. (2019). Cyber attribution: Can a new institution achieve transnational credibility? *The Cyber Defense Review*, 4(1), 107–122.

Nietzsche, F. (2012). *Beyond good and evil*. Andrews UK. http://ebookcentral.proquest.com/lib/jhu/detail.action?docID = 977667

Nimmo, B., Eib, C., & Tamora, L. (2019). *Cross-platform spam network targeted Hong Kong protests: "Spamouflage dragon" used hijacked and fake accounts to amplify video content.* Grafika. https://public-assets.graphika.com/reports/graphika_report_spamouflage.pdf

Nye, J. (1990a). *Bound to lead: The changing nature of American power.* Basic Books.

(1990b). Soft power. *Foreign Policy*, 80, 153–171. https://doi.org/10.2307/1148580

(2002). The information revolution and American soft power. *Asia-Pacific Review*, 9(1), 60–76. https://doi.org/10.1080/13439000220141596

(2008). Public diplomacy and soft power. *The Annals of the American Academy of Political and Social Science*, 616(1), 94–109. https://doi.org/10.1177/0002716207311699

(2019). Soft power and public diplomacy revisited. In J. Melissen & J. Wang (Eds.), *Debating public diplomacy: Now and next* (pp. 7–20). Brill Nijhoff. http://brill.com/view/book/edcoll/9789004410824/BP000006.xml

(2021). Soft power: The evolution of a concept. *Journal of Political Power*, 14(1), 196–208. https://doi.org/10.1080/2158379X.2021.1879572

Parycek, P., & Sachs, M. (2010). Open government – Information flow in Web 2.0. *European Journal of ePractice*, 9, 57–68.

Piper, J. (2023, September 24). Anti-vaxxers are now a modern political force. *Politico*. https://politico.com/news/2023/09/24/anti-vaxxers-political-power-00116527

QAnon | ADL. (2022, October 28). https://adl.org/resources/backgrounder/qanon

Quarles, C. (1999). *The Ku Klux Klan and related American racialist and antisemitic organizations: A history and analysis*. McFarland.

Raddaoui, A. (2012). Democratization of knowledge and the promise of Web 2.0: A historical perspective. In H. Beldhuis (Ed.), *Proceedings of the 11th European Conference on E-Learning* (pp. 435–441). Acad. Conferences Ltd. https://webofscience.com/wos/woscc/full-record/WOS:000321613000053

Reddick, C., & Aikins, S. (2012). Web 2.0 technologies and democratic governance. In C. Reddick & S. Aikins (Eds.), *Web 2.0 technologies and democratic governance: Political, policy and management implications* (pp. 1–7). Springer. https://doi.org/10.1007/978-1-4614-1448-3_1

Rosenzweig, R. (1998). Wizards, bureaucrats, warriors, and hackers: Writing the history of the internet. *The American Historical Review*, 103(5), 1530–1552. https://doi.org/10.2307/2649970

Schradie, J. (2011). The digital production gap: The digital divide and Web 2.0 collide. *Poetics*, 39(2), 145–168. https://doi.org/10.1016/j.poetic.2011.02.003

Seduce, v. (2023). *OED online* (3rd ed.). Oxford University Press. https://oed.com/view/Entry/174721

Siekmeier, J. (2014, June 6). *Bolivia shows how Andean nations can be punished by US neoliberal soft power if they refuse to assist in the 'war on drugs'*. https://blogs.lse.ac.uk/usappblog/2014/06/06/bolivia-shows-how-andean-nations-can-be-punished-by-u-s-neoliberal-soft-power-if-they-refuse-to-assist-in-the-war-on-drugs/

Sjoberg, L. (2018). Jihadi brides and female volunteers: Reading the Islamic State's war to see gender and agency in conflict dynamics. *Conflict Management and Peace Science*, 35(3), 296–311. https://doi.org/10.1177/0738894217695050

Skow, M., & Stumphauzer, N. (Directors). (2022, November 21). *Died suddenly*. Stew Peters Network; https://stewpeters.com/video/2022/11/live-world-premiere-died-suddenly/. https://rumble.com/v1wcs70-died-suddenly-2022-full-documentary.html

Szabla, M., & Blommaert, J. (2020). Does context really collapse in social media interaction? *Applied Linguistics Review*, 11(2), 251–279. https://doi.org/10.1515/applirev-2017-0119

Taggart, J., & Abraham, K. (2023). Norm dynamics in a post-hegemonic world: Multistakeholder global governance and the end of liberal international order. *Review of International Political Economy*, 1–28. https://doi.org/10.1080/09692290.2023.2213441

Tapscott, D., & Williams, A. (2006). *Wikinomics: How mass collaboration changes everything*. Portfolio.

(2010). *MacroWikinomics: Rebooting business and the world*. Portfolio Penguin.

Tella, O. (2023). The diaspora's soft power in an age of global anti-Nigerian sentiment. *Commonwealth & Comparative Politics, 61*(2), 177–196. https://doi.org/10.1080/14662043.2022.2127826

The Economist. (2023, March 30). Both America's political camps agree that TikTok is troubling. *The Economist*. https://economist.com/united-states/2023/03/30/both-americas-political-camps-agree-that-tiktok-is-troubling

The RAND Corporation. (2019). *Accountability in cyberspace: The problem of attribution*. The RAND Corporation. https://youtube.com/watch?v=ca9xomGmZPc

Tiffany, K. (2023, January 24). Twitter has no answers for #DiedSuddenly. *The Atlantic*. https://theatlantic.com/technology/archive/2023/01/died-suddenly-documentary-covid-vaccine-conspiracy-theory/672819/

Topinka, R. (2018). Politically incorrect participatory media: Racist nationalism on r/ImGoingToHellForThis. *New Media & Society, 20*(5), 2050–2069. https://doi.org/10.1177/1461444817712516

Unkelbach, C., Koch, A., Silva, R., & Garcia-Marques, T. (2019). Truth by repetition: Explanations and implications. *Current Directions in Psychological Science, 28*(3), 247–253. https://doi.org/10.1177/0963721419827854

Van Dijck, J., & Nieborg, D. (2009). Wikinomics and its discontents: A critical analysis of Web 2.0 business manifestos. *New Media & Society, 11*(5), 855–874. https://doi.org/10.1177/1461444809105356

Verhage, A. (2009). Between the hammer and the anvil? The anti-money laundering-complex and its interactions with the compliance industry. *Crime, Law & Social Change, 52*(1), 9–32. https://doi.org/10.1007/s10611-008-9174-9

Vidgen, B., Margetts, H., & Harris, A. (2019). *How much online abuse is there? A systematic review of evidence for the UK* (Policy Briefing, Hate Speech: Measures and Counter Measures). Alan Turing Institute. https://turing.ac.uk/sites/default/files/2019-11/online_abuse_prevalence_full_24.11.2019_-_formatted_0.pdf

Whittaker, J., Looney, S., Reed, A., & Votta, F. (2021). Recommender systems and the amplification of extremist content. *Internet Policy Review, 10*(2). https://doi.org/10.14763/2021.2.1565

Wilson, E. (2008). Hard power, soft power, smart power. *Annals of the American Academy of Political and Social Science, 616*(1), 110–124. https://doi.org/10.1177/0002716207312618

Wilson, S., & Wiysonge, C. (2020). Social media and vaccine hesitancy. *BMJ Global Health, 5*(10). https://doi.org/10.1136/bmjgh-2020-004206

Yang, J., & Counts, S. (2010). Predicting the speed, scale, and range of information diffusion in Twitter. *Proceedings of the International AAAI Conference on Web and Social Media, 4*(1) 355–358. https://aaai.org/papers/00355-14039-predicting-the-speed-scale-and-range-of-information-diffusion-in-twitter/

Zaharna, R. (2010). The soft power differential: Mass communication and network communication. In R. Zaharna (Ed.), *Battles to bridges: U.S. strategic communication and public diplomacy after 9/11* (pp. 92–114). Palgrave Macmillan. https://doi.org/10.1057/9780230277922_6

Zahran, G., & Ramos, L. (2010). From hegemony to soft power: Implications of a conceptual change. In *Soft power and US foreign policy* (1st ed., pp. 12–31). Routledge.

Zhong, W. (2023, May 3). Who gets the algorithm? The bigger TikTok danger. *Lawfare*. https://lawfaremedia.org/article/who-gets-the-algorithm-the-bigger-tiktok-danger

Zuquete, J., & Marchi, R. (2023). Postscript. In *Global identitarianism*. Routledge.

5

Cyber Disinformation Risk Perception and Control

Integration of the Extended Theory of Planned Behavior and a Structural Equation Model

Małgorzata Pańkowska and Ioana Vasiu

The extensive use of digital platforms and services has expanded widely the range of potential attacks and targets, rendering individuals and the democratic values and institutions vulnerable to a substantial number of cyber-enabled threats. These threats can be sophisticated, conducted on a large scale, and capable of producing significant, viral consequences. Among these threats, cyber disinformation is regarded as a major threat. The phenomenon is widespread and complex, in certain cases, part of hybrid warfare, involving various cyberattacks by nefarious actors, which deceptively distribute fake or incomplete materials, with a view to influencing people's opinions or behavior.

Disinformation can involve numerous vectors and take several forms. The goal of disinformation campaigns is to promote or sustain certain economic or political interests, discrimination, phobia, hate speech, or harass individuals (European Parliament, 2022). Instances of alleged disinformation can be encountered with respect to a large variety of aspects, such as food (Diekman, Ryan, & Oliver, 2023); migrants (Culloty et al., 2022); fossil fuel;[1] sexual preferences (Carratalá, 2023); health hazards;[2] politics;[3] and so on.

Successful disinformation campaigns can negatively affect fundamental freedoms, undermine trust, subvert attention, change attitudes, sow confusion, exacerbate divides, or interfere with decision-making processes. Consequently, such campaigns can rightly be considered attacks on knowledge integrity (Pérez-Escolar, Lilleker, & Tapia-Frade, 2023, p. 77). The potential consequences can be disquieting, negatively affecting democratic values and institutions (Jungherr & Schroeder, 2021; Schünemann, 2022). The concerns over cyber disinformation are notable worldwide and received significant attention from researchers (Buchanan & Benson, 2019; Nenadić, 2019; Olan et al., 2022; Pierri, Artoni, & Ceri, 2020; Tenove

1 *District of Columbia v. Exxon Mobil Corp.*, Civil Action No. 20 1932 (TJK) (D.C. 2022).
2 *RJ Reynolds Tobacco Co. v. Rouse*, 307 So.3d 89 (Fla. Dist. Ct. App. 2020).
3 *Nat'l Coal. on Black Civic Participation v. Wohl*, 498 F. Supp. 3d 457 (S.D.N.Y. 2020).

& Tworek, 2019; Ternovski, Kalla, & Aronow, 2022; Vaccari & Chadwick, 2020; Weikmann & Lecheler, 2022).

While there are laws that address the phenomenon (e.g., 18 U.S. Code § 35, the German Network Enforcement Act, the French Law on the fight against the manipulation of information), strengthened codes of practice (e.g., the European Commission's Strengthened Code of Practice on Disinformation 2022), assignment of anti-disinformation attributions to governmental agencies (e.g., the U.S. Department of Homeland Security's Cybersecurity and Infrastructure Security Agency), awareness campaigns, and implementation of disinformation detection and blocking algorithms or filters, the control of the phenomenon still poses significant challenges.

The control of the cyber disinformation phenomenon plays a significant role in the protection of democratic values and systems. This chapter argues that an essential role in the control of the phenomenon is played by the individual behavior of users and aims to identify factors that impact on Behavioral Intentions (BIs) and Cyber Hygiene Behavior (CHB), in the circumstances of cyber disinformation. The chapter integrates the Extended Theory of Planned Behavior (ETPB) and a Structural Equation Model. The research data were collected using a questionnaire. The model's parameters were processed using the SmartPLS software.

The rest of this chapter is organized as follows. The next section outlines the phenomenon's main attributes and explains how cyber-enabled means can threaten democratic values and institutions. The third section discusses aspects regarding structural equation modeling (SEM), applied to disinformation. The fourth section presents the conceptual model and the proposed hypotheses. Finally, the fifth section presents the model evaluation. The chapter concludes with implications of findings.

CYBER DISINFORMATION ATTRIBUTES

"Disinformation" is a term difficult to define because the phenomenon is complex (Ó Fathaigh, Helberger, & Appelman, 2021) and covers many forms, such as "fabrications, fakeness, falsity, lies, deception, misinformation, disinformation, propaganda, conspiracy theory, satire or just anything with which one disagrees" (Andersen & Søe, 2020, p. 6). Wardle and Derakhshan (2017), for instance, contrast "disinformation," referred to as intentionally false or deceptive communication, with "misinformation," understood as communications that may contain false claims, however, not intended to cause or inflict harm. The European Commission (2020, p. 18) clearly distinguishes between misinformation, information influence operation, foreign interference in the information space, and disinformation, defining the latter as "false or misleading content that is spread with an intention to deceive or secure economic or political gain and which may cause public harm."

Disinformation can be orchestrated by individuals or by organized groups (state or non-state) and involve various sources, such as regular citizens, political leaders or officials, attention-seeking trolls, profiteers, or propagandistic media (Watson, 2021). Several factors were identified that favor the phenomenon, such as the tendency to believe unreliable statements (European Parliamentary Research Service, 2020) or people's difficulties in identifying disinformation (Machete & Turpin, 2020), the identity confirming problems, and deficiencies in platform filtering (Krafft & Donovan, 2020).

According to Bontcheva et al. (2020, pp. 22–23), disinformation can take various formats, such as false claims or textual narratives; altered, fake, or decontextualized audio and/or video; and fake websites and manipulated datasets. Cyber disinformation campaigns can involve, for example, deceptive advertising, propaganda, or the dissemination of forged materials, such as videos, photographs, audios, documents (including, for instance, fake web pages or maps), created through image altering or airbrushing or cover-up, or by audio camouflage.

One of the characteristics of disinformation campaigns regards the existence of deceptive goals. According to Fallis (2014, pp. 142–146), the deceptive goals can be classified as regarding the accuracy of the content, the source believing the content, the content source identity, and the content accuracy implication. Disinformation can cause significant harm, as it has the real potential to confuse or manipulate people, suppress the truth or critical voices, generate distrust in democratic institutions or norms, and even disrupt democratic processes (Bontcheva et al., 2020).

Social media is often regarded as a highly effective vector to promote political goals via disinformation campaigns (Aïmeur, Amri, & Brassard, 2023). Twitter, now called "X," for example, was used to spread misleading election memes and graphics, designed to demoralize opponent's voters, and even deter them from exercising their right to vote, which went viral.[4] For an illustration of the importance attached to X as a disinformation vector, according to Statista research, the number of disinformation and pro-Russian posts in Poland via X amounted, in January 2022, to 25,910 disinformation and pro-Russian posts on X, increasing to 358,945 during the year (Statista, 2023).

In practice, disinformation campaigns employ an impressive array of tactics, including the impersonation of organizations or real people; creation of fake or misleading online personas or websites; creation of deepfakes or synthetic media; devise or amplification of certain theories; astroturfing and flooding; exploitation of gaps in information; manipulation of unsuspecting people; and spread of targeted content (Cybersecurity and Infrastructure Security Agency, 2022). Of particular concern, given their massive disinformation potential, are the deepfakes. In video and/or audio form, deepfakes nowadays are very realistic, allowing morphing attacks and the creation of unreal faces or voices, allowing personalized messages to

[4] *United States v. Mackey*, No. 21-CR-80 (AMD)(SB) (E.D.N.Y. Oct. 17, 2023).

individuals. Deepfakes can negatively affect the credibility of individuals, disrupt markets, facilitate frauds, manipulate public opinions, incite people to various forms of violence, and support extremist narratives, social unrest, or political polarization (Mattioli et al., 2023; Trend Micro, 2020). Moreover, deepfakes undermine conversations about reality and can disrupt democratic politics (Chesney & Citron, 2019).

Personalization algorithms can be employed to facilitate the spreading of disinformation, potentially making it thrive on digital platforms (Borges & Gambarato, 2019). The techniques or means employed in disinformation campaigns may also include, for instance, bots. These are increasingly difficult to distinguish from humans and can be effectively used to produce disinformation content, targeted at predetermined or general users (Edwards et al., 2016). For instance, bots are used to disseminate election disinformation (Knight Foundation, 2018) or disinformation regarding health issues (Benson, 2020).

Artificial neural network (ANN) and deep learning methods can be used in disinformation campaigns, with unlawful or nefarious potential (Rana et al., 2022). Amplifiers, such as influential people or artificial intelligence tools, via, for instance, cross-platform coordination or the manipulation of engagement metrics, can be used to maximize engagement or the spread of disinformation through networks, to retweet or to follow X accounts or to share Facebook, now called Meta, posts (European Commission, 2023; Michaelis, Jafarian, & Biswas, 2022). Clickbait is another disinformation method used to attract online users to click on disinformation links (Collins et al., 2021).

STRUCTURAL EQUATION MODELING OF DISINFORMATION

The original approach to SEM assumed that the use of technical systems could be explained and predicted by user motivation directly influenced by external factors (i.e., the functionalities and capabilities of those technical systems) (Chuttur, 2009; Davis, 1985). The Technology Acceptance Model (TAM) theory was proposed to explore behavior and user acceptance of Information Communication Technology (ICT) based on the social psychology perspective. The TAM theory assumes that two factors determine users' acceptance of a technology: (1) perceived usefulness and (2) perceived ease of use. The first refers to the user's belief in the degree to which they think that using the technology enhances their job performance, productivity, or overall effectiveness. The second represents the user's perception of how easy it is to apply the technology. In general, the acceptance of technology is a critical element and a necessary condition in the implementation of ICT in everyday life. An extensive literature survey was conducted utilizing the Scopus database, which covers 18,639 papers on TAM, published between 1964 and 2023.

Over decades, several theoretical models have been developed to understand the acceptance and the use of ICT. Researchers have been hesitant in selecting the appropriate theoretical model for the evaluation of the acceptance and usage of

ICT. Recognition of the ICT needs and the ICT acceptance by individuals in business organizations is usually the beginning stage of any business activity and this understanding can be helpful to find the way of future implementation of the ICT.

In general, TAM models are estimated through the SEM, which is an approach for testing the hypotheses on relations among observable and latent variables (Sabi et al., 2016). The SEM is a statistical method applied in various fields of social sciences to estimate relationships among specified variables and verification of hypotheses if those relations are statistically dependable and valid. In this study, the SEM is realized through the Partial Least Square–Structural Equation Modeling (PLS_SEM), which represents the composite-based SEM method (Hair Jr. et al., 2017). Partial Least Square (PLS) is a statistical method for estimation of relationships between independent variables and dependent variables.

For the past thirty years, the research community has been strongly involved in the identification of the factors that have an impact on technology acceptance. The theory of reasoned action (TRA) and the theory of planned behavior (TPB) were predecessors of the TAM (Marikyan & Papagiannidis, 2021; Park & Park, 2020). The TRA explains and predicts human behaviors considering their attitudes and Subjective Norms (SN). That theory assumes that individuals make rational decisions based on their attitudes and social norms.

The TPB is an extension of the TRA, also provided by Ajzen (2005). The TPB explains and predicts individual behavior based on human intentions, which are dependent on three factors, that is, attitude identified with personal beliefs, SN referring to the social pressure, and Perceived Behavioral Control (PBC) encompassing self-efficacy, perceived obstacles, and facilitators. The TAM had further modifications (i.e., TAM2, TAM3); however, researchers have utilized the Unified Theory of Acceptance and Use of Technology (UTAUT) model, which suggests that the actual use of technology is determined by BI. The perceived BI is dependent on four key constructs: performance expectancy, effort expectancy, social influence, and facilitating conditions. The effect of variables is moderated by age, gender, experience, and voluntariness of use (Venkatesh et al., 2003). Further, researchers have noticed the importance of factors reflecting the costs and benefits of behavior, as well as the context of use.

Venkatesh, Thong, and Xu (2012) proposed the UTAUT2 model, which was developed to examine technology use in organizational settings. The authors of the UTAUT2 argue that the use of technology by individuals is determined by the following constructs: performance expectancy, effort expectancy, social influence, facilitating conditions, hedonic motivation, price value, and habit, moderated by age, gender, and experience. In the UTAUT and UTAU2 models, BI has an impact on use behavior.

This study aims to identify factors having an impact on Behavioral Intentions (BIs) and Cyber Hygiene Behavior (CHB) in the circumstances of wide dissemination of disinformation in cyberspace. The BIs comprise an individual's predispositions and willingness to behave in a specific way. This concept is included in various human behavior theories to analyze and predict human actions. CHB covers all practices that allow avoiding the risk to be a victim of cyberattacks and reduce cyber vulnerabilities.

This study considered state-of-the-art research work on disinformation attitudes. The Scopus literature survey revealed 4,526 publications on the "disinformation" keyword search. These papers were published between 1974 and 2023. However, there are only nineteen publications on the "disinformation" AND "structural equation modelling," query, all between 2020 and 2023. Certain countries (i.e., China, Russia, and Turkey) have professionalized operations online to support social media campaigns and create an alternative informational space and effectively disseminate persuasive messages through symbols and emotions. Therefore, their action monitoring as well as online trolling are subjects of research (Alieva, Moffitt, & Carley, 2022; Uyheng, Moffitt, & Carley, 2022).

Several researchers examine the phenomenon of disinformation as a threat in the sphere of cybersecurity (Caramancion et al., 2022; Carrapico & Farrand, 2021). Hence, cybersecurity issues have been included as observable variables (i.e., Security (SEC) items) in the proposed survey. Arayankalam and Krishnan (2021) formulated some hypotheses, which were positively verified, concerning disinformation, as follows:

- Disinformation through social media is positively associated with online media development.
- Online media are positively associated with its social media-induced offline violence.
- The government control negatively moderates disinformation.

In social psychology, the TPB is one of the most influential behavioral models. The TPB links beliefs to behavior and assumes that the user's behavior is determined by their intentions to perform that behavior. In the conceptual model proposed by Jia et al. (2022), for example, several factors have an impact on Behavioral Attitudes (BA), Subjective Norm (SN), and Perceived Behavioral Control (PBC). Further, the three variables determine BI. Moreover, Shirahada and Zhang (2022) argue that TPB is used to predict and explain human intentions in a particular context. Intentions are influenced by SN, attitudes, and PBC. SN concern the expectations of other people and social pressures regarding desirable behavior. Attitude refers to evaluations of behavior, and PBC refers to the ease of performing a behavior.

Maheri, Rezapour, and Didarloo (2022) argue that the Perceived Risk (PR) refers to subjective assessments of the risk of disinformation and its potential consequences. SN refer to respondents' beliefs that significant others think they should or should not engage in a particular behavior. PBC concerns participants' perceptions of their ability to do verification.

Romero-Galisteo et al. (2022) consider that TPB explains the degree of correlation between variables, that is, entrepreneurial intention, perceived feasibility, and perceived desirability. Beyond that, Savari, Mombeni, and Izadi (2022) develop an Extended Theory of Planned Behavior (ETPB) including the variables, that is, Descriptive Norms (DN), Moral Norms (MN), Habits (HA), and Justification (JU). In their theoretical framework, Attitude, SN, DN, and PBC have impacts on Intention, while PBC, MN, and variables such as HA and JU influence Behavior.

MN define a sense of inherent moral commitment, according to a value system. The concept of DN explains personal attitude about how much other people exhibit a certain behavior. The norms are introduced as people learn not only from their own experiences but also from analyses of behaviors of others. Comparable extension of TPB was provided by Khani Jeihooni et al. (2022), who included attitude, among others, PBC, SN, and BIs in their survey.

According to Ababneh, Ahmed, and Dedousis (2022), the TPB proposes four major predictors of human behavior (i.e., attitude toward the behavior, SN, BI, and PBC). Ajzen (1991, p. 183) argues that attitude, norms, and control determine intentions and behavior. Cabeza-Ramirez et al. (2022) notice that literature has rarely considered the possible perception of risk associated with desirable behavior. Similarly, the risk is included in the TPB model proposed by Zhang et al. (2022). Security is considered in the TPB model developed by Al-Shanfari et al. (2022). Using the SEM method, they revealed factors having an impact on information security behavior adoption and employees' training.

THE CONCEPTUAL MODEL AND HYPOTHESES

Considering the literature survey on latent variables included in the TPB models, this study noticed that there is no standardized approach: The models are formulated according to the preferences of researchers and some extensions are possible. Therefore, this study focuses on the application of the ETPB model; however, additional constructs are added, which are expected to present the context of behavior.

This study defines the BA as the degree to which a person believes that they can properly recognize disinformation. The BA influences the decision on whether to accept or reject the information. The BA reveals the extent to which a person believes that the use of information is needed and not harmful. BA refers to personal predispositions to act in a specific way, regarding a particular object, person, situation, concept, or technology.

Beyond that, this study proposes to include three types of norms, that is, MN, SN, and DN. MN result from personal internal beliefs not to tolerate disinformation. In general, MN are principles or rules that govern human behavior and establishing what is right or wrong in a social community. SN concern a personal perception of social pressure or influence to perform or not perform a particular action. SN result from personal motivation, normative beliefs, individuals' knowledge, and impacts and experiences of third-party people, who may have influence on the questionnaire recipient. DN concern the perceptions that individuals have about behaviors exhibited by others in a community.

In this study, DN reveal the degree to which the recipient creates themselves as the image of a person who knows how to avoid disinformation. PBC means personal beliefs that an individual has capabilities, that is, competencies and resources, to control factors that may influence their behavior. In this study, PBC refers to the degree to which the recipient believes in their abilities to self-control and avoid disinformation. Therefore, this study proposes the following hypotheses:

H1: Behavioral Attitude (BA) has an impact on Behavioral Intention (BI).

H2: Moral Norms (MN) have a positive impact on Behavioral Intention (BI).

H3: Subjective Norms (SN) have a positive impact on Behavioral Intention (BI).

H4: Descriptive Norms (DN) have a positive impact on Behavioral Intention (BI).

H5: Perceived Behavioral Control (PBC) has a positive impact on Behavioral Intention (BI).

H6: Perceived Behavioral Control (PBC) has a positive impact on Cyber Hygiene Behavior (CHB).

H7: Behavioral Intention (BI) has a positive impact on Cyber Hygiene Behavior (CHB).

Beyond variables considered in the TPB model, this study added other variables. Two of them, that is, HA and JU, have been introduced to the ETPB model by Savari, Mombeni, and Izadi (2022). HA are repetitive actions, which are performed regularly or automatically in human lives. They can be positive (i.e., good habits, e.g., teeth cleaning) and negative (i.e., unhealthy habits, e.g., avoiding physical activities). In this paper, HA includes individual practices and routines applied by the recipients, particularly avoiding internet news. JU refers to collecting and revealing the reasons for a particular action, decision, or belief. JU means a personal explanation of regulations, policies, and administrative practices to avoid disinformation.

This study also considered the impact of variables combined with security, Anxiety (AN), and risk. Hence, the conceptual model covers the impact of three additional factors that may influence CHB, which covers practices and habits to maintain an elevated level of cybersecurity and protection of digital assets. It may also include prevention to maintain mental health and avoiding unreliable and untested, unchecked, and malicious information. Cyber AN is a degree to which a person hesitates to use internet information because of its harmfulness. PR is defined as a degree of risk recognition by an individual. SEC means level of knowledge on Information Technology (IT) tools to protect in case of a human agent or software attack. Hence, the next hypotheses are as follows:

H8: Justification (JU) has an impact on Cyber Hygiene Behavior (CHB).

H9: Habits (HA) have an impact on Cyber Hygiene Behavior (CHB).

H10: Perceived Risks (PRs) have an impact on Cyber Hygiene Behavior (CHB).

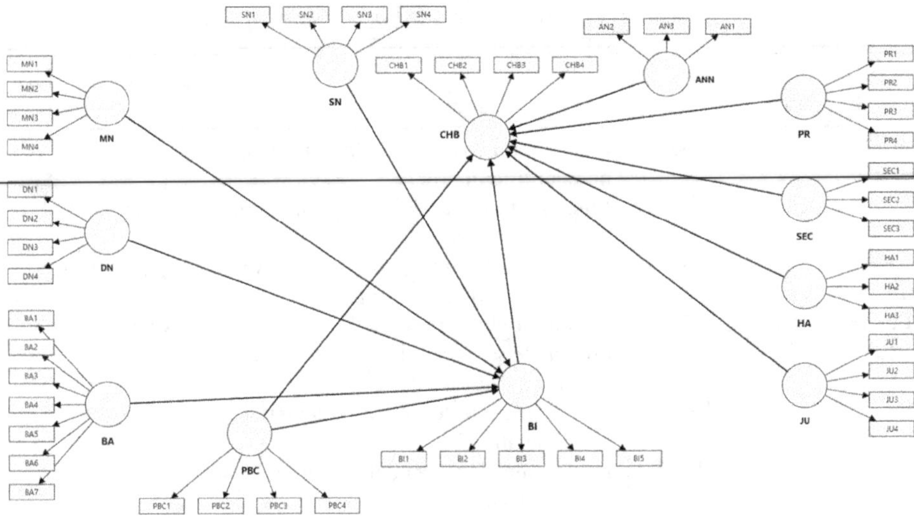

FIGURE 5.1 Conceptual model.

H11: Security (SEC) has an impact on Cyber Hygiene Behavior (CHB).

H12: Anxiety (AN) has an impact on Cyber Hygiene Behavior (CHB).

Figure 5.1 includes the conceptual model of variables having an impact on CHB. In this theoretical framework, relationships among constructs, that is, latent variables, as well as between constructs and their assigned indicators, that is, items or observable variables, are shown with arrows.

OBSERVABLE INDICATORS FOR CYBER HYGIENE BEHAVIOR MODEL

For the past thirty years, ICT, in general, and the internet have played a significant role in communications among people in all sectors of life (i.e., education, administration, business, health care, and agriculture). The benefits of ICT do overcome risks and wastes caused by disinformation. To evaluate young peoples' behavior and recognize factors having an impact on their BIs and actions, the TPB model has been specified and estimated. The literature survey on TAM, UTAUT, and the TPB models led to observations that researchers focus on the latent variable's identification. However, the specification of observable items, such as indicators, should also be discussed.

Considering the items identified in literature and proposed by other researchers, this study items are included in Table 5.1.

The research data were collected using a questionnaire and analyzed using SEM. The survey respondents were students at the University of Economics in Katowice (Poland) and the Babeş-Bolyai University (Romania). The questionnaires were

TABLE 5.1 *Items included in the survey*

Latent variables		Items	Mean RO	Mean PL
Anxiety (AN)	**AN1**	I feel apprehensive about finding fake news on the internet	4.115	3.245
	AN2	I hesitate to use social media for fear of finding fake news	2.285	1.685
	AN3	Fake news are threats to democratic values and democratic institutions	5.394	4.925
Perceived Risk (PR)	**PR1**	Buying products promoted by an unreliable source adds to the uncertainty about the results	5.782	5.780
	PR2	Disinformation destroys a positive image and reputation	5.842	5.890
	PR3	I accept the risk to enable learning from uncertain sources	3.194	5.080
	PR4	I think there is no risk in using social media to meet new people	2.291	2.900
Security (SEC)	**SEC1**	Anti-spamming software allows me to avoid fake news	3.982	4.070
	SEC2	Internet service provider warns me about fake news	2.327	3.500
	SEC3	I pay consideration to website artifacts, i.e., Padlock/https	4.024	4.755
Moral Norms (MN)	**MN1**	Avoiding fake news dissemination is a matter of conscience for me	5.600	4.040
	MN2	I feel compelled by my conscience to punish fake news providers	4.279	5.040
	MN3	I feel uncomfortable when I observe that other people tolerate fake news dissemination	5.497	4.660
	MN4	I feel responsible for the true information inserted by me on the internet	6.115	5.110
Behavioral Attitude (BA)	**BA1**	I like to be engaged in the activity for fake news recognition	4.121	2.830
	BA2	I believe that constant monitoring of COVID-19 news has a positive impact on my mental health	2.521	3.410
	BA3	I have enough responsibility not to read fake news	5.370	4.995
	BA4	I think it is better to verify the information provenance	6.467	5.825
	BA5	I think that unreliable sources of data may provide fake news	5.697	4.660
	BA6	I think that losers and crazy people provide fake news on the internet	3.618	3.940
	BA7	I think fake news is like a joke	2.455	3.685

Latent variables		Items	Mean RO	Mean PL
Subjective Norms (SN)	**SN1**	Some of my colleagues have been deceived by fake news	5.091	4.620
	SN2	Public opinion will affect my choice of the internet news	3.303	4.300
	SN3	People whom I work with help each other to recognize fake news	4.327	4.360
	SN4	People whom I trust warn me and explain to me the fake news	5.164	4.930
Descriptive Norms (DN)	**DN1**	I think most of my friends know how to avoid fake news	4.709	4.875
	DN2	I am sure that people around me do not read unreliable news	3.273	3.895
	DN3	I believe that most of my family thinks that reading unreliable news is unreasonable and wrong	4.685	5.040
	DN4	Reading fake news is disgusting to the people around me	4.006	4.120
Perceived Behavioral Control (PBC)	**PBC1**	My technical ability is sufficient to avoid disinformation	5.079	5.270
	PBC2	I purposefully avoid nonverified information	5.364	5.005
	PBC3	I know how to avoid fake news	5.267	5.335
	PBC4	I think I have good self-control	5.818	5.175
Behavioral Intention (BI)	**BI1**	I would like to know more about the possibilities of verifying internet information	6.236	4.945
	BI2	I will recommend my friends/relatives to verify information from uncertain/ unknown sources	6.073	4.890
	BI3	Post COVID-19, I carefully check information on it	5.442	4.435
	BI4	I will take good care of myself, particularly when I am browsing unsafe portals	5.933	5.525
	BI5	I am still looking for news that allows me to verify the information received earlier	5.418	4.655
Habits (HA)	**HA1**	I do not think about the fake news on the internet because I do not read internet news	2.539	3.450
	HA2	I habitually always pay attention to reliability of news and always check the source of information	5.273	4.910
	HA3	I always read reliable information on the internet because it has become a habit for me	4.836	4.570

(*continued*)

TABLE 5.1 (*continued*)

Latent variables		Items	Mean RO	Mean PL
Justification (JU)	JU1	Due to the fake news dissemination, people do not trust each other and the internet is not reliable source of information	4.685	4.855
	JU2	Governmental activities to punish and reduce fake news are small and hard to notice	5.685	5.050
	JU3	The habit of reducing fake news on the internet is usually forgotten when people need to receive important information, e.g., on COVID-19 risks	5.333	4.550
	JU4	Increasing the punishment for fake news is often overlooked because there is so much everyday news and people do not remember nor recognize what is false or true	5.497	4.985
Cyber Hygiene Behavior (CHB)	CHB1	I avoid constantly studying the news on gossip portals	5.358	5.135
	CHB2	I will not encourage others to study the gossip portal news	5.430	5.545
	CHB3	I immediately remove emails from unknown senders	4.873	4.610
	CHB4	I do not click on links or attachments from unsolicited emails or texts	6.515	5.970

distributed to bachelor, master, and doctoral-level students. The responses to the questionnaire were voluntary and anonymized. This research collected 200 questionnaires from the University of Economics in Katowice and 165 questionnaires from the Babeş-Bolyai University.

The students were asked to express their degree of agreement or disagreement with the statements in Table 5.1 by marking the answers on the seven-grade Likert scale, considering the following meanings: 1 – absolutely disagree; 2 – disagree; 3 – rather disagree; 4 – irrelevant; 5 – rather agree; 6 – agree; and 7 – definitely agree.

Table 5.1 contains the items included in the survey and presents a list of questions with acronyms and a set of latent variables. The last column in Table 5.1 includes average (Mean) values of these research indicators. The Pearson correlation rate for the two last columns in Table 5.1 is 0.7854; hence, authors conclude on high comparability of responses of recipients from these two populations under research.

TABLE 5.2 *Construct reliability and validity – preliminary model estimated (sample size: 200 records from Poland)*

Construct	Cronbach's Alpha	rho_A	Composite Reliability	Average Variance Extracted (AVE)
AN	0.454	0.553	0.696	0.447
BA	0.373	0.485	0.618	0.234
BI	0.678	0.704	0.795	0.442
CHB	0.609	0.617	0.775	0.468
DN	0.592	0.543	0.673	0.389
HA	0.272	0.521	0.508	0.404
JU	0.647	0.678	0.779	0.473
MN	0.599	0.697	0.752	0.443
PBC	0.685	0.70	0.806	0.512
PR	−0.115	0.267	0.005	0.321
SEC	0.325	0.226	0.533	0.356
SN	0.410	0.717	0.638	0.377

THE TPB MODEL EVALUATION

The presented conceptual model (see Figure 5.1) consists just of items connected to the variables. SmartPLS3 was used to calculate the model (Ringle, Hair, & Sarstedt, 2014). In the first run, the model was calculated with the PLS algorithm. The number of iterations was set to 1,000 and the stop criterion to 10^{-X} with selected 7. Then the model was calculated with the Bootstrap algorithm, in which the number of samples was set to 5,000 for the full version with bias-corrected and accelerated in two-tailed distribution. The significant level was equal to 0.05.

The conceptual model (Figure 5.1) was estimated twice. Firstly, data were gathered in Poland, then in Romania. The reliability of the variables was evaluated using Cronbach's Alpha and Composite Reliability (CR). The results for reliability and validity are presented for the overall sample. Cronbach's Alpha is a way of assessing reliability by comparing the amount of shared variance, or covariance, among the items in a psychological test or questionnaire (Collins, 2007). CR is an "indicator of the shared variance among the observed variables used as an indicator of a latent construct" (Fornell & Larcker, 1981). In psychology, all of Cronbach's Alpha and CR values are recommended to be higher than 0.600. Cronbach's Alpha values of 0.60 to 0.70 are acceptable in exploratory research, while values between 0.70 and 0.90 are regarded as satisfactory (Nunally & Bernstein, 1994). The Average Variance Extracted (AVE) and CR values are to be higher or close to 0.500 and 0.700, respectively, which corroborates convergent validity. Fornell and Larcker (1981) said that if AVE is less than 0.5, but CR is higher than 0.6, the validity of the construct is still adequate. The results for reliability and validity for the overall sample of 200 records from Poland are included in Tables 5.2 and 5.3. Unfortunately, in the first estimation, the chosen observed variables have not

TABLE 5.3 *Construct reliability and validity – secondary model estimated (sample size: 200 records from Poland)*

Construct	Cronbach's Alpha	rho_A	Composite Reliability	Average Variance Extracted (AVE)
BI	0.678	0.703	0.795	0.442
CHB	0.609	0.626	0.774	0.467
DN	0.592	0.540	0.665	0.386
JU	0.647	0.677	0.779	0.473
MN	0.599	0.695	0.751	0.443
PBC	0.685	0.701	0.806	0.512

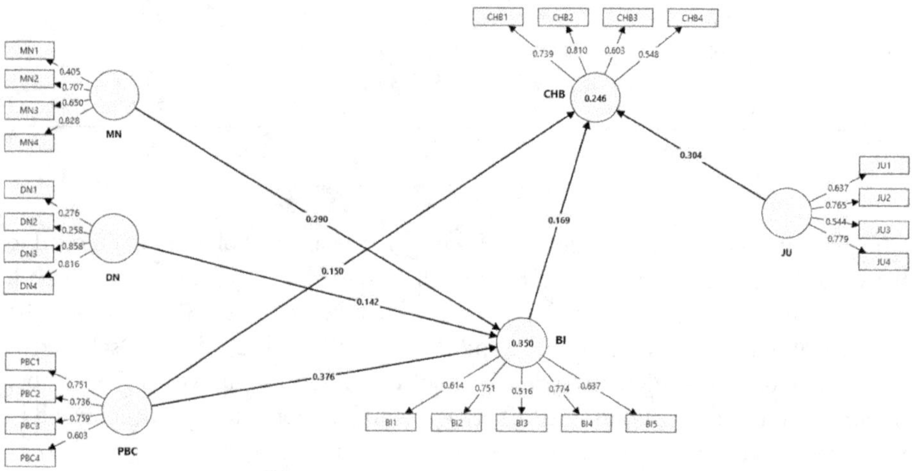

FIGURE 5.2 The final model with estimated coefficients (sample size: 200 records from Poland).

explained well the latent variables; therefore, model fitting was necessary. The preliminary conceptual model as unreliable has been changed, and Figure 5.2 includes the secondary estimated model covering the following hypotheses:

H1: Behavioral Intention (BI) has a positive impact on Cyber Hygiene Behavior (CHB).

H2: Descriptive Norms (DN) have a positive impact on Behavioral Intention (BI).

H3: Justification (JU) has an impact on Cyber Hygiene Behavior (CHB).

H4: Moral Norms (MN) have a positive impact on Behavioral Intention (BI).

H5: Perceived Behavioral Control has a positive impact on Behavioral Intention (BI).

H6: Perceived Behavioral Control has a positive impact on Cyber Hygiene Behavior (CHB).

Path coefficients and R^2 constructs are included in Table 5.4.

TABLE 5.4 *PLS Algorithm R^2 and Path Coefficients (sample size: 200 records from Poland)*

	R^2	BI	CHB	DN	JU	MN	PBC
BI	0.350		0.169				
CHB	0.246						
DN		0.142					
JU			0.304				
MN		0.290					
PBC		0.376	0.150				

TABLE 5.5 *Bootstrapping Path Coefficients for final model (sample size: 200 records from Poland)*

Hypothesis No	Hypothesis (impact direction à)	Original sample	Sample mean	Standard deviation	T-statistics	*P* values	Decision
H1	BI à CHB	0.169	0.174	0.078	2.175	0.030	Accepted
H2	DN à BI	0.142	0.156	0.085	1.673	0.094	Rejected
H3	JU à CHB	0.304	0.316	0.068	4.453	0.000	Accepted
H4	MN à BI	0.290	0.293	0.065	4.476	0.000	Accepted
H5	PBC à BI	0.376	0.378	0.063	6.019	0.000	Accepted
H6	PBC à CHB	0.150	0.150	0.075	1.994	0.046	Accepted

The goodness of the model is estimated by the strength of each structural path, determined by the R^2 value for the dependent variables (Jankelová, Joniaková, & Skorková, 2021). Generally, R^2 is a statistical measure of the goodness of the fit of a regression model. For the dependent variables, the R^2 value should be equal to or over 0.125 (Falk & Miller, 1992). The results in Table 5.4 show that all R^2 values are over 0.1.

The R^2 ranges from 0 to 1, higher values indicating stronger explanatory power. As a general guideline, R^2 values of 0.75, 0.50, and 0.25 can be considered substantial, moderate, and weak, respectively, in many social science disciplines (Hair Jr. et al., 2021). But acceptable R^2 values are based on the research context, and in some disciplines, an R^2 value as low as 0.10 is considered satisfactory, that is, for the large sample size research, it is statistically significant, but substantively meaningless (Falk & Miller, 1992).

Table 5.5 covers the Bootstrapping Path Coefficients values for the final model as well as the decisions on the proposed hypotheses' acceptance or rejection.

The results of the tests indicate that the proposed constructs (i.e., JU, MN, PBC) have a weak impact on the intention and behavior of students (expressed as BI, CHB) to avoid the disinformation. If a *P* value is below a certain threshold, then the corresponding hypothesis is assumed to be supported. The threshold is

TABLE 5.6 *Construct reliability and validity – preliminary model estimated (sample size: 165 records from Romania)*

Construct	Cronbach's Alpha	rho_A	Composite Reliability	Average Variance Extracted (AVE)
AN	0.453	0.461	0.733	0.480
BA	0.294	0.553	0.416	0.244
BI	0.707	0.721	0.808	0.459
CHB	0.487	0.505	0.703	0.381
DN	0.612	0.624	0.774	0.463
HA	0.045	0.711	0.508	0.593
JU	0.640	0.642	0.786	0.480
MN	0.705	0.726	0.819	0.535
PBC	0.674	1.104	0.711	0.400
PR	0.019	0.383	0.091	0.304
SEC	0.459	−0.254	0.177	0.309
SN	0.470	0.537	0.674	0.391

usually 0.05 (Kock, 2014). Therefore, in this research, hypotheses H1, H3, H4, H5, and H6 are supported, but hypothesis H2 is rejected. This means that: (1) Behavioral Intention (BI) impacts on Cyber Hygiene Behavior (CHB); (2) Justification (JU) has a positive impact on Cyber Hygiene Behavior; (3) Moral Norms (MN) have a weak impact on Behavioral Intention (BI); (4) Perceived Behavioral Control (PBC) has a positive impact on Behavioral Intention (BI); and (5) Personal Behavioral Control (PBC) has an impact on Cyber Hygiene Behavior (CHB).

Next, the study estimated the conceptual model considering data from Romania. However, for these data also, the reliability and validity measures have low values (Table 5.6), and authors eliminated some variables from that model.

Since the chosen observed variables have not explained well the latent variables, model fitting was necessary. The preliminary conceptual model as unreliable has been changed, and Figure 5.3 includes the secondary estimated model covering the following hypotheses:

H1: Behavioral Intention (BI) has a positive impact on Cyber Hygiene Behavior (CHB).

H2: Descriptive Norms (DN) have a positive impact on Behavioral Intention (BI).

H3: Justification (JU) has an impact on Cyber Hygiene Behavior (CHB).

H4: Moral Norms (MN) have a positive impact on Behavioral Intention (BI).

H5: Perceived Behavioral Control (PBC) has a positive impact on Behavioral Intention (BI).

H6: Perceived Behavioral Control (PBC) has a positive impact on Cyber Hygiene Behavior (CHB).

TABLE 5.7 *Construct reliability and validity – secondary model estimated (sample size: 165 records from Romania)*

Construct	Cronbach's Alpha	rho_A	Composite Reliability	Average Variance Extracted (AVE)
BI	0.707	0.726	0.808	0.458
CHB	0.543	0.559	0.812	0.685
DN	0.612	0.622	0.774	0.463
JU	0.640	0.677	0.783	0.476
MN	0.705	0.726	0.819	0.535
PBC	0.674	1.239	0.688	0.382

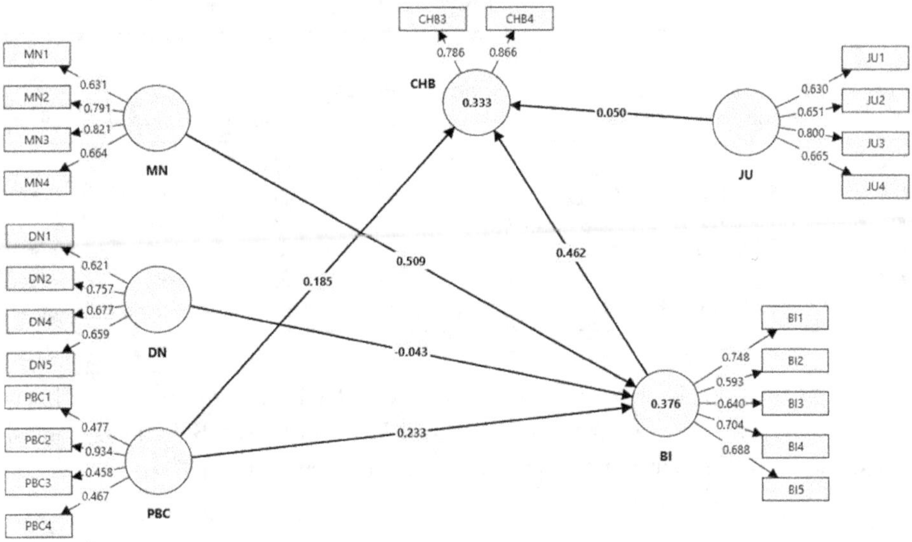

FIGURE 5.3 The final model with estimated coefficients (sample size: 165 records from Romania).

The same reliability and validity verification was done for the Romania model (Table 5.7).

Path Coefficients and R^2 constructs are included in Table 5.8.

Table 5.9 covers the Bootstrapping Path Coefficients values for the final model as well as the decisions on the proposed hypotheses acceptance or rejection.

The results of the tests indicate that the proposed constructs (i.e., MN, PBC) have a weak or moderate impact on the intention and behavior of students (expressed as BI, CHB) to avoid the disinformation. In this research, the threshold of the *P* value is also 0.05. Therefore, in this research, hypotheses H1, H4, H5, and H6 are supported, but hypotheses H2 and H3 are rejected. This means that: (1) Behavioral Intention (BI) impacts on Cyber Hygiene Behavior (CHB); (2) Moral Norms (MN) have a moderate

TABLE 5.8 *PLS Algorithm R^2 and Path Coefficients (sample size: 165 records from Romania)*

	R^2	BI	CHB	DN	JU	MN	PBC
BI	0.376		0.462				
CHB	0.333						
DN		−0.043					
JU			0.050				
MN		0.509					
PBC		0.233	0.185				

TABLE 5.9 *Bootstrapping Path Coefficients for the final model (sample size: 165 records from Romania)*

Hypothesis No	Hypothesis (impact direction à)	Original sample	Sample mean	Standard deviation	T-statistics	*P* values	Decision
H1	BI à CHB	0.462	0.450	0.101	4.578	0.000	Accepted
H2	DN à BI	−0.043	−0.007	0.098	0.434	0.665	Rejected
H3	JU à CHB	0.050	0.076	0.085	0.589	0.556	Rejected
H4	MN à BI	0.509	0.519	0.071	7.131	0.000	Accepted
H5	PBC à BI	0.233	0.232	0.090	2.591	0.010	Accepted
H6	PBC à CHB	0.185	0.191	0.077	2.413	0.016	Accepted

impact on Behavioral Intention (BI); (3) Perceived Behavioral Control (PBC) has a weak positive impact on Behavioral Intention (BI); (4) Perceived Behavioral Control (PBC) has a weak positive impact on Cyber Hygiene Behavior (CHB).

CONCLUSION

Cyber disinformation is a complex and concerning phenomenon. Successful disinformation campaigns can have a significant negative effect on democratic values and institutions. Defending democracy in the digital age requires a complex approach. The individual behavior of users can influence the spread and effects of the phenomenon.

This chapter argued that users' behavior plays an essential role in this phenomenon and aimed to identify factors that impact on users' BIs and CHB. The chapter integrated the ETPB and a Structural Equation Model, realized through PLS–SEM, applied to the cyber disinformation phenomenon. The analysis of the self-assessment survey on disinformation risk perception and control revealed that responses are highly similar, with a correlation rate of 0.7854. The research revealed the applicability of the TPB model and found that MN and PBC have an impact on BI and CHB.

The findings of this chapter provide valuable insights that can be used to improve the overall responses to the phenomenon, such as policies, programs, and clinics, and to elaborate educational materials. To effectively address the phenomenon's relevant vectors, tactics, or methods, there is a clear need for a complex strategy, with multiple components, including research, to better understand the phenomenon's attributes and the behavior of users; frequent risk assessments; increased empowerment of people to detect and report disinformation; improved fact-checking procedures; enhanced international anti-disinformation enforcement and cooperation; technical assistance programs; better defined responsibility for secondary liability; awareness raising and education programs, with a view to improve the critical thinking abilities of people.

REFERENCES

Ababneh, K. I., Ahmed, K., & Dedousis, E. (2022). Predictors of cheating in online exams among business students during the Covid pandemic: Testing the theory of planned behavior. *International Journal of Management Education*, 20(3), 1–15. https://doi.org/10.1016/j/ijme.2922.100713

Aïmeur, E., Amri, S., & Brassard, G. (2023). Fake news, disinformation and misinformation in social media: a review. *Social Network Analysis and Mining*, 13(1), 30. https://link.springer.com/article/10.1007/s13278-023-01028-5

Ajzen, I. (1991). The theory of planned behavior. *Organizational Behavior and Human Decision Processes*, 50(2), 179–211. https://doi.org/10.1016/0749-5978(91)90020-T

(2005). *Attitudes, personality, and behavior*. New York: Open University Press.

Al-Shanfari, I., Yassin, W., Tabook, N., Ismail, R., & Ismail, A. (2022). Determinants of information security awareness and behaviour strategies in public sector organizations among employees. *International Journal of Advanced Computer Science and Applications*, 13(8), 479–490.

Alieva, I., Moffitt, J. D., & Carley, K. M. (2022). How disinformation operations against Russian opposition leader Alexei Navalny influence the international audience on Twitter. *Social Network Analysis and Mining*, 12(1), 1–13. https://doi.org/10.1007/s13278-022-00908-6

Andersen, J. & Søe, S. O. (2020). Communicative actions we live by: The problem with fact-checking, tagging or flagging fake news – The case of Facebook. *European Journal of Communication*, 35(2), 126–139. https://doi.org/10.1177/0267323119894489

Arayankalam, J. & Krishnan, S. (2021). Relating foreign disinformation through social media, domestic online media fractionalization, government's control over cyberspace, and social media-induced offline violence: Insights from the agenda-building theoretical perspective. *Technological Forecasting and Social Change*, 166, 1–14. https://doi.org/10.1016/j.techfore.2021.120661

Benson, T. (2020, July 29). *Twitter bots are spreading massive amounts of COVID-19 misinformation*. IEEE Spectrum. https://spectrum.ieee.org/twitter-bots-are-spreading-massive-amounts-of-covid-19-misinformation

Bontcheva, K., Posetti, J., Teyssou, D., Meyer, T., Gregory, S., Hanot, C., & Maynard, D. (2020). *Balancing act: Countering digital disinformation while respecting freedom of expression*. United Nations Educational, Scientific and Cultural Organization

(UNESCO). https://unesco.org/en/articles/balancing-act-countering-digital-disinformation-while-respecting-freedom-expression

Borges, P. M. & Gambarato, R. R. (2019). The role of beliefs and behavior on Facebook: A semiotic approach to algorithms, fake news, and transmedia journalism. *International Journal of Communication*, 13, 603–618. https://ijoc.org/index.php/ijoc/article/view/10304/2550

Buchanan, T. & Benson, V. (2019). Spreading disinformation on Facebook: Do trust in message source, risk propensity, or personality affect the organic reach of "fake news"? *Social Media+ Society*, 5(4), 1–9. https://doi.org/10.1177/2056305119888654

Cabeza-Ramirez, L. J., Sanchez-Canizares, S. M., Santos-Roldan, L. M., & Fuentes-Garcia, F. J. (2022). Impact of the perceived risk in influencers' product recommendations on their followers' purchase attitudes and intention. *Technological Forecasting and Social Change*, 184, 1–16. https://doi.org/10.1016/j.techfore.2022.121997

Caramancion, K. M., Li. Y., Dubois, E., & Jung E. S. (2022). The missing case of disinformation from the cybersecurity risk continuum: A comparative assessment of disinformation with other cyber threats. *Data*, 7(4), 1–18. https://doi.org/10.3390/data7040049

Carrapico, H. & Farrand, B. (2021). When trust fades, Facebook is no longer a friend: Shifting privatisation dynamics in the context of cybersecurity as a result of disinformation, populism and political uncertainty. *JCMS: Journal of Common Market Studies*, 59(5), 1160–1176. https://doi.org/10.1111/jcms.13175

Carratalá, A. (2023). Disinformation and sexual and gender diversity in Spain: Twitter users' response, and the perception of LGBTQI+ organisations. *Social Sciences*, 12(4), 1–19. https://doi.org/10.3390/socsci12040206

Chesney, B., & Citron, D. (2019). Deep fakes: A looming challenge for privacy, democracy, and national security. *California Law Review*, 107, 1753–1820.

Chuttur, M. (2009). Overview of the technology acceptance model: Origins, developments and future directions. *Sprouts: Working Papers on Information Systems*, 9(37), 1–22.

Collins, B., Hoang, D. T., Nguyen, N. T., & Hwang, D. (2021). Trends in combating fake news on social media – A survey. *Journal of Information and Telecommunication*, 5(2), 247–266. https://doi.org/10.1080/24751839.2020.1847379

Collins, L. M. (2007). Research design and methods, encyclopedia of gerontology. In *Encyclopedia of gerontology* (pp. 433–442). Elsevier. https://doi.org/10.1016/B0-12-370870-2/00162-1

Culloty, E., Suiter, J., Viriri, I., & Creta, S. (2022). Disinformation about migration: An age-old issue with new tech dimensions. In *World migration report* (pp. 1–23). International Organization for Migration.

Cybersecurity and Infrastructure Security Agency (CISA). (2022). *Tactics of disinformation*. CISA. https://cisa.gov/sites/default/files/publications/tactics-of-disinformation_508.pdf

Davis, F. D. (1985). A *technology acceptance model for empirically testing new end-user information systems: Theory and results*. Doctoral dissertation, Massachusetts Institute of Technology. https://researchgate.net/publication/35465050

Diekman, C., Ryan, C. D., & Oliver, T. L. (2023). Misinformation and disinformation in food science and nutrition: Impact on practice. *Journal of Nutrition*, 153(1), 3–9. https://doi.org/10.1016/j.tjnut.2022.10.001

Edwards, C., Beattie, A. J., Edwards, A., & Spence, P. R. (2016). Differences in perceptions of communication quality between a Twitterbot and human agent for information seeking and learning. *Computers in Human Behavior*, 65, 666–671. https://doi.org/10.1016/j.chb.2016.07.003

European Commission. (2020). On the European Democracy Action Plan, COM (2020), 790. EU Monitor.

(2023). *Digital services act: Application of the risk management framework to Russian disinformation campaigns*. Publications Office of the European Union.

European Parliament. (2022). Resolution of 9 March 2022 on foreign interference in all democratic processes in the European Union, including disinformation (2020/2268 (INI)) (2022/C 347/07). European Parliament. https://europarl.europa.eu/doceo/document/TA-9-2022-0064_EN.html

European Parliamentary Research Service. (2020, April 9). *Disinformation and science: A survey of the gullibility of students with regard to false scientific news*. European Parliament, Panel for the Future of Science and Technology (STOA). https://europarl.europa.eu/RegData/etudes/STUD/2020/656300/EPRS_STU(2020)656300_EN.pdf

Falk, R. F., & N. B. Miller (1992). *A primer for soft modeling*. The University of Akron Press.

Fallis, D. (2014). The varieties of disinformation. In Floridi, L., & Illari, P. (Eds.), *The philosophy of information quality* (pp. 135–161). Synthese Library.

Fornell, C., & Larcker, D. F. (1981). Evaluating structural equation models with unobservable variables and measurement error. *Journal of Marketing Research*, 18(1), 39–50. https://doi.org/10.2307/3151312

Hair, J. F., Jr., Hult, G. T. M., Ringle, C. M., & Sarstedt, M. (2017). *A primer on partial least squares structural equation modeling (PLS-SEM)*. Sage.

Hair, J. F., Jr., Hult, G. T. M., Ringle, C. M., Sarstedt, M., Danks, N. P., & Ray, S. (2021). *Partial least squares structural equation modeling (PLS-SEM) using R: A workbook*. Springer Nature.

Jankelová, N., Joniaková, Z., & Skorková, Z. (2021). Perceived organizational support and work engagement of first-line managers in healthcare – The mediation role of feedback seeking behavior. *Journal of Multidisciplinary Healthcare*, 14, 3109–3123. https://doi.org/10.2147/JMDH.S326563

Jia, H., Yu, J., Feng, T., Ning, L., Cao, P., Shang, P., Gao, S., & Yu, X. (2022). Factors influencing medical personnel to work in primary health care institutions: An extended theory of planned behavior. *International Journal of Environmental Research and Public Health*, 19(5), 1–15. https://doi.org/10.3390/ijerph19052785

Jungherr, A., & Schroeder, R. (2021). Disinformation and the structural transformations of the public arena: Addressing the actual challenges to democracy. *Social Media+ Society*, 7(1), 1–13. https://doi.org/10.1177/2056305121988928

Khani Jeihooni, A., Layeghiasl, M., Yari, A., & Rakhshani, T. (2022). The effect of educational intervention based on the theory of planned behavior on improving physical and nutrition status of obese and overweight women. *BMC Women's Health*, 22(1), 1–9. https://doi.org/10.1186/s12905-022-01-01593-5

Knight Foundation. (2018, October). *Disinformation, 'fake news' and influence campaigns on Twitter*. Knight Foundation. https://s3.amazonaws.com/kf-site-legacy-media/feature_assets/www/misinfo/kf-disinformation-report.0cdbb232.pdf

Kock, N. (2014). *Stable P value calculation methods in PLS-SEM*. ScriptWarp Systems. https://researchgate.net/publication/269989910_Stable_P_value_calculation_methods_in_PLS-SEM

Krafft, P. M., & Donovan, J. (2020). Disinformation by design: The use of evidence collages and platform filtering in a media manipulation campaign. *Political Communication*, 37(2), 194–214. https://doi.org/10.1080/10584609.2019.1686094

Machete, P., & Turpin, M. (2020). The use of critical thinking to identify fake news: A systematic literature review. In M. Hattingh, M. Matthee, H. Smuts, I. Pappas, Y. K.

Dwivedi, & M. Mantymaki (Eds.), *Responsible design, implementation and use of information and communication technology* (pp. 235–246). Springer International Publishing. https://doi.org/10.1007/978-3-030-45002-1_20

Maheri, M., Rezapour, B., & Didarloo, A. (2022). Predictors of colorectal cancer screening intention based on the integrated theory of planned behavior among the average-risk individuals. *BMC Public Health*, 22(1), 1–11. https://doi.org/10.1186/s12889-022-14191-9

Marikyan, M., & Papagiannidis, P. (2021). *Unified theory of acceptance and use of technology*. TheoryHub Book.

Mattioli, R., Malatras, A., Hunter, E. N., Biasibetti Penso, M. G., Bertram, D., & Neubert, I. (2023). *Identifying emerging cyber security threats and challenges for 2030*. ENISA.

Michaelis, M., Jafarian, J. H., & Biswas, A. (2022). The dangers of money and corporate power relating to online disinformation. In *2022 23rd IEEE international conference on mobile data management (MDM)* (pp. 470–475). IEEE.

Nenadić, I. (2019). Unpacking the "European approach" to tackling challenges of disinformation and political manipulation. *Internet Policy Review*, 8(4), 1–22. https://doi.org/10.14763/2019.4.1436

Nunnally, J. C., & Bernstein, I. H. (1994). *Psychometric theory*. McGraw-Hill.

Ó Fathaigh, R., Helberger, N., & Appelman, N. (2021). The perils of legally defining disinformation. *Internet Policy Review*, 10(4), 1–25. https://doi.org/10.14763/2021.4.1584

Olan, F., Jayawickrama, U., Arakpogun, E. O., Suklan, J., & Liu, S. (2022). Fake news on social media: The impact on society. *Information Systems Frontiers*, 26, 443–458. https://doi.org/10.1007/s10796-022-10242-z

Park, E. S., & Park, M. S. (2020). Factors of the technology acceptance model for construction IT. *Applied Sciences*, 10(22), 1–15. https://doi.org/10.3390/app10228299

Pérez-Escolar, M., Lilleker, D., & Tapia-Frade, A. (2023). A systematic literature review of the phenomenon of disinformation and misinformation. *Media and Communication*, 11(2), 76–87. https://doi.org/10.17645/mac.v11i2.6453

Pierri, F., Artoni, A., & Ceri, S. (2020). Investigating Italian disinformation spreading on Twitter in the context of 2019 European elections. *PLOS One*, 15(1), 1–23. https://doi.org/10.1371/journal.pone.0227821

Rana, M. S., Nobi, M. N., Murali, B., & Sung, A. H. (2022). Deepfake detection: A systematic literature review. *IEEE Access*, 10, 25494–25513.

Ringle, C. M., Hair, J. F., & Sarstedt, M. (2014). PLS-SEM: Looking back and moving forward. *Long Range Planning*, 47(3), 132–137. https:/doi.org/10.1016/j.lrp.2014.02.008

Romero-Galisteo, R.-P., Gonzalez-Sanches, M., Galvez-Ruiz, P., Palomo-Carrion, R., Casuso-Holgado, M. J., & Pinero-Pinto E. (2022). Entrepreneurial intention, expectations of success and self-efficacy in undergraduate students of health sciences. *BMC Medical Education*, 22(1), 1–7. https://doi.org/10.1186/s12909-022-03731-x

Sabi, H. M., Uzoka, F. M. E., Langmia, K., & Njeh, F. N. (2016). Conceptualizing a model for adoption of cloud computing in education. *International Journal of Information Management*, 36(2), 183–191. https://doi.org/10.1016/j.ijinfomgt.2015.11.010

Savari, M., Mombeni, A. S., & Izadi, H. (2022). Socio-psychological determinants of Iranian rural households' adoption of water consumption curtailment behaviors. *Scientific Reports*, 12(1), 1–12. https://doi.org/10.1038/s41598-022-17560-x

Schünemann, W. J. (2022). A threat to democracies?: An overview of theoretical approaches and empirical measurements for studying the effects of disinformation. In M. D. Cavelty & A. Wenger (Eds.), *Cyber security politics* (pp. 32–47). Routledge.

Shirahada, K., & Zhang, Y. (2022). Counterproductive knowledge behavior in volunteer work: Perspectives from the theory of planned behavior and well-being theory. *Journal of Knowledge Management*, 26(11), 22–41. https://doi.org/10.1108/JKM-08-2021-0612

Statista. (2023). Number of disinformation and pro-Russian Twitter posts in Poland 2023. *Statista*. https://statista.com/statistics/1365122/number-of-disinformation-and-pro-russian-twitter-posts-poland/

Tenove, C., & Tworek, H. J. S. (2019). Online disinformation and harmful speech: Dangers for democratic participation and possible policy responses. *Journal of Parliamentary and Political Law*, 13, 215–232.

Ternovski, J., Kalla, J., & Aronow, P. (2022). The negative consequences of informing voters about deepfakes: Evidence from two survey experiments. *Journal of Online Trust and Safety*, 1(2), 1–16. https://doi.org/10.54501/jots.v1i2.28

Trend Micro. (2020). *Malicious uses and abuses of artificial intelligence*. United Nations Interregional Crime & Justice Research Institute. https://unicri.it/sites/default/files/2020-11/AI%20MLC.pdf

Uyheng, J., Moffitt, J. D., & Carley, K. M. (2022). The language and targets of online trolling: A psycholinguistic approach for social cybersecurity. *Information Processing and Management*, 59(5), 1–15. https://doi.org/10.1016/j.ipm.2022.103012

Vaccari, C. & Chadwick, A. (2020). Deepfakes and disinformation: Exploring the impact of synthetic political video on deception, uncertainty, and trust in news. *Social Media and Society*, 6(1), 1–13. https://doi.org/10.1177/2056305120903408

Venkatesh, V., Morris, M. G., Davis, G. B., & Davis, F. D. (2003). User acceptance of information technology: Toward a unified view. *MIS Quarterly*, 27(3), 425–478. https://doi.org/10.2307/30036540

Venkatesh, V., Thong, J. Y. L., & Xu, X. (2012). Consumer acceptance and use of information technology: Extending the unified theory of acceptance and use of technology. *MIS Quarterly*, 36(1), 157–178. https://doi.org/10.2307/41410412

Wardle, C., & Derakhshan, H. (2017, September 27). *Information disorder: Toward an interdisciplinary framework for research and policy making*. Council of Europe. https://rm.coe.int/information-disorder-toward-an-interdisciplinary-framework-for-researc/168076277c

Watson, A. (2021). Main sources of disinformation as ranked by journalists worldwide as of June 2020. *Statista*. https://statista.com/statistics/1249671/journalists-cite-sources-disinformation-worldwide/

Weikmann, T., & Lecheler, S. (2022). Visual disinformation in a digital age: A literature synthesis and research agenda. *New Media & Society*, 25(12), 3696–3713. https://doi.org/10.1177/14614448221141648.

Zhang, H., Shi, Z., Chen, J., & Zhang, Z. (2022). Understanding combined health and business risk behavior: Small tourism firm owners reopening amid Covid-19 in Pingyao, China. *Behavioral Sciences (Basel)*, 12(10), 1–18. https://doi.org/10.3390/bs12100358

PART II

Case Studies

6

Innovative Frontrunner or Delayed by Political Gridlock?

Israel's Attempts at Countering Disinformation

Gabrielle Dora Beacken and Inga Kristina Trauthig

On October 7, 2023, Hamas and Palestinian Islamic Jihad launched a terrorist attack inside Israel that resulted in over 1,200 Israelis killed, over 3,300 wounded, and over 200 people – including Israelis and foreign nationals – taken hostage (Haaretz, 2023; *The Economist*, 2023). The attack's unprecedented scale caught the Israeli government and defense forces off-guard (Harding, 2023). Subsequently, the Israeli government's excessive military response to the terror attacks resulted in thousands of Palestinians killed, displaced, and in dire need of humanitarian assistance (Pamuk, 2023). As with other contemporary military conflicts, information warfare is integrated into offensive capabilities by all actors (Mueller et al., 2023). The attacks on October 7 incorporated coordinated use of video and audio content by Hamas fighters, who subsequently uploaded their content to digital messaging channels, such as the encrypted messaging app Telegram (Frenkel & Myers, 2023; Klempner, 2023). Graphic videos and images consequently circulated on popular platforms with insufficient content moderation on X (formerly Twitter), YouTube, Instagram, Facebook, TikTok, and more (Frenkel & Myers, 2023; Klempner, 2023).

In line with this, disinformation enters the fray – deployed by official but also commercial actors. Analysts have argued that Israel was not prepared for the resulting information warfare on social media, including Hamas allegedly being aided by Iran and Russia, and to a lesser extent, China (Benjakob, 2023; Institute for Strategic Dialogue, 2023; Myers & Frenkel, 2023). From denying the existence of the October 7 attacks and claiming the Israel Defense Forces (IDF) orchestrated the attacks themselves to the fake or misleading images of explosions in buildings and the hateful provocations that ignore the history of the Israeli–Palestinian conflict (Nechin, 2023), social media feeds have been flooded with misleading or false information around the Israel–Hamas War – and actors on both sides contributed (Nechin, 2023).

This chapter explores Israel's public and private sector capabilities to counter disinformation, focusing on the period between March and June 2023 through qualitative interviews and thematic analysis. We argue that Israel has not prioritized countering disinformation – mainly because of internal political division and legislative gridlock, but also due to overshadowing security concerns related to Iran, as well as unresolved internal conflicts related to the West Bank and Gaza Strip. Most importantly, we argue that the fight against disinformation has been deprioritized by the ruling Likud party's Prime Minister Benjamin Netanyahu who benefits from the divides sewn and support bolstered from the spread of internal disinformation. We review Israel's mechanisms – both absent and present – to counter disinformation *before* October 7.

BACKGROUND: ISRAELI JUDICIAL REFORMS, DEMOCRACY, AND DISINFORMATION

In May 2023, in Israel, wide-scale protests ultimately forced Prime Minister Benjamin Netanyahu to abandon judicial reforms, which would have threatened the independence of the Israeli judiciary – at least for now (Smith, Chuck, & Zelenko, 2023). Israel is a relatively young democracy, and arguably, a troubled one (Gavison, 2011). The modern state grew out of Jewish movements that came to the Middle East in search of a safe place for all Jewish people. It was established in 1948 and has regularly fought wars and displaced local populations, as well as countered internal skirmishes over the preceding decades (Jones & Murphy, 2002). Cyberspace has increased in importance since 2000 – it is not only an added dimension during warfare but also a space where Israel exploits its capabilities to preemptively act against potential threats, exemplified, for example, in the targeted killings of Iranian nuclear scientists or inserting "cyber worms" into the computer systems of Iranian nuclear facilities (Farwell & Rohozinski, 2011) – those actions are regularly criticized by international human rights lawyers (International Bar Association, 2020).

When shifting focus from external to internal threats, disinformation continues as a cyber-enabled aspect that challenges Israeli democracy. Disinformation is understood as false or misleading information that is intentionally composed and spread – however, it can lose its intention if people, who were not part of the targeted campaign originally, start spreading it themselves, and hence turn it into misinformation (Wardle, 2018). Disinformation can be especially potent in the lead-up to elections when large parts of the population are trying to figure out whom to vote for – and in extension lead their country for the next years (Bader, 2018). Israel had five national elections in three years (from 2019 to 2022) (Jewish Virtual Library, 2023). When compared to, for example, the United Kingdom (UK) – a state that aligns with Israel as both political systems do not have a formal, written constitution, but differentiates itself from Israel as Britain (or better, England), traces its democracy to the Magna Carta in the thirteenth century and hence is considered one of the world's oldest republics (Kiser & Barzel, 1991). Israel's recent political upheavals outplay the UK. While the UK has been derided for having three different prime ministers in one year by domestic and international observers (Langfitt, 2022), Israel has not been able to solve its cabinet quarrels internally – but instead needed to call on voters repeatedly. This is all to say that Israel can be considered a nascent democracy simply given its short time of existence but also due to the outlined political instabilities, especially since 2020. Some argue that these political instabilities (or in other words, the repeated need for irregular elections) are mainly tied to one person – Prime Minister Benjamin Netanyahu (Berg, 2023). The seventy-three-year-old is an Israeli politician who was elected to the office of prime minister for the sixth time in 2022 (Berg, 2023). While acting as prime minister, he has also been the center of a criminal trial in which he is accused of bribery, fraud, and breach of trust – charges he fiercely denies (Freidson, 2023). Over the past years, he has grown into a polarizing and divisive figure – most recently because of his decision to form a government with the most right-wing Israeli parties. This coalition is joined at the hip due to:

> Their unbridled passion to circumscribe the authority of the courts which, by their narrative, have intervened illegitimately to obstruct the democratic will of the citizenry as it would be implemented by the Knesset majority – i.e., them. Secondary villains on their most-wanted list include the state attorney, the media and the academy, although none of these institutions is a monolith. (Lipner, 2023, p. 2)

Not only do many Israelis consider themselves surrounded by enemies (alluding to the notion that bordering countries either do not accept the Israeli state formally like Syria or actively attack the country like Hezbollah from Lebanon) but Israelis are also astutely aware of internal divisions (Hermann & Anabi, 2023). The *Times of Israel* defined Netanyahu as "indefatigable and ultra-divisive" (Horovitz, 2022). In the words of one our interviewees, Ofir Barel, who researches Israeli information warfare at an independent institute and has collaborated with the Ministry of Foreign Affairs in the past:

> [the] political discourse [is] already tense because in general Netanyahu himself is a very emotional political issue. If any one entity would like to sow chaos here during election or after or between election, [they] just need to mention Netanyahu and it will just work.

He was convinced that previous disinformation campaigns related to recent elections originated domestically and were designed to exploit existing polarizations in the Israeli society. The challenges associated with this type of disinformation ring familiar to other democracies around the world. For example, in the United States domestic disinformation cumulated in the storming of the Capitol on January 6, 2021, a deeply disturbing event for both US citizens and international allies of the United States from around the world (Freedman, 2022). Disinformation should not be shoehorned into a niche, disconnected phenomenon – instead, it should be understood as a cross cutting issue of cyberspace with imminent offline repercussions. It therefore also needs various actors to work together to counter it most effectively. In other words, both the private and public actors, both within and between nations, should come together to maintain democracy. In the case of Israel, an ambivalent picture emerges regarding the value of public actors' interventions or even legislative actions aiming to diminish (the effects of) disinformation. This is mainly due to the divided political landscape in the country specifically and the reactive nature of legislative actions generally. However, it is questionable if private actors of the (quite capable) Israeli information technology (IT) sector are useful or even benign forces in this regard. As recent journalistic investigations uncovered, Israeli firms have been involved in developing and selling spy software (spyware), as well as offering propagandists for hire (Kirchgaessner et al., 2023).

We therefore examine specific challenges to the Israeli (dis-)information environment to distill in how far its lessons learned are useful for other democracies around the world. We address the presence – or absence – in legislative policy concerning disinformation and analyze the usability of public–private partnerships for countering disinformation and argue that democracy relies on different parts of society to function in a healthy manner; governmental actors can but should not control everything, and certainly not the information environment. Finally, we address how Israeli insights can be transferred to initiatives in other democracies (or not). The analysis relies on primary sources in Hebrew and English, such as committee hearings in the Knesset (Israel's parliament), as well as interviews with Israeli stakeholders, such as former officials or currently active private actors addressing disinformation, supplemented by secondary sources on the topic.

DISINFORMATION IN ISRAEL: AN EXTERNAL AND INTERNAL THREAT

Israel's geographic location and geopolitics in the region have shaped and continue to shape its fight against disinformation campaigns. External information threats allegedly stemming from Iran – considered Israel's main antagonist in the region – have been studied and monitored by the Israeli government and Israeli research institutes. According to Barel, Iran reportedly launched information campaigns that attempted to further divide Israeli citizens along political lines during the recent prime minister elections. However, the origins of numerous recent disinformation campaigns launched in Israel are speculated to have launched *internally*. Yet, it is important to remember that internal and external threats in Israel are difficult to disentangle, according to Lt. Col. (res.) David Siman-Tov, a Senior Researcher at the Institute for National Security Studies (INSS) and deputy head of the Institute for the Research of the Methodology of Intelligence (IRMI). As is oftentimes the case within information warfare, internal disinformation campaigns echo sentiments that typically derive from external actors. Even so, there are key characteristics that give away the identity of externally launched disinformation campaigns in Israel, observed interviewee *Haaretz* journalist Omer Benjakob, whose journalistic work covers technology and disinformation. Firstly, Hebrew is both a difficult language to master and is rarely spoken as a first language outside of Israel (BBC, 2014). Therefore, disinformation campaigns employing Hebrew draw attention to themselves by including grammatical errors, typos, or awkward phrases that a native speaker would immediately spot. Secondly, Israel is a small country – approximately the size of the state of New Jersey in the United States – and it is logistically difficult to blatantly fabricate news about events that are supposedly taking place (Nations Online, 2023). As Benjakob described it:

> [It's] very hard to lie at a big level. I can't say there are riots in a certain part of town because everyone has a cousin who lives in that part of town. [I] can't say Arabs are murdering people in droves when it's a twenty-minute drive from your house. That undermines the ability to do a lot of fake news.

Yet, disinformation campaigns targeting Arab voters do exist, even though it is more difficult to spread due to the intricacies of Hebrew and Israel's small size (Benjakob, 2021). For example, according to our interviewee Guy Lurie, an attorney and researcher at the Israel Democracy Institute, an independent and nonpartisan center for research in Israel, campaigns aiming to disenfranchise Arab voters were disseminated during Israel's recent elections. As Lurie described:

> Very targeted campaigns we saw in Israel during election ... for example in 2015 there was a targeted campaign saying that Arab voters are coming in droves to election booths and delegitimizing Arab citizens ... trying to charge the public atmosphere with this kind of tension that would lead supporters of the Right to [the] election booth.

Disinformation campaigns created to rally supporters from right-wing parties – such as current Prime Minister Netanyahu's Likud party – were popular during recent Israeli elections. According to Lurie, there are popular conspiracy theories claiming Netanyahu's corruption charges are instituted by a "leftist deep state." These conspiracies have been popular since 2016 when Netanyahu was charged for, as *The New York Times* described it, "a habit of performing official favors for wealthy businessmen in exchange for gifts both material and intangible" (Joseph & Kingsley, 2022). These conspiracies claim that Israel's top law and enforcement ministers charged Netanyahu with corruption because they are attempting to preserve their power and bring down a popular elected leader. As Lurie observes, this "witch hunt" conspiracy is a very powerful rhetorical tool that has sparked distrust and anger from the Israeli people toward public institutions. Furthermore, recent judicial reform protests in Israel have provided fertile ground for disinformation campaigns. Via the social media platform X (previously Twitter) but also messaging app WhatsApp, actors supporting the judicial reforms created fake accounts that encouraged protestors to engage in violence against police officers in the hope of discrediting the protest. Likewise, fake accounts on X spread malicious information against senior Likud member of the Knesset Yuli Edelstein. Edelstein, one of the few Likud members who have voiced opposition to the judicial reform legislation, was targeted by accounts who claimed that he was "a betrayer, a Ukrainian, born in the Soviet Union," observed Barel (Hauser-Tov, 2023).

It is unsurprising that the most popular social media platforms in Israel are beholden to the spread of the most noted disinformation since political disinformation's global presence is often studied and analyzed on social media platforms. X and Facebook have been sources of fake accounts spreading disinformation and WhatsApp has been cited as a place where group chats are infiltrated by malicious actors. Accounts created by actors who support the judicial reforms reportedly entered activist group chats on WhatsApp to sow chaos and create factions within the anti-judicial reform movement. For example, research conducted at Tel Aviv University found an instance where these actors posted provocative material in these activist groups, such as comparing Netanyahu to Hitler, that was then pointed to by the prime minister to claim that "radical left activists" were comparing him to Hitler, observed Barel. While disinformation campaigns are identified and analyzed by researchers in Israel, the question of what measures currently or should exist to stop the spread of this malicious content remains open-ended and complex.

Countering Disinformation in Israel: Lacking Coherence, Planning, and Responsiveness

There is existing, yet limited, legislature enabling the Israeli government to counter internal disinformation swiftly and effectively. Specifically, the Knesset Elections Law, otherwise known as the Propaganda Methods Law, was created in 1959 to define campaign advertising regulations during Israeli elections (Shwartz Altshuler & Lurie, 2015). Elements of the 1959 law are outdated and require updated amendments that address the powerful effects of social media and the internet during campaign seasons, though the law remains an important regulatory baseline for modern political elections (Shwartz Altshuler & Lurie, 2015). Finding and securing an opportune occasion to remediate these flaws has been a difficult task for the Israeli judiciary and legislature, as compressed and fast-changing results of five elections in three years offered few periods of enough political stability to craft and establish such improved legislation. Israel's Central Election Committee proposed recommendations to the Propaganda Methods Law in 2017 that included a principle of transparency, which required political advertisements to identify themselves as such. Under this principle of transparency, political actors or parties must identify themselves within political adverts, including ones on social media (TOI Staff, 2019). This principle was transferred into a judiciary ruling led by then Supreme Court Justice and Chairman of the Central Elections Committee Hanan Melcer (Surkes, 2019; TOI Staff, 2019). This ruling followed insistent objections from the Likud party to ban anonymous political ads online via legislation in 2019 (Surkes, 2019; TOI Staff, 2019). Even without solid legislative backing, new transparency processes enabled the chairperson of the Election Committee to give out injunctions during the 2019 and 2022 campaign season for campaign advertising posing as news stories on social media channels, such as Facebook and WhatsApp. However, Lurie noted that while this principle of transparency is a positive effort toward stopping the spread of political disinformation, more needs to be done:

> It's not enough. Need to include more of transparency, obligation, ability [of the Chairperson] to enforce transparency especially in light of new media, social media and its ability to disseminate information in a very quick manner . . . Need to create more robust regulatory landscape that allow enforcement of these issues.

However, as noted by Lurie and additional experts, the government's ability to curb disinformation through legislation enters the sensitive, important realm of freedom of speech debates.

> In terms of actual content of election campaigns, even if they seem to be misleading or seem to be disinformation, they [Election Committee] are very restrained and very reluctant to enter the fray in terms of freedom of speech. Even when they are intervening, evidentiary basis must be very strong.

In this regard, CEO and co-founder of tech company ActiveFence, Noam Schwartz, believes that the most effective fight against disinformation cannot be from the government because of the potential for freedom of speech violations. If the government were to aggressively fight disinformation, they would be "rightly so accused of censorship. The only way to curb disinformation is to go to where the disinformation is being distributed." Illiberal and authoritarian figures can claim political speech from opponents as disinformation to silence and deter dissent and plurality of voices, such as examples in Egypt or Russia have shown (Jack, 2022; Jumet, 2022). Researchers invested in preserving Israeli democracy strive to imagine a balance of freedom of political speech while still holding malicious parties accountable. Additionally, Schwartz contemplated what the Israeli government would look like if it did block swaths of domains from the internet because they deemed it "disinformation." "We'll have a very different regime if they do that," said Schwartz. "All of the sudden the government is not a democracy anymore. They are deciding for you." Who needs to regulate, what should be regulated, and how to regulate are complex and universal questions for any democratic government approaching legislation toward fighting disinformation. Even the plausible applications of government interference in the disinformation fight are questioned by Schwartz:

> Israel can't tell Facebook what to do. They have no teeth, the government. What will they say? 'You are not allowed to operate in this country anymore.' They can't really because Facebook's power is so much business.

Even with the creation of a more robust landscape for countering disinformation, deciding who is responsible to create and enforce legislation is unclear. "The problem is Israel cannot find a dedicated team to countering disinformation," said Barel. "Efforts are ad hoc, not systematic." It is also unclear what is appropriate to regulate and how to regulate it. For example, campaign advertising and campaign finance laws are entirely different domains in Israel that would both need to be addressed through robust regulatory efforts. The recent flux of governments, minister officials, and civil servants in Israel has left a noted void in both expertise about and legislative enthusiasm to counter internal disinformation.

Countering Disinformation in Israel: What About the Private Sector?

Benjakob, defeatedly, believes that the only real solutions currently on the table are stemming from social media companies who are primarily concerned with attracting eyeballs to screens for advertising dollars.

> At the legislation level it's really a game of whack-a-mole. You reach the really sad conclusion that the only mechanism we actually have against disinformation is social media platforms user guidelines, which to me is tantamount to saying we have nothing in place.

Placing the responsibility on the tech companies to counter internal disinformation in Israel is a double-edged sword. On the one hand, the tech companies have the technological accessibility into their platforms and the expertise to find, identify, report, and remove harmful content online. According to Schwartz, platforms have vastly improved the identification and removal of harmful content online over Israel's past five election campaigns in three years. Online disinformation surrounding these recent, reiterative elections has served as an optimal test ground for tech companies to improve their strategies to fight disinformation. However, while technologists at platforms are improving, so are the producers of disinformation:

> The tricks that used to be common are not that common anymore . . . What actors are getting better at is creating a more believable narrative. So, they can actually create a deep conviction among the people in what they are saying is true (Noam Schwartz).

Within the past five elections, political parties across the spectrum – including the ruling right Likud party and the opposition centrist party Yesh Atid – have reportedly employed disinformation campaigns that attempted to emotionally resonate with Israeli citizens, observed Schwartz. For example, recent and ongoing judicial reform protests in the first half of 2023 are complex, deeply resonant political fights that have wide-ranging implications for the democratic institutions within Israel. As Schwartz and his team monitored the online space, he commented that:

> The Right will say, "Hey, protestors on the right you need to go to demonstrations because the anarchists on the left are ruining this country" . . . and the Left will say "the Right is trying to make Israel a dictatorship and take it back 1,000 years."

Since the judicial reforms and the charged debates over Prime Minister Netanyahu spark an intimate, emotional touchpoint for many Israelis, much disinformation – particularly one party lying about what another party said – is propagated through social media channels that hold personal family chats, such as WhatsApp. Thus, these encrypted messaging apps that host private conversations are much more difficult to monitor by content moderators at tech companies. The extent to which these social media platforms can help fight internal disinformation is limited. On the other hand, tech companies do not exist to serve the best interest of the public. As a corporate entity, naturally tech companies aim to grow profit and appease stakeholders. "I don't think the platforms owe you anything. It's not a public service. It's not a penchant fund," commented Schwartz. While partnerships between the Israeli government and social media companies exist to help fight election season disinformation, for example, Facebook banned certain political ads that aggressively discouraged people to vote in Israel in the November 2022 election, their effectiveness and reach are short term (Jerusalem Post Staff, 2022). As previously noted, the social media companies' accessibility and expertise toward their tech is not comprehensively understood or effectively regulated by constantly fluctuating government workers. Therefore, Israel's private spaces – with advanced tech expertise and limited regulation – can flourish in ways that best serve their entrepreneurial interest, rather than prioritizing the public good. Israel's high-tech culture and expertise in cybersecurity threats also pose reasons for both pessimism and optimism in the fight against disinformation. Often coined as a "start-up nation," Israel has advanced technological skills to fight external information threats, most notably from Iran. "The capabilities of the intelligence community – with an emphasis on the cyber field – can be a reason for optimism regarding the attempts of foreign campaigns," noted Siman-Tov. While Israel may be adept at pinpointing information threats from foreign entities, this privatization of intelligence is seen as worrisome by Siman-Tov who noted, "At the same time, in front of the internal processes there are not many reasons for optimism."

According to Benjakob, the privatization of Israel's high-tech culture and expertise is noticeably increasing, specifically within the past fifteen to twenty years. Journalistic investigations in Israel within the past year have exposed privatized and professional Israeli-led disinformation operations, for example, the infamous Team Jorge's undemocratic influence and information operations were exposed by journalistic teams at Haaretz and TheMarker in 2023 (Megiddo & Benjakob, 2023). Privatized, for-hire intelligence efforts in Israel complicate the systematic fight against disinformation. Benjakob compared Israel's disinformation boutiques to a larger country like the United States:

> The way we've turned our high-tech stuff and the way we think about it and do it is a bit leaner … That's what's so dangerous within the Israeli space, where you have misinformation plus high tech culture.

However, the rapid development of artificial intelligence (AI) tools may prove to be more dangerous than high-tech boutique disinformation firms in Israel. Organized, coherent fights against internal disinformation in Israel have been complicated by limited jurisdiction over tech platforms, legislative gridlock, and lack of regulative fervor from the Likud government. Therefore, it is unclear whether swift, effective governmental regulation or other advocacy movements will be created to fight against AI tools spreading disinformation, for example, generative AI or robocalls. Schwartz observed the criticalness and long-term nature of the future of disinformation campaigns in Israel:

> This is a constant fight. This is an arms race. This is not a fight over regulation. It's way bigger than that. I don't think regulation is necessarily the answer. If it is the answer, it needs to move fast.

Governmental regulation and overreliance on tech companies to counter disinformation in Israel are not the only solutions. Interviewees suggested that Israel seriously partake in a movement already enacted within other democracies, such as the UK or the United States: systemic investment in information and media digital literacy (Horrigan, 2016). Promoting and investing in digital literacy, specifically media or information digital literacy, may help cultivate helpful habits in social media users, such as critically analyzing the source material (i.e., news outlet, sources) and reporting malicious activity online.

However, the responsibility of teaching digital literacy to help counter disinformation in Israel should not just be allocated toward the schools or parents. An onus on the tech platforms to help their users navigate and not believe whatever they read, hear, or see is critical. Just as efforts in the United States have recently put the onus on social media platforms to help young users' mental health, so should governments put the onus on the platforms to encourage digital literacy (Richtel, Pearson, & Levenson, 2023). Digital and media literacy research have demonstrated mixed results, as some scholars emphasize the "disconnect between accuracy judgments and sharing intentions" (Sirlin et al., 2021). However, interviewees believed in the value of using their "conscience and their brain," as interviewee Schwartz put it. For example, when news articles filled with propaganda about recent judicial reforms are shared within family group chats on WhatsApp, it is up to the individual to assess the information presented to them. Information literacy contributes to a healthy, safe online lifestyle. As Schwartz described it:

> If there's an incident [offline], there is something that will help you solve it ... people don't expect that level of security and safety online. This is a bug. There is no difference between our online presence and our offline presence anymore.

CONCLUSION

While countering disinformation can promote a safer online environment, it's a very "non-sexy topic" in Israel, as Schwartz described it. Generally, the public discourse surrounding disinformation in Israel deprioritizes the topic. Israel considers itself surrounded by adversaries; in its seventy-five-year history, the country has at points been at war with neighbors Egypt, Jordan, Lebanon, and Syria and has yet to come to a peaceful solution about Palestinian statehood, which affects discouraged Palestinians in the West Bank and Gaza Strip (Waxman, 2019). Priorities in Israeli society include terrorist threats and potential nuclear weapons in Iran. In comparison, a fake news account created on X, for example, is considered little threatening, according to Barel. Interviewees agreed that disinformation is indeed a danger for Israeli democracy and should be of high public concern. Yet, there were varied accounts of where the Israeli public should look to see the detriments of disinformation. Barel argued that all Israel needs to do is look at the Capitol riots of January 6, 2021, in the United States to see the consequences of Russian information warfare. Barel compares the political tensions of the United States to the political instability that has been brewing in Israel over many years. "So, if it's something we don't take care of today effectively, we may create a monster that will hurt us in, I don't know, a few years ahead in the future," observed Barel. Benjakob disagrees and instead points toward smaller, former Soviet Union countries to predict Israel's future. The way false news and disinformation manifests in Israel is more aligned with the quasi-liberal and increasingly illiberal democracies of Hungary and Poland, rather than the United States. Benjakob made the comparison:

> In the US, UK you have this implicit assumption that truth reigns supreme and that people are not lying to you . . . the rest of the world attuned to that not actually ever being true. If you talk for example to Polish people, Hungarian people, Israelis feel the same, you're kind of used to living in a world where you accept that there's kind of some level of manipulation going on . . . it's a young country and everyone was on board with the national project early on.

Whether Israel's future attempts at countering internal disinformation more similarly mirrors older, established democracies – such as the UK or the United States – or younger, evolving democracies – such as Hungary and Poland – is disputed. Yet, a commonly shared belief is that Israel's current government headed by Netanyahu is not interested in leading the charge against internal disinformation. Coordinated disinformation campaigns that disseminate conspiracies around Netanyahu's corruption charges and attacks against judicial reform protestors and Likud political opponents work in favor of Netanyahu's government. Evidence for Netanyahu's willingness to strike down legislative efforts of transparency in political advertising is evidence of this disinterest. As of this writing, it remains to be seen what action the Netanyahu government will take in response to the Israeli Supreme Court striking down key portions of its judicial reform bill in January 2024.

Furthermore, juggling emerging normalization efforts with Middle Eastern countries such as Saudi Arabia (Berman, 2023), maintaining a strategic relationship with the United States among recent criticism over judicial reforms (Pinkas, 2023), and aims to halt Iran's nuclear program are governmental priorities that attract media headlines. And the terrorist attack of October 7, coupled with Israel's aggressive response, will have far-reaching domestic and international political consequences that are yet to be determined. With a strong victory in the winter of 2022, the Right finally has the opportunity to set and push through its agenda in the Knesset. Barel commented on the overarching significance of Netanyahu's proposed judicial reforms:

> This is not just the case of let's elect a justice in one way or the other, not something like this. The story behind it is much, much bigger. The right-wing in Israel for years felt that it cannot implement its policy . . . After 4 elections without a clear cut result, now November election finally resulted in a clear cut resolution. The Right wing in Israel sees a historic opportunity to make changes that would service for the long term . . . When you speak in those terms . . . disinformation . . . is secondary for making this historic change.

An outlook for the future of Israeli efforts to counter internal disinformation is mixed. Expert capabilities that its high-tech culture and start-up entrepreneurial spirit brings to the table could be reason for hope – however, those same capabilities have been used for harmful purposes in the past. Persistent protests against judicial reforms speak to Israeli citizens' desire to protect their democratic institutions. Yet, the disinterest of the government to counter disinformation due to its beneficial value and the public's redirected attention to critical issues of Iran's nuclear program and relations with Palestinians deprioritizes the disinformation fight. A hopeful step toward prioritizing disinformation and preserving Israeli democracy is to remember that "Attempts of Iran and other entities make us [Israel] divided," commented Barel. "We need to remember what makes us [Israel] united." After the terrorist attacks of October 7, perceived threats and consequences of disinformation in Israel are materialized and being played out across the social media landscape. Similar to other political systems around the world, Israeli tech representatives, government actors, and citizens interested in a prospering democracy need to counter internal and external challenges – among them disinformation.

REFERENCES

Bader, M. (2018). Disinformation in elections. *Security and Human Rights*, 29(1–4), 24–35. https://doi.org/10.1163/18750230-02901006

BBC. (2014). *A guide to Hebrew – 10 facts about the Hebrew language*. BBC. https://bbc.co.uk/languages/other/hebrew/guide/facts.shtml

Benjakob, O. (2021, March 23). Israeli election: This time, Arabs are the target – not the subject – of disinformation. *Haaretz*. https://haaretz.com/israel-news/elections/2021-03-23/ty-article/.premium/israeli-election-this-time-arabs-are-the-target-not-subject-of-disinformation/0000017f-da7b-d938-a17f-fe7ba5940000

(2023, October 15). Musk's X and Hamas' digital offensive: Gaza is a perfect storm of disinformation. *Haaretz*. https://haaretz.com/israel-news/security-aviation/2023-10-15/ty-article/musks-x-and-hamas-digital-offensive-gaza-is-a-perfect-storm-of-disinformation/0000018b-3331-d450-a3af-7b3d6a050000

Berg, R. (2023, March 27). *Benjamin Netanyahu, Israel's defiant leader*. BBC News. https://bbc.com/news/world-middle-east-18008697

Berman, L. (2023, May 28). Deal between Israel and Saudi Arabia is 'absolutely possible,' says ex-Mossad chief. *The Times of Israel*. https://timesofisrael.com/deal-between-israel-and-saudi-arabia-is-absolutely-possible-says-ex-mossad-chief/

Farwell, J. P., & Rohozinski, R. (2011). Stuxnet and the future of cyber war. *Survival*, 53(1), 23–40. https://doi.org/10.1080/00396338.2011.555586

Freedman, R. O. (2022). The Trump Administration's threat to American democracy. In T. Ketko, H. Bor, & K. Arar (Eds.), *Enhancing values of dignity, democracy, and diversity in higher education* (pp. 55–68). Routledge.

Freidson, Y. (2023, February 10). Three years in, Netanyahu's trial has no end in sight. *Haaretz*. https://haaretz.com/israel-news/2023-02-10/ty-article-magazine/.highlight/three-years-in-netanyahus-trial-has-no-end-in-sight/00000186-37c0-dfa7-afee-ffeb9fd10000

Frenkel, S., & Myers, S. L. (2023, October 10). Hamas seeds violent videos on sites with little moderation. *The New York Times*. https://nytimes.com/2023/10/10/technology/hamas-violent-videos-online.html

Gavison, R. E. (2011). *Can Israel be both Jewish and democratic?* SSRN Scholarly Paper 1862904. https://papers.ssrn.com/abstract=1862904

Haaretz. (2023, October 22). Hostages held by Hamas: The names of those abducted from Israel. *Haaretz*. https://haaretz.com/haaretz-explains/2023-10-22/ty-article-magazine/hostages-held-by-hamas-the-names-of-those-abducted-from-israel/0000018b-55f8-d5d2-afefd5fdd04e0000

Harding, E. (2023). *How could Israeli intelligence miss the Hamas invasion plans?* Center for Strategic and International Studies. https://csis.org/analysis/how-could-israeli-intelligence-miss-hamas-invasion-plans

Hauser-Tov, M. (2023, March 6). Four Likud MKs press for dialogue, flexibility in judicial overhaul. *Haaretz*. https://haaretz.com/israel-news/2023-03-06/ty-article/.premium/four-likud-mks-press-for-dialogue-flexibility-in-judicial-overhaul/00000186-b39a-d2fe-a7be-ff9beade0000

Hermann, T., & Anabi, O. (2023). *National mood unrestful*. The Israel Democracy Institute. https://en.idi.org.il/articles/48985

Horovitz, D. (2022, October 19). Why this election is a defining moment for Israel, how it's run, what it stands for. *The Times of Israel*. https://timesofisrael.com/why-this-election-is-a-defining-moment-for-israel-how-its-run-what-it-stands-for/

Horrigan, J. (2016, September 20). *Digital readiness gaps*. Pew Research Center: Internet, Science & Tech. https://pewresearch.org/internet/2016/09/20/digital-readiness-gaps/

Institute for Strategic Dialogue. (2023, October 25). *Capitalising on crisis: Russia, China and Iran use X to exploit Israel-Hamas information chaos*. Digital Dispatches. https://isdglobal.org/digital_dispatches/capitalising-on-crisis-russia-china-and-iran-use-x-to-exploit-israel-hamas-information-chaos/

International Bar Association. (2020, December 3). *IBAHRI condemns extrajudicial killing of Iran's nuclear scientist, Mohsen Fakhrizadeh*. International Bar Association. https://ibanet.org/article/E60E1F31-47B3-433A-B009-FC91DF00F44C

Jack, V. (2022, March 22). Russia expands laws criminalizing 'fake news'. *Politico*. https://politico.eu/article/russia-expand-laws-criminalize-fake-news/

Jerusalem Post Staff. (2022, October 6). Facebook to ban certain political ads before elections. *The Jerusalem Post*. https://jpost.com/israel-news/article-718994

Jewish Virtual Library. (2023). *Israeli electoral history*. https://jewishvirtuallibrary.org/israeli-electoral-history

Jones, C., & Murphy, E. (2002). *Israel: Challenges to identity, democracy, and the state*. Routledge.

Joseph, Y., & Kingsley, P. (2022, November 3). Netanyahu will return with corruption charges unresolved. Here's where the case stands. *The New York Times*. https://nytimes.com/2022/11/03/world/middleeast/netanyahu-corruption-charges-israel.html

Jumet, K. (2022). Authoritarian repression under Sisi: New tactics or new tools? In F. Cavatorta, M. Mekouar, & O. Topak (Eds.), *New authoritarian practices in the Middle East and North Africa* (pp. 73–91). Edinburgh University Press. https://cambridge.org/core/books/new-authoritarian-practices-in-the-middle-east-and-north-africa/authoritarian-repression-under-sisi-new-tactics-or-new-tools/95E4E25E59C9542CEDA39C3D633A189E

Kirchgaessner, S., Ganguly, M., Pegg, D., Cadwalladr, C., & Burke, J. (2023, February 15). Revealed: The hacking and disinformation team meddling in elections. *The Guardian*. https://theguardian.com/world/2023/feb/15/revealed-disinformation-team-jorge-claim-meddling-elections-tal-hanan

Kiser, E., & Barzel, Y. (1991). The origins of democracy in England. *Rationality and Society*, 3(4), 396–422. https://doi.org/10.1177/1043463191003004002

Klempner, U. (2023, October 23). *Emojis of terror: Telegram's role in perpetuating extremism in the October 2023 Hamas-Israel War*. Global Network on Extremism and Technology. https://gnet-research.org/2023/10/23/emojis-of-terror-telegrams-role-in-perpetuating-extremism-in-the-october-2023-hamas-israel-war/

Langfitt, F. (2022, December 30). *3 prime ministers, 2 monarchs, 1 year: This was Britain's tumultuous 2022*. NPR. https://opb.org/article/2022/12/30/3-prime-ministers-2-monarchs-1-year-this-was-britain-s-tumultuous-2022/

Lipner, S. (2023, February 1). Netanyahu's coalition isn't built to last: Expect high sparks within and fragile prospects for Israel's incoming government. *Atlantic Council*. https://atlanticcouncil.org/in-depth-research-reports/issue-brief/netanyahus-coalition-isnt-built-to-last-expect-high-sparks-within-and-fragile-prospects-for-israels-incoming-government/

Megiddo, G., & Benjakob, O. (2023). The Israelis destabilizing democracy and disrupting elections worldwide. *Haaretz*. https://haaretz.com/israel-news/security-aviation/2022-11-16/ty-article-static-ext/the-israelis-destabilizing-democracy-and-disrupting-elections-worldwide/00000186-461e-d80f-abff-6e9e08b10000

Mueller, G. B., Jensen, B., Valeriano, B., Maness, R. C., & Macias, J. M. (2023). *Cyber operations during the Russo-Ukrainian War*. CSIS. https://csis.org/analysis/cyber-operations-during-russo-ukrainian-war

Myers, S. L., & Frenkel, S. (2023, November 3). In a worldwide war of words, Russia, China and Iran back Hamas. *The New York Times*. https://nytimes.com/2023/11/03/technology/israel-hamas-information-war.html

Nations Online. (2023). *List of US states by area – Nations Online Project*. https://nationsonline.org/oneworld/US-states-by-area.htm#:~:text=New%20Jersey%20is%20the%20most,the%20same%20number%20of%20inhabitants

Nechin, E. (2023, November 14). 'Similar to a virus': Disinformation becomes deadly new front in Israel-Hamas war. *Haaretz*. https://haaretz.com/israel-news/2023-11-14/ty-article-magazine/.premium/similar-to-a-virus-disinformation-becomes-deadly-new-front-in-israel-hamas-war/0000018b-cde9-dd11-a19f-edfd51180000

Pamuk, H. (2023, November 10). *Blinken says "far too many" Palestinians killed as Israel battles Hamas in Gaza*. Reuters. https://reuters.com/world/middle-east/blinken-says-far-too-many-palestinians-killed-israel-battles-hamas-gaza-2023-11-10/

Pinkas, A. (2023, March 29). Biden no longer buys Netanyahu's lies, and Israel will pay the price. *Haaretz*. https://haaretz.com/israel-news/2023-03-29/ty-article/.highlight/not-being-invited-to-washington-is-bad-not-being-trusted-there-is-far-worse/00000187-2d13-d6f0-af9f-7d5775f00000

Richtel, M., Pearson, C., & Levenson, M. (2023, May 23). Surgeon General warns that social media may harm children and adolescents. *The New York Times*. https://nytimes.com/2023/05/23/health/surgeon-general-social-media-mental-health.html

Shwartz Altshuler, T., & Lurie, G. (2015). *Reforming Israel's campaign advertising laws*. The Israel Democracy Institute, Policy Paper 109.

Sirlin, N., Epstein, Z., Arechar, A. A., & Rand, D. G. (2021). Digital literacy is associated with more discerning accuracy judgments but not sharing intentions. *Harvard Kennedy School Misinformation Review*, 2(6). https://doi.org/10.37016/mr-2020-83

Smith, P., Chuck, E., & Zelenko, A. (2023, March 27). *Netanyahu agrees to pause judicial overhaul following widespread unrest*. NBC News. https://nbcnews.com/news/world/netanyahu-israel-judicial-reforms-engulf-gallant-protests-rcna76759

Surkes, S. (2019, February 27). Experts implore elections chief to appoint anti-cyber meddling czar. *The Times of Israel*. https://timesofisrael.com/experts-implore-elections-chief-to-appoint-coordinator-to-fight-cyber-meddling/

The Economist. (2023, October 12). Hamas's attack was the bloodiest in Israel's history. *The Economist*. https://economist.com/briefing/2023/10/12/hamass-attack-was-the-bloodiest-in-israels-history

TOI Staff. (2019, February 28). Election judge bars anonymous internet ads despite Likud objection. *The Times of Israel*. https://timesofisrael.com/election-judge-bars-anonymous-internet-adds-despite-likud-objection/

Wardle, C. (2018). The need for smarter definitions and practical, timely empirical research on information disorder. *Digital Journalism*, 6(8), 951–963. https://doi.org/10.1080/21670811.2018.1502047

Waxman, D. (2019). *The Israeli-Palestinian conflict: What everyone needs to know®*. Oxford University Press. http://ebookcentral.proquest.com/lib/utxa/detail.action?docID=5738713

7

Israeli Information Strategies and Maneuvers

David Amsellem

INTRODUCTION

On Saturday, October 7, 2023, Hamas, a Palestinian political and military movement considered a terrorist organization by the European Union, launched a massive and unprecedented attack against Israel from the Gaza Strip, which it has controlled since 2006: Operation Al Aqsa Deluge.

Through meticulous intelligence work, preparation, and training, the Izz al-Din al-Qassam Brigades, the military wing of the movement, managed to thwart Israel's extensive surveillance apparatus and introduce nearly 3,000 of its men into Israeli territory. The simultaneous attacks by these heavily armed fighters targeted military (military outposts on the outskirts of Gaza) and, more importantly, civilian (kibbutzim and nearby towns, music festival) targets, resulting in numerous casualties: 1,150 deaths, including 775 civilians.[1]

The strategic surprise created by Hamas caught the Israeli state off guard, taking several hours to organize a response and regain control of the territories held by Palestinian terrorists, due to insufficient resources on the ground. In addition to the security forces in the sector who were killed in the early hours of the operation (308 soldiers and 57 policemen), some active soldiers were on leave on this Sabbath and religious holiday, while for several months, the army had been more mobilized in the West Bank where clashes with the Palestinian population are escalating.

For several hours, Hamas thus managed to control large swaths of Israeli territory bordering the Gaza Strip, allowing its members to organize the kidnapping of dozens of Israelis, mostly civilians, with – for the first time – a high proportion of women and children. In total, around 240 people were captured in a matter of hours.

[1] For figures provided by the State of Israel on its online platform, see *Israel War Database* (n.d.).

An Unprecedented Attack

Hamas' attack on October 7 is unprecedented in Israel's history. Never before has an armed group belonging to a non-state organization penetrated Israeli territory so massively and for so long and carried out such acts. Except for its War of Independence (1948), Israel has always managed to shift the theater of operations outside its national territory: into Egypt during the Suez War (1956), then into the Sinai, West Bank, and Golan Heights during the Six-Day War (1967), and even during the surprise attack that was the Yom Kippur War in 1973. Arab armies penetrated territories occupied by Israel since 1967, but never entered Israeli territory.

Hamas' attack is therefore unprecedented in every respect: its scale, its number of victims and hostages, the identity of the dead (mostly civilians, including women, the elderly, and children), and the atrocities committed (rape, torture, and decapitated and burned bodies). The fact that this occurred within Israeli territory, in supposedly inviolable places (secure rooms), plunges society into terror and revives the trauma of antisemitism persecution in Europe, against which the State of Israel, created following the Holocaust, was meant to be a bulwark.

Internally, a Tense Moment

Hamas' attacks come at a time of very high political tensions in Israel, as the country has been undermined for several years by the rise of identity and cultural claims, reflecting the diversity of the Israeli society.[2] This explosion of the political field is exacerbated by an institutional and electoral system[3] that prevents the emergence of a stable majority. Since 2019, the country has therefore experienced no less than five elections in just four years[4] (compared to one every four years usually), either due to a lack of majority or due to too short majorities or coalitions too disparate to hold over time.

Since 2022, however, a coalition seems to have emerged: that between the Israeli right-wing party (Likud) led by Benjamin Netanyahu and various religious and nationalist parties, which crystallize strong opposition due to their radicalism. However, this coalition has been pushing for institutional reform for several months,

[2] Despite the overwhelming majority of the country's citizens being of Jewish culture or religion, there are numerous identity and cultural subgroups, including among Jews: between secular and religious; among the religious there are also many currents: between Sephardim and Ashkenazim; between the various countries of Western, Eastern, or Russian immigration. In addition to the Jewish population, there are other cultural and religious minorities, notably Arabs (who make up almost 20 percent of the population), Druze, and Christians.

[3] Israel is a parliamentary democracy: The head of the executive is appointed by the parliamentary majority. However, the single-round system is based on full proportional representation, which favors the emergence of small parties that obtain at least 3.25 percent of the vote.

[4] Two elections in 2019 (April and September), one each in 2020, 2021, and 2022.

which, according to the opposition, threatens the democratic foundation of the state. For over a year, hundreds of thousands of people have been gathering every Saturday in Tel Aviv to oppose this project, which deeply divides society.

All these internal tensions have contributed to weakening the very heart of the Israeli security apparatus: Throughout 2023, more than 12,000 reservists have announced their refusal to serve voluntarily in the army, especially in elite units (commandos, intelligence, air force), supported by former senior officials of the Shin Bet (internal intelligence) (Bateman, 2023). Such was the situation in the months preceding the Hamas attack.

Internationally, a Crucial Moment

Beyond internal politics, the attacks on October 7 occurred at a crucial moment for Israeli diplomacy. At the end of 2020, Israel normalized its relations with several Arab countries (United Arab Emirates and Bahrain in September, Sudan in October, and Morocco in December) as part of the Abraham Accords, concluded under the auspices of the United States. Israel was thus reviving its normalization policy toward Arab countries, which had been at a standstill since the peace agreement with Jordan in 1996.

For several months, negotiations had been taking place behind the scenes for Saudi Arabia, a major oil power and a major Sunni Islamic site with the presence of the two holy sites (Medina and Mecca), to join the Abraham Accords. On October 4, 2023, three days before the Hamas attacks, an Israeli minister attended a conference organized by a United Nations (UN) agency in Riyadh, a visit that was unthinkable a few months earlier.

These diplomatic successes for Israel validate the strategy initiated by Benjamin Netanyahu, who has been in power almost uninterrupted since 2009.[5] It can be summarized as follows: militarily contain the security threat posed by certain Palestinian groups; politically obscure the Palestinian issue; and focus on the Iranian threat, deemed existential, and regional partnerships with Sunni powers.

The sudden return of the Palestinian issue on October 7 thus challenges Netanyahu's strategy and undermines the entire Israeli foreign policy.

Communication as a Political Weapon

It was in this internal and international context that Israel launched its military response against the Gaza Strip on October 7. In the hours following the attacks, intense bombings targeted infrastructure presumed to belong to Hamas while the

[5] With the exception of the period from June 2021 to December 2022, when the opposition managed, in a very short space of time, to build a slim majority to remove him from power before finally breaking up.

country declared a state of war with the recall of over 300,000 reservists, the largest mobilization ever launched by the state. Israeli authorities warned from the outset that the war would be long-lasting, intense, massive, and destructive with a dual objective: to destroy the operational, political, and military capabilities of Hamas in Gaza; and to bring the hostages back to Israel. There is another objective that has not been clearly stated but is evident: to restore Israel's deterrent capacity vis-à-vis its regional competitors (Hezbollah and Iran). To achieve all these objectives, Israel must ensure it has the military, financial, and political means necessary. For this, the role of communication is fundamental, especially since Israeli authorities are aware of the fractures within their society, know they are being closely watched, and suffer from a degraded image among a portion of global public opinion due to their occupation policy in the West Bank. Therefore, to wage its war against Hamas, Israeli authorities must ensure two conditions at two different geographical levels: (1) internally, securing long-term support from the population, some of whom will go to the front line and risk their lives, while all will be more or less economically affected – a complex objective given the strong divisions and distrust toward the government in the country – and (2) internationally, obtaining diplomatic, financial, and/or military support from its traditional allies within the Western Bloc (Europe and the United States), and the most neutral or least hostile posture possible from partners within the Arab world, whose public opinions are particularly sensitive to the Palestinian cause.

The success of these objectives requires the implementation of an adapted communication strategy that can address them. And indeed, on October 8, the Israeli state deployed a large communication campaign. From afar, this all-encompassing communication strategy, on social networks, in the media, with political leaders, in French, English, and Arabic, may seem haphazard, opportunistic, and ill-suited. However, it has been finely crafted at the highest levels of the politico-military scale and is the result of several decades of doctrinal evolution within the state apparatus. It is coordinated and responds to specific and targeted political and strategic objectives. It is hybrid, as it is designed to reach different targets. It sometimes appears ineffective due to the unpopularity or ridicule it incites, but this does not mean it has not reached its target audience and thus its objectives. In nearly four months of conflict (October 7, 2023–January 27, 2024), Israel thus produced several complementary narratives, published countless informational materials, mobilized thousands of channels within its state apparatus, its civil society, and also in the Israeli and Jewish diaspora worldwide, as well as among its supporters within Arab societies. This chapter aims to understand the informational maneuvers deployed by the State of Israel in the context of its war against Hamas since October 7, but also, and above all, how and why they were implemented.

The first part explains how Israel's informational and communication apparatus has been structured in recent decades and how the state has evolved its doctrine to face new challenges. It shows that the communication efforts of the Israeli army, initiated in the 1970s, struggled to lead to a coherent strategy and results until the advent of digital and social networks, which have radically changed the game. Without this, it is not possible to understand the scope and speed of the informational actions carried out by Israel immediately after the Hamas attacks.

The second part presents the political objectives sought by Israel and the narratives deployed to achieve them. These narratives are adapted to target audiences, whether they are intended for the Israeli public or for Western public opinion. Finally, Israel has adapted its communication strategy for Arabic-speaking populations, both in terms of content and channels, to reach its target audience.

BEFORE OCTOBER 7: PERFECTING ISRAEL'S INFORMATION SYSTEM

In Israel, the Hebrew word Hasbara is generally used to designate the state's communication strategy (Goodman, 2011, p. 22). The literal translation of this word means "explanation,"[6] but its use by Israel refers more to terms such as "justification" or even "propaganda" in its original sense (to persuade).

For half a century, Hasbara was the reference concept in Israel for thinking about the communication strategy that could be implemented by state institutions such as the government, ministries, embassies, the army, or nongovernmental organizations (NGOs) affiliated to the state; in the framework of a very vertical communication.

However, Hasbara as a doctrine failed to adapt properly to the changing international context, the changing nature of Israel's conflicts, and the transformation of the means of communication. This is why, from the 2000s onwards, two new, complementary concepts began to emerge within the state: "public diplomacy" and "psychological warfare."

The Limited Successes and Failures of Hasbara

As a concept, Hasbara involves producing and disseminating a narrative to target audiences with the aim of influencing public opinion on a specific political issue related to Israel. Its aim is to win public support and legitimize Israel's action and creation. But Hasbara's effectiveness has produced little effect, except perhaps before the creation of Israel.

The Early Years: A Lack of Vision, Will, and Means

Paradoxically, it was before the creation of the State of Israel that Hasbara was at its strongest in the world on the part of the Zionist movement and its representatives, who were seeking the support of the Western powers with a view to creating a state

[6] The word "Hasbara" comes from the Hebrew root LéHasbire, meaning "to explain."

in Palestine under British mandate. Once the state had been created, it invested little in its communications for reasons of means and priority: The country, which was supported by all the major powers, was more concerned with absorbing waves of immigrants, some of whom were Holocaust survivors, developing the Negev desert, and building egalitarian communities (kibbutz); all actions that required no justification for the Israeli authorities, since they seemed so just and moral to them.

The creation of a Hasbara Office within the Ministry of Foreign Affairs, envisaged as early as 1948, did not materialize, and was not finally realized until the late 1960s, but within the Army Spokesman's Unit (Dover Tsahal); a change which is not insignificant and shows the new preoccupations of the Israeli Hasbara. Indeed, Israel's image changed radically with the Six-Day War (1967). The perception of a small state surrounded by threatening enemies collapsed after Israel's lightning victory and conquest of vast territories. It was also at this time that many Arab and Muslim states were newly created as a result of the decolonization movement, intensifying international criticism of Israeli policy to such an extent that Israel decided to create a Ministry of Hasbara in 1974 (one year after the Yom Kippur War). Its main aim was to coordinate all the players involved in the state's strategic communications. However, a year after its creation, the Ministry was abolished due to excessive competition and intense interministerial rivalry (Shai, 2013, p. 116).

Hasbara's Repeated Failures from the 1970s Onwards

The year 1975 was Israel's first major diplomatic slap in the face on the world stage, when the UN General Assembly passed a resolution regarding Zionism as a form of racism (supported by seventy-two states, against thirty-five opposed and thirty-two abstaining; United Nations General Assembly, 1975). Unquestionably, this episode marked the failure of Israel's communication policy, which had been unsuccessful at winning sufficient international support. It is also the origin of Israel's mistrust of international bodies such as the UN: The Israeli authorities began to display a frank contempt for international criticism, which they consider to be biased.

At the same time, the nature of the conflicts in which Israel was engaged began to change in the 1980s, marking the end of conventional warfare between enemy armies. The outbreak of the First Intifada (1987–1993) pitted the Israeli army against the Palestinian population of the territories Israel had occupied since 1967 (West Bank and Gaza Strip). The information that Israel communicated to explain its actions in the territories was disrupted by the Palestinians, who maintain a close relationship with the foreign journalists who are on the ground, enabling them to tell their own story of the ongoing conflict. Israel's communication strategy began to show its lack of effectiveness in the field, due to a lack of adaptability.

The same situation arose during Operation Grapes of Wrath (1996), which pitted the Israeli army against Hezbollah, a Shiite militia from southern Lebanon (Razoux, 2006). As a result, the government decided to create a National Hasbara Forum with the same objective as the ministry created two decades earlier; but this initiative met with the same end for the same reasons: Interministerial rivalry prevented concrete progress.

This lack of coordination would prove to be Israel's undoing during the Second Intifada (2000–2005). The State of Israel, faced with an unprecedented wave of attacks on its soil, found that Palestinian actions were perceived as legitimate resistance to Israelis seen as oppressors. More importantly, the interaction between the Israeli army and the foreign media had changed radically. Foreign journalists were no longer content with reports and briefings from army spokesmen but went directly to officers in the field who had not been trained in communication skills; hence the incoherent and often contradictory messages (Eiland, 2010, pp. 27–37).

Acknowledged Ineffectiveness and a Failed Attempt to Change Doctrine

With the Intifada barely over, the Israeli army found itself in a new theater of operations, in southern Lebanon (2006). Hezbollah leader Hassan Nasrallah's well-crafted communications, and above all the ineffectiveness of the Israeli Hasbara, helped spread the idea that the conflict had been lost by the army, despite Israel's military successes on the ground. Israeli communications were so chaotic that a special report was produced by the state comptroller in Israel. This pointed to the absence of a strong conceptual approach to Hasbara and a lack of institutional coordination, leading to the absence of clear guidelines issued by the government and the failure of Israel's communication (State Comptroller of Israel, 2007).

To remedy the situation, a special commission was set up under the Prime Minister's Office. To avoid repeating the mistakes of the past, it brought together all the parties involved in the subject: the National Information Board, the Ministerial Committee for National Security, various ministers, as well as the spokesman for the army, and the Police and Internal Intelligence (Shin Bet). However, despite a strong will, the players involved were unable to develop a more precise overall conceptual approach.

According to former Tsahal general Avi Benayahou, the Hasbara concept lacks the sophistication to change and refine the perception of reality (Benayahu, 2012, pp. 4–9). One of the reasons for this failure is its temporality: Hasbara comes into play just after the fact (post factum), that is, once the action has taken place. However, in the age of digital communication, smartphones, and social networks, this approach of explaining and justifying facts is often useless. Today's communication requires a complex complementarity between political and military activities and the manipulation of emotions to arouse empathy and support, regardless of the veracity of the facts.

Public Diplomacy and Cognitive Campaigning: Two Complementary Approaches to Hasbara

It was in the early 2000s that Israel realized its inefficiency and inability to transform Hasbara into an operational communication doctrine. The evolution of conflicts combined with the transformation of means of communication, in a strong desire for doctrinal renewal, led to the emergence of two other approaches that were to become fully integrated into Israel's communication strategy: public diplomacy and the cognitive campaign or psychological warfare (discussed later in the chapter).

Public Diplomacy: The Revival of Communication

Public diplomacy emerged in the mid-2000s at the initiative of the Ministry of Foreign Affairs, which wished to renew the Hasbara approach that had shown its limitations. This new communication doctrine also came at a time when the means of communication were evolving rapidly, and traditional Hasbara channels seemed outdated.

Its objective is radically different: Public diplomacy must not be a post-factum communication, but on the contrary, a long-term policy, whose objective is no longer the dissemination of an Israeli narrative on the ongoing conflict, but a permanent dialogue with foreign and critical players, beyond security issues. It is conceived as a response to the increasingly palpable criticism in Israel and abroad of the very notion of Hasbara, which is translated by the pejorative term propaganda.

In 2012, the Ministry of Foreign Affairs renamed its communications division Hasbara to Public Diplomacy with an evolving objective: no longer just to defend Israel's legitimacy and policy abroad, but to present the Israeli narrative in all its diversity. In order to disseminate it more widely, a "digital diplomacy" department was created to promote Israeli narratives on all social platforms and in all languages (English, French, Spanish, Russian, Persian, and Arabic).

Another major difference is that, unlike Hasbara, which is conducted solely by state bodies, public diplomacy includes the participation and mobilization of public or para-public agencies, NGOs, opinion leaders and, more broadly, the whole of civil society, in Israel and beyond. Indeed, Israeli public diplomacy intends to rely on the Israeli and Jewish diasporas around the world to relay its messages.

The Various Concentric Circles of the System

At the heart of the system is the Army Spokesman's Unit, which has been strengthened and supported by other state bodies. These include the Coordination of Government Activities in the Territories (COGAT), responsible for communicating Israeli policy in the occupied territories; the Government Press Office and the National Information Directorate, which report to the Prime Minister's Office; and, of course, the Ministry of Foreign Affairs, which can rely on its network of embassies and consulates to amplify the Israeli narrative abroad. These institutions form the first circle of actors in public diplomacy.

Next come pro-Israeli NGOs, which are not necessarily Israeli. Among the most active are American NGOs. These are the ones with the biggest budgets, influence, and resources. Some have been around for a long time, such as the American Israel

Public Affairs Committee (AIPAC), the main American Jewish pro-Israeli lobby, or the American Jewish Committee (AJC).

Others have been created more recently, precisely to respond in their own way to the failures of Israeli communication and to fight against the intense boycott campaign of Israel initiated by the pro-Palestinian boycott movement BDS (Boycott Divestment Sanction). One of the most active is undoubtedly Stand with Israel, a Los Angeles-based NGO founded in 2001 by three Jewish Americans. With an annual budget in excess of $20 million and offices in eighteen different countries, this NGO carries out actions in favor of Israel in the digital field and on the ground, particularly on campuses. There are many others,[7] and most of them are now organized into networks to amplify their action. All these NGOs are thus, in one way or another, integrated and taken into account in Israel's global communications system.

Finally, a third circle has been devised for individuals, opinion leaders or influential Israelis, or people with strong ties to Israel, who live outside Israel and are encouraged to improve Israel's image and disseminate pro-Israeli narratives to their entourage abroad. To structure these individual initiatives, the Israeli government launched the Masbirim ("explanations"[8]) project in 2010, which aimed to provide ready-to-use narratives on various topics concerning Israel. The initiative was not as successful as had been hoped, but it does demonstrate the willingness shown some fifteen years ago to integrate diaspora personalities, who will play an important role from October 7, 2023, onwards, as discussed later in the chapter.

Expanding the Scope of Psychological Warfare

Psychological warfare is not a new communications concept in Israel. It can be defined as the means of influencing enemy perceptions through the dissemination of false information or disinformation (Galili, 2019, pp. 75–91). Given its nature, psychological warfare was mainly used on a confidential basis by the army's intelligence units for enemy state agencies, and not integrated within the army's communications services to produce mainstream narratives.

The Failed Beginnings of the Psychological Approach

Things changed with the Second Intifada (2000–2005), when Israel realized that Palestinians were making abundant use of this communication tactic, producing narratives and images for foreign journalists that amplified or distorted reality.[9]

7 Examples include the Anti-defamation League (ADL), Israel on Campus Coalition, AMCHA Initiative, David Project, Christians United for Israel, and others.

8 The word is a declension of the verb LéHasbire, which gave rise to the term Hasbara.

9 One of the most emblematic cases is certainly the episode of the "Jenin massacre" from April 3 to 11, 2002, right at the heart of the Intifada. After a suicide bombing in Israel killed thirty people, Israel launched a ground operation in the Jenin camp, considered a base for

In 2005, the Center for Cognitive Operations was created. Its primary objective is to develop a doctrine and concepts for cognitive campaigns within the army in order to influence the perception, political position, and feelings and sentiments of a target audience. It is within this center that influence methods and various tools for evaluating the impact of campaigns are developed. These concepts were immediately put into practice the following year, with the war against Lebanon (2006). The challenge was to document the war "from the inside," so as to accompany Israeli victories with a communications campaign tailored to reach the Israeli and Lebanese public. For example, the town of Bint Jbeil in Lebanon was chosen as a target by the Israeli army, which succeeded in occupying it; six years earlier, it was from this town that Hezbollah leader Hassan Nasrallah had given a victorious speech after Israel's withdrawal from the subject of Lebanon (2000). As part of a cognitive warfare operation, an Israeli colonel decided to hold a speech there after the capture of the town, in front of his soldiers, some of whom filmed and photographed with their own equipment, immortalizing the installation of an Israeli flag replacing that of Hezbollah. But, the doctrine of psychological warfare had not yet been fully integrated: The army spokesman decided not to broadcast the images, which were deemed too amateurish, leaving foreign journalists with no images of the event other than those eventually supplied by Hezbollah.

A first consequence to be drawn from this: Tsahal decided to reinforce its control over information from war zones by preventing the deployment of journalists, particularly foreign journalists, in contact with soldiers. But this strategy quickly backfired, as Tsahal found out during its next conflict: Operation Cast Lead in Gaza against Hamas, in December 2008–January 2009. Israel banned foreign journalists from entering the country, leaving them dependent on sources and correspondents in Gaza, some of whom were working under the control and threat of Hamas. As a result, foreign journalists found themselves inundated with images of Israeli attacks, while Israel, on the defensive, spent most of its communication time minimizing civilian casualties.

The publication of the Goldstone[10] report in September 2009 was yet another political setback for Israel, as the document drew up a long list of accusations against the Israeli authorities (and, to a lesser extent, Hamas), accusing them of having committed acts that could constitute war crimes or even crimes against humanity.

Palestinian suicide bombers. The operation was poorly communicated by the IDF, which left little doubt as to the scale of the attack. Palestinian fighters, in contact with journalists on the ground, quickly spoke of a "massacre" with between 400 and 500 dead. The Tsahal spokesman mentioned dozens of deaths, but not hundreds; too late. The vagueness of the media gives equal, if not greater, weight to Palestinian estimates. Finally, the UN Secretary-General's report in August 2002 confirmed the deaths of dozens of people (fifty-two), not hundreds.

[10] The report is named after a South African judge, Richard J. Goldstone, who chaired a commission, at the request of the UN Human Rights Council, to establish whether actions during the conflict were in violation of international law.

This shows that, despite the Israeli government's manifest determination, its communication strategy, even when incorporating new concepts, is still faltering.

The Use of Social Networks

Even so, the army continues its mission and adapts to new means of communication. The early 2000s saw the development of the internet, social networks, and smartphones, revolutionizing the means of communication. In 2009, the Israel Defense Forces (IDF) Spokesman's Unit opened its own Facebook page, Twitter (rebranded as X since July 2023) account, and YouTube channel to communicate information directly to internet users. A dedicated "new media" unit was created (Amsellem, 2020).

The first effects were quickly felt. First, during the Gaza flotilla episode (May 2010).[11] In reaction to the incriminating images provided by the pro-Palestinian activists aboard the flotilla and widely relayed by the mainstream media, Tsahal decided to broadcast its own images just a few hours after the operation. This time, they showed militants armed with iron bars attacking the soldiers as soon as they arrived on the ship. The army had thus chosen to bypass the traditional media to give its perspective on the facts by broadcasting its own content; a procedure which was not common ten years ago and which paid off: international newsrooms were broadcasting the army's images, which presented the pro-Palestinian militants as violent aggressors, faced with victimized soldiers.

With its new capabilities, Israel is breaking new ground in the digital field of warfare. During the Operation Pillar of Defense (November 2012), the IDF was the first army in the world to use Twitter to announce an imminent attack against an enemy actor on foreign soil. It was during this new conflict that psychological warfare was massively extended on social networks. It was possible to follow, minute by minute, the progress of Israel's operations, testifying to its determination to impose its information content and combat its critics.

At the same time, and in order to wage psychological warfare, Israel was broadcasting on its networks videos of Palestinian rockets aimed at civilian targets in Israel; Hamas' executions of Palestinians regarded as collaborators; and, in parallel, other content showing the army's efforts to avoid civilian deaths. Each of these informational materials served a clear political purpose: to justify the Israeli attack, criminalize Hamas, and defend Israeli tactics on the ground. Noting the effects of its new communication, the IDF Spokesman's Unit decided to create a unit

[11] At dawn on May 31, 2010, units of the Shayetet 13 (Marine Commandos) intercepted a flotilla of pro-Palestinian activists on the high seas, attempting to break the blockade of the Gaza Strip. The boarding of the ship *Mavi Marmara*, carrying 700 passengers, turned into a hand-to-hand confrontation. The intervention left nine activists dead and twenty-eight injured, and ten Israeli soldiers wounded.

dedicated to combat documentaries, to produce professional images directly from the battlefield.

Undoubtedly, Israel's communication strategy was better. The Israeli authorities were able to produce and disseminate their narratives from their images, which were picked up massively on social networks and by foreign media. Psychological warfare worked this time, prompting Israel to strengthen this pole within its army: In 2018, a Department of Influence was created and placed under the control of the Operations Directorate, responsible for force deployment, reflecting a desire to integrate this aspect of Israel's strategic communication at the very heart of its military operations.

Strong Digital Presence

The digital world is clearly a new theater of operations for Israeli communications. To maximize its influence, Tsahal does not hesitate to break with the reserve of other armies around the world, which are more circumspect when it comes to using social networks. Indeed, for some of its publications, the army seems to have adopted the language, codes, and vocabulary of social networks, sometimes even using ironic and sarcastic humor on sensitive subjects.[12] This surprising tone is, in fact, a clever strategy on the part of the "new media" unit to broaden its audience beyond its subscribers and detractors. This style of publication, which no other similar player takes on so frankly, is often widely relayed on social networks, precisely because they seem inappropriate – even if it means being criticized.

And it works. The Israeli army accumulates tens of millions of subscribers on various social networks (3.8 million on Facebook, nearly a million on YouTube), sometimes surpassing the US army's account (on Twitter, e.g., with nearly 2.5 million subscribers); a considerable audience for a country of less than 9 million inhabitants, which also demonstrates the extent to which it is observed.

The advent of social networks radically changes the game for Israel. The traditional tools used by the Hasbara are not adapted to new needs and new ways of communicating. By the 2010s, Israel understood that its operations in the Palestinian territories were difficult to justify to an international audience. At the same time, groups and organizations hostile to Israel continued their work of delegitimization and virulent criticism, themselves producing biased information to broaden their audience via social networks. Where Hasbara used to campaign on university campuses and in international organizations, psychological warfare and public diplomacy are now being deployed more massively in the infosphere, with the aim of producing its

[12] In March 2019, the army's Facebook account hijacked a viral Facebook video to wish a happy birthday to Qasem Soleimani, the Iranian general commanding the Al-Quds force of the Revolutionary Guards Corps. At the end of the video, the cake explodes, a situation that leaves one wondering when one remembers that the person concerned was killed a few months later (January 2020) by an American drone strike in Syria.

own narrative to attack its adversaries head-on and disseminate its own version of the conflict, and more broadly, of Israeli society. All these doctrines have been put to the test in real-life conditions, during armed conflicts whose succession in recent years has required the Israeli authorities to be highly agile in measuring problems, evaluating successes and, finally, continually adapting. This experience proved invaluable for the vast campaign that the country launched on October 7.

ISRAEL'S COMMUNICATION FROM OCTOBER 7 ONWARDS: AN ALL-OUT STRATEGY WITH SPECIFIC OBJECTIVES

Since the advent of social networks, the State of Israel has greatly evolved its doctrine in terms of strategic communication in order to anticipate, with the creation of a variety of narratives. To achieve this, the state has considerably increased its resources, both in terms of recruitment, with the creation of dedicated units or departments within the army or the Ministry of Foreign Affairs, and in terms of distribution channels, since it is present on just about every major social media platform and in the main languages spoken. A whole ecosystem of public and para-public agencies is also functional to distribute varied and targeted information to different audiences.

From October 7 onwards, a new element was added to Israel's communication strategy, particularly abroad: The Jewish and Israeli diasporas started massively acting as relays for Israeli narratives, so shocked were they by the nature of the attacks. Associations and influential figures mobilized their networks and expertise to relay and even produce information content.[13] The approach itself is not new, and indeed a number of associations and organizations around the world had set themselves the task of relaying this information; but the scale of the effort is totally unprecedented and has never before reached the level of commitment seen since October 7 among leading figures in the diaspora.

In the wake of the Hamas attacks, the Israeli government's communications system will be able to deploy all its levers to achieve a number of political objectives aimed at target audiences that differ from one region to another. The number of initiatives, publications, information materials, and actions, both in the physical world and in the cyber field, has been so great that it is not possible to give an exhaustive presentation. Nevertheless, in order to understand them all, we have chosen to structure our approach around the "major informational actions" that bring together the bulk of these initiatives and meet two clear political objectives: raising public awareness and justifying the military response.

[13] An anecdotal example is indicative of the spontaneous individual initiatives that ultimately serve the Israeli narrative: Simply Piano, a famous mobile and tablet piano application developed in Israel, offered all its subscribers the chance to discover a whole range of Israeli music free of charge, as a show of solidarity with the Hebrew state.

Raising Public Awareness

To raise international public awareness of the attacks of October 7, Israel will carry out four informational actions to produce and disseminate its narratives. For the Hebrew state, this communication has several sub-objectives: Internally, the aim is to unite and mobilize the country, whose unity has been weakened, while responding to the high expectations of the population following the attacks; internationally, the challenge is to raise public awareness of the unprecedented nature of the attacks to create a feeling of empathy and support. The ambitions are therefore immense, which explains the extensive resources deployed by the Israeli authorities and their relays around the world.

Intense Digital Campaign

On October 8, Israel launched an intense social networking campaign to raise awareness among Western public opinion. Through hundreds of publications, the Hebrew state hammered home several messages that helped to raise awareness among international public opinion. We have identified three main messages:

- **Hamas is equivalent to the Islamic State**. Many of its publications are accompanied by the hashtag #hamasIsis or #hamasisIsis. The aim is to elicit the same rejection from Western opinion as the macabre acts of Islamic State fighters did a decade ago.
- **Hamas is the embodiment of Islamist terrorism, which will also target Western countries**. Several visuals show armed men in tunnels under the Eiffel Tower or the Louvre Pyramid. The message is clear: Israel is the West's outpost, and the fight it will wage against Hamas is part of a global struggle by Islamist terrorism against Western countries.
- **Hamas' actions are a continuation of the antisemitism acts perpetrated by the Nazis**. It can no longer be considered a political or even a terrorist organization. A number of publications have pointed out the anti-Jewish passages in the Hamas charter, while a telephone conversation between a terrorist on October 7 calling his parents to boast that he had killed "10 Jews" – not Israelis – with his own hands was broadcast. In this context, to support the Hamas project, which aims not at a two-state solution, but at "liberating Palestine from the river [Jordan] to the sea [Mediterranean]," is tantamount to supporting this antisemitism project.

The Means Deployed

To support these narratives, Israel chose, for the first time in such a rapid and massive way, to sponsor content, photos, or videos, to enable its messages to be pushed before viewing YouTube videos or directly into the newsfeeds of social network accounts (see Figure 7.1). Thus, all over the world, thousands (if not

FIGURE 7.1 Screenshots from social media showing content promoted by Israel through purchased advertising space ("ads") displayed on users' accounts, before their video (YouTube) or in their newsfeed (X/Twitter).

millions) of internet users found themselves with commercials warning of Hamas attacks. The commercials were also tailored to the target audience: For adults, violent, barely blurred images showed certain Hamas attacks, while before the YouTube videos for children under six (who couldn't read) were broadcast, a message addressed to parents explained that dozens of Israeli minors had been killed or kidnapped, and that Israel would do whatever was necessary to get them back.

A journalist (Galer Smith, S. [@sophiasgaler]) on X (previously Twitter) revealed that between October 7 and 19, 2023, eighty-eight different commercials were broadcast in some twenty countries, at a cost of over $7 million. France was by far the most targeted country, with spending estimated at €3.8 million, which would have resulted in almost 445 million screen impressions (number of times the ad was displayed on a screen); followed by Germany (€1.9 million for 231 million impressions). For the period from October 7 to November 6, Google's advertising transparency center lists around 200 spots paid for by the Israeli Ministry of Foreign Affairs. Interestingly, the same pro-Israeli content received relatively little sponsorship in the United States (around €50,000). Does this mean that Israel takes the support of the US government for granted, as does a large part of its public opinion? If this is the reasoning, it could be considered partly false, given the unprecedented mobilization for Gaza, particularly on American campuses. It would also mean that Israel considers Europe to be a politically uncertain partner, given the considerable financial efforts made by the major European powers.

This advertising campaign organized by Israel is just one part of Israel's vast digital strategy on social networks. Indeed, since the 2010s, we have seen how the state has strengthened its resources to be more effective on social networks, with the recruitment of people dedicated to "new media" within the army or ministries.

Thus, the official accounts of the State of Israel, its Ministry of Foreign Affairs or Tsahal on the networks (7 million on TikTok; 215,000 on YouTube; 1.5 million on X; 1 million on Instagram; 890,000 on Facebook) accumulate several million subscribers and publish dozens of messages, photos, and videos to disseminate Israeli narratives, even if this is strongly criticized. Indeed, the comments on these publications regularly generate far more negative and pro-Palestinian comments, but this doesn't stop Israel from continuing to publish in order to get its messages across.

David Sarangua, Director of the Ministry of Foreign Affairs' Digital Office, estimates that in the first month of the conflict (October 8–November 8, 2023), Israel had published over 2,500 messages in English on its networks, reaching over a billion people, thanks to innovative content and sponsored publications.

The Israeli authorities have also authorized the broadcast of interrogations of Palestinian terrorists arrested on October 7. In an exchange in Arabic with the Israelis who questioned them, the latter declared that their organization, in committing the acts of October 7, had behaved worse than the Islamic State and had the objective of killing civilians and raping women.

The state and its various entities are not the only players. Israeli society has also mobilized to produce original, viral content. Such is the case of the famous Israeli TV show, Eretz Nehederet ("A Wonderful Country"), a comedy program broadcast weekly for the past twenty years. Since October 7, comedians have been staging satirical episodes to denounce the use of civilians by Hamas and antisemitism acts by students on American campuses. These videos have been viewed millions of times on YouTube and relayed massively on social networks.

There's plenty more content and narratives to criticize Hamas and its supporters, or the silence of certain international organizations in the wake of the attacks. We can't list them all, but let's end with the initiative of a rather art-oriented Israeli content creator, Hila Yerushalmi, who produced and broadcast a video on YouTube to denounce the silence of international organizations against the rape of Israeli women. Her content was then relayed by thousands of people as part of a social networking campaign entitled "Rape is not resistance."

The Israeli Hostage Campaign

Another key aspect of Israel's communications strategy was the vast campaign for the release of the hostages. Their exceptional numbers and profiles (very young children, women, and the elderly) created a shock in Israel and in the diasporas, which mobilized to demand their release.

Objective and Strategy

This mobilization was not specifically aimed at the Israeli government, whose war aims to secure their release. It was aimed, above all, at the Western world, to arouse emotion and solidarity with the families in their fight for the hostages' release. One initiative proved particularly successful: the one originally organized by hostage families who wanted to appeal to the world and publicize the victims. Via WhatsApp groups, these families distributed posters with the photos and main details (including age) of all the hostages, framed by large, easily identifiable red stripes and accompanied by a message in English: "Bring them home." Pages and accounts on social networks were created on October 10 with this name, and the hashtag of the same name was quoted in publications.

The initiative aroused a great deal of interest in Israel, where hundreds of volunteers were taking part in collage campaigns featuring photos of the hostages. It's interesting to see how digital action produces real-world effects, as the files with the hostages' photos circulated in various Signal, Telegram and WhatsApp groups, and were then printed and pasted on city walls. Very quickly, the group became structured, collected donations, and benefited from the support of professional figures such as David Meidan, a former Mossad officer who led the negotiations for the release of Israeli soldier Guilad Shalit (2006–2011).

International Relays

The campaign provoked a huge international response, particularly in Western countries, where a number of organizations and personalities, mostly from Jewish communities or the Israeli diaspora, were organizing poster campaigns in various public places or relaying the photos on their social networks. The National Council of Jewish Women in the United States was the first (October 19) to take up this initiative and organize collages in the United States; the Union des étudiants juifs did the same in Belgium, then in France.

Still within the Jewish community, and notably within associative networks, other initiatives accompanied the movement, with the creation of dedicated groups ("the October 7 collective") and the organization of occasional actions beyond the collages (e.g., weekly gatherings). Various town councils in France relayed the campaign; in Nice, for example, the town council financed street billboards.

The element that certainly contributed most to the popularity of this campaign was the negative reaction of supporters of the Palestinian cause. Believing that these actions amounted to propaganda, or at least failed to shed light on the Palestinian victims of the conflict, dozens of people were filmed tearing down the posters, provoking widespread indignation and helping to amplify the campaign.

Aware of the communicative potential of this campaign for Israel's image, the Israeli authorities are also investing time and resources to finance larger scale poster campaigns. We learned that the Israeli government had prepared a large-scale campaign to display photos of the hostages in the Netherlands a few days before the International Court of Justice (ICJ) hearings requested by South Africa, which accuses Israel of genocide in Gaza (January 2024). The official aim of the poster campaign was to "raise awareness of the need to free the hostages held captive by Hamas"; but the political maneuvering, given the timing and choice of location, is beyond doubt. However, a dozen poster companies in the Netherlands turned down the contract with the Israeli government, which nevertheless promised to organize several other awareness-raising campaigns in the country.

Field Visits

Israel's other major communications initiative to raise public awareness of the October 7 attacks was the organization of visits to Israel, sometimes to the scene of the attack.

Traditional Channels and Channels of Communication

While the military response had already begun and the ground operation was being prepared, the State of Israel was organizing visits by foreign delegations who wished to express their solidarity or who had come to see what had happened. These visits were a crucial moment for Israel, as they could raise awareness among a very broad public.

Throughout the month of October, a number of leading political figures (the US president, the German chancellor, the British prime minister, the Italian prime minister, the Dutch prime minister, and the French president) came to Israel to meet politicians, hostage families, and victims. Other politicians (MPs, senators, mayors, presidents of opposition parties) have also visited Israel, and sometimes even the sites of the massacres. In a moment of palpable emotion, several leaders made political statements that met the expectations of the Israeli authorities, but also provoked criticism in their own countries. For example, during her visit to Israel on October 13, the President of the European Commission, Ursula Von Der Leyen, affirmed her unconditional support for Israel, which irritated some European countries concerned about the situation in Gaza. During his visit to Israel on October 24, President Emmanuel Macron spoke of mobilizing the international coalition against the Islamic State to combat Hamas, a statement that upset some 100 French diplomats, who denounced in an internal memo a risk to France's position in the Arab world.

Beyond the political world, Israel also wanted to show the violence of the attacks to delegations of journalists, so that they too could relay what happened that day. Several of them were invited to visit the scene of the attack, while the army and rescue services were still working in some areas to recover bodies from burned-out houses and blood-covered rooms. Live broadcasts were organized from the scene, sometimes behind trucks filled with unidentified bodies. By mobilizing foreign journalists, Israel is enabling foreign newsrooms to produce and broadcast news content to raise global awareness of the scale of the destruction.

Digital Influence

Israel also mobilized social network influencers to communicate about the attacks. The Israeli Ministry of Foreign Affairs organized visits to the attacked kibbutz by a number of Israeli influencers, whose interests had absolutely nothing to do with politics; the aim was to enable the dissemination of images on various social platforms such as Instagram, X, or TikTok and to reach a wider audience not necessarily interested in political news. The two most talked-about influencers at the time, Maja Kravarusic and Alina Rabinovich, who specialize in fashion and cooking, published a number of images usually reserved for journalists.

Israel, through its Ministry for the Diaspora and the Fight against Antisemitism (The Ministry for Diaspora Affairs and Combating Antisemitism, 2023), explains that it has mobilized Israel's biggest influencers (TV presenters, models, and actors with tens of millions of subscribers worldwide) for visits to the field to tell, document, broadcast, and bear witness to the October 7 attacks.

This strategy was not limited to Israel. Several French influencers, including one of the best-known, Magalie Berdah, visited Israel at the invitation of an Israeli rescue

NGO (Zaka). Although this visit was made possible with the agreement of the Israeli army, it was nonetheless the initiative of a non-state actor, confirming the ability of the Israeli system to rely on relays other than its state institutions, in line with its doctrine of public diplomacy.

Another visit was far more strategic for Israel in terms of digital influence: that of Elon Musk, head of X, who visited a kibbutz near Gaza on November 27 in the presence of the Israeli prime minister. His visit to Israel is significant for several reasons: In addition to his position at X, he is one of the most followed personalities on this network (170 million subscribers), making him a particularly influential intermediary. He is also the head of StarLink, a company that provides internet connection to territories where none exists. However, at the end of October, Israel decided to cut off all internet connections to the Gaza Strip in order to hinder terrorist activity; Musk announced that he would deploy his satellite network to reestablish the connection to Gaza, which greatly concerned the Israeli Minister of Communications, Shlomo Karhi. After Musk's visit, the same minister proudly announced that he had signed an agreement in principle with StarLink to deploy its satellite network in Gaza only with Israel's agreement.

Since then, Elon Musk has been a strong supporter of Israel, proudly wearing a "Bring them home" necklace in the shape of a military identification tag, given to him by the mother of a hostage who showed him a video of her son being kidnapped by Hamas.

The Video of the October 7 Attacks

The final key element in Israel's communication strategy was the broadcast, from October 23 onwards, of a forty-minute film, edited by the Israeli army from video recordings made at the time of the attack. These videos were recovered from several sources, both Israeli (security cameras, witnesses' and victims' telephones) and Palestinian (terrorists' GoPro).

From Communication Object to Political Object

What's most interesting about this video is not so much its content, most of which can be viewed on various Telegram channels, but the fact that it has become a political communication tool in its own right. Indeed, rather than broadcasting it widely, the Hebrew state chose to include extremely violent sequences (decapitation, execution at close range, violence against children, etc.) to show some of the atrocities perpetrated against its population. Out of respect for the victims and in order to comply with platform distribution rules, the Israeli authorities decided to target the film's viewers. This decision lends political weight to the video, access to which becomes rare. Indeed, only a handful of people were invited to participate in these viewing sessions, which were usually supervised by an Israeli representative. The effect of scarcity immediately made it a political phenomenon in the media, where a handful of journalists recounted part of what they had seen, using words that amplified the phenomenon ("unbearable images," "unspeakable horrors," etc.).

The video was first shown in Israel, to a limited number of foreign journalists who were told that it was forbidden to film the screen; the only images they were allowed to shoot were those showing the journalists' faces during the broadcast, some of whom were covering their eyes or leaving the room. From a purely communications point of view, these images of distraught journalists were perhaps more effective in achieving the desired effect than broadcasting the gruesome scenes themselves.

The same scenes occurred in other circles: in front of American senators, in the French National Assembly or Senate. The network of Israeli embassies around the world was also mobilized to broadcast the video to selected audiences within their walls. Although the exact list is not known, we do know that screenings of the film were held in Geneva, Berlin, Brussels, and Madrid, as well as in Latin America (Santiago de Chile) and at the UN.

Invited by the French Embassy in Israel, as part of a screening reserved for French researchers, we also viewed this video. Before doing so, we were asked to sign an undertaking – later given to embassy staff – to not film the scenes out of respect for the victims. More interestingly, the document recalled the political objective of this viewing: The video aims to show and prove the atrocities of the October 7 attacks, at a time when voices were being raised around the world to contest their veracity.

Another interesting element: The text submitted explained that Israel's aim was precisely to target opinion leaders, influential people in political, media, and intellectual circles, so that they could bear witness to what they had seen. In a quick exchange with embassy staff, we learned that screenings had been carried out in Russia and China; we didn't get any precise answers about the Arab world, where Holocaust denial is most widespread.

International Relays

As with these other campaigns, the Hebrew state was also able to mobilize the Israeli and Jewish diaspora around the world to relay the video. The most emblematic case is that of Israeli actress Gal Gadot. Famous around the world for playing the iconic Wonder Woman character, now based in the United States where she is pursuing her career, Gal Gadot gathers tens of millions of followers on her various social networks (over 100 million on the Instagram platform alone). Sensitized by the attacks of October 7, she managed to get a copy of the video from the Tsahal spokesperson, so that it could be shown at her home to a private circle of personalities from the American film industry.

A few days later, renowned American film director Steven Spielberg announced an initiative to collect video testimonies from survivors of the October 7 event. In France, it was host and producer Arthur who produced and broadcast on CNews a report on these events ("Supernova–massacre at the rave party") at the end of December 2023. More than a simple assembly of previously published images, this report features previously unpublished content, obtained directly from Israelis present at the scene or from videos of the assailants; all elements that suggest this report could not have been made without authorizations or direct contacts with the Israeli authorities.

As you can see, Israel has succeeded in using filmed scenes of the massacres to create an object of political communication, relayed by its network of embassies abroad and by various players in the diaspora.

Justifying the Military Response

In addition to the various awareness campaigns organized by Israel, the authorities have also organized a dedicated communication campaign to justify and defend its military response. Here, we have identified two main mechanisms implemented mainly by the army, which has absolute control over communications in the military arena.

Here too, the objectives are twofold: to assure the Israeli population that the sacrifice they are making is necessary and worthwhile; and at the same time, to provide proof to the world that Israel is deploying proportionate force to achieve its war aims, while protecting Palestinian civilians as far as possible.

The Army Spokesman's Press Briefing

Ever since the early days of the conflict, Israelis have been waiting for a live television report on the security situation in the country. Initially scheduled to last just a few minutes, this press briefing had expanded to become a full-fledged press conference, lasting between 20 and 30 minutes. Occasionally, journalists were invited to take the floor to question the spokesman, who presented a whole range of visual representations (maps, satellite images, sound recordings, and videos) to explain current operations and demonstrate Israel's ability to destroy the threat posed by Hamas.

Explaining the War

The content of this daily news item has evolved with the conflict: Initially confined to the domestic situation, it now presents the situation on all the fronts on which Israel is engaged (West Bank, the North, Syria, Yemen, etc.). Its news content will then be picked up and commented on by all the media in the country, enabling the army's narrative to spread to the whole of Israeli society and beyond. An English version is also available to enable international newsrooms to directly retrieve information produced by the army. This is a classic Hasbara system: Information is produced and distributed directly by the military authorities to journalists, who then pick it up and distribute it.

On the domestic front, this appointment is a political success, thanks in particular to the stature and personality of the spokesperson, Daniel Hagari, a former commander of the IDF's most prestigious unit, the Shayetet 13, the elite commandos renowned for carrying out perilous and secret actions in enemy territory. According to a poll carried out five weeks after the start of the conflict, almost three-quarters of Israelis (73.7 percent) consider Daniel Hagari to be the most reliable source of information on the conflict, an interesting figure given that only 4 percent put Prime Minister Netanyahu in first place (Bagno, 2023). Despite the political crisis and Benjamin Netanyahu's low popularity, Israelis still have confidence in the army and therefore in the state in this war.

Showing Success

The second strong expectation Israelis have of their leaders is their ability to secure the release of the hostages. To achieve this, the Israeli government's strategy has been to intensify its attacks on Hamas in order to corner it and force it to negotiate a truce in exchange for the release of hostages. This position was not easy to maintain in the face of public opinion, which was very strongly committed to and mobilized for the release of the hostages. Various informational maneuvers by Hamas were aimed precisely at increasing the pressure on Israeli civil society via the hostages, so that it would demand a ceasefire from its government.[14]

The release of around a hundred hostages under an agreement concluded at the end of October between Israel and Hamas via Qatar was seen as a victory for the Israeli government, justifying its military strategy. The state's communication apparatus therefore used and staged these releases, producing videos and images in which the symbols of the state were omnipresent: Once freed, the families were photographed in front of a large Israeli flag, surrounded by sympathetic soldiers. The images made the rounds on social networks and in the Israeli media.

Videos from the Field

To justify the war, the Hebrew state was not content with producing information from a command center or hospitals in Israel; it organized the production of informational material directly from the combat zones to justify the army's action.

Live Warfare: Images from the Field

To ensure control of the war news, the army completely closed the Gaza territory to the foreign press; only Al Jazeera, which has correspondents on the spot and is fully

[14] This chapter focuses on Israel's maneuvers and strategies in its war against Hamas. But, it should be pointed out that Hamas, in a strategy of psychological warfare, has recorded and broadcast videos of hostages criticizing Benyamin Netanyahu and demanding an end to the fighting for their release.

established in the territory, could continue to broadcast its own images. The aim is not to make ongoing operations opaque, but, on the contrary, to be able to broadcast information produced and/or controlled by the Israeli army.

The two main producers of content are the Israeli army and foreign journalists authorized to film in areas designated by Tsahal. To be effective, the army deployed troops from the Spokesman's Unit to film and photograph war scenes. At the same time, several soldiers were equipped with front-facing cameras to capture first-person footage of battle scenes; some of these videos were then retrieved and posted on the army's various social networks. Finally, reports from occupied areas will be produced entirely by the army, which takes every step to make this production as professional as possible (cameras, no smartphones, drones for large fields, microphones, etc.). The spokesperson, Daniel Hagari, was on hand to show, camera in hand, the Hamas tunnels under Palestinian hospitals.

All these means and devices are aimed at documenting the war and putting across several messages to justify Israel's action and denounce Hamas' actions. The main Israeli narrative aims to criminalize Hamas, not just for its actions against Israel but for its attitude that dangerously exposes Gaza's civilian population. To this end, Israel provides images from the field showing weapon caches, tunnel entrances, and rocket launchers installed directly in schools, mosques, or hospitals. In its videos, Israel also shows how the equipment of international organizations benefits (intentionally or not) Hamas, with the presence of United Nations Relief and Works Agency (UNRWA)[15] or Red Cross stamped equipment in the terrorists' caches in the tunnels.

The other aim of these communications operations from the field is also psychological warfare. Israel wants to show its competitors that it is winning the war, that defections and arrests of militants are multiplying, and ultimately that Hamas is completely losing control of the territory. Videos of dozens of Palestinians posing as Hamas members are posted on the networks, with some accusing their leaders of betraying them.

Finally, there's another source of information from the field that Israel exploited to its advantage: films produced by Hamas fighters themselves who, in a reverse psychological campaign, film their surprise attacks on Israeli tanks or soldiers. On social networks, images from these films are extracted and broadcast by Israel to show that Hamas fighters are purposely dressed as civilians to deceive soldiers and expose real civilians.

Protecting Palestinian Civilians

The other aim of these images from the field is to show that Israel is making considerable efforts to protect the civilian population of Gaza, and that its war is

[15] At the end of January, the UNRWA announced the dismissal of several of its employees suspected of involvement in the October 7 attacks. See Lazzarini (2024).

directed exclusively against Hamas. This communication work is not so important for the Israeli population, which is more concerned about the hostages and soldiers involved. On the other hand, it is of vital importance to international leaders, both in the West and among Israel's Arab partners. Their position of support or moderate criticism of Israel would be more difficult to maintain in the eyes of public opinion if these states did not have guarantees and material proof that Israel is implementing a policy aimed at minimizing civilian casualties and protecting the Palestinian population as much as possible.

To this end, Israel produces a whole series of elements to justify itself: leaflets thrown from an airplane, audio clips of telephone calls advising inhabitants to leave, organization of population movements via secure corridors, resumption of humanitarian truck deliveries, and so on. In addition to protecting civilians, the army is also keen to show how it is helping the population by distributing food and water. All these actions will be relayed on social networks by the army's official accounts, then by Israel's entire digital ecosystem.

CONCLUSION

During this new war, Israel demonstrated it had learned from its previous communication mistakes in past conflicts. Indeed, we can see that the Israeli communication apparatus has been working at full speed, deploying numerous strategies to reach very different target audiences.

This chapter focuses on Israeli actions, all of which have been deployed for Israel and the world, mainly in English-language versions. However, given the nature of the conflict, the historical relationship between Israel and the Arab world, and recent political agreements with a number of Muslim countries (the Abraham Agreement), Israel has also deployed a specific communications strategy aimed at the Arab world. It goes beyond the major Arab media, most of which are believed to deliver a biased discourse according to the Israeli government; this is particularly true of the Qatari channel Al Jazeera, long known for its almost absolute support of the Palestinian cause. Israel's efforts have not focused specifically on producing content dedicated to the Arab world – although this has been done too – but more on adapting the way this content was broadcast and presented.

Since October 7, and perhaps for the first time in decades, Israel had an urgent need to get its narratives across to wage its war against Hamas. It had to mobilize its deeply divided society around a widely criticized government and, at the same time, provide sufficiently convincing elements for Tsahal to be able to carry out its response with the support (or silence) of its allies and partners.

Was Israel's communication strategy effective? It all depends on whose objectives. According to a study carried out in mid-December 2023 and broadcast by an Israeli channel, the overwhelming majority of publications on social networks and articles in the major international media concerning the war against Hamas were unfavorable to the Hebrew state. Of the nearly 2 million publications that received at least 500 likes, shares, and comments, 83 percent were against the Hebrew state, compared with 9 percent in support of Israel. So, if Israel had set itself the goal of convincing the majority of internet users of the merits of its military action, the answer is clearly "no."

But the effectiveness of a communications strategy must be assessed in relation to the political objectives that have been defined. And the question is whether this unpopularity on the internet and the hundreds of pro-Gaza demonstrations around the world have prevented Israel from taking action on the ground and led the government to lose the support of its population.

On the contrary, what has been observed since October 7 is that, thanks to its communications campaigns, Israel has succeeded in massively rallying its population, which, despite its losses, continues to strongly support the military action, and in creating a wave of solidarity on the part of all Western countries. This situation has had very concrete political consequences: military and economic support from the United States, which has released a special envelope of $14 billion and dispatched an imposing naval air fleet to the region; political support from European leaders, despite criticism and calls for restraint in the face of the death toll in Gaza. As for the Arab countries, many of which were planning to break their normal ties with Israel, none have done so to date. Better still, Israel can count on certain influential members of these countries to relay its narratives.

In the months following October 7, we can therefore consider that the political objectives of Israel's strategic communication have been achieved. However, as the conflict is taking hold, the effects of this communication strategy could have been challenged by further geopolitical developments, including digital influence campaigns launched by other major players in the conflict such as Qatar. But since then, Israel's political objectives appear to have evolved as well. The prime minister can rely on a decline in the pro-Palestinian mobilization worldwide, while the return of Donald Trump to power in the United States ensure him strengthened support.

REFERENCES

Amsellem, D. (2020). Le Cyberespace Israélien, un Enjeu de Puissance [Israeli cyberspace, a power issue]. *Hérodote*, 177/178(2/3), 281–296.

Bagno, Y. (2023, November 14). Israelis overwhelmingly trust IDF spox over PM Netanyahu – poll. *The Jerusalem Post.* https://jpost.com/israel-news/article-773276

Bateman, T. (2023, March 6). *Israel's elite fighter pilots escalate judicial reform protest.* BBC News. https://bbc.com/news/world-middle-east-64866873

Benayahu, A. (2012). Milkhemet Ha'asbara be'idan Hadigitali' [The Hasbara War in the Digital Age]. *Ma'archot*, 445, 4–9.

Eiland, G. (2010). The IDF in the Second Intifada. *Strategic Assessment*, 13(3), 27–37.

Galer Smith, S. [@sophiasgaler]. [X profile]. https://twitter.com/sophiasgaler

Galili, R. (2019). Ha'Ma'araha She'bein Milkhamot Ve'ha'ma'amatz Ha'ne'elam [The campaign between the wars and the invisible effort]. *Bein Haktavim, 22/23*, 75–91.

Goodman, G. (2011). Palestine's Best: The Jewish Agency's press relations, 1946–1947. *Israel Studies*, 16(3). https://doi.org/10.2979/israelstudies.16.3.1

Israel War Database. (n.d.). *Israel's Defense and Security Forum (IDSF)*. https://warinisrael.org/

Lazzarini, P. (2024, January 26). *Serious allegations against UNRWA staff in the Gaza strip.* United Nations Relief and Works Agency for Palestine Refugees in the Near East. https://unrwa.org/newsroom/official-statements/serious-allegations-against-unrwa-staff-gaza-strip

Razoux, P. (2006). *Tsahal: nouvelle histoire de l'armée israélienne [IDF: New history of the Israeli army]*. Éditions Perrin.

Shai, M. (2013), Milkhamedia [Media War]. *Yediot Ahronot.*

State Comptroller of Israel. (2007). *Aspects of preparedness of Hasbara bodies and their functioning in the Second Lebanon War.* State Comptroller of Israel.

The Ministry for Diaspora Affairs and Combating Antisemitism. (2023, August 11). *Social media influencers' tour to the Gaza envelope*. Swords of Iron, Information for the Public from Government Offices. https://gov.il/en/departments/news/news-gaza080123

United Nations General Assembly. (1975). *Resolution 3379: Declaration that Zionism is a form of racism and racial discrimination.* Resolution adopted on November 10, 1975, A/RES/3379. https://undocs.org/A/RES/3379(XXX)

8

Ukraine's Support Coalition and the Long (Info) War

Mitigating the Disinformation Threat to Democratic Collaboration

Jaclyn A. Kerr

In February 2022, when Russia mounted its full-scale invasion of Ukraine, Western democracies came together in a remarkable show of unity in support of Ukraine and of democratic principles. They referred to Ukraine's fight as a fight for democracy and a global rules-based order. They imposed sanctions on the aggressor, undertook massive shifts in energy independence and military spending, welcomed large numbers of Ukrainian refugees, and collaborated to provide the beleaguered country with financial assistance, intelligence and strategic support, and military aid – all critical to its survival in its David versus Goliath struggle with its larger, and more powerful, neighbor. As of this writing, two years into the fighting, the situation looks bleaker. In late 2023, Ukraine's then top general publicly lamented the state of fighting as reaching a "stalemate" in which no major breakthrough was immediately likely. While the two armies stand bogged down in an attritional phase of war where lines move little, Ukraine's military now runs low on munitions. In the absence of some course correction, observers increasingly point to a long-term Russian advantage. At the same time, discussions of continued aid on both sides of the Atlantic have faced intensified political challenges.

The fight on the battlefield will be crucial to Ukraine's future – as well as to transatlantic security and democracy, and global order. But this fight itself hinges on the continued unity and collaboration across Western democratic partners that have provided critical aid and assistance to enable Ukraine's remarkable show of resistance until this point. This coalition is premised on trust and shared values across Ukraine and its democratic partners. It depends upon electoral outcomes, domestic politics, and multinational organization processes across Europe, the United States, and beyond. As such, it has many seams of vulnerability – even without deliberate adversarial action. It has also been targeted persistently by Russian information and influence campaigns throughout the war and before, seeking to undermine unified

The views expressed in this chapter are those of the author and do not reflect the official policy or position of the National Defense University, the Department of Defense, or the US government.

support for Ukraine's war effort across Western democracies. In so doing, Moscow seeks also to undermine future confidence in one of the West's greatest strengths – its strength in numbers of allies and partners willing to collaborate around a shared vision.

In recent years, democracies have faced fundamental challenges in addressing the threat of adversarial disinformation aimed at undermining trust in and functioning of key democratic institutions and processes. These challenges are sufficiently daunting at the national level. They have led to significant, if nascent, innovations to mitigate impacts, foster trust and resilience, and simultaneously protect core democratic values. But the challenge does not stop at national borders. Nondemocratic competitors frequently use coordinated cyber-enabled disinformation and influence campaigns strategically at a regional or international level. They aim to undermine cooperation between democracies, break alliance cohesion, and otherwise use interference in the democratic politics of individual countries to foster broader geopolitical and strategic gains. No event in the past decade better illustrates this challenge than the war in Ukraine and Russia's multipronged efforts to influence transatlantic cooperation in support of Ukraine. But the war has also fostered new forms of strategic awareness and adaptation.

This chapter examines the role of cyber-enabled information and influence in relation to transatlantic support for Ukraine as a case study of the challenge of addressing transnational coordinated strategic disinformation campaigns. Specifically, the chapter examines Russia's uses of multipronged disinformation and influence campaigns in attempts to influence transatlantic support for Ukraine by democratic partners and allies, scrutinizing how the Kremlin has targeted within- and cross-national vulnerabilities as part of broader strategic goals. Investigating what has been done by democratic target countries, individually *and collaboratively*, to mitigate the worst outcomes and potential strategic impacts, this chapter in turn examines existing mechanisms of coordination and cooperation by which democracies have sought to address this strategically motivated threat, their current adequacy to the task, as well as ongoing learning and adaptation in this area.

The remainder of the chapter is divided into three sections. The first section, "Democracies and the Transnational Disinformation Challenge," examines the nature of today's strategic, transnational, cyber-enabled information and influence campaigns as a challenge to democracy writ large, and as a particularly complex challenge to international unity and collaboration across democratic partners and allies. The Ukraine war has made this threat more obvious than ever before, demonstrating how such campaigns can seek to undermine critical strategic collaboration between democratic countries. The second section, "Support for Ukraine and Russian Strategic Information Campaigns," considers the role of a broad coalition of democratic partners in support for Ukraine's quest for self-determination and democracy, examining how Russian efforts to thwart Ukraine's defense have extended well beyond the battlefield through extensive orchestrated information and influence campaigns across countries and audiences. These campaigns have targeted not only specific actors or countries but also relationships, institutions, and mechanisms of cooperation across democracies that enable the collaborative support effort. The final section, "Conclusion: Defensive Progress and Challenges," considers the challenge of democratic defenses and resilience to such strategic disinformation campaigns. While democracies have indeed made some progress, the challenge of addressing complex, transnationally orchestrated campaigns remains particularly daunting. The chapter concludes with a call for more robust and strategically aligned collaboration across democracies and in defense of collaborative institutions.

DEMOCRACIES AND THE TRANSNATIONAL DISINFORMATION CHALLENGE

Since revelations of Russian efforts to influence the 2016 United States presidential election, democratic countries have been increasingly aware of the threat posed to their domestic political systems from adversarial cyber-enabled information and influence operations and campaigns. Such operations involve the deliberate use of information and narrative to target individuals, groups, or large segments of society, influence perceptions and decision-making processes, and ultimately gain desired strategic outcomes – often utilized during peacetime or gray zone confrontation without resorting to direct military conflict, but also used to complement above-threshold clashes, both within and outside of the theater of armed conflict (Lin & Kerr, 2019).

By no means entirely new, this form of competition bears deep commonalities with forms of information competition and deception common during earlier historical periods, with Russian use of these techniques particularly bearing similarity to the Soviet "active measures" of the Cold War period (Rid, 2020). But the renewed use of such aggressive information confrontation was nonetheless novel in the post–Cold War environment, and the possibilities were also transformed by the fundamentally different twenty-first-century information environment, including the rise of the global internet, online media and social media ecosystems, and ubiquitous data, digital tools, and algorithms. The new forms of operations drew not only on earlier operational techniques but also on rapidly developing cyber domain capabilities, covert manipulations of online media and social media systems, and the multi-vector spread of false, misleading, or manipulative information and narratives. The variety of techniques demonstrated a degree of flexibility, low cost, and scalability that could potentially be much more widely utilized and emulated – particularly by nondemocratic states.

Adversarial disinformation poses particularly salient challenges for democracies. Efforts to sway and polarize public opinion, spread uncertainty and confusion about factual events, influence or undermine faith in the outcomes of elections, and otherwise weaken trust in key institutions and public figures all constitute challenges to core elements of democratic systems. These states share deep commitments to freedoms of expression, association, and information. They support a free and open internet. And they base their governments' legitimacy on the sanctity of free and fair elections. The online platforms, digital tools, and media outlets utilized in disinformation campaigns often fall under private ownership, cut across multiple jurisdictions, and have their own interests, rules of service, and technical challenges. Foreign hostile disinformation campaigns frequently interact with existing echo chambers, social cleavages, polarized media, fringe politics, divisive conspiracy theories, home-grown mis- and disinformation currents, and other domestic societal dynamics that are vulnerable to further exploitation and manipulation. The problem, therefore, has not been prone to an easy and immediate solution, despite serious efforts by democracies on both sides of the Atlantic.

While a variety of approaches have been attempted to address these challenges at governmental, whole of society, and even intergovernmental levels, the examination of the *long-term strategic goals* of adversarial campaigns has often been somewhat underdeveloped. Given the types of granular forensic data necessary to track and attribute disinformation operations, the focus has sometimes necessarily dwelt on specific adversarial behaviors or content forms such as the targeting of particular platforms, audiences, or events, the use of particular techniques of manipulation, or the spread of specific false, biased or misleading narratives, pictures, or other content forms. This is critical and challenging analytical work. But its focus is often necessarily at an operational or a tactical level rather than on strategic analysis. Insofar as specific campaign objectives are identified, these often have focused on local and chronologically proximate events, communities, and institutions. Adversarial uses of disinformation might be tied to efforts to generate an in-person protest event, exacerbate local animus between social groups, or undermine support for a political candidate. But the longer term follow-on effects of these coordinated actions and their impacts beyond the given country's political system are often not the primary focus of inquiry.

The goals of uncovered operations are often broadly characterized in relation to efforts to undermine elections, sow distrust or confusion, and otherwise weaken democracy. While these broad high-level objectives are likely frequently correct, the focus on domestic politics sometimes has obfuscated attention to likely regional, transnational, or global strategic dimensions of adversarial efforts. By interpreting operations in terms of the local political context, issues, and threats to domestic democratic institutions, there has sometimes been inadequate attention to the wider orchestration of campaigns across multiple national political jurisdictions. In some cases, such campaigns might amount simply to efforts to achieve similar outcomes at scale across larger regions or sets of countries. But, in other cases, the attempt to influence dynamics between countries or regions is also critical – whether aimed at affecting foreign policies toward third parties, bi- or multilateral relations between states, the cohesion or policies of alliances or of regional or international organizations, or some other specific system-level interaction or outcome.

We can discern various examples of such higher level strategic logic at work in Russian uses of disinformation campaigns over more than a decade. While often characterized as efforts to create chaos and uncertainty, impart a sense of nihilism, and stand against something rather than for anything, there is also ample evidence that Russian information and influence campaigns have sought specific regional and international outcomes, including to secure influence across the historic region of the Russian Empire and Soviet Union, undermine European Union (EU) and transatlantic unity and North Atlantic Treaty Organization (NATO) alliance cohesion, diminish international accountability for chemical weapons use, limit uptake of Western COVID-19 vaccines, counter Western security roles in Africa and the Middle East, diminish trust in Western countries across the Global South, win broad support for positions in the United Nations (UN) Global Assembly, and bolster global pro-Russia "conservative" movements and organizational networks.

Russia's multidimensional use of cyber-enabled information and influence campaigns in relation to efforts to undermine Ukrainian independence stands out as a particularly longstanding and egregious example of such coordinated and long-term efforts across many national jurisdictions. Russia has persistently used a mix of information operations to target Ukraine in support of its own strategic goals since at least the 2013–2014 Euromaidan demonstrations and 2014 Crimea annexation and instigation of conflicts in the Donbas and other regions of Ukraine. This has included direct operations against specific Ukrainian targets and populations such as the 2014 hacking of the Central Election Commission of Ukraine and the attempt to spread doubt and undermine legitimacy of electoral results, the use of non-demarcated military personnel to reduce certainty and speed of attribution processes, and the use of propaganda to sow ethnic tensions and stoke conflict. Efforts have frequently focused on shifting narratives concerning specific events in or pertaining to the conflict with Ukraine, such as the rapid online spread of numerous alternative explanations following the July 2014 downing of the Malaysian Airlines flight MH17 over Ukraine.

Even these efforts focused directly on the Ukraine conflict have utilized a variety of operations and techniques to pursue interrelated goals. A number of digitally enabled techniques have been used, including, for example, the use of spear phishing to gain unauthorized access, hack-and-leak operations – as well as the release of forged documents – to influence public understanding of the conflict, distributed denial of service (DDoS) attacks to block access to information at key moments, and the release of wiper malware and cyberattacks destroying data, damaging the economy, and shutting down parts of the power grid. These technical operations have had informational and psychological elements, aiming to affect public opinion or decision-making dynamics – within Ukraine and Russia, but also sometimes beyond. Narratives have also explicitly been weaponized to exacerbate conflict and undermine support for Kyiv, including discussion of "being 'brother nations' with a shared history, religion, and culture; mistreatment of Russian-speaking communities in Ukraine and fear of supposed Ukrainian Naziism, portraying the elected government in Kyiv as illegitimate and violent 'Banderites' [or fascists]; and nostalgia for and possibility of reclaiming the former Soviet greatness" (Kerr, 2023). A variety of platforms and channels have been utilized to disseminate these messages, ranging from social media to television to official public statements and involving everything from fake online personas to supposedly independent expert speakers and official state sources and outlets.

The Kremlin's use of information and influence campaigns in its efforts to subjugate Ukraine has also long involved international components. Operations targeting US and European elections, public opinion, or political decisions have often been examined mostly as threats to domestic political systems, potentially damaging to the targeted country's national security and democracy. But collectively, many of these efforts have also aimed to support Moscow's broader objectives in Ukraine, clearly supporting politicians, parties, or agendas viewed as most commensurate with these goals. Even the 2016 election interference, often seen as the origin point of Western concern about democratic vulnerability to disinformation, can also be understood as related closely to Moscow's efforts to achieve desired outcomes in Ukraine, with the former Republican campaign chief Paul Manafort having specifically served as an advisor to Ukraine's pro-Russia former president Viktor Yanukovych, and the source of the Robert Mueller investigation and first impeachment trial of former US president Donald Trump relating to his handling of relations with Russia and military aid to Ukraine.

Since Russia's full-scale invasion of Ukraine in February 2022, the global and multifaceted scope of these efforts has only increased, utilizing coordinated, multi-front, often transnational and cyber-enabled disinformation and influence campaigns to achieve its desired objectives in the conflict. This has become all the more important given the complexity and criticality of coordinated Western support for Kyiv's war effort.

SUPPORT FOR UKRAINE AND RUSSIAN STRATEGIC DISINFORMATION CAMPAIGNS

In the opening days of Russia's war against Ukraine, a broad coalition of democratic countries – including the United States, members of the EU and NATO, and other partners and allies – came together to condemn the invasion and to offer military and economic aid and other forms of assistance. This support has been critical to Ukraine's ability to defend itself and withstand further Russian conquest during two years of full-scale war. It has involved major contributions by many countries of the transatlantic region and beyond. It has also involved efforts to reinforce and expand

European and transatlantic institutions, embrace nonaligned, like-minded countries, and provide pathways toward greater security and integration into the community of democratic states for Ukraine and other non-EU and non-NATO member countries vulnerable to Russian coercion and aggression. All of this has been undertaken against a backdrop of concerns about potential escalation risks, economic and energy interdependencies, and differing levels of military stockpiles, defense industry readiness, and existing policies and cultural attitudes. These efforts have been remarkable, but they also have exposed additional vulnerabilities to Russian disinformation and influence campaigns – which the Kremlin has diligently sought to exploit.

A Transformative Coalition

In the first two years of the war, over forty-one countries have contributed to the support of Ukraine – whether through the sending of arms and ammunition, support for military training, financial assistance, logistic support, acceptance and support of refugees, or other means. These efforts have involved significant financial and economic burdens, changes in policy, and overcoming a panoply of domestic, regional, intraorganizational, and transatlantic obstacles and tensions. Some countries have pledged large percentages of their national heavy weapons and ammunition stockpiles or committed to rapidly producing more as part of their support for Ukraine. Others have accepted large numbers of refugees, served as major logistics and supply hubs, or fundamentally changed aspects of their domestic economies or foreign policies. In addition to the United States and EU and NATO members, this has included G7 countries and others from across Europe and beyond – including contributions, for example, by Japan, South Korea, Australia, New Zealand, and Taiwan (Bomprezzi et al., n.d.).

As of January 15, 2024, partners have committed some $278 billion in aid since the beginning of the war, including $141.06 billion in financial assistance, $19.01 billion in humanitarian assistance, and $117.99 billion in military commitments (Antezza et al., 2024). While the United States has committed $75.4 billion ($46.33 billion of it military aid), Europe (through the EU and bilateral commitments by individual countries) has collectively committed $183.43 billion ($102.499 billion of it financial and $67.68 billion military aid) (O'Hanlon, Stelzenmüller, & Wessel, 2024). According to the Kiel Institute's "Ukraine Support Tracker" statistics, thirty European countries as well as Canada have actually committed higher percentages of gross domestic product (GDP) than the United States (0.32 percent), though these come as proportions of smaller overall economies. A total of fifteen countries have committed more than 1 percent of their total GDP to the aid effort, led by Estonia (4.09 percent), Denmark (3.06 percent), Lithuania (2.04 percent), Norway (1.72 percent), and Latvia (1.67 percent) (Bomprezzi et al., n.d.). Eastern European countries formerly dominated by Russia have made particularly large proportionate commitments. Of the top fifteen contributors by GDP percentage, seven were former communist states.[1] European countries have also provided significant support in the form of accepting and assisting Ukrainian refugees – led by Germany, Poland, and the Czech Republic, but with fourteen countries accepting refugee numbers greater than 1 percent of their prewar populations.[2] These countries have also spent substantial amounts on support for the refugees they have taken in, led by Poland spending 3.35 percent of its GDP on this support, followed by the Czech Republic and Bulgaria (each 2.08 percent), Slovakia (1.68 percent), Latvia (1.51 percent), Lithuania (0.98 percent), and Estonia (0.94 percent) (Antezza et al., 2024).

These efforts have involved particularly significant undertakings or dramatic changes in policy by a number of countries critical to the support collaboration. For example, Germany – which has committed the second-most total ($24.2 billion) and military ($19.42 billion) aid of any individual country behind the United States, and a total worth 1.06 percent of its GDP – had to dramatically alter its approach to defense and military production, as well as overturning its trade and energy dependence relations with Russia (Antezza et al., 2024). In his February 27, 2022 speech to the Bundestag, German Chancellor Olaf Scholz called the Russian attack on Ukraine a "*Zeitenwende*," or "historic turning point," and announced significant changes in German defense policy and military spending. While gaps remain between commitments and what has actually been delivered to date, this represents a generationally important change in German defense policy. France has also made some substantial changes to its foreign policy as a result of the war effort. Some observers ridiculed French President Emmanuel Macron's prewar shuttle diplomacy charm offensive and open line to Putin during the first year of the war, seeing these efforts as potentially placating Russia or pressuring Ukraine into negotiation. But, by December 2022, Macron had declared France's support for Ukraine "all the way to victory" and France had begun heavy arms deliveries to Ukraine. Subsequent changes suggest an increasing support for inclusive European defensive hardening, including a 40 percent increase in France's defense budget announced in January 2023. Perhaps more significantly, there is also evidence of a changing French approach to European security – including a more positive stance toward further enlargement of the EU and NATO.[3]

[1] In addition to the three Baltic states, this includes Slovakia, Croatia, Bulgaria, and the Czech Republic (see Bomprezzi et al., n.d.).

[2] As of January 15, 2024, Germany had accepted over 1.1 million refugees or 1.35 percent of its population, followed by Poland with over 956,000, the Czech Republic with over 375,000, and the United Kingdom with 250,000. In total, nine – mostly East European – countries have accepted larger proportions than Germany relative to their national populations, including: Montenegro (7.84 percent), Moldova (4.46 percent), the Czech Republic (3.51 percent), Poland (2.52 percent), Latvia (2.30 percent), Slovakia (2.09 percent), Ireland (2.05 percent), Lithuania (1.87 percent), and Cyprus (1.51 percent) (see Antezza et al., 2024).

[3] Not only did France support the Ukrainian and Moldovan moves to EU candidate status but it also lifted prior vetoes on membership talks for Albania and North Macedonia, with Macron

Former Soviet Bloc and nonaligned countries on Europe's Eastern flank have also undertaken dramatic changes in policy and critical supportive efforts. In addition to the substantial aid contributions and refugee support relative to their GDPs and populations, Baltic and East European states have loudly pressured partners for greater supportive efforts. Poland has played a particularly essential role, serving as a hub for logistics – including the transfer of military and humanitarian aid – with its city Rzeszow providing the closest airport to the Ukrainian border. It has also taken in one of the largest total refugee populations with many more transiting through the country to further destinations. Ukraine's closest European neighbors have also become conduits for shipment of its agricultural products, while Turkey has played an intermittent role in pressuring Russia to allow their Black Sea export.

In addition to specific efforts to provide immediate aid and support for Ukraine, another significant element of the response by democratic partners has involved efforts to consolidate and reinforce structures of cooperation and security across Europe and the transatlantic region. In the first months of the war, Sweden and Finland – which had long maintained a neutral status in relation to NATO – declared their desire to join the alliance and were formally invited at the Madrid Summit in July 2022. Despite intra-alliance tensions that held up the actual accessions, most NATO members rapidly embraced the further integration of these two partner countries, seen as capable of quickly becoming important contributors to the alliance's defense posture. Western democracies have also come together in an effort to provide pathways forward to secure democratic futures for Ukraine and other non-NATO and non-EU member countries vulnerable to Russian aggression. At NATO's Vilnius summit in July 2023, the alliance affirmed language that "Ukraine's future is in NATO" and agreed that, after the war, Ukraine would not be required to go through the formal process of a "membership action plan," or MAP.[4] On December 14, 2023, the EU's current members voted to begin membership accession negotiations with Ukraine and Moldova, also advancing Georgia to candidate status.[5]

suggesting that EU expansion should occur "as fast as possible" and calling for a Ukrainian "path to NATO membership" in 2023 (*The Economist*, 2023a; *The Economist*, 2023b).

4 Though this did not provide Ukraine with as strong a guarantee of rapid accession as the country desired, with some friction between members, it was accompanied by discussion of additional assistance in training and interoperability and an additional pledge of "enduring" support from the G7 countries – the United States, UK, Canada, France, Germany, Italy, and Japan – promising that each state would offer "specific, bilateral, long-term security commitments and arrangements" (*The Economist*, 2023c).

5 Ukraine, Georgia, and Moldova had each submitted applications for EU membership in the opening weeks of the war in February and March 2022. In June 2022, the European Council conferred Ukraine and Moldova with candidate status and named Georgia as a potential candidate. During this same period, the EU has also reinvigorated engagement around the path to membership with six Western Balkan countries that had long seemed bogged down in

Vulnerabilities and Targeting of Ukraine's Support

The outpouring of support for Ukraine in the face of Russian hostility has marked an impressive, coordinated response, but it has also demonstrated new seams of vulnerability to Russian information and influence campaigns. While some relate to core democratic institutions and protections and processes across democracies, others are due to the historic, cultural, or political specificities of particular states critical to the support efforts – or capable of playing spoilers in those efforts, such as through the EU or NATO. While the individual support of key states is vital in and of itself, some vulnerabilities are explicitly inter- or transnational, related to alliance or regional institutions, bi- or multilateral dynamics, coordination, trust, and cohesion. Russia has made extensive strategic use of cyber-enabled information and influence campaigns during the first two years of the war, including targeting these vulnerabilities in Ukraine's support coalition. Coordinated campaigns across different national and regional audiences have targeted not only specific countries key to the support effort but also the very relationships, organizations, and mechanisms that have been most critical in enabling a collective unified response.

A review of several known instances of Russian disinformation and influence operations since the start of the full-scale war with Ukraine readily demonstrates this strategic sophistication, both in target selection and often also in coordination of tactics and narratives across jurisdictions. We see this first, for example, in operations targeting countries that are leading providers of military, financial, or humanitarian support. Operations across these countries use similar but tailored tactics, aiming to bolster challenges to support for Ukraine and increase conciliatory positions toward Russia across the right and left extremes of the political spectrum, and spread narratives undermining public support for Ukraine or emphasizing associated risks and harms to national well-being. These efforts began long before the full-scale invasion, cultivating networks of relationships with extreme political parties and movements, fringe media outlets, organizations, politicians, journalists, activists, influencers, and other public figures. They also long involved cultivating digital ecosystems for the laundering and spread of interrelated but tailored disinformation across many platforms.

Since the invasion, not only has the intensity of these efforts increased but they have also focused much more explicitly on the goal of undermining support for Ukraine. Russian cyber-enabled information and influence campaigns seeking to affect the course of the war have targeted numerous audiences, including within Ukraine itself, the Russian public, the Global South, and the West. Building on the relationships, audiences, and techniques cultivated through earlier campaigns and operations, they have sought to "amplify divisive local issues and voices," "tailor[ing] disinformation and narratives for specific audiences." They have used a

different stages of the membership process. In December 2023, it was announced that negotiations might begin in 2024 with Bosnia and Herzegovina (*The Economist*, 2023d).

combination of official channels, "state-backed media outlets," "Russia-linked actors," and organizations, and "coordinated inauthentic activity on social media platforms." They have leveraged techniques such as "hack-and-leak operations," "falsified imagery," fake copies of trusted websites, and automated systems for the dissemination, laundering, and amplification of fake stories across multiple media ecosystems (Atlantic Council Digital Forensic Research Lab (DFRLab), 2023; Huntley, 2023; Insikt Group, 2022; Kerr, 2023, p. 17). Through a mix of narratives and covert influence campaigns across numerous countries, they have aimed to discredit the legitimacy or capability of the Ukrainian government and military, spread doubt and fear concerning pro-Ukraine policies, encourage conciliatory approaches to Russia, and foment grievances and division between Ukraine's supporters (Bronk, Collins, & Wallach, 2022; Kerr, 2023). Narratives of particular prevalence have included those seeking to stoke hostility, fear, and resentment toward Ukrainian refugees; blame Russian sanctions and aid to Ukraine for local economic and social hardships; legitimize Russian actions and blame Ukraine, NATO, or the United States for the war; raise the specter of military escalation to involve supporting countries, nuclear, or other catastrophic threats; and sow distrust in mainstream parties and media of Western democracies as "biased or untruthful" (Aleksejeva, 2023; Kerr, 2023).

Studies both prior to and during the full-scale war show Russia building vast networks for the distribution of targeted disinformation and cultivation and manipulation of supportive actors and publics across Europe and the United States, often appearing to particularly emphasize those countries most critical to the Ukraine support effort. For example, the EUvsDisinfo Database – a project of the European External Action Service (EEAS) East StratCom Taskforce – found that Germany was the European country most targeted by disinformation campaigns recorded in their data for the 2015–2021 period leading up to the war, with 700 cases collected. During this same period, their data showed France as the second-most targeted, with 300 cases. Comparative studies by the EU DisinfoLab since the full-scale invasion likewise point to Germany as the most-targeted EU member state during the conflict, while major leaks of Kremlin correspondence and investigative studies have demonstrated explicitly planned efforts to target both French and German public opinion and politics to undermine support for Ukraine.

Operations in both Germany and France have sought to instrumentalize fringe political parties and movements to spread narratives undercutting support for Ukraine across receptive audiences and promote policies serving Russia's strategic goals. In Germany, for example, leaks and traced online campaigns show Moscow attempting to utilize pro-Russian media and social media as well as networks of collaborative relationships and clandestine operatives to mobilize both left- and right-wing activists, political parties, and sympathetic segments of the population around opposition to support for Ukraine – in some cases specifically seeking to bring together both ends of the political spectrum around common narratives and grievances. Some of these operations have long roots going back well before the 2022 invasion. Prior to the full-scale war, German-language Russian state-backed media had an established presence in the German media system, including outlets such as RT Deutsch and Sputnik, which focused their coverage on polarizing issues such as immigration and EU skepticism, producing content that was often picked up by – and frequently supportive of – extreme populist political parties and campaigns (Hadeed & Sus, 2023; Spahn, 2020). By mid-decade, Russian disinformation often targeted Angela Merkel and her policies, including her stance on migration. In the infamous 2016 "Lisa F." case, a hoax about a thirteen-year-old Russian–German girl having allegedly been kidnapped and assaulted by men of Arab origin was amplified by Russian media leading to anti-migrant demonstrations and an attack on a refugee reception center by German neo-Nazis.

Since Germany's blocking of RT shortly prior to the Russian invasion of Ukraine in February 2022, a number of pro-Russian German blogs and independent media sources on platforms such as Telegram have achieved wide audiences spreading Kremlin narratives (DW, 2022; Kastner & Hewson, 2023). Analysis by Reuters has identified twenty-seven Telegram channels that "reshare and boost pro-Kremlin messages to a combined audience of about 1.5 million subscribers," including flattering images of Putin and warnings about the risk of nuclear escalation (Nikolskaya et al., 2023). German researchers have also shown the Russian government is more often using official channels of communication such as Foreign Ministry and Embassy websites, social media, and press releases to spread disinformation (Organisation for Economic Co-operation and Development (OECD), 2022). In one prominent August 2022 example of the use of these mechanisms to spread inflammatory disinformation against support for Ukraine, an out-of-context video clip of German Foreign Minister Annalena Baerbock portrayed her as declaring her intention to continue support for Ukraine even against the will and interests of German voters. The clip was picked up first on pro-Russian Telegram accounts and then propagated further across mainstream social media platforms, spread by accounts connected with extremists and fringe political party members, and leading to a trending hashtag on German-language Twitter (now X) calling for Baerbock's resignation (Delcker, 2022).

The Kremlin has long sought to build closer relations with German fringe politicians and activists. The hard-right Alternative für Deutschland (AfD) party has been a particularly pronounced beneficiary of Moscow's largess. Prior to and since the beginning of the full-scale war, several AfD members have been invited on trips to meet with Kremlin or Kremlin-aligned figures in Moscow, Belarus, Kyiv, and Russian-occupied regions of Ukraine. At the same time, Kremlin efforts also have aimed to stoke support for left-wing activism such as peace and anti-NATO movements. Investigations have traced Kremlin efforts to encourage alliance between the AfD and the far-left party, Die Linke, specifically appearing to target Die Linke parliamentarian Sahra Wagenknecht, who has led protests opposed to supplying arms to Ukraine.[6] Reuters investigations have also indicated that the Russian agency *Rossotrudnichestvo* is also directly coordinating a "network of agents" – some under false German identities – involved in promoting Kremlin narratives in protests and civil society events within Germany (Nikolskaya et al., 2023). After the beginning of the war, the AfD's popularity has soared nationally, doubling between fall 2022 and 2023 an average of 22 percent, with much higher numbers in some Eastern regions.[7] Berlin's Center for Monitoring, Analysis, and Strategy (CeMAS) research also showed a significant increase in "approval of pro-Russian propaganda narratives" between spring and fall of 2022 (Kastner & Hewson, 2023). The exact impact of Russian information and influence campaigns on such shifts in polling and public opinion is difficult to establish, as these efforts often target already vulnerable populations and seek to exacerbate preexisting grievances and dynamics. But these trends could prove concerning in relation to long-term support for Ukraine.

In France, Russian disinformation and influence operations have also sought to leverage fringe parties, organizations, and public opinion to influence policy. Campaigns targeting France since the start of the full-scale war, similarly to those in Germany, have built on longstanding efforts. Russia has, for example, long cultivated a relationship with Marie Le Pen's far-right party, the National Rally (formerly National Front), with past loan interactions suggesting financial support from Russia, Le Pen's rhetoric emphasizing negative impacts of sanctions on the French economy, and the party voting against or abstaining from support for Ukraine and advocating better relations with Russia. National Rally member and European parliamentarian, Thierry Mariani, also leads the Association for Franco-Russian Dialogue, an organization which promotes pro-Russian positions in Paris. Mariani has made frequent trips to Russia, served as an election observer in the Donbas in 2018, and led National Rally delegations to Crimea. He pushes against Western support for Ukraine and sanctions of Russia, promoting negative views of

6 The Kremlin has invited Wagenknecht's ex-husband, Ralph Niemeyer, on trips to Moscow, for example, and encouraged him to help bridge the left and right coalitions. Leaked Kremlin emails show numerous, sometimes lavish, all-expenses-paid trips to Moscow by AfD members since at least 2017, with some paid for through the "Russian Peace Foundation," which is run by the head of the Duma's Foreign Affairs Committee, Leonid Slutsky (Belton, Mekhennet, & Harris, 2023; DW, 2021; Kastner & Hewson, 2023).

7 Parts of the former East Germany appear to be particularly vulnerable to Russian disinformation due to long-simmering residual resentments of the West, greater economic difficulties, and shared communist history. An October 2022 survey showed 40 percent of Germans "fully or partially" agreeing with the argument "that NATO provoked Russia into invading Ukraine" – an already alarming number – but 59 percent agreed in former East German provinces. Extremist and separatist groups have had more sway in this region, including the "Free Saxons" movement who aim for their own "Säxit" – an idea of "far-reaching autonomy or secession" based on the British "Brexit." Saxony was also home to a planned coup attempt – led by the far-right group *Reichsbürger* and Prince Heinrich XIII Reuss, a member of the regional aristocracy – conspirators involved in which were arrested by German authorities in December 2022 (Kastner & Hewson, 2023; Morris, Mekhennet, & Bisset, 2022).

the Ukrainian government and the United States. Jean-Luc Schaffhauser, a former member of the European Parliament for Le Pen's party, has sought to "[launch] a foundation with Moscow's backing that would advocate for a cease-fire in Ukraine, with the Kremlin maintaining its grip on the country's eastern regions" (Belton, 2023). Schaffhauser, who arranged the loans to support Le Pen's prior presidential bid, also plans to back a slate of far-right candidates to the 2024 EU Parliament who seek closer relations with Russia.[8]

Russian efforts in France appear to have been tailored to emphasize particular narratives thought to be most resonant and play off of existing divisions and vulnerabilities in French society. In 2023, a French parliamentary inquiry issued a report noting Russia's "long-term disinformation campaign" and efforts to "defend and promote Russian interests" and "polarize [France's] democratic society" (Belton, 2023). A December 2023 *The Washington Post* investigative report examined how leaked Kremlin documents demonstrate explicit plans in this regard led by First Deputy Chief of Staff to the Putin Administration, Sergei Kiriyenko. The documents show an effort to utilize social media, politicians, activists, and other public figures to heighten domestic political tension, challenge NATO cohesion, and weaken support for Ukraine. Leaked 2022 Kremlin presentations give a window into the strategic thinking, expressing a belief that France would be "vulnerable to political turmoil." They cited polling numbers showing the French public – at 30 percent – had the second-highest positive view of Russia[9] of any country in Western Europe (behind Italy), with "[40 percent] inclined not to believe reporting on Ukraine by France's own mass media." Kiriyenko's team encouraged promoting narratives about the negative impacts of the sanctions on Russia leading to "social and economic crisis," the inappropriateness of "paying for another country's war," suggesting nefarious US use of the war "as an instrument to weaken Russia's position in Europe," the risk of European embroilment in a "World War III," and the need for "dialogue with Russia" to develop a "common European security architecture" (Belton, 2023). Other investigations suggest ongoing Russian efforts to exacerbate tensions around immigrants and ethno-religious difference in French society.[10]

[8] According to a December 2023 *The Washington Post* report, this was a topic Schaffhauser planned to discuss directly with Sergei Naryshkin, the head of Russian foreign intelligence, during a January 2024 meeting in Moscow. His activities, furthermore, are supported by renting a floor of his home to Russia's second-highest ranked diplomat in Paris, Ilya Subbotin (Belton, 2023).

[9] French society's connections with Russia go back many years, potentially helping to explain some reservoir of positive sentiment. Among other connections was the large influx of "White Russian" immigrants settling in France in the 1920s (Nabozhniak et al., 2023).

[10] Russian interference has also been tied to efforts to exacerbate tensions in French society between Muslim and Jewish communities. In June 2023, pro-Russian social media accounts played an outsized role in commentary around riots in response to the killing of an Arab French teenager by Paris police, and in November 2023, in the wake of onset of the Israel–Gaza war, an antisemitic campaign to paint Stars of David around Paris and amplify pictures on

Use of digital platforms and tools has been critical in Russia's efforts to spread disinformation and influence in France, as it has been in Germany and elsewhere. The leaked Kremlin documents showed direct instructions for the use of troll farms and false French personas in targeting French society (Belton, 2023). In June 2023, French authorities announced the discovery of a broad Russian disinformation campaign, dubbed "Doppelgänger," involving the production of fake duplicates of official government and media websites – including those of the French Foreign Ministry and the newspaper *Le Monde* – then using these impersonations to disseminate false content supportive of Russia and critical of Ukraine and its support. The French Foreign Ministry attributed the operation to Russia, pointing to "numerous elements revealing the involvement of Russian or Russian-speaking individuals and many Russian companies . . . [and] many state [or state-affiliated] entities." The Russian companies Struktura and Social Design Agency were identified as "running [the] operation," while an anonymous news agency, Recent Reliable News (RRN), provided a repository of propaganda content for its use (EU Disinfo Lab, n.d.). The operation similarly targeted Germany, Italy, Ukraine, and the United Kingdom (Reynaud & Leloup, 2023).

In early February 2024, in another major revelation concerning Russia's at-scale use of digital tools to spread disinformation, the French government revealed a vast network of Russian sites that were "structured and coordinated" to spread Kremlin propaganda across multiple countries supporting Ukraine, including France, Germany, Poland, and the United States.[11] The network, dubbed "Portal Kombat" had been discovered by Viginum, the French government organization tasked with confronting foreign disinformation. The network included 193 sites set up to disseminate materials in multiple languages and jurisdictions. A sub-portion of the network had spread over 150,000 articles during a three-month period of June–September 2023, tracked by researchers. The materials disseminated primarily focused on justifying Russia's war against Ukraine and spreading false or misleading information and narratives to do so (Le Temps, 2024; Willsher & O'Carroll, 2024).

Russian campaigns to undermine support for Ukraine have also targeted Poland, one of Ukraine's most invaluable supporters and closest neighbors. As with other cases, the prehistory of the recent disinformation and influence efforts stretches back well before the full-scale invasion. While a significant wariness of Russia and potential Kremlin interference or aggression has long been a hallmark of Polish domestic politics – including on the far-right[12] –evidence suggests that Russia has

social media was traced to Russia-connected individuals and bot social media accounts (Belton, 2023; Caulcutt, 2023).

11 Spain, Austria, Switzerland, and the United Kingdom were also targeted (Le Temps, 2024).

12 In July 2023, Poland's then-ruling conservative Law and Justice party (PiS) passed a law creating a commission (appointed in August 2023) to investigate alleged Russian influence (particularly targeting political opposition), in a move which critics lamented as unconstitutional, "McCarthyist" and a threat to democracy. Conspiratorial theories about Russian involvement

attempted a similar cultivation of fringe political party connections and exploitation of local grievances as it has in the other countries it has targeted. Leaked emails have shown Russian cultivation of relationships with some fringe Polish politicians at least as far back as 2015, utilizing connections with the *Zmiana* ("Change") party, for example, to prompt demonstrations of support for Russia's annexation of Crimea (Agence France-Presse in Warsaw, 2016; Foy, 2015; Glos Koszalinski, 2023; Morozova & Szczygieł, 2023; Pacula, 2015). In 2019, only three months after its formation, *Konfederacja* ("Confederation") – "an openly pro-Russia party" – won 4.6 percent of the vote for Polish representation in the European Parliament. While this meant it did not reach the 5 percent threshold to win seats, it finished as the fourth strongest party and its fortunes have continued to grow.[13]

Pre-2022 Russian information and influence campaigns in Poland leveraged both overt state-backed sources and covert networks – often involving social media.[14] They also used illicit cyber campaigns involving phishing and hack-and-leak operations.[15] Particularly prominent themes, which have had continuing relevance during the war, included Polish loss of sovereignty to the EU, US, or other foreign actors; Polish "'Russophobia' and anti-Russian actions"; "Polish aggressiveness and imperialist intentions," including desires to turn Belarus and Ukraine into "vassals"; "economic difficulties" resulting from this subservience, hatred, and aggression; and

in the April 2010 plane crash in Smolensk, Russia, that killed then-President Lech Kaczynski and over ninety leading members of the Polish government and political elite have been credited with contributing to a consolidation of power under PiS between 2015 and 2023 that was seen by many analysts as contributing to democratic decline in the country (Applebaum, 2020; Franz, 2023; NFP, 2023; Schmitz, 2023; Shotter & Foy, 2020).

[13] Prominent members and associates of these and other fringe Polish parties have traveled to Crimea (in 2014), Grozny, and Moscow (including in late 2022), worked with the outlet Sputnik Polska, and published a book by Russian nationalist philosopher Alexander Dugin. Since the start of the full-scale Russia–Ukraine war, some members of the Confederation have called for not opening Polish borders to Ukrainian refugees, refused to support NATO accession for Finland and Sweden, promoted the slogan "Stop Ukrainization of Poland," and invoked narratives suggesting that the massacre in Bucha, Ukraine, was staged and that Polish support for Ukraine might prompt a Russian nuclear retaliation against Warsaw (Alan-Lee, 2013; Mierzyńska, 2023; Zaborowski, 2019).

[14] Until Russia's state-sponsored Sputnik and RT outlets were blocked across the EU in 2022, these outlets openly promoted Polish-language news with Kremlin narratives. These sites themselves were not so popular with Polish audiences, but other Polish websites copied their content without attribution, putting it into broader circulation (Kozłowski, 2022).

[15] A major 2021 hack-and-leak incident targeted the private email of the then-head of the office of the Polish Prime Minister, Michał Dworczyk, with emails later being posted to Telegram. The broader "Ghostwriter" cyber espionage campaign targeted thousands of additional Polish email accounts, including those of 100 public officials. These phishing attacks were later publicly attributed to Russia, with the Polish government noting that they had targeted both the ruling party and opposition as well as Polish civil society, and that they were "part of the disinformation operation that the Russian side is conducting against Poland, but also against other countries on NATO's eastern flank." As disinformation investigator Anna Gielewska pointed out in June 2023, much of the data obtained through the Ghostwriter campaign appeared to have been held for future use (Gielewska, 2023; NFP, 2021).

amplifying historical grievances and false or misleading "history-related claims," including about Polish responsibility for World War II, and inadequate Polish gratitude for the Soviet liberation of Poland (Nemečkayová, 2023). Other prominent narratives of Russian pre-2022 disinformation in Poland included those about the COVID-19 pandemic[16] and migration and refugees.[17]

Since February 2022, Russian information and influence operations in Poland have built on these earlier efforts. In a rapid shift following the start of the full-scale war, many of the social media accounts and group pages that had been most active in promoting COVID-19 disinformation (or other themes such as conspiracies around 5G) rapidly switched to align against Ukraine and the war support effort. Hundreds of new anonymous accounts also appeared suddenly and began to comment on content related to Russia and Ukraine.[18] Disinformation about the war has focused with particular intensity on undermining Polish relations with Ukraine and attitudes toward Ukrainian immigrants, but also justifying Russian actions, questioning economic and social consequences of support for Ukraine, promoting pacifism and anti-war sentiment, and amplifying tensions between East and West European allies. Narratives about Ukrainian refugees have suggested that the refugees are usurping privileges of Polish citizens such as access to jobs, housing, hospitals or schools, stirring resentment. They also have sought to induce fear and anger by falsely suggesting that the refugees are mostly young men rather than women and children, and that they are dangerous, engaging in criminal activities.[19] Some propaganda narratives play up historical grievances and ethnic tensions (Insikt Group, 2022, p. 5) – such as recalling unresolved animosities around the World War II Volhynian massacre, or even suggesting Polish imperialist ambitions in Ukraine.[20] Other content seeks to amplify

16 During the COVID-19 pandemic, Poland was bombarded by – as well as fairly vulnerable to – COVID-19- and vaccine-related disinformation. Much of this was disseminated by a network of pro-Russian online portals that targeted Western and pro-Western countries. The content was further picked up by networks inclined to believe and spread conspiracy theories. The EUvsDisinfo database tracked 800 "fake news" items related to the subject "distributed by Russian and pro-Russian portals" (EUvsDisInfo, n.d.; Pawela, 2021; Zadroga, 2022).

17 During the 2021 refugee crisis provocation on the Polish–Belarusian border, Russian state media outlets as well as social networks (particularly Telegram) sought to portray Poland and the European Union as not respecting the human rights of migrants, using this coverage in multiple languages to seek to damage perceptions of Poland (as well as Lithuania and Latvia), but also seeking to fan the flames of divisive internal tensions around migration and immigration policies within EU countries – and Poland itself. In Poland in 2015, this issue had been an important element in the rise of the Law and Justice (PiS) party (Gönczi, 2023; Legucka & Bryjka, 2021).

18 Research showed some social media group pages changed their names, in one example going from "We don't believe in COVID-19 Pandemic" to "STOP Ukrainization of Poland" (Kozłowski, 2022).

19 In one infamous case, Russian disinformation claimed that a murder committed in Warsaw was perpetrated by Ukrainian refugees – whereas the perpetrators charged were in fact Polish nationals (Rogalewicz, 2023; Texty, 2022; Tyburski, 2023; Zadroga, 2023).

20 In late November 2022, following shortly after the incident of a Ukrainian air defense missile accidentally landing in Poland and killing two civilians, Russian media outlets began running

broader anti-Ukrainian sentiments – whether through suggesting that Ukrainians are all "Banderites," Nazis, fascists, nationalists, or extremists, seeking to discredit the Ukrainian government, or blaming Ukraine and NATO for inciting the conflict (Tymińska, Korpal, & Sek, 2023; Zadroga, 2023). Research on Ukrainian social media since the start of the war shows some of the anti-Ukrainian rhetoric to be taking off – including the popularization of the hashtag #StopUkrainizacjiPolski ("#Stop UkrainizationPoland"), driven in part by the at-scale deployment of inauthentic, automated, Russian disinformation-spreading accounts.[21]

Recent shifts in public opinion polling, political rhetoric, and protest dynamics within Poland suggest that – though support for Ukraine is still relatively strong – the audience for some of these Kremlin messages may be growing. Public opinion studies conducted in the fall of 2022 and early 2023 already found Poles – particularly in poorer regions of the country – growing more critical of the economic effects of support for Ukrainian refugees, with approximately a third of the population believing that "the war in Ukraine was the result of [the same] global liberal conspiracy [. . .] that caused the COVID-19 pandemic," and that "Ukrainians residing in Poland were not refugees but economic migrants." Approximately two-thirds of respondents thought that Poland "'cannot afford' the presence of war exiles" (Mazzini, 2024). In 2022–2023, polling showed the right-wing party Confederation's popularity rising rapidly, polling third with 10 percent support by April 2023, and reaching 16.9 percent by July, prompting much speculation that they would prove "kingmakers" in Poland's October 15, 2023, parliamentary elections, potentially helping then-ruling Law and Justice party (PiS) form a coalition government. While this did not occur,[22] the

stories suggesting a Polish plan to annex part of Ukraine's territory. In an interview, Russia's Director of Foreign Intelligence, Sergey Naryshin, stated that the Polish government was planning annexation followed by referendums in three western regions of Ukraine with the goal of preventing a NATO–Russia agreement over Ukraine's future (Salvo, 2022).

21 The April 2023 "Anti-Ukrainian Hate Speech on Polish Twitter" report by the Helsinki Foundation for Human Rights in collaboration with Polish civil society organizations the Gremek Foundation and Securlex, highlighted an uptick in hate speech targeting Ukrainian migrants on Polish Twitter. Examining the period from February 23, 2022, to January 1, 2023, the study found that "far-right politicians," "leaders and activists of radical political movements," "extremist publicists," and "some internet creators" played prominent roles in spreading xenophobic narratives. The research also found evidence of coordinated inauthentic activity on the Twitter (now X) platform driven by automated "bot" accounts including a "network of accounts duplicating Russian propaganda." The report found that this at-scale republishing was able to rapidly create trends, including popularization of the #StopUkrainizacjiPolski hashtag. While "anti-Ukrainian hate speech and disinformation were present in Polish social media even before the Russian aggression," the research found that "its scale increased significantly after February 24, 2022." The research indicated "content hostile to Ukrainians is contained in tens of thousands of posts" and "identif[ied] 90,019 posts potentially containing hate narratives against Ukrainians" (Tymińska, Korpal, & Sek, 2023).

22 Ultimately, a relative underperformance by both Confederation (garnering approximately 10 percent of the vote to only expand their parliamentary presence from eleven to eighteen seats) and PiS (35.38 percent) allowed for Donald Tusk's liberal Civic Platform (30.7 percent) to form a ruling coalition with smaller partners Third Way and the Left party, ending eight

campaign saw the Confederation and PiS candidates competing to be the loudest "defenders of Polish sovereignty," with slogans of "no more welfare for Ukrainians" and that "the needs of Polish citizens need to come first." The year 2023 also saw the emergence of the *Polski Ruch Antywojenny* (Polish Anti-War Movement) or PRA, which led a march in Warsaw in May 2023 and popularized the hashtag/slogan "#niemojawojna" (Not My War).[23] Poland has also seen several waves of mass protests by farmers, angered by the competition created by the import of inexpensive Ukrainian grain. The apparent role of the Confederation party in orchestrating these protests as well as some pro-Russia displays suggest potential growing alignment between the galvanized farming communities and Russian narratives.[24]

Equally important to the targeting of key countries to Ukraine's support, Russia's campaigns appear to also target key relationships between countries, cohesion of and trust in multinational organizations, and mechanisms of cooperation playing critical roles in the support processes. These have included efforts, for example, to sow discord in bi- and multilateral relations between parts within Europe, to diminish trust and cooperation in the transatlantic relationship between Europe and the United States, to weaken the cohesion and amplify distrust in the EU and NATO, and to reduce the confidence of supporters in Ukrainian leadership and capability. Such campaigns often make use of multiple coordinated operations across different countries, stressing parallel themes of discord, leveraging transnational networks, and laundering disinformation through fringe media and social media ecosystems across different languages.

We see this, for example, in the Kremlin's efforts to amplify rifts between Eastern-Central and Western Europe. Already by July 2022, Recorded Futures had tracked RT stories "repeatedly stressing extreme political divisions between Poland and Germany or insoluble disagreements between Poland and the Baltics versus Germany, France, and Turkey, suggesting radically different stakes or positions in

years of PiS's increasingly illiberal rule (Chiappa, 2023; Faiola & Chapman, 2023; Koper & Wlodarczak-Semczuk, 2023).

[23] The PRA and a related new political party *Bezpieczna Polska* (Secure Poland) are both led by political scientist Leszek Sykulski. Sykulski, who has posted pictures on social media showing himself with the Russian ambassador to Poland Sergei Andreyev and the Russian nationalist philosopher Alexander Dugin, has over 105,000 subscribers for his YouTube channel. He endorses a "multi-vector" approach to foreign policy, including a closer embrace of Russia and a possible future "Polexit" from European and transatlantic institutions. Polish journalist and expert on Russian disinformation Anna Mierzynska has drawn attention to the alignment between these efforts' rhetoric and Kremlin disinformation as well as to the potential of more direct connections through Sykulski and associates (Harper, 2023; Mierzyńska, 2023).

[24] In April 2023, Poland's PiS party agriculture minister resigned in protest following a European Commission decision requiring the extension of "duty free imports" on Ukrainian grain until June of 2024. Though farming communities are a traditional PiS constituency, the protests appear to have closer connections to the Confederation and the rhetoric has grown increasingly hostile to Ukraine. In further protests in February 2024, in which farmers blocked roads and railroad tracks, there have been incidents of Soviet flags and pro-Russia banners displayed on tractors (Alan-Lee, 2013; Harper, 2024; Reuters, 2023a; NFP, 2024).

relation to the war."[25] Also noteworthy are attempts to undermine European trust for the United States and its motives in rallying transatlantic support for Ukraine. An incident in September 2022 involving efforts to publicize a fake RAND Corporation report shows the lengths that Russian operations have gone to in order to launder disinformation and help it to gain traction in relevant echo chambers across countries and language barriers. The inauthentic report was a document supposedly prepared at the behest of the US government and laid out a plan for using the pretext of a US-provoked war between Russia and Ukraine as a mechanism to weaken Germany and the EU, while strengthening the United States. The report and stories about it were publicized by fringe outlets in Germany and then Sweden, discussed in connected YouTube videos, and then written about by RT and promoted by social media of the Russian Embassy in Sweden.[26]

Equally complex Russian disinformation and influence campaigns have sought to disrupt NATO and EU processes and cohesion. Sweden's and Finland's 2022 decisions to apply for NATO membership and the subsequent accession processes became targets of opportunity for such campaigns. Russian disinformation narratives tracked in Finland have, for example, "argue[d] that Finland has been pressured by the United States to apply to the alliance and that the majority of Finns oppose the NATO membership."[27] The campaigns to slow or undermine Sweden's NATO bid appear to have been particularly complex, spanning several languages and countries,

[25] While the upsurge in anti-German rhetoric in the lead-up to the fall 2023 elections has not been directly tied to Russian disinformation, this resonated with and drew on core themes of threats to Polish sovereignty and distrust of European institutions, which Kremlin messaging campaigns have amplified (Insikt Group, 2022; Kerr, 2023; Minder & Pitel, 2023; Strzelecki, Siebold, & Koper, 2023).

[26] On September 6, 2022, the multilingual mis- and disinformation outlet *Weltexpress* published a German-language article describing the supposedly leaked report. On September 8, it published a copy of the fake report with further discussion. Subsequent YouTube videos continued discussion of the topic, gaining over 16,000 views. (The PDF of the fake report contained basic errors of grammar, spelling, and fact.) On September 13, a fringe Swedish outlet, *Nya Dagbladet* ("The New Daily Post"), picked up coverage of the false report, declaring in their Swedish-language headline "Shocking document: How the US planned the war and energy crisis in Europe" ("*Chockerande dokumentet: Så planerade USA kriget och energikrisen i Europa*"). This was followed on September 15 by an English-language translation of the story by the same outlet, and on September 16 by an RT story about the *Nya Dagbladet* article. On September 17, Russia's Embassy in Sweden posted to Twitter (now X) about the story. After RAND Corporation itself published a September 14 statement refuting the report as a fake, *Nya Dagbladet* continued to argue that this dismissiveness further suggested the report's veracity. The outlet *Nya Dagbladet* was founded in 2012 by members of an extreme right-wing nationalist party and has become known for being a bridge between "conspiratorial" and "far-right milieu[s]," playing a major role in the spread of anti-lockdown and anti-vaccine content during the pandemic. It also is known for consistently espousing pro-Kremlin views (Haag, 2022; NYA Dagbladet, 2022; RAND Corporation, 2022).

[27] The EU Disinfo Lab also reported on "multiple Russian-linked media outlets falsely report[ing] that Finland is moving its tanks to the Eastern border" in an apparent effort to bolster accusations by far-right parties blaming the "Finnish government and mainstream media" for "war-mongering" and "inciting hysteria" (Moilanen, Hautala, & Saari, 2023).

and plausibly involving covert encouragement of Koran burnings and other protest actions in Sweden as well as online campaigns. In July 2023, the Swedish government announced that Sweden had been targeted by "Russia-backed actors [...] amplifying incorrect statements such as that the Swedish state is behind the desecration of holy scriptures."[28] Sweden's Psychological Defence Agency drew attention to the fact that RT and Sputnik had published numerous articles in Arabic about the Koran burnings, and that their agency had tracked millions of social media posts in Arabic and other languages, apparently part of a campaign to portray Sweden as an "Islamophobic" country that supports Koran burning, to create tensions with domestic minorities and backlash in Muslim-majority countries (protesters stormed and vandalized the Swedish Embassy in Baghdad). Most significantly, these campaigns amplified a pretext for continued Turkish (and to a lesser extent Hungarian) resistance to Sweden's NATO accession bid.[29]

CONCLUSION: DEFENSIVE PROGRESS AND CHALLENGES

In February 2024, when the French government issued an announcement about its discovery of a vast network of sites disseminating disinformation about the war in Ukraine in multiple languages across Europe, it did not do so alone. Instead, the "Portal Kombat" discovery was revealed in a joint press conference of the French, Polish, and German foreign ministers. In this collaborative "Weimar Triangle" format, the three countries – each key actors in support for Ukraine – also announced the launch of a joint alert mechanism to enable intelligence sharing and coordination around "unacceptable interference," such as Russian disinformation campaigns. The countries also agreed to each do more to "pressure online platforms to counter these influence operations." "We are in a period of vulnerability with the European elections," noted the French Foreign Minister Stephane Sejourne, drawing attention to the June vote for the European Parliament (Irish, 2024; Le Temps, 2024). While this recent move is certainly not the first effort by Western democracies to find common cause in fighting transnational flows of

[28] These statements followed a spate of highly divisive protest demonstrations in Stockholm in January through June 2023. These included the hanging in effigy of Turkish President Recep Tayyip Erdogan from a lamppost and burning of a Koran outside of the Turkish embassy in January, which prompted Turkey to cancel a state visit by Sweden's Defense Minister, Pal Jonson, as well as a subsequent summer Koran burning after which Turkey's government stated that their decision on the NATO accession ratification might be further delayed "if these attacks on the things we hold sacred continue." Investigations by open-source analysts and journalists have further pointed to plausible connections between individuals involved in staging the Koran burnings and the Kremlin (AftonBladet, 2023; Armstrong, 2023; Braw, 2023; Bryant, 2023; Haag, 2022; Henley, 2023; Reuters, 2023b; Robert Lansing Institute, 2023).

[29] These campaigns also demonstrate apparent Russian orchestration across several countries, utilizing disinformation and influence campaigns in combination with leveraging of countries with which they have closer political ties or alignment as spoilers within EU and NATO processes.

foreign disinformation, much more such coordination will be necessary to succeed in mitigating the threat.

Western threat perceptions around cyber-enabled disinformation have developed gradually since at least 2016, prompting various forms of experimentation to address the problem. Following initial surprise, states were relatively quick to recognize the strategic nature of the threat with its potential to undermine democratic elections and decision processes. But much of the initial focus fell on developing the necessary capabilities and collaborative relationships to enable tracking and, where possible, disrupting particular operations on single or multiple platforms. This included developing research centers focused on identification and tracking, building mechanisms for multistakeholder and whole-of-society engagement, ironing out relevant areas of law many of which differ across jurisdictions, and, in some cases, creating government entities tasked with oversight on the issue.

While a full review of these developments is beyond the scope of this chapter, we see examples of the significant headway that has been made in addressing the disinformation challenge in the various governmental and nongovernmental institutions, private sector reports, open-source intelligence trackers, and other data sources cited. We are no longer operating in the dark with regard to many of the ongoing operations and campaigns. The number of trustworthy organizations engaged in researching and publicizing information concerning cyber-enabled disinformation operations has skyrocketed in Europe and the United States over the past eight years. This includes programs dedicated to tracking, exposing, and counteracting foreign disinformation campaigns, from think tank and university centers to investigative media outlets and civil society organizations, and from private sector entities to government bodies. Several countries have dedicated government bodies focused on addressing the issue at home or abroad.

But we also see here some of the gaps that have developed in Western efforts to address the problem. At first by necessity, much of this work has happened at a highly granular and forensic level – concerned with tracking particular identified operations. Also, because of the early focus on known operations targeting either domestic elections or destabilizing areas of domestic politics, the lion's share of attention has examined these national-level dynamics as end-goal targets of the cyber-enabled influence campaigns tracked. This has been challenging enough, furthermore, with national government responses often hamstrung to some degree by the phenomenon's intersection with thorny areas of domestic politics and the entanglement of foreign disinformation campaigns with domestic actors and their freedoms of expression and organizing. In other words, identifying and attempting to mitigate national and subnational operational and tactical dimensions of disinformation campaigns have posed sufficient challenges. So, the strategic orchestration of campaigns across multiple national jurisdictions – including to impact long-term interactive outcomes beyond the particular countries targeted – was, at first at least, an underappreciated dimension of the threat.

Democratic countries have thus made substantial progress in building innovative institutions and mechanisms to address the problem of foreign disinformation – including innovative defensive measures by governments, the private sector, and civil society. But these efforts still face many significant difficulties even at the national level. At the same time, evident transnational dimensions of disinformation campaigns around the COVID-19 pandemic and the war in Ukraine have drawn growing attention to the criticality of coordination on this issue across democracies in order to protect common interests, relationships, and capacity to successfully collaborate to achieve shared strategic goals.

It is not too late to better protect these objectives vis-à-vis Ukraine, but the timing is urgent. Finding adequate collaborative solutions to protect Ukraine's support coalition from adversarial disinformation will also prove broadly applicable and critical in the next phases of global strategic competition that will shape the future success of the international rule-based order and democracy.

REFERENCES

AftonBladet. (2023, January 31). SD's Russian connections are an acute security risk. *AftonBladet*. https://aftonbladet.se/debatt/a/jlKMyn/sd-s-ryska-kopplingar-ar-en-akut-sakerhetsrisk

Agency France-Presse in Warsaw. (2016, May 19). Poland detains pro-Kremlin party leader for 'spying'. *The Guardian*. https://theguardian.com/world/2016/may/19/poland-detains-pro-kremlin-party-leader-mateusz-piskorski-spying

Alan-Lee, N. (2013, April 13). *Poland's far-right advances on anti-Ukraine sentiment*. Center for European Policy Analysis (CEPA). https://cepa.org/article/polands-far-right-advances-on-anti-ukraine-sentiment/

Aleksejeva, N. (2023, February). *Narrative warfare: How the Kremlin and Russian news outlets justified a war of aggression against Ukraine*. Atlantic Council. https://atlanticcouncil.org/wp-content/uploads/2023/02/Narrative-Warfare-Final.pdf

Antezza, A., Bushnell, K., Dyussimbinov, Y., Frank, A., Frank P., Frank, L., et al. (2024, February). *Data set: Ukraine support tracker data*. Kiel Institute for the World Economy. https://ifw-kiel.de/publications/ukraine-support-tracker-data-20758/

Applebaum, A. (2020). *Twilight of democracy: The seductive lure of authoritarianism*. Doubleday.

Armstrong, K. (2023, January 21). *Turkey condemns 'vile' Sweden Quran-burning protest*. BBC. https://bbc.com/news/world-europe-64360528

Atlantic Council Digital Forensic Research Lab (DFRLab). (2023). *Undermining Ukraine: How the Kremlin employs information operations to erode global confidence in Ukraine*. Atlantic Council. https://atlanticcouncil.org/in-depth-research-reports/report/undermining-ukraine/

Belton, C. (2023, December 30). Russia is working to subvert French support for Ukraine, documents show. *The Washington Post*. https://washingtonpost.com/world/2023/12/30/france-russia-interference-far-right/

Belton, C., Mekhennet, S., & Harris, S. (2023, April 21). Kremlin tries to build antiwar coalition in Germany, documents show. *The Washington Post*. https://washingtonpost.com/world/2023/04/21/germany-russia-interference-afd-wagenknecht/

Bomprezzi, P., Dyussimbinov, Y., Frank, A., Kharitonov, I., & Trebesch, C. (n.d.). *Ukraine support tracker: A database of military, financial and humanitarian aid to Ukraine*. Kiel

Institute for the World Economy. https://ifw-kiel.de/topics/war-against-ukraine/ukraine-support-tracker/

Braw, E. (2023, September 7). A curious Quran burning in Sweden. *The Wall Street Journal*. https://wsj.com/articles/a-curious-quran-burning-in-sweden-iran-iraq-disinformation-d838afbe

Bronk, C., Collins, G., & Wallach, D. (2022, September 6). *Cyber and information warfare in Ukraine: What do we know seven months in?* Baker Institute. https://bakerinstitute.org/research/cyber-and-information-warfare-ukraine-what-do-we-know-seven-months

Bryant, M. (2023, August 6). Russia spreading false claims about Qur'an burnings to harm NATO bid, says Sweden. *The Guardian*. https://theguardian.com/world/2023/aug/06/russia-spreading-false-claims-about-quran-burnings-to-harm-nato-bid-says-sweden

Caulcutt, C. (2023, November 9). France condemns Russian disinformation campaign linked to Stars of David graffiti. *Politico*. https://politico.eu/article/france-condemns-russia-involvement-stars-of-david-graffiti/

Chiappa, C. (2023, December 11). Donald Tusk wins parliament's backing to be new polish PM. *Politico*. https://politico.eu/article/donald-tusk-parliament-backing-poland-government-vote/

Delcker, J. (2022, September 12). *Russian disinformation looms large over German writer*. DW. https://dw.com/en/russian-disinformation-threat-looms-large-over-cold-german-winter/a-63096336

DW. (2021, March 10). *Germany's far-right AfD lawmakers visit Moscow*. DW. https://dw.com/en/germanys-far-right-afd-lawmakers-visit-moscow/a-56829773

(2022, February 2). *Russia's RT blocked by German regulators*. DW. https://dw.com/en/russias-rt-channel-blocked-by-german-regulators/a-60635397#:~:text=The%20channel%2C%20called%20RT%20DE,down%20from%20Europe's%20satellite%20network

EU Disinfo Lab. (n.d.). *Doppelganger operation*. EU Disinfo Lab. https://disinfo.eu/doppelganger-operation/

EUvsDisInfo. (n.d.). *Database*. EUvsDisInfo. https://euvsdisinfo.eu/disinformation-cases/

Faiola, A., & Chapman, A. (2023, October 17). Poland election results favor the opposition in a political earthquake. *The Washington Post*. https://washingtonpost.com/world/2023/10/16/poland-elections-2023-donald-tusk/

Foy, H. (2015, March 16). Poland's pro-Russia Zmiana party urges embrace of Putin. *Financial Times*. https://ft.com/content/a088379e-cbdb-11e4-beca-00144feab7de

Franz, M. (2023, June 8). *Poland's phoney war on 'Russian saboteurs': The government commission is a McCarthyite ploy*. UnHerd. https://unherd.com/2023/06/polands-phoney-war-on-russian-saboteurs/

Gielewska, A. (2023, June 5). *Confusing smoke and fire: Russian influence in Polish politics*. VSquare. https://vsquare.org/russian-influence-poland-tusk-pis-democracy-march/

Glos Koszalinski. (2023, February 5). *Siatka prorosyjskich agentów w Europie. Wśród nich wymieniany jest Mateusz Piskorski [A network of Pro-Russian agents in Europe. Mateusz Piskorski is mentioned among them]*. Glos *Koszalinski*. https://gk24.pl/siatka-prorosyjskich-agentow-w-europie-wsrod-nich-wymieniany-jest-mateusz-piskorski/ar/c1-17263255

Gönczi, R. (2023, September 28). *Disinformation as a tool of hybrid warfare at the Polish-Belarusian border*. Warsaw Institute. https://warsawinstitute.org/disinformation-as-a-tool-of-hybtid-warfare-at-the-polish-belarusian-border/

Haag, C. (2022, September 22). *Double check: NYA Dagbladet publishes fake RAND document about Ukraine*. Logically Facts. https://logicallyfacts.com/en/analysis/double-check-nya-dagbladet-publishes-fake-rand-document-about-ukraine

(2023, February 6). *Double check: Was the Quran burning in Stockholm a Russian intelligence operation*. Logically Facts. https://logicallyfacts.com/en/analysis/double-check-was-the-quran-burning-in-stockholm-a-russian-intelligence-operation

Hadeed, M., & Sus, M. (2023). Germany and the Baltic Sea Region. *Prism*, 10(2), 149–165.

Harper, J. (2023, August 3). *Kremlin disinformation campaign targets Polish pacifist groups, analysts say*. Anadolu Ajansi. https://aa.com.tr/en/europe/kremlin-disinformation-campaign-targets-polish-pacifist-groups-analysts-say/2840124#

(2024, February 21). *Poland's farmers' leaders linked with far-right, pro-Russian party*. Anadolu Ajansi. https://aa.com.tr/en/europe/poland-s-farmers-leaders-linked-with-far-right-pro-russian-party/3143889#

Henley, J. (2023, June 28). Turkish fury as Sweden allow Qur'ran burning risks further delays to NATO bid. *The Guardian*. https://theguardian.com/world/2023/jun/28/turkey-rebuke-of-quran-burning-poses-risk-to-sweden-nato-application

Huntley, S. (2023, February 16). *Fog of war: How the Ukraine conflict transformed the cyber threat landscape*. Google Blog. https://blog.google/threat-analysis-group/fog-of-war-how-the-ukraine-conflict-transformed-the-cyber-threat-landscape/

Insikt Group. (2022, July 7). *Russian information operations aim to divide the western coalition on Ukraine*. Recorded Future. https://recordedfuture.com/blog/russian-information-operations-divide-western-coalition-ukraine

Irish, J. (2024, February 12). *European powers warn of spike in Russian propaganda before EU elections*. Reuters. https://reuters.com/world/europe/european-powers-warn-spike-russian-propaganda-before-eu-elections-2024-02-12/

Kastner, J., & Hewson, J. (2023, September 17). *Why does Eastern Germany love Putin so much?* Foreign Policy. https://foreignpolicy.com/2023/09/17/east-germany-putin-afd-misinformation/

Kerr, J. (2023, November). *Assessing Russian cyber and information warfare in Ukraine: Expectations, realities, and lessons*. CNA Corporation. https://cna.org/reports/2023/11/assessing-russian-cyber-and-information-warfare-in-ukraine

Koper, A., & Wlodarczak-Semczuk, A. (2023, December 11). *Donald Tusk appointed Polish PM, setting stage for warmer EU ties*. Reuters. https://reuters.com/world/europe/all-eyes-polish-parliament-tusk-set-become-pm-2023-12-11/

Kozłowski, A. (2022, June 1). *Disinformation in Poland on the war in Ukraine*. Casimir Pulaski Foundation. https://pulaski.pl/pulaski-policy-paper-disinformation-in-poland-on-the-war-in-ukraine/

Le Temps. (2024, February 12). Les Autorités Françaises Dévoilent un Vaste Réseau de Sites de Propagande Russe Vers l'Europe et les Etats-Unis [French authorities unveil a vast network of Russian propaganda sites to Europe and the US]. *Le Temps*. https://letemps.ch/monde/les-autorites-francaises-devoilent-un-vaste-reseau-de-sites-de-propagande-russe-vers-l-europe-et-les-etats-unis.

Legucka, A., & Bryjka, F. (2021, December 9). *Russian and Belarusian disinformation and propaganda in the context of the Polish-Belarusian border crisis*. Polish Institute of International Affairs. https://pism.pl/publications/russian-and-belarusian-disinformation-and-propaganda-in-the-context-of-the-polish-belarusian-border-crisis

Lin, H., & Kerr, J. (2019). On cyber-enabled information warfare and information operations. In P. Cornish (Ed.), *Oxford Handbook of Cybersecurity* (pp. 251–272). Oxford Handbooks.

Mazzini, M. (2024, February 1). *How the Polish anti-war movement's message entered mainstream politics*. Balkain Insight Reporting Democracy. https://balkaninsight.com/2024/02/01/how-the-polish-anti-war-movements-message-entered-mainstream-politics/

Mierzyńska, A. (2023, June 1). Rosyjskie wpływy w Polsce? Do ich odkrycia nie trzeba lex Tusk! [Russian influence in Poland? It doesn't take Lex Tusk to discover them!]. *Oko Press*. https://oko.press/rosyjskie-wplywy-lex-tusk-lista

Minder, R., & Pitel, L. (2023, May 2). The feud at the heart of Europe. *Financial Times*. https://ft.com/content/81825290-29a2-48b2-8e69-73e897dafe9d

Moilanen, P., Hautala, M., & Saari, D. (2023, May 8). *The disinformation landscape in Finland*. EU DisInfo Lab. https://disinfo.eu/publications/disinformation-landscape-in-finland/

Morozova, A., & Szczygieł, K. (2023, March 14). Skrzynka z planami Kremla [A box with Kremlin plans]. *Frontstory*. https://frontstory.pl/mateusz-piskorski-mejle-rosja-szpiegostwo-mirzakhanian/

Morris, L., Mekhennet, S., & Bisset, V. (2022, December 7). German police arrest 25 over far-right plot to overthrow government. *The Washington Post*. https://washingtonpost.com/world/2022/12/07/germany-coup-arrests-reichsbuerger-heinrich/

Nabozhniak, O., Tsekhanovska, O., Castagna, A., Khutkyy, D., & Melenchuk, A. (2023). *Revealing Russian influence in Europe: Insights from Germany, France, Italy and Ukraine*. Kyiv Institute of Innovative Governance. https://gmfus.org/sites/default/files/2024-01/revealing-russian-propaganda-3%5B71%5D.pdf

Nemečkayová, N. (2023, June 26). *Major pro-Kremlin disinformation narratives and their transmitters in Poland, Czechia, and Slovakia*. Association for International Affairs (AMO). https://amo.cz/en/strengthening-the-resilience-of-czech-slovak-and-polish-societies-prior-to-the-2024-european-parliament-elections/major-pro-kremlin-disinformation-narratives-and-their-transmitters-in-poland-czechia-and-slovakia/

NFP. (2021, June 24). *Hacking of Polish officials linked to Russian security services, says Poland*. NFP. https://notesfrompoland.com/2021/06/24/hacking-of-polish-officials-linked-to-russian-security-services-says-poland/

(2023, August 31). *Polish parliament forms Russian influence commission despite boycott and EU warning*. NFP. https://notesfrompoland.com/2023/08/31/polish-parliament-picks-members-of-russian-influence-commission-amid-opposition-boycott/

(2024, February 22). *Polish farmers' protests "possibly influenced by Russian agents," says Foreign Ministry after pro-Putin banner*. NFP. https://notesfrompoland.com/2024/02/22/polish-farmers-protests-possibly-influenced-by-russian-agents-says-foreign-ministry-after-pro-putin-banner/

Nikolskaya, P., Saito, M., Tsvetkova, M., & Zverev, A. (2023, January 3). *Pro-Putin operatives in Germany work to turn Berlin against Ukraine*. Reuters. https://reuters.com/investigates/special-report/ukraine-crisis-germany-influencers/

NYA Dagbladet. (2022, September 13). Chockerande Dokumentet: Så planerade USA Kriget Och Energikrisen i Europa [Shocking document: How the US planned the war and energy crisis in Europe]. *NYA Dagbladet [New Dagbladet]*. https://nyadagbladet.se/utrikes/chockerande-dokumentet-sa-planerade-usa-kriget-och-energikrisen-i-europa/

O'Hanlon, M. E., Stelzenmüller, C., & Wessel, D. (2024, February 20). *Ukraine index: Tracking developments in the Ukraine war*. Brookings Institution. https://brookings.edu/articles/ukraine-index-tracking-developments-in-the-ukraine-war/

Organisation for Economic Co-operation and Development (OECD). (2022, November 3). *Disinformation and Russia's war of aggression against Ukraine*. Organisation for Economic Co-operation and Development (OECD). https://oecd.org/ukraine-hub/policy-responses/disinformation-and-russia-s-war-of-aggression-against-ukraine-37186bde/

Pacula, P. (2015, March 23). New pro-Russia party emerges in Poland. *Parlementaire Monitor*. https://parlementairemonitor.nl/9353000/1/j9vvij5epmj1eyo/vjsggqulopxt?ctx=vgax lcr1jzm0&tab=1

Pawela, M. (2021, March 23). Ujawniamy: Skala Rosyjskiej Dezinformacji o COVID-19 w Polsce [We reveal: The scale of Russian misinformation about COVID-19 in Poland]. *FakeNews.pl.* https://fakenews.pl/badania/ujawniamy-skala-rosyjskiej-dezinformacji-o-covid-19-w-polsce/

RAND Corporation. (2022, September 14). *Fake RAND report on 'weakening Germany'.* RAND Corporation. https://rand.org/news/press/2022/09/14.html

Reynaud, F., & Leloup, D. (2023, June 13). 'Doppelganger': The Russian disinformation campaign denounced by France. *Le Monde.* https://lemonde.fr/en/pixels/article/2023/06/13/doppelganger-the-russian-disinformation-campaign-denounced-by-france_6031227_13.html

Reuters. (2023a, April 5). *Polish agriculture minister resigns amid anger over Ukrainian grain imports.* Reuters. https://reuters.com/world/europe/polish-agriculture-minister-resigns-amid-anger-over-ukrainian-grain-imports-2023-04-05/

(2023b, July 26). *Sweden says its target of Russia-backed disinformation over NATO, Koran burnings.* Reuters. https://reuters.com/world/europe/sweden-says-its-target-russia-backed-disinformation-over-nato-koran-burnings-2023-07-26/

Rid, T. (2020). *Active measures: The secret history of disinformation and political warfare.* Farrar, Straus, and Giroux.

Robert Lansing Institute. (2023, January 24). *Russian military intelligence operation in Sweden, besides blocking the nation's NATO membership bid, could raise the level of terrorist threat in the county.* Robert Lansing Institute. https://lansinginstitute.org/2023/01/24/russian-military-intelligence-operation-in-sweden-besides-blocking-the-nations-nato-membership-bid-could-raise-the-level-of-terrorist-threat-in-the-country/

Rogalewicz, M. (2023, September 11). *Russian disinformation about Ukranian refugees in Poland.* Warsaw Institute. https://warsawinstitute.org/russian-disinformation-about-ukrainian-refugees-in-poland/

Salvo, D. (2022, December 5). *Oh, the irony...Russia spreads disinformation about Polish annexation of Western Ukranian regions.* German Marshall Fund (GMF) Alliance for Securing Democracy. https://securingdemocracy.gmfus.org/oh-the-ironyrussia-spreads-disinformation-about-polish-annexation-of-western-ukrainian-regions/

Schmitz, R. (2023, June 14). *Poland's new Russian influence law gets flak as an attack on democracy.* NPR. https://npr.org/2023/06/14/1181674873/poland-russian-influence-law-polish-democracy

Shotter, J., & Foy, H. (2020, April 3). Ten years after the Smolensk Air Disaster, political scars remain. *Financial Times.* https://ft.com/content/41e31f96-73ac-11ea-95fe-fcd274e920ca

Spahn, S. (2020, October). *Russian media in Germany: How Russian information warfare and disinformation have affected Germany.* Friedrich Naumann Foundation for Freedom. https://freiheit.org/east-and-southeast-europe/russian-media-germany

Strzelecki, M., Siebold, S., & Koper, A. (2023, October 5). *Poland election turns Germany into punching bag, straining Western alliance.* Reuters. https://reuters.com/world/europe/poland-election-turns-germany-into-punchbag-straining-western-alliance-2023-10-05/

Texty. (2022, December 1). *The Germs of the Russian world.* Texty. https://texty.org.ua/projects/108323/germs-russian-world-who-supports-russia-europe/

The Economist. (2023a, June 1). Europe makes a show of unity with Ukraine and other neighbours. *The Economist.* https://economist.com/europe/2023/06/01/europe-makes-a-show-of-unity-with-ukraine-and-other-neighbours

(2023b, June 20). France's foreign-policy revolution. *The Economist.* https://economist.com/europe/2023/07/20/frances-foreign-policy-revolution

(2023c, July 12). NATO did not give Volodymyr Zelensky everything he wanted. *The Economist*. https://economist.com/europe/2023/07/12/nato-did-not-give-volodymyrzelensky-everything-he-wanted

(2023d, September 28). The EU is finally rebooting the enlargement machine. *The Economist*. https://economist.com/europe/2023/09/28/the-eu-is-finally-rebooting-the-enlargement-machine

Tyburski, M. (2023, October 27). *Russian disinformation war against Poland after the invasion of Ukraine*. Warsaw Institute. https://warsawinstitute.org/russian-disinformation-war-against-poland-after-the-invasion-of-ukraine/

Tymińska, A., Korpal, P., & Sek, M. (2023, April). *Przyjdą i zabiorą: Antyukraińska Mowa nienawiści na Polskim Twitterze [They will come and take: Anti-Ukrainian hate speech on Polish Twitter]*. Helsinki Foundation for Human Rights. https://hfhr.pl/publikacje/raport-przyjda-i-zabiora-antyukrainska-mowa-nienawisci-na-polskim-twitterze-

Willsher, K., & O'Carroll, L. (2024, February 12). French security experts identify Moscow-based disinformation network. *The Guardian*. https://theguardian.com/technology/2024/feb/12/french-security-experts-identify-moscow-based-disinformation-network

Zaborowski, M. (2019, May 28). The Kremlin's influence reaches Warsaw. *Visegrad Insight*. https://visegradinsight.eu/the-kremlins-influence-reaches-warsaw/

Zadroga, M. (2022, September 2). The anti-vaccine movement and pro-Russian propaganda in social media – A summary report. *Fakenews.pl*. https://fakenews.pl/en/analyzes/the-anti-vaccine-movement-and-pro-russian-propaganda-in-social-media-a-summary-report/

(2023, December). *Disinformation landscape in Poland*. EU Disinfo Lab. https://disinfo.eu/publications/disinformation-landscape-in-poland/

9

Weapons of Mass Derision

Humor, War, and Democracy

Jean Camp, Julia R. Fox, Inna Kouper, Sandra Kübler, and Maria Shardakova

In contemporary societies, the pursuit of democratic ideals is a common theme, yet the practical implementation of democracy can vary significantly, especially in non-Western cultures. This chapter delves into the Russian context, where the struggle for democracy persists in a pervasive totalitarian environment. Although Russia's attempts at democracy, initiated in the early 1990s following the dissolution of the Soviet Union, have largely failed (Graham, 2023; McFaul, 2021), many Russian citizens, particularly the younger generations, maintain hope for shedding the yoke of totalitarian rule. They engage in political activism, often through innovative means. This chapter examines how Russian citizens leverage cyber technologies, participatory media, and humor in their pursuit of democratic change. Focusing on their use of cyber humor on social media, particularly in relation to the 2022 Russian invasion in Ukraine, we aim to understand how citizens engage in democratic practices despite severe constraints on freedom of speech and dynamic information sharing. Our investigation is guided by the following research questions:

- How do Russian citizens employ humor as a vehicle for democratic change?
- What political functions does humor serve in the context of the ongoing Russo-Ukrainian war?
- How does the nature of humor differ between individuals advocating for democratic change and those supporting the autocratic regime?

This project received partial funding from the Indiana University Faculty Research Support Program, Cellular Telecommunications Industry Association (CTIA), and the Comcast Innovation Fund. The opinions, findings, and recommendations expressed in this material are solely those of the authors and do not necessarily reflect the views of Indiana University, CTIA, or Comcast. Additionally, we acknowledge support from the U.S. Department of Defense under Contract No. W52P1J2093009. This material is based on work supported by the U.S. Department of Homeland Security under Grant Award Number 17STQAC00001-07-00. The views and conclusions in this document are the authors' own and should not be interpreted as representing the official policies of the U.S. Department of Homeland Security or the U.S. Department of Defense.

We postulate that prodemocratic actors employ humor in three key ways: (1) to challenge the regime by countering its propaganda and disinformation; (2) to create a space for broad political engagement and discussion; and (3) to nurture a digital community that upholds democratic values and mitigates the sense of isolation and loneliness among its members.

THE VALUE AND FUNCTIONS OF HUMOR AND SATIRE

As Nietzsche observed, "Man alone suffers so excruciatingly in the world that he was compelled to invent laughter" (as quoted in Gruner, 1978, p. 2). Humor has evolved in humans as a means of coping with stress and adversity; by laughing at threatening events and stressful situations, we are able to displace feelings of anxiety, depression, and anger (Martin, 2007). Many humor theorists have pointed generally to the relief provided through humor, be it from physiological, psychological, or social constraints (Derks, 1996; Holland, 1982; Koller, 1988; Martin, 2007; Mulkay, 1988). Release theories of humor suggest it relieves tension and suffering by providing physiological restoration as well as psychological and emotional relief (Chafe, 2007; Davis, 1993; Hurley, Dennett, & Adams, 2011; Keith-Spiegel, 1972; Meyer, 2000).

Comic relief can keep us from acting or thinking seriously when serious responses would be counterproductive (Chafe, 2007), possibly risky (Martin, 2007), or socially restricted (Keith-Spiegel, 1972). Cohen (1999) considers this response an expression of humanity to "keep us from dying of fear or going mad" (p. 41), and Highet (1962) likens it to a medicinal effect, both in healing the wounds of social injustice and providing inoculation against further painful truths. As Koller (1988) noted, "Humor is viewed as a powerful mechanism to help individuals endure, to cope with, and to move beyond – in a word, survive – those difficulties, problems, and issues confronting them because humanity has contrived social systems and procedures that are inadequate and imperfect in meeting human needs" (p. 1).

Humorous responses also can create a safe space for social groups to confront difficult circumstances and build solidarity (Fox, 2011; Boxman-Shabtai & Shifman, 2014; Martin, 2007), particularly in times of stress when competing with other groups (Giles et al., 1996). In this way, humor can serve a dual purpose of uniting and building solidarity among those who share it while targeting others outside the group (Boxman-Shabtai & Shifman, 2014). Humor targeting others, particularly out-group members, is often used to establish the in-group's superiority, a response that not only unites but also mobilizes and creates a stronger sense of identity (La Fave, Hadddad, & Maesen, 1996; Martin, 2007; Zillmann & Cantor, 1996).

Jokes targeting others in positions of power will likely employ satire rather than superiority. By criticizing, undermining, challenging, and devaluing people or institutions in power, satire aims to fix social and political problems by using humor to hold those in power accountable (Martin, 2007; Fox & Steinberg, 2020; Highet,

1962). Satire helps to resolve structural tensions (Mulkay, 1988) and to restore social norms and values and a sense of morality (Davis, 1993; Koller, 1988).

While humor has been studied in the context of civil uprisings and repressive regimes, such as the Arab Spring and the uprisings in Syria (Anagondahalli & Khamis, 2014; Elsayed, 2016; Hatab, 2016), and historically throughout the former Soviet empire (Davies, 2007, 2010), neither its impact on information behavior nor humor as a distinguishing feature specifically of Russian propaganda and anti-war resistance narratives have been subject to the same level of examination. Such studies have not been done in the context of the Russian-speaking public sphere. Considering the hyper-connected nature of digital environments and the attempts of the Russian government to exert more control over both its domestic and international cyberspace (Wilde & Sherman, 2022), it becomes crucial to capture and understand its patterns of domestic communication and resistance to it in attempts to limit the spread of disinformation and, broader, to enable cyber peace. Identifying distinguishing features of humor in Russian online spaces will create better knowledge of the role of humor in countering propaganda and may help identify opportunities to subvert undesirable messages and amplify desirable ones.

Our core underlying hypotheses are that (1) pro- and anti-war narratives will have marked differences in their use of humor-related techniques and (2) those differences can be leveraged to detect propaganda and counternarratives and increase the effectiveness of communication responding to disinformation.

POLITICAL SPEECH IN RUSSIA

The current political situation in Russia is characterized by a high concentration of power in the hands of President Vladimir Putin and the increasing crackdown on any form of dissent, which began soon after the start of the Russo-Ukrainian war in 2014 (Freedom House, n.d.). Attempts to suppress and manipulate public opinion have been observed in Russia since the 2010s, when over fifty new laws were passed to expand censorship and surveillance, restrict freedom of speech, and prevent citizens from demanding free and transparent elections (International Federation for Human Rights, 2018). The laws enabled the government, among other things, to block websites without a court decision, monitor users of messaging services, prosecute citizens for their opinions, and suppress activities of any organization or individual under the “foreign agent” label (FIDH, n.d.).

In 2012, the law restricted the right of Russian citizens to gather in public places and introduced stricter punishment for organizing such gatherings, particularly if it leads to the disturbance of public order or interferes with traffic. Loose interpretations of public events provided law enforcement with greater freedom to detain, arrest, and fine Russian citizens, creating more fear and reluctance to participate in any public expression of opinion. The law aimed to punish not only organizers and participants but also those who disseminated information about the event (OVD-Info, n.d.).

In 2016, another round of legislation changes further restricted political and religious freedom by expanding interpretations of and punishments for extremism and terrorism and requiring telecom companies to store data on Russian servers and providing the state with access to it. The arrest and detention of leading opposition figure Alexei Navalny in January 2021 resulted in some of the largest protests in Russia and thousands of people were detained and arrested daily (Human Rights Watch, 2021). The police have also detained and threatened journalists who reported on the events, and pressured students and activists to withdraw from participation in protests and further actions (OVD-Info, 2021).

The political situation worsened in February 2022, when Russia initiated a full-scale invasion of Ukraine. Calling it a special military operation (SVO) to downplay the scale and intent, Russia occupied the eastern Ukrainian territories, launched air and missile attacks on various Ukrainian cities, including Kyiv, Odesa, Kherson, and Zaporizhzhia, and caused thousands of casualties, massive displacement, and a humanitarian crisis. Days after Russia invaded Ukraine, the Russian government made it a crime to oppose the war in public and introduced large fines and up to fifteen years in prison for spreading "false" information about Russia, its actions abroad, and its army (Tsvetkova, 2023).

"Foreign agent" legislation is used to suppress dissent – many independent media organizations and intellectuals have been designated as foreign agents, which cuts their funding, undermines their reputation and effectively removes them from the public sphere. In May 2023, the list contained almost 600 entries and included many prominent nongovernmental organizations (NGOs) as well as journalists, politicians, writers, and artists (Gogov.ru, 2022). In addition, a new national facial recognition database was expanded, increasing Russia's digital surveillance power over its citizens (Salaru, 2022). Since then, it continues to repress dissent, putting Russian citizens in jail for such offenses as holding a poster, sharing a news article on social media, or even organizing a theater performance.

In 2022 and 2023, the Russian government continued to undercut the prominent voices of opposition. In addition to arresting Navalny, they arrested Ilya Yashin and Vladimir Kara-Murza, sentencing them to eight and twenty-five years in prison, respectively (de Vogel, 2023). In March 2022, the homes of the former leaders of "Memorial," an international human rights organization founded in Russia, were raided and cases were opened against them for discrediting and rehabilitating Nazism. *Novaya Gazeta*, an independent newspaper, ceased publication in March 2022 and had its license revoked. International NGOs including Amnesty International, Human Rights Watch, and Transparency International have ended operations in Russia, and in 2022 at least twenty-two organizations were classified as "undesirable," which functionally forces them to cease operations or move abroad.

Protest exists, but in small and subversive forms. Within Russia they are most likely taking the form of a "dissident kitchen," a quasi-protest form coming from the 1950s to the 1960s Soviet times, when intelligentsia used to gather in apartments in small kitchens for a free exchange of ideas and information, including arts, scientific knowledge, and political information (Sakharov Center, n.d.). The Telegram platform and its personal channels that multiple people can subscribe to have become a form of "digital kitchen" as most other Western social media platforms have been banned in Russia. Outside of Russia, many movements try to organize and use digital platforms to protest, but their voices are rather weak and decentralized, with a significant amount of internal disagreement (Ziener, 2023).

Humor as a Political Tool in Russia

Humor can function as a form of resistance in attacking the status quo, from institutions to individuals in power (Lynch, 2002), including, specifically, communist leaders and political parties (Davies, 2007). Humor has played an important role in resistance and political activism in Russia in the context of authoritarian rule and restrictions on freedom of expression. Political activists use satire, irony, performative art, ridicule, and humorous withdrawal as ways to reconcile incongruent realities or counteract propaganda and oppression.

Satirical content in cartoons, memes, and parody videos is used as an overt tool to criticize political leaders and their policies. Russian political satire has a long tradition, dating back to the Soviet era, when humor was often used to expose the absurdities of the regime. Today, satirical content is often shared on social media platforms, where it can reach a wide audience.

Irony and sarcasm are used to subvert official narratives and highlight contradictions in government statements. For example, during the COVID-19 pandemic, Russian activists used irony to criticize the government's response to the crisis, pointing out the discrepancies between official statistics and the reality on the ground.

Performative art is also used to draw attention to political issues. For example, the feminist punk rock group Pussy Riot gained international attention in 2012 when they staged a protest performance in Moscow's Cathedral of Christ the Savior, criticizing the Orthodox Church's support for Putin and his election campaign. The performance had absurdist, mocking, and satirical elements as five female group members entered the cathedral, put on colorful balaclavas and began jumping around and punching the air on the altar steps. Later they combined the video with the song, which they entitled "Punk Prayer: Mother of God Drive Putin Away." The song invoked the name of the Virgin Mary, urging her to get rid of the then Russian Prime Minister Vladimir Putin. The song used crude analogies and obscenities to point to the connections between the Church and the government. The performance led to the arrest and prosecution of three members of Pussy Riot.

Under severe restrictions and threats of punishment and arrest, citizens in Russia developed humorous forms of protest as a way to express themselves and challenge authority while minimizing the danger. Thus, in 2011–2020, citizens organized "nanoprotests" or "toy protests" in various cities in Russia, a form of action where political participation of humans was replaced by toys (e.g., Lego toys, soft toys, or toys from Kinder eggs), and the toys were expressing their political views through slogans such as "I'm for fair elections!" and "This referendum is even more toy-like than ours" (Gogitidze, 2012). The terms and this form of action were an ironic reaction to the inability to organize "real" human protests and a reference to the ubiquitous claims that Russia is the country of advanced nanotechnologies (Nim, 2016).

Another case of ridiculing the authorities was the words auction, an online event organized by the student magazine "DOXA" to support its journalists who were arrested and charged with the involvement of minors in protests. The auction invited subscribers of DOXA channels to donate money and send editors random words. Words that received the most donations were to be included in the speeches that arrested students would give in court (@doxajournal, 2021). The money was intended for paying fines and fees for the arrested journalists (and others). The goals of this act included emphasizing the randomness of the arrests and charges and exposing the absurdity of the court and its procedures (Tyshkevich et al., 2021; random words selected by online users are in bold):

> My **freedom** of movement is limited. I can't even go to **Reutov** – my friend **honey badger** lives there, and I miss him a lot. I cannot freely go out into the city in the evening, even though for me it is critically important, because I am a **brewerosaurus**.
>
> [Ogranichena **svoboda** moego peredvizheniia. Ia ne mogu dazhe s"ezdit' v **Reutov** – tam zhivet moi drug-**medoed**, ia sil'no skuchaiu po nemu. Ia ne mogu svobodno vyiti vecherom v gorod, a dli amenia eto kriticheski vazhno, ved' ia **pivozavr**.]

The authorities understand the power of humor and try to stifle it using legal measures, surveillance, intimidation and harassment, and discreditation. Several Russian comedians were included in the list of foreign agents and had to leave the country (e.g., Galkin, Shatz). Satirical publications and websites have been shut down, and individuals have been fined or imprisoned for their satirical content. Increased surveillance and persecution also increased self-censorship, as individuals fear the consequences of sharing humorous or critical content. The Russian government has also employed disinformation and propaganda campaigns to undermine the credibility of activists and satirists. They use state-controlled media outlets to portray dissenters as unpatriotic, foreign agents, or as promoting harmful ideologies. By discrediting and marginalizing those who use humor as a tool of resistance, the authorities aim to undermine their influence and discourage others from following their lead.

Overall, despite the evidence of extensive use of humor and ridicule in the political context, it is not clear how effective humor is as a tool for resistance and political activism in Russia. It allows activists and citizens to express dissent in creative and subversive ways, but so far, its impact has not been shown to effectively challenge authority and promote change. In the context of repressive measures and violent crackdown, humor can be seen more as an individual coping mechanism rather than a tool of collective political action. Humor is an attempt to fight against the absurdity of Russian reality and counteract a sense of helplessness and defeat, information overload, and collective guilt.

Whether jokes use satire as a form of protest and resistance to harsh regimes or provide only relief rather than resistance may depend on circumstances dictating which is possible (Davies, 2007).

Russian Humor after the 2022 Invasion of Ukraine

Even before the full-scale invasion of Ukraine in 2022, the Russian media waged an information war, ridiculing the other side, undermining the legitimacy of Ukraine as a state, and portraying Ukrainians as subhuman. The media introduced and amplified the use of ethnic slurs for Ukraine and Ukrainians, one of them being a reference to the dill plant because it bears a phonetic similarity to the Russian word for Ukrainians (Berdy, 2014). In addition to the state media, thousands of regular users and hired trolls have been involved in creating and disseminating pro-Kremlin humorous content on social media.

Political dissenters have also leveraged humor to counter the Kremlin's offensive. In the wake of the invasion, wherein the Russian government enforced strict limitations on all expressions of dissent, the role of cyber humor has become increasingly pivotal. It now plays a central role in countering propaganda and disinformation, challenging the autocratic regime, trying to erode its grip on freedom of expression and human rights, and nurturing a sense of community among those who resist the government, offering them reassurance that they are not alone in their opposition efforts.

In this section, we illustrate patterns of humor use and dissemination by both Kremlin supporters and those who oppose its policies, its ideology, and its war. Additionally, we propose strategies for bolstering and amplifying the use of humor as a tool of resistance in Russia and, more broadly, as a means to foster democratic transformation.

Propaganda Humor

The Russian authorities never underestimated the effectiveness of humor in manipulating public opinion. After the invasion, the media sphere has become a battlefield where all means are fair, with war-fueled humor taking on a more acerbic

FIGURE 9.1 Post on VKontakte from Mozalevsky, D. (September 22, 2018).[1]

character. The illegitimacy of Ukraine as a state is among the central themes being pushed through humorous content by pro-Kremlin actors. Prior to the invasion, Ukraine's geopolitical borders were repeatedly called into question when countless images of a map of Ukraine flooded social media and captions urged Ukraine to follow through on its decommunization policy[2] and give up territories "gifted" to it by communist Russia. Such a map is shown in Figure 9.1. The caption under the map image of Ukraine mockingly inquires: "As part of decommunization, shouldn't gifts be returned?" The regions of Ukraine shaded in different colors are marked as "Gifts from Russian tzars 1654–1917," "A gift from Lenin, 1922," "Gifts by Stalin, 1939, 1945," "A gift by Khrushchev, 1954." The small section in the middle colored in red is identified as "Ukraine within the borders of 1654."

This example is similar to many others, as it comes from a popular Russian humorous site, fishki.net, and has been shared multiple times. However, the author of this post adds his own rich framing context by mockingly responding to another user who has the "real, authentic, 25th generation purebred representative of the Ukrainian nation with a truly Ukrainian name 'Vanya'." This exaggeratedly ironic

1 @Dmitry Mozalevsky, X (Sept. 22, 2018, 12:05 AM), https://vk.com/wall11198583_25910.

2 In 2015, the Ukrainian government passed "decommunization laws" criminalizing both the communist and Nazi totalitarian regimes and banning their symbols. The implementation of these laws included the removal of monuments, street names, and other vestiges of the communist past (Cherviatsova, 2020).

FIGURE 9.2 Post on Twitter from Lada [@_LadyLidiya] (March 21, 2022).[3]

subject line already hints at the content of the appeal: Just as the name "Vanya" is not "truly Ukrainian," but rather is often claimed to be the most authentic Russian name, so is Ukraine not a separate country, but rather a part of Russia. In a nearly 400-word appeal in this post, the author ridicules his opponent for being brainwashed and not understanding that Ukraine is the creation of "Bolshevik idiots" who arbitrarily "drew on the map with a pencil" a territory inhabited by "a bunch of different nationalities" and called it Ukraine. The author continues: "With the same success – from a hangover or, having smoked a little [weed], the Bolsheviks could unite, for example, the Pskov, Novgorod and Tver provinces – into one republic !!!))))) And name it – 'UKRAINE'!!!"

After the invasion, the tone of these messages became more ominous as the authors cynically sneered that Russia was simply implementing a decommunization program for Ukraine when it seized Ukrainian territories. Thus, in a tweet from February 2022, the user Lada provided the following retort to criticisms of Russia's aggression: "I'm sorry, but Russia is acting strictly within the framework of decommunization" (Figure 9.2). The user shared a map similar to the one in Figure 9.1 with regions of Ukraine marked as "Gifts of the Russian Tsars 1654–1917," "Lenin's gift, 1922," "Stalin's gifts, 1939, 1945," and "Khrushchev's gift, 1954."

[3] @_LadyLidiya, X (Mar. 21, 2022, 1:28 PM), https://twitter.com/_LadyLidiya/status/1505959618715004932.

FIGURE 9.3 Post on ok.ru from user "1-2nd platforms-admin dwelling. Donetsk. DNR. RF" (August 23, 2022).[4]

Other themes of pro-Kremlin humor reinforce the idea of Ukraine as a failing state. The inadequacy of Ukrainian leaders and the military, the country's servile admiration for the West, and grotesque Russophobia have become the most common topics with their own rhetoric and tropes. President Zelenskyy's comedic past has provided a rich source for comparing Ukraine to a circus. Thus, a post on the Russian platform ok.ru (Figure 9.3) shared a picture of a traveling circus colored in yellow and blue (the colors of the Ukrainian flag) with the statement "All the world's a stage, only Ukraine is a circus. Circus with clowns."

The posts on social media mocked president Zelenskyy as a clown who is under the influence of drugs (Figure 9.4) or is thirsty for blood after the invasion (Figure 9.5). In the example from Figure 9.4, the subject line is a play on words: the word "agony" is made up of two words "fire" and "I," which can be interpreted as if the author is burning with anger or as if Zelenskyy is on fire. Zelenskyy is portrayed

[4] @1-2-ая Площадки-Админпосёлок. Донецк. ДНР. РФ, X (Apr. 21, 2022), https://ok.ru/pervayaplo/topic/154090801629959.

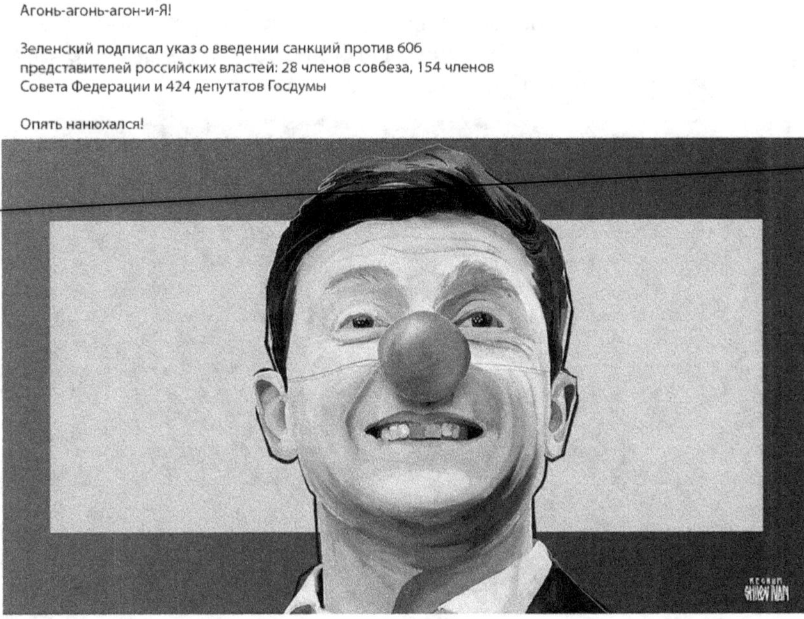

FIGURE 9.4 Post on Twitter from user Dusia Niushina [@DNusina] (September 9, 2022).[5]

as a clown high on cocaine. The text with the picture reads: “Zelenskyy signed a decree imposing sanctions against 606 representatives of the Russian authorities: 28 members of the Security Council, 154 members of the Federation Council and 424 deputies of the State Duma. Got sniffed again!”

In the example from Figure 9.5, Zelenskyy is depicted in a clown wig with a red nose added to his face, but he has bloodstains on his suit. Behind him is a war scene with a firing tank and a destroyed building. The text reads: “The bloody clown, for the sake of victory, put more than 1,200 soldiers into fertilizer, but the victory did not happen. More than 3,000 tons of scrap metal is now scattered on the outskirts of the Kherson region.”

A clown, who is supposed to make people laugh and (mostly) is considered a benign figure, is juxtaposed against the horrors of war and made into a “bloody clown” who terrorizes and kills. Zelenskyy the comedian is not funny anymore, as he is being blamed for Ukrainian suffering.

The “expectation vs reality” framing is deployed by Russian users to ridicule the Ukrainian army. The pictures shared online often put together a positive military image, such as an army of disciplined soldiers or a victorious soldier, and a mocking

5 Дуся Нюшина (@Dnusina), X (Sept. 9, 2022, 11:10 AM), https://twitter.com/dnusina/status/1568255617919328256.

FIGURE 9.5 Post on Twitter from user Saint Francesco [@saint_francesco] (August 31, 2022).[6]

negative image of impoverished destitutes or draft-dodging cowards (Figures 9.6 and 9.7).

Ukraine's relations with the West and its aspirations to become a member of the European Union (EU) and North Atlantic Treaty Organization (NATO) are regularly depicted in crude sexual clichés, as in the following joke: "Ukraine will never be a member of NATO or a member of the EU. It will only be a hole for all kinds of members."

Even a cursory analysis shows that pro-Kremlin actors weaponize humor to create a certain representation of reality and justify the Kremlin's actions. Crude and denigrating jokes depict Ukrainians as inferior, ungrateful people who betrayed their Russian brothers and sold out to the West. Easy-to-grasp, pro-Kremlin humor builds on familiar stereotypes that existed in Russia before and advances the Kremlin's political agenda while hiding the atrocities committed by the Putin regime and the Russian army or justifying them as necessary to restrain Ukraine and its people.

Resistance Humor

At the outset of the invasion, cyber humorists waged a battle against Kremlin propaganda by exposing the true nature of the incursion. Despite authorities

[6] @saint_francesco, X (Aug. 21, 2022, 5:29 AM), https://twitter.com/saint_francesco/status/1564908113630732288.

FIGURE 9.6 "Ukrainian Army. Expectation vs reality."

FIGURE 9.7 "Expectation vs reality."

consistently labeling it as a "special operation" and prohibiting the use of war-related terminology to downplay the scale of the invasion, anti-war social media channels were inundated with memes humorously advocating for the renaming of Leo Tolstoy's novel *War and Peace* to *Special Operation and Peace*. Similarly, a tweet that humorously questioned why Kremlin supporters opted for the Latin letters Z or V instead of the genuine Cyrillic "Ы" in reference to the special operation was recognized as the top ironic comment by a contributor on the Russian humor site fishki.net in 2022 (Figure 9.8). Without exploring the origins of Z and V as symbols of support for Russia's war in Ukraine (see Dean, 2022), it is important to note that the letter Ы is linked to the iconic Soviet comedy *Operation Y and Shurik's Other Adventures*, which follows a naive student Shurik and his wins over bungling criminals. The parallel between Operation Z and Operation Y exemplified in the accompanying tweet mocks the special military operation as a failed criminal scheme: "I don't fully understand why they took Z and V as symbols, two least cyrillic letters. Why not Ы?"

President Putin's speech on February 24, which marked the beginning of the invasion, has faced ongoing ridicule through satirical memes, sarcastic comments,

FIGURE 9.8 Post on Twitter from user Ladno, ya Archet [@sir_Archet] as cited on Fishki.net.[7]

and pointed jokes (anecdote). The following joke involving Russia's Defense Minister, Sergei Shoigu, and President Putin satirizes one of the central arguments of Putin's speech, specifically the call for de-Nazification in Ukraine ("Volodya" is a short pet name for "Vladimir"):

- Sergei, why are we retreating from Kherson?
- Volodya, you yourself ordered the liberation of Ukraine from fascists and Nazis.

The joke flips President Putin's argument, exposing the invasion's illegitimate and aggressive character while drawing a parallel between Russian forces and the Nazis.

Another much-derided point in Putin's speech was that Ukraine had committed genocide in the Donbas region while Russia had spent "eight long years" trying to resolve the conflict peacefully (Putin, 2022). The widely shared meme features an animated ape passionately discussing "eight years" in colloquial incorrect spelling, so much so that it has now become part of meme-arsenal.com, a Russian meme-generating site. The irreverent comparison of the President to an ape highlights the argument's absurdity, effectively discrediting it (Figure 9.9).

As Putin's leadership has come to symbolize authoritarianism, the strategy of democratic forces opposing his rule has been to constantly mock the Russian president, aiming to undermine his authority. Even minor slipups provide ample material for satirists. For example, when Putin commented at the All-Russian Youth Environmental Forum "Ecosystem. Protected Land" that Russia was the true land of the rising sun, it triggered a wave of sarcastic tweets where Russia was humorously referred to as "the land of the rising sun and setting hopes" (Figure 9.10).

7 Richard, Accurately Noted: Twitter Users Talk About Special Operations and Sanctions, *Fishki* (Mar. 9, 2022; 7:00 PM), https://fishki.net/4095110-tochno-podmecheno-polyzovateli-tvittera-rassuzhdajut-na-temu-specoperacii-i-sankcij.html.

FIGURE 9.9 Post on Pikabu.ru from user victor545.[8]

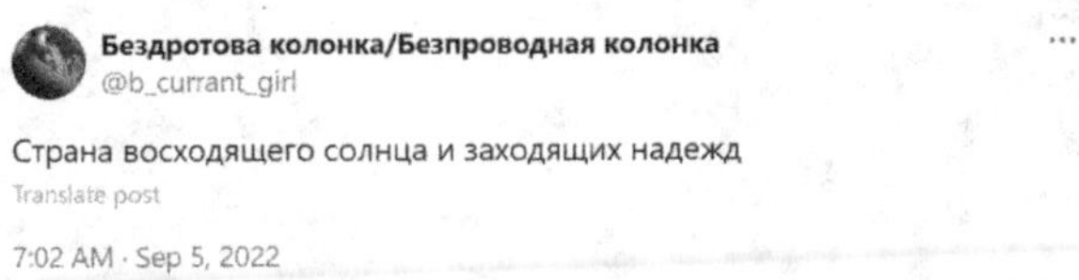

FIGURE 9.10 Post on Twitter from user Bezdrotova kolonka/Besprovodnaia kolonka [@b_currant_girl] (September 5, 2022).[9]

Some playfully accused Japan of stealing the title from Russia, along with the notion of an eternal emperor. As the text on Figure 9.11 says in response to Putin's comment, "Japan stole from Russia both the rising sun and the idea of the eternal emperor."

While personal attacks may provide entertainment and provoke strong social media reactions, opponents of Putin's autocratic regime recognize the need to target the key pillars of his power that stifle democratic processes. These include institutions, propaganda and disinformation, and constraints on freedom of speech. These subjects regularly appear in reports on the popular opposition YouTube channel "Superpower News." The channel's founder, Maxim Maltsev, is known for his unique news reporting style, characterized by irreverent gallows humor and deadpan delivery. For example, in his video posted on November 2, 2023, and titled "Thank you to those who die for Putin – Simonyan mocks Russians" (Figure 9.12), Maltsev employs gallows humor to critique the position of Russian authorities and propaganda purveyors, such as Margarita Simonyan, the editor-in-chief of the

8 @victor545, X, https://pikabu.ru/@victor545?page=2.

9 Bezdrotova kolonka/Besprovodnaia kolonka, (@b_currant_girl), X (Sept. 5, 2022), https://twitter.com/b_currant_girl/status/1566743689258569728?s=20&t=CL_8j724ubrRiasc6oWhuQ.

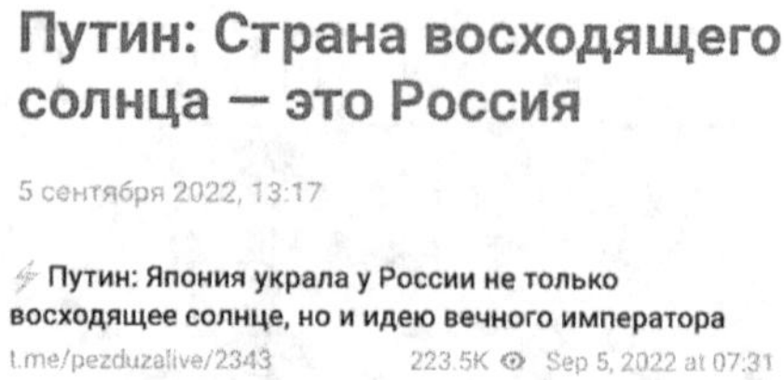

Путин: Страна восходящего солнца — это Россия

5 сентября 2022, 13:17

Путин: Япония украла у России не только восходящее солнце, но и идею вечного императора

t.me/pezduzalive/2343 223.5K Sep 5, 2022 at 07:31

FIGURE 9.11 Post on the Telegram channel "Pezduzalive" (September 5, 2022).[10]

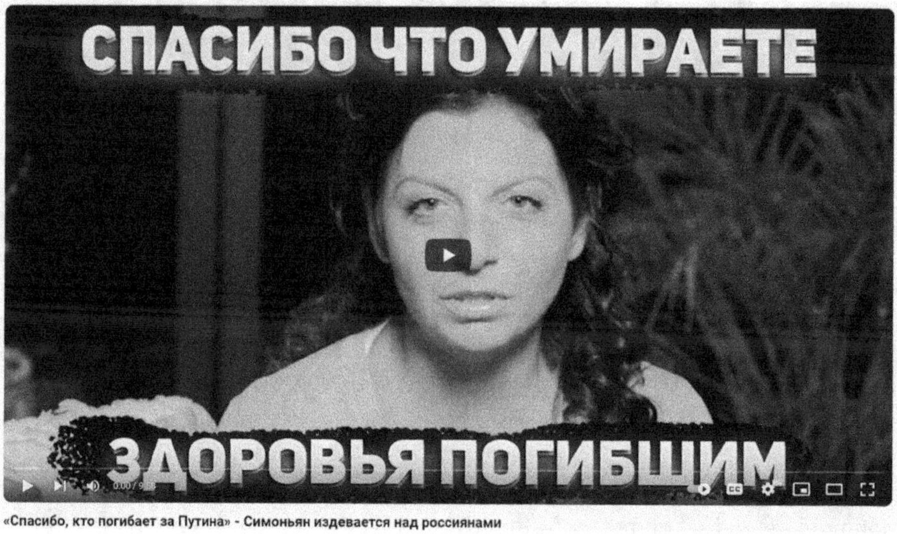

FIGURE 9.12 YouTube video "Thank you to those who die for Putin – Simonyan mocks Russians" on the channel Superpower News.[11]

state-controlled Russian broadcaster RT, often referred to as a "Kremlin mouthpiece" (e.g., see U.S. Department of State, 2022).

Simonyan justifies the war in Ukraine, claiming that everything is going according to plan and expresses gratitude to Russian citizens, including those who have given their lives for the war effort. Maltsev ironically questions the nature of the plan that requires the sacrifice of numerous Russian and Ukrainian lives. The video's title provocatively reads, "Thank you for dying. The fallen, stay healthy."

In another video (Maltsev, 2023), Maxim criticizes new Russian high school history textbooks, which he argues follow the principles of propaganda and will turn

[10] @Пездуза, X (Sept. 5, 2022, 7:31 AM), https://t.me/pezduzalive/2343.

[11] Новости СВЕРХДЕРЖАВЫ [New Superpowers], Спасибо, кто погибает за Путина Симоньян издевается над россиянами [Thank You to Those Who Die for Putin; Simonyan Mocks Russians], YouTube (Nov. 2, 2023), https://youtube.com/watch?v=RV7dsCF75WA.

FIGURE 9.13 Post on Telegram from user Ivan B. (April 2, 2022).[12]

a new generation of Russians into zombies ready to serve as cannon fodder in the Kremlin's protracted war. He wryly remarks that parents must now worry about their children getting "A" grades in history classes; poor grades, according to Maxim, are no less troublesome, because students failing history courses may find themselves promptly dispatched to the front lines.

The theme of widespread deception is a recurring one, with blame extending beyond just the Russian president, propagandists, and elites. Those who don't oppose the regime are also viewed as complicit in perpetuating lies. In April 2022, a widely popular meme was shared on the Telegram channel "Most na Zhepi," targeting those who refuse to acknowledge the truth. The image features a cat that obviously has eaten a good chunk from a tray of cold cuts and yet the captions read "Not everything is so clear" and "We don't know the whole truth," referring to very common retorts against the statements that Russia invaded Ukraine and waged a brutal unfair war (Figure 9.13).

Since its posting, this image has been widely shared and adapted across various social media platforms. In one follow-up, a post mockingly deployed propaganda tropes, claiming that if we get to the bottom of it, there are at least five plausible explanations: (1) the ham took a bite of itself; (2) the cat defended the ham from the owner by eating it; (3) picture is a fake and represents an information war between the cat and the ham; (4) we are not experts in ham and therefore it is difficult to say what the picture shows; and (5) they said on TV that it was not the cat (Figure 9.14).

[12] @Мост на Жепи, Telegram (Apr. 2, 2022, 1:22 AM), https://t.me/most_na/7212.

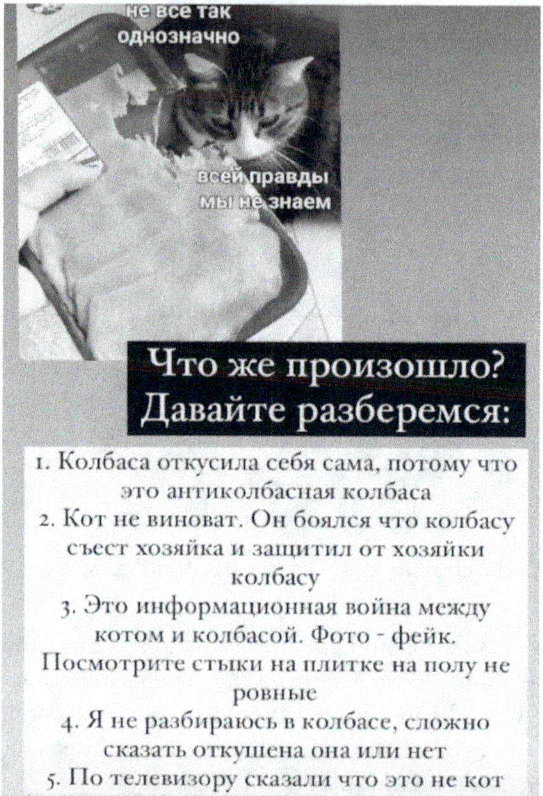

FIGURE 9.14 Post on Twitter from user Helgi Oiisac [@HelgiOiisac] (April 5, 2022).[13]

As the war continues, there is an increasing trend of humorous posts targeting ordinary Russian citizens (Arkhipova, 2023). This upsurge in self-deprecating humor represents a strategic shift in the efforts of prodemocratic forces. They aim to dissuade people from complying with the Kremlin's orders by publicly shaming them for their complicity. An example of this self-deprecating humor is a joke about Russian soldiers supposedly fighting alongside the Nazis, subverting the commonly held patriotic trope of victory over fascism. This joke irreverently challenges Putin's narrative of de-Nazification in Ukraine while simultaneously accusing ordinary Russians of supporting an unlawful war:

- Good afternoon! You are summoned to the military recruiting office.
- And with whom will we fight?

[13] Анна Красюк [Anna Krasiuk], «Все не так однозначно»: хозяева «не знают всей правды» о краденой еде и порванных обоях ["Everything Is Not So Simple": The Owners "Don't Know the Whole Truth" About Stolen Food and Torn Wallpaper], *Afisha Daily* (Apr. 12, 2022, 3:37 PM), https://daily.afisha.ru/infoporn/22793-vse-ne-tak-odnoznachno-hozyaeva-ne-znayut-vsey-pravdy-o-kradenoy-ede-i-porvannyh-oboyah/.

- With the Nazis, of course!
- And against whom?

Stalin-era self-deprecating jokes that emphasized the powerlessness of the common person have been recycled to reflect the new Russian realities. To cope with the fear of being rounded up, labeled "foreign agents," or thrown in jail, people invoke the jokes from World War II:

- Tell me, what concentration camp are we being taken to?
- I don't know, I'm not interested in politics.

The joke mocks the neutrality of those citizens who claim that they are not interested in politics to avoid discussions about collective responsibility and civic duties. The person who is not interested in politics ignores what is going on around them and eventually ends up in a concentration camp, one of the most horrendous places where humans are tortured and killed in large numbers. Lack of interest in politics can eventually lead to one's own demise.

This self-deprecating humor serves multiple social functions, primarily offering humorists and those who share their content a feeling of cognitive independence in a political environment where such independence is unattainable (cf., Wisse, 2013). Although this diverse online community may not directly confront the regime, it unmistakably and audibly rejects the regime's values and ideology, and it also mobilizes new followers.

The ongoing struggle for democratic change in Russia, involving both pro- and anti-war forces, is incomplete without considering the Russian émigré community, which has grown significantly as many Russians leave the country (van Brugen, 2022). Unburdened by the fear of persecution for criticizing the regime, this expanding Russian diaspora openly mocks Russian authorities, including President Putin, underscoring the groundlessness of the official Russian narrative.

An example of this irreverent humor is the Propaganda Review series hosted on the YouTube Navalny Live channel. In this series, presenter Anton Pikuli (Ustimov) gives sarcastic reviews of Russian news, mocking the absurdity of Putin's regime. In a video posted on March 26, 2022 (Figure 9.15), Anton Pikuli reports on the official rally "For a World Without Nazism" that took place in Moscow three weeks after the invasion to commemorate the eighth anniversary of the annexation of Crimea. More than 200,000 people attended the event, as Putin delivered a speech praising Russian troops fighting in Ukraine. Pikuli ridicules the event, commenting that "tens of thousands of civil servants" were forcibly rounded up by the authorities "to create the illusion of support for Putin." These people "were under the gunpoint of snipers, who apparently protected Putin from excessive support from the Russians." In his series, Pikuli creates an advantageous subjective position for his viewers, who, at least for a moment, are freed from their fear and frustration and can laugh at authority. The episode was viewed by 1.4 million people, which is the average for

FIGURE 9.15 Anton Pikuli (Ustimov) hosts the YouTube series Propaganda Review on the Navalny Live channel.[14]

this series. The blogger has been declared a "foreign agent" by the Russian Federation Ministry of Justice.

The irreverent irony culminates in the widely popular animated online series *Masyanya*, in which the female protagonist comes to Putin, showers elaborate profanity on the president for attacking Ukraine, and leaves him a Japanese sword so he can kill himself (Figure 9.16). The audience experiences cathartic relief when Masyanya returns safely to her apartment, where her boyfriend shares with her the happy news that the war is over. Over 6 million people watched the episode within a few weeks of its release, marveling at the possibility of Russia freeing itself from Putin's tyranny and ending the war. The Russian media regulator Roskomnadzor banned the series, claiming that it "contains false information" and "discredits the Russian armed forces" (Current Time, 2022).

When viewed through the prism of democratic processes, cyber humor serves multiple functions, ranging from attempts at eroding autocratic structures to facilitating the broader dissemination of information and fostering a digital community of individuals who might otherwise have experienced a sense of fragmentation and isolation – precisely the conditions totalitarian regimes seek to impose on their citizens (Desmet, 2022).

DISCUSSION

Our analysis reveals that prodemocratic forces in Russia persist in their struggle against autocracy amid Russia's ongoing war with Ukraine. Faced with increasingly

[14] Навальный LIVE [Navalny LIVE], Концерт «Za Voйну» и биолаборатории НАТО | Обзор Пропаганды [Concert "For Voynu" and NATO Biological Laboratories | Propganda Review], YouTube (Mar. 26, 2022), https://youtube.com/watch?v=mQp_bRqVgOY&t=605s.

FIGURE 9.16 *Masyanya*, Episode 160 on YouTube. "Masyanya is trying to solve the war situation."[15]

strict censorship laws and the criminalization of dissent against the Russian authorities, this conflict between pro- and antidemocratic forces has shifted to the online sphere, with social media evolving into a battleground where humor is wielded as a potent weapon in a high-censorship environment, as its seemingly shallow surface reveals underlying truths (Fox, 2011).

Humor creates opportunities for political engagement in Russia. Both pro-Kremlin actors and their opponents use humor to construct social reality, connect with people on an emotional level, and influence the audience's political behavior. Recognizing the power of humor, the Russian authorities are trying to maintain a monopoly on political humor through heavy censorship and legal restrictions. Despite significant obstacles, dissent is still audible on Russian social media, and the postwar Russian diaspora is leading the way, openly challenging Russian official discourse and propaganda.

The creators of both propaganda humor and resistance humor are equally adept at recycling and generating Soviet-style jokes (anekdots) originally intended for oral distribution, while also adopting the styles and formats of modern social networks, including images, videos, and multimedia. The two most popular media spaces for sharing humor are Twitter (now called "X") and VKontakte.

The key differences between propaganda humor and resistance humor lie in their themes, targets, preferred types, and the subject positions afforded by humorous narratives. Propaganda humor is directed outward, dealing aggressive blows to the enemies of the state – Ukraine, its leaders, military, and people. Disaffiliating,

[15] Masyanya Kuvaeva, *Masyanya*. Episode 160. Wakizashi, YouTube (Mar. 21, 2022), https://youtube.com/watch?v=kzx_N8AJiKw.

aggressive humor helps the Russian regime divide society and dehumanize its opponents. The preferred types of propagandistic humor are mockery and parody, as these forms of humor provide a position of superiority for propagandists to cast judgment upon the targets of their humor.

We found two types of resistance humor in our data – inwardly directed and outwardly directed. Inwardly directed, self-deprecating humor makes up a large part of the political humor shared on Twitter and VKontakte. People laugh at themselves to cope with a harsh reality when their lives are uprooted, their sons are drafted into the army, and they find themselves in a police state worse than the USSR. Self-deprecating humor draws on a long tradition of Soviet oral jokes, repurposing them for new media; this humor provides temporary relief and creates a sense of camaraderie between people. This humor also shames people for their passivity and complicity with the regime, thereby encouraging the audience to oppose the regime, even if not overtly.

The combative outward humor has become a staple of the political humor of the Russian diaspora, actively challenging and subverting government pro-war narratives and propaganda. This humor attacks Putin, Russian authorities and institutions, mobilizing people and giving them hope.

CONCLUSION AND FUTURE STEPS

Many reports detail Russia's use of algorithms, bots, trolls, and other technical means to manipulate global narratives, disrupt democratic processes, meddle in elections, distort information sharing, and normalize cyberbullying and disinformation. Less documented is the ongoing struggle by democratic forces within Russia, the human impact of information warfare, or the sociocultural aspects of competing narratives surrounding the war, including nuanced patterns of Russian discussions about the war across multimodal social media, in particular the use of humor in those competing narratives.

Understanding communication tactics and the interplay between actors, their messages, and behaviors within Russian-speaking social media spaces is crucial. Such understanding can help refine strategies and increase precision in countering Russian (mis)information power, ultimately amplifying dissenting voices in Russia and advancing the democratic agenda. The interplay of censorship, language dependencies, and historical preferences has created a unique information ecosystem in Russia. Knowledge of communication patterns among Russian-speaking users, including the use of humor, will guide the development of counternarratives to combat Russian propaganda. As Ukraine President Volodymyr Zelenskyy, himself a former comedian, said in a 2022 interview, Russian President Vladimir Putin is afraid of humor because comedy is a "powerful weapon" for spreading truth.

Further understanding of the role of humor in defeating misinformation and advancing the goals of democracy will contribute not only to creating models that assess the expected outcomes of online propaganda and resistance techniques in

Russian-speaking social media spaces, but, more broadly, will also expand understanding of how various information ecosystems shape narratives. As a clandestine instrument, humor can be particularly effective in resisting propaganda and promoting democratic processes in a high-censorship environment of authoritarian, restrictive nondemocratic systems as well as in emergent democracies, including former Soviet states such as Georgia, where many Ukrainian refugees and Russian draft evaders fled after the invasion. Although there has been strong public support in Georgia for joining the EU and NATO, there is growing pessimism there about democratic backsliding and Russian influence has increased there since the invasion of Ukraine (Fix & Kapp, 2023). Russian-speaking citizens in Georgia and other emerging democracies in that region are exposed to Russian propaganda and may also be reading Russian-language posts resisting official narratives. Humor in those messages may support Russian-speaking citizens in emerging democracies in the region by showing solidarity, thus fostering global cyber communities against authoritarianism. This line of research may also suggest different ways in which humor can be used in various misinformation contexts in American and other democratic societies' low-censorship social media environments.

Finally, while humor has the potential to bolster resistance to propaganda and thus promote cyber peace and the resilience of democratic institutions, it should be noted, as demonstrated here, that it can also be used for nefarious purposes as a tool to manipulate opinion in support of pro-war and antidemocratic propaganda, particularly as it operates on an emotional rather than a rational level.

REFERENCES

@doxajournal. (2021). [Post]. https://t.me/doxajournal/8817

Anagondahalli, D., & Khamis, S. (2014). Mubarak framed! Humor and political activism before and during the Egyptian Revolution. *Arab Media & Society*, 19, 1–16. https://files.ethz.ch/isn/184970/20140924113801_Khamis_HumorandPoliticalActivism_Final.pdf

Arkhipova, A. (2023, December 22). *The humor of the "Russian hanged men" in 2022: How anecdotes and jokes have changed after February 24 [Iumor russkikh visel'nikov v 2022: kak izmenilis' anekdoty i shutki posle 24 fevralia]* Cherta. https://cherta.media/interview/anekdoty-i-yumor-vo-vremya-vojny/

Berdy, M. A. (2014, July 24). Talking smack about Ukrainians and Russians. *The Moscow Times*. https://themoscowtimes.com/2014/07/24/talking-smack-about-ukrainians-and-russians-a37647

Boxman-Shabtai, L., & Shifman, L. (2014). Evasive targets: Deciphering polysemy in mediated humor. *Journal of Communication*, 64(5), 977–998. https://doi.org/10.1111/jcom.12116

Chafe, W. (2007). *The importance of not being earnest: The feeling behind laughter and humor*. John Benjamins.

Cherviatsova, A. (2020). On the frontline of European memory wars: Memory laws and policy in Ukraine. *European Papers*, 5(1), 119–136.

Cohen, T. (1999). *Jokes: Philosophical thoughts on joking matters*. The University of Chicago Press.

Current Time. (2022, March 29). *Russian media regulator bans cartoon about war in Ukraine*. RadioFreeEurope/RadioLiberty. https://rferl.org/a/roskomnadzor-bans-cartoon-ukraine-war/31776410.html

Davies, C. (2007). Humour and protest: Jokes under communism. *International Review of Social History*, 52(S15), 291–305. https://jstor.org/stable/26405495

(2010). Jokes as the truth about Soviet socialism. *Folklore*, 46, 9–32. https://doi.org/10.7592/FEJF2010.46.davies

Davis, M. S. (1993). *What's so funny? The comic conception of culture and society*. The University of Chicago Press.

Dean, J. (2022, March 9). *The letter Z is becoming a symbol of Russia's war in Ukraine. But what does it mean?* NPR. Special Series: Ukraine invasion – explained. https://npr.org/2022/03/09/1085471200/the-letter-z-russia-ukraine

Derks, P. (1996). Introduction to the transaction edition – Twenty Years of humor: A view from the edge. In A. J. Chapman and H. C. Foot (Eds.), *Humor and laughter: Theory, research, and applications* (pp. vii–xxv). Transaction Publishers.

Desmet, M. (2022). *The psychology of totalitarianism*. Chelsea Green Publishing.

de Vogel, S. (2023, April 28). Russia: A war with no end. *Dissent Magazine*. https://dissentmagazine.org/online_articles/russia-war-with-no-end

Elsayed, Y. (2016). Laughing through change: Subversive humor in online videos of Arab youth. *International Journal of Communication*, 10, 5102–5122. https://ijoc.org/index/php/ijoc/article/view/4795/1816

FIDH. (n.d.). *Table illustrating legislative crackdown on rights and freedoms of the civil society in Russia since 2012*. FIDH. https://fidh.org/IMG/pdf/tableau_russie_web_paysage_v2-2.pdf

Fix, L., & Kapp, C. (2023, June 21). *The dangers of democratic backsliding in Georgia*. Council on Foreign Relations. https://cfr.org/article/dangers-democratic-backsliding-georgia

Fox, J. R. (2011). Wise fools: Jon Stewart and Stephen Colbert as modern-day jesters in the American court. In A. Amarasingam (Ed.), *The Stewart/Colbert Effect: Essays on the real impacts of fake news* (pp. 136–148). McFarland & Co.

Fox, J. R., & Steinberg, E. (2020). News you can't use: Jon Stewart's Daily Show media critiques. *Journalism & Mass Communication Quarterly*, 97(1), 235–256. https://doi.org/10.1177/1077699019851228

Freedom House. (n.d.). *Russia*. Freedom House. https://freedomhouse.org/country/russia

Giles, H., Bourhis, R. Y., Gadfield, N. J., Davies, G. J., & Davies, A. P. (1996). Cognitive aspects of humor in social interaction: A model and some linguistic data. In A. J. Chapman and H. C. Foot (Eds.), *Humor and laughter: Theory, research, and applications* (pp. 139–154). Routlege.

Gogitidze, K. (2012, January 27). *Authorities take interest in toy rallies [Vlasti zainteresovalis' igrushechnymi mitingami]*. BBC News Russian Service. https://bbc.com/russian/russia/2012/01/120127_barnaul_nanomeeting_toys_rally

Gogov.ru. (2022, April 21). *Register of foreign agents in Russia*. [*Reestr inostrannykh agentov v Rossii*]. Gogov.ru. https://gogov.ru/articles/inagenty-21apr22https://gogov.ru/articles/inagenty-21apr22

Graham, T. (2023, March 7). *The precarious future of Russian democracy*. Council on Foreign Relations. https://cfr.org/article/precarious-future-russian-democracy

Gruner, C. R. (1978). *Understanding laughter: The workings of wit & humor*.Nelson-Hall.

Hatab, W. A. (2016). The Arab spring: A new era of humor consumption and production. *International Journal of English Linguistics*, 6(3), 70–87. https://doi.org/10.5539/ijel.v6n3p70

Highet, G. (1962). *The anatomy of satire*. Princeton University Press.

Holland, N. N. (1982). *Laughing*. Cornell University Press.

Human Rights Watch. (2021, January 25). *Russia: Police detain thousands in pro-Navalny protests*. Human Rights Watch. https://hrw.org/news/2021/01/25/russia-police-detain-thousands-pro-navalny-protests

Hurley, M. M., Dennett, D. C., & Adams, R. B. (2011). *Inside jokes: Using humor to reverse-engineer the mind*. The MIT Press.

International Federation for Human Rights. (2018, November 3). *Russia: 2012–2018: 50 anti-democracy laws entered into force*. International Federation for Human Rights. https://fidh.org/en/region/europe-central-asia/russia/russia-2012-2018-50-anti-democracy-laws-entered-into-force-within

Keith-Spiegel, P. (1972). Early conception of humor: Varieties and issue. In J. H. Goldstein and P. E. McGhee (Eds.), *The psychology of humor: Theoretical perspectives and empirical issues* (pp. 4–39). Academic Press.

Koller, M R. (1988). *Humor and society: Explorations in the sociology of humor*. Cap and Gown Press.

La Fave, L., Hadddad, J., & Maesen, W. A. (1996). Superiority, enhanced self-esteem, and perceived incongruity humour theory. In A. J. Chapman and H. C. Foot (Eds.), *Humor and laughter: Theory, research, and applications* (pp. 63–91). Transaction Publishers.

Lynch, O. (2002). Humorous communication: Finding a place for humor in communication research. *Communication Theory*, 12(4), 423–445. https://doi.org/10.1111/j.1468-2885.2002.tb00277.x

Maltsev, M. (2023, August 11). *If you don't pass history, you go to the front. Propaganda came to school*. Superpower News. YouTube. https://youtube.com/shorts/VQ19JQH1UmM

Martin, R. A. (2007). *The psychology of humor: An integrative approach*. Elsevier Academic Press.

McFaul, M. (2021). Russia's road to autocracy. *Journal of Democracy*, 32(4), 11–26. https://journalofdemocracy.org/articles/russias-road-to-autocracy/

Meyer, J. (2000). Humor as a double-edged sword: Four functions of humor in communication. *Communication Theory*, 10(3), 310–331. https://doi.org/10.1111/j.1468–2885.2000.tb00194.x

Mulkay, M. (1988). *On humor: Its nature and its place in modern society*. Basil Blackwell.

Nim, E. (2016). "I Can Haz Toy Protezt": In search of a theory of social movement mediatization ["Igrushko mitingue": v poiskakh teorii mediatizatsii grazhdanskogo protesta]. *Journal of Social Politics Research [Zhurnal issledovaniy sotsialnoy politiki]*, 14(1), 55–70.

OVD-Info. (2021). *Suppression of rallies in support of Alexei Navalny: January 17 and 18, 2021*. OVD-Info. https://en.ovdinfo.org/suppression-rallies-support-alexei-navalny-january-17-and-18-2021

(n.d.). *Freedom of assembly in the digital age*. OVD-Info. https://en.ovdinfo.org/freedom-of-assembly-in-the-digital-age-en

Putin, V. (2022, February 24). *Text of the address by Russian President Vladimir Putin [Tekst obraschenia presidenta Rossii Vladimira Putina]*. RIA Novosti. https://ria.ru/20220224/obraschenie-1774658619.html

Salaru, D. (2022). *Russia: Facial recognition software used to target journalists*. International Press Institute. https://ipi.media/russia-facial-recognition-software-used-to-target-journalists/

Sakharov Center. (n.d.). *Resistance to unfreedom in the USSR [Soprotivlenie nesvobode v SSSR]*. Sakharov Center. https://sakharov-center.ru/node/11682

Tsvetkova, M. (2023, May 18). Russia expands laws to criminalize fake news. *Politico*. https://politico.eu/article/russia-expand-laws-criminalize-fake-news/

Tyshkevich, N., Gutnikova, A., Metelkin, V., Aramyan, A. & chitatel_nitsy DOXA (2021, October 12). *Brewerosaurus from Lytkarino [Pivozavr is Lytkarino]*. https://web.archive.org/web/20240131154805/https://doxajournal.ru/pivozavr_from_lytkarino

U.S. Department of State. (2022, August 31). *Faces of Kremlin Propaganda: Margarita Simonyan*. U.S. Department of State. https://state.gov/disarming-disinformation/faces-of-kremlin-propaganda-margarita-simonyan/

van Brugen, I. (2022. October 4). Putin's mobilization backfires as 370,000 flee Russia in two weeks. *Newsweek*. https://newsweek.com/putin-mobilization-backfires-russians-flee-kazakhstan-georgia-eu-1748771

Wilde, G., & Sherman, J. (2022). *Putins internet plan: Dependency with a veneer of sovereignty*. Brookings Institution. https://coilink.org/20.500.12592/hgcvhn

Wisse, R. (2013). *No joke: Making Jewish humor*. Princeton University Press.

Ziener, M. (2023, February 22). *Russia's opposition is united against Putin but divided over basically everything else*. NBC News. https://nbcnews.com/news/world/russia-putin-navalny-opposition-divided-ukraine-war-rcna71242

Zillmann, D., & Cantor, J. R. (1996). A disposition theory of humour and mirth. In A. J. Chapman and H. C. Foot (Eds.), *Humor and laughter: Theory, research, and applications* (pp. 93–115). Transaction Publishers.

10

Election Cyber Threats in Central Asia

A Multistakeholder Approach to Tackling Election Interference and Increasing Resilience

Pavlina Pavlova

INTRODUCTION

The Central Asian region comprises a complex historical, political, social, and cultural landscape. The five countries – Kazakhstan, Kyrgyzstan, Tajikistan, Turkmenistan, and Uzbekistan – are located at the nexus of Russia, China, South Asia, and the Middle East. Having been part of the Soviet Union, Central Asian republics entered the Commonwealth of Independent States after the bloc's disintegration in 1991. Turkmenistan reduced its involvement to an associate membership in 2005 and the country maintained a status of permanent neutrality (Mite, 2005). Kazakhstan, Kyrgyzstan, Tajikistan, and Uzbekistan have participated in the security and economic Russia-led organizations. The Collective Security Treaty Organization (CSTO) currently comprises Kazakhstan, Kyrgyzstan, and Tajikistan. Uzbekistan suspended its membership in 2012 (RFE/RL, 2012). The Eurasian Economic Union (EAEU) has Kazakhstan and Kyrgyzstan as full members and Uzbekistan gained observer status to the EAEU in 2020 (Aidarkhanova, 2023). The region's traditionally strong relations with Russia have seen competing interests and prominently a shift towards closer cooperation with China and diversification of international partnerships. Economic ties and trade with China have intensified with the Belt and Road Initiative, alongside security cooperation, including in the Shanghai Cooperation Organization (SCO). Kazakhstan, Kyrgyzstan, Tajikistan, and Uzbekistan are among CSO members, together with China, Russia, and more recently India, Pakistan, Iran and Belarus (Kassenova, 2022). The US deepened its engagement in Central Asia as a response to the war in Afghanistan, and the region has been dealing with the fallout from the Taliban takeover (Putz, 2023; Temnycky, 2023). The US commitment has transitioned from primarily security-focused interests to a broader diplomatic and economic strategy, such as the C5+1 diplomatic platform serving as a multilateral dialogue initiative (U.S. Department of State, 2023).

Central Asia is at a critical demographic juncture with a combined population of more than 78 million people, which is young and growing. Young people under thirty years old constitute more than 50 percent of the population, which is set to form a strong labor force in a growingly digitalized society (UNODC, 2023). The strategically positioned region has unequally distributed oil and gas reserves, Kazakhstan and Turkmenistan possess the majority of the hydrocarbon resources, and deposits of critical minerals that attract international cooperation. The armed conflict in Ukraine reinforced the diversification of economic and security alliances and catalyzed reconsiderations about Russia's role in the region. While the regional dependencies remain strong, Moscow is viewed with increased suspicion (Freeman, Helf, & McFarland, 2023; Hess, 2023). The Central Asian leaders have distanced their rhetoric from Russia concerning the war against Ukraine. The countries declined to recognize the annexation of Ukrainian territories, officially complied with sanctions against Russia, and declared support for Ukraine's territorial integrity (Freedom House, 2023b).

After more than three decades since gaining independence, efforts toward democratic reforms in Central Asia have shown limited progress. Regional approaches to the rule of law, democratic institutions and processes, and the protection of human rights and fundamental freedoms remain distorted. The Central Asian republics move on the spectrum from authoritarian-leaning countries to consolidated autocracies. According to Freedom House's "Freedom in the World" (2023b) report, all five states are considered "not free." Kyrgyzstan is regarded as the only democracy in the region, but the country has gradually shifted towards authoritarianism. On the other side of the democratic spectrum is Turkmenistan, a repressive authoritarian state where political rights and civil liberties are largely denied. Governing structures reflect in online spaces. Assessing internet freedom status, Freedom House (2023c) categorizes Kyrgyzstan as "partly free," Kazakhstan and Uzbekistan as "not free," and no data is available for Tajikistan or Turkmenistan.

Despite the negative outlook, some democratic processes have become more pluralistic, mainly because countries prioritize economic modernization, development of digital infrastructure and services, and attracting foreign investments. However, elections as critical markers of democratic progress remain uncontested. The incumbent administrations use various forms of suppression, including digital repression, to ensure that opposition candidates and parties do not gain viable support or political traction. Prospects for a grassroots change are negligible, which translates into the voting results. The key election questions remain the size of the regime-chosen candidates winning the vote and the size of the turnout. For illustration, in the November 2022 presidential election in Kazakhstan, incumbent President Kassym-Jomart Tokayev won with over 81.3 percent of the votes, with turnout reported at 69.4 percent (OSCE & ODIHR, 2022b), while in Uzbekistan's presidential election in July 2023, incumbent President Mirziyoyev won with an 87.1 percent share and voter turnout of 79.8 percent (OSCE & ODIHR, 2023). Turkmen presidential elections in March 2022 saw the office passed from father to son when Serdar Berdimuhamedow was elected with 73 percent of the votes and a 97.2 percent voter turnout (Vershinin, 2022).

Amid the efforts to exert control over election results, the digital environment has emerged as a vital operational domain. In this respect, the Central Asian republics are part of a broader trend present in authoritatively leaning countries. Information autocracies, as observed by Sergei Guriev and Daniel Treisman (2019), use technology to control the online information space. These regimes display a track record of restrictive policies, especially around elections and referendums, leveraging the state control of the internet infrastructure and the influence governments exercise over digital service providers operating in their jurisdictions. While tendencies toward digital authoritarianism are present in all five countries, Central Asia is not a monolithic space. States display several national specifics depending on the available tools and resources, sociopolitical contexts, and strategic objectives. Kazakhstan, Kyrgyzstan, and Uzbekistan enjoy comparably open online space in contrast to Tajikistan, where online information and communication are heavily restricted and subject to government control, and Turkmenistan, which has pursued a stringent and centralized approach to internet control through a combination of offline and online measures that maintain a highly sterilized online environment (Muhamedov & Buralkiyeva, 2023).

Electoral processes worldwide are increasingly vulnerable to cyber-enabled interference originating from abroad. Perpetrators harness the power of social media and messaging platforms to disseminate fake news and disinformation, conduct disruptive attacks on governmental services, electoral and related critical infrastructure, breach and leak data, penetrate candidates' online accounts or conduct espionage to gain strategic advantage (ASPI, 2019; Van der Staak & Wolf, 2019). Such interference can impact elections both directly and indirectly, by eroding trust in democratic processes and institutions over the long term. The 2016 US presidential election stress-tested the influence of online intrusion, particularly when carried out by threat actors affiliated or sponsored by adversarial states (United States Senate, 2017). Reports on foreign interference have been growing ever since with malicious actors expanding tactics, techniques, and targets. For example, in a statement from December 2023, the British government condemned Russia's attempts to target high-profile individuals and entities through cyber operations with the intent to use hacked information to interfere in the national democratic processes. The data breach was attributed to a group within Russia's intelligence services, and reportedly involved several years of spear-phishing campaigns prominently targeting parliamentarians, as well as universities, think tanks, journalists, public sector, and civil society organizations (UK Government, 2023).

The second section examines the domestic and foreign cyber-enabled election interference in the region in further detail. National case studies are analyzed and positioned against the backdrop of global trends and regional practices. The presented examples are not exhaustive and serve as a representative snapshot. The third section considers potential incentives for governments to secure electoral infrastructure and wider democratic processes, including strengthening respective digital ecosystems. The final section offers policy recommendations to protect electoral integrity, enhance cyber resilience, and bolster accountability, which extend to states, international and regional bodies, the private sector, and civil society.

CYBER THREATS TO ELECTION INTEGRITY

Network Interference

The Central Asian republics control, monitor, and manipulate online information around elections and other politically charged events. As early as February 2005, the Citizen Lab (Deibert, 2005) reported that Kyrgyz websites belonging to political parties and independent media were subject to hacking during the parliamentary election. The pattern of recorded failures pointed to deliberate interference with access to online sources (OpenNet Initiative, 2005). Influenced by the Russian and Chinese models of information control (Weber, 2019), governments in the region employ a plethora of restrictive measures to silence political dissent or discontent and censor the media and civil society voices. Several connected tactics are used to restrict access to online information, including blocking content and throttling or shutting down networks (Muhamedov & Buralkiyeva, 2023).

Internet shutdowns are an extreme form of digital censorship. Authorities in Turkmenistan have been particularly prone to imposing large-scale blackouts. The country is a repeated offender using censorship when the electorate votes and keeping tight control over the online information space as a preventive measure. Recent incidents were reported by Access Now (2023b) around protests in December 2021 and during the March 2022 presidential elections when the citizens were plunged into digital darkness. Kazakhstan has also repeatedly switched off the internet amid elections and protests. The most severe internet shutdowns to this date were imposed as a reaction to the massive protests in January 2022 when Kazakhstani authorities initiated a country-wide blackout to curb the unrest. The government also disrupted internet access around extraordinary presidential elections in November 2022, accompanied by targeted blocking of social media and communications platforms (Access Now, 2023a). From a legal perspective, governments justify internet shutdowns with provisions on anti-terrorism and public security under their domestic law. On the technical level, close to complete shutdowns are enabled by centralized state control and influence over large segments of telecommunication infrastructure providing internet services (Pavlova, 2022).

Selectively blocking access to online content is a widespread practice across Central Asia. According to Freedom House (2023a), Turkmenistan exerts the tightest control over the online information space, where the state-run internet service provider permanently blocks websites that carry independent news coverage or critical content. A key election in Kazakhstan in June 2019, when the country voted for a successor to then-president Nursultan Nazarbayev, was also accompanied by excessive network disruption on election day and restrictions on streaming services and several social media platforms (NetBlocks, 2019). The authorities justified the network interference with concerns over the spread of false information (Freedom House, 2020). During the January 2021 parliamentary election, media freedoms were curtailed with social media restrictions and distributed denial of service (DDoS) attacks designed to disrupt or block websites. According to the country's officials, the targeted censorship intended to prevent the spread of false information and maintain public order (Freedom House, 2022). Kazakhstan repeated similar tactics in the extraordinary presidential elections in November 2022 (Access Now, 2023a; RSF, 2022) and again in the parliamentary election in March 2023 (RFE/RL, 2023). The region's practice of suppressing free speech extends into censorship in online spaces. For illustration, Uzbekistan amended its criminal code to make insults against the president illegal and added penalties for online offences. These provisions, infringing on freedom of expression, entered into force ahead of the presidential elections in October 2021 (Freedom House, 2021).

DDoS attacks disrupt the traffic of a server, service, or network by overwhelming the target or its surrounding infrastructure. These disruptive attacks are simple to deploy and difficult to prevent, especially for small and under-resourced entities, which makes them a popular tool to censor media outlets and websites of civil society organizations and political candidates (Korosteleva, 2022). For example, Kazakhstani news site *Vlast* reported suffering a persistent targeted DDoS attack in January 2021 (Freedom House, 2022). DDoS attacks were also targeted against several news sites, including *KazTAG* and *Orda.kz* prior to the presidential elections in November 2022 (Justice for Journalists, 2024). Disruptive cyber operations have been playing an increasingly political role. In September 2022, Kazakhstan experienced a series of primarily DDoS attacks that interfered with internet connectivity across the country, allegedly linked to the upcoming presidential elections scheduled for November 2022. The intent behind these incidents was unknown, but President Kassym-Jomart Tokayev blamed foreign actors seeking to destabilize the country during a sensitive political period (Eurasianet, 2022; Khassenkhanova, 2022). Considering the regional context, the cyberattacks might have been connected to the war in Ukraine. According to the CyberPeace Institute's database "Cyber Attacks in Times of Conflict Platform #Ukraine," government websites in Kazakhstan were targeted by Russia-affiliated groups deploying DDoS attacks on three different occasions in October 2022.

It is noteworthy that Russia employed DDoS attacks as a coercive measure around politically charged events in the past, including state-orchestrated DDoS attacks on Estonia during the bilateral conflict throughout April and May 2007 and in the Russo-Georgian War in August 2008 (Kozłowski, 2020). Another early example was the use of DDoS attacks as part of Russian mounting pressure to persuade the Kyrgyz president to close the US base in Manas (Bradbury, 2009). According to the Electoral Knowledge Project, in January 2009, DDoS attacks targeted the country's internet infrastructure, lasting for approximately ten days and eliminating 80 percent of the country's limited online capacity.

Cyberattacks Targeting Electoral Infrastructure

Malicious cyber activities against electoral infrastructure, including electronic voting systems and voter registration databases, with the intent to obstruct voting or erode trust in election results have been observed worldwide (ASPI, 2019). Central Asian countries have experimented with e-voting systems. Kazakhstan actively used e-voting technology between 2004 and 2011 but discontinued this practice and returned to paper ballots due to concerns over the integrity of e-voting procedures (Kassen, 2020). Uzbekistan piloted biometric identification during the referendum on constitutional amendments in April 2023 (Gazeta.uz, 2023). The Kyrgyz authorities view the digitalization of electoral infrastructure as a step toward enhancing transparency and increasing electoral participation through biometrics registration, biometric identification of voters, and ballot scanning and reporting technology. The e-system prevents common election fraud in the form of vote buying, carousel voting, and group or family voting (Sheranova, 2020). This technology was piloted in the 2015 parliamentary election to increase the integrity of voting stations (Goyal, 2017; Putz, 2015). In 2016, the Osh City Council introduced e-voting after repeated violent political uprisings in the region. Kyrgyzstan has conducted e-counts since 2017, where optical scanners are used to verify counts (International IDEA, 2023). The United Nations Development Programme (UNDP) (2021) reported a large-scale voters' biometric data collection campaign prior to local council elections in March 2021 to increase the reliability of the vote count during elections and referendums. In April 2023, the Central Election Commission of Kyrgyzstan presented a pilot electronic voting project and an upgraded voter identification device for local elections (Kharizov, 2023).

Public concerns about the integrity and reliability of electoral infrastructure, whether based on suspected external interference or internal manipulation, can have serious repercussions. Such disruption erodes public trust, impacts voter turnout, and challenges the legitimacy of election outcomes. The Kyrgyz parliamentary elections in November 2021 were accompanied by allegations of interference, and opposition leaders called for the results to be annulled after technical difficulties appeared to have affected the vote count (OSCE & ODIHR, 2022a; RFE/RL, 2021). The Central Election Commission's tabulation monitor experienced a blackout, and when the system restarted, different results appeared on the monitor. The discrepancy resulted in several opposition parties falling below the 5 percent threshold required for entering the Parliament (Pannier, 2021). Technical failures can be destabilizing especially in countries with contested election outcomes. The 2021 Kyrgyz elections in question followed a failed parliamentary vote in October 2020. In that case, the Central Election Commission declared the results of voting in all polling stations invalid amid protests over alleged campaign violations and unfair voting practices. Concerning potential foreign interference in the 2021 repeated elections, the Kyrgyz Security Council registered cyber incidents targeting the Central Election Commission's servers from twenty countries without affecting the elections (Kabar, 2021b; Orlova, 2021). The Commission reported on the attempted cyberattacks against national servers while stating that the current level of protection sufficiently defends the country's electoral infrastructure (Kabar, 2021a).

Data Leaks and Cyber Espionage

Central Asia has witnessed a shift toward digitalizing government services driven by digital economy initiatives and international support. However, as pointed out in the Electoral Knowledge Project (n.d.), rapid digitalization can increase the attack surface for malicious activities if coupled with massive data collection and insufficient safeguards that would ensure privacy, transparency, and effective oversight to handle citizens' personal information securely. Sensitive data can be hacked, leaked, or otherwise exploited for the purpose of fraud, jeopardizing people's security, or undermining trust in democratic processes and institutions. For illustration, the Kazakhstani Central Election Commission experienced an extensive data breach in July 2019. Data from the election database, comprising information on 11 million Kazakhstanis, which constitutes approximately 60 percent of the total population, was published online, exposing names, identification numbers, passport numbers, and residence addresses (Vlast, 2019). The Ministry of Internal Affairs launched an investigation into the unlawful dissemination of confidential data in the same month. However, the investigation did not find anyone accountable for the incident. The official report cited insufficient evidence of a crime as the leaked personal data was neither further used nor caused harm. Still, the mere publication of personal data suggests malicious intent and poses risks to citizens, including the potential for identity theft, targeted scams, and social engineering to exploit the targets. The decision taken by the Kazakhstani Ministry of Internal Affairs to close the investigation highlights the lack of accountability for data breaches – even when national security and the democratic process are at stake (U.S. Bureau of Democracy, Human Rights, and Labour, 2020).

Data exfiltration and cyber espionage can also constitute election interference. Primary targets of such operations are government agencies, officials, and political candidates, but hacking extends to research and civil society organizations, journalists, and private companies (O'Connor et al., 2020). Although the known cases of targeted hacking do not conclusively prove an objective to interfere in democratic processes, threat intelligence reports increasingly point to political motivation of state-affiliated groups operating in Central Asia. Microsoft's reporting (2022) suggests that China utilizes cyber espionage as a tool for advancing the country's political, economic and military influence, including in Kazakhstan. A Chinese cybersecurity vendor further reported on Russian-speaking actors deploying malware to surveil a wide range of individuals and organizations in Kazakhstan, extending to government agencies, military personnel, researchers, journalists, private companies, educational organizations, and dissidents (Cimpanu, 2019). Securelist by Kaspersky (2018c) reported on a Chinese threat actor detected behind a targeted campaign linked to a high-level meeting in Central Asia pursuing a regional political agenda and another campaign targeting a national data center in the region that allowed access to a wide range of government sources (Securelist, 2018a). Another report by Securelist (2019) detailed Zebrocy malware, primarily associated with Russian state-sponsored hacking groups, spearphishing Central Asian government-related targets, both in-country and in remote locations. A Russia-affiliated group was also reported to use the potential Telegram ban in Kazakhstan to distribute malware in an alternative communication software for the political opposition (Securelist, 2018b). In yet another case, a hacking group deployed a novel backdoor against international governmental targets located in Kazakhstan, with low confidence indicators pointing to Moscow (Chakravarti, 2023). While not directly interfering with the elections, these incidents point to an active engagement of Russia- and China-affiliated actors in politically motivated hacking in the region, targeting critical components of democratic processes.

Disinformation Campaigns, Inauthentic Accounts, and Synthetic Content

Disinformation deployed to deliberately share false narratives and information with the aim of manipulating opinion and discrediting the opposition intensifies around elections. Online disinformation campaigns target a wide array of political candidates, media organizations, individual journalists, and civil society representatives. Malicious actors leverage social media and messaging platforms to sway voters, amplify the content via inauthentic accounts, and deploy trolls to harass individuals and distort online discourse (Lee Myers, 2022). In Central Asia, the coordinated online attacks provide the basis for a high incidence of online and offline abuse aimed at deterring candidates and independent reporting (Pavlova, 2023). Networks of fake accounts promoting pro-government narratives have been observed in Kazakhstan around elections, including in the presidential election campaign in November 2022 (Du Boulay, 2023). These accounts are commonly referred to as "nurbots," after the ruling Nur Otan Party (Kozhanova, 2019). Kyrgyz activists reported on fake accounts spreading disinformation, allegedly coordinated by national ministries and operated by a combination of government agencies and individuals (Bradshaw, Bailey, & Howard, 2021). The Committee to Protect

Journalists (2020) and Reporters Without Borders (2020) observed that law enforcement agencies in Kyrgyzstan instructed a troll farm to discredit critics. The practice of using fake accounts has also been observed in Uzbekistan, where online trolls derail discussions and undermine the reputation of journalists and news organizations (Bradshaw, Bailey, & Howard, 2021).

As documented by the Australian Strategic Policy Institute (ASPI) (2019), Russia frequently deploys coordinated information operations abroad. The government and state-affiliated groups exploit the online information space to sway public narratives. These efforts persist beyond elections, forming part of a broader, long-term strategy to manipulate public opinion and erode trust in democratic institutions. Networks of accounts originating in Russia and targeting Central Asian states are regularly detected on popular social media platforms (Bradshaw, Bailey, & Howard, 2021). Online disinformation campaigns have intensified in the aftermath of the international armed conflict in Ukraine (Cabar, 2023). Disinformation finds a fertile ground amid the expanding social media landscape and low trust in traditional media. The commercialization of advanced artificial intelligence tools is set to facilitate further abuse and empower malicious actors to spread fake and harmful content (Khashimov, 2021; Neudert, 2018; Stanley-Becker & Nix, 2023; Tiku, 2022).

Online Surveillance and Intimidation

Politically motivated surveillance is pervasive throughout Central Asia, with governments employing sophisticated technologies to monitor citizens' communications and online activities. Invasive data collection practices are facilitated by the adoption of Russian-style legislation and tools, increasing use of Chinese surveillance and censorship technologies, and adaptation of domestic legal frameworks to authorize state overreach (Weber, 2019). The Kazakhstani authorities intercept internet traffic and internet users are required to install digital security certificates designed to generate detailed logs of their online activity (Kumenov, 2020; Raman, 2019). Human Rights Watch (2021) reported that the "false information" bill in Kyrgyzstan, which came into power in August 2021, compels internet service providers to register their clients in a unified identification system and provides authorities with complete information related to users if a court or a state agency requests such data. Without adequate transparency and independent oversight, these intrusive practices are weaponized against the opposition, the media, and civil society, violating individuals' rights to privacy and participation in civil society as well as freedom of expression, assembly, and association.

Both Kazakhstan and Uzbekistan have repeatedly engaged in the targeted surveillance of media, dissidents and activists (Kumenov, 2018; Marczak et al., 2023; RFE/RL, 2016; Securelist, 2023). Already in 2015, WikiLeaks published an exchange of documents linking state agencies and a surveillance software company indicating that the government might have obtained software to monitor and interfere with online traffic, including encrypted communications, as well as to perform targeted attacks against certain users and devices (Freedom House, 2020, 2023b). In 2021, Amnesty International's Security Lab conducted forensic analysis on the phones of Kazakhstani human rights activists – confirming four individuals had their devices infected with the Pegasus spyware (Amnesty International, 2021). A Justice for Journalists (2020) report highlights how online surveillance goes hand in hand with arbitrary arrests of opposition figures and journalists, creating a climate of self-censorship and preventing genuine political participation.

INCENTIVES FOR IMPROVEMENT

States have obligations under international law to uphold and protect the right to vote and to ensure that citizens can exercise their fundamental right without interference, intimidation, or coercion. Free and fair elections are protected under the Universal Declaration of Human Rights and the International Covenant on Civil and Political Rights. Complementary international and regional obligations, such as the Organization for Security and Cooperation in Europe (OSCE) commitments, further mandate Central Asian states to respect and protect freedom of expression, association, and assembly online, and the right to freely seek and impart information (Human Rights Council, 2022; Democracy Reporting International, 2012). In principle, governments should secure their legislative frameworks and enforcement mechanisms against abuse and exploitation of the online information space for political ends, guarantee the independence of digital infrastructure and services, and refrain from repressive practices such as internet shutdowns or throttling, censoring online content, or surveillance that violate the principles of necessity and proportionality and the right to seek, receive, and impart information. However, in practice, Central Asian countries justify restrictive practices as an intrinsic prerogative derived from sovereign state authority, appealing to the need to safeguard national security and maintain constitutional and public order (Muhamedov & Buralkiyeva, 2023).

While incentives are missing for the regimes to ease their digital authoritarian practices, the economic ramifications of interference with internet connectivity and service restrictions are significant and could potentially influence countries' behavior (Lamensch, 2021; Rakhmetov & Valeriano, 2022). Internet shutdowns and near-complete blackouts disrupt access to financial and public services and, in their consequences, harm populations as well as the private and public sectors (Muhamedov & Buralkiyeva, 2023). Network interference inflicts reputational damage, discourages foreign investments, erodes citizens' trust in digital services, and hinders digital transition (Woodhams & Migliano, 2023). Some states have shown an interest in minimizing the risks associated with shutting down the internet. However, this comes alongside exerting control over the online information space through more sophisticated approaches to allow monitoring of online space and circumscribing access to information. The Kazakhstani government has acknowledged that the nationwide internet shutdowns during the January 2022 unrest were an excessively harsh response, however, the authorities did not denounce the practice of internet shutdowns. The Ministry of Digital Development informed about a more refined approach, proposing the creation of a list of resources that would remain accessible during such crises (Zakon.kz, 2023). These were expected to be pro-government media. Turkmenistan proposed developing an autonomous national network. In December 2022, the Ministry of Foreign Affairs announced plans to develop an autonomous national digital network that would disconnect the country from the global internet (Chronicle of Turkmenistan, 2022). The project aims to create a separate digital infrastructure for tighter censorship, potentially resembling China's Great Firewall.

Central Asian governments collect extensive data on their citizens without implementing adequate data security measures. This raises significant cybersecurity and human rights concerns. The countries have laws intended to protect personal and biometric data, and work on improving the data protection standards. However, substantial loopholes allow government access to sensitive information under the guise of national security or public order. By compromising data integrity, as well as users' anonymity and privacy, Central Asian countries increase their potential attack surface and risk exposing domestic digital ecosystems to foreign interference. Both Russia and China are active powers in the region with a track record of hacking elections for political influence. These threats only intensify with the growing geopolitical polarization.

Central Asian countries largely fail to increase cyber resilience and preparedness. The Global Cybersecurity Index (GCI) by the International Telecommunication Union (ITU) measures the commitment of 182 countries to cybersecurity at a global level. In the 2024 Index, Kazakhstan and Uzbekistan are ranked as advancing. Kyrgyzstan, Tajikistan, and Turkmenistan remain in low tiers. The ITU figures show that Central Asia has been digitalizing without adequate legal frameworks, cybersecurity measures, and the necessary capacity in place. Nation-state actors and organized cybercriminal groups can exploit these vulnerabilities, especially around elections, referendums, and protests, and position to exert political or financial pressure on governments. Election interference benefits the perpetrators, while regional responses remain inadequate to deter malicious behavior and ensure meaningful accountability. With the growing use of cyber operations and disinformation campaigns as a political tool and large-scale participation of non-traditional and non-state actors in a domain that has traditionally seen an exclusive engagement of states, foreign threats to the region's elections and fragile democratic processes are set to increase. In response to the worsening threat landscape, the Central Asian republics have more incentives to double down on extended cooperation and alignment with international partners. Although optimism for revitalizing democracy remains limited in the short to medium term, certain aspects of cyber policy and cybersecurity offer promising opportunities for multistakeholder collaboration.

RECOMMENDATIONS

Reduce the Risk of Information Compromise

- Central Asian governments must curb the mass collection of personal data to what can reasonably be justified, following the principles of legality, necessity, and proportionality, while increasing the cybersecurity, transparency, and oversight measures for how data is processed, transmitted, and stored to secure the systems that are custodians of sensitive and personal data. Excessive data collection creates weaknesses in the digital ecosystem that can be exploited for malicious purposes, such as unauthorized access to personal data, resulting in severe privacy violations with little accountability.
- Broad surveillance powers violate international human rights standards, undermine data security, and induce self-censorship. States must refrain from intrusive practices such as mass surveillance, real-time collection of traffic data, and targeted interception of online communications without legal authorization and a legitimate purpose, adhering to the principles of necessity and proportionality in line with international human rights standards.
- Internet service providers and online platforms must help secure digital ecosystems, especially in regard to transparency about their operations as well as trust and safety practices and potential threats to users' privacy. Digital service providers must ensure privacy by design, including end-to-end encryption, data protection safeguards, and fact-checking mechanisms that include trusted and verified partners in the loop of accuracy verification and limit the virality of disinformation and other harmful content. Priority should be given to improving verification techniques to combat manipulated content and inauthentic coordinated behavior online, especially amid the commercialization and rapid proliferation of AI tools for language generation, image creation, and content amplification.
- Procurement and deployment of dual-use technologies such as commercial cyber intrusion capabilities by states should be conditional and subject to a human rights and impact assessment that informs and guides such activities and their scope, aligns them with the international human rights law, and subjects them to independent and transparent oversight. Governments should commit to imposing international controls to

prevent commercial cyber intrusion tools from being exported to countries with poor human rights records and prevent vendors from bypassing regulations.

Improve the Understanding of the Cyber Threat Landscape

- Countering foreign cyber-enabled election interference requires effective technical and legal attribution to identify threat actors and address malicious behavior. States should invest in building their national capacities and extend international and bilateral cooperation aimed at information exchange and forensic and legal capacity building. Proactive measures such as conducting regular cybersecurity assessments and simulations can help identify vulnerabilities within electoral systems.
- Central Asian governments should advance the implementation of confidence-building measures on structured and transparent exchange of information between states and private companies. International partnerships, such as the International Counter Ransomware Initiative, and operational collaboration between the public and private sectors facilitate gathering timely, comprehensive, and actional intelligence and allow states and affected entities to protect themselves against attacks. For example, the OSCE confidence-building measures include threat information sharing among participating states, public–private partnerships, critical infrastructure protection, and vulnerability disclosure (OSCE, 2016). Common baselines for sharing intelligence and recognizing the impacts of cyber incidents are key for effective mitigation and response, and OSCE delivers programs in Central Asia that support the development and implementation of the classification of cyber incidents in terms of scale and seriousness, emphasizing critical infrastructure protection (Cybil Portal, n.d.).
- Donor countries and organizations should prioritize funding for civil society initiatives, research and investigative organizations, and independent media providing transparent data collection, investigation, and analysis. Such efforts help build data-driven understandings of the threat landscape, including the knowledge of cyber threats affecting elections and democratic processes. Information about cyber-enabled election interference is currently reliant on the fragmented work of organizations operating with limited resources. To evidence cyber threats and their impacts on infrastructure, services, and populations, authorities and research organizations should conduct rigorous data collection and pilot data-driven methodologies to enhance cyber preparedness, improve accountability, and inform effective victim redress.

Strengthen Accountability and Legal Frameworks

- Central Asian governments must increase transparency around elections by allowing independent election observation and reporting. Electoral observation missions should advance their reporting on cyber incidents, information campaigns, online intimidation, and other cyber-enabled tactics threatening free and fair elections. By incorporating detailed assessments of cyber threats into their reports, electoral observation missions can provide critical insights into how cyber-enabled tactics undermine electoral integrity.
- States should advance normative and legal frameworks to strengthen international provisions safeguarding electoral infrastructure, namely under the United Nations framework of responsible state behavior in cyberspace. In the consensus report of the United Nations Open-Ended Working Group on information and communications technologies (ICTs) (United Nations General Assembly, 2021), states acknowledged that malicious cyber activities against critical infrastructure and critical information infrastructure that undermine trust and confidence in political and electoral processes, public institutions, or that impact the general availability or integrity of the internet, are a real and growing concern, and that public–private cooperation may be necessary to protect its integrity, functioning, and availability. However, progress on these commitments remains uneven and stakeholder engagement inadequate. States should advance cyber norm implementation and clarify the application of international law, including international human rights law, in cyberspace through targeted capacity building to strengthen accountability measures for state-sponsored interference in elections and democratic processes.
- Governments should develop policy and legal frameworks through inclusive consultative processes. Multistakeholder platforms such as the Oxford Process on International Law in Cyberspace provide expert guidance and support for states. "The Oxford Statement on International Law Protections against Foreign Electoral Interference through Digital Means" (The Oxford Process, 2020) reaffirms that the body of existing international law applies to cyber operations by states, including those that have adverse consequences for the electoral processes of other states. Other multistakeholder initiatives, such as the Paris Call for Trust and Security in Cyberspace (2018), have called on stakeholders to strengthen their capacity to prevent malign interference by foreign actors aimed at undermining electoral processes through the malicious use of cyber capabilities.
- State response to cyberattacks must be timely and transparent, extending to informing citizens, reporting on detected cyber threats, and following

up with accountability measures to deter malicious behavior. Detailing which norms or laws have been violated by a cyber incident can enhance the transparency of attributions and build state capacity to recognize and penalize malicious behavior. For instance, the EU Cyber Diplomacy Toolbox includes a cyber sanctions regime that addresses persons and entities involved in cyberattacks or attempted cyberattacks with a significant effect (EEAS) (Cyber Diplomacy Toolbox, n.d.).

Increase Cyber Resilience of Electoral Infrastructure and Processes

- Cybersecurity measures must be prioritized already at the inception phase of building or upgrading electronic election systems and digitizing election administration. State agencies relevant to election processes must act transparently and ensure election results are verifiable to be accepted by the electorate. Such measures hold particular significance for the Central Asian region, where several countries have experimented with e-voting systems. For instance, Kazakhstan initially embraced e-voting technology but later abandoned the system due to concerns about the reliability of e-voting procedures, or Kyrgyzstan, where technical difficulties appeared to have affected the vote count.
- Central Asian authorities should increase and incentivize cyber capacity building, including sharing best practices and promoting dialogue with stakeholders. Many existing initiatives facilitated by states or intergovernmental organizations are open only to government representatives. Capacity building needs to be more inclusive to build trust and leverage the strengths of diverse groups of stakeholders. Similarly, international and regional platforms dealing with cybersecurity and cybercrime must enable and support multistakeholder cooperation.
- Civil society is critical in fostering transparency and accountability during the election process. To support these efforts, funding from international organizations, donor countries, and private companies should be directed toward organizations with a track record of capacity-building initiatives that can raise cybersecurity awareness, provide training programs, and help combat disinformation, such as those promoting independent fact-checking or supporting investigative journalistic initiatives.
- Securing free and fair elections, including by refraining from network interference and information campaigns that influence election results, must be an integral part of multilateral and bilateral agendas that democratic countries pursue in their engagement with Central Asian governments. Cybersecurity cooperation and capacity building presents a viable

platform to enhance the region's overall resilience against internal and foreign cyber threats to elections (European Commission, 2023).

CONCLUSION

Central Asian governments tightly control their online information space. Elections in the region, albeit in varying degrees, are marked by a combination of internet shutdowns, network restrictions, deployment of inauthentic accounts to amplify pro-government narratives, extensive mass and targeted surveillance, and intimidation. Digital authoritarianism takes place amid intensifying disruptive and stabilizing cyberattacks, data extortion, cyber espionage, and foreign disinformation campaigns. The multiple and connected cyber threats require a coordinated response to enhance election integrity and resilience of the digital ecosystem. Governments must curb domestic censorship and surveillance practices to enable free and fair elections while mitigating the risk of cyber-enabled foreign interference. State-affiliated actors will continue to target electoral processes to plant distrust and project power as long as rewards outweigh the risks. The cyber domain presents promising opportunities for international and multistakeholder collaboration to reduce the risk of information compromisation, improve understanding of the cyber threat landscape, strengthen accountability and legal frameworks, and increase cyber resilience of electoral infrastructure and processes – steps that are increasingly urgent in light of the growing geopolitical polarization.

REFERENCES

Access Now. (2023a, March 23). *#KeepItOn: 2022 elections and internet shutdowns watch*. Access Now. https://accessnow.org/elections-internet-shutdowns-watch-2022

(2023b). *2023 elections and internet shutdowns to watch*. Access Now. https://accessnow.org/campaign/2023-elections-and-internet-shutdowns-watch/#Turkmenistan

Aidarkhanova, E. (2023, November 23). Why Is the Eurasian Economic Union Broken? *The Diplomat*. https://thediplomat.com/2023/11/why-is-the-eurasian-economic-union-broken/

Amnesty International. (2021, December 9). *Kazakhstan: Four activists' mobile devices infected with Pegasus Spyware*. Amnesty International. https://amnesty.org/en/latest/news/2021/12/kazakhstan-four-activists-mobile-devices-infected-with-pegasus-spyware

Australian Strategic Policy Institute (ASPI). (2019, May 15). *Hacking democracies*. Australian Strategic Policy Institute (ASPI). https://aspi.org.au/report/hacking-democracies

Bradbury, D. (2009, February 5). The fog of cyberwar. *The Guardian*. https://theguardian.com/technology/2009/feb/05/kyrgyzstan-cyberattack-internet-acces

Bradshaw, S., Bailey, B., & Howard, P. N. (2021, January 13). *Country case studies industrialized disinformation: 2020 global inventory of organized social media manipulation* (Working Paper 2021.1). University of Oxford. https://demtech.oii.ox.ac.uk/wp-content/uploads/sites/12/2021/01/CyberTroop-Report-2020-v.2.pdf

Central Asian Bureau for Analytical Reporting (CABAR). (2023, October 10). *International expert panel: Investigating the influence of Russian propaganda in Central Asia*. Central

Asian Bureau for Analytical Reporting (CABAR). https://cabar.asia/en/international-expert-panel-investigating-the-influence-of-russian-propaganda-in-central-asia

Chakravarti, J. (2023, May 10). *Russian group possibly behind cyberespionage in Central Asia*. Bank Info Security. https://bankinfosecurity.com/russian-group-possibly-behind-cyberespionage-in-central-asia-a-22032

Chronicle of Turkmenistan. (2022, December 10). *The Cabinet of Ministers: Embassy in Qatar, propaganda information center and autonomous network, "not connected to the Internet."* Chronicle of Turkmenistan. https://hronikatm.com/2022/12/propaganda-autonomous-internet

Cimpanu, C. (2019, November 23). *Extensive hacking operation discovered in Kazakhstan*. ZDNET. https://zdnet.com/article/extensive-hacking-operation-discovered-in-kazakhstan

Committee to Protect Journalists (CPJ). (2020, January 9). *Investigative journalist Bolot Temirov assaulted in Kyrgyzstan*. Committee to Protect Journalists (CPJ). https://cpj.org/2020/01/investigative-journalist-bolot-temirov-assaulted-i

Cyber Diplomacy Toolbox. (n.d.). *The cyber diplomacy toolbox*. Cyber Diplomacy Toolbox. https://cyber-diplomacy-toolbox.com

CyberPeace Institute. (2023). *Cyber attacks in Times of Conflict Platform #Ukraine*. CyberPeace Institute. https://cyberconflicts.cyberpeaceinstitute.org

Cybil Portal. (n.d.). *Development and implementation of National Cyber Incident Severity Scales (NCISS) and related measures to protect critical infrastructures*. Cybil Capacity Knowledge Portal. https://cybilportal.org/projects/facilitation-of-the-development-and-implementation-of-national-cyber-incident-severity-scales-nciss-and-related-measures-to-protect-critical-infrastructures

Deibert, R. (2005, March 7). *More Kyrgyz internet hacking and DDOS attacks*. Citizen Lab. https://deibert.citizenlab.ca/tag/kyrgyzstan

Democracy Reporting International. (2012). *Overview of state obligations relevant to democratic governance and democratic elections*. Democracy Reporting International. https://aceproject.org/ero-en/misc/overview-of-state-obligations-relevant-to

Du Boulay, S. (2023, May 26). *Fake accounts and presidential elections in Kazakhstan*. Global Voices. https://advox.globalvoices.org/2023/05/26/fake-accounts-and-presidential-elections-in-kazakhstan

Electoral Knowledge Project. (n.d.). *Cybersecurity in elections: Developing a Holistic Exposure and Adaptation Testing (HEAT) process for election management bodies. Types of exposure that can impact cybersecurity*. ACE. https://aceproject.org/ace-en/focus/heat/types-of-exposure-that-can-impact

Eurasianet. (2022, September 30). *Kazakhstan: President pins week-long cyberattacks on foreign-based plotters*. Eurasianet. https://eurasianet.org/kazakhstan-president-pins-week-long-cyberattacks-on-foreign-based-plotters

European Commission. (2023, October 26). *Global Gateway Forum: The EU reaffirms a high level of cooperation with the Kyrgyz Republic on digital development*. https://global-gateway-forum.ec.europa.eu/news/global-gateway-forum-eu-reaffirms-high-level-cooperation-kyrgyz-republic-digital-development-2023-10-26_en

Freedom House. (2020). *Freedom on the net 2020: Kazakhstan*. Freedom House. https://freedomhouse.org/country/kazakhstan/freedom-net/2020

(2021). *Freedom on the net 2021: Uzbekistan*. Freedom House. https://freedomhouse.org/country/uzbekistan/freedom-net/2021

(2022). *Freedom on the net 2022: Kazakhstan*. Freedom House. https://freedomhouse.org/country/kazakhstan/freedom-net/2022

(2023a). *Freedom on the net 2023: Turkmenistan*. Freedom House. https://freedomhouse.org/country/turkmenistan/freedom-world/2023

(2023b). *Freedom in the world 2023*. Freedom House. https://freedomhouse.org/sites/default/files/2023-03/FIW_World_2023_DigtalPDF.pdf

(2023c). *Internet freedom status*. Freedom House. https://freedomhouse.org/explore-the-map?type = fiw&year = 2023

Freeman, C., Helf, G., & McFarland, A. (2023, May 25). *China looks to fill the void in Central Asia*. United States Institute of Peace. https://usip.org/publications/2023/05/china-looks-fill-void-central-asia

Gazeta.uz. (2023, April 17). *Biometric voting and live video broadcasts planned for Uzbekistan's constitutional amendments referendum*. Gazeta.uz. https://gazeta.uz/en/2023/04/17/refer

Goyal, A. (2017, October 18). Kyrgyz election brings high expectations, but mixed results for voters. *The Diplomat*. https://thediplomat.com/2017/10/kyrgyz-election-brings-high-expectations-but-mixed-results-for-voters

Guriev, S. & Treisman, D. (2019). Informational autocrats. *Journal of Economic Perspectives*, 33(4), 100–127. https://aeaweb.org/articles?id = 10.1257/jep.33.4.100

Hess, M. (2023, February 17). *Russia is down but not out in Central Asia*. Foreign Policy Research Institute (FPRI). https://fpri.org/article/2023/02/russia-is-down-but-not-out-in-central-asia

Human Rights Council. (2022, June 3). *Reinforcing media freedom and the safety of journalists in the digital age*. ReliefWeb. https://reliefweb.int/report/world/reinforcing-media-freedom-and-safety-journalists-digital-age-report-special-rapporteur-promotion-and-protection-right-freedom-opinion-and-expression-irene-khan-ahrc5029-enarruzh

Human Rights Watch. (2021, November 18). *How are the authorities in Central Asia trying to control the internet?* Human Rights Watch. https://hrw.org/news/2021/11/18/how-are-authorities-central-asia-trying-control-internet

International IDEA. (2023). *ICTs in elections database*. International IDEA. https://idea.int/data-tools/question-view/742

International Telecommunications Union (ITU). (2024). *Global Cybersecurity Index 2024*. International Telecommunications Union (ITU). https://itu.int/en/ITU-D/Cybersecurity/Documents/GCIv5/2401416_1b_Global-Cybersecurity-Index-E.pdf

Justice for Journalists. (2020, May 22). *Attacks on journalists, bloggers and media workers in Central Asia and Azerbaijan (2017–2019)*. Justice for Journalists. https://jfj.fund/attacks-on-journalists-bloggers-and-media-workers-in-central-asia-and-azerbaijan-2017-2019

(2024, June 27). *Attacks on media workers in Kazakhstan 2022–2023*. Justice for Journalists. https://jfj.fund/attacks-on-media-workers-in-kazakhstan-in-2022-2023

Kabar. (2021a, November 20). *Technical problems at CEC website did not affect elections results: Secretary Council*. Kabar. http://en.kabar.kg/news/technical-problems-at-cec-website-did-not-affect-elections-results-secretary-council

(2021b, November 29). *CEC website attacked by hackers from 20 countries: Security Council of Kyrgyzstan*. Kabar. http://en.kabar.kg/news/cec-website-attacked-by-hackers-from-20-countries-security-council-of-kyrgyzstan

Kassen, M. (2020, May 5). Politicization of e-voting rejection: Reflections from Kazakhstan. *Transforming Government: People, Process and Policy*, 14(2), 305–330. https://doi.org/10.1108/TG-11-2019-0106

Kassenova, N. (2022, December 7), *How China's foreign aid fosters social bonds with Central Asian ruling elites*. Carnegie Endowment for International Peace. https://carnegieendowment.org/research/2022/12/how-chinas-foreign-aid-fosters-social-bonds-with-central-asian-ruling-elites?lang = en

Kharizov, R. (2023, April 6). *Local elections: CEC presents pilot e-voting project*. 24KG. https://24.kg/english/262725_Local_elections_CEC_presents_pilot_e-voting_project

Khashimov, S. (2021, July 12). *Kazakhstan's alternative media is thriving – and in danger*. Foreign Policy. https://foreignpolicy.com/2021/07/12/kazakhstan-alternative-media-thriving-danger

Khassenkhanova, G. (2022, October 7). Kazakhstan's officials and experts advocate for more cybersecurity funding and establishment of cybersecurity agency. *Astana Times*. https://astanatimes.com/2022/10/kazakhstans-officials-and-experts-advocate-for-more-cybersecurity-funding-and-establishment-of-cybersecurity-agency

Korosteleva, Y. (2022, November 11). *Kazakhstan's broken internet*. Vlast. https://vlast.kz/english/52525-kazakhstans-broken-internet.html

Kozhanova, N. (2019, February 20). Finding Kazakhstan's troll farms. *The Diplomat*. https://thediplomat.com/2019/02/finding-kazakhstans-troll-farms

Kozłowski, A. (2020). Comparative analysis of cyberattacks on Estonia, Georgia and Kyrgyzstan. *European Scientific Journal*, 3, 1–14 https://doi.org/10.19044/esj.2014.v10n7p%25p

Kumenov, A. (2018, December 21). *Report: Hackers detect online protest-sniffing software in Kazakhstan*. Eurasianet. https://eurasianet.org/report-hackers-detect-online-protest-sniffing-software-in-kazakhstan

(2020, December 7). *Kazakhstan: As election beckons, authorities tighten control on internet*. Eurasianet. https://eurasianet.org/kazakhstan-as-election-beckons-authorities-tighten-control-on-internet

Lamensch, M. (2021, March 9). *The cost of an internet shutdown*. Centre for International Governance Innovation. https://cigionline.org/articles/cost-internet-shutdown

Lee Myers, S. (2022, November 6). Russia reactivates its trolls and bots ahead of Tuesday's midterms. *The New York Times*. https://nytimes.com/2022/11/06/technology/russia-misinformation-midterms.html

Marczak, B., Scott-Railton, J., Perry, A., Al-Kizawi, N., Anstis, S., Panday, Z., et al. (2023, April 11). Sweet QuaDreams a first look at spyware vendor QuaDream's exploits, victims, and customers. *Citizen Lab*. https://citizenlab.ca/2023/04/spyware-vendor-quadream-exploits-victims-customers

Microsoft. (2022). *Microsoft Digital Defense Report 2022*. Microsoft. https://query.prod.cms.rt.microsoft.com/cms/api/am/binary/RE5bUvv?culture = en-us&country = us

Mite, V. (2005, August 29) *CIS: Turkmenistan reduces ties to "associate member."* RadioFreeEurope/RadioLiberty (RFE/RL). https://rferl.org/a/1061002.html

Muhamedov, R. & Buralkiyeva, D. (2023, March 8). How, and why, Kazakhstan and Turkmenistan shut down the internet. *The Diplomat*. https://thediplomat.com/2023/03/how-and-why-kazakhstan-and-turkmenistan-shut-down-the-internet

NetBlocks. (2019, June 9). *Internet and streaming services blocked in Kazakhstan on election day*. NetBlocks. https://netblocks.org/reports/internet-and-streaming-services-blocked-in-kazakhstan-on-election-day-dAmOP7y9

Neudert, L. M. (2018, August 22) *Future elections may be swayed by intelligent, weaponized chatbots*. MIT Technology Review. https://technologyreview.com/2018/08/22/104087/future-elections-may-be-swayed-by-intelligent-weaponized-chatbots

O'Connor, S., Hanson, F., Currey, E., & Beattie, T. (2020, October 28). *Cyber-enabled foreign interference in elections and referendums*. Australian Strategic Policy Institute (ASPI). https://aspi.org.au/report/cyber-enabled-foreign-interference-elections-and-referendums

OpenNet Initiative. (2005, April 15). *Special report: Kyrgyzstan: Election monitoring in Kyrgyzstan*. OpenNet Initiative. https://opennet.net/special/kg

Organization for Security and Co-operation in Europe (OSCE). (2016, March 10). *Permanent council decision No. 1202*. OSCE. https://osce.org/pc/227281

Orlova, M. (2021, November 29). *Security Council Secretary of Kyrgyzstan announces cyber-attacks on CEC server*. 24KG. https://24.kg/english/215336_Security_Council_Secretary_of_Kyrgyzstan_announces_cyber_attacks_on_CEC_server

OSCE & ODIHR. (2022a). *Kyrgyz Republic, parliamentary elections*. ODIHR Election Observation Mission, Final Report. https://osce.org/files/f/documents/2/f/519087.pdf

(2022b). *Republic of Kazakhstan, early presidential election*. ODIHR Election Observation Mission, Final Report. https://osce.org/files/f/documents/8/d/548593.pdf

(2023). *Uzbekistan, early presidential election, 9 July 2023*. ODIHR Election Observation Mission, Final Report. https://osce.org/odihr/elections/uzbekistan/544495

Pannier, B. (2021, November 29). *Democratic "blackout"? latest Kyrgyz parliamentary elections can't escape controversy*. Radio Free Europe/Radio Liberty (RFE/RL). https://rferl.org/a/kyrgyzstan-elections-democratic-blackout/31585579.html

Paris Call for Trust and Security in Cyberspace. (2018). *The 9 principles*. Paris Call for Trust and Security in Cyberspace. https://pariscall.international/en/principles

Pavlova, P. (2022, January 31). *How Kazakhstan's control of information can turn into a regime weakness*. Open Global Rights. https://openglobalrights.org/how-kazakhstans-control-of-information-can-turn-into-a-regime-weakness

(2023, February 27). Gendered disinformation and connected cyber threats: Historical patterns, new battlefields, and the implications for international security. *Global Policy Journal*. https://globalpolicyjournal.com/blog/27/02/2023/gendered-disinformation-and-connected-cyber-threats-historical-patterns-new

Putz, C. (2015, August 13). Kyrgyzstan set to use biometric registration in next election. *The Diplomat*. https://thediplomat.com/2015/08/kyrgyzstan-set-to-use-biometric-registration-in-next-election

(2023, November 21). Central Asia faces challenges and sees opportunities amid complex geopolitical outlook. *The Diplomat*. https://thediplomat.com/2023/11/central-asia-faces-challenges-and-sees-opportunities-amid-complex-geopolitical-outlook

RadioFreeEurope/RadioLiberty (RFE/RL). (2012, June 28). *Uzbekistan Suspends Membership in CSTO*. RadioFreeEurope/RadioLiberty (RFE/RL). https://rferl.org/a/uzbekistan-csto-suspends-membership/24629244.html

(2021, November 29). *Kyrgyz opposition protests against parliamentary election results, citing alleged fraud*. RadioFreeEurope/RadioLiberty (RFE/RL). https://rferl.org/a/kyrgyzstan-parliamentary-vote-rally-protest-fraud/31585124.html

(2023, April 28). *Internet monitor says Kazakhstan 'throttling' RFE/RL sites to limit access to information*. RadioFreeEurope/RadioLiberty (RFE/RL). https://rferl.org/a/kazakhstan-rferl-internet-throttling-ooni/32383892.html

Rakhmetov, B., & Valeriano, B. (2022, February 24). *The consequences of internet shutdowns in Kazakhstan*. Council for Foreign Relations (CFR). https://cfr.org/blog/consequences-internet-shutdowns-kazakhstan

Raman, R. S., Evdokimov, L., Wurstrow, E., Halderman, J. A., & Ensafi, R. (2019, July 23). *Investigating large scale HTTPS interception in Kazakhstan*. ACM Digital Library. https://censoredplanet.org/kazakhstan

Reporters Without Borders (RSF). (2020). *Kyrgyzstan*. Reporters Without Borders (RSF). https://rsf.org/en/kyrgyzstan

(2022). *Heading for reelection, Kazakhstan's Tokayev must respect press freedom obligations*. Reporters Without Borders (RSF). https://rsf.org/en/heading-reelection-kazakhstan-s-tokayev-must-respect-press-freedom-obligations

RFE/RL. (2016, August 3). *Uzbekistan, Kazakhstan said to be hacking, spying on dissidents*. RFE/RL. https://rferl.org/a/uzbekistan-kazakhstan-said-hacking-spying-dissidents/27897226.html

Securelist. (2018a, June 13). *LuckyMouse hits national data center to organize country-level waterholing campaign*. Securelist. https://securelist.com/luckymouse-hits-national-data-center/86083

(2018b, October 15). *Octopus-infested seas of Central Asia*. Securelist. https://securelist.com/octopus-infested-seas-of-central-asia/88200

(2018c, September 10). *LuckyMouse signs malicious NDISProxy driver with certificate of Chinese IT company*. Securelist. https://securelist.com/luckymouse-ndisproxy-driver/87914

(2019, January 11). *A zebrocy go downloader*. Securelist. https://securelist.com/a-zebrocy-go-downloader/89419

(2023, March 8). *The state of stalkerware in 2022*. Securelist. https://securelist.com/the-state-of-stalkerware-in-2022/108985

Sheranova, A. (2020, March 26). Cheating the machine: E-voting practices in Kyrgyzstan's local elections. *European Review*, 28(5), 793–809. https://doi.org/10.1017/S1062798720000241

Stanley-Becker, I. & Nix, N. (2023, March 22). Fake images of Trump arrest show 'giant step' for AI's disruptive power. *The Washington Post*. https://washingtonpost.com/politics/2023/03/22/trump-arrest-deepfakes

Temnycky, M. (2023, September 6). *The United States must strengthen its engagement with Central Asia*. Atlantic Council. https://atlanticcouncil.org/blogs/new-atlanticist/united-states-engagement-central-asia

The Oxford Process. (2020). *The Oxford statement on international law protections against foreign electoral interference through digital means*. The Oxford Process. https://elac.ox.ac.uk/the-oxford-process/the-statements-overview/the-oxford-statement-on-international-law-protections-against-foreign-electoral-interference

Tiku, N. (2022, September 28). AI can now create any image in seconds, bringing wonder and danger. *The Washington Post*. https://washingtonpost.com/technology/interactive/2022/artificial-intelligence-images-dall-e/?itid = lk_inline_manual_3

U.S. Bureau of Democracy, Human Rights, and Labor. (2020). *2020 country reports on human rights practices: Kazakhstan*. U.S. Department of State. https://state.gov/reports/2020-country-reports-on-human-rights-practices/kazakhstan

U.S. Department of State. (2023, February 27). C5+1 *diplomatic platform*. U.S. Department of State. https://state.gov/c51-diplomatic-platform

UK Government. (2023, December 7). *UK exposes attempted Russian cyber interference in politics and democratic processes*. Gov.uk. https://gov.uk/government/news/uk-exposes-attempted-russian-cyber-interference-in-politics-and-democratic-processes

United Nations Development Programme (UNDP). (2021, March 3). *A large-scale voters' biometric data collection campaign will take place prior to local council elections*. United Nations Development Programme (UNDP). https://undp.org/kyrgyzstan/press-releases/large-scale-voters'-biometric-data-collection-campaign-will-take-place-prior-local-council-elections

United Nations General Assembly. (2021, March 10). *Open-ended Working Group on developments in the field of information and telecommunications in the context of international security*. Final Substantive Report. A/AC.290/2021/CRP.2. https://front.un-arm.org/wp-content/uploads/2021/03/Final-report-A-AC.290-2021-CRP.2.pdf

United Nations Office on Drugs and Crime (UNODC). (2023). *Empowering Central Asian youth for positive change: UNODC ROCA's regional initiative*. United Nations Office on Drugs and Crime (UNODC). https://unodc.org/centralasia/en/news/empowering-central-asian-youth-for-positive-change_-unodc-rocas-regional-initiative.html#:~:text= The%20Central%20Asian%20region%20is,the%20region%20has%20ever%20had

United States Senate. (2017, June 21). *Russian interference in the 2016 U.S. elections. Hearing Before the Select Committee on Intelligence*. United States Senate. https://intelligence.senate.gov/sites/default/files/hearings/Russian%20Interference%20in%20the%202016%20U.S.%20Elections%20S.%20Hrg.%20115-92.pdf

Van der Staak, S., & Wolf, P. (2019). *Cybersecurity in elections models of interagency collaboration*. International IDEA. https://idea.int/sites/default/files/publications/cybersecurity-in-elections-models-of-interagency-collaboration.pdf

Vershinin, A. (2022). *Turkmenistan leader's son wins presidential election*. Associated Press News. https://apnews.com/article/central-asia-asia-turkmenistan-presidential-elections-elections-3d13e95fe055bf53525141c351708488

Vlast. (2019, August 8). *The leak of Kazakhstani data to the network occurred from the Central Election Commission*. Vlast. https://vlast.kz/novosti/34706-utecka-dannyh-kazahstancev-v-set-proizosla-iz-centrizbirkoma-carka.html

Weber, V. (September 2019). *The worldwide web of Chinese and Russian Information controls* (Working Paper Series No. 11). University of Oxford. https://ctga.ox.ac.uk/article/worldwide-web-chinese-and-russian-information-controls

Woodhams, S. & Migliano, S. (2023, October 10). Government *internet shutdowns have cost $50 billion since 2019*. TOP10VPN. https://top10vpn.com/research/cost-of-internet-shutdowns

Zakon.kz. (2023, January 16). *Kazakhstan will create a "White List" of sites that will not be blocked in case of emergency*. Zakon.kz. https://zakon.kz/6382621-v-kazakhstane-sozdadut-belyy-list-saytov-kotorye-ne-budut-blokirovat-pri-chs.html

11

Stacking Up for Resilience

Digital Public Infrastructure: The India Way

Ravi Nayyar

The word "democracy" literally means "rule by the people" (Dahl & Shapiro, 2024, para. 1). Democracy is underpinned by the right and power of people in a jurisdiction to shape their collective destiny. This is enshrined in international law. Article 21 of the *Universal Declaration of Human Rights* (1948) defines the authority of government as stemming from the will of the people who elected it, the right of the people to participate in their government, as well as the right of the people "of equal access to public service" in their country.[1] Article 1 of the *International Covenant on Civil and Political Rights* (1976) similarly enshrines the right of all to self-determination and thus their right to "freely pursue their economic, social and cultural development."[2] The United Nations generally advocates for democracy as a system of governance where the "freely expressed will of people is exercised," and which enables greater security and human development (United Nations, 2019, para. 4). Therefore, democratic rights comprise both specific human rights such as freedom of expression and peaceful assembly and association (United Nations, 2019, para. 5) and, more generally, to enable the people of a jurisdiction to determine how they are governed and how they pursue the development of their society and economy.

Economic development – the process followed by an economy in becoming more advanced, "especially when both economic and social conditions are improved" ("Economic development," 2023) – and the promotion of human rights, including democratic rights, share a symbiotic relationship. For example, Articles 23 and 25(1) of the *Universal Declaration of Human Rights* (1948) protect one's entitlement to what are arguably the fruits of economic development, including the

The author profusely thanks Associate Professor Chinmayi Sharma for advising him of the opportunity to be a part of this wonderful project on defending democracy in the digital age and for her help in conceptualizing this chapter.

[1] Universal Declaration of Human Rights, GA Res 217A (III), UN GAOR, UN Doc A/810 (December 10, 1948).

[2] International Covenant on Civil and Political Rights, opened for signature December 16, 1966, 999 UNTS 171 (entered into force March 23, 1976).

right to an appropriate standard of living, food, the best of health and certain employment protections (Feldman et al., 2016, p. 7). Sen (2001, p. 36, emphasis in original) argues that conferral of human rights (the "expansion of freedom") functions "as both . . . the *primary end* and . . . the *principal means* of development." In underpinning economic growth, economic development is among "the most reliable means for advancing human rights," which include democratic rights (Feldman et al., 2016, pp. 6–7; Marslev & Sano, 2016, p. 15). For instance, economic development enables richer participation in societies by citizens, given that they feel more secure in their ability to express their political views if they are confident about their financial and food security, and having a home to go back to. Therefore, economic development (and subsequent economic growth) can bolster the trust and confidence of citizens of democracies in democracy itself as a means of delivering tangible benefits for them; and thus, the capacity of democratic institutions to promote and preserve their human rights through their roles in the making and/or adjudication of law and/or policy concerning economic development.

As enablers of economic development, and thus growth by providing essential services for citizens to live and flourish, critical national infrastructure (CNI) assets play a vital role in the promotion of citizens' human rights, including their democratic rights. Indeed, citizens' ability to do anything in modern societies depends on the availability of, for instance, electricity, telecommunications, and water treatment that are provided by CNI assets (Parliamentary Joint Committee on Intelligence and Security, 2022). Their protection is a "sovereign necessity," given the relevance of the assets' functioning to these societies' national security (Parliamentary Joint Committee on Intelligence and Security, 2022, p. 6). Indeed, the very definition of CNI assets under national laws invokes their key role in the preservation of social or economic stability, national defense, and security (see, e.g., *Security of Critical Infrastructure Act 2018* (Cth) s 51(c); *Critical Infrastructures Protection Act of 2001* (2001) 42 USC § 5195(e)).

A species of CNI is digital public infrastructure (DPI). Given that this chapter is focused on the Indian approach to DPI, it will define DPI as per the definition agreed upon by the G20 under India's presidency of the multilateral grouping, that is, a "set of shared digital systems, built and leveraged by both the public and private sectors, based on secure and resilient infrastructure, and can be built on open standards and specifications," and open-source software (OSS), as well as an enabler of "delivery of services at societal-scale" (G20 Leaders, 2023, para. 55). The systems used to operate DPI (that this chapter refers to as "DPI Backbones") are CNI assets that are delivering digitally native essential services, promoting the human rights of users of those services and thus, if regulated by democratic systems of government, helping maintain the citizenry's confidence in democracy itself and the resilience of their democratic institutions. One should also note, for instance, the G20 countries' call in 2023 for DPI to be "human-centric, development-oriented" and be governed in a way that "respect[s] human rights and fundamental freedoms" (G20 Digital Economy Ministers, 2023, paras. 6, 7, Annexure 1, para. 6.j). These calls reflect the role of DPI as an enabler of the preservation and promotion of human rights, including democratic rights, of citizens reliant on the services delivered through DPI.

In this vein, any threat to the operational resilience, including the cyber resilience, of CNI assets, such as DPI Backbones, is a threat to the human rights of the population they serve, including their democratic rights (see, e.g., Newbill, 2019, pp. 766, 771). Indeed, such a threat is also to their confidence and trust in the ability of democratic systems of government to regulate the functioning of CNI assets and thus promote their human rights. The United States acknowledges this in referring to cybersecurity as "essential to … the operation of our critical infrastructure, [and] the strength of our democracy and democratic institutions" (The White House, 2023, p. i). Similarly, the G7 Digital and Tech Ministers (2023, para. 15) defined "secure and resilient digital infrastructure" as "a key foundation for … an open and democratic society."

One should also note that two of the norms of responsible state conduct in cyberspace, approved by the United Nations General Assembly (UNGA) by consensus, called on states to appropriately protect their CNI assets, which would include DPI Backbones, from cyber-enabled threats, and – in ensuring they respect specific UN Human Rights Council resolutions on human rights in the digital age – to "guarantee full respect for human rights, including the right to freedom of expression," a democratic right (United Nations, 2021, pp. 8, 11, 13). This is complemented by how CNI assets themselves enable human rights promotion, as mentioned, and the implementation of international law and norms by which elected governments would give their citizens confidence in democracy as a mode of government itself. Therefore, work by governments to tackle cyber-enabled threats to CNI assets and thus boost their cyber resilience would promote and operationalize the UNGA-approved cyber norms, one of the themes of this book which adopts a wide, holistic approach to exploring how to defend democracy.

The conceptual relationships outlined in the preceding paragraphs are summarized in Figure 11.1.

This chapter focuses on India's DPI, the platforms and systems that deliver a range of digitally native essential services to the citizens of the world's largest democracy (Guterres, 2022, para. 10). As it highlights, Indian DPI has enabled an extraordinary level of economic development and growth. The cyber resilience of DPI Backbones is vital to Indians' trust in the democratic institutions that define, run, and/or oversee this infrastructure (such as the elected federal government) as bodies meant to promote their welfare and thus their human rights. This feeds directly into the resilience of Indians' faith in democracy as a concept. Any work by the Indian government to ensure the cyber resilience of DPI Backbones would also be implementing the aforementioned UNGA-approved norms for responsible state conduct in cyberspace.

In exploring Indian DPI, this chapter also argues that the bedrock of India's DPI, the actual open Application Programming Interfaces (APIs) and protocols called the "India Stack," make the latter fundamental to India's resilience as an increasingly digitally enabled democracy (iSPIRT, 2021). The chapter hones in on how the software dependencies of the India Stack and DPI Backbones invite systemic cyber

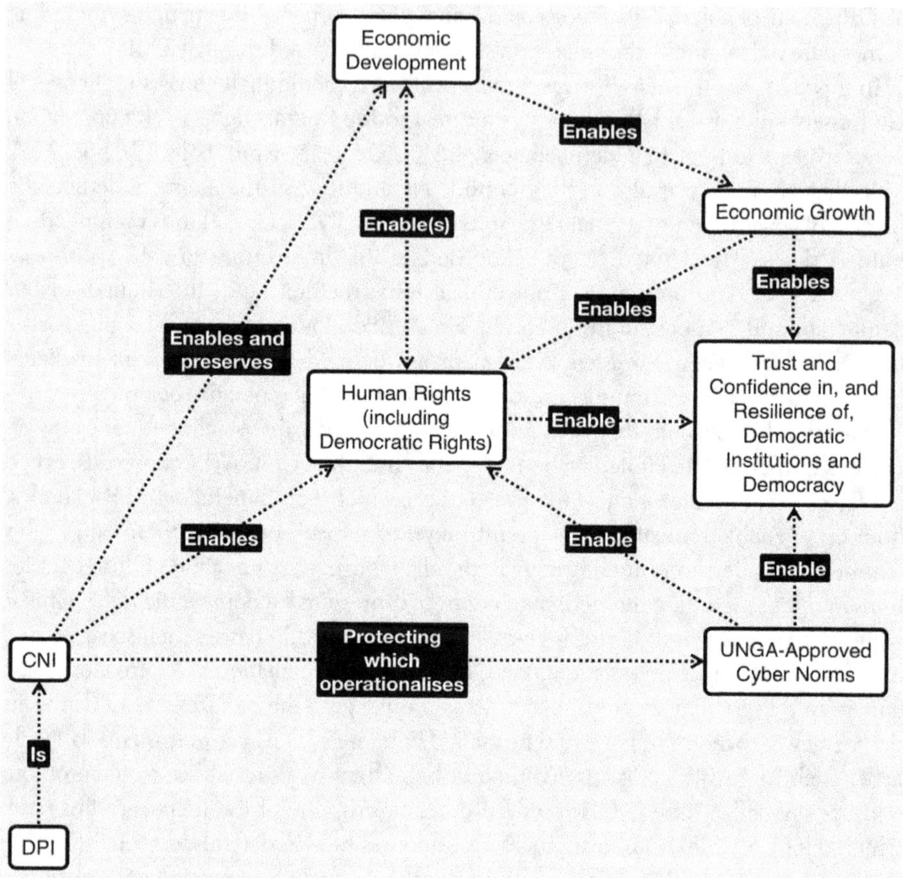

FIGURE 11.1 The relationships between critical national infrastructure (CNI; including digital public infrastructure (DPI)); economic development and growth; human rights; citizens' trust and confidence in democratic institutions and the resilience of those institutions; and United Nations General Assembly (UNGA)-approved norms for responsible state conduct in cyberspace (composed by the author)

risks for India as a democracy. In particular, it calls for India to prosecute systemic cyber risks that its DPI, built with the India Stack, faces via critical software which runs on India's DPI Backbones. This is justified with reference to the sheer complexity of (critical) software supply chains, the greater intent and capability of malicious cyber actors to target software supply chains, and the (recent) history of CNI assets more generally being attacked via vulnerabilities in, or misconfigurations of, critical software. There is also a recommendation that India closely scrutinize cyber risks invited by the use of OSS in building DPI, especially since the India Stack itself uses OSS (Alonso et al., 2023, p. 8). The chapter closes by exploring how India can take the India Stack, as well as its approach to building and deploying DPI more generally, to the world, particularly democracies in the Global South. It calls on India to, as part of sharing its open standards-based approach to DPI, help its democratic Global South partners deploy DPI in a cyber-resilient manner to make it harder for malicious actors to disrupt the provision of essential services and thus undermine their citizens' faith in democratic systems of government as guarantors of economic development and human rights, as well as threaten efforts by these Global South partners to implement the aforementioned UNGA-approved cyber norms, per Figure 11.1.

This chapter defines "critical software" as software, the execution of which, broadly speaking, can seriously impact the cyber resilience of a computer running it, drawing inspiration from the National Institute of Standards and Technology (NIST)'s (2021) definition.

WHAT ARE DIGITAL PUBLIC GOODS AND DIGITAL PUBLIC INFRASTRUCTURE?

Before exploring the India Stack, two foundational concepts must be understood: digital public goods (DPGs) and DPI. DPGs are "types of open-source software, models and standards that countries can use to operationalize their [DPI]" (OECD, 2021, p. 257). DPI comprises "platforms such as identification (ID), payment and data exchange systems that help countries deliver vital services to their people" (OECD, 2021, p. 257). In this manner, DPGs are the building blocks of DPI and thus the essential services that the latter provide in societies and economies. DPGs and DPI are ever more crucial in light of the move of social and economic activity online since the pandemic (OECD, 2022, p. 5). DPGs thus democratize the ability to "participate fully in social, financial, and political life," given that said ability is technologically dependent (Behrends et al., 2021, p. 3). DPGs are, like the DPI they underpin, fundamental to democratic resilience in the societies where they are provided, given the relationships between DPI, CNI, economic development and growth, human rights, as well as the trust and confidence in democratic institutions and democracy as a concept (per Figure 11.1).

DPGs are defined by their open format, adaptable for different populations and contexts (OECD, 2021, p. 257). The underlying code and standards can be audited by the (government) organizations deploying DPGs in DPI, enabling the identification and management of vulnerabilities in the code and other potential shortcomings of the relevant DPGs before they are deployed widely across a population (OECD, 2021, p. 260). This transparency enables more effective and inclusive consultation of relevant stakeholders by (government) organizations deploying DPI, helping drive a better, more inclusive deployment that respects democratic values and helps inspire confidence in the ability of democratic systems of government to deliver economic development via DPGs and DPI.

Indeed, the role of DPGs as enablers of the flourishing of societies and democracies is well recognized. The United Nations Secretary-General (2020, pp. 6–7) pointed to their critical role "in unlocking the full potential of digital technologies and data to attain the Sustainable Development Goals, in particular for low- and middle-income countries." In addition to the technical infrastructure on which DPGs are deployed, what are essential to their deployment are common standards that enable open access to datasets that themselves become available as DPGs, as well as "robust human rights and governance frameworks to enhance trust in technology and data use, while ensuring inclusion" (United Nations Secretary-General, 2020, p. 7). These factor into efforts to ensure that DPI itself is developed and deployed in a manner that respects human rights, per the calls of the G20 (G20 Digital Economy Ministers, 2023, paras. 6, 7, Annexure 1, para. 6.j). Therefore, the safely calibrated deployment of DPGs as part of DPI is vital to trust and confidence in democratic institutions running and/or overseeing that deployment and the resilience of the democracies where that deployment occurs.

The nature of DPGs can also be understood by contrasting their reflection of an open approach to the digital delivery of essential services to citizens with the closed approach of private companies. Historically, private companies have often provided these digitally delivered services because of their having the capacity to build and deploy the necessary infrastructure at (population) scale and in an economical manner (Burt, 2018, as cited in OECD, 2021, p. 257; ID4D, 2020, as cited in OECD, 2021, p. 257). Since they own the intellectual property underlying these services and infrastructure – and set the terms and conditions of their use – these companies have substantial influence, if not control, over whether and how these services are delivered, including over their benefits to citizens (Burt, 2018, as cited in OECD, 2021, p. 257; ID4D, 2020, as cited in OECD, 2021, p. 257). These companies are powerful gatekeepers and, given the centrality of these services to the ability of citizens to meaningfully participate in their societies and economies, have great influence over the conduct of affairs in a democracy (Behrends et al., 2021, p. 5). In this manner, the digital delivery of essential services by private companies threatens the digital sovereignty of democracies, that is, their governments' "power and authority . . . to make free decisions affecting citizens and businesses within the digital domain" (Gawen et al., 2021, as cited in OECD, 2021, p. 257). These companies threaten the ability of democratically elected governments to act in the interests of the people who elect them, the very essence of democracy, including by working toward their economic development by achieving the Sustainable Development Goals (OECD, 2021, p. 257). Conversely, this underlines the criticality of DPGs as pillars of the collective ability of the people of a democracy, via the governments that they elect, to act in their interests; and thus, their trust in democracy as a concept.

As with DPGs, DPI operates under an open paradigm governed by frameworks built on transparency and participatory governance (Alonso et al., 2023, p. 8). DPI comprises the "networks, systems or platforms that allow programmatic and secure access to the underlying data and business logic [of DPGs] through [APIs]" (Alonso et al., 2023, p. 8). DPI is "public" if its operator provides equal access to the relevant services to all users, and if its underlying standards and platforms are publicly available, making the subsequent enjoyment of these services by users non-rivalrous (Alonso et al., 2023, p. 8). This is combined with the positive externalities for populations where the DPI is deployed in an open, interoperable manner, which also points to the nature of DPI as providing public goods (Alonso et al., 2023, pp. 8–9). It is the interoperability of DPI (such as payments services with identity verification services) that enables these externalities to be "foundational and cross-cutting" at the public policy and operational levels (Desai et al., 2023, paras. 6–10). Indeed, DPI reaches across sectoral and policy siloes "to create population scale digital ecosystems that promote inclusive development," including the acceleration of progress toward achieving the 2030 Agenda for Sustainable Development and Sustainable Development Goals (European Union & Government of India, 2023, p. 2; see also G20 Digital Economy Ministers, 2023, para. 7). Therefore, just like the DPGs that underpin DPI, it is the "foundational infrastructure" for a democracy and goes to the ability of its people to choose their own destiny (Alonso et al., 2023, p. 8). DPI enables the efficient, convenient, and transparent delivery of a range of essential services and provides all stakeholders with a platform to innovate on top of the DPI itself, facilitating further economic development (Alonso et al, 2023, p. 12). In this vein, the cyber and operational resilience of DPI Backbones are critical to the resilience of the democracy where DPI is deployed. Much like how protecting CNI assets has been termed a "sovereign necessity" in light of the criticality of the essential services these assets provide to the national security and social stability of the jurisdiction where these assets are deployed (Parliamentary Joint Committee on Intelligence and Security, 2022, p. 6), so is protecting DPI Backbones from a range of threats, especially in the cyber domain, vital to the resilience of the democracy where DPI is deployed.

In the same vein, India's DPI, like the India Stack that India's DPI is built with, is the "foundational infrastructure" for Indian democracy, given that the operational resilience of its DPI Backbones enables Indians to participate in their society and economy in the manner in which they collectively see fit (Alonso et al., 2023, p. 8). India's DPI and DPI Backbones go to India's digital sovereignty, the ability of the government elected by the Indian people to make decisions affecting their participation in the burgeoning Indian digital economy, rather than that of (overseas) malicious cyber actors looking to undermine their confidence in their democratic system of government (Gajbhiye et al., 2022; Gawen et al., 2021, as cited in OECD, 2021, p. 257). As per Figure 11.1, if the Indian government takes steps to ensure the cyber resilience of Indian DPI Backbones (CNI assets), it implements the UNGA-approved cyber norms, promotes economic development and growth, Indians' human rights, including their democratic rights, and thus their trust that democracy truly delivers for them.

WHAT ARE THE INDIA STACK AND INDIA'S DPI?

The India Stack can be defined as follows:

> India Stack is the moniker for a set of open APIs [Application Programming Interfaces] and digital public goods that aim to unlock the economic primitives

> of identity, data, and payments at population scale . . . [T]his project was conceptualized and first implemented in India, where its rapid adoption by billions of individuals and businesses has helped promote financial and social inclusion and positioned the country for the Internet Age. (iSPIRT, 2021, para. 1)

Therefore, the India Stack comprises the DPGs that enable the provision of digitally native essential services by India's DPI, the platforms that are built with the India Stack. The India Stack has three layers (Alonso et al., 2023, pp. 3, 10, 20, 22; D'Silva et al., 2019, p. 8):

- identity, which includes Aadhaar (a "12-digital unique identification number that is linked to biometric [identifiers]"), eKYC (Electronic Know Your Customer, that is, identity authentication using Aadhaar), eSign (legally binding digital signatures that are linked with the signatories' respective Aadhaar numbers), GSTN (Goods and Services Tax Network, that is, 15-digit identifiers for businesses registered under the federal goods and services tax regime) and Udyam (a framework for Indian Micro, Small, and Medium Enterprises);
- payments, which include the Unified Payments Interface ('UPI', fast payments rails), Aadhaar-Enabled Payment System (enabling transitions between bank accounts authenticated by the parties' Aadhaar identities), Aadhaar Payment Bridge (digitally transferring government benefits and subsidies to the Aadhaar-linked bank accounts of payees) and Bharat Bill Payment System (a platform through which citizens can pay utility, telephone, and other types of bills); and
- data, which includes DigiLocker (a credential and document management platform for Aadhaar holders) and Account Aggregator (a consent-based data portability framework for Indians' financial information that is handled by federally regulated financial institutions).

This is an extensive catalog of services that are delivered by Indian public sector entities via India's DPI, enabled by the India Stack. The scope of these services speaks to the importance of the India Stack and thus India's DPI to the ability of hundreds of millions of Indians to participate fully in social and economic activities. Some key examples of these services and platforms are Aadhaar (digital identity), the UPI (digital payments), the Account Aggregator Framework (open banking), and DigiLocker (management of government-issued documents and credentials) (Alonso et al., 2023, pp. 10, 20, 22).

One should also note the additional delivery mechanisms for services that India's DPI comprises, including the following:

- Open Network for Digital Commerce (ONDC), a set of open protocols which seeks to democratize e-commerce and replace a "platform-centric" model with a "transaction-centric" one where buyers and sellers can find each other across e-commerce applications that are hosted on the ONDC network and built using those protocols (Gupta, 2022, paras. 28–29; Open Network for Digital Commerce, 2022, pp. 10, 13);

- Direct Benefit Transfer (DBT) mechanism for transferring funds and other benefits under 312 Indian social welfare programs run by fifty-three government departments directly to the bank accounts of beneficiaries (over half of which are linked with their Aadhaar numbers), and which is part of India's Public Financial Management System (PFMS), itself integrated with over 600 banks for verification of bank accounts and with the National Payments Corporation of India (NCPI) for verification of Aadhaar-linked bank accounts (Alonso et al., 2023, p. 8; Government of India, 2023a; Ministry of Finance, 2023, p. 212). The DBT is fundamentally enabled by the "JAM Trinity," that is: the opening of over 530 million bank accounts (as of late August 2024) for formerly unbanked Indians under the "Pradhan Mantri Jan Dhan Yojana" program; Aadhaar, the means by which the identity of most DBT beneficiaries is verified; and the sheer penetration of mobile telephony in India, namely, over 960 million phones that enable phone and/or online banking (Alonso et al., 2023, pp. 15–16; Department of Financial Services, 2023; Ministry of Finance, 2023, pp. 30, 156; MyGovIndia, 2023; Modi, 2024);
- COVID Vaccine Intelligence Network (CoWIN), which was developed as an extension of India's electronic Vaccine Intelligence Network and is a cloud-based solution that ran India's COVID-19 vaccination program (Ministry of Finance, 2023, p. 198). This served all stakeholders, be it vaccine recipients (booking appointments and receiving vaccination certificates), vaccinators, or logistics providers (such as through real-time visibility into the vaccine supply chain at the national, state, and even district levels) (Ministry of Finance, 2023, p. 198).

To understand the sheer scale of India's DPI, the following statistics and developments are instructive:

- India's success with the JAM Trinity in advancing financial inclusion is such that, had the country not used DPI solutions, it was estimated that India would have taken forty-seven years to open bank accounts for over 80 percent of Indian adults; much longer than the nine years taken to lift it to that level from 25 percent in 2008 (World Bank Group, 2023, p. 3, citing D'Silva et al., 2019, p. 4).
- In the case of the UPI:
  - In 2022, India processed the most real-time digital payments in the world, the number growing over 76 percent year-on-year in 2021–2022 and the country representing over 46 percent of all the world's real-time digital payments in 2022 (ACI Worldwide, 2023, pp. 5–6). This

has been complemented by the shrinking of the informal economy in India, estimated in 2021 to represent 15–20 percent of India's gross domestic product (GDP), down from 52 percent in the fiscal year 2018 (Ghosh, 2021, pp. 1–2).

  - The number of UPI transactions grew in fiscal year 2023–2024 by a record 57 percent to a record 131 billion (Jacob, 2024, paras. 1–3).
  - As a signal of the value of the UPI as a digital payments paradigm, Google even presented the UPI to the U.S. Treasury Department as an example of how to deploy an open standards-based payments network (Wadhwa, Amla, & Salkever, 2022, paras. 2, 9).

- As of November 2022, there had been over 1.35 billion unique Aadhaar numbers generated; 8.6 billion identity authentications done with Aadhaar; over 1.3 billion eKYC checks done; 754 million bank accounts linked with Aadhaar; and over 1.549 billion transactions done through payment systems simply reliant on counterparties' Aadhaar numbers to identify them (Ministry of Finance, 2023, pp. 155–156).
- Between 2013 and January 2023, the DBT was used to transfer over 3.2 trillion dollars' worth of social security benefits directly to the bank accounts of hundreds of millions of Indians (Ministry of Finance, 2023. pp. 212–213). This was alongside the PFMS transferring COVID relief payments to around 500 million Indians during the pandemic (Alonso et al., 2023, p. 18). Separately, a major benefit of the DBT, enabled by welfare recipients' bank accounts being linked to citizens' Aadhaar numbers, is the substantial reduction in monies being paid to phantom beneficiaries. The Indian government has estimated that it has saved over Rs 2.73 trillion between 2015 and 2022 by plugging these leakages (Choudhary & Singh, 2023, para. 3).
- As at December 31, 2022, twenty-three Indian banks had joined the Account Aggregator framework, enabling Indians, holding 1.1 billion bank accounts collectively, to share their banking data with eligible financial institutions through this open banking framework. Already, 3.3 million Indians have linked their accounts to the framework and 3.28 million of them have shared their data under it (Ministry of Finance, 2023, pp. 308–309). In June 2023, citizens had cumulatively raised 13.46 million consents (representing a monthly growth of over a quarter) while 2.9 million new consents were fulfilled in the same month (World Bank Group, 2023, p. 12).
- The ONDC platform, which went live in September 2022, has expanded to pilot programs in over 180 cities and saw over 5,000 orders daily in the retail category of goods and services (mostly food and beverages) as at April 2023 (Choudhury, 2023, para. 5). This constituted a twenty-five-fold growth in the period March–April 2023 (Choudhury, 2023, para. 1).

- CoWIN was the backbone of India's COVID-19 vaccination program, the world's largest, and critical to the distribution, administration, and tracking of over 2.2 billion doses of vaccines given to 1.04 billion Indians (847 million of whom were identified by their Aadhaar numbers) between January 2021 and September 2022 (Ministry of Finance, 2023, p. 198; World Health Organization, 2021).

These factors suggest the criticality of DPI, built with the India Stack, to the ability of the citizens of India, the world's largest democracy, to participate fully in their society and economy (Guterres, 2022, para. 10). This is reinforced by the sheer quantum of citizens served by India's DPI and the vitality of the services it provides – from digital identity to payments, data portability, social welfare, and vaccination – to their collective ability to live their lives as they see fit. Given that several of these services are operated by the public sector, India's DPI is vital to the ability of Indian citizens to shape their collective destiny via the government they elect – the very essence of democracy – and have faith in that system of government as a means of driving their economic development, growth, and promotion of their human rights, including their democratic rights, as flagged in the opening paragraphs of this chapter and in Figure 11.1.

The importance of India's DPI and the India Stack to India's ability to drive the economic development of its people, and thus their confidence in its democratic institutions as enablers of this development (given in Figure 11.1), is also underlined by the praise these have received from senior officials in governments and international organizations. The President of the UNGA referred to India as "leading in the field of digital public infrastructure" with the world having "much to learn from [India]" (Ministry of External Affairs, 2022a). The Secretary-General of the United Nations labeled India's DPI as "world-class" and implementing a "whole-of-society approach to development [which] combines old-fashioned community outreach with cutting-edge technology" (Observer Research Foundation, 2022). The German Ambassador to New Delhi referred to India's journey as a growing digital economy, including through the digital delivery of services, as an example for Germany to learn from (ANI, 2022c). The United States' then-Deputy National Security Advisor for Cyber and Emerging Technology praised Aadhaar as an enabler of "critical services" for Indian citizens – "often to sets of a population who were illiterate so that they could get their rations, they could get their access" – and for its "thoughtful" approach to preserving the privacy of citizens through data minimization (Inglis & Neuberger, 2021, pp. 16–17). The Deputy Director of the International Monetary Fund's Fiscal Affairs Department, termed the DBT as a "logistical marvel, seeking to help people at low-income levels, reaching hundreds of millions of people" (ANI, 2022b).

Industry and civil society actors have also praised India's DPI, enabled by the India Stack, as an example for the world. The Chief Technology Officer and a

Senior Vice-President of PayPal at the time, Sri Shivananda, spoke of the uniqueness of India's achievement:

> There is no technical stack in the world with a country's name as a prefix. What the Indian government and regulators have done together with the common national identity through a digital system and a common national API for payments, is nothing but brilliant. India is one of the first countries that has a platform first approach, with the platform being secure, robust and reliable. It is a role model for many other countries to follow. (Via & Sanghi, 2021, para. 104)

Philanthropist and technology luminary, Bill Gates, was similarly effusive in his remarks:

> No country has built [a] more comprehensive platform than India ... Because of the pioneering investment including creating the basic Aadhaar identity, India was in the lead in getting out (relief) payments ... during the pandemic ... We would like to see all countries, particularly developing countries, adopt these things. (PTI, 2023, paras. 3, 5, 10)

These words of praise for India's DPI, built atop the India Stack, underline the criticality of both to the ability of India's people to independently run their affairs through the government they elected to further their digital sovereignty. It also reinforces the nature of India's DPI as a guarantor of their economic development and thus, ultimately, their trust and confidence in the democratic system of government to advance their interests through tools such as DPI and the India Stack, given in Figure 11.1. Therefore, (praise for) the substantial track record of DPI stresses its importance as a pillar of the resilience of India's increasingly digital democracy (explored earlier).

This makes India's prosecution of systemic cyber risks that its DPI, especially its DPI Backbones, face via critical software all the more important, which the chapter now explores.

PROSECUTING SYSTEMIC CYBER RISKS FROM CRITICAL SOFTWARE

Given that India's DPI, like the India Stack itself, is digitally native, the security of the software that is deployed on DPI Backbones is paramount for its operational resilience. The weaponization of vulnerabilities in that software by malicious cyber actors – be they criminals, hacktivists, or state(-affiliated) actors – ultimately weaponizes the "digital dependence" of over a billion Indians on these CNI assets to verify their identity, as well as make and receive digital payments, among other things (OECD Council, 2022, Preamble para. 6). These are systemic cyber risks for India as the world's largest democracy (Guterres, 2022, para. 10).

Governments generally recognize the need to prosecute such risks. Under India's presidency, the G20 Leaders (2023, para. 57) recognized the increasing importance of a "secure digital economy" for all stakeholders. The G20 Digital Economy

Ministers (2023) repeatedly used the word "secure" to describe the digital economy and technologies, including DPI, that their governments seek to foster. The Ministers "reaffirm[ed] the importance of security in the digital economy as a key enabling factor" (G20 Digital Economy Ministers, 2023, para. 5). Given the vitality of secure digital technologies to how citizens of democracies conduct their lives, as flagged above, software security goes directly to how they collectively shape their destinies and, flowing from that, their confidence in democratic institutions as protectors of their democratic rights such as freedom, assembly, expression, privacy, and association in the increasingly digital societies they inhabit.

Given that most of the services provided by India's DPI are provided by the public sector (Alonso et al., 2023, p. 10; D'Silva et al., 2019, p. 8), the weaponization of vulnerabilities affecting the underlying DPI Backbones has the very real potential to undermine Indians' confidence in their democratically elected government to protect their collective ability to shape their own destiny, and thus their confidence in democracy itself. This echoes the implications of the cyber-enabled disruption of the functioning of physical CNI assets for social and economic stability that were flagged in the earlier sections of this chapter, and thus the relationships visualized by Figure 11.1 between CNI (including DPI) cyber resilience, economic development, growth, as well as the trust and confidence of citizens generally in democratic institutions, and the implementation of the UNGA-approved cyber norms.

India's G20 Sherpa, Amitabh Kant, pointed to how "Cybersecurity is paramount and will be the key to the future," including in managing "the whole DPI framework" (Digital India, 2023, para. 7). In particular, India needs to be mindful of the systemic cyber risks to its DPI and the India Stack via critical software running on its DPI Backbones. This is because critical software is identified in terms of performing functions critical to the cyber resilience of the computer that the software is running on (National Institute of Standards and Technology, 2021, p. 10). NIST (2021, pp. 1–3) defines critical software:

> as any software that has, or has direct software dependencies upon, one or more components with at least one of these attributes:
>
> - is designed to run with elevated privilege or manage privileges;
> - has direct or privileged access to networking or computing resources;
> - is designed to control access to data or operational technology;
> - performs a function critical to trust [that is, the cyber resilience of the device running the software]; or,
> - operates outside of normal trust boundaries with privileged access.

NIST specifies categories of such software, including access management, device security, operating systems, web browsers, remote access and scanning, and operational and network monitoring (National Institute of Standards and Technology, 2021, pp. 3–8). Given these factors, critical software represents an attractive attack vector for malicious cyber actors to leverage in targeting DPI Backbones.

In this context, India must take steps to appropriately incentivize the vendors of critical software running on DPI Backbones to invest in the security of their software development life cycles (SDLCs), that is, the "formal or informal methodology for designing, creating, and maintaining software" (Souppaya, Scarfone, & Dodson, 2022, p. 1).

Each SDLC can be viewed as being vulnerable to eight categories of threat vector that malicious cyber actors can exploit in order to, for instance, insert malware and thus compromise the, in this case, critical software produced by that SDLC (SLSA, 2023). These threat vectors in each SDLC are multiplied across each developer and vendor populating the software supply chain(s) for that critical software product. In general, a software supply chain comprises the "entire sequence of events that impacts software from the point of origin where it is designed and developed, to the point of end-use," and each event can be a means of ultimately targeting the end-user of a piece of software (U.S. Department of Commerce & U.S. Department of Homeland Security, 2022, p. 34). If successful, that targeting is defined as a software supply chain attack, that is, the "compromise of software code … at any phase of the supply chain to infect an unsuspecting [end-user]" (Clancy et al., 2021, p. 1; NTIA Multistakeholder Process on Software Component Transparency Framing Working Group, 2021, p. 24).

Given that critical software can be weaponized to directly compromise the cyber resilience of the computer running it, it becomes all the more crucial for India to take steps to incentivize the vendors of critical software deployed on DPI Backbones – not just ensure the security of their own SDLCs but also manage risks from their software supply chains. If they do not do so, they open up India's DPI Backbones to software supply chain attacks and thus make the delivery of a range of essential services to hundreds of millions of Indians by Indian DPI ever more prone to disruption.

The imperative for India to drive critical software vendors to perform software supply chain risk management (SCRM) in particular is enlivened by the increasingly hostile threat environment for software supply chains. Herr et al. (2020, p. 8), for example, have compiled a list of eighty-two software supply chain attacks, involving different elements of software supply chains, from 2010 to 2020. Similarly, Australian agencies have warned that threat actors are "increasingly looking to compromise multiple victims across a range of sectors via a single entry point" and targeting "products commonly found in ICT supply chains" (Australian Cyber Security Centre, 2022, p. 65; Australian Signals Directorate, 2023, p. 53). The Cybersecurity and Infrastructure Security Agency (2021b, p. 5) similarly pointed to the threat to software supply chains from highly sophisticated threat actors. The Agence Nationale de la Sécurité des Systèmes d'Information (2023, p. 30) referred to the targeting of software supply chains as "[continuing] to pose a systemic risk." The Quad, a diplomatic grouping of four democracies (Japan, Australia, India and the United States), signed joint principles for software security in May 2023 that began with an explicit recognition of "the security risks posed by lack of adequate controls to prevent tampering with the software supply chain by adversarial and non-adversarial threats" (Commonwealth of Australia et al., 2023, p. 2). Indeed, the severity of the threat landscape for software supply chains is underlined by, apart from the relative recency of these warnings from governments, the frankness of tone in these quotes (Nayyar, 2023, p. 19).

The impetus for India to act with respect to combating critical software risk to its DPI Backbones, including the risk via the software supply chains of critical software vendors, is bolstered by the past few decades of instances where CNI assets around the world have been successfully targeted via critical software running on their systems. The United States and Israel exploited vulnerabilities in software controlling Iranian uranium centrifuges (in the Iranian defense industrial base) to sabotage them (Perlroth, 2021, pp. 122–130). The Russian state manipulated supervisory control and data acquisition (SCADA) software used by three Ukrainian electricity utilities to open circuit breakers remotely, taking dozens of substations offline and causing blackouts that affected hundreds of thousands of citizens in 2015 (Cybersecurity & Infrastructure Security Agency, 2021a, paras. 2, 8–9; Zetter, 2016, pp. 2–3, 8, 19). Additionally, the Russian state gained access to the KA-SAT satellite internet network via, in part, a misconfigured virtual private network appliance to disrupt it at the start of the war in Ukraine (Blinken, 2022, para. 2; Viasat, Inc., 2022, para. 10). The NotPetya and WannaCry attacks both exploited vulnerabilities in the Windows operating system to cripple the Ukrainian government's ability to function and the country's CNI, and European and British CNI assets, respectively (Greenberg, 2018, paras. 28, 34; 2019, p. 1; Perlroth, 2021, pp. 389, 402; Romine, 2017, p. 3; Smart, 2018, pp. 8, 10; Trautman and Ormerod, 2019, p. 528). Such attacks are possible with respect to India's DPI Backbones, part of India's CNI, given that they are entirely dependent on software to function. These attacks would also occur within the context of India being the second-most targeted of all countries by malicious cyber actors in 2021 and 2022, with attacks reported to have increased by 24.3 percent in 2022 (CloudSEK, 2023, pp. 8–9).

India has made some progress on the world stage in tackling software security risks, which includes tackling critical software security risks. As G20 President, it forged consensus among the world's largest economies on the need to uplift software security. The *G20 High-Level Principles to Support Businesses in Building Safety, Security, Resilience, and Trust in the Digital Economy* (*G20 High-Level Principles*), endorsed by the G20 Leaders, include principles regarding "Security and Trust" (G20 Digital Economy Ministers, 2023, Annexure 2, para. 1; G20 Leaders, 2023, para. 57.i). As part of "develop[ing] a human-centric culture of security and trust in the digital economy," these principles seek to promote a "security by design" approach in relation to digital technologies (G20 Digital Economy Ministers, 2023, Annexure 2, para. 1.c). Specifically for DPI, developed under India's presidency and endorsed by the G20 Leaders, the G20 Framework for Systems of Digital

Public Infrastructure (G20 DPI Framework) calls for stakeholders to incorporate "security features within the core design" (G20 Digital Economy Ministers, 2023, Annexure 1, para. 6.e; G20 Leaders, 2023, para. 56.i). Though these are political commitments with respect to building security into the digital economy and DPI, they are welcome. Fulfilling them would require the G20 countries – including the world's largest software markets, and developer and innovation centers (see, e.g., U.S. Department of Commerce & U.S. Department of Homeland Security, 2022, p. 35) – to incentivize software developers and vendors in their jurisdictions to harden their SDLCs and perform robust software SCRM, having positive externalities for cyber resilience generally, not just that of India's DPI Backbones. Given the relationships between DPI, human rights promotion, trust, and confidence in democratic institutions described by Figure 11.1, these positive externalities ultimately reinforce the resilience of democratic institutions and drive the implementation of UNGA-approved cyber norms.

Alongside work to incentivize the vendors of critical software running on DPI Backbones to invest in the security of their SDLCs, including to perform robust software SCRM, India must closely scrutinize cyber risk invited by the use of OSS. In general, this is because of the sheer pervasiveness of OSS in modern computing (European Commission, 2020, p. 2). It has been estimated that OSS comprises dependencies for 97 percent of all software (Scott et al., 2023, p. 2). The India Stack itself uses OSS (Alonso et al., 2023, p. 8). If one looks at critical software, per a 2020 assessment by the U.S. Department of Commerce of 389 American technology companies that produce "security-related products," OSS was "frequently" incorporated in software running tools such as firewalls, logging programs, network management devices and (62 percent of) SCADA systems (National Institute of Standards and Technology, 2021, pp. 5–7; U.S. Department of Commerce & U.S. Department of Homeland Security, 2022, pp. 36–37). Furthermore, attack surfaces are multiplied by the sheer number of dependencies of commercial software's OSS dependencies themselves; meaning that vendors using OSS in their products are inheriting risks transmitted through multiple tiers of OSS developers and maintainers, (potentially) resulting in those OSS dependencies being "deeply buried" within their products (Scott et al., 2023, pp. 10–11). The sheer size of the resultant attack surface for critical software vendors that incorporate OSS into their products, therefore, should give urgency to scrutiny by India of OSS-borne risk to critical software and thus DPI Backbones.

Indeed, that attack surface is evident in the huge number of vulnerabilities in the OSS ecosystem and, therefore, in the dependencies of commercial software. Synopsys (2023, p. 7) found that 84 percent of 1,730 commercial codebases that it analyzed "contained at least one known open-source vulnerability" in 2022, a 4 percent increase on the equivalent figure yielded from analysis of over 2,409 codebases in 2021. Malicious cyber actors have seized on this, with Sonatype (2023, p. 4) finding that software supply chain attacks increased 633 percent year-on-year in 2022, marking a 742 percent average annual increase over the three years to 2023. An egregious example of malicious cyber actors seeking to exploit vulnerabilities in OSS is the exploitation of a critical vulnerability in the Log4j package, which was first seen in December 2021 (Silvers et al., 2022, p. 3). Merely five days after the vulnerability was disclosed, threat actors were observed trying to exploit it 400 times per second (Prince, 2021, as cited in Silvers et al., 2022, p. 4). Such was the severity of the vulnerability, including because of its being a(n enigmatic) transitive dependency for an innumerable amount of OSS and commercial software, that it triggered a multinational response by public and private sectors alike, scrambling to "identify and mitigate hundreds of millions of potentially affected devices" (Silvers et al., 2022, pp. 5–9, 11). The Director of the Cybersecurity and Infrastructure Security Agency (CISA) went as far as terming the vulnerability as "one of the most serious I've seen in my entire career, if not the most serious" (Starks, 2021, para. 1).

Therefore, the immense number of vulnerabilities in OSS ecosystems that are inherited by commercial software products, including critical software products that are deployed on DPI Backbones, as well as the greater intent of malicious cyber actors to exploit those vulnerabilities as part of software supply chain attacks makes it all the more vital for India to pay greater attention to the OSS risk to its DPI and the India Stack. While India should thus be applauded for the G20, under its presidency, recognizing "the importance of promoting open-source software" to enable (cross-border) DPI interoperability, India must not lose sight of the need to drive work to uplift the security of OSS, in line with the G20 calling for security to be built into the digital economy and DPI, as flagged earlier (G20 Digital Economy Ministers, 2023, para. 9). Its resilience as a democracy, the world's largest, is at stake, given the criticality of its DPI generally (as CNI) to Indians' trust in democratic institutions and the democratic mode of government as the ideal means to advance their economic development, growth and human rights, including their democratic rights, per Figure 11.1 (Guterres, 2022, para. 10). Similarly, critical software- and OSS-borne risks to India's DPI Backbones threaten its efforts to implement the UNGA-approved cyber norms outlined in the opening paragraphs of this chapter.

These are the sort of issues that India must especially be mindful when it looks to share its open standards-based approach to DPI through the India Stack, particularly with democratic partners in the Global South. It is imperative that India helps fellow democracies deploy DPI in a cyber-resilient manner that makes it harder for malicious actors to weaponize their technological dependencies and undermine citizens' trust and confidence in their democratic modes of government, as detailed in the next section.

TAKING INDIA'S APPROACH TO DPI AND THE INDIA STACK TO THE WORLD

Given the success of India's DPI in advancing India's economic development (as detailed in the introduction to the India Stack and Indian DPI), India's exporting its approach can enable other countries, especially democracies in the Global South, to benefit like it has. These benefits include the strengthening of the trust and confidence of their citizens in democracy as a system of government to drive economic development and growth, per the relationships described in Figure 11.1. This will be reinforced by advice from India on how to deploy DPI in a cyber-resilient manner, informed by the G20 *High-Level Principles* and *G20 DPI Framework* enacted under India's G20 presidency, and especially if India implements the recommendations in the immediately preceding section of this chapter ("Recommendations") on prosecuting systemic cyber risks from critical software. India, the world's largest democracy, can thus enable its fellow democracies, especially among developing countries, to implement the UNGA-approved cyber norms, per Figure 11.1, and better ensure their national (cyber) resilience amid a deteriorating threat landscape detailed in the previous section of this chapter (Guterres, 2022, para. 10).

India's experience as G20 President holds it in good stead. DPI was among its core priorities, including the facilitation of more sharing of expertise on DPI (Ministry of External Affairs, 2022c, paras. 35–37). India followed this up by forging "groundbreaking" international consensus on DPI (Gates, 2023). It successfully pushed for the creation of the *G20 DPI Framework*, endorsed by the G20 Leaders (as mentioned in the previous section of this chapter) who also "recognize[d] that safe, secure, trusted, accountable and inclusive digital public infrastructure, respectful of human rights, personal data, privacy and intellectual property rights can foster resilience, and enable service delivery and innovation" (G20 Leaders, 2023, para. 56). Indeed, the Indian G20 presidency produced the first "multilaterally agreed language and detail on DPI" (Chaudhuri, 2023, para. 14). With governments and donors around the world seeking to invest in DPI deployment (versus little prior multilateral work on DPI), the championing of DPI by the G20 in 2023 was pathbreaking, a "centerpiece of India's G20 presidency," and has helped forge India's "digital revolution" as a source of soft power (Chaudhuri, 2023, paras. 11, 16; Mehta, 2023, para. 2). India is indeed poised to share its approach, particularly with democratic developing countries for them to, as the Indian prime minister put it, "unlock the power of inclusive growth" (Modi, 2023, para. 21), which would enable them to better promote their democratic resilience, given in Figure 11.1.

Indeed, Indian efforts will be aided by New Delhi's general reputation as a trusted development partner, particularly for the Global South (Banerji, 2023).

Firstly, its G20 presidency was and wider foreign policy is animated by "Vasudhaiva Kutumbakam," a Sanskrit phrase from the *ślokas* [VI.71–73] of the ancient Hindu text, the *Maha Upanishad*, which roughly translates to "the world is one family" (Ministry of External Affairs, 2022b, para. 21; Vivekananda International Foundation, 2019, p. 7). One of the priorities of its G20 presidency was "accelerated, inclusive and resilient growth" (Ministry of External Affairs, 2022b, para. 32).

Secondly, as part of its prioritization of inclusive growth and development, India devoted special attention to uplifting that of the Global South and its role in international governance. India hosted two virtual "Voice of the Global South Summits" where countries from the Global South provided their views on matters such as economic development and DPGs, matters that go directly to the promotion of human rights and democratic resilience, given in Figure 11.1 (Government of India, 2023b; Ministry of External Affairs, 2023a, paras. 1–2, 9–17). As G20 President, India placed the "Global South squarely at the center of the global governance agenda," having successfully proposed the permanent G20 membership of the African Union, which it considers "the most satisfying outcome" of its Presidency (Jaishankar, 2023a, para. 5; Pant, 2023, paras. 1–2). As the Indian External Affairs Minister put it, India pushed for solutions to global challenges from the Global South itself as G20 President (Jaishankar, 2023a, para. 4). This is combined with the Indian prime minister "firmly" believing that "that the success of our G20 presidency is the success of the Global South" (Jaishankar, 2023b, para. 6).

Thirdly, India has an excellent reputation for public goods delivery, for instance, as a trusted health care partner. Under its COVID-19 vaccine diplomacy initiative, "Vaccine Maitri," it gifted over 14.85 million doses of locally manufactured COVID-19 vaccines to fifty countries and provided close to 51.52 million doses to forty-eight countries in the Global South under the COVAX facility until November 30, 2022 (Ministry of External Affairs, 2023b, p. 309). Jamaica actually received its first batch of COVID-19 vaccines from India, with the Jamaican Foreign Minister saying that, "From the very onset, India was a reliable partner whose assistance was critical to our pandemic response" (ANI, 2022a, paras. 2–3). Similarly, India co-led with South Africa the international push for a waiver of intellectual property rights for COVID-19 vaccines and is now working to extend the waiver to drugs used to treat the disease (Kumar, 2021, para. 1; The Pharma Letter, 2023).

These factors add to the attractiveness of India's offering in terms of DPI and the India Stack, especially for fellow democracies in the Global South. The goodwill India thus enjoys will be reinforced by how it is not looking to weaponize the India Stack. Rather, India seeks to empower other countries to use an open standards-based approach to the digital delivery of essential services, which prioritizes cyber resilience, per the *G20 High-Level Principles* and *G20 DPI Framework* enacted under India's G20 presidency and if India implements the Recommendations. As seen with CoWIN (Sansad TV, 2023), recipient countries are free to customize and build with the India Stack and India's approach as they see fit, "no strings attached," to quote the head and co-founder of the Digital India Foundation (Sansad TV, 2023). With the international community confident in DPI being "a critical accelerator" of the achievement of the Sustainable Development Goals (Gates, 2023), the Indian approach to DPI will enable recipient democracies, especially in the Global South, to promote their citizens' faith in democracy itself as a means of driving their economic development, growth, and thus preservation of their human rights, combined with implementing UNGA-approved cyber norms, as per Figure 11.1.

This is in stark contrast with China's Belt and Road Initiative and Digital Silk Road that constitute the blatant weaponization of Chinese technology vendors to influence and/or interfere in the affairs of recipient countries (Lewis, 2023, p. 7). Instead, India, the world's largest democracy, seeks to help these countries build their digital sovereignty and strengthen their overall democratic resilience through robust, cyber-resilient DPI and DPI Backbones in line with their needs, rather than "weaponise their interdependence" with the India Stack (Guterres, 2022, para. 10; Narlikar, 2021, pp. 289–290). This echoes how India characterizes its development cooperation with the Global South as "demand driven, outcome oriented, transparent and sustainable" (Jaishankar, 2023b, para. 9).

Further differentiating India's efforts from China's on digital economy diplomacy is its bilateral cooperation with leading democratic partners on DPI projects (in the Global South), such as the European Union, United States, France, Germany and Japan (Choudhury, 2023, paras. 20, 28; European Union & Government of India, 2023, p. 2; Government of India & Government of France, 2023, para. I.6.1.7; Ministry of External Affairs, 2023c, para. 3; The White House & Government of India, 2023; The White House & Government of India, 2024 para. 39, para. 37; Government of India & Republic of Germany, 2024, para. 32). India and the United States have incorporated DPI into their bilateral Initiative on Critical and Emerging Technologies (Government of India, 2023c, para. 5). Both countries also cooperate on DPI with the Republic of Korea through a "trilateral technology dialogue," looking to "expand cooperation on ... [among other things,] delivering technology solutions for the broader Indo-Pacific region" (U.S. Mission Korea, 2024, paras. 1–2). Furthermore, the world's largest democracy and France's championing of DPI as an enabler for "open, free, democratic and inclusive digital economies and digital societies" (Government of India & Government of France, 2023, para. I.6.1.7; Guterres, 2022, para. 10) will help project India as a trusted, democratic technology partner for fellow developing country democracies that look to bolster their citizens' faith in democracy and democratic institutions as drivers of economic development and uphold UNGA-approved cyber norms by developing and deploying robust, cyber-resilient DPI, per Figure 11.1. India's reputation as such is key to the success of its work to share its DPI expertise because "trust and transparency" are valuable commodities in foreign policy, especially in digital economy diplomacy, as defined by the Indian External Affairs Minister (Ministry of External Affairs, 2022b).

Indeed, amid technological contestation and balkanization, those very commodities will underwrite India's efforts to lead "an international architecture of collaboration" on DPI (Carnegie India, 2022; Ministry of External Affairs, 2022b). India has established the Global Digital Public Infrastructure Repository (GDPIR, welcomed by the G20 Leaders), a virtual library for DPI that countries and organizations have deployed at scale (at the time of writing, the GDPIR features over fifty projects from sixteen countries) (G20 Leaders, 2023, para. 56.ii; Ministry of Electronics and Information Technology, 2023, para. 3; https://dpi.global). India has created the One Future Alliance (OFA), a voluntary capacity building initiative for DPI targeted at low- and middle-income countries (LMICs) (G20 Leaders, 2023, para. 56.iii). India's credibility is also enhanced by its forming a Social Impact Fund (SIF), having pledged 25 million dollars to this government-led, multistakeholder capacity-building and financing initiative for DPI deployment in the Global South (Ministry of Electronics and Information Technology, 2023, para. 4).

The GDPIR, OFA, and SIF can underpin an India-anchored international architecture for DPI. The GDPIR provides a knowledge base for DPI. The OFA can structure DPI internationalization (Choudhury, 2023, para. 26), financially backed by the Global South-focused SIF. In potentially leading the OFA and SIF and already hosting the GDPIR, India can build on its credentials as a trusted hub for DPI expertise while working with its democratic partners, as mentioned earlier, and other stakeholders such as industry and academia to streamline DPI capacity-building efforts around the world and thus, at least indirectly, streamline the promotion of democracy as a sustainable means of driving economic development (Choudhury, 2023, para. 27; see Figure 11.1). India can also include the Global South in its DPI diplomacy by linking the OFA, GDPIR, and SIF with the DAKSHIN "global centre of excellence dedicated to [the Global South]," which the Indian prime minister launched in November 2023 (DD News, 2023, paras. 1–2). Such efforts would most likely implement the vision of the G20 Digital Economy Ministers (2023, para. 10) under the Indian presidency, which called for coordinated capacity building, technical assistance as well as "global multistakeholder approaches ... for implementing robust, inclusive, human-centric, and sustainable DPI in LMICs."

India can weave its aforementioned bilateral cooperation with democratic partners on DPI – including through a U.S.–India Global Digital Development Partnership suggested by both countries in June 2023 – as well as its aforementioned trilateral cooperation with the United States and Republic of Korea into its multilateral DPI diplomacy via the OFA and SIF so that the latter initiatives receive further credibility from the backing of major democracies (The White House & Government of India, 2023, para. 39). An example of such crossover from bilateral or trilateral cooperation to multilateral cooperation is how, in January 2024, France "expressed its support to join [OFA]" in order to "further synergize global efforts on building DPI capacities" (Government of India & Government of France, 2024, para. 24). In terms of concrete multilateral cooperation, India itself has pledged $10 million to the World Health Organization's Global Initiative on Digital Health, which includes capacity building for countries in the Indo-Pacific region seeking to adopt India's approach to DPI to aid cancer diagnosis and treatment (Commonwealth of Australia, Government of India, Government of Japan, & United States Government, 2024a, para. 9).

Indeed, such cooperation would be aided by increased momentum for DPI cooperation at the multilateral (and multistakeholder) level more broadly since India's G20 presidency. The following are key examples of this momentum in 2024 alone:

- In September, the UNGA approved the *Global Digital Compact* (United Nations, General Assembly, 2024, Annex I), which recognized: DPGs and "Resilient, safe, inclusive and interoperable" DPI as "key drivers of inclusive digital transformation and innovation"; and the necessity for greater investment in their deployment (United Nations, General Assembly, 2024, Annex I, paras. 14–16). The UNGA even committed to, among other things, establish safeguards "for inclusive, responsible, safe, secure and user-centred [DPI]," and grow finance for DPGs and DPI development (particularly in developing countries) by 2030 (United Nations, General Assembly, 2024, Annex I, paras. 17(c), (e)).
- In October, the "Global DPI Summit 2024" featured representatives across stakeholder groups from over 100 countries (Global DPI Summit 2024, 2024, para. 1). In addition to highlighting "the extraordinary progress" in the rollout of DPI around the world, attendees called for greater collaboration in areas like ecosystem-building, "safeguards to ensure that DPI is people-centric, transparent, accountable, and fair of all users"; ensuring adequate "support for the widespread implementation of DPI"; and driving adoption of robust technical standards to drive better interoperability and security of DPI (Backbones) (Global DPI Summit 2024, 2024, paras. 2, 5–8, 11–12, 15–18).
- In November, India cosponsored the *Declaration on Digital Public Infrastructure, AI and Data for Governance* with Brazil (G20 President for 2024) and South Africa (G20 President for 2025), which was endorsed by several G20 governments (Government of India, Government of Brazil, & Government of South Africa, 2024).

Such momentum certainly helps India's cause as it seeks to lead international efforts to develop and adopt DPI. That world leaders, particularly through the UN, endorsed the value of DPGs and DPI as instruments of economic and digital development, and called for greater investment in their development and deployment is highly consequential. After all, consensus at the UN level not merely validates but also significantly builds upon the pioneering multilateral consensus engineered by New Delhi on DPI and DPGs as G20 President in 2023.

Furthermore, India's being a trusted DPI partner and its leadership in DPI development and deployment will be aided by its work through the Quad. In September 2024, the Quad released the *Quad Principles for Development and Deployment of Digital Public Infrastructure*, including inclusivity, security (such as by incorporating "security features into the core design to ensure … resilience") and

"Governance for Public Benefit, Trust, and Transparency" (Commonwealth of Australia, Government of India, Government of Japan, & United States Government, 2024b, paras. 3.i, v, vii).

This is combined with the work of the Quad on uplifting software security, particularly through the *Joint Principles for Software Security* that it released in May 2023 and that seek to "promote and strengthen a culture where software security is by design and default" (Quad Senior Cyber Group, 2023, p. 2). These joint principles lay down "high-level secure software development practices" that echo the recommendations of NIST (Quad Senior Cyber Group, 2023, p. 2; Souppaya, Scarfone & Dodson, 2022, p. 4). Apart from committing to acquire software from vendors meeting these practices (thereby pledging to use their collective purchasing power to uplift software security), the Quad countries aim to "where necessary . . . build policy frameworks" that "encourage" software developers and suppliers to follow said software development practices (Quad Senior Cyber Group, 2023, p. 2).

Given the fundamental dependence of any DPI and DPGs on secure software (as mentioned earlier), work by the Quad to uplift software security under these joint principles underpins the ability of India to implement the Recommendations at home and help build and deploy cyber-resilient DPI in other (Global South) democracies; thereby helping the latter boost the confidence of their citizens in democratic institutions as effective vehicles for their economic development, per Figure 11.1. This is particularly significant in light of the deteriorating threat landscape for software supply chains, as per the previous section of this chapter on prosecuting systemic cyber risks. Given that DPI Backbones are CNI assets (see the opening paragraphs of this chapter), India's work to uplift software security through the Quad would also help fellow democracies implement the UNGA-approved cyber norms, as well as deliver public goods for their people such as national cyber resilience and national security (Nayyar, 2023, pp. 28–30).

One should note that India has already taken several concrete steps to export its approach to DPI.

For example, it cooperates with a number of countries when it comes to internationalizing the UPI.

- As part of its engagement with over thirty countries, including Japan, Australia, and Saudi Arabia, the NPCI has connected the UPI with France's Lyra Network, as well as the Bhutanese, Mauritian, Singaporean, and Sri Lankan payments networks (Ministry of Commerce & Industry, 2022, para. 6; Rudra, 2023, para. 1; Sibal, 2022, 2023, paras. 1–3; Wadhwa, Amla, & Salkever, 2022, para. 2; Prime Minister's Office, 2023; Ministry of External Affairs, 2024a, para. 1; PIB India, 2024).
- The Reserve Bank of India cofounded Project Nexus, a multilateral program to link the national 'Fast Payments Systems' of India with

Malaysia, Philippines, Singapore, and Thailand, in June 2024, and it is expected to be launched by 2026 (Pancholy, 2024, paras. 1–4).

- The Indian and Emirati governments have signed agreements on "cooperation in digital infrastructure projects" and on linking the UPI with the United Arab Emirates' (UAE's) AANI payments network, while UPI payments can already be made through the PhonePe payments app at Mashreq's NEOPAY Terminals in the UAE (Ministry of External Affairs, 2024b, para. 3; HT News Desk, 2024).
- Just in October 2024, the Maldivian president decided to establish "a consortium to introduce [the] UPI in the Maldives" (The President's Office, 2024, para. 3).

India's economic statecraft with respect to exporting the UPI also features the work of the NPCI International (the "international arm" of the NPCI) with a growing number of overseas partners.

- The body signed a memorandum of understanding (MoU) with Google Pay India to expand the acceptance of UPI payments outside India; export the approach to digital payments that the UPI represents; and "[ease] the process of remittances between countries" through use of the UPI's infrastructure (NPCI International, 2024a, paras. 2, 8).
- It signed an MoU with the major Greek bank, Eurobank, to create a "strategic alliance" for upgrading India–Greece payments flows and "streamlining remittances from Greece to India" using UPI technology (NPCI International, 2024b, paras. 1, 3).
- It partnered with the Bank of Namibia and Central Reserve Bank of Peru to help their respective countries develop and deploy UPI analogues (NPCI International, 2024c; NPCI International, 2024d).

If one moves from payments to health care, CoWIN's success as a component of India's DPI to fight the pandemic attracted so much international interest that India's virtual "CoWIN Global Conclave" was attended by representatives from 142 countries (Chandna, 2021; Ministry of Health and Family Welfare, 2021). By early February 2023, India had open-sourced CoWIN and shared it with over twenty-seven countries, enabling them to customize the platform as per their needs (Sansad TV, 2023).

When it comes to digital identity, the Philippines and Morocco became the first countries to adopt an Aadhaar-based digital identity system in March 2023 (Lele, 2023).

In terms of sharing India's approach to DPI more generally, there have been a number of such initiatives in train in the past few years alone.

- India signed MoUs with Armenia, Sierra Leone, Suriname, and Antigua and Barbuda on building DPI based on the India Stack (Kant & Sudke, 2023, para. 9).

- Sri Lanka plans to tailor India's DPI approach to enable the "effective and efficient delivery of citizen-centric services" (Government of India & Government of Sri Lanka, 2023, para. 4.IV.e). This is in addition to both countries agreeing to establish a Joint Working Group on implementing DPI, including by adapting India's DigiLocker and Aadhaar for Sri Lanka (Government of India & Government of Sri Lanka, 2024, paras. 15.iii, v).
- Google India and the EkStep Foundation launched "DPI in a Box," an initiative providing countries with "a readily deployable model" of India's DPI, including Aadhaar (Google India Team, 2024, paras. 13–18).
- In September 2024, the Secretary of Papua New Guinea's (PNG's) Department of Information Communication Technology observed that PNG's bilateral cooperation with India informed the former's own projects on digital identity, payments, and building DPI ecosystems (ASPICanberra, 2024). The Secretary stressed the need for development partners more generally to see the value in (financing) DPI projects (ASPICanberra, 2024).
- India and the Maldives agreed to cooperate on DPI, including by enabling the Maldives to adopt an Aadhaar analogue (Government of India & Republic of Maldives, 2024, para. 4.IV.ii).

In light of factors such as India's expertise and experience in DPI development and deployment, its growing cooperation with international partners in a variety of contexts, and the strengthening multilateral and multistakeholder consensus on the need for greater investment in DPI around the world, the world looks to India to lead. Indeed, India is well-positioned to lead the way on DPI, particularly in advising fellow democracies (in the Global South) on how to develop and deploy cyber-resilient DPI solutions and thus implement the UNGA-approved cyber norms (see Figure 11.1). In doing so, India will not only help fellow democracies better assure their national (cyber) resilience amid a worsening risk landscape but also help them strengthen the faith of their own polities in democracy as a force multiplier for their own development, much like DPI itself.

CONCLUSION

This chapter began by defining democracy, including with reference to international law, as the right of a people to shape their collective destiny, as well as including specific human rights such as peaceful assembly, expression, and association. It pointed to the relationship between economic development, economic growth, and the promotion of human rights, including democratic rights. Threats to the ability of democratic institutions such as elected governments to drive their citizens' economic development and thus promote their human rights are threats to their democracies themselves, given that the manifestation of these threats can undermine their citizens' confidence in democracy as a system of government under which they can flourish. In this context, the cyber resilience of CNI assets, which enable and preserve economic development, was argued to be a pillar of their democracies and indeed their governments' ability to implement UNGA-approved cyber norms with respect to human rights and CNI protection. The example of DPI Backbones as CNI assets provided the lens for this chapter on defending democracy in a digital age featuring a worsening cyber threat landscape, with India's approach to DPI and the India Stack serving as a case study.

After introducing DPI and DPGs (the essential ingredients for DPI) as enablers for the delivery of digitally native essential services at scale via open standards-based paradigms unconstrained by the closed paradigms of private technology companies, this chapter explored the DPI of the world's largest democracy and the India Stack. It highlighted the sheer quantum of service delivery by India's DPI, built on the three layers of the India Stack: identify, payments, and data. India's DPI has accelerated financial inclusion, empowered citizens through reliable digital public services, greatly reduced leakages of social security expenditures, and made its COVID-19 vaccination program quite efficient and transparent. In this respect, India's DPI, built atop the India Stack, is crucial to the world's largest democracy driving the economic development of its people and thus their confidence in their democratic system of government as the ideal means of advancing their interests, attracting the praise of world leaders and international organizations alike.

Given that DPI and DPGs are digitally native, and Indians are extremely dependent on the latter for a number of digitally native essential services, the chapter then called for India to prosecute systemic cyber risks to its DPI Backbones that stem from the critical software running on them. With India's G20 presidency forging multilateral consensus on the foundational importance of security to the digital economy, there is a need for India to incentivize the vendors of critical software to invest in the security of their SDLCs, perform robust software SCRM, and manage OSS risks appropriately. India has made progress in doing so, including as G20 President. The G20 *DPI Framework* and G20 *High-Level Principles*, endorsed by the G20 Leaders in 2023 and calling for security to be built into all software and DPI alike, are a testament to India's efforts.

The chapter concluded with a discussion of how India, the world's largest democracy, can export its approach to DPI and the India Stack, especially to fellow democracies in the Global South. Given India's success in advancing its citizens' economic development through DPI and the India Stack, other democracies stand to gain from what it has learned, including by strengthening the trust and confidence of their citizens in democracy as a system of government to drive their development and growth, as well as implementing the UNGA-approved cyber norms. This will be reinforced by advice from India on how to deploy DPI in a cyber-resilient manner, informed by the G20 *High-Level Principles* and G20 *DPI*

Framework and if India implements the Recommendations, all the more important amid a deteriorating cyber threat landscape.

India is poised to share its approach to DPI and the India Stack for a number of reasons, particularly that: its G20 presidency forged the first multilateral consensus on DPI policy; India is known for being a trusted development partner (for the Global South), which continues to be enhanced by how it is not seeking to weaponize its DPI expertise and the India Stack against smaller democracies (in the Global South); and India is increasingly cooperating on DPI (in the Global South) with leading democracies, which lends its own efforts more credibility. This is backed by the building of momentum at the multilateral and multistakeholder levels since India's G20 presidency on the value of DPI as an instrument of economic and digital development, and the need for greater investment in the development and deployment of DPI around the world.

These factors hold the world's largest democracy in good stead also in its plans to lead "an international architecture of collaboration" on DPI (Carnegie India, 2022) through initiatives such as the OFA, SIF, and GDPIR, potentially integrated with the DAKSHIN global center of excellence for the Global South. Its leadership and partnership with other countries will be aided by its work through the Quad on DPI and on uplifting software security in general, given that DPI and DPGs are digitally native, and this work will help *all countries* implement the UNGA-approved cyber norms, as well as deliver public goods for their people such as national cyber resilience and national security. This is complemented by India's strides in exporting its approach to DPI, including through the linkage of the UPI with overseas payments networks, the sharing of an open-sourced version of CoWIN with a few dozen countries for their vaccination programs, as well as its agreeing to work bilaterally with a range of Global South countries on their development and deploying DPI.

Whether it is deploying DPI at home in a cyber-resilient manner or capacity-building fellow democracies on how to do so in order to bolster their polities' confidence in democracy itself, the world looks to India to lead.

And the world is indeed India's oyster.

REFERENCES

ACI Worldwide. (2023). *It's prime time for real-time 2023*. GlobalData. https://go.aciworldwide.com/rs/030-ROK-804/images/2023-Prime-Time-for-Real-Time-Report.pdf

Agence Nationale de la Sécurité des Systèmes d'Information. (2023, January 15). *Cyber threat overview 2022*. French Government. https://cert.ssi.gouv.fr/uploads/CERTFR-2023-CTI-002.pdf

Alonso, C., Bhojwani, T., Hanedar, E., Prihardini, D., Uña, G., & Zhabska, K. (2023). *Stacking up the benefits: Lessons from India's digital journey* (Working Paper No. 2023/078). International Monetary Fund. https://imf.org/en/Publications/WP/Issues/2023/03/31/Stacking-up-the-Benefits-Lessons-from-Indias-Digital-Journey-531692

ANI. (2022a, September 25). *"India is a reliable partner", says Jamaican Foreign Minister in New York*. ThePrint. https://theprint.in/world/india-is-a-reliable-partner-says-jamaican-foreign-minister-in-new-york/1142442/

ANI [@ANI]. (2022b, October 13). *#WATCH | Paolo Mauro, Deputy Director of International Monetary Fund speaks on India's digital cash transfer scheme* [Video attached] [Tweet]. Twitter. https://twitter.com/ANI/status/1580366069780615168

ANI [@ANI]. (2022c, December 1). *We will look very closely and intensely at how India has done in order to promote digitisation. I think India…* [Post]. X. https://twitter.com/ANI/status/1597977439451635712

ASPICanberra. (2024, September 19). *Digital public infrastructure in the Indo-Pacific: security, privacy and accessibility* [Video]. YouTube. https://youtu.be/8A3xloF-SuM

Australian Cyber Security Centre. (2022, November 4). *Annual cyber threat report: July 2021 to June 2022*. Australian Government. https://cyber.gov.au/sites/default/files/2023-03/ACSC-Annual-Cyber-Threat-Report-2022_0.pdf

Australian Signals Directorate. (2023, November 14). *ASD annual cyber threat report: 2022–2023*. Australian Government. https://cyber.gov.au/sites/default/files/2023-11/asd-cyber-threat-report-2023.pdf

Banerji, E. (2023, January 26). *Opinion | India: The voice of the global south*. News18. https://news18.com/news/opinion/opinion-india-the-voice-of-the-global-south-6917011.html

Behrends, J., Simons, J., Troy, K., & Gupta, H. (2021). *Digital public goods: Guidance for development, governance, and stewardship*. Harvard University. https://ethics.harvard.edu/publications/digital-public-goods-guidance-development-governance-and-stewardship

Blinken, A. J. (2022, May 10). *Attribution of Russia's malicious cyber activity against Ukraine* [Press release]. U.S. Department of State. https://state.gov/attribution-of-russias-malicious-cyber-activity-against-ukraine

Burt, C. (2018, June 13). *Vendor lock-in hindering African identity projects*. Biometric Update. https://biometricupdate.com/201806/vendor-lock-in-hindering-african-identity-projects

Carnegie India. [Carnegie India]. (2022, November 30). *Panel: The Next Decade of India Stack* [Video]. YouTube. https://youtu.be/sfInBUOgIcQ

Chandna, H. (2021, November 15). *CoWIN set to go global as over 12 countries in talks with govt to borrow technology*. News18.com. https://news18.com/news/india/cowin-set-to-go-global-as-over-12-countries-in-talks-with-govt-to-borrow-technology-4443131.html

Chaudhuri, R. (2023, September 1). *Decoding the G20 consensus on digital public infrastructure: A key outcome of India's presidency*. Carnegie India. https://carnegieindia.org/2023/09/01/decoding-g20-consensus-on-digital-public-infrastructure-key-outcome-of-india-s-presidency-pub-90467

Choudhary, S., & Singh, N. (2023, August 27). *9 years on, Jan-Dhan helps govt seal leaks and purge bogus accounts: About 6.26 PMJDY account holders receives DBT*. Business Standard. https://business-standard.com/india-news/jan-dhan-helps-centre-tackling-corruption-in-direct-benefits-transfers-123082700732_1.html

Choudhury, D. (2023, April 26). *ONDC grows 25 times in 2 months to cross 5,000 food, grocery orders a day*. moneycontrol. https://moneycontrol.com/news/business/startup/ondc-grows-25-times-in-2-months-to-cross-5000-food-grocery-orders-a-day-10478711.html

Clancy, C., Ferraro, J., Martin, R., Pennington, A., Sledjeski, C., & Wiener, C. (2021, January). *Deliver uncompromised: Securing critical software supply chains: Proposal to establish an end-to-end framework for software supply chain integrity*. The MITRE Corporation. https://mitre.org/sites/default/files/2021-11/prs-21-0278-deliver-uncompromised-securing-critical-software-supply-chain.pdf

CloudSEK TRIAD Team. (2023, February 8). *Global threat landscape report 2021–2022*. CloudSEK. https://cloudsek.com/whitepapers-reports/global-threat-landscape-report-2021-2022

Commonwealth of Australia, Government of India, Government of Japan, & United States Government. (2023, May 20). *Quad Cybersecurity Partnership: Joint principles for secure software*. PMC.gov.au. https://pmc.gov.au/sites/default/files/resource/download/quad-joint-principles-secure-software.pdf

Commonwealth of Australia, Government of India, Government of Japan, & United States Government. (2024a, September 21). *The Wilmington Declaration Joint Statement from the Leaders of Australia, India, Japan, and the United States* [Joint statement]. https://whitehouse.gov/briefing-room/statements-releases/2024/09/21/the-wilmington-declaration-joint-statement-from-the-leaders-of-australia-india-japan-and-the-united-states/

Commonwealth of Australia, Government of India, Government of Japan, & United States Government. (2024b, September 22). *Quad Principles for Development and Deployment of Digital Public Infrastructure* [Media Note]. https://state.gov/quad-principles-for-development-and-deployment-of-digital-public-infrastructure/

Cybersecurity & Infrastructure Security Agency. (2021a, April). *Defending against software supply chain attacks*. United States Government. https://cisa.gov/sites/default/files/publications/defending_against_software_supply_chain_attacks_508_1.pdf

Cybersecurity & Infrastructure Security Agency. (2021b, July 20). *Cyber-attack against Ukrainian critical infrastructure* (ICS Alert No IR-ALERT-H-16-056-01). United States Government. https://cisa.gov/news-events/ics-alerts/ir-alert-h-16-056-01

D'Silva, D., Filková, Z., Packer, F., & Tiwari, S. (2019, December). *The design of digital financial infrastructure: Lessons from India* (BIS Paper No. 106). Bank for International Settlements. https://bis.org/publ/bppdf/bispap106.pdf

Dahl, R. A., & Shapiro, I. (2024, December 18). Democracy. In The Editors of Encyclopaedia Britannica (Eds.), *Encyclopaedia Britannica*. Encyclopaedia Britannica. https://britannica.com/topic/democracy

DD News. (2023, November 17). *PM Modi unveils DAKSHIN at Global South Summit*. DD News. https://ddnews.gov.in/international/pm-modi-unveils-dakshin-global-south-summit

Department of Financial Services. (2023, May). *Pradhan Mantri Jan Dhan Yojana (PMJDY)*. Mission Office, Department of Financial Services, Ministry of Finance, Government of India. https://pmjdy.gov.in/

Desai, V. T., Markskell, J., Marin, G., & Varghese, M. (2023, March 15). *How digital public infrastructure supports empowerment, inclusion, and resilience*. World Bank Blogs. https://blogs.worldbank.org/digital-development/how-digital-public-infrastructure-supports-empowerment-inclusion-and-resilience

Digital India [@_DigitalIndia]. (2023, November 5). *#KeyHighlights Address by G20 Sherpa Shri Amitabh Kant (@amitabhk87) at the Workshop on Transformative Technology – Promoting Development, Growth and Innovation…* [Post]. X. https://x.com/_DigitalIndia/status/1721099269413683237

Economic development. (2023). *Cambridge Dictionary*. Cambridge University Press.

European Commission. (2020, October 21). *Communication to the Commission: Open Source Software Strategy 2020–2023* (Communication No C(2020) 7149). European Union. https://commission.europa.eu/system/files/2023-02/en_ec_open_source_strategy_2020-2023.pdf

European Union & Government of India. (2023, May 16). *EU–India Joint Statement 1st meeting of the Trade and Technology Council* [Joint statement]. European Commission. https://digital-strategy.ec.europa.eu/en/library/eu-india-ttc-joint-statement

Feldman, M., Hadjimichael, T., Lanahan, L., & Kemeny, T. (2016). The logic of economic development: A definition and model for investment. *Environment and Planning C: Government and Policy*, 34(1), 5–21. https://doi.org/10.1177/0263774X156 14653

G7 Digital and Tech Ministers. (2023). *Ministerial Declaration: The G7 Digital and Tech Ministers' Meeting* [Ministerial Declaration]. University of Toronto. https://g7.utoronto.ca/ict/2023-declaration.html

G20 Digital Economy Ministers. (2023). *Digital Economy Ministers Meeting: Outcome document & chair's summary*. G20. https://g7g20-documents.org/database/document/2023-g20-india-sherpa-track-digital-economy-ministers-ministers-language-g20-digital-economy-ministers-meeting-outcome-document-and-chair-summary

G20 Leaders. (2023). *G20 New Delhi Leaders' Declaration*. G20. https://g20.in/content/dam/gtwenty/gtwenty_new/document/G20-New-Delhi-Leaders-Declaration.pdf

Gajbhiye, D., Arora, R., Arham, N., Yangdol, R., & Thakur, I. (2022). *Measuring India's digital economy*. Reserve Bank of India. https://rbidocs.rbi.org.in/rdocs/Bulletin/PDFs/05ART2012202221265B8E871824B98970F03E87228C0FE.PDF

Gates, B. [@BillGates]. (2023, September 12). *The #G20 reached a groundbreaking consensus on the role of digital public infrastructure as a critical accelerator of the Sustainable* [Post]. X. https://twitter.com/BillGates/status/1701318146878218667

Gawen, E., Hirschfeld, A., Kenny, A., Stewart, J., & Middleton, E. (2021). *Open source in government: Creating the conditions for success*. Public Digital. https://assets.public.digital/Open_Source_Exec_Summary.pdf

Ghosh, S. K. (2021). *Share of informal economy may have shrunk to no more than 20% from 52% in FY18* (Ecowrap Issue No. 43, FY22). State Bank of India. https://sbi.co.in/documents/13958/10990811/01112021_Ecowrap_20211101.pdf/a4a69fed-e227-6da0-d217-a8474a5ae982?t=1635764900143

Global DPI Summit 2024. (2024). *Global DPI Summit Outcome Statement* [Outcome statement]. https://globaldpisummit.org/page/4280934/outcome-statement

Google India Team. (2024, October 3). *Driving large-scale impact for businesses and individuals through Gemini and Google Cloud* [Blog post]. Google. https://blog.google/intl/en-in/company-news/outreach-initiatives/driving-large-scale-impact-for-businesses-and-individuals-through-gemini-and-google-cloud/

Government of India. (2023a). *Direct benefit transfer*. Direct Benefit Transfer Mission, Government of India. https://dbtbharat.gov.in/

(2023b, November 15). *2nd voice of Global South Summit* [Press release]. Ministry of External Affairs, Government of India. https://mea.gov.in/press-releases.htm?dtl/37261/2nd_Voice_of_Global_South_Summit

(2023c, December 4). *Visit of US Principal Deputy National Security Adviser to India (December 04, 2023)* [Press release]. Ministry of External Affairs, Government of India. https://mea.gov.in/press-releases.htm?dtl/37333/Visit_of_US_Principal_Deputy_National_Security_Adviser_to_India_December_04_2023

Government of India, Government of Brazil, & Government of South Africa. (2024, November 20). *Declaration on Digital Public Infrastructure, AI and Data for Governance* [Declaration]. Ministry of External Affairs, Government of India. https://mea.gov.in/bilateral-documents.htm?dtl/38551/Declaration+on+Digital+Public+Infrastructure+AI+and+Data+for+Governance++Joint+Communiqu233+by+the+G20+Troika+India+Brazil+and+South+Africa+endorsed+by+several+G20+countries+guest+countries+and+international+organizations

Government of India, & Government of France. (2024, January 26). *India – France Joint Statement on the State Visit of H.E. Mr. Emmanuel Macron, President of French Republic, to India (25 26 January 2024)* [Joint statement]. https://mea.gov.in/bilateral-documents.htm? dtl/37534/India__France_Joint_Statement_on_the_State_Visit_of_HE_Mr_Emmanuel_Macron_President_of_French_Republic_to_India_25__26_January_2024

(2023, July 14). *Horizon 2047: 25th Anniversary of the India-France Strategic Partnership, Towards A Century of India-France Relations* [Joint statement]. https://mea.gov.in/bilateral-documents.htm?dtl/36806/Horizon_2047_25th_Anniversary_of_the_IndiaFrance_Strategic_Partnership_Towards_A_Century_of_IndiaFrance_Relations

Government of India, & Republic of Germany. (2024, October 25). *Joint Statement: 7th India-Germany Inter-Governmental Consultations (IGC)* [Joint statement]. Ministry of External Affairs, Government of India. https://mea.gov.in/bilateral-documents.htm?dtl/38467/Joint_Statement_7th_IndiaGermany_InterGovernmental_Consultations_IGC

Government of India, & Republic of Maldives. (2024, October 7). *India and Maldives: A Vision for Comprehensive Economic and Maritime Security Partnership* [Joint statement]. Ministry of External Affairs, Government of India. https://mea.gov.in/bilateral-documents.htm?dtl/38384/India_and_Maldives_A_Vision_for_Comprehensive_Economic_and_Maritime_Security_Partnership

Government of India, & Government of Sri Lanka. (2023, July 21). *Promoting connectivity, catalysing prosperity: India-Sri Lanka Economic Partnership Vision* [Joint statement]. Ministry of External Affairs, Government of India. https://mea.gov.in/bilateral-documents.htm?dtl/36864/Promoting_Connectivity_Catalysing_Prosperity_IndiaSri_Lanka_Economic_Partnership_Vision

(2024, December 16). *India – Sri Lanka Joint Statement: Fostering Partnerships for a Shared Future* [Joint statement]. Ministry of External Affairs, Government of India. https://mea.gov.in/press-releases.htm?dtl/38797/India__Sri_Lanka_Joint_Statement__Fostering_Partnerships_for_a_Shared_Future

Greenberg, A. (2018, August 22). The untold story of NotPetya, the most devastating cyberattack in history: Crippled ports. Paralyzed Corporations. *Wired*. https://wired.com/story/notpetya-cyberattack-ukraine-russia-code-crashed-the-world

(2019). *Sandworm: A New Era of Cyberwar and the Hunt for the Kremlin's Most Dangerous Hackers*. Doubleday.

Gupta, T. (2022, May 11). Explained: How the ONDC Is all set to democratise e-commerce in India. *Swarajya*. https://swarajyamag.com/technology/explained-how-the-ondc-is-all-set-to-democratise-e-commerce-in-india

Guterres, A. (Speaker). (2022, October 19). *Secretary-General's remarks on the partnership between India and the United Nations on India's 75th anniversary* [Speech Transcript]. United Nations. https://un.org/sg/en/content/sg/speeches/2022-10-19/secretary-generals-remarks-the-partnership-between-india-and-the-united-nations-india%E2%80%99s-75th-anniversary

Herr, T., Lee, J., Loomis, W., & Scott, S. (2020, July). *Breaking trust: Shades of crisis across an insecure software supply chain*. Atlantic Council. https://atlanticcouncil.org/wp-content/uploads/2020/07/Breaking-trust-Shades-of-crisis-across-an-insecure-software-supply-chain.pdf

HT News Desk. (2024, March 29). *PhonePe users can now make UPI payments in UAE: All you need to know*. Hindustan Times. https://hindustantimes.com/business/phonepe-users-can-now-make-upi-payments-in-uae-all-you-need-to-know-101711681533321.html

ID4D. (2020). *Open source for global public goods*. World Bank Group. https://documents1.worldbank.org/curated/en/672901582561140400/pdf/Open-Source-for-Global-Public-Goods.pdf

Inglis, C., & Neuberger, A. (2021, October 28). *A conversation with Chris Inglis and Anne Neuberger (J. A. Lewis, interviewer)* [Interview transcript]. Centre for Strategic and International Studies. https://csis-website-prod.s3.amazonaws.com/s3fs-public/publication/211028_Lewis_Inglis_Neuberger.pdf

International Covenant on Civil and Political Rights, opened for signature 16 December 1966, 999 UNTS 171 (entered into force 23 March 1976).

iSPIRT. (2021, December 15). *IndiaStack*. IndiaStack. https://indiastack.org

Jacob, S. (2024, 1 April). *In a first, yearly transactions through UPI cross 100 billion in FY24*. Business Standard. https://business-standard.com/finance/news/upi-transactions-cross-100-billion-mark-in-fy24-clock-131-billion-124040100655_1.html

Jaishankar, Dr. S. [@DrSJaishankar]. (2023a, November 17). *Addressed the first Foreign Ministers' session of the Voice of Global South Summit. Made the following points: India walked the…* [Post]. X. https://twitter.com/DrSJaishankar/status/1725457015051608130

(2023b, November 17). *Addressed the second Foreign Ministers' session of the Voice of Global South Summit. Made the following points: India took over…* [Post]. X. https://twitter.com/DrSJaishankar/status/1725489700381893077

Kant, A., & Sudke, A. (2023, November 22). *Lessons for Africa, from India: Africa can achieve quick and inclusive growth by Replicating India's DPI model*. Financial Express. https://financialexpress.com/opinion/lessons-for-africa-from-india/3313459/lite/

Kumar, M. (2021, November 26). *India to push for patent waiver for COVID-19 vaccines at WTO*. Reuters. https://reuters.com/world/india/india-push-patent-waiver-covid-19-vaccines-wto-2021-11-26

Lele, S. (2023, March 23). *Philippines and Morocco start the adoption of Aadhaar architecture*. Business Standard. https://business-standard.com/article/international/philippines-and-morocco-start-the-adoption-of-aadhaar-architecture-123032201100_1.html

Lewis, J. (2023, April 10). *An overview of global cloud competition*. Centre for Strategic & International Studies (CSIS). https://csis-website-prod.s3.amazonaws.com/s3fs-public/2023-04/230410_Lewis_Overview_Cloud_1.pdf

Marslev, K., & and Sano, H.-O. (2016). *The Economy of Human Rights: Exploring potential linkages between human rights and economic development* (Human Rights Research Paper No 2016/2, 2016). The Danish Institute for Human Rights. https://humanrights.dk/sites/humanrights.dk/files/media/migrated/the_economics_of_human_rights_2016.pdf

Mehta, N. (2023, September 9). G20: India's new soft power is digital public infrastructure. *The Times of India*. https://timesofindia.indiatimes.com/blogs/academic-interest/g20-indias-new-soft-power-is-digital-public-infrastructure/

Ministry of Commerce & Industry. (2022, September 19). *Shri Piyush Goyal concludes fruitful visit to Saudi Arabia* [Press release]. Ministry of Commerce & Industry. https://pib.gov.in/PressReleasePage.aspx?PRID = 1860633

Ministry of Electronics and Information Technology. (2023, November 23). *Prime Minister announces completion of Global Digital Public Infrastructure Repository and creation of a Social Impact Fund to advance Digital Public Infrastructure in Global South* [Press release]. https://pib.gov.in/PressReleasePage.aspx?PRID = 1979113

Ministry of External Affairs. [Ministry of External Affairs, India]. (2022a, September 24). *India@75: Showcasing India UN Partnership in Action (Sep 24, 2022)* [Video]. YouTube. https://youtube.com/live/8fvQ1X1g-eU

(2022b, November 29). *EAM: Global Technology Summit 2022* [Video]. YouTube. https://youtube.com/live/MR-ebRUHMCU

(2022c, December 9). *G-20 and India's Presidency* [Press release]. https://pib.gov.in/PressReleaseIframePage.aspx?PRID = 1882356

(2023a, January 13). *Summary of Deliberations: Voice of Global South Summit 2023 (January 12–13, 2023)* [Statement]. Government of India. https://mea.gov.in/bilateral-documents.htm?dtl/36119/Summary_of_Deliberations_Voice_of_Global_South_Summit_2023_January_1213_2023

(2023b, February 23). *Annual Report 2022*. Government of India. https://mea.gov.in/Uploads/PublicationDocs/36286_MEA_Annual_Report_2022_English_web.pdf

(2023c, July 27). *15th India-Japan Foreign Ministers' Strategic Dialogue* [Press release]. Government India. https://mea.gov.in/press-releases.htm?dtl/36913/15th+India Japan+Foreign+Ministers+Strategic+Dialogue

(2024a, February 12). *Prime Minister jointly inaugurates UPI services with Mauritius Prime Minister & Sri Lankan President* [Press release]. https://mea.gov.in/press-releases.htm?dtl/37616/Prime_Minister_jointly_inaugurates_UPI_services_with_Mauritius_Prime_Minister_amp_Sri_Lankan_President

(2024b, February 13). *Prime Minister's meeting with the President of the UAE* [Press release]. https://mea.gov.in/press-releases.htm?dtl/37620/Prime_Ministers_meeting_with_the_President_of_the_UAE

Ministry of Finance. (2023, January). *Economic Survey 2022–23*. Government of India. https://indiabudget.gov.in/economicsurvey/

Ministry of Health and Family Welfare. (2021, July 5). *Prime Minister Shri Narendra Modi inaugurates the Co-WIN Global Conclave* [Press release]. https://pib.gov.in/PressReleaseIframePage.aspx?PRID=1732897

Modi, N. (2023, September 6). Narendra Modi: India's G20 is a chance for the world to unite. *The Times*. https://thetimes.co.uk/article/narendra-modi-indias-g20-is-a-chance-for-the-world-to-unite-gpp6jgfjn

[@narendramodi]. (2024, August 28). *Today, we mark a momentous occasion—#10YearsOfJanDhan. Congratulations to all the beneficiaries and compliments to all those who worked to* [Post]. X. https://x.com/narendramodi/status/1828640493737054688

MyGovIndia [@mygovindia]. (2023, August 28). *Banking for all paves the way for a brighter tomorrow. With a rising number of Jan Dhan Accounts, we're forging…* [Image attached] [Tweet]. X. https://x.com/mygovindia/status/1696003775012413487

Narlikar, A. (2021). Must the weak suffer what they must? In D. W. Dresser, H. Farrell, & A. L. Newman (Eds.), *The uses and abuses of weaponized interdependence* (pp. 289–304). Brookings Institution Press.

National Institute of Standards and Technology. (2021, October 13). *Definition of Critical Software Under Executive Order (EO) 14028*. United States Government. https://nist.gov/system/files/documents/2021/10/13/EO Critical FINAL.pdf

Nayyar, R. (2023). *The quad: Carved in code: Collaborating to deliver the greatest public good*. German Institute for Global and Area Studies. https://giga-hamburg.de/assets/tracked/pure/48834609/GIGA_DigitalDiplomacyStatecraft_WP_01_Nayyar_update2307.pdf

Newbill, C. M. (2019). Defining critical infrastructure for a global application. *Indiana Journal of Global Legal Studies*, 26(2), 761–779. https://repository.law.indiana.edu/ijgls/vol26/iss2/11

NPCI International. (2024a, January 17). *Google Pay India signs MoU with NPCI International for Global Expansion of UPI* [Press release]. https://npci.org.in/PDF/npci/press-releases/2024/NPCI-Press-Release-Google-Pay-India-signs-MoU-with-NPCI-International-for-Global-Expansion-of-UPI.pdf

(2024b, February 29). *NPCI International and Eurobank Sign MoU in View of Forming a Strategic Alliance on Foreign Inward Remittances* [Press release]. https://npci.org.in/PDF/npci/press-releases/2024/NIPL-Press-Release-NPCI-International-and-Eurobank-Sign-MoU-in-View-of-Forming-a-Strategic-Alliance-on-Foreign-Inward-Remittances.pdf

(2024c, May 2). *NPCI International Partners with Bank of Namibia for Deploying India's UPI Stack in Namibia* [Press release]. https://npci.org.in/PDF/npci/press-releases/2024/NPCI-International-Partners-with-Bank-of-Namibia-for-Deploying-India's-UPI-Stack-in-Namibia.pdf

(2024d, June 5). *NPCI International and the Central Reserve Bank of Peru Partner to Develop UPI-Like Real-Time Payments System in Peru* [Press release]. https://npci.org.in/PDF/npci/press-releases/2024/NIPL-Press-Release-NPCI-International-and-the-Central-Reserve-Bank-of-Peru-Partner-to-Develop-UPI-Like-Real-Time-Payments-System-in-Peru.pdf

NTIA Multistakeholder Process on Software Component Transparency Framing Working Group. (2021, October 21). *Framing Software component transparency: Establishing a common software bill of materials (SBOM)*. United States Government. https://ntia.gov/files/ntia/publications/ntia_sbom_framing_2nd_edition_20211021.pdf

Observer Research Foundation. [ORF]. (2022, October 19). *India @ 75 || India-UN Partnership: Strengthening South-South Cooperation ||* [Video]. YouTube. https://youtube.com/live/bItbHTPBE_4

OECD. (2021). *Development Co-operation Report 2021: Shaping a just digital transformation*. OECD Publishing. https://doi.org/10.1787/ce08832f-en

(2022). *OECD policy framework on digital security*. OECD Publishing. https://doi.org/10.1787/a69df866-en

OECD Council. (2022, September 26). *Recommendation of the Council on National Digital Security Strategies* [OECD Legal Instrument No OECD/LEGAL/0480]. OECD. https://legalinstruments.oecd.org/en/instruments/OECD-LEGAL-0480

Open Network for Digital Commerce. (2022, January). *Open network for digital commerce: Democratizing digital commerce in India*. https://ondc-static-web-bucket.s3.ap-south-1.amazonaws.com/res/daea2fs3n/image/upload/ondc-website/files/ONDCStrategyPaper_ucvfjm/1659889490.pdf

Pant, H. V. (2023, September 14). *Rediscovering the centrality of the Global South*. Observer Research Foundation. https://policycommons.net/artifacts/4825715/rediscovering-the-centrality-of-the-global-south/5662432/

Parliamentary Joint Committee on Intelligence and Security. (2022). *Advisory report on the Security Legislation Amendment (Critical Infrastructure Protection) Bill 2022*. Parliament of Australia. https://parlinfo.aph.gov.au/parlInfo/download/committees/reportjnt/024898/toc_pdf/AdvisoryreportontheSecurityLegislationAmendment(CriticalInfrastructureProtection)Bill2022.pdf;fileType = application/pdf

Perlroth, N. (2021). *This is how they tell me the world ends*. Bloomsbury Publishing.

PIB India. [@PIB_India]. (2024, December 14). *Driving the #DigitalPayment revolution, #UPI achieved 15,547 crore transactions worth Rs. 223 lakh crore from January to November, 2024, showcasing* [Post]. X. https://x.com/PIB_India/status/1867834028487020946

Prime Minister's Office. (2023, February 21). *PM Narendra Modi and Prime Minister of Singapore Lee Hsien Loong participate in the Virtual Launch of UPI-PayNow Linkage between India and Singapore* [Press release]. https://pib.gov.in/PressReleseDetail.aspx?PRID = 1900976

Pancholy, P. (2024, July 1). *Reserve Bank of India and ASEAN Countries to Create a Platform to Facilitate Instantaneous Cross-Border Retail Payments* [Press release]. https://rbi.org.in/Scripts/BS_PressReleaseDisplay.aspx?prid = 58197

Prince, M. [@eastdakota] (2021, December 14). *Correction: Seeing >1000 per second instances of ${, of those 400 per second are confirmed attempts at exploit* [Tweet]. Twitter. https://twitter.com/eastdakota/status/1470819030155993089

PTI. (2023, March 1). *Bill Gates praises India's digital public networks, payment systems; says this will be cheapest 5g market*. Outlook. https://business.outlookindia.com/news/bill-gates-praises-india-s-digital-public-networks-payment-systems-says-this-will-be-cheapest-5g-market-news-266464

Quad Senior Cyber Group. (2023, May 20). *Quad cybersecurity partnership: Joint principles for secure software*. Department of the Prime Minister and Cabinet. https://pmc.gov.au/sites/default/files/resource/download/quad-joint-principles-secure-software.pdf

Romine, C. H. (2017, June 15). *Testimony of Charles H. Romine, Ph.D.* U.S. Department of Commerce. https://ogc.commerce.gov/sites/default/files/media/files/2017/20170615_house_science_-_romine.pdf

Rudra, T. (2023, July 14). *UPI enters France following NPCI's MoU agreement with Lyra Network last year*. Inc42. https://inc42.com/buzz/upi-enters-france-following-npcis-mou-agreement-with-lyra-network-last-year/

Sansad TV. [Sansad TV]. (2023, February 4). *Diplomatic Dispatch: India's Leadership in Digital Public Goods | 03 February, 2023* [Video]. YouTube. https://youtu.be/HZNOT2tq4vo

Scott, S., Brackett, S. A., Herr, T., & Hamin, M. (2023, February). *Avoiding the success trap: Toward policy for open-source software as infrastructure*. Atlantic Council. https://atlanticcouncil.org/wp-content/uploads/2023/02/Avoiding-the-success-trap-Toward-policy-for-open-source-software-as-infrastructure.pdf

Security of Critical Infrastructure Act 2018 (Cth).

Sen, A. (2001). *Development as freedom*. Oxford University Press.

Sibal, S. [@sidhant] (2022, July 29). *Statement in Parliament* [Image attached] [Tweet]. Twitter. https://twitter.com/sidhant/status/1552962784224153600/photo/1

(2023, May 19). *Exclusive | Japan considering joining India's UPI payment system, says Japanese Minister Kono Taro*. WION. https://wionews.com/world/exclusive-japan-considering-joining-indias-upi-payment-system-says-japanese-minister-kono-taro-593773

Silvers, R., Adkins, H., Alperovitch, D., Carlin, J., DeRusha, C., Inglis, C., et al. (2022, July 11). *Review of the December 2021 Log4j Event*. United States Government. https://cisa.gov/sites/default/files/publications/CSRB-Report-on-Log4-July-11-2022_508.pdf

SLSA. (2023). *Introduction*. https://slsa.dev/spec/v0.1/#supply-chain-threats.

Smart, W. (2018). *Lessons learned review of the WannaCry ransomware attack*. Department of Health & Social Care. https://england.nhs.uk/wp-content/uploads/2018/02/lessons-learned-review-wannacry-ransomware-cyber-attack-cio-review.pdf

Sonatype. (2023). *8th Annual State of the Software Supply Chain*. Sonatype. https://sonatype.com/hubfs/8th%20Annual%20SSCR%20-%202023.pdf

Souppaya, M., Scarfone, K., & Dodson, D. (2022, February). *Secure Software Development Framework (SSDF) Version 1.1: Recommendations for Mitigating the Risk of Software Vulnerabilities* (NIST Special Publication No 800-218). United States Government. https://doi.org/10.6028/NIST.SP.800-218

Starks, T. (2021, December 13). *CISA warns 'most serious' Log4j Vulnerability likely to affect hundreds of millions of devices*. CyberScoop. https://cyberscoop.com/log4j-cisa-easterly-most-serious

Synopsys. (2023, February 22). 2023 *Open source security and risk analysis report*. Synopsys. https://synopsys.com/content/dam/synopsys/sig-assets/reports/rep-ossra-2023.pdf

The Pharma Letter. (2023, March 22). *India and South Africa renew push for extending TRIPS waiver beyond Covid vaccines*. https://thepharmaletter.com/article/india-and-south-africa-renew-push-for-extending-trips-waiver-beyond-covid-vaccines

The President's Office. (2024, October 20). *President decides to introduce India's Unified Payment Interface in Maldives, paving the way for improved financial transactions* [Press Release]. Republic of Maldives. https://presidency.gov.mv/Press/Article/31921

The White House. (2023, March). *National cybersecurity strategy*. The United States Government. https://whitehouse.gov/wp-content/uploads/2023/03/National-Cybersecurity-Strategy-2023.pdf

The White House & Government of India. (2023, June 22). *Joint statement from the United States and India* [Joint statement]. The White House. https://whitehouse.gov/briefing-room/statements-releases/2023/06/22/joint-statement-from-the-united-states-and-india/

(2024, September 21). *Joint Fact Sheet: The United States and India Continue to Expand Comprehensive and Global Strategic Partnership* [Joint Fact Sheet]. The White House. https://whitehouse.gov/briefing-room/statements-releases/2024/09/21/joint-fact-sheet-the-united-states-and-india-continue-to-expand-comprehensive-and-global-strategic-partnership/

Trautman, L. J., & Ormerod, P. C. (2019). WannaCry, ransomware, and the emerging threat to corporations. *Tennessee Law Review*, 86(2), 503–556. https://ir.law.utk.edu/cgi/viewcontent.cgi?article = 1080&context = tennesseelawreview

United Nations. (2019, November 26). *Democracy*. United Nations. https://un.org/en/global-issues/democracy

(2020). *Road map for digital cooperation: Implementation of the recommendations of the high-level panel on digital cooperation: Report of the Secretary-General*. United Nations. https://un.org/en/content/digital-cooperation-roadmap/

United Nations, General Assembly, *The Pact for the Future*, A/79/L.2 (20 September 2024), available from https://docs.un.org/A/79/L.2.

United Nations, General Assembly, *Report of the Group of Governmental Experts on Advancing Responsible State Behaviour in Cyberspace in the Context of International Security*, A/76/135 (14 July 2021), available from https://docs.un.org/A/76/135.

Universal Declaration of Human Rights, GA Res 217A (III), UN GAOR, UN Doc A/810 (10 December 1948).

U.S. Department of Commerce & U.S. Department of Homeland Security. (2022, February 23). *Assessment of the critical supply chains supporting the U.S. information and communications technology industry*. United States Government. https://dhs.gov/sites/default/files/2022-02/ICTSupplyChainReport_0.pdf

U.S. Mission Korea. (2024, March 13). *Readout of the United States–India–Republic of Korea Trilateral Technology Dialogue* [Press release]. U.S. Embassy & Consulate in the Republic of Korea. https://kr.usembassy.gov/031324-readout-of-the-united-states-india-republic-of-korea-trilateral-technology-dialogue/

Viasat, Inc. (2022, March 30). *KA-SAT Network cyberattack overview*. Viasat. https://viasat.com/about/newsroom/blog/ka-sat-network-cyber-attack-overview/

Vir, A. & Sanghi, R. (2021, January 15). The internet country: How India created a digital blueprint for the economies of the future. *Tigerfeathers*. https://tigerfeathers.substack.com/p/the-internet-country

Vivekananda International Foundation. (2019, March 25). *Vasudhaiva Kutumbakam: Relevance of India's ancient thinking to contemporary strategic reality*. https://vifindia.org/sites/default/files/Vasudhaiva-Kutumbakam-Conference-Proceedings.pdf

Wadhwa, V., Amla, I., & Salkever, A. (2022, June 30). *As Silicon Valley fantasizes about Web3, India leaps ahead on payments*. Fortune. https://fortune.com/2022/06/30/blockchain-india-upi-payments-global-reach/

World Bank Group. (2023). *G20 policy recommendations for advancing financial inclusion and productivity gains through digital public infrastructure*. World Bank Group. https://openknowledge.worldbank.org/entities/publication/b8d6b107-3e97-41be-886d-1c46ee906042

World Health Organization. (2021, January 16). *India rolls out the world's largest COVID-19 vaccination drive* [Press release]. World Health Organization. https://who.int/india/news/feature-stories/detail/india-rolls-out-the-world-s-largest-covid-19-vaccination-drive.

Zetter, K. (2016, May 3). Inside the cunning, unprecedented hack of Ukraine's power grid. *Wired*. https://wired.com/2016/03/inside-cunning-unprecedented-hack-ukraines-power-grid/

12

The Domestication of Cybersecurity in Authoritarian Regimes

China's Media Narrative on Cybersecurity and Its Challenge to Democracy

Jun Liu

CYBER THREATS AND AUTHORITARIAN REGIMES: CHALLENGES TO DEFENDING CYBERSECURITY

The disruptive and damaging cyber threats and attacks carried out by authoritarian regimes and their proxies toward both domestic and international entities is a long-standing issue, although one that has become increasingly prominent in recent years (e.g., Bradshaw & Howard, 2019; Morgan, 2018; Schünemann, 2022; Woolley & Howard, 2017). Scholars have examined diverse cyber threats and attacks ranging from, for instance, internet shutdowns (e.g., Majeed, 2022; Mare, 2020) to opinion manipulation (e.g., Alyukov, 2022; Bradshaw & Howard, 2017; King, Pan, & Roberts, 2017), from content blockage and filtering (e.g., Greitens, 2013; Roberts, 2018; Ververis, Marguel, & Fabian, 2020) to fake news and disinformation campaigns (e.g., Abrahams & Leber, 2021; Jones, 2022). As authoritarian regimes are actively shaping cyberspace at home and on the global stage to their own strategic advantage, understanding their cyber threats not only explains their resilience but, more importantly, monitors their capacity for *resurgence* (Deibert, 2015, p. 64, emphasis as in original) and subsequent challenges to cybersecurity.

Among authoritarian countries, China's cyber or internet policies and threats have attracted significant attention, especially in recent years (e.g., Hung & Hung, 2022; Lindsay, Cheung, & Reveron, 2015; Myers & Mozur, 2019; Shackelford et al., 2020). Without denying their contributions, extant scholarship still has not captured the full gamut of cyber policies and politics that could generate threats to democracies. More specifically, existing studies have either presented the overall picture of internet governance and policies in China (e.g., Miao, Jiang, & Pang, 2021; F. Yang & Mueller, 2014) or elaborated on individual policies and regulations that cater to specific subject matter (e.g., Lindsay, Cheung, & Reveron, 2015; Qi, Shao, & Zheng, 2018). Few studies, however, have analyzed the media narratives and discourses of those policies and regulations that cater to specific subject matter and that bring about a broader influence on society beyond the policy domain. To fill this gap, this chapter tracks the media narrative and discourse centered on the term "cybersecurity" to uncover how China, "a latecomer on the global cybersecurity scene" (Qi, Shao, & Zheng, 2018, p. 1343), has oriented the domestic discursive constructions of cybersecurity toward the perceived national context of the audience.

In the following sections, I first present a general review of studies on China's internet policies. Second, I explain "domestication" (Clausen, 2004) as the theoretical framework to scrutinize the media narrative of cybersecurity in China's internet policy. The third section presents the method for data collection and computer-assisted semantic network analysis as the analytical strategy. In the fourth section, the analysis and discussion explain how the discourse on cybersecurity in media coverage legitimizes the regime's role in enacting internet policy, including its control over the free flow of information, while accusing democracies of cyberattacks. The chapter concludes with implications for the domestication of cybersecurity and challenges to cybersecurity.

LITERATURE REVIEW

Since China established its connection to the internet in 1994, internet policies have become one of the key topics in the debate on the transformation created by the internet to (the authoritarian) China (e.g., Taubman, 1998; Wu, 1996). Despite the then popular utopian vision of the internet (or cyberspace) as a facilitator of a radically democratic form of participation from its inception (Barlow, 2019), several scholars remind us that from the beginning of its connection with the internet, the party-state in China was engaged in "a multipronged effort" (Taubman, 1998, p. 267) with resources and regulations to prevent the internet from being "a disruptive force in the domestic area" (Taubman, 1998, p. 268), with the mostly well-known tactic being to build a self-contained intranet national network with a firewall (Barme & Ye, 1997; Griffiths, 2021).

Generally speaking, extant scholarship has investigated China's internet policies and politics from both a top-down and a bottom-up approach. The top-down approach encompasses macro-level policy, as well as the legal and technological aspects of internet control, surveillance, and censorship (e.g., Deibert, 2002; MacKinnon, 2009; Roberts, 2018; Xiaoming, Zhang, & Yu, 1996). For instance, some studies have scrutinized regulatory control (e.g., Esarey & Kluver, 2014; MacKinnon, 2008, 2009; Pan, 2017), while others have looked at the technical infrastructure of the "Great Firewall of China" (Barme & Ye, 1997), such as techniques of filtering, domain name system poisoning, and virtual private network blocking (e.g., Clayton, Murdoch, & Watson, 2007; Deibert et al., 2008; Lowe, Winters, & Marcus, 2007; for a review, see, e.g., Keremoğlu & Weidmann, 2020). Some, like Pan (2017), have revealed how the dominance of domestic internet platforms that "comply with China's censorship requirements" in the market allows "the Chinese regime to engage in content censorship that quickly removes online content pertaining to collective action while retaining a great deal of information, including criticisms of the government, online" (p. 182; see also, e.g., Weber & Jia, 2007). Others, such as Liang and Lu (2010), with their term "multidimensional regulatory system," have offered a holistic view to describe multiple agencies with various laws and regulations to establish comprehensive control over the infrastructure and commercial and social use of the internet in China.

The bottom-up approach, which can mostly be seen in studies on internet control and censorship, involves understanding the mechanisms behind censorship by analyzing which elements are censored or not (e.g., Bamman, O'Connor, & Smith, 2012; Crandall et al., 2013; King, Pan, & Roberts, 2013, 2017; Liu & Zhao, 2021; Qin, Strömberg, & Wu, 2017). In bottom-up studies, large-scale datasets are harvested through application programming interfaces and analyzed via complex computational and statistical approaches to depict nuanced pictures of how the control, surveillance, manipulation, and censorship program is implemented on the ground (e.g., King, Pan, & Roberts, 2013, 2017; Liu & Zhao, 2021; Lu & Pan, 2021; Roberts, 2018). Yet, without denying its significance, the bottom-up approach suffers from the lack of a holistic view of policies, as well as the discourse and narratives revolving around these policies, that would better draw a full picture of the evolving internet politics in China.

In recent years, more and more studies have looked beyond policy as relatively stable to track a combination of policy change and policy stability in the internet policies, given the complexity of "allowing access and giving a fair amount of freedom to non-political and less-political information exchange in this country … [while] resisting with firewall solutions and regulations" (Zhang, 2006, p. 285) in China. F. Yang and Mueller (2014), for example, used the content analysis approach with the laws and regulations on internet governance between 1994 and 2012 to track how these policies changed over time, identify different policymaking agencies, and ascertain various scopes of application and topical focuses for these policies. Among the many issues and themes, content regulation and cybersecurity have occupied significant and substantial parts of internet policies (57 percent and 41 percent, respectively, see F. Yang & Mueller, 2014, p. 458). Similarly, the study by Miao, Jiang, and Pang (2021, p. 2021) on Chinese internet policies issued between 1994 and 2017 uncovered the paramount concern over cybersecurity that exemplifies the state's "deep-seated insecurity over regime stability" in numerous internet regulations. Still, in comparison to the extensive scholarship on content regulation and moderation in China, as discussed earlier, the topic of cybersecurity seems to be relatively understudied, despite its emerging visibility in recent years (but see Lindsay, Cheung, & Reveron, 2015; Mueller, 2011). This chapter aims to enrich the discussion with the concept of "domestication."

DOMESTICATION: NATIONAL LENS ON CROSS-BORDER EVENTS AND BEYOND

A key concept in journalistic practice, domestication (Gurevitch, Levy, & Roeh, 1993) refers to the framing of foreign or international events to render them comprehensible, compatible, appealing, and relevant to national or local audiences (e.g., Alasuutari, Qadir, & Creutz, 2013; Clausen, 2004; Huiberts & Joye, 2018). The fundamental idea, as Gurevitch, Levy, and Roeh (1993) explain, is that "the 'same' events are told in divergent ways, *geared to the social and political frameworks and sensibilities of diverse domestic audiences*" (p. 217, emphasis added). A substantial amount of work has been conducted to interrogate different discursively adaptive ways in which cross-border news is domesticated to make it suited for different audiences nationally and locally (e.g., Clausen, 2004; Joye, 2015; Lee, Chan, & Zhou, 2011). Olausson (2014) further differentiates three discursive modes of domestication: "(1) introverted domestication, which disconnects the domestic from the global; (2) extroverted domestication, which interconnects the domestic and the global; and (3) counter-domestication, a de-territorialized mode of reporting that lacks any domestic epicenter" (p. 715). In short, domestication entails a deliberate choice in how one talks about and understands the world.

The research on domestication beyond cross-border events has been expanded by a growing body of studies. Domestication as the process of discursive appropriation and transformation occurs not only in the genre of cross-border news, which has been extensively studied, but also in other genres, such as entertainment (Adamu, 2010), technology (Matassi, Boczkowski, & Mitchelstein, 2019), education (Alasuutari & Alasuutari, 2012), popular culture (H. Fu, Li, & Lee, 2023), and the implementation of exogenous policy (Alasuutari, 2009). H. Fu, Li, and Lee (2023), for instance, expand the term to examine the process "in which a non-native cultural artifact or practice becomes embedded in and tamed by a techno-cultural arena in a receiver country" (p. 77). In other words, broadly speaking, domestication research should pay attention to the strategies that could generate resonance with national or local audiences and contexts beyond the genre of foreign news. By doing so, domestication not only makes events and artifacts meaningful for the domestic audience but it could also be utilized by various actors to reinforce "nation-state discourse and identity" (Olausson, 2014, p. 711).

Following this argument, in this study, we ask the following research question: *How does news coverage domesticate "cybersecurity" in internet regulations and policies in China?*

METHODS

To answer the research question, this study explored the semantic meaning in media narratives and frames as units of analysis. Gamson and Modigliani (1989) refer to such narratives and frames as "media packages" – that is, as "interpretive packages that give meaning to an issue" (p. 3). Media frames denote structured semantic representations of associated contextual and cultural information (Werner & Cornelissen, 2014). Examining media frames detects the background structure of a shared reality and identifies "the role of political culture and practices in stabilizing particular imaginaries" (Jasanoff & Kim, 2009, p. 121). Given the idea of "associative framing" (Ruigrok & van Atteveldt, 2007, p. 72), this study operationalizes media narratives and frames as complex patterns of associations between different concepts, with the main associations in a message being its "central organizing idea" (Gamson & Modigliani, 1989, p. 3). In other words, media narratives and frames involve not only the selection of concepts but also their mutual associations that stand for schemata of interpretation. Such associative framings and narratives – recognized as domestication, or discursive appropriation and transformation to local context – are therefore examined through semantic networks derived from the occurrences and co-occurrences of concepts.

Semantic Network Analysis

This study employed computer-assisted semantic network analysis to explore media narratives and frames of cybersecurity in news coverage in the Chinese mainland. With its origin in cognitive science, semantic network analysis argues that human memory contains a structural meaning system (Collins & Quillian, 1972). Semantic network studies have thus suggested that the frequency, co-occurrence, and distances among words and concepts allow researchers to explore a text's embedded meaning (Danowski, 1993; Doerfel, 1998). This study adopted the word association (concept co-occurrence) method, which maps the relationships among words by indexing pairs of concepts. Extending beyond the standard content analysis of texts and frequencies of concepts, semantic network analysis reveals the manifest meaning structure of the text and thus indirectly represents the discursive appropriation among the text's creators (Danowski, 1993). The analysis, with second-hand data from news sources, followed the research question proposed earlier.

Data Collection

To identify and collect data, we first performed an extensive search of news coverage in the Chinese mainland. Before 2017, China enacted several laws and regulations in response to cybersecurity problems (Miao, Jiang, & Pang, 2021, p. 2004). These laws and regulations were nevertheless insufficient in dealing with the increasing challenges facing cyberspace. Against this backdrop, China formally introduced the *Cybersecurity Law of the People's Republic of China* ("the Cybersecurity Law" in short), which came into effect on June 1, 2017. Accordingly, the time span for the data search and collection was set after June 1, 2017, the date of the enactment of the

Cybersecurity Law, until May 1, 2023. We used the keyword-screening method in the Huike News Database (WiseNews, http://wisesearch.wisers.net.cn/), the most professional Chinese media content database. The keywords "网络安全 (cybersecurity)" and "互联网安全 (internet security)" were used in all fields to locate news articles covering issues related to cybersecurity, which yielded a total of 6,362 news articles and commentaries (1,268 pieces in 2017; 1,196 in 2018; 1,056 in 2019; 814 in 2020; 962 in 2021; 748 in 2022; and 318 in 2023 through the end of April).

Data Cleaning and Analysis

The next step was to conduct semantic network analysis and explore the discursive network of cybersecurity in news coverage through the following four steps.

- The corpus of 6,362 news articles and commentaries was first preprocessed and cleaned. Raw texts were segmented into words using the Chinese lexical analyzer *Jieba*. Punctuation, numbers, common Chinese stop words, and nonwords were then filtered.
- Second, the corpus consisting of space-spliced words was submitted to a Python script that counted the frequency of each word and the co-occurrence of word pairs. Word pairs with a raw co-occurrence frequency higher than five were retained for further analysis, following the suggestion of Church and Hanks (1990), who noted that the mutual information score becomes unstable and meaningless when the count is smaller than five.
- Third, the semantic network of news coverage on cybersecurity was visualized using Gephi (https://gephi.org/). The ego-network of the terms "cybersecurity" and "internet security" were identified and extracted, given that we focused on the semantic meaning and narrative strategies of the term "cybersecurity."
- Fourth, the modularity partition algorithm in Gephi (Newman, 2006) was employed to detect concept communities for the semantic networks. The generated semantic network identified cybersecurity-related concepts in the text data as nodes linked together by the frequencies with which each concept co-occurred with other concepts.

MAPPING OUT SEMANTIC NETWORKS ABOUT "CYBERSECURITY" IN NEWS NARRATIVES

There are 41,053 words and 578,008 edges in the whole news articles' semantic network. The semantic networks for Chinese news articles were visualized using Gephi (Bastian, Heymann, & Jacomy, 2009). We then filtered the ego-network for the term "cybersecurity" that consists of 990 words (2.4 percent of the total number of words) and 84,801 edges (14.7 percent of the total number of edges) (Figure 12.1).

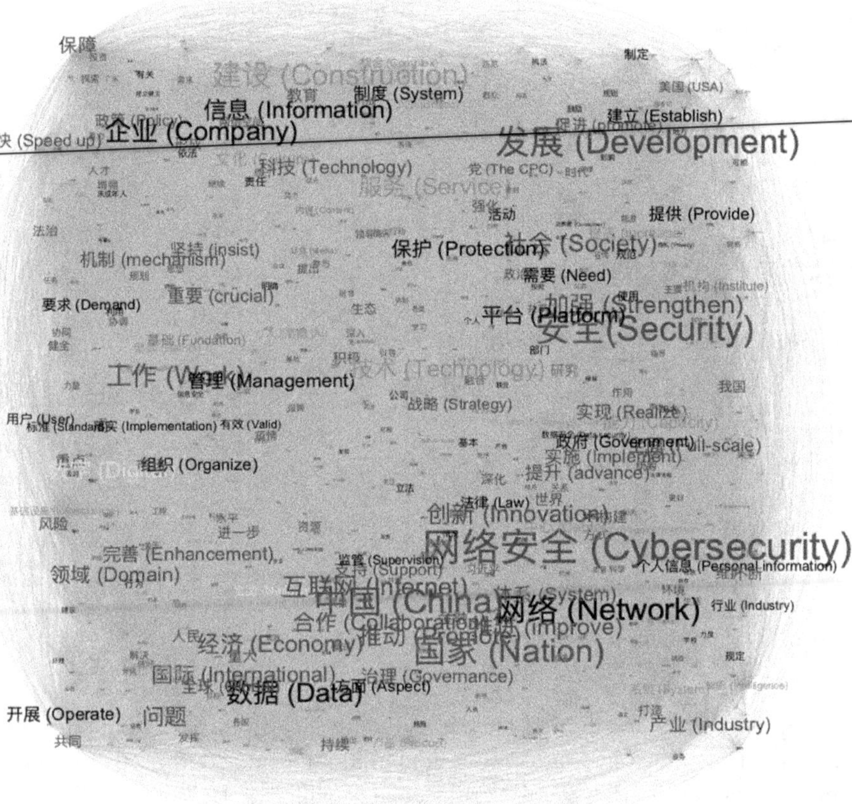

FIGURE 12.1 Ego-network of cybersecurity in news coverage in the Chinese mainland, 2017–2023

We ran the average degree to calculate the node strength for each word, which is determined as the number of edges that are incident on that node; the average degree (85.658) refers to the average number of edges per node. Each node represents a word, and the size of the label indicates the node strength, which is calculated by summing the weights of the edges belonging to the node. Edges are undirected and weighted. The modularity partition algorithm suggested that the network could be divided into eight communities, with a modularity score of 0.231.

We identified topics for each word community by their top words and inductively summarized those topics into different themes. Six main clusters could be identified from the semantic network, in ranking order: control and contestation, development and collaboration, personal information, infrastructure, governing actors, and mass media. Figure 12.1 presents the themes and top words for the semantic networks.

FIGURE 12.2 Control and contestation cluster

Control and contestation (Figure 12.2) is the largest cluster (283 nodes, or 28.6 percent of the total words) in the semantic network. Within the cluster, the word "cybersecurity (网络安全)" is associated with "中国 (China)," "国家nation (al)," "安全 (security)," and "主权 (sovereignty)." Terms such as "党 (the CPC, i.e., the Communist Party of China)," "习近平(Xi Jinping)," "法治 (rule of law)," "领导 (leadership)," "统一 (unity)," "意识形态 (ideology)," and "防火墙 (firewall)" encapsulate control over cybersecurity. The contestation of the term "cybersecurity" is specifically delineated through the use of words such as "保障 (safeguard)," "风险 (risk)," "维护 (maintain)," "防控 (prevention and control)," "挑战 (challenge)," "破坏(undermine)," and "威胁 (threat)." Threats to cybersecurity are epitomized through specific terms such as "恐怖主义 (terrorism)," "反恐 (anti-terrorism)," and "反间谍(counterintelligence)." Notably, this cluster is the only one that includes foreign entities, such as "美国 (the USA)," "欧盟 (European Union)," "美方 (the US)," "英国 (Britain)," "俄罗斯 (Russia)," and "乌克兰 (Ukraine)."

The second largest cluster, development and collaboration (Figure 12.3), involves 258 nodes (or 26.1 percent of the total words) that address cybersecurity in concert with economic development, technological innovation, and international collaboration. This cluster involves key terms related to the theme of development, such as "发展 (development)," "加强 (strengthen)," "创新 (innovation)," "推进 (improve)," and "完善 (enhancement)," while specifying different "domains (领域)," including

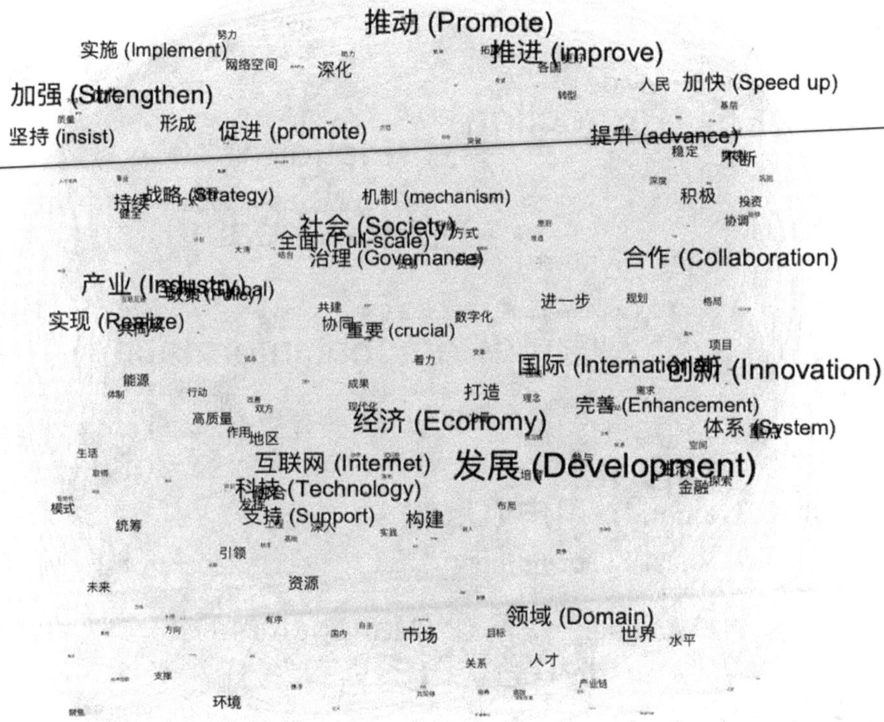

FIGURE 12.3 Development and collaboration cluster

"经济 (economy)," "科技 (technology)," "产业 (industry)," "政策 (policy)," and "战略 (strategy)." It also contains words describing the scope of "collaboration (合作)" in cybersecurity, such as "国际 (international)," "全球 (global)," "世界 (world)," "各国 (different countries)," "地区 (regional)," and "双方 (bilateral)."

Next is the personal information cluster (Figure 12.4), with 246 nodes (or 24.8 percent of the total words), which in essence discusses issues related to personal "data (数据)" in business. Terms such as "企业 (enterprise)," "平台 (platform)," "政府 (government)," "法律 (law)," "用户 (user)," "行业 (industry)," "公司 (company)," "未成年人 (juvenile)," "个人 (individual)," and "消费者 (consumer)" allude to various actors involved in the processes of, for instance, "管理 (manag[ing])," "保护 (protect[ing])," "规范 (standardiz[ing])," and "监管 (supervis[ing])."

Following the personal information cluster, the infrastructure cluster (Figure 12.5), with 109 nodes (16.5 percent of the total words), addresses aspects of technological and infrastructural applications in cybersecurity with keywords such as "建设 (construction)," "服务 (service)," "技术 (technology)," "系统 (system),"

FIGURE 12.4 Personal information cluster

"人工智能 (AI)," "智能 (intelligence)," "基础设置 (infrastructure)," and "智慧 (smart)."

The governing actors cluster (Figure 12.6) consists of fifty-five nodes (5.6 percent of the total words) that allow us to pin down concrete agencies involved in cybersecurity issues. More specifically, the included words identify the national- and local-level actors and agencies that handle cybersecurity, including, for instance, "中央 (central government)"; different levels of "人民政府 (people's government[s])," "有限公司 (Company Limited)," "公安部 (Ministry of Public Security)," and "网信(办) ([office of] Cyberspace Affairs Commission)"; municipal- and provincial-level public security bureau such as the "北京市公安局 (Beijing public security bureau)" and "信息化(办) ([office of] informationalization)"; and public health agencies ("卫生 [public health]" and "健康 [health]"). Most importantly, a critical group of governing actors are the various levels and divisions of party organizations, such as the "省委 (provincial CPC committee)," "市委 (municipal CPC committee)," "书记 (party secretary)," and

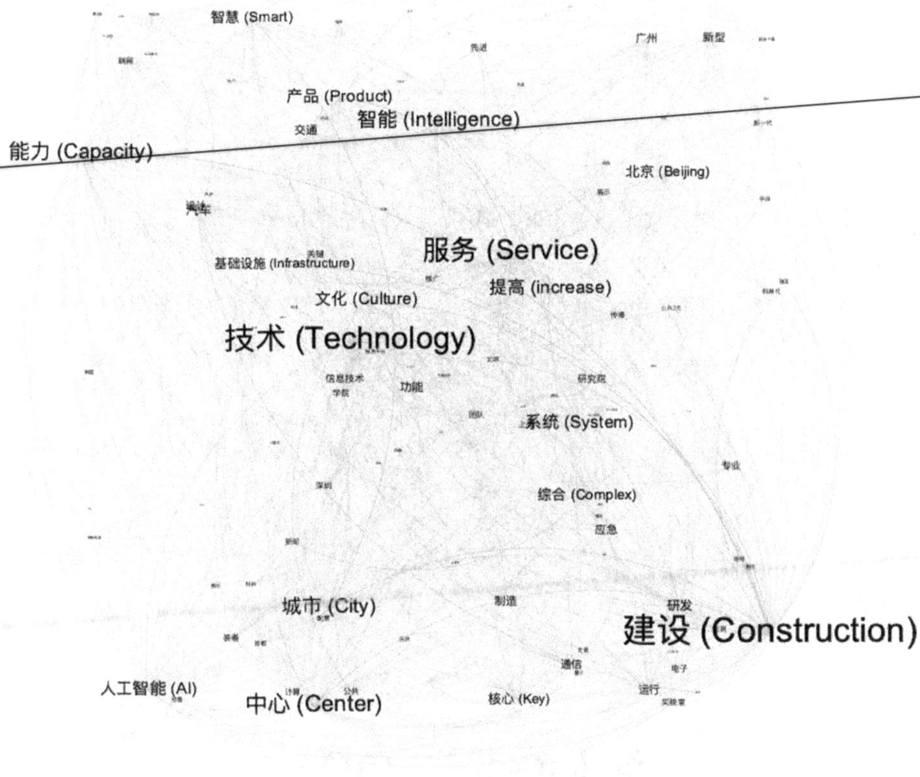

FIGURE 12.5 Infrastructure cluster

"宣传部 (propaganda department)," to mention just a few. In other words, these terms signify the essential role of the CPC as well as its in-depth, multidimensional control in the governing of cybersecurity.

The three remaining clusters (Figure 12.7), with a total of thirty-seven nodes (3.7 percent of words), involve words that narrate the relationship between news industries and cybersecurity, as demonstrated in terms such as "媒体 (media)," "要闻 (hard news)," and the names of news organizations, including "新华社 (Xinhua News Agency)," "人民日报 (*People's Daily*)," "新京报 (*Beijing News*)," "环球时报 (*Global Times*)," and "南方都市报 (*Southern Metropolis Daily*)."

Domesticating Cybersecurity

Although extant scholarship has presented an overall picture of internet governance and policies in China (e.g., Miao, Jiang, & Pang, 2021; F. Yang & Mueller, 2014),

FIGURE 12.6 Governing actors cluster

FIGURE 12.7 Mass media cluster

few studies have yet analyzed how those policies and regulations that cater to specific subject matter have been constructed and appropriated for the national context of the audience – that is, the domestication that this study examines. In particular, our research reveals that the domestication of cybersecurity in mainland China highlights the CPC's pivotal role in controlling, safeguarding, and advancing cybersecurity measures against the supposedly malicious cyber activities of the democracies. Such domestication not only reinforces the CPC's comprehensive control over cybersecurity but also frames democracies as the source of unfounded cyber threats to China's national and societal well-being. By doing so, we recognize the cultural construction of cybersecurity "through which common sense understandings are constructed and the foundations are laid" (Bernal, 2021, p. 612) for national consciousness of cybersecurity. This study, for the first time, fills the gap by tracking the narrative and discourse on "cybersecurity" in news coverage in the Chinese mainland since the enactment of the Cybersecurity Law in 2017.

Similar to the contested discourse on cybersecurity elsewhere – for instance, the discourse in the United States uses metaphors of cybersecurity as a war and makes analogies to the Cold War between the United States and China (e.g., Bernal, 2021; Lawson, 2012; also see the Swedish case in Boholm, 2021) – the media narrative and frame in the Chinese mainland underlines contestations between China and the democracies – that is, the United States and beyond – as a key part of domestication. The most striking feature is that the domestication of cybersecurity in the Chinese context reiterates the CPC's domination at the heart of the management, operationalization, and development of cybersecurity and, further, national security. By domesticating cybersecurity to the leadership of the CPC and ascribing cyber threats involving cyberattack and cyberterrorism to democracies, the Chinese regime not only legitimizes and consolidates its control over cyberspace but also utilizes cybersecurity to place blame on the democracies.

Our question asks how news coverage domesticates "cybersecurity" in the Chinese mainland. The findings revealed four features. The first, and most prominent one, is the political imperative of highlighting, ensuring, and protecting the dominant role of the CPC in decision-making, developing, maintaining, and executing cybersecurity issues. As illustrated in the analysis, two of the six clusters, or themes – the control and contestation and the governing actors' clusters – highlighted the hegemonic role of the CPC in cybersecurity. More specifically, in the control and contestation cluster, the CPC, together with the names of the leadership like President Xi Jinping, are articulated as the pivotal actor(s) in safeguarding national sovereignty, societal security, and rule of law and in countering cyber threats from the West. Terms such as "保障 (safeguard)," "强化 (reinforce)," "维护 (maintain)," and "统一 (unit)" further legitimize the hegemonic role of the CPC in cybersecurity through the evaluation of government policies dealing with cyber threats and challenges.

While the CPC's domination stays as the foundation of cybersecurity in China (as articulated in the control and contestation theme), the governing actors theme adds nuance to the multiplicity of agencies involved in the operationalization of cybersecurity issues. Here, the complexity has a two-fold meaning. For one thing, it refers to the engagement of multisectoral, or what Liang and Lu (2010) describe as the "multidimensional regulatory system" – that is, multiple government departments and agencies, such as public security, public health, Cyberspace Affairs Commission, but also the businesses (as illustrated in "有限公司 [Company Limited]") that establish comprehensive control over the commercial, public interest, and social dimensions of cybersecurity in China. For another thing, and more importantly, multiplicity indicates the essential involvement of the CPC organizations at all levels – from central to municipality and provincial and from the CPC committee to its propaganda department – in the management of cybersecurity.

Second, as signified in the control and contestation theme, the domestication of cybersecurity capitalizes on blaming cyber challenges and threats on democracies, including the United States, the European Union, and Japan, among others, to promote antagonism toward these countries. As shown in the control and contestation theme, the use of terms such as "terrorism," "counterterrorism," and "counterintelligence" is quite common in the narrative of cybersecurity. Moreover, the term "force (势力)" – quite often being adopted together with "foreign (境外)" and "hostile (敌对)" to launch allegations of foreign interference – has frequently been used by domestic media as flag-waving, despite the lack of real instances of external meddling. In other words, the use of cyber threat-related terms, alongside vague references to democratic countries such as the United States and Japan, indicates that a narrative of foreign interference has become a regular feature of cybersecurity in the media discourse, with a wide range of (unspecified) individuals, groups, and countries denounced as counterparts to underscore the tensions between China and the democracies and to facilitate antidemocracy sentiment and assertive nationalism, both online and offline (e.g., Lehman-Ludwig et al., 2023).

The first two features encapsulate what scholars observe as the reemergence of *ideology* (which is also a keyword in the control and contestation theme) in China's development and outreach, which has dramatically shaped its internet policy. Ideology is, as Pieke (2012) points out, "an indispensable aspect in the creation of regime support, no longer intending to generate 'belief' in the party, but to cultivate responsible, trusting, and 'high-quality' citizens who inhabit an active, autonomous, and governable society" (p. 150). The ideological turn and its further "marriage" with digital technologies exemplify not only the effort expended "on channeling and containing Internet expression through ideological work and cultural governance more broadly" (G. Yang, 2014, p. 112), as we can observe in other initiatives, such as "Telling China's Story" to shape global narratives (Huang & Wang, 2019). It further involves "an increasingly visible ideological thread vying to give coherence to an expanding system of Internet control" (G. Yang, 2014, p. 109), which promotes domestic ideology on a global scale via the internet (Martin, 2021) and drives nationalistic sentiments, including a "wolf-warrior diplomacy" that seeks to aggressively defend China's national interests (Zhu, 2020) and a series of nationalistic portrayals in Chinese cinema to convey the ideologies of the Chinese government and epitomize the state's changing foreign policies (X. Yang, 2023). In the case of cybersecurity and politics, the reemergence of ideology, with the risk of overreaction and arbitrariness, serves as a strategy to defend the CPC's hold on power and overarching rule, leading to a state of hypervigilance with wide-reaching effects on China's domestic and, especially, international policies. Such a reemergence is further illustrated in, for instance, China being a major advocate for cyber sovereignty in recent years (e.g., Hong & Goodnight, 2020; Zeng, Stevens, & Chen, 2017).

Third, the domestication of cybersecurity also points to both the global development of and international collaboration on cybersecurity issues (the development and collaboration cluster) and personal data security, mostly in business but also beyond it (the personal information cluster) (see similar discussions in Kuner et al., 2017). Nevertheless, both narratives – through the keywords identified in the semantic network – remain general (but vague) and thereby have not made their way into the dominant discourse of the domestication of cybersecurity. For instance, despite the emphasis on strengthening international collaboration on cybersecurity, no specific country or international organization was named in the development and collaboration cluster, which implies that this initiative might be more of a political slogan than evidence-based policymaking.

Fourth, although the narrative of cybersecurity further includes topics such as technological and infrastructural applications (the infrastructure cluster) and media relationships, these topics that are crucial to cybersecurity elsewhere (e.g., Haber & Zarsky, 2016) occupy rather marginal positions in the semantic network and thus in the domestication of cybersecurity in the Chinese mainland, as displayed in the number of words in the cybersecurity's ego-network.

In summary, our analysis brings to the forefront the discursive strategies used in news coverage related to the domestication of cybersecurity in mainland China, which seek to validate and strengthen the CPC's authority and control over cybersecurity. This narrative often portrays Western democracies as the culprits behind cyberattacks, posing a significant threat to China's national and societal security. Consequently, our analysis underscores the importance of understanding the regime's cyber policies, going beyond the call to dismantle the Great Firewall or circumvent censorship. It highlights the unique role of mass media in shaping the domestication of cyber policies within the broader context of national discourse and identity.

CONCLUSION

This chapter enriches extant scholarship on internet governance and policies by focusing on media narratives on cybersecurity in authoritarian China. It delineates the specific way in which the term cybersecurity has been implicated and domesticated in local politics since the enactment of the Cybersecurity Law in 2017. The findings indicate that, although China was initially "a latecomer on the global cybersecurity scene" (Qi, Shao, & Zheng, 2018, p. 1343), the regime has strategically crafted and propagated cybersecurity narratives to resonate ideologically with the domestic audience, notably by portraying democracies as sources of cyber threats, including cyberterrorism. This domestic framing of cybersecurity serves to reinforce the CPC's control over the internet and engenders anti-Western and anti-democratic sentiment. This study highlights at least two further implications. First, the concept of domestication could reconcile the false binary between inward- and outward-focused internet policies (e.g., X. Fu, Woo, & Hou, 2016), recognizing their interdependent nature as shaped by domestic narratives. Second, this lens reveals a significant shift in discourse over a decade, from sporadic mentions of cyber warfare (Cai & Dati, 2015) to positioning cybersecurity as a critical issue that, if mismanaged, poses a threat to both national security and internal stability, including terrorism and territorial disputes in domestic Chinese politics. Recognizing this evolution is essential for a comprehensive understanding of China's ascent and its approach to global cyber governance.

REFERENCES

Abrahams, A., & Leber, A. (2021). Comparative approaches to mis/disinformation | Electronic armies or cyber knights? The sources of pro-authoritarian discourse on Middle East Twitter. *International Journal of Communication*, 15, 1173–1199.

Adamu, A. U. (2010). The muse's journey: Transcultural translators and the domestication of Hindi music in Hausa Popular Culture. *Journal of African Cultural Studies*, 22(1), 41–56.

Alasuutari, P. (2009). The domestication of worldwide policy models. *Ethnologia Europaea*, 39(1), 66–71. https://doi.org/10.16995/ee.1046

Alasuutari, P., & Alasuutari, M. (2012). The domestication of early childhood education plans in Finland. *Global Social Policy*, 12(2), 129–148. https://doi.org/10.1177/1468018112443684

Alasuutari, P., Qadir, A., & Creutz, K. (2013). The domestication of foreign news: News stories related to the 2011 Egyptian Revolution in British, Finnish and Pakistani newspapers. *Media, Culture & Society*, 35(6), 692–707. https://doi.org/10.1177/0163443713491299

Alyukov, M. (2022). Propaganda, authoritarianism and Russia's invasion of Ukraine. *Nature Human Behaviour*, 6(6), 763–765.

Bamman, D., O'Connor, B., & Smith, N. A. (2012). Censorship and deletion practices in Chinese social media. *First Monday*, 17(3–5). https://doi.org/10.5210/fm.v17i3.3943

Barlow, J. P. (2019). A declaration of the independence of cyberspace. *Duke Law & Technology Review*, 18, 5–7.

Barme, G. R., & Ye, S. (1997, June 1). The great firewall of China. *Wired*. https://wired.com/1997/06/china-3

Bastian, M., Heymann, S., & Jacomy, M. (2009). Gephi: An open source software for exploring and manipulating networks. *ICWSM*, 8(2009), 361–362.

Bernal, V. (2021). The cultural construction of cybersecurity: Digital threats and dangerous rhetoric. *Anthropological Quarterly*, 94(4), 611–638.

Boholm, M. (2021). Twenty-five years of cyber threats in the news: A study of Swedish newspaper coverage (1995–2019). *Journal of Cybersecurity*, 7(1), tyab016.

Bradshaw, S., & Howard, P. (2017). *Troops, trolls and troublemakers: A global inventory of organized social media manipulation*. Computational Propaganda Research Project. https://ora.ox.ac.uk/objects/uuid:cef7e8d9-27bf-4ea5-9fd6-855209b3e1f6/files/m3ca8c4558 52611e82d0fb182445a471f

Bradshaw, S., & Howard, P. N. (2019). *The global disinformation order: 2019 global inventory of organised social media manipulation* [White Paper]. Working Paper 2019.2. Oxford Project on Computational Propaganda.

Cai, C., & Dati, D. (2015). Words mightier than hacks: Narratives of cyberwar in the United States and China. *Asian Perspective*, 39(3), 541–553.

Church, K., & Hanks, P. (1990). Word association norms, mutual information, and lexicography. *Computational Linguistics*, 16(1), 22–29.

Clausen, L. (2004). Localizing the global: 'Domestication' processes in international news production. *Media, Culture & Society*, 26(1), 25–44.

Clayton, R., Murdoch, S. J., & Watson, R. N. (2007). Ignoring the great firewall of China. *I/S: A Journal of Law and Policy*, 3(2), 271–296.

Collins, A. M., & Quillian, M. R. (1972). How to make a language user. In E. Tulving & W. Donaldson (Eds.), *Organization of memory* (pp. 310–351). Academic Press.

Crandall, J. R., Crete-Nishihata, M., Knockel, J., McKune, S., Senft, A., Tseng, D., et al. (2013). Chat program censorship and surveillance in China: Tracking TOM-Skype and Sina UC. *First Monday*, 18(7). https://doi.org/10.5210/fm.v18i7.4628

Danowski, J. A. (1993). Network analysis of message content. *Progress in Communication Sciences*, 12, 198–221.

Deibert, R. J. (2002). Dark guests and great firewalls: The Internet and Chinese security policy. *Journal of Social Issues*, 58(1), 143–159.

(2015). Authoritarianism goes global: Cyberspace under siege. *Journal of Democracy*, 26(3), 64–78.

Deibert, R. J., Palfrey, J. G., Rohozinski, R., & Zittrain, J. (2008). *Access denied: The practice and policy of global Internet filtering*. The MIT Press.

Doerfel, M. L. (1998). What constitutes semantic network analysis? A comparison of research and methodologies. *Connections*, 21(2), 16–26.

Esarey, A., & Kluver, R. (Eds.). (2014). *The Internet in China: Cultural, political and social dimensions (1980–2000s)*. Berkshire Publishing Group.

Fu, H., Li, Y., & Lee, F. L. (2023). Techno-cultural domestication of online Tarot reading in contemporary China. *Media, Culture & Society*, 45(1), 74–91.

Fu, X., Woo, W. T., & Hou, J. (2016). Technological innovation policy in China: The lessons, and the necessary changes ahead. *Economic Change and Restructuring*, 49, 139–157.

Gamson, W. A., & Modigliani, A. (1989). Media discourse and public opinion on nuclear power: A constructionist approach. *American Journal of Sociology*, 95(1), 1–37.

Greitens, S. C. (2013). Authoritarianism Online: What can we learn from Internet data in nondemocracies? *PS: Political Science & Politics*, 46(2), 262–270.

Griffiths, J. (2021). *The great firewall of China: How to build and control an alternative version of the Internet*. Bloomsbury.

Gurevitch, M., Levy, M. R., & Roeh, I. (1993). The global newsroom: Convergences and diversities in the globalization of television news. In P. Dahlgren & C. Sparks (Eds.), *Communication and citizenship* (pp. 195–216). Routledge.

Haber, E., & Zarsky, T. (2016). Cybersecurity for infrastructure: A critical analysis. *Florida State University Law Review*, 44, 515.

Hong, Y., & Goodnight, G. T. (2020). How to think about cyber sovereignty: The case of China. *Chinese Journal of Communication*, 13(1), 8–26.

Huang, Z. A., & Wang, R. (2019). Building a network to "tell China stories well": Chinese diplomatic communication strategies on Twitter. *International Journal of Communication*, 13, 2984–3007.

Huiberts, E., & Joye, S. (2018). Close, but not close enough? Audience's reactions to domesticated distant suffering in international news coverage. *Media, Culture & Society*, 40(3), 333–347.

Hung, T.-C., & Hung, T.-W. (2022). How China's cognitive warfare works: A frontline perspective of Taiwan's anti-disinformation wars. *Journal of Global Security Studies*, 7(4), ogac016.

Jasanoff, S., & Kim, S.-H. (2009). Containing the atom: Sociotechnical imaginaries and nuclear power in the United States and South Korea. *Minerva*, 47(2), 119.

Jones, M. O. (2022). *Digital authoritarianism in the Middle East: Deception, disinformation and social media*. Hurst.

Joye, S. (2015). Domesticating distant suffering: How can news media discursively invite the audience to care? *International Communication Gazette*, 77(7), 682–694.

Keremoğlu, E., & Weidmann, N. B. (2020). How dictators control the Internet: A review essay. *Comparative Political Studies*, 53(10–11), 1690–1703. httsp://doi.org/10.1177/0010414020912278

King, G., Pan, J., & Roberts, M. E. (2013). How censorship in China allows government criticism but silences collective expression. *American Political Science Review*, 107(2), 326–343.

(2017). How the Chinese government fabricates social media posts for strategic distraction, not engaged argument. *American Political Science Review*, 111(3), 484–501.

Kuner, C., Svantesson, D. J. B., Cate, F. H., Lynskey, O., & Millard, C. (2017). The rise of cybersecurity and its impact on data protection. *International Data Privacy Law*, 7(2), 73–75.

Lawson, S. (2012). Putting the "war" in cyberwar: Metaphor, analogy, and cybersecurity discourse in the United States. *First Monday*, 17(2). https://doi.org/10.5210/fm.v17i7.3848

Lee, F. L., Chan, J. M., & Zhou, B. (2011). National lenses on a global news event: Determinants of the politicization and domestication of the prelude to the Beijing Olympics. *Chinese Journal of Communication*, 4(3), 274–292.

Lehman-Ludwig, A., Burke, A., Ambler, D., & Schroeder, R. (2023). Chinese anti-Westernism on social media. *Global Media and China*, 8(2), 119–137. https://doi.org/10.1177/20594364231166541

Liang, B., & Lu, H. (2010). Internet development, censorship, and cyber crimes in China. *Journal of Contemporary Criminal Justice*, 26(1), 103–120.

Lindsay, J. R., Cheung, T. M., & Reveron, D. S. (2015). *China and cybersecurity: Espionage, strategy, and politics in the digital domain*. Oxford University Press.

Liu, J., & Zhao, J. (2021). More than plain text: Censorship deletion in the Chinese social media. *Journal of the Association for Information Science and Technology*, 72(1), 18–31.

Lowe, G., Winters, P., & Marcus, M. L. (2007). *The great DNS wall of China*. https://censorbib.nymity.ch/pdf/Lowe2007a.pdf

Lu, Y., & Pan, J. (2021). Capturing clicks: How the Chinese government uses clickbait to compete for visibility. *Political Communication*, 38(1–2), 23–54.

MacKinnon, R. (2008). Flatter world and thicker walls? Blogs, censorship and civic discourse in China. *Public Choice*, 134, 31–46.

(2009). China's censorship 2.0: How companies censor bloggers. *First Monday*, 14(2) https://doi.org/10.5210/fm.v14i2.2378

Majeed, T. (2022). Embedded authoritarianism: The politics of poor press freedom in Indian Kashmir. *Media, Culture & Society*, 44(3), 613–624.

Mare, A. (2020). Internet shutdowns in Africa| state-ordered Internet shutdowns and digital authoritarianism in Zimbabwe. *International Journal of Communication*, 14, 20.

Martin, P. (2021). *China's civilian army: The making of wolf warrior diplomacy*. Oxford University Press.

Matassi, M., Boczkowski, P. J., & Mitchelstein, E. (2019). Domesticating WhatsApp: Family, friends, work, and study in everyday communication. *New Media & Society*, 21(10), 2183–2200.

Miao, W., Jiang, M., & Pang, Y. (2021). Historicizing Internet regulation in China: A meta-analysis of Chinese Internet policies (1994–2017). *International Journal of Communication*, 15, 24.

Morgan, S. (2018). Fake news, disinformation, manipulation and online tactics to undermine democracy. *Journal of Cyber Policy*, 3(1), 39–43.

Mueller, M. L. (2011). China and global Internet governance: A tiger by the tail. In R. Deibert, J. Palfrey, R. Rohozinski, & J. L. Zittrain (Eds.), *Access contested: Security, identity, and resistance in Asian cyberspace* (pp. 177–194). The MIT Press.

Myers, S. L., & Mozur, P. (2019, August 13). China is waging a disinformation war against Hong Kong protesters. *The New York Times*. https://nytimes.com/2019/08/13/world/asia/hong-kong-protests-china.html

Newman, M. E. (2006). Modularity and community structure in networks. *Proceedings of the National Academy of Sciences*, 103(23), 8577–8582.

Olausson, U. (2014). The diversified nature of "domesticated" news discourse: The case of climate change in national news media. *Journalism Studies*, 15(6), 711–725.

Pan, J. (2017). How market dynamics of domestic and foreign social media firms shape strategies of Internet censorship. *Problems of Post-Communism*, 64(3–), 167–188.

Pieke, F. N. (2012). The Communist Party and social management in China. *China Information*, 26(2), 149–165.

Qi, A., Shao, G., & Zheng, W. (2018). Assessing China's cybersecurity law. *Computer Law & Security Review*, 34(6), 1342–1354.

Qin, B., Strömberg, D., & Wu, Y. (2017). Why does China allow freer social media? Protests versus surveillance and propaganda. *Journal of Economic Perspectives*, 31(1), 117–140.

Roberts, M. E. (2018). *Censored: Distraction and diversion inside China's great firewall*. Princeton University Press.

Ruigrok, N., & van Atteveldt, W. (2007). Global angling with a local angle: How US, British, and Dutch newspapers frame global and local terrorist attacks. *Harvard International Journal of Press/Politics*, 12(1), 68–90.

Schünemann, W. J. (2022). A threat to democracies? An overview of theoretical approaches and empirical measurements for studying the effects of disinformation. In M. D. Cavelty & A. Wenger (Eds.), *Cyber security politics* (pp. 32–47). Routledge.

Shackelford, S. J., Raymond, A., Stemler, A., & Loyle, C. (2020). Defending democracy: Taking stock of the global fight against digital repression, disinformation, and election insecurity. *Washington and Lee Law Review*, 77, 1747.

Taubman, G. (1998). A not-so World Wide Web: The Internet, China, and the challenges to nondemocratic rule. *Political Communication*, 15(2), 255–272.

Ververis, V., Marguel, S., & Fabian, B. (2020). Cross-country comparison of Internet censorship: A literature review. *Policy & Internet*, 12(4), 450–473.

Weber, I., & Jia, L. (2007). Internet and self-regulation in China: The cultural logic of controlled commodification. *Media, Culture & Society*, 29(5), 772–789.

Werner, M. D., & Cornelissen, J. P. (2014). Framing the change: Switching and blending frames and their role in instigating institutional change. *Organization Studies*, 35(10), 1449–1472.

Woolley, S. C., & Howard, P. (2017). *Computational propaganda worldwide: Executive summary*. Oxford Internet Institute.

Wu, W. (1996). Great leap or long march: Some policy issues of the development of the Internet in China. *Telecommunications Policy*, 20(9), 699–711.

Xiaoming, H., Zhang, K., & Yu, H. (1996). The Internet and information control: The case of China. *Javnost-the Public*, 3(1), 117–130.

Yang, F., & Mueller, M. L. (2014). Internet governance in China: A content analysis. *Chinese Journal of Communication*, 7(4), 446–465.

Yang, G. (2014). The return of ideology and the future of Chinese Internet policy. *Critical Studies in Media Communication*, 31(2), 109–113.

Yang, X. (2023). The "wolf warrior cycle": Chinese blockbusters in the age of the belt and road initiative. *The China Quarterly*, 2003, 1–15. https://doi.org/10.1017/S0305741023000693

Zeng, J., Stevens, T., & Chen, Y. (2017). China's solution to global cyber governance: Unpacking the domestic discourse of "Internet sovereignty". *Politics & Policy*, 45(3), 432–464.

Zhang, L. L. (2006). Behind the 'great firewall' decoding China's Internet media policies from the inside. *Convergence*, 12(3), 271–291.

Zhu, Z. (2020). Interpreting China's 'wolf-warrior diplomacy'. *The Diplomat*, 15(5), 2020.

13

Defending Taiwan's Democracy in the Internet Commons

Simon Sun

CHINA'S CYBER WARFARE AGAINST TAIWAN

Taiwan, officially known as the Republic of China (ROC), is a self-governing democracy situated across the Taiwan Strait from the People's Republic of China (PRC) ("Taiwan: Political and Security Issues," 2023). Taiwan stood as an exemplar during the global "third wave" of democratization in the 1980s and 1990s, successfully transitioning from an authoritarian regime to a representative electoral system in a gradual and peaceful manner (Diamond, 2009; Myers & Chao, 2003). At the heart of Taiwan's democratic system lies its electoral process, through which 23 million citizens exercise their right to vote in the selection of presidents, Congress members, and local government officials (Fell, 2018). As described by Freedom House, "Taiwan's vibrant and competitive democratic system has allowed for regular peaceful transfers of power since 2000, and protections for civil liberties are generally robust" (Freedom House, n.d.).

However, the ongoing efforts by the PRC to exert influence over policymaking, media outlets, and the foundational pillars of democracy pose persistent challenges to Taiwan's democratic system (Freedom House, n.d.). The PRC's Anti-Secession Law, enacted in 2005, stipulates that non-peaceful means may be employed to protect China's sovereignty and territorial integrity in the event of Taiwan's secession or when peaceful unification options are deemed exhausted (Mainland Affairs Council, Republic of China (Taiwan), 2005). In line with this stance, at the Chinese Communist Party (CCP)'s 20th Party Congress in October 2022, the party's leader, Xi Jinping, emphasized the necessity of unification with Taiwan for the rejuvenation

The author would like to thank Scott Shackelford, Michael D. McGinnis, Dan Cole, Fred Cate, Kenny Huang, Tim Waters, Craig Jackson, Oscar Engelbrektsson, and Mar Diez. Henao for their valuable comments. The author is also thankful for all the feedback received during the Defending Democracy Colloquium, the 2023 Asian Law School Association (ALSA) conference, the Maurer School of Law Graduate Colloquium, and the Young Digital Law Conference 2024.

of the Chinese nation and reiterated that the CCP would not renounce the use of force if deemed necessary (Ministry of Foreign Affairs of the People's Republic of China, 2022). Beyond these official pronouncements, Taiwan has also come under increasing digital assault. In the early months of 2023, it emerged as the most targeted country in terms of cyberattacks, experiencing an average of over 15,000 attacks per second (Fortinet, 2023). These orchestrated interventions, strategically implemented by China, are intended to systematically undermine civilians' trust in Taiwan's democratic processes.

The Chinese Cyber Warfare

China's cyber warfare against Taiwan is conducted in a systematic and methodical manner. Influenced by the Gulf War, the PRC began establishing digitized forces and researching novel aspects of cyber warfare (劉 & 張, 2021, p. 122). In November 1999, the concept of a "cyber army" (网军) was first mentioned in the *Liberation Army Daily*, becoming a new branch alongside the Army, Navy, Air Force, and Second Artillery Corps (劉 & 張, 2021). The People's Liberation Army (PLA) began the task of establishing "information warriors" (信息战士), with the goal of identifying talent within the information industry across various regions (林, 2016, p. 59). In 2002, Major General Dai Qingmin, who served as the Director of the Fourth Department (Electronic Countermeasures and Radar) of the General Staff Department of the PLA, revealed in an internal report that the PLA had consolidated ten major patterns of "information warfare" (信息战), with a specific focus on "integrated network-electronic warfare" (网电一体战). This refers to the use of electronic warfare, computer network operations, dynamic targeting, and other methods to disrupt the enemy's battlefield network information systems that support combat operations and force projection. The PLA believed that achieving electromagnetic superiority during the initial stages of a battle was paramount to ensuring victory on the battlefield (林, 2016).

The overarching strategy employed by the Chinese cyber army involves the utilization of advanced persistent threats (APTs), which leverages the intricacies of human nature and employs sophisticated "social engineering" tactics (林, 2013, pp. 102–103). These orchestrated and meticulously planned espionage activities distinguish themselves from conventional cybersecurity attacks. In pursuit of their objectives, attackers navigate through various stages of attack, employing diverse tactics to evade detection. These stages include the establishment of initial footholds, internal network scanning, and lateral movement between systems within the network, all aimed at reaching the ultimate target system. Upon carrying out their malicious activities on the target system, attackers reach a decision point. They may opt to remain within the network, continuing their harmful actions on other systems, or they may choose to exit the system after eliminating any traces, depending on the directives of their funding source. These multistage attacks typically initiate with the infiltration of one of the network's systems. Subsequently, privilege escalation techniques are executed as needed to reach the ultimate target system, gain access to sensitive systems, and transmit status updates or information back to the attackers' command and control center (Alshamrani et al., 2019, p. 2). APTs demonstrate the meticulous planning, organization, and coordination among cyber army units (曾, 2020, p. 22). They exhibit characteristics of organized crime, often with the backing of adversarial governments, and are particularly adept at concealing their tracks (曾, 2020).

Taiwan's Regulatory Response and Its Limitations

Although Taiwan boasts one of the most liberated online environments in Asia, the proliferation of cyberattacks has prompted the nation to embrace a top-down approach to shaping its cybersecurity policy. The Cybersecurity Management Act (資通安全管理法) serves as the primary legislation for cybersecurity. This is part of the strategy of "cybersecurity-as-national-security strategy" (資安即國安) (國家資通安全辦公室, 2021). The law, passed in 2018, applies to government agencies and specific nongovernmental entities, including critical infrastructure providers, state-owned enterprises, and government-funded foundations (資通安全管理法,全國法規資料庫, 2022). The requirements for government agencies are modeled after the Federal Information Security Management Act of 2004 (FISMA). Moreover, specific nongovernmental entities must develop and implement cybersecurity maintenance plans in accordance with their respective cybersecurity responsibility levels and establish incident reporting and response mechanisms. These guidelines should include references to and recommendations for the relevant requirements under the International Organization for Standardization/International Electrotechnical Commission (ISO/IEC) 27001 international information security management standard. The broad application of this provision to nongovernmental entities has drawn criticism from scholars and certain members of Congress for its perceived lack of specificity (劉 & 徐, 2018, pp. 122–125; "「資通安全管理法」何去何從?," 2018, p. 158).

To counteract the APTs from China, significant legislative advancements have been made. First, the National Security Act (國家安全法) was updated to include "cyberspace" as the "fifth domain" of national security protection (國家安全法,全國法規資料庫, 2022; 國家安全法異動條文及理由, 立法院法律系統, 2019). This amendment reflects the reality that national security threats have transcended physical boundaries, with organized cyber criminals posing significant risks by targeting and compromising national critical information infrastructure through internet connections. However, the legal definition of cyberspace remains ambiguous, lacking clarity and precision (蔡, 2019, p. 37).

Second, in 2022, the National Communications Commission (NCC) proposed a draft act called the Digital Intermediary Service Act (數位中介服務法) to combat disinformation. The draft legislation included provisions establishing liability for internet intermediaries, modeled after the Digital Service Act. It also includes provisions for an "access restriction order," inspired by Section 125 of the United Kingdom's "Draft Online Safety Bill" from 2022 ("數位中介服務法草案總說明," n.d.). However, the law faced extensive criticisms for infringing on freedom of expression and allegations of unconstitutionality (陳, 2023). In response, the NCC announced its decision to refer the entire draft back to the internal digital convergence working group for thorough deliberation and examination of the contentious issues. (Shan, 2022)

Third, in consideration of data breaches involving nongovernmental organizations, the Administrative Yuan passed an amendment to the Personal Data Protection Act (個人資料保護法) (新聞傳播處, 2023). The proposed legislation establishes an autonomous entity dedicated to data protection and significantly raises the penalty (up to NT$10 million) for private enterprises that fail to ensure the security of personal data. According to the National Development Council (國家發展委員會), this is part of the key strategies outlined in the "New Generation Anti-Fraud Strategy Action Plan" by the Executive Yuan, which focuses on strengthening the cybersecurity obligations of all stakeholders involved under the "Prevention of Fraud" initiative (新聞傳播處, 2023).

Taiwan remains committed to upholding a free and open internet. However, the prevalence of cyberattacks from China has led to the adoption of a top-down approach, involving increased government intervention and the establishment of national boundaries within the internet sphere. Taiwan faces a critical challenge: safeguarding its democratic institutions while navigating the pressures of cyber warfare. This situation reflects broader discussions about the normative behavior of governments and private parties online. This research will explore the underlying norms and metaphors shaping internet governance over time, gaining valuable insights to address the complex challenges of the digital age.

NORM DEVELOPMENTS OF THE INTERNET

Norms and Metaphors

The internet was conceived in the late 1960s as a groundbreaking project by the U.S. Department of Defense (Leiner et al., 1997). Designed to interconnect research institutions and universities, it emerged as a sophisticated network for communication and resource sharing. Since its inception, the internet has undergone remarkable transformations, becoming the ubiquitous global network that defines our modern era. One of the internet's most important features is its ability to construct virtual reality, which has sparked a wide range of perspectives (Kerr, 2003, p. 357). Building on these perspectives, scholars have increasingly emphasized the idea of a "norm" in the digital context, focusing on how it is defined and established within the internet.

According to political scientist Martha Finnemore and Kathryn Sikkink, a norm is "a standard of appropriate behavior for actors with a given identity" (Finnemore & Sikkink, 1998, p. 891). The discourse surrounding norms in the digital realm is commonly referred to as "cyber norm," with its primary focus on defining the expected conduct of governments in relation to global security and the stability of the internet (Finnemore & Hollis, 2016). A norm life cycle consists of three stages: norm emergence, norm cascade, and norm internalization. Norm emergence may potentially result in a norm cascade, once the tipping point has been reached, which is then followed by the norm's internalization. The fundamental mechanism of the initial stage, norm emergence, entails the persuasive efforts of norm entrepreneurs who strive to sway a critical mass of states toward the adoption of novel norms. This process relies on the art of persuasion and the strategic influence wielded by these entrepreneurial actors to foster the acceptance and endorsement of emerging norms (Finnemore & Sikkink, 1998, p. 897). In short, the development of norms is linked to the active engagement of norm entrepreneurs.

At its core, the development of norms in internet governance revolves around the metaphors promoted by norm entrepreneurs. These metaphors not only present legitimate regulatory functions and drive policy changes but also possess remarkable cognitive power, as they help us conceptualize complex ideas or phenomena (Frischmann, 2007; Hunter, 2003). They serve as bridges between the technical complexities of the internet's infrastructure and the sociopolitical dynamics that shape its governance. Moreover, metaphors encapsulate specific visions of the internet, rendering the abstract realities of the digital world more tangible and relatable.

In the subsequent sections, I will analyze the two influential norm entrepreneurs in the digital realm – the United States and China – to glean perspectives on the evolution of behavioral norms and their significant contributions to this process. I will specifically explore how these norm entrepreneurs have used two distinct metaphors to shape internet policies. This analysis could offer valuable insights into the governance of international relations, where the interplay of law and politics influences the actions of states and other relevant entities (Finnemore & Sikkink, 1998, p. 916).

The United States and Cyberspace

The US' norm development was influenced by the "cyberspace" metaphor, popularized by William Gibson, a science fiction novelist, to describe a new place created by worldwide networks (Hunter, 2003, p. 441; Lemley, 2003, p. 524). According to traditional cyberlibertarianism, cyberspace is its own entity and therefore not subject to territorial regulation (Barlow, 1996). This vision depicted a free and open place where "land could be taken, explorers could roam, and communities could form with their own rules" (Hunter, 2003, pp. 442–443).

Notably, David Johnson and David Post argued in a 1996 article that cyberspace should be left to develop its own self-regulatory structure, as there was no longer an obvious method to connect an electronic transaction communication to a particular nation-state jurisdiction (Johnson & Post, 1996, p. 1367). Among the various proposals on self-governance, some theorists believe that online transactions should be governed by norms similar to those in the Lex Mercatoria – a set of norms that governed merchant transactions in medieval times (Hardy, 1994, pp. 1015–1025; Hunter, 2003, p. 448; Perritt, Jr., 1997, p. 461–463; Reidenberg, 1998, p. 553).

While the internet has never been as independent or sovereign as early idealists believed, the "cyberspace" metaphor strongly influenced the US legal academic discourse, judicial pronouncements, and legislative enactments (Hunter, 2003, pp. 446–447). The concept of cyberspace as an unrestricted virtual realm is deeply rooted in the American philosophy of free speech (Bradford, 2023, pp. 33–68; Lessig, 2000, p. 6). It embodies the conviction that individuals possess the liberty to articulate their thoughts without censorship or unwarranted intervention, akin to the safeguards enshrined in the First Amendment of the U.S. Constitution (Bradford, 2023, p. 41). Most significantly, the cyberspace metaphor resulted in favoring a bottom-up rather than top-down approach to internet governance. This philosophy contributes to an evolving legal landscape in the United States shaping how online activities are governed and influencing the protection of user data and online security. For instance, the United States lacks a comprehensive cybersecurity law. Meanwhile, US legal discourse on cyber policy has been closely monitoring the density of regulations over the cyber world, with the goal of keeping it free and open (Lessig, 1996, p. 869; Mueller, 2020, p. 779).

The metaphor of "cyberspace" has significantly shaped the trajectory of the US international norm development in cybersecurity, particularly by emphasizing constraints on government actions in the digital domain. Since 2005, the United States has actively engaged in the United Nations (UN) Group of Governmental Experts (GGE), prioritizing the development of responsible state behavior to prevent interstate conflict and limit the use of cyberattacks during cyber conflicts (Lotrionte, 2013, p. 75; Mueller, 2020, pp. 786–787). The GGE's efforts fostered constructive progress that culminated in the formation of a 2013 working group whose participants reached a consensus that the principles of the UN Charter principles, as well as international law, apply to the digital domain.

In 2015, the GGE released a report that acknowledged eleven voluntary norms – a significant milestone in advancing both the understanding of relevant international laws applicable to information and communications technologies (ICTs) and the imperative of safeguarding critical infrastructure (United Nations General Assembly, 2015). These principles were reaffirmed in the 2021 report by the UN Open-Ended Working Group (OEWG), an initiative originally seen as the GGE's counterpart and sponsored by Russia (Broeders, 2021, p. 278; United Nations General Assembly, 2021).

Overall, the United States has promoted its norms through the "cyberspace" metaphor, emphasizing minimal government intervention in the digital realm and prioritizing voluntary measures to protect free speech. This approach has influenced US cybersecurity policies abroad and has been effectively championed in international forums such as the UN GGE, where similar norms appear in the UN OEWG, the Paris Call, and the Global Commission ("The 9 Principles," n.d.; The Hague Centre for Strategic Studies, n.d.).

China and Internet Sovereignty

China views the internet as an extension of its territorial sovereignty, shaping its metaphorical perspective on how the internet should be governed (Bradford, 2023, p. 70). This notion was first introduced in the Chinese State Council Information Office's 2010 publication, *The internet in China* (Wang, 2020, p. 397). The "internet sovereignty of China" in this context refers to the assertion that the internet within Chinese territory falls under Chinese jurisdiction – a significant statement to partitioning the internet along national boundaries. The Chinese government has spearheaded legitimation and adoption of "internet sovereignty" through its 2017 Chinese Cybersecurity Law, representing the nation's intent to assert control over the internet within its jurisdiction (Creemers, Webster, & Triolo, 2018). Central to this framework are measures such as "public opinion guidance" and requirements for data localization by foreign companies (McKune & Ahmed, 2018, p. 3835; E. Wu, 2021, p. 1).

Acting as a norm entrepreneur, China has promoted internet content control norms in regional and international institutions under the principle of internet sovereignty. The Shanghai Cooperation Organization (SCO), jointly led by China and Russia, exemplifies this successful multilateral adoption of digital authoritarian norms and practices (McKune & Ahmed, 2018, p. 3841). Formed in 2001, the SCO consisted of China, Russia, Kazakhstan, Kyrgyzstan, Tajikistan, and Uzbekistan. Over time, the organization has developed a robust normative framework and gained international prominence. In 2009, SCO member states adopted the Yekaterinburg Agreement, which established core principles for "international information security" and paved the way for proposing an "International Code of Conduct for Information Security" to the UN in 2011 and 2015 (Ministry of Foreign Affairs of the People's Republic of China, 2011). This Code of Conduct emphasizes sovereignty, territorial integrity, and political independence, urging UN members to refrain from using ICTs to interfere in the internal affairs of other states or undermine their political, economic, and social stability (McKune & Ahmed, 2018, p. 3841). Meanwhile, President Xi Jinping underscored the importance of "respect for cyber sovereignty" at the second World Internet Conference (WIC) held in Wuzhen in December 2015 (McKune & Ahmed, 2018, p. 3845).

The concept of "sovereignty" has gained traction, resonating not only in authoritarian regimes but also in liberal democracies such as those in Europe (C.-H. Wu, 2021, p. 659). The European Union (EU) has begun using the terms "technological sovereignty" and "digital sovereignty," driven by the aim of enhancing its competitiveness in the digital realm and ensuring economic independence (Burwel & Propp, 2020, p. 1; European Commission, 2019, p. 3; von der Leyen, 2020). This concept encompasses preserving strategic autonomy and safeguarding security interests, as highlighted by the European Commission (European Commission, 2019, p. 3). The Digital Silk Road (DSR) extends the opportunity to propagate similar ideologies to African nations, potentially importing principles of "internet sovereignty." One noteworthy policy proposition is "data localization," which rests on government control, self-determined economic advancement, and societal structuring. This idea holds substantial appeal worldwide, extending well beyond nondemocratic governments (Erie & Streinz, 2021). The internet appears to be moving toward greater balkanization, marked by the creation of national boundaries that restrict the flow of information within specific jurisdictions (Lemley, 2021, p. 1399).

In general, China's norm development in the cybersecurity realm has advanced significantly, with one notable achievement being the increased awareness among nations of their sovereignty in the digital sphere. As a result, there has been a growing inclination to implement regulations and policies that exercise state control over the internet. By consistently using the term "sovereignty," President Xi has emphasized the importance of upholding the principle of internet sovereignty, highlighting the need for nations to assert their authority over their respective digital domains and establish governance mechanisms aligned with their national interests.

Taiwan's Metaphorical Choice: The Internet as Commons

The main implications of the two norm developments, each driven by a distinct metaphor, center on differing cybersecurity strategies. The US conception of "cyberspace" emphasizes voluntary measures, whereas China treats the internet as an extension of its national territory and favors regulatory controls. However, both perspectives face significant challenges. Under the "cyberspace" metaphor, the notion of a free and open internet, while aligned with the original vision of the internet, leaves democratic institutions vulnerable to attacks. As a result, the National Cybersecurity Strategy, published by the White House in March 2023, calls for coherent regulations in critical sectors, signaling a shift toward a model more akin to China's (The White House, 2023). Meanwhile, the "internet sovereignty" metaphor – by endorsing stringent regulatory measures – risks creating a "splinternet," characterized by regulatory conflicts and the potential for authoritarian regimes to curtail online freedoms (Lemley, 2021, pp. 1418–1421).

An alternative path for developing internet norms can be fostered by adopting the metaphor of the internet as "commons." This approach is not without theoretical foundations – scholars and politicians have long used the term "commons" to characterize the internet, with some referencing concepts such as the "global commons," "semi-commons," "pseudo commons" or commons within the economic context (111th Congress, 2010; Benkler, 2003; Chertoff, 2014; Frischmann, 2013; Hess, 1996; Hess & Ostrom, 2003; Lessig, 2001; Mueller, 2020; Shackelford, 2013, 2020; Shiffman & Gupta, 2013). Embracing the "commons" metaphor to depict the internet offers two primary advantages.

First, the metaphor of the "commons" aptly captures the shared nature of the internet (Hess, 1996). The term "commons" generally refers to a resource shared by a group of people subject to social dilemmas (Hess & Ostrom, 2007, pp. 3–4). One specific type of shared resource system, known as a "common-pool resource," combines the subtractability characteristic of private goods with the difficulty of exclusion typically associated with public goods (Ostrom, 2010, pp. 644–645). Forests, fisheries, and irrigation systems are prominent examples of common-pool resources worldwide (Ostrom, 2010, p. 645).

Given the internet's intricacies, the levels of subtractability and exclusivity vary depending on the aspect of the resource system under examination. The exclusion of internet resources is highly fragmented and piecemeal. When many users access the internet simultaneously, congestion can arise, highlighting the issue of subtractability (Hess, 1996). However, the attribute of difficulty of exclusion and high subtractability do not fully encompass the diverse resources of the internet. Accordingly, this research focuses on the notion of the "commons" to capture the internet's shared nature and highlights three shared resources:

- The cable commons: The internet relies on a vast physical infrastructure, with a network of high-performance submarine cables carrying 99 percent of global traffic between countries and continents (Takeshita et al., 2019, p. 36). This infrastructure can be referred to as the cables commons, comprising more than 552 submarine cables that span the ocean floor and linking to over 1,300 distinct coastal landing stations (McDaniel & Zhong, 2022; TeleGeography, n.d.). Ownership of submarine cables is heavily concentrated in the private sector, with about 99 percent privately owned by prominent telecom carriers, content delivery providers, and investor groups (Burnett, 2021). While network operators have traditionally been the primary investors, content providers such as Google, Amazon, Microsoft, and Meta have also expanded their investments to ensure seamless interconnection between their data centers (Wall & Morcos, 2021). Excluding others from using the same submarine cables can be challenging, given their shared nature. Congestion may occur due to high demand, technical issues, underinvestment, or geopolitical factors.
- The communications commons: The internet's most significant accomplishment is its standardized means of communication, enabled by a set

of globally accepted protocols. The communications commons refers to the shared, interoperable, and equitable nature of internet communication. This commons is primarily maintained by several organizations, including the Internet Engineering Task Force (IETF), Internet Corporation for Assigned Names and Numbers (ICANN), and Institute of Electrical and Electronics Engineers (IEEE). A foundational conceptual framework for coordinating the development of interconnection standards is the Open Systems Interconnection (OSI) model, developed by the ISO. This model consists of seven abstraction layers, including physical, data link, network, transport, session, presentation, and application layers (ISO, 1994). Each layer represents a specific aspect of the communication process in a computing system. These standards are designed to be open and universal, enabling anyone, anywhere, to build software or hardware that connects to the internet. Because of these open standards and the interoperable nature of the internet, excluding others can be difficult. However, congestion may occur due to network architecture, peak usage, heavy users, or distributed denial of service (DDoS) attacks.

- The content commons: The "content commons" refers to the collective body of information and speech that flows across the internet, shaping the virtual world. It encompasses content created by both users and organizations such as governments, corporations, and academic institutions. Much of this commons is hosted on platforms controlled by large US and Chinese corporations – ranging from social networking to search engine services and e-commerce (CompaniesMarketCap, 2023). Within these platforms, diverse social groups establish various sub-commons, each with unique functions, thereby fostering distinct communities. Sharing content on the web remains relatively easy due to low costs, wide reach, and the prevalence of social media platforms. However, congestion can occur because of information overload, the tendency to prioritize quantity over quality, and the lack of effective content discoverability.

Second, Ostrom's scholarly inquiry into the governance of commons offers profound insights that can significantly enhance internet governance, particularly regarding cybersecurity strategies. Ostrom's main contribution to the commons theory lies in her formulation of eight institutional design principles, which are strongly tied to the effectiveness of institutions in managing common-pool resources. These principles were the successful commons management systems she identified among the cases examined in *Governing the Commons* (Ostrom, 2015). The eighth design principle, which addresses larger and more complex systems of common-pool resources, specifies that various governance activities associated with robust institutions should be organized across multiple layers of nested enterprises. In subsequent work, Ostrom and others have sometimes used the term "polycentric" interchangeably with, or in reference to, the "nested" requirement of the eighth design principle – though polycentricity implies more than nestedness (Carlisle & Gruby, 2017, p. 930).

While there is no unified definition of "polycentric governance," at the heart of nearly every discussion is the notion of multiple centers of decision-making, where none of them has ultimate authority for making collective decisions (Stephan, Marshall, & McGinnis, 2019, p. 31). This mirrors the structure of the internet, wherein the decision-making centers encompass national authorities, international organizations, private companies, and individuals. Recognizing this, when governance systems are structured in a polycentric manner – from the smallest to the largest scales – they become capable of addressing collective action problems across multiple levels (Ostrom, 2012, p. 107). This arrangement inherently fosters the development of norms among participants through a variety of mechanisms, all interconnected and mutually reinforcing. It emphasizes the potential for effective cooperation, conflict resolution, fruitful competition, and shared learning (Bruns, 2019, p. 237). As a result, polycentricity highlights the organic and self-organizing nature of internet governance – where multiple centers of decision-making interact and collaborate – and stands in contrast to a purely market- or state-centric approach (Stephan, Marshall, & McGinnis, 2019).

The Taiwan–China conflict illustrates the clash between two different internet metaphors. The US concept of "cyberspace" encourages minimal regulatory intervention and is less effective in mitigating cyberattacks, whereas China's "sovereignty" perspective prioritizes stricter regulations and enhanced security, often at the expense of freedom of expression. Embracing the metaphor of the "internet as a commons" offers Taiwan valuable insights for formulating its cybersecurity strategy. It directs the attention toward identifying shared resources and decision-making centers within the internet. This metaphor serves as a critical tool for interpreting, shaping, and navigating the intricate landscape of policies and protocols that underpin Taiwan's cybersecurity frameworks. It also promotes meaningful dialogue among diverse stakeholders – policymakers, technologists, academics, civil society, and businesses – that often transcends disciplinary and cultural boundaries. By adopting this approach, Taiwan gains a strategic advantage without veering toward an overly idealized "cyberspace" metaphor or fully embracing "internet sovereignty." Individuals can safeguard and coordinate the management of shared resources without relying on centralized rulemaking, thereby enhancing security and fostering norm development (Shiffman & Gupta, 2013, p. 100).

DEFENDING TAIWAN'S DEMOCRACY IN THE INTERNET COMMONS UNDER POLYCENTRIC GOVERNANCE

Tragedy of the Internet Commons

V. Ostrom, Tiebout, and Robert Warren (1961) introduced the concept of polycentricity in their endeavor to ascertain the nature of activities undertaken by numerous public and private agencies involved in the provision and production of public services within metropolitan areas (Carlisle & Gruby, 2017, p. 928). V. Ostrom's idea of polycentricity goes beyond specific domains and encompasses various aspects of societal organization, including economic markets, legal systems, scientific disciplines, and multicultural societies. In the realm of politics, federalism stands as a key example of polycentricity (Stephan, Marshall, & McGinnis, 2019, p. 24). As mentioned earlier, Elinor Ostrom adopted the term in her work on *governing the commons*, making it a central pillar of the Bloomington School of Political Economy (Carlisle & Gruby, 2017, p. 930).

The main purpose of Ostrom's polycentric governance is to mitigate the risk of the "tragedy of the commons" (Hardin, 1968). In valuable open-access resources, the absence of an effective governance regime – either by involved parties themselves or external authorities – may lead to suboptimal outcomes. As internet usage increases, it introduces more threat vectors and provides malicious actors with an expanded range of networks to target, creating a scenario akin to the "tragedy of the commons." While the broader China–Taiwan conflict resembles a vibrant threat system, the emergence of APTs and activities such as undersea cable disruptions, DDoS attacks, and disinformation campaigns within the internet context are analogous to overexploitation of resources across different internet commons. These developments present a collective action problem that falls within the realm of classic social dilemmas (Shackelford, 2013, p. 1293).

Tragedy of the Cable Commons

The tragedy of the "cable commons" refers to intentional interference with submarine cables and their use as tools for intelligence gathering. Despite their pivotal role in the digital economy, submarine cables remain surprisingly vulnerable, and the regulations governing their security are antiquated (McDaniel & Zhong, 2022). The governance of the cable commons occupies a gray area, which some phrase as "the orphans of international law" (Beckman, 2014, p. 281). Relevant conventions, including the 1884 Convention for the Protection of Submarine Telegraph Cables, the 1958 Convention on the Continental Shelf, and the 1982 United Nations Convention on the Law of the Sea (UNCLOS), only provide a limited degree of peacetime protection for submarine cables. Their applicability during times of conflict, however, remains contested (McDaniel & Zhong, 2022).

Intentional interference can originate from state or non-state actors, serving various objectives. These may include disrupting military or government communications in the early stages of a conflict, cutting off internet access for a targeted population, sabotaging economic competitors, or causing economic disruptions for geopolitical reasons (Davenport, 2015; Wall & Morcos, 2021). Taiwan is connected by fifteen submarine cables (McDaniel & Zhong, 2022). This network – protected by advanced encryption – has landing points in Toucheng, Taiwan, Baler, Philippines; and El Segundo, California, yet it poses a significant vulnerability to the nation's cybersecurity. For instance, in February 2023, two submarine cables connecting Taiwan and Matsu were severed, disrupting internet access for residents in Matsu Island. In an invasion scenario, beyond physically cutting these cables, China could deploy submarines or unmanned underwater vehicles (UUVs) to locate and sever cables, launch cyberattacks that result in data disruption, and use devices that generate electromagnetic pulses (EMPs) to damage cables or their connected infrastructure (陳, 2023).

It is also possible to tap cables to intercept and steal data for espionage. Edward Snowden revealed that the United States and the United Kingdom have been directly intercepting the internet backbone (Davenport, 2015). Moreover, the need for cable tapping in espionage may become redundant when a state owns the infrastructure. One important feature of the DSR involves Chinese technology firms partnering with non-Chinese counterparts to construct undersea cables (Erie & Streinz, 2021). China's ongoing efforts to assert control over various islands in the South China Sea further exacerbate the issue, allowing it to lay its own network cables away from international scrutiny. With ambitions to expand 5G networks – led by Huawei – the Chinese government stands to exert even greater influence over the flow of information entering and exiting the country (Martin, 2019).

Tragedy of the Communications Commons

Cyberattacks predominantly take place within the "communications commons" and take various forms. Their primary goal is to disrupt the shared internet communication. A common type is the DDoS attack, which involves flooding the network's communications channels. In one method, an attacker sends a continuous stream of packets to a target, depleting critical resources and rendering the system inaccessible to legitimate clients. Another tactic uses a few maliciously crafted packets to disrupt an application or a protocol on the victim's machine, causing it to freeze or require a reboot. Such attacks are feasible because internet security is highly interdependent and internet resources are finite (Mirkovic & Reiher, 2004, p. 40). Other cyberattacks include malware, phishing, ransomware, spoofing, and eavesdropping (Fortinet, n.d.). One major consequence of cyberattacks is a data breach, in which unauthorized entities gain access to sensitive or confidential information (Kosinski, 2024).

Taiwan experiences persistent daily DDoS attacks from China. For instance, in 2018, the computer systems of Taiwanese government departments were subjected to frequent cyberattacks and vulnerability probing, exceeding 10 million incidents per month – more than half of which originated from Chinese information warfare units. In 2022, following a visit to Taiwan by U.S. House Speaker Nancy Pelosi, Taiwan's Ministry of National Defense reported a DDoS attack that took down its network for about two hours (Miller, 2022). Hackers have also targeted the websites of the Presidential Office, Ministry of Foreign Affairs, and Ministry of National Defense.

Additionally, Taiwan has experienced numerous significant data breaches, affecting both government agencies and private sectors across various industries (李, 2023). Reports indicate that personal data from key intelligence systems, including the National Security Bureau and Military Intelligence Bureau, have been compromised and traded in overseas markets (李, 2023). Also, domestic and international cybersecurity agencies have repeatedly found Trojan programs in devices produced by well-known Chinese smartphone brands. These programs covertly transmit users' personal information, captured photos, and network communications to specific addresses, enabling surveillance of smartphone users and creating a "cybersecurity black hole" (國防部政治作戰局, 2017).

Tragedy of the Content Commons

The tragedy of the content commons refers to the disruption of a shared content ecosystem. It can arise from "information warfare," a strategy that involves controlling information to gain a competitive advantage. This strategy encompasses both offensive and defensive operations. Strategy, in this context, refers to the process of planning to achieve national objectives and goals, while operations serve as the bridge between strategic objectives and specific tactics, techniques, and procedures. This linkage is facilitated through information operations (IO). Categories of information used in IO include propaganda, misinformation, and disinformation. Notably, the Russian government has been accused of employing bots to spread disinformation and sow discord in various contexts, including the 2016 US presidential election (Theohary, 2018).

Beijing's information warfare targeting Taiwan has been focused on promoting the PRC's model of governance and fostering polarization, aiming to undermine confidence in Taiwan's democratic process (Faust, 2023). Doublethink Lab, a Taiwanese organization researching the impact of digital authoritarianism, has identified several methods used by Chinese actors. These include social media influencers amplifying disinformation from CCP-backed content farms and operations involving collaboration with actors who often recruit Taiwanese agents to carry out influence campaigns originating from the mainland (Lee et al., 2020, pp. 22–39).

The task of preserving the content commons through regulations has been arduous due to the inherent risk of "collateral censorship" associated with any form of speech regulation (Balkin, 1999, p. 2298). When the state holds one private party, "A," liable for the speech of another private party, "B," A has an incentive to avoid any potential liability by restricting even fully protected speech. This dynamic often leaves the content commons largely unregulated, especially in democratic states. Meanwhile, authoritarian regimes have enacted laws to censor online speech, ostensibly in the interest of national security. These measures include dictating the permissible forms of speech on websites, exemplified by the 2017 Chinese Cybersecurity Law (Creemers, Webster, & Triolo, 2018). In summary, striking a delicate balance between protecting free speech and upholding national security remains a significant challenge.

Taiwan's Polycentric Governance in the Internet Commons

Within the internet commons, global problems involve a diverse array of actors, extending beyond governments to include corporate entities that serve as agents for complex publics and exhibit significantly intricate behavior (McGinnis & Ostrom, 1992). As mentioned, nearly every discussion of polycentric governance revolves around the concept of multiple "decision-making centers" (Stephan, Marshall, & McGinnis, 2019, p. 31). This concept highlights the distributed nature of governance, where power and decision-making are dispersed across various institutions. Jurisdictions of authority may overlap, with many centers of decision-making operating formally independent of each other (Ostrom, Tiebout, & Warren, 1961). The goal of polycentric governance is to facilitate the use of local knowledge and build mutual trust (Cole, 2015). Local communities possess the skills, local knowledge, and capacity to overcome many challenges, making it essential to resolve problems as close to these communities as possible. This approach effectively addresses the challenges posed to traditional models of democracy centered on the nation-state (Scholte, 2017, p. 167). Polycentricity challenges the belief that either the state or markets alone hold the solution to addressing complex challenges (Shackelford, 2013, p. 1333). Instead, it creates an effective mechanism for cooperation, coordination, conflict resolution, and the utilization of local knowledge.

Taiwan's Role as a Public Entrepreneur in the Cable Commons

To effectively address collective action problems, it is critical to foster entrepreneurship and innovation across local, regional, national, and international domains. Taiwan, as a decision-making center, has the potential to act as a public entrepreneur in the cable commons, calling for policy changes on maintaining the cable commons among governments, cable operators, and cable owners. As explained by Elinor Ostrom, "Entrepreneurship is a particular form of leadership focused primarily on problem solving and putting heterogeneous processes together in complementary and effective ways, rather than simply making public speeches and being charismatic" (Ostrom, 2012, p. 107). Entrepreneurship can be further understood as "acts performed by actors who seek to punch above their weight," distinguishing them from those who merely perform their duties and act appropriately (Boasson, 2018, p. 119). In relation to the concept of "norm entrepreneurs," as discussed in international relations theory, both norm and public entrepreneurs serve as agents of change. While the former concentrates on shaping norms and values, the latter seeks to drive policy change.

The governance of the cable commons, as mentioned, is a gray zone that poses significant concerns due to its vulnerability to disruption and penetration. Taiwan's role as a public entrepreneur in this domain should focus on promoting best practices, including diversification, cable installation, operation and maintenance, information sharing among allies and contingency planning, and the development of a variety of regulatory regimes and international legal frameworks (European Agency for Cybersecurity, 2023). This role is particularly important given the ongoing competition between China and the United States over control of undersea cables.

Specifically, regional and international cooperation on information sharing should be established as a mechanism for interorganizational, intersectoral, and intergovernmental exchanges of data deemed relevant by the sharers for resolving collective action problems (Housen-Couriel, 2022). Taiwan and its allies can formulate joint patrols or task forces with regional partners to share intelligence and coordinate countermeasures. The goal is to strengthen infrastructure by investing in cable armoring, deep burial, and decoy cables, while collaborating with international organizations to establish accountability systems (陳, 2023).

The Industry's Role of Fostering a Security Culture in the Communications Commons

In the communications commons, each company within the industry serves as a decision-making center to maintain internet communication by fostering a cybersecurity culture. The concept of cybersecurity culture can be understood as a set of rules regarding best cybersecurity practices expressed through either formal regulations or informal social norms and values. It refers to the norms spanning industries, individuals, governments that promote best cybersecurity practices, given that human error is one of the biggest security threats. Under polycentric governance, companies, as local communities, inherently harbor a wealth of valuable skills, indigenous knowledge, and capacity to surmount multifarious challenges, serving as a decision-making center. Therefore, it is essential to address problems at the community level, recognizing the potential for localized solutions.

The industry can cultivate a cybersecurity culture in two ways: by nurturing it within individual companies and by collectively developing a cybersecurity framework. Fundamentally, security cultures should be rooted in and aligned with the broader organizational culture (Nasir et al., 2019; Uchendu et al., 2021). Studies have shown that critical factors in fostering security culture include top management support, clear policies and procedures, and information security awareness and training. Specifically, without management support, cybersecurity initiatives may not appear significant to employees when weighed against their daily responsibilities (Uchendu et al., 2021). It is critical to establish a community and an environment of trust to effectively implement and sustain a cybersecurity culture (Batteau, 2011). As mentioned, adversaries utilize APTs to execute precise and covert cyberattacks on organizations, often remaining concealed within enterprise networks for extended periods, sometimes months or even years (Mahmoud, Mannan, &

Youssef, 2023). Research indicates that people are often the weakest point in the cybersecurity chain. Internal users may either intentionally disclose sensitive information to external entities or inadvertently provide valuable information to adversaries with sophisticated expertise and significant resources. Fostering a strong security culture becomes a crucial step in raising awareness to reduce the likelihood of APTs (Alshamrani et al., 2019, p. 1873). The ultimate goal is to build a "solid and effective human firewall" (Marotta & Pearlson, 2019, p. 9).

Furthermore, the Taiwanese industry and government can coordinate to establish a cybersecurity framework. Ideally, industry groups most familiar with best practices should be allowed to craft local rules, which can then be augmented and enforced (Shackelford, 2013, p. 1353). Such a framework can be voluntary, at least in the beginning. One example is the cybersecurity framework developed by the National Institute of Standards and Technology (NIST). In response to Executive Order 13636, NIST employed a year-long process involving active dialogue with multiple stakeholders, establishing a bottom-up approach to cybersecurity (Peng, 2018, p. 451; Shackelford et al., 2015). A voluntary cybersecurity framework for Taiwan should also be created through an inclusive and transparent process, involving stakeholders from the private sector, civil society, and government. This would complement the Taiwanese government's top-down approach. Different frameworks may address different risks, such as those related to cybersecurity, privacy, and artificial intelligence (AI). By promoting collaboration and drawing on best practices from both the public and private sectors, such an initiative would foster a culture of proactive and voluntary cyber defense measures.

The Community's Role in Content Moderation in the Content Commons

In the content commons, online communities – including fact-checking initiatives – play a key role in maintaining the shared content ecosystem. Individuals within each community can collaborate to create a network for verifying and disseminating accurate information. The Taiwanese online community, in particular, ought to foster a strong sense of collective responsibility for content moderation, empowering individuals to actively shape and maintain a healthy online environment. Their goal is to counter information warfare at the local level. This approach should center on two key elements: first, fostering both cooperation and competition between professional and crowdsourced fact-checking initiatives and, second, implementing a multilevel governance framework.

First, professional and crowdsourced fact-checking initiatives can be perceived as decision-making centers within the context of polycentric governance. The proliferation of professional fact-checking outlets around the globe has experienced a remarkable growth, increasing from just eleven sites in 2008 to 424 in 2022 (Stencel, Ryan, & Luther, 2023). Taiwan, in particular, boasts a robust environment for fact-checking centers, with organizations such as MyGoPen and Taiwan FactCheck Center. At the same time, Cofacts, a crowdsourced fact-checking center, focuses on local and daily matters, helping to mitigate the effects of everyday misinformation. Research indicates that Cofacts plays a complementary role alongside professional fact-checkers. It leverages the global, cross-language perspectives offered by professional fact-checking organizations while offering faster responses to fact-checking needs (Saeed et al., 2022). The overlapping jurisdictions between these two types of fact-checking initiatives are integral to the dynamic of polycentric governance, which guarantees competition and cooperation among themselves (Stephan, Marshall, & McGinnis, 2019, p. 33).

A key aspect of a polycentric system is the concept of "nested enterprises," where governance activities are organized in multiple layers of related governance regimes. Large tech companies and local administrators can be perceived as part of a nested ecosystem. Given that one of the central challenges within the content commons is the centralization of platforms, an approach to decentralizing platform power involves introducing intermediary layers of local administration. Research suggests several design implications for local administrators – platforms should support them in experimenting with community guidelines, sanctioning criteria, and automation settings; allowing for cross-cutting membership so users can participate in multiple communities; fostering healthy competition; holding decision-makers accountable for poor performance; and providing mechanisms for conflict resolution (Jhaver, Frey, & Zhang, 2021). This approach could be particularly impactful for local administrators on popular social media platforms in Taiwan, such as Facebook.com, Line.me, Instagram.com, ptt.cc, and dcard.tw. The goal is to involve volunteers of subcommittees in Taiwan to actively enforce platform moderation policies and help establish local community norms.

CONCLUSION

In conclusion, the development of internet governance has been driven by two distinct metaphors – the "cyberspace" metaphor and the "sovereignty" metaphor. The United States holds significant influence in promoting responsible state behaviors in the UN rooted in the "cyberspace" metaphor. This approach reflects the belief that voluntary measures provide greater flexibility and adaptability to address the multifaceted challenges of cyberspace. In contrast, China has made notable advancements in raising global awareness about the notion of "sovereignty." This progress has contributed to a growing trend of nations adopting regulations and policies that emphasize state authority and control over the internet.

By embracing the metaphor of the internet as "commons," the focus of internet governance can be directed toward governing various shared resources, including the "cable commons," the "communications commons" and the "content commons." This approach allows Taiwan to navigate the delicate balance between national and private control of the internet to protect its democratic system. Grounded in compelling evidence, Ostrom's research on commons highlights that individuals from all walks of life possess the ability to voluntarily organize and establish rules to protect shared resources.

Polycentric governance offers a pathway to address the various challenges posed by cyberattacks. This approach acknowledges the benefits and constraints of multi-level regulation, underscores the importance of self-organization, and recognizes the vital role of internet governance from the local level. Taiwan's efforts to defend its democracy in the digital realm extend beyond its borders, offering a blueprint for other nations navigating similar threats. Ultimately, Taiwan's success in this endeavor will not only strengthen its own democratic system but also contribute to a more resilient, inclusive, and cooperative global digital ecosystem.

REFERENCES

中華民國 [Republic of China]. (2018, June 6). 資通安全管理法 *[Information Security Management Law]*. 全國法規資料庫 [Law & Regulation Database of The Republic of China (Taiwan)]. https://law.moj.gov.tw/LawClass/LawAll.aspx?pcode=A0030297

(2022, June 8). 國家安全法 *[National Security Law]*. 全國法規資料庫 [Law & Regulations Database of The Republic of China (Taiwan)]. https://law.moj.gov.tw/LawClass/LawAll.aspx?pcode=A0030028

中華民國 [Republic of China]. (2019, June 19). 國家安全法 異動條文及理由 *[National Security Law Amendments to the National Security Act and Explanatory Notes]*. 立法院法律系統 [Legislative Yuan Law Database of the Republic of China (Taiwan)] https://lis.ly.gov.tw/lglawc/lawsingle?000918C97866000000000000000000014000000004FFFFFD^01441108061900^00000000000

(2023, June 28). 增訂並修正電信管理法條文-全國法規資料庫 *[Update and amendments to the provisions of the Telecommunications Management Law]*. 全國法規資料庫 [Laws & Regulations Database of The Republic of China (Taiwan)]. https://law.moj.gov.tw/News/NewsDetail.aspx?msgid=176197

數位中介服務法草案總說明 [General explanation of the draft Digital Intermediary Services Law]. (n.d.). https://ncc.gov.tw/chinese/files/22081/5542_47882_220811_1.pdf

國防部政治作戰局 [Department of Defense, Political Operations Bureau]. (n.d.). 中共網軍襲臺的案例與效應 *[Cases and effects of the CCP's cyber army's attack on Taiwan]*. 國防部政治作戰局 [Department of Defense, Political Operations Bureau]. https://gpwd.mnd.gov.tw/Download_File.ashx?id=2327

謝銘洋 [Mingyan, S.], 蔡易餘 [Yiyu, T.], 余宛如 [Wanju, Y.], 劉靜怡 [Jingyi, L.], 林明昕 [Minghsin, L.], 黃居正 [Chucheng, H.], & 邱文聰 [Wentsong, C.]. (2018, April). 「資通安全管理法」何去何從? [Where does the "Information Security Management Law" go from here?]. 月旦法學雜誌 *[The Taiwan Law Review]*, 275, 156–167. https://doi.org/10.3966/102559312018040275012

國家資通安全辦公室 [National Information Security Office]. (2021, September). 國家資通安全戰略報告: 資安即國安2.0 [National Information Security Strategy Report: Information Security is National Security]. https://scribd.com/document/679477578/資安及國安

新聞傳播處 [Press and Communication Department, Executive Yuan]. (2023, April 13). 政院通過「個人資料保護法」第1條之1、第48條、第56條修正草案設置個資保護獨立監督機關並提高個資外洩罰責. 行政院 [The political Yuan passed the draft amendments to Articles 1-1 48, and 56 of the "Personal Data Protection Las" to establish an independent supervision agency for personal information protection and increase penalties for personal information leakage]. 行政院 [Executive Yuan]. www.ey.gov.tw/Page/9277F759E41CCD91/2d6bb590-fa47-435f-818e-c196c25733e0

林穎佑 [Yingyou, L.]. (2013, March). 大陸網軍與APT攻擊 [Mainland CyberArmy and APT attacks]. 展望與探索 *[Perspective and Exploration Monthly]*, *11*(3), 95–110.

(2016, Fall). 中國近期網路作為探討:從控制到攻擊 (Discussion of recent China cyber operations: From control to attack). 台灣國際研究季刊, *12*(3), 51–68.

蔡震榮 [Zhenrong, C.]. (2019, July 14). 間諜罪防制修法之探討 [Discussion on the amendment to the prevention and control of espionage crime]. 台灣法學雜誌 *[Taiwan Law Journal]*, *371*, 25–38.

曾于臻 [Yuzhen, Z.]. (2020, January 1). 網路安全對國家安全之重要性:以台灣的網路安全為例 [The importance of cybersecurity to national security: Taking Taiwan's cybersecurity as an example]. 發展與前瞻學報 *[Journal of Development and Prospect]*, *30*(1), 5–26. https://doi.org/10.6737/JDP.202012_(30).01

李佳琪 [Jiaqi, L.]. (2023, February 24). 國安大漏洞！中國駭客盜賣台灣2300萬筆個資(圖) - 在地見聞- - (移動版) [Big national security loophole! Chinese hackers stole and sold 23 million pieces of personal information in Taiwan]. 看中国 [*Vision Times*]. www.secretchina.com/news/b5/2023/02/24/1029710.html

陳成良 [Chengliang, C.]. (2023, March 23). 中國黑手伸向海底電纜 外媒：台灣應反擊 [China's black hands extend to undersea cables. Foreign media; Taiwan should fight back]. 自由時報 *[The Liberty Times]*. https://news.ltn.com.tw/news/life/paper/1573543

陳俐蓉 [Lirong, C.]. (2023, November 4). 數位中介服務法草案爭議問題 [Controversial Issues in the Draft Digital Intermediary Services Law]. Taiwan Artificial Intelligence Wise Agent Network. https://ai.iias.sinica.edu.tw/controversial-draft-digital-intermediary-service-act/

劉靜怡 [Jingyi, L.], & 徐彪豪 [Xu, B.]. (2018, January). 行政院版資通安全管理法草案評析 [Commentary on the Draft Information Security Management Law of the Executive Yuan]. 月旦法學雜誌 [*The Taiwan Law Review*], 272, 111–132. https://doi.org/10.3966/102559312018010272009

劉嘉偉 [Jiawei, L.], & 張家瑍 [Jiayuan, Z.]. (2021, June 1). 面對中共網軍威脅國家資訊網路安全之探討 [Discussion on the Security of the National Military Information Network in the Face of the Threat from the Chinese Communist Party's Cyber Army]. 海軍學術雙月刊 *[Naval Academic Bimonthly]*, 55(3), 118–131. https://doi.org/10.6237/NPJ.202106_55(3).0008

111th Congress. (2010, February 23). *Cybersecurity: Next steps to protect our critical infrastructure*. GovInfo.

Alshamrani, A., Myneni, S., Chowdhary, A., & Huang, D. (2019, January). A survey on advanced persistent threats: Techniques, solutions, challenges, and research opportunities. *IEEE Communications Surveys & Tutorials*, *21*, 1851–1877. https://doi.org/10.1109/COMST.2019.2891891

Balkin, J. M. (1999). Free speech and hostile environments. *Columbia Law Review*, 99(8), 2295–2320. https://doi.org/10.2307/1123612

Barlow, J. P. (1996, February 8). *A declaration of the independence of cyberspace*. Electronic Frontier Foundation (EFF). https://eff.org/cyberspace-independence

Batteau, A. W. (2011). Creating a culture of enterprise cybersecurity. *International Journal of Business Anthropology*, *2*(2). https://doi.org/10.33423/ijba.v2i2.1179

Beckman, R. (2014). Protecting Submarine Cables from intentional damage – The security gap. In D. R. Burnett, R. C. Beckman, & T. Davenport (Eds.), *Submarine cables: The handbook of law and policy* (pp. 281–297). Martinus Nijhoff.

Benkler, Y. (2003). The political economy of commons. *The European Journal for the Informatics Professional*, 4(3), 6–9.

Boasson, E. L. (2018). Entrepreneurship: A key driver of polycentric governance? In A. Jordan, D. Huitema, H. van Asselt, & J. Forster (Eds.), *Governing climate change: Polycentricity in action?* (pp. 117–134). Cambridge University Press. https://doi.org/10.1017/9781108284646.008

Bradford, A. (2023). *Digital empires: The global battle to regulate technology*. Oxford University Press.

Broeders, D. (2021). The (im)possibilities of addressing election interference and the public core of the internet in the UN GGE and OEWG: A mid-process assessment. *Journal of Cyber Policy*, 6(3), 277–297 https://doi.org/10.1080/23738871.2021.1916976

Bruns, B. (2019). Practicing polycentric governance. In A. Thiel, D. E. Garrick, & W. A. Blomquist (Eds.), *Governing complexity: Analyzing and applying polycentricity*. Cambridge University Press. https://doi.org/10.1017/9781108325721

Burnett, D. R. (2021). Submarine cable security and international law. *International Law Studies*, 97, 1659–1682.

Burwel, F., & Propp, K. (2020, June). *The European Union and the search for digital sovereignty: Building "Fortress Europe" or preparing for a new world?* Atlantic Council: Future Europe Initiative. https://atlanticcouncil.org/wp-content/uploads/2020/06/The-European-Union-and-the-Search-for-Digital-Sovereignty-Building-Fortress-Europe-or-Preparing-for-a-New-World.pdf

Carlisle, K., & Gruby, R. L. (2017). Polycentric systems of governance: A Theoretical model for the commons. *Policy Studies Journal*, 47(4), 927–952. https://doi.org/10.1111/psj.12212

Chertoff, M. (2014). The strategic significance of the internet commons. *Strategic Studies Quarterly*, 8(2), 10–16.

Cole, D. H. (2015). Advantages of a polycentric approach to climate change policy. *Nature Climate Change*, 5, 114–118. https://doi.org/10.1038/nclimate2490

CompaniesMarketCap. (2023). *Largest internet companies by market cap*. Companies Market Cap. https://companiesmarketcap.com/internet/largest-internet-companies-by-market-cap/

Creemers, R., Webster, G., & Triolo, P. (2018, June 29). *Translation: Cybersecurity Law of the People's Republic of China (Effective June 1, 2017)*. DigiChina. https://digichina.stanford.edu/work/translation-cybersecurity-law-of-the-peoples-republic-of-china-effective-june-1-2017/

Davenport, T. (2015). Submarine cables, cybersecurity and international law: An intersectional analysis. *Catholic University Journal of Law and Technology*, 24(1), 57–109, https://scholarship.law.edu/jlt/vol24/iss1/4

Diamond, L. (2009). *The spirit of democracy: The struggle to build free societies throughout the world*. St. Martin's Publishing Group.

Erie, M. S., & Streinz, T. (2021). The Beijing effect: China's 'Digital Silk Road' as transnational data governance. *New York University Journal of International Law and Politics*, 54(1), 1–92.

European Agency for Cybersecurity. (2023, August 31). *Dive into the deep sea: A view of the subsea cable ecosystem*. The European Union Agency for Cybersecurity (ENISA). https://enisa.europa.eu/news/dive-into-the-deep-sea-a-view-of-the-subsea-cable-ecosystem

European Commission. (2019). *Questionnaire to the Commissioner-Designate Thierry Breton*. European Parliament. https://europarl.europa.eu/resources/library/media/20191113RES66410/20191113RES66410.pdf

Faust, R. (2023, September 12). *Taiwan on the Frontline of China's Information Operations*. Power 3.0. Retrieved December 16, 2024, from https://power3point0.org/2023/09/12/taiwan-on-the-frontline-of-chinas-information-operations/

Fell, D. (2018). *Government and politics in Taiwan*. Routledge.

Finnemore, M., & Hollis, D. B. (2016). Constructing norms for global cybersecurity. *The American Journal of International Law*, 110(3), 425–479.

Finnemore, M., & Sikkink, K. (1998). International norm dynamics and political change. *International Organization*, 52(4), 887–917.

Fortinet. (2023, August 23). Global Threat Landscape Report: A Semiannual Report by FortiGuard Labs. https://fortinet.com/content/dam/fortinet/assets/threat-reports/threat-report-1h-2023.pdf

(2023, August 23). *Fortinet report: Taiwan was attacked an average of nearly 15,000 times per second in the first half of 2023, ranking first in the Asia-Pacific*. Fortinet.

(n.d.). *Top 20 most common types of cyber attacks*. Fortinet. https://fortinet.com/resources/cyberglossary/types-of-cyber-attacks

Freedom House. (n.d.). *Taiwan: Country Profile*. Freedom House. https://freedomhouse.org/country/taiwan

Frischmann, B. M. (2007). Cultural environmentalism and the wealth of networks. *The University of Chicago Law Review*, 74(3), 1083–1143.

(2013). *Infrastructure: The social value of shared resources*. Oxford University Press.

Hardin, G. (1968). The tragedy of the commons. *Science*, 162(3859), 1243–1248. https://doi.org/10.1126/science.162.3859.1243

Hardy, T. (1994). The proper legal regime for 'cyberspace'. *University of Pittsburgh Law Review*, 55, 993–1055.

Hess, C. (1996, March). *Untangling the web: The internet as a commons*. Indiana University. https://dlc.dlib.indiana.edu/dlc/bitstream/handle/10535/327/Untangling_the_Web96.pdf?sequence = 1&isAllowed = y

Hess, C., & Ostrom, E. (2003, Winter). Ideas, artifacts, and facilities: Information as a common-pool resource. *Law and Contemporary Problems*, 66, 111–146.

(2007). Introduction: An overview of the knowledge commons. In C. Hess & E. Ostrom (Eds.), *Understanding knowledge as a commons: From theory to practice*. MIT Press.

Housen-Couriel, D. (2022). Information sharing as a critical best practice for the sustainability of cyber peace. In S. J. Shackelford, F. Douzet, & C. Ankersen (Eds.), *Cyber peace: Charting a path toward a sustainable, stable, and secure cyberspace* (pp. 39–63). Cambridge University Press. https://doi.org/10.1017/9781108954341.003

Hunter, D. (2003). Cyberspace as place and the tragedy of the digital anticommons. *California Law Review*, 91(2), 439–519. https://doi.org/10.2307/3481336

ISO. (1994, November). *ISO.IEC 7498-1:1994 – Information technology – open systems interconnection – basic reference model: The basic model*. ISO. https://iso.org/standard/20269.html

Jhaver, S., Frey, S., & Zhang, A. (2021). Decentralizing platform power: A design space of multi-level governance in online social platforms. *Journal of the ACM*, 47(4), 1–10. https://doi.org/10.48550/arXiv.2108.12529

Johnson, D. R., & Post, D. (1996). Law and borders: The rise of law in cyberspace. *Stanford Law Review*, 48(5), 1367–1402. https://doi.org/10.2307/1229390

Kerr, O. S. (2003). The problem of perspective in internet law. *Georgetown Law Journal*, 91, 357–362. https://dx.doi.org/10.2139/ssrn.310020

Kosinski, M. (2024, May 24). What is a Data Breach? IBM. Retrieved July 3, 2025, from https://ibm.com/think/topics/data-breach

Lee, L. M.-C., Tseng, P.-Y., Kao, S.-S. W., Wu, M.-H., & Shen, P. (2020). *Deafening Whispers China's Information Operation and Taiwan's 2020 Election*. Doublethink Lab. https://drive.google.com/file/d/1FW35t93GvMJ3W61qLPhAm6lNZ4uy66jD/view

Leiner, B. M., Cerf, V. G., Clark, D. D., Kahn, R. E., Kleinrock, L., Lynch, D. C., et al. (1997). *Brief history of the internet*. Internet Society. https://internetsociety.org/wp-content/uploads/2017/09/ISOC-History-of-the-Internet_1997.pdf

Lemley, M. A. (2003). Place and cyberspace. *California Law Review*, 91, 357–405.

(2021). The splinternet. *Duke Law Journal*, 70(6), 1397–1427. https://dx.doi.org/10.2139/ssrn.3664027

Lessig, L. (1996). Reading the constitution in cyberspace. *Emory Law Journal*, 45(3), 869–910. https://dx.doi.org/10.2139/ssrn.41681

(1999). *Code: And other laws of cyberspace*. Basic Books.

(2001). *The future of ideas: The fate of the commons in a connected world*. Knopf Doubleday Publishing Group.

Lotrionte, C. (2013). A better defense: Examining the United States' new norms-based approach to cyber deterrence. *Georgetown Journal of International Affairs, (2013–14)*, 75–88.

Mahmoud, M., Mannan, M., & Youssef, A. (2023, March 31). APTHunter: Detecting advanced persistent threats in early stages. *Digital Threats: Research and Practice*, 4(1), 1–31 https://doi.org/10.1145/3559768

Mainland Affairs Council, Republic of China (Taiwan). (2005, March 29). *The Official Position of the Republic of China (Taiwan) on the People's Republic of China's Anti-Secession (Anti-Separation) Law*. General Policy Archives (1994–2008). https://mac.gov.tw/en/News_Content.aspx?n = 8A319E3 7A32E01EA&sms = 2413CFE1BCE87E0E&s = D1B0D66D5788F2DE

Marotta, A., & Pearlson, K. E. (2019, July). A *culture of cybersecurity at Banca Popolare di Sondrio* (Working Paper No. CISL# 2019-07). MIT Management Sloan School. https://web.mit.edu/smadnick/www/wp/2019-07.pdf

Martin, H. (2019, September 29). *Undersea espionage: Who owns underwater internet cables?* The McGill International Review. https://mironline.ca/undersea-espionage-ownership-of-underwater-internet-cables/

McDaniel, C., & Zhong, W. (2022, August 29). *Submarine cables and container shipments: Two immediate risks to the US economy if China invades Taiwan*. Mercatus Center, George Mason University. https://mercatus.org/research/policy-briefs/submarine-cables-and-container-shipments-two-immediate-risks-us-economy-if.

McGinnis, M., & Ostrom, E. (1992). Design principles for local and global commons. *Conference on "Linking Local and Global Commons"*. Harvard Center for International Affairs. https://researchgate.net/profile/Muhammad_Rafique15/post/Is_there_any_research_and_articles_that_assess_Ostrom_principles_by_statistical_approach_or_econometrics/attachment/59d64158c49f478072eaacca/AS%3A273795674247171%401442289384859/download/design+principles.pdf

McKune, S., & Ahmed, S. (2018). Authoritarian practices in the digital age: The contestation and shaping of cyber norms through China's internet sovereignty agenda. *International Journal of Communication*, 12, 3835–3855.

Miller, M. (2022, August 2). Taiwan presidential office website hit by cyberattack ahead of Pelosi visit. *Politico*. https://politico.com/news/2022/08/02/taiwan-presidential-office-website-hit-by-cyberattack-ahead-of-pelosi-visit-00049255

Ministry of Foreign Affairs of the People's Republic of China. (2011, September 12). *International Code of Conduct for Information Security*. Ministry of Foreign Affairs of the People's Republic of China. https://fmprc.gov.cn/eng/wjdt_665385/2649_665393/201109/t20110913_679318.html

(2022, October 25). *Full text of the report to the 20th National Congress of the Communist Party of China*. Ministry of Foreign Affairs of the People's Republic of China. https://mfa.gov.cn/eng/xw/zyjh/202405/t20240530_11341666.html

Mirkovic, J., & Reiher, P. (2004). A taxonomy of DDoS attack and DDoS defense mechanisms. *ACM SIGCOMM Computer Communications Review*, 34(2), 39–54.

Mueller, M. L. (2020, December). Against sovereignty in cyberspace. *International Studies Review*, 22(4), 779–801. https://doi.org/10.1093/isr/viz044

Myers, R. H., & Chao, L. (2003). *The first Chinese democracy: Political life in the Republic of China on Taiwan*. Johns Hopkins University Press.

Nasir, A., Arshah, R. A., Ab Hamid, M. R., & Fahmy, S. (2019). An analysis on the dimensions of information security culture concept: A review. *Journal of Information Security and Applications*, 44, 12–22. https://doi.org/10.1016/j.jisa.2018.11.003

Ostrom, E. (2010). Beyond markets and states: Polycentric governance of complex economic systems. *American Economic Review*, 100(3), 641–672. https://doi.org/10.1257/aer.100.3.641

(2012). 5 polycentric systems: Multilevel governance involving a diversity of organizations. In E. Brousseau, T. Dedeurwaerdere, P.-A. Jouvet, & M. Willinger (Eds.), *Global environmental commons: Analytical and Political challenges in building governance mechanisms* (pp. 105–125). Oxford University Press. https://doi.org/10.1093/acprof:oso/9780199656202.003.0005

(2015). *Governing the commons: The evolution of institutions for collective action*. Cambridge University Press https://doi.org/10.1017/CBO9781316423936

Ostrom, V., Tiebout, C. M., & Warren, R. (1961). The organization of government in metropolitan areas: A theoretical inquiry. *The American Political Science Review*, 55(4), 831–842. https://doi.org/10.2307/1952530

Peng, S. (2018). "Private" cybersecurity standards? Cyberspace governance, multistakeholderism, and the (ir)relevance of the TBT regime. *Cornell International Law Journal*, 51(2), 445–469.

Perritt, H. H., Jr. (1997). Cyberspace self-government: To democracy or rediscovered royalism? *Berkeley Technology Law Journal*, 12(2), 413–482.

Reidenberg, J. R. (1998). Lex informatica: The formulation of information rules through technology. *Texas Law Review*, 76(3), 553–593.

Saeed, M., Traub, N., Nicolas, M., Demartini, G., & Papotti, P. (2022). Crowdsourced fact-checking at Twitter: How does the crowd compare with experts? *CIKM '22: Proceedings of the 31st ACM International Conference on Information & Knowledge Management*, 1736–1746. https://doi.org/10.1145/3511808.3557279

Scholte, J. A. (2017). Polycentrism and democracy in internet governance. In Kohl, U. (Ed.), *The net and the nation state: Multidisciplinary perspectives on internet governance* (pp. 165–184). Cambridge University Press. https://doi.org/10.1017/9781316534168.012

Shackelford, S., Proia, A. A., Martell, B., & Craig, A. (2015). Toward a global cybersecurity standard of care? Exploring the implications of the 2014 NIST cybersecurity framework on shaping reasonable national and international cybersecurity practices. *Texas International Law Journal*, 50, 303–330.

Shackelford, S. J. (2013). Toward cyberpeace: Managing cyberattacks through polycentric governance. *American University Law Review*, 62(5), 1273–1364.

(2020). *Governing new frontiers in the information age: Toward cyber peace*. Cambridge University Press. https://doi.org/10.1017/9781108604000

Shan, S. (2022, September 8). NCC halts drafting of controversial online legislation. *Taipei Times*. https://taipeitimes.com/News/taiwan/archives/2022/09/08/2003784968

Shiffman, G., & Gupta, R. (2013). Crowdsourcing cyber security: A property rights view of exclusion and theft on the information commons. *International Journal of the Commons*, 7(1), 92–112. https://doi.org/10.18352/ijc.343

Stencel, M., Ryan, E., & Luther, J. (2023, June 21). *Misinformation spreads, but fact-checking has leveled off*. Duke Reporters' Lab https://reporterslab.org/misinformation-spreads-but-fact-checking-has-leveled-off/

Stephan, M., Marshall, G., & McGinnis, M. (2019). An introduction to polycentricity and governance. In A. Thiel, D. Garrick, & W. A. Blomquist (Eds.), *Governing complexity: Analyzing and applying polycentricity* (pp. 21–44). Cambridge University Press. https://doi.org/10.1017/9781108325721

Taiwan: Political and Security Issues. (2023, June 13). CRS Report No. IF10275, Version 76. https://crsreports.congress.gov/product/pdf/IF/IF10275/76

Takeshita, H., Sato, M., Inada, Y., de Gabory, E. L. T., & Nakamura, Y. (2019). Past, current and future technologies for optical submarine cables. *2019 IEEE/ACM Workshop on Photonics-Optics Technology Oriented Networking, Information and Computing Systems (PHOTONICS)*, 36–42. https://doi.org/10.1109/PHOTONICS49561.2019.00011

TeleGeography. (n.d.). *Submarine Cable FAQs*. TeleGeography. https://telegeography.com/submarine-cable-faqs-frequently-asked-questions

The 9 principles. (n.d.). *Paris Call for Trust and Security in Cyberspace*. https://pariscall.international/en/principles

The Hague Centre for Strategic Studies. (n.d.). *Global Commission on the Stability of Cyberspace: Norms: The rules of the road*. The Hague Centre for Strategic Studies. https://hcss.nl/gcsc-norms/

The White House. (2023, March 1). *National cybersecurity strategy*. The White House https://whitehouse.gov/wp-content/uploads/2023/03/National-Cybersecurity-Strategy-2023.pdf

Theohary, C. A. (2018, March 5). *Information warfare: Issues for Congress* (CRS Report No. R45142). https://crsreports.congress.gov/product/pdf/R/R45142

Uchendu, B., Nurse, J. R. C., Bada, M., & Furnell, S. (2021). Developing a cyber security culture: Current practices and future needs. *Computers & Security*, 109 https://doi.org/10.1016/j.cose.2021.102387

United Nations General Assembly. (2015). *Group of governmental experts on developments in the field of information and telecommunications in the context of international security*. United Nations Digital Library https://digitallibrary.un.org/record/799853#record-files-collapse-header

(2021). *Open-ended working group on developments in the field of information and telecommunications in the context of international security: Final Substantial Report*. United Nations General Assembly. https://front.un-arm.org/wp-content/uploads/2021/03/Final-report-A-AC.290-2021-CRP.2.pdf

von der Leyen, U. (2020, February 19). *Shaping Europe's digital future: Op-ed by Ursula von der Leyen, President of the European Commission*. European Commission. https://ec.europa.eu/commission/presscorner/detail/es/ac_20_260

Wall, C., & Morcos, P. (2021, June 11). *Invisible and vital: Undersea cables and transatlantic security*. CSIS. https://csis.org/analysis/invisible-and-vital-undersea-cables-and-transatlantic-security

Wang, A. (2020). Cyber sovereignty at its boldest: A Chinese perspective. *The Ohio State Technology Law Journal*, 16(2), 395–466. http://hdl.handle.net/1811/92276

Wu, C.-H. (2021). Sovereignty fever: The territorial turn of global cyber order. *Heidelberg Journal of International Law*, 81(3), 651–676. https://doi.org/10.17104/0044-2348-2021-3-651

Wu, E. (2021, July). *Sovereignty and data localization*. The Cyber Project, Belfer Center for Science and International Affairs, Harvard Kennedy School. https://live-hksbelfer.pantheonsite.io/sites/default/files/2021-07/SovereigntyLocalization.pdf

PART III

Policy Responses

14

Some Truths About Lies

Misinformation and Inequality in Policymaking and Politics

Barbara Allen and Lindsay B. Flynn

How do the dual trends of increased misinformation in politics and increased socioeconomic inequality contribute to an erosion of trust and confidence in democratic institutions? In an era of massive misinformation, voters bear the burden of separating truth from lies as they determine how they stand on important issue areas and which candidates to support. When candidates engage in misinformation, it uncouples the already weak link among vote intentions, candidate choice, and policy outputs. At the same time, high levels of economic inequality and social stratification may contribute to lower levels of institutional trust, and the correspondingly more insular socioeconomic groups may experience misinformation differently. Social policy, as a policy area intentionally designed to alleviate risk and redistribute resources, thus becomes a special case where the effects of misinformation and socioeconomic inequality may be cross-cutting and heightened.

We examine the potential for this amplification by drawing on the Institutional Analysis and Development (IAD) framework. This framework, a product of policy analysis and public sector performance evaluation scholarship undertaken at the Ostrom Workshop, offers a metatheoretical approach to understanding diverse institutions in which the normative value of democratic self-governance is paramount. Information and, more generally, language are among the core features of the framework, as are individual decision-makers' (officials and ordinary participants alike) capacities (e.g., legal, social, economic, positions, and capabilities) and the distribution of outcomes (e.g., costs and benefits) from the decisions under study. While the framework makes no assumptions about the veracity of information in use or the homogeneity of capacities or equality of disbursed costs or benefits, the normative goals of democratic self-governance emphasize the necessity of warrantable information claims and the adverse effects of fixed inequalities, whether concerning decision-making authority or distributions of a policy's costs and benefits. Regarding authority, fixed inequalities suggest an unlimited capacity to

This work was supported by the Luxembourg National Research Fund [14345912].

dominate; fixed inequalities in the distribution of costs or benefits may indicate normative harms – injustice – and policy failures.

We start by examining the place of information and inequality in the IAD framework. We then discuss the differences between policy *framing* and more aggressive forms of *misinformation* and *disinformation*, and how they relate to trust. Next, we review the negative relationship between socioeconomic inequality and trust, identifying a number of potential mechanisms linking the two. We conclude by suggesting that mis- and disinformation exacerbate the challenges of democratic self-government not only on their own but also through its interactions with inequality and (dis)trust.

IAD FRAMEWORK: INFORMATION AND INEQUALITY

In 1982, Larry Kiser and Elinor Ostrom described what they called a "metatheoretical synthesis of institutional approaches." Their picture of "three worlds of action," the arenas of operational, collective, and constitutional choices, offered a foundational frame for understanding these distinct levels of analysis, each characterized by a set of "working parts" generally found in any theoretical explanation: attributes of (1) individual decision-makers (e.g., participants of varying positions and associated capacities to act in a given situation); (2) events (e.g., goods, services or collective acts to be produced or consumed); (3) communities affected by the decision; (4) institutions (e.g., rules and norms) guiding individual choices; and (5) the decision situation in which choices are made (Kiser & Ostrom, 1982, p. 58). The authors suggested that these broad domains of the kinds of variables contained in institutional theories could be used to explain two main phenomena: the actions and strategies of decision-makers and the aggregated results of their activities. The picture of cause and effect was "meta" in that any theory might be described in this way, since the framework covered the general elements found in any and all specific theories of diverse institutions. In the same year, Vincent Ostrom wrote "Institutional Analysis, Policy Analysis, and Performance Evaluation" as an extension of his earlier work on the normative contexts and limitations of institutions. These working papers became the basis of the IAD framework, a widely used approach to policy analysis.

Information and the IAD Framework

Vincent Ostrom's scholarship, particularly, offered a critique and correction to traditional policy analysis through an institutional analysis that turned to constitutional choice and the broader problem of language, itself understood as an institution, as a basis for rule-ordered relations. Indeed, Kiser and Ostrom (1982) started their discussion of a meta-framework of institutional analysis by amplifying Vincent Ostrom's (1982) insights about the uncertainties produced by our reliance on language to create and implement policies that are mere instructions, often with little guidance or metrics for goal achievement.

The ever-present problem of imprecise language is one among many communication failures at the heart of social dilemmas. Language, as Vincent Ostrom pointed out, using the terminology of John Searle (1969), is an "institutional fact." Language depends not only on shared understandings but also on the choices we make in constituting and using (humanly created) rules for articulating our individual experiences. The creation of shared understanding presumes a common desire to come to mutually beneficial conceptions of cause and effect. While language and knowledge may be imperfect, the common aim of fallible humans presumably involves a choice to pursue more, rather than less, accurate representations of "brute facts" – the facts of our physical existence. At every step in the effort to articulate what an individual makes of experiencing "brute facts," and what the audience takes from this articulation, lie the many traps of misunderstanding, ranging from mere mistakes to intentionally false representations. Nevertheless, the assumption made in the IAD approach to policy analysis is that a self-governing people have a stake in correcting errors rather than amplifying the consequences of their mistakes.

This assumption is neither naive nor ignorant of the fact that individuals may gain advantage not only by acceptable strategies of contextualizing information – framing – but also by misrepresentation. In appraising the vulnerabilities of democracy, V. Ostrom (1997) detailed the uses of Orwellian rhetorical strategies of "doublespeak" and deceptive "glittering generalities" (V. Ostrom, 1982), staples in political discourses. The many studies of self-managed commons (e.g., E. Ostrom, 1990) document the capacities of communities to come to a shared understanding in facing collective choice dilemmas – and the consequences of failing to do so. Effective, self-managed commons generally use highly participatory, egalitarian strategies for reaching these understandings. Democratic self-governance requires striving for accurate representations of cause and effect. Or, put another way, assuming the opposite – that we strive to dissemble and deceive – is a nonstarter for self-governance. By assuming fallibility and a capacity for learning, the question becomes one of the institutional arrangements that promote a drive for accuracy, including corrections to misinformation, and policies that foster trust in constitutional and collective choices and outcomes.

In the IAD framework, information, as well as its availability and accuracy, reflect the foundational dilemmas posed by human fallibility, particularly our limitations when it comes to producing shared understandings, given the institutional fact, language. The IAD framework sets out information as a feature of policy decisions in two ways. First, the constraints bounding and motivating choice and action focus on the characteristics of an action situation governed by eight types of rules, including "information rules, that specify channels of communication among actors and what information must, may, or must not be shared" (E. Ostrom, 2010, p. 810). Second, information about the decision at hand, the participants and their capacities, the expected effects of a decision, the measurement and evaluation of these effects influence actions in the arena of choice designated as the "action situation," which is the core of the IAD framework.

Prior to these worlds of action is a world of ideas; Vincent Ostrom argued that constitutional choice is preceded by the public articulation of values and beliefs that may be called "epistemic choice" (V. Ostrom, 1993). These shared understandings include an agreed-upon framework of inquiry, for example; orientations to our ways of evaluating choices and their effects; values such as respect, reciprocity, and fairness; and, germane to this chapter, beliefs about the degree of equality, inequality, liberty, and so forth. Misinformation, disinformation, and inequality not only affect our desire to coordinate, cooperate – or even compete – in a shared Action Arena but, indeed, to continue to believe in shared standards of value, or even conceptions of biophysical existence.

The concept of an action situation allows researchers to identify the variables generic to policymaking about any type of good or service. Empirical investigations using the framework revealed design principles conducive to well-functioning, sustainable self-managed communities (E. Ostrom, 1990).[1] More broadly, the framework can help us compare institutional arrangements, with a focus on a diversity of variables (Kiser & Ostrom, 1982; E. Ostrom, 2010). In the generic framework, "the amount of information available to a participant," is among the relevant structural elements of the action situation. While not explicitly stated, the term "amount" necessarily exceeds "quantity," to cover the quality, scope, scale, and accuracy of information as well.

Likewise, the framework does not assume perfect information, but it necessarily assumes a desire to improve the accuracy of information. The motivation to improve (minimally, to abandon behaviors that do not produce desirable outcomes) can be seen in Ostrom's (2005) discussion of the action situation:

> Within a particular situation, individuals can attempt to choose only in light of their beliefs about the opportunities and constraints of that situation. In an open society, individuals may be able eventually to affect the structure of action situations in which they repeatedly find themselves by changing the rule configurations affecting the structure of these situations. To do so, they move to deeper analytical levels (collective-choice or constitutional-choice action situations) where the outcomes generated are changes in the rules of other action situations. (p. 33)

We underscore the variability that language and, more generally, ideation, brings to the framework and the implications for taking action to move to "deeper analytical

[1] Ostrom's design principles (1990) are clear group boundaries, rules of governance match local conditions, those affected by the rule can participate in rule amendment procedures, self-organizing capacities recognized by outside authorities, local monitoring procedures, graduated sanctions for rule violators, accessible low-cost means of dispute resolution, and nested enterprises.

levels" to affect beneficial changes. The framework assumes that an open society can pursue accurate information, and that we ask about the motivation and effectiveness of that pursuit. Framing, misinformation, and disinformation emerge as specific concerns in treating information in the IAD framework. Differences of many kinds may lead to individuals existing in diverse circumstances but the basis of collective action assumes capacities to enter arenas of action characterized by at least a minimal degree of common ground. In a context of disinformation, heterogeneities, including inequalities, may inhibit the comity required for constitutional and collective choice and action, and, more fundamentally, the epistemic choices preceding the three arenas of action.

Inequality and the IAD Framework

Research has focused on the heterogeneity of motives and resources in collective action situations as these diversities characterize the positions and consequent actions of decision-makers in the IAD framework. Early theoretical work considered the potential for highly motivated individuals with greater resources to provide common goods, even if they contributed more than those with fewer resources (Olson, 1965). Heterogeneity often characterizes the endowments of resource users, yielding several types of inequalities, including social, political, and economic inequalities (Andersson & Agrawal, 2006). Most of the research engaging the IAD framework and heterogeneities of actors concern the governance of common-pool resources. In studies of collective actions to secure natural resources (or produce their protection through allocation decisions), there is some support for the hypothesis that participants with greater resources may be willing to contribute a larger share of the initial costs of a management regime in exchange for a greater share of the benefits (Baland & Platteau, 1999). More generally, economic and status inequalities have also been associated with unequal political power (Neupane, 2003), lower levels of trust in the decision-making methods as well as the decisions themselves (Ruttan, 2006), lower levels of commitment, and decreased capacities for monitoring implemented policies (Schlager & Blomquist, 1998), that undermine cooperation and collective action. Experiments in common-pool resource management show that communication is vital to producing efficient resource use but heterogeneities among actors (e.g., differences in resources enabling contributions to collective action) impede self-governance (Hackett, Schlager, & Walker, 1994); inequalities likewise impede communication across groups, often a necessary condition for collective action (E. Ostrom, 2005).

Heterogeneities are ubiquitous and may be found in each element of the IAD framework, including rules governing contributions (who pays) and allocation rules (who benefits). In addition to helping researchers create a taxonomy of solutions to commons dilemmas created by myriad heterogeneities, the IAD framework alerts us to information asymmetries (including the effects of misinformation) and their relationship to economic, social, and political inequalities. Heterogeneities, asymmetries in information, and limited communication also impede trust among groups of different statuses. Related to the emphasis on open communication and warrantable claims is the overall necessity of credible commitments that lead to cooperative actions over several iterations. As people see the outcome of their choices and know the choices and actions of others, trust becomes increasingly possible. It turns out that trust is a major component in surmounting the obstacles that heterogeneities raise (e.g., E. Ostrom, 2005).

INFORMATION FRAMING, MISINFORMATION, DISINFORMATION, AND TRUST

Information "framing" most generally means putting information into a context and has long been accepted as a legitimate rhetorical strategy: Credible contextualization and analysis are staples of journalism. Aristotle's "rhetorical triangle" of pathos (frames engaging belief, value, experience, imagination, and feelings), logos (appeals to reason and logic), and ethos (appeals using authoritative, credible sources) mark normatively acceptable strategies of persuasive speech. Framing and appeals to feelings and imagination may be acceptable when linked to the other sides of the metaphorical triangle. But framing, in this logic has generally referred to accurate, truthful information. Disinformation and misinformation bring us to a different place in the deployment of affective rhetorical strategies.

Framing and Framing Effects

Over the fifty years of its evolution as a concept crossing a broad array of scientific disciplines, "framing" has come to indicate many different, albeit occasionally related, phenomena. In communications theory, political psychology, media studies, and related disciplines, the term "framing" has been used to indicate ways of organizing information and social realities (Cowart, Blackstone, & Riley, 2022; Goffman, 1974), types of narrative and their effects (Bennett, 2016; Iyengar, 1991; Iyengar & Kinder, 1987), and efforts or means of influencing opinion and choices by directing attention toward some consequences, risks, benefits, or values and away from other plausible concerns (Chong, 2000; Chong & Druckman, 2007a; Druckman, 2001, 2004; Tversky & Kahneman, 1981).

Framing effects occur when "logically equivalent (but not transparently equivalent) statements of a problem lead decision makers to choose different options" (Rabin, 1998, p. 36). In initial research on framing effects, for example, Tversky and Kahneman (1981, 1986) showed that framing the expected consequences of a choice in terms of a chance of loss rather than the logically equivalent chance of gain caused participants in their experiments to take the riskier of two options, framed as a chance for gain, the safer bet was the dominant choice. In political communication, "comparability" rather than "logical equivalence" may better describe the various considerations influencing choices (Chong & Druckman, 2007b): Framing effects occur when the contextualization of information elevates some considerations – including principles and values – over others. For example, Druckman (2001) finds either of two valued principles, freedom or security, may be highlighted by framing and used as the basis of a policy choice. Experiments on the effects of news narrative styles show how framing influences attributions of responsibility for public problems as either the fault of the government, or of the person who is featured as an example of the social concern (Iyengar, 1991; Iyengar & Kinder, 1987); news broadcasters overwhelmingly hew to the latter narrative style (Allen et al. 2023; Stevens et al. 2006).

Framing also makes an appeal to our emotional intelligence, but absent logic or source credibility, the resulting appeals cross a line into propaganda and may be perceived as unsound. Indeed, weak frames (generally those lacking value or logical relevance) demonstrably fail to influence decisions and in some cases increase the efficacy of strong frames (Chong & Druckman, 2007a). Source credibility can constrain the use of frames to manipulate public opinion (Druckman, 2001), but the credibility of the source matters most when message recipients lack either prior knowledge or preexisting attitudes toward the message topic (Kumkale, Albarracín, & Seignourel, 2010). Early work in framing effects broadly assumed the veracity of the information to be framed and investigated the effects of placing truthful information into various contexts. In an online context, "message credibility" is a result of evaluations of source credibility, the message frame, and social endorsement (Borah & Xiao, 2018). This research suggests that the veracity of information is perhaps only one of the many factors influencing perceptions of message credibility, although truthfulness remains a critical dimension in distinguishing framing from misinformation and disinformation as well as our analysis of the effects of each rhetorical style.

Misinformation and Disinformation Definitions and Dimensions

It might seem that the definitions of misinformation and disinformation are self-evident, but our excursion into the meaning and effects of framing signals that matters are more complex. We start our discussion of information, by focusing on the well-researched topic of news representations and the conception of "fake news" and suggesting that much of the theorizing in this area of communication studies can be applied to discussion of "information" more broadly. Fake news is a term that has recently been appropriated by office holders in the United States as meaning simply information with which the official disagrees. Here, we consider the attributes described by Newman et al. (2017, p. 20), writing for the annual Reuters Digital Report: Information invented for the purpose of discrediting others or for monetary gain (e.g., "clickbait") or news with a basis in fact that is spun to fit a particular agenda. Martens et al. (2018) discuss information that is suspect because of its source, its dissemination method, and its intention, while the European Union (EU) Commission for Communications Networks, Content and Technology (2018) similarly describes fake news as disinformation: "false, inaccurate, or misleading information that is designed, presented, and promoted" for profit or to cause intentional public harm (p. 3). In contrast to the characteristics of fake news, Newman et al. (2017) measure consumer perceptions of four qualities sought in online news: information of high accuracy and reliability, enabling better understanding of complex issues, communicating strong viewpoints and opinions, and providing entertaining content.

Unpacking these definitions reveals several dimensions to be used in evaluating information, with two that stand out in much of the literature: purpose and truthfulness. Wardle and Derakhshan (2017) focus on these dimensions to define three terms: misinformation as false information, where no harm is meant; disinformation as false information knowingly shared to cause harm; and mal-information as factual information shared to cause harm (e.g., doxing, disclosing private information in public forums to enable harm). The purpose of distributing the information is central to these definitions in which intentions to deceive, harm, or profit signal disinformation, exempting errors (which news outlets make and correct), satire, parody, and partisan commentary from this category. The idea of combining mistakes, parody, and partisan news spin in one category deserves greater scrutiny.

The broader definition of misinformation allows for framing, "spin," and ideological slant as a matter of consumer trust in a news brand. The Reuters' definition of quality news insists that news outlets meet consumers' expectations of a given editorial slant and partisan perspective, framing, and filtering of information in reporting. Filtering and slanting news to establish a commercial position in a news market is expected, and consumers want to be presented with the topics, types, slants, and agendas – partisan, ideological, and so on – that they intended to buy when tuning in or clicking on (Martens et al., 2018). Following this broad view of news products, we can imagine misinformation and disinformation on these continua (see Figure 14.1).

In contrast, the narrow view of misinformation confines the definition of misinformation to the misrepresentation of facts such as omissions and additions that mislead and outright lies. Recent work on US voters' responses to political advertising (Allen & Stevens, 2019; Stevens et al., 2008) and news coverage of elections (Allen et al., 2007) show that inaccurate claims in political advertising along with news framing influence voter attitudes toward candidates and voter participation in elections (Stevens et al., 2006). Inaccurate political advertising claims not only result in inaccurate understandings of candidates' issue positions but also lead to more general confusion about policies, candidates' partisanship and ideologies, and the issues that are targets of the false claims (Allen & Stevens, 2019). Distrust of politics and news media increase the likelihood that news consumers will believe online mis- or disinformation (Zimmermann & Kohring, 2020).

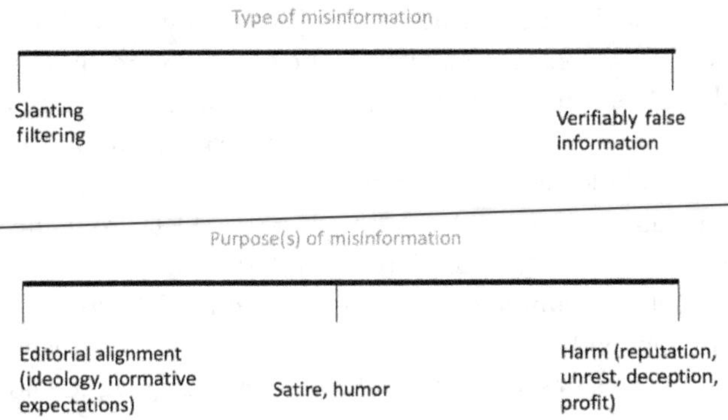

FIGURE 14.1 Misinformation continua – purpose and accuracy

Critics of fact-checking (e.g., Park et al., 2021) show how evidence that is open to interpretation or claims that seem to elude evidentiary evaluations encourage information spin on the part of fact-checkers themselves. Building on research studying partisan perceptions of ad claim accuracy and fairness (Allen & Stevens, 2015; Allen et al., 2016; Stevens et al., 2008), Allen and Stevens (2019) offered two measures of claim accuracy: an absolute measure of the accuracy of each ad claim (accurate or not) and an evaluation of the degree of accuracy specifying truthfulness on a scale ranging as follows – a wholly accurate representation of facts, majority accurate representation of facts, and/or inferences drawn logically from facts, mildly misleading from a factual basis, omissions and misleading representation of facts, major distortions with little clear basis in facts, gross untruths (i.e., lies).

Efforts to combat lies in political communication do not correct misinformation (Allen et al., 2016; Allen & Stevens, 2019; Nyhan & Reifler, 2010) and may in fact cause decision-makers to double down and hew to errant information that comports with a preexisting bias (Nyhan & Reifler, 2010). In the United States, motivated information processing driven mainly by partisanship led significantly more Republicans than Democrats to reject reports of independent fact-checkers stating that the advertising claims of their favored candidate was false (Allen et al., 2016; Stevens et al., 2008). It may be that these partisan differences are associated with diminished trust in news media, particularly fact-checkers, in an increasingly polarized political climate.

Trust in News Media, Institutions, and Support for Democracy

Trust in news media, worldwide, has indeed declined from 2015 to 2023 (Newman et al., 2023). In the United States, trust in news media declined significantly between 2018 and 2022 and, while recovering to 2015 levels, remains in the bottom half of forty-six democratic countries whose citizens were surveyed in YouGov polling. Worldwide, around 40 percent of respondents say they "trust most news most of the time" (p. 10). Social media information sources are viewed as generally less trustworthy than traditional news platforms; news consumers have grown increasingly skeptical of algorithm-based information selection. Although news consumers generally trust social media less than traditional news media as an information source, trust in social media has been gaining on traditional news media, especially in younger generations (Liedke & Gottfried, 2022). Data from this time period document the rising anxiety caused by misinformation (Newman & Fletcher, 2017), a trend that has continued along with record high distrust of algorithm-driven news in the post-pandemic media environment (Newman et al., 2023). While news consumers say they value reliable branding (e.g., ideological orientations) in news analysis, "bias, spin, and agendas" are the main causes of distrust in news media (Newman & Fletcher, 2017, p. 5).

Distrust of social media as an information source appears to influence attitudes toward news media in general. In a twenty-six-country survey conducted between 2016 and 2019, Park et al. (2020) show that increased accesses to news through social media is linked to a decline in trust in media. Other spillover effects of social media use are also well documented by evidence that internet use increases voter uncertainty (Sudulich, Wall, & Baccini, 2015), partisan polarization (Bail et al., 2018; Newman et al., 2023), as well as eroding trust in institutions and politics (Kiratli, 2023).

Recent work indicates that support for democratic norms and prodemocracy candidates for office is in decline in Europe and the United States (Bartels, 2020; Claassen & Magalhães, 2023; Drutman, Goldman, & Diamond, 2020; Foa & Mounk, 2017). In the United States, this erosion of support for democracy is shown in a greater than 20 percent drop in those agreeing that democracy "is better than any other form of government," over the thirteen years from 2006 to 2019, and a decline from 75 percent to 62 percent between 1995 and 2017 of those rejecting a political system headed by a "strong leader who does not have to bother with Congress and elections" (Claassen & Magalhães, 2023). As survey research shows, support for democracy appears to be in decline, while electoral support for illiberal candidates for office appears on the assent (e.g., Cohen et al., 2022), not, perhaps, as a move against democratic norms, per se, but simply because voters' policy preferences converge with those stated by antidemocratic candidates (Lewandowsky & Jankowski, 2022). In experimental research (Lewandowsky & Jankowski, 2022) and survey research (Rydgren, 2008) in Germany, these preferences converged on the topic of immigration, an issue that has been the focus of considerable disinformation on social media (Newman & Fletcher, 2017). In the United States, partisanship is associated with lower support for democratic norms, which include greater belief in the illegitimacy of the 2020 election results among Republicans than among Democrats as well as a higher percentage of Republicans than Democrats who support the former president refusing to vacate the office based on these claims (Drutman, Goldman, & Diamond, 2020).

The weakening attachment to democratic norms and institutions is strongest among younger citizens (e.g., Foa & Mounk, 2017). Research suggests this trend is not a function of life cycle effects in which youthfulness accounts for a cohort's skepticism of democracy, with the expectation that attachments to this form of government grow with age and experience. Rather, younger generations seem less inclined to support democratic norms, institutions, or candidates (Claassen & Magalhães, 2023). In the United States, this decline occurs across each age cohort since World War II.

Younger cohorts are also those who are more likely to avoid news altogether (Eddy, 2022). Reasons for avoiding news consumption include not only disinterest but also concerns for mental well-being and avoidance of caustic, divisive political debates and perspectives with which the consumer disagrees (Newman et al., 2023). News avoidance is a matter of partisan preferences. In the United States, 70 percent of right-leaning news consumers avoid social justice news, while 64 percent avoid climate change and environmental news, for example, while avoidance of these topics among left-leaning news media users is 22 percent and 12 percent, respectively. Reported avoidance among left-leaning consumers of crime and personal security news is 30 percent, compared to 14 percent of right-leaning news users, and 25 percent of left-leaning respondents report avoiding news of business, financial, and economic activities, compared to 9 percent of right-leaning respondents (Newman et al., 2023). The online media landscape has also changed news consumption patterns, particularly in younger age cohorts. Instead of accessing news through such platforms as Facebook or Twitter (now known as X), where mainstream journalists lead news conversations, video-led networks such as TikTok have emerged as an information medium of choice for consumers under thirty-five years old. Coupled with the decline in voice among mainstream news organizations on X, the "new, new media" of TikTok, Instagram, and Snapchat is the domain of influencers (Newman et al., 2023). From celebrities to sports personalities, views of policies, wars, and current events vie with news analysts for attention and credibility.

No definitive statement of cause can be taken from these patterns, but the trend approaching the eve of the U.S. General Elections and EU Parliamentary Elections in 2024 can be summarized: Increased misinformation, disinformation, and anxieties about discerning fact and fiction join decreased trust in news organizations, institutions, and government; support for democracy and prodemocracy candidates; and engagement with news, particularly among partisans seeking to avoid topics and viewpoints with which they disagree and, more broadly, younger cohorts. These trends are associated with increased polarization of viewpoints in the United States, as is the ascendance of misinformation and disinformation, generally.

We began this discussion by observing that no one thinks that the "information" influencing policy choices is perfect or that all participants in policymaking will adhere to norms of truth, including making warrantable claims. Nevertheless, we suggested the importance, if not necessity, of assuming a general orientation to truth-seeking rather than lie-mongering for the survival of democratic processes. Our look into the practice, prevalence, and consequences of lies supports this conjecture. We now turn to a second trend in politics, increasing inequality, which also hampers policymaking efforts in democracies.

INEQUALITIES AND TRUST: SUSTAINING DEMOCRACY

Socioeconomic inequality is one of the primary sources of heterogeneity in actors' resources and motivations, making the increase in income and wealth inequality important attributes of actors in the IAD framework – and of concern to the framework's underlying social theory. Just as some level of truth-seeking is necessary for the survival of democratic processes, so is trust in those processes. Growing levels of inequality may lead to lower levels of social and political trust (e.g., Bienstman, Hense, & Gangl, 2024; Bobzien, 2023), jeopardizing such core IAD principles as claim warrantability and truth-seeking. If neither participants nor processes can be trusted, an Orwellian world of "double speak" (2003 [1949]) signals a critical vulnerability of democracies (V. Ostrom, 1997).

Trust can be placed in many politically relevant objects and constructs, with political trust and social trust serving as two primary dimensions of analysis. Political trust captures the trust that people have in institutions such as governments, politicians, the legal system, and parties. Goubin and Hooghe (2020) view political trust as capturing the latent concept of political legitimacy, a necessary condition for democratic governments that rely on voluntary adherence to rules and shared norms to maintain social order. Social trust denotes the belief that "most people" (i.e., the broad group of people not personally known in a society) can be trusted. The concept can extend to related beliefs about whether most people try to be fair or try to be helpful most of the time. Drawing from the vast literature on political and social trust (Uslaner, 2018), we focus specifically on the links between inequality and each dimension of trust.

Inequality also exists along multiple dimensions such as income, wealth, or social status. These dimensions can be conceptualized and gauged objectively using measures like the Gini coefficient or through a subjective measure such as perceptions of inequality or normative beliefs about the fairness of inequality. Economically rich democracies have witnessed remarkable changes in income and wealth inequality over the past three decades. While income inequality dominated the discourse in the second half of the twentieth century, it is wealth inequality that increasingly takes center stage today. Housing equity is a primary determinant of cross-national differences in wealth inequality (Pfeffer & Waitkus, 2021). While wealth comes in many forms for the richest, for most people it comes in the form of housing, where wealth is increasingly concentrated among high-income households (Dewilde & Flynn, 2021). A global real estate firm recently put the scope of housing wealth into perspective: The value of global real estate is larger than global equities and debt securities combined, and three-quarters of that value is in residential real estate (Savills News, 2023). The relevance of housing to wealth inequality extends particularly to younger generations who are locked out of housing markets, and who increasingly rely more on their parents than governments for resources (Flynn, 2020; Flynn & Schwartz, 2017). Such re-familialization has important policy implications, especially given the role of governments in redistributing resources and risk through social policy.

Inequality can also exist at various levels of the individual, regional, national, or even the supranational tier. Inequalities in resource distribution in any of these often-nested arenas may have an impact on social or political trust. For researchers studying the relationship between either dimension of trust and inequality, the different levels of experience produce diverse forms of the inequality–trust nexus, and diverse scholarly views of the mechanisms driving the identified relationships.

Inequality and Political Trust

Income inequality is commonly measured at the national level, and scholars focused on the United States or Europe have found that a relationship between income inequality and political trust exists across countries and over time (Bienstman, 2023; Bienstman, Hense, & Gangl, 2024; Bobzien, 2023). Studies that fail to find a relationship between *income* inequality and political trust often instead find a relationship between *social* inequality and political trust (e.g., Kim et al., 2022). These results point to the importance of adopting a broad understanding of both forms of inequality.

People are situated in smaller regional subunits and larger supranational units, and inequality at these levels is also associated with political trust; these levels are nested, leading to interrelated assessments of trust in relevant institutions. Researchers find that both income inequality and regional wealth inequality affect trust in national institutions and in the EU. At the micro-level, lower levels in inequality correspond to higher levels of trust in national institutions; higher levels of inequality similarly depress trust in the EU, a so-called extrapolation effect. At the macro-level, countries with high inequality have lower levels of national trust, a situation that can prompt individuals to place their trust outside national institutions, a so-called compensation effect that corresponds to higher levels of EU trust (Lipps & Schraff, 2021). Regional wealth differences may have an additional impact. Economically vibrant urban areas may see more visible EU infrastructure development that prompts more trust than poorer areas where people consider themselves left behind (Lipps & Schraff, 2021). This relationship may not be linear, with regions in the middle of the wealth distribution less trusting of the EU than poorer or richer regions (Vasilopoulou & Talving, 2023).

What drives such relationships between socioeconomic inequality and political trust? Important factors can exist at the individual level – individual income or individual characteristics like social status – or can be more sociotropic in nature (Bienstman, 2023; Kim et al., 2022). The latter refers to the context in which a person lives (including social norms concerning relationships and autonomy) and its ability to affect the effects of inequality on trust, independent from the impact of any individual characteristics. People can respond to inequality in either a rational, evaluative manner or through a more affective social–psychological response (or some degree of each cognitive style) (Bienstman, Hense, & Gangl, 2024; Goubin & Hooghe, 2020, Greenwood-Hau, 2021). When evaluating degrees of inequality through either rational–evaluative or social–psychological channels, a person's perception of inequality, rather than the actual distribution of inequality, may more accurately predict trust levels (Bobzien, 2023; Scheidegger & Staerklé, 2011). Lower levels of political trust are associated with higher gaps between inequality perceptions and preferences (Bobzien, 2023). Scheidegger and Staerklé (2011) find that it is not objective markers like income, but subjective markers like the perception of being at material risk that affect threats to the social order (including the threat that inequality could bring), which in turn affects political trust.

At first glance, the logic for an evaluative mechanism emphasizing individual socioeconomic characteristics seems straightforward. Whether inequality is a matter of perception or a matter of facts (i.e., Gini index based), people evaluate whether the current system works for them, and those who evaluate the system more positively will be more likely to trust the institutions that create the system. This reasoning implies that high-income individuals – who stand to benefit the most from inequality – are the most trusting. A closer look shows several potential caveats to this formulation, given the diverse criteria that define the system that "works for them."

Greenwood-Hau (2021) emphasizes that people can attribute inequality to structural reasons such as government policy, or to individual reasons such as hard work, positing that those who emphasize reasons like hard work are more likely to have system-justifying beliefs. The study finds that people who attribute inequality to government policies (that benefit high-income workers) have lower levels of political trust. Bienstman et al. (2023) similarly find that citizens' trust in government is predicated on their evaluation of government policy and performance, with inequality as one outcome used in that evaluation. The study also finds support for a "process-based evaluation" whereby inequality affects people's belief that they can influence the political process, and this sense of external (in)efficacy influences trust.

Sociotropic explanations of the inequality–trust link contend that the criteria for evaluating a given context include values and beliefs, for instance, regarding the moral acceptability of high inequality (Goubin & Hooghe, 2020). Social–psychological explanations maintain that such individual attributes as status anxiety, or even social trust, lead to more visible status differences in a high-inequality society, thereby lowering trust in institutions.

These individual and sociotropic explanations all advance an evaluative logic. Each account also helps explain the otherwise puzzling finding that someone in an economically advantageous position in a high-inequality society nevertheless has lower levels of political trust. In this case, a person may employ a notion of social justice, judging the morality of high inequality in their society and adjusting their trust in government accordingly (Goubin & Hooghe, 2020). Bienstman (2023) finds support for both sociotropic explanations. Individuals living in countries with greater inequality have lower trust in democratic institutions, regardless of their own socioeconomic status. Although social–psychological characteristics affect levels of political trust, this research finds that evaluation-based processes (e.g., a performance evaluation based on the individual's expectations and preferences and the regime's economic performance) better explain the link between inequality and political trust.

The link between socioeconomic inequality and political trust is confirmed in many studies and empirically supported through plausible accounts featuring either individual characteristics or sociotropic orientations as the main explanation. The association between inequality and political trust is complex, with perceived institutional performance (expectations and evaluations), values, and beliefs about equality and social justice mediating the relationship between these two terms. Examining the contextual and social–psychological sides of the relationship encourages us to pinpoint just exactly what kind of information and beliefs people have in mind when they think about inequality.

Inequality and Social Trust

Researchers accept the near-consensus finding of a relationship between inequality and political trust, moving on to consider explanatory mechanisms for this link. In contrast, scholars currently debate the nature, scope, and scale of the inequality–social trust relationship. Much of the social trust research emphasizes the difference between analyses conducted at the regional level versus the national level, and differences when using objective measures of inequality such as the Gini index versus subjective measures.

Scholars regularly measure social trust (stated also as interpersonal trust or generalized trust) with either a one-item scale asking whether most people can be trusted, or a three-item scale additionally including whether most people try to be fair and whether most of the time people try to be helpful (Hastings, 2018; Kanitsar, 2022; Kim et al., 2022; Knell & Stix, 2021; Olivera, 2015; Stephany, 2017). Using these measures, researchers have found lower levels of social trust correlate with high-income inequality, especially when making the comparison across countries (see Buttrick & Oishi, 2017 for a review).

As with the nexus of inequality and political trust, the relationship of social trust and inequality is complex. Fairbrother and Martin (2013) show that inequality has increased while social trust has declined between 1970 and 2002 in all US states, but states (and counties) with the greatest increase in inequality have not shown a significantly greater loss of social trust. Similarly, in a study using panel data from thirty-two EU countries, Olivera (2015) confirms the conventional relationship between social trust and inequality, but also shows that country-specific factors including institutions and culture, discrimination, and ethnic and linguistic fractionalization may play a bigger role than growing income inequality in explaining declining social trust.

Testing a claim put forward in a review by Wilkinson and Pickett (2009), Kanitsar (2022) confirms that the relationship between income inequality and social trust exists at the cross-national level but not at the regional level within countries. Using US tax return data at the state level, Hastings (2018) similarly finds no evidence for the state-level relationship, but some evidence that an overtime increase in inequality correlates with a decline in trust. Using large, cross-national surveys, Kim et al. (2022) find that social class is a better predictor of social trust than income inequality at the regional level. These studies all use Gini coefficients as their measure of income inequality. Studies emphasizing perceptions of inequality more consistently find a relationship between inequality and social trust (Gallego, 2016; Larsen, 2013; Loveless, 2013).

Larsen (2013) finds that social trust increased in socially democratic welfare states of Denmark and Sweden in the three decades leading up to 2010, but declined in the liberal welfare states of the United Kingdom and United States. Larsen attributes these changes to cognitive perceptions of inequality. In the United Kingdom and the United States, people began to perceive others as more likely to be in the "bottom" of society with untrustworthy, undeserving, or dangerous personas. Conversely, people in Denmark and Sweden formed perceptions of others in the "middle" of society with trusting and deserving personas.

Perceptions of inequality have also continued to play an important role in theory building. Knell and Stix (2021) argue that when responding to survey questions about "most people" (the wording of social trust questions), respondents will use a reference group that may be biased in some way, and which can only be captured by using direct measures of perceptions of inequality as opposed to calculations that are based on the actual income distribution. To capture perceptions of inequality, Stephany (2017) uses age-specific Gini coefficients and finds that the relationship between income inequality and trust does extend to within-country regions, where it can be attenuated or intensify based on the spread of the age-specific indicators. This finding offers a promising line of study connecting objective and subjective measures of inequality. In sum, the research on inequality and social trust generally points to a relationship, but the boundaries of that relationship are still under review. Differences in findings are often explained by measurement differences, with many emphasizing the importance of perceptions. This review brings us full circle, pointing to the key role that information – shared understandings, perceptions, beliefs, and framing – plays in policymaking and democratic self-governance.

INFORMATION AND INEQUALITY AS AMPLIFYING FACTORS

Growing inequality and growing misinformation are two major trends in contemporary democracies. Both act as depressive forces on trust and confidence in democratic institutions. The research on the misinformation–trust link and the inequality–trust link are in separate fields, but there are reasons to expect that misinformation might amplify the corrosive effects of inequality on trust. We suggest two such amplification channels, linking each back to the IAD framework and noting their policy relevance with respect to social policy as an important equalizing policy tool.

First, high levels of inequality are thought to lead to less social mixing, more insular groups, and more cursory interactions with those beyond a given socioeconomic circle. As the logic goes, fewer and more cursory interactions lead to decreased trust. Second, perceptions and beliefs around inequality are just as important as the actual distribution of inequality.

The studies that demonstrate these two paths offer a departure from Robert Putnam's (2000) thesis that social trust is conditioned on civic associations and volunteering; Rothstein and Uslaner (2005) argue, in contrast, that inequality is the important factor. In fact, in Hochschild's (2016) sociological study of a community in Louisiana that is plagued by the effects of fracking yet distrusts regulators, political institutions in general, and mainstream news media, she finds highly participatory, yet insular, groups. Her interviews show individuals attuned to media brands and political leaders that support their worldview, reinforcing their distrust and detachment from other social groups.

It is a kind of activism and engagement that democratic theorist Tocqueville describes as collective individualism (Allen, 2005). As Vasilopoulou and Talving (2023) point out, people living in place-based communities share experiences and take informational cues from one another. Income and especially wealth inequality likewise have important spatial dimensions. Growing income and wealth inequality, especially through its housing- and community-based dimensions, lead to increased insularity. The increased potential for insularity – as much as the conviviality that place-based groups are assumed to have – again points to the importance of communities and information, as highlighted in the IAD framework. Misinformation may reinforce or amplify this insularity: people may not only have fewer interactions with outsiders but also receive messaging with spin, ideological slant, or even verifiably false information about policies, ideologies, and the issues that are targets of false claims.

As more people hold incomplete or incorrect information, this condition may influence their perceptions of inequality levels or shift their tolerance, or intolerance, for inequality. Such effects may extend to more innocuous forms of framing. Initial evidence of the latter can be found in the Yellow Vest movement in France, where evidence exists that the historic collective framing of inequality, which is at odds with fundamental values of solidarity and equality, drives the movement (Jetten, Mols, & Selvanathan, 2020). Experimental evidence exists indicating that citizens trust institutions less when they are led to believe that there is greater inequality (Guinjoan & Rico, 2018). This research, too, points to the importance of information in potential processes of amplification.

These two potential amplification channels, along with the effects that both inequality and misinformation have on trust in democratic institutions, have important implications for social policy and the welfare state. As some have noted (e.g. Gärtner & Prado, 2016; Habibov, Cheung, & Auchynnikava, 2018), inequality and trust shape support for social policies, and inequality is associated with a decline in prosocial attitudes among the poor, an important target group of social policies (Gallego, 2016). In other words, support for the very policies designed to redistribute risk and promote greater equality may hinge on levels of inequality and trust, which themselves are at risk because of increased misinformation. People who do not interact, who receive their news from different sources, and who lack social and political trust may not only be less likely to support one another in interactions that necessitate collective action but also in supporting policies that would lead to greater risk sharing.

CONCLUSION

We have argued that the IAD framework alerts us to the problems of distrust and disaffection from democracy that go far beyond the correction of misinformation and disinformation. Heterogeneities and inequalities teamed with disinformation may today prevent us from reaching collective agreement on the methods of discerning warrantable information, if we no longer share common understandings to enable a collective epistemic choice, or we now live in distinct epistemes (or all of these).

The methodologies of productive contestation and, broadly, individual and collective inquiry, deliberation, reflection, and choice as well as other aspects of the iterative learning and amendment process (action-outcome-observation-institutional development-action) found in the IAD framework are imperiled by disinformation and the erosion of trust in facts, social and political institutions, and fellow community members. What is to be done to defend democracy in an inequality-centric, digital age?

When it comes to information, in several US states and in the EU, various campaigns aim to educate children and adults in ways to spot spin, reporter error, and demonstrably false claims. In the EU and the United Kingdom, slander and libel laws put the onus on those making claims to warrant their validity, enabling regulations prohibiting false statements in, for example, election advertising, while in the United States, constitutionally protected political speech presently includes misleading and even false claims in political advertising (Allen & Stevens, 2019).

The prevailing belief in the United States is that truth will prevail over falsehoods in an unregulated arena of public speech. Yet, the evidence is decidedly against this conventional view (Allen & Stevens, 2019).

Structural interventions in the United States will necessarily encounter challenges of First Amendment claims against the regulation of political speech. Yet, we suggest – particularly as artificial intelligence (AI)-generated manipulated images and manipulated speech emerge in social media and mainstream media commentary on this novel form of misinformation – regulation is necessary. EU high commissions have begun such policy investigations; in the United States, regulation is left to social media and cable news platforms.

Inequality, in turn, is both place-based and perception-based. This points to two fronts that need to be addressed. Policies in Europe and the United States have enabled and indeed encouraged the marketization and re-familialization of risk, which reinforce growing inequality trends. Such trends occur in communities through both employment sectors and housing markets (or in other words, both income and wealth), two policy areas where governments have introduced greater precarity instead of security. Increased precarity extends beyond low-income households and other socially marginalized groups who have always experienced it, to also include younger generations who have lived their entire lives during an era of state retreat. Policies must be redesigned to open more opportunities for locked-out groups, which almost certainly requires a stronger state role in re-pooling risk.

Given that cognitive perceptions of deservingness, trustworthiness, and fairness vary across countries, it is likely that some countries will meet greater resistance in this endeavor and have further to go in rebuilding trust. This points to the importance of supranational channels in encouraging risk sharing. The EU has indicated some willingness to move in this direction, including through the European Pillar of Social Rights and by further embedding social policy into the European Semester. However, such tools could be used to greater effect. In the United States, the idea of Franklin D. Roosevelts' second bill of rights – emphasizing the importance of social rights and risk pooling at the societal level – seems a far cry from current political rhetoric. The first step might be to consider the degree to which communities really are operating in distinct epistemes, and if so, at which action level trust rebuilding initiatives might have the best chance of taking hold.

REFERENCES

Allen, B. (2005). *Tocqueville on covenant and the democratic revolution: Harmonizing earth with heaven*. Lexington Books.

Allen, B., Lawrence, E., Stevens, D., & Sullivan, J. (2016). Partisanship and perceptions of fairness: Ignoring the facts. *Journal of Experimental Political Science*, 3(1), 32–43.

Allen, B., & Stevens, D. (2015). What is negative about negative ads? In A. Nai & A. S. Walter (Eds.), *New perspectives on negative campaigning: Why attack politics matters* (pp. 47–61). ECPR Press.

(2019). *Truth in advertising? Lies in political advertising and how they affect the electorate.* Lexington Books.

Allen, B., Stevens, D., Fox-Arnold, D., Holtey, B., Vincent, M., & Woollen, B. (2023). Local news in a social capital sixteen years later. Paper presented at the 2023 *Annual Conference of the Elections, Public Opinion & Political Parties (EPOP)*, Southampton University, Southampton, UK, 8–9 September 2023.

Allen, B., Stevens, D., Marfleet, G., Sullivan, J., & Alger, D. (2007). Local news and perceptions of the rhetoric in political advertising *American Politics Research*, 35(4), 506–540.

Andersson, K. P., & Agrawal, A. (2006). Equity, institutions, and the environment: Socioeconomic aspects of local forest governance. Paper presented at the *11th Conference of the International Association for the Study of Common Property*, Bali, Indonesia, June 19–23.

Bail, C. A., Argyle, L. P., Brown, T. W., Bumpus, J. P., Chen, H., Hunzaker, M. B. F., et al. (2018). Exposure to opposing views on social media can increase political polarization. *Proceedings of the National Academy of Sciences of the United States of America*, 115, 9216–9221. https://doi.org/10.1073/pnas.1804840115

Baland, J., & Platteau, J. P. (1999). The ambiguous impact of inequality on local resource management. *World Development*, 27(5), 773–788. https://doi.org/10.1016/S0305-750X(99)00026-1

Bartels, L. M. (2020). Ethnic antagonism erodes Republicans' commitment to democracy. *Proceedings of the National Academy of Sciences of the United States of America*, 117, 22752–22759. https://doi.org/10.1073/pnas.2007747117

Bennett, W. L. (2016). *News: The politics of illusion* (10th ed.). University of Chicago Press.

Bienstman, S. (2023). Does inequality erode social trust? *Frontiers in Political Science*, 5, 1–19. https://doi.org/10.3389/fpos.2023.1197317

Bienstman, S., Hense, S., & Gangl, M. (2024). Explaining the "democratic malaise" in unequal societies: Inequality, external efficacy and political trust. *European Journal of Political Research*, 63, 172–191. https://doi.org/10.1111/1475-6765.12611

Bobzien, L. (2023). Income inequality and political trust: Do fairness perceptions matter? *Social Indicators Research*, 169(1–2), 505–528. https://doi.org/10.1007/s11205-023-03168-9

Borah, P., & Xiao, X. (2018). The importance of 'likes': The interplay of message framing, source, and social endorsement on credibility perceptions of health information on Facebook. *Journal of health communication*, 23(4), 399–411. https://doi.org/10.1080/10810730.2018/1455770

Buttrick, N. R., & Oishi, S. (2017). The psychological consequences of income inequality. *Social and Personality Psychology Compass*, 11(3). https://doi.org/10.1111/spc3.12304

Chong, D. (2000). *Rational lives: Norms and values in politics and society*. University of Chicago Press.

Chong, D., & Druckman, J. (2007a). Framing public opinion in competitive democracies. *American Political Science Review*, 101(4), 637–655.

(2007b). Framing theory. *Annual Review of Political Science*, 10, 103–126.

Claassen, C., & Magalhães, P. C. (2023). Public support for democracy in the United States has declined generationally. *Public Opinion Quarterly*, 87(3), 719–732. https://doi.org/10.1093/poq/nfad039

Cohen, M. J., Smith, A. E., Moseley, M. W., & Layton, M. L. (2022). Winners' consent? Citizen commitment to democracy when illiberal candidates win elections. *American Journal of Political Science*, 67(2), 261–276. https://doi.org/10.1111/ajps,12690

Cowart, H. S., Blackstone, G. E., & Riley, J. K. (2022). Framing a movement: Media portrayals of the George Floyd protests on Twitter. *Journalism and Mass Communication Quarterly*, 99(3), 676–695. https://doi.org/10.1177/10776990221109232

Dewilde, C., & Flynn, L. B. (2021). Post-crisis developments in young adults' housing wealth. *Journal of European Social Policy*, 31(5), 580–596. https://doi.org/10.1177/09589287211040443

Druckman, J. N. (2001). On the limits of framing effects: Who can frame? *Journal of Politics*, 63(4), 1041–1066.

(2004). Political preference formation: Competition, deliberation, and the (ir)relevance of framing effects. *American Political Science Review*, 98, 671–686.

Drutman, L., Goldman, J., & Diamond, L. (2020, June). *Democracy maybe: Attitudes on authoritarianism in America*. Voter Study Group. https://voterstudygroup.org/publication/democracy-maybe

Eddy, K. (2022, June 15). *The changing news habits and attitudes of younger audiences*. Reuters Institute for the Study of Journalism. https://reutersinstitute.politics.ox.ac.uk/digital-news-report/2022/young-audiences-news-media

European Commission. (2018). A multi-dimensional approach to disinformation: Report of the independent High Level Group on fake news and online disinformation. Publications Office of the European Union. https://digital-strategy.ec.europa.eu/en/library/final-report-high-level-expert-group-fake-news-and-online-disinformation

Fairbrother, M., & Martin, I. W. (2013). Does inequality erode social trust? Results from multilevel models of US states and counties. *Social Science Research*, 42(2), 347–360. https://doi.org/10.1016/j.ssresearch.2012.09.008

Flynn, L. B. (2020). The young and the restless: Housing access in the critical years. *West European Politics*, 43(2), 321–343. https://doi.org/10.1080/01402382.2019.1603679

Flynn, L. B., & Schwartz, H. M. (2017). No exit: Social reproduction in an era of rising income inequality. *Politics & Society*, 45(4), 471–503. https://doi.org/10.1177/0032329217732314

Foa, R. S., & Mounk, Y. (2017). The signs of deconsolidation. *Journal of Democracy*, 28(1), 5–15. https://doi.org/10.1353/jod.2017.0000

Gallego, A. (2016). Inequality and the erosion of trust among the poor: Experimental evidence. *Socio-Economic Review*, 14(3), 443–460. https://doi.org/10.1093/ser/mww010

Gärtner, S., & Prado, S. (2016). Unlocking the social trap: Inequality, trust and the Scandinavian welfare state. *Social Science History*, 40(1), 33–62. https://doi.org/10.1017/ssh.2015.80

Goffman, E. (1974). *Frame analysis: An essay on the organization of experience*. Harper & Row.

Goubin, S., & Hooghe, M. (2020). The effect of inequality on the relation between socio-economic stratification and political trust in Europe. *Social Justice Research*, 33(2), 219–247. https://doi.org/10.1007/s11211-020-00350-z

Greenwood-Hau, J. (2021). The system works fine: The positive relationship between emphasis on individual explanations for inequality and external political efficacy. *Frontiers in Political Science*, 3, 1–17. https://doi.org/10.3389/fpos.2021.643165

Guinjoan, M., & Rico, G. (2018). How perceptions of inequality between countries diminish trust in the European Union: Experimental and observational evidence. *Political Psychology*, 39(6), 1289–1303. https://doi.org/10.1111/pops.12541

Habibov, N., Cheung, A., & Auchynnikava, A. (2018). Does institutional trust increase willingness to pay more taxes to support the welfare state? *Sociological Spectrum*, 38(1), 51–68. https://doi.org/10.1080/02732173.2017.1409146

Hackett, S., Schlager, E., & Walker, J. (1994). The role of communication in resolving commons dilemmas: Experimental evidence with heterogeneous appropriators. *Journal of Environmental Economics and Management*, 27(2), 99–126. https://doi.org/10.1006/jeem.1994.1029

Hastings, O. P. (2018). Less equal, less trusting? Longitudinal and cross-sectional effects of income inequality on trust in U.S. states, 1973–2012. *Social Science Research*, 74, 77–95. https://doi.org/10.1016/j.ssresearch.2018.04.005

Hochschild, A. (2016). *Strangers in their own land: Anger and mourning on the American right.* The New Press.

Iyengar, S. (1991). *Is anyone responsible?: How television frames political issues.* University of Chicago Press.

Iyengar, S., & Kinder, D. (1987). *News that matters.* University of Chicago Press.

Jetten, J., Mols, F., & Selvanathan, H. P. (2020). How economic inequality fuels the rise and persistence of the Yellow Vest movement. *International Review of Social Psychology*, 33(1), 2. https://doi.org/10.5334/irsp.356

Kanitsar, G. (2022). The inequality-trust nexus revisited: At what level of aggregation does income inequality matter for social trust? *Social Indicators Research*, 163(1), 171–195. https://doi.org/10.1007/s11205-022-02894-w

Kim, Y., Sommet, N., Na, J., & Spini, D. (2022). Social class – not income inequality – predicts social and institutional trust. *Social Psychological and Personality Science*, 13(1), 186–198. https://doi.org/10.1177/1948550621999272

Kiratli, O. (2023). Social media effects on public trust in the European Union. *Public Opinion Quarterly*, 87(3), 749–763. https://doi.org/10.1093/poq/nfad029

Kiser, L., & Ostrom, E. (1982). The three worlds of action: A metatheoretical synthesis of institutional approaches. In E. Ostrom (Ed.), *Strategies of political inquiry* (pp. 179–222). Sage.

Knell, M., & Stix, H. (2021). Inequality, perception biases and trust. *The Journal of Economic Inequality*, 19(4), 801–824. https://doi.org/10.1007/s10888-021-09490-x

Kumkale, G. T., Albarracín, D., & Seignourel, P. J. (2010). The effects of source credibility in the presence or absence of prior attitudes: Implications for the design of persuasive communication campaigns. *Journal of Applied Social Psychology*, 40(6), 1325–1356. https://doi.org/10.1111/j.1559-1816.2010.00620.x

Larsen, C. A. (2013). *The rise and fall of social cohesion: The construction and de-construction of social trust in the US, UK, Sweden and Denmark*. Oxford University Press.

Lewandowsky, M., & Jankowski, M. (2022). Sympathy for the devil? Voter support for illiberal politicians. *European Political Science Review*, 15, 39–56. https://doi.org/10.1017/S175577392200042X

Liedke, J., & Gottfried, J. (2022, October 27). *U.S. adults under 30 now trust information from social media almost as much as from national news outlets*. PEW Research Center. https://pewrsr.ch/3DF4dn1

Lipps, J., & Schraff, D. (2021). Regional inequality and institutional trust in Europe. *European Journal of Political Research*, 60(4), 892–913. https://doi.org/10.1111/1475-6765.12430

Loveless, M. (2013). The deterioration of democratic political culture: Consequences of the perception of inequality. *Social Justice Research*, 26(4), 471–491. https://doi.org/10.1007/s11211-013-0198-7

Martens, B., Aguiar, L., Gomez-Herrera, E., & Mueller-Langer, F. (2018, April). *The digital transformation of news media and the rise of disinformation and fake news* (JRC Digital Economy Working Paper 2018-02). Joint Research Centre, the European Commission's In-house Science Service. https://joint-research-centre.ec.europa.eu/document/download/08432650-f418-4b6e-94f7-61d2ba1cba1e_en?filename=jrc111529.pdf

Neupane, H. (2003). Contested impact of community forestry on equity: Some evidence from Nepal. *Journal of Forest and Livelihood*, 2(2), 55–61.

Newman, N., & Fletcher, R. (2017). *Bias, bullshit and lies: Audience perspectives on low trust in the media*. Reuters Institute Digital News Project. https://reutersinstitute.politics.ox.ac.uk/sites/default/files/2017-11/Nic%20Newman%20and%20Richard%20Fletcher%20-%20Bias%2C%20Bullshit%20and%20Lies%20-%20Report.pdf

Newman, N., Fletcher, R., Kalogeropoulos, A., Levy, D. A. L., & Nielsen, R. K. (2017). *Reuters Institute digital news report 2017*. Reuters Institute for the Study of Journalism. https://reutersinstitute.politics.ox.ac.uk/sites/default/files/Digital%20News%20Report%202017%20web_0.pdf

(2023). *Reuters Institute digital news report 2023*. Reuters Institute for the Study of Journalism. https://reutersinstitute.politics.ox.ac.uk/sites/default/files/2023-06/Digital_News_Report_2023.pdf

Nyhan, B., & Reifler, J. (2010). When corrections fail: The persistence of political misperceptions. *Political Behavior*, 32, 303–330. https://doi.org/10.1007/s11109-010-9112-2

Olivera, J. (2015). Changes in inequality and generalized trust in Europe. *Social Indicators Research*, 124(1), 21–41. https://doi.org/10.1007/s11205-014-0777-5

Olson, M. (1965). *The logic of collective action: Public goods and the theory of groups*. Harvard University Press.

Ostrom, E. (1990). *Governing the commons*. Cambridge University Press.

(2005). *Understanding institutional diversity*. Princeton University Press.

(2010). The institutional analysis and development framework and the commons response. *Cornell Law Review*, 95(3), 807–815.

Ostrom, V. (1982). Institutional analysis, policy analysis, and performance evaluation. Paper presented at the *Workshop for the Study of Interorganizational Arrangements in the Public Sector, International Institute of Management*, Berlin, Germany, 26–28 July 1982.

(1993). Epistemic choice and public choice. *Public Choice*, 77(1), 163–176. https://jstor.org/stable/30027217

(1997). *The meaning of democracy and the vulnerability of democracies*. University of Michigan Press.

Park, S., Fisher, C., Flew, T., & Dulleck, U. (2020). Global mistrust in news: The impact of social media on trust. *International Journal on Media Management*, 22(2), 83–96.

Park, S., Park, J. Y., Kang, J.-H., & Cha, M. (2021). The presence of an unexpected bias in online fact checking. *Harvard Kennedy School Misinformation Review*, 2(1). https://doi.org/10.37016/mr-2020-53

Pfeffer, F. T., & Waitkus, N. (2021, July 30). The wealth inequality of nations. *American Sociological Review*, 86(4), 567–602. https://doi.org/10.1177/00031224211027800

Putnam, R. (2000). *Bowling alone*. Simon & Schuster.

Rabin, M. (1998). Psychology and economics. *Journal of Economic Literature*, 36(1), 11–46.

Rothstein, B., & Uslaner, E. M. (2005). All for all: Equality, corruption, and social trust. *World Politics*, 58(1), 41–72. https://doi.org/10.1353/wp.2006.0022

Ruttan, L. M. (2006). Sociocultural heterogeneity and the commons. *Current Anthropology*, 47(5), 843–853.

Rydgren, J. (2008). Immigration sceptics, xenophobes or racists? Radical right-wing voting in six West European countries. *European Journal of Political Research*, 47(6): 737–765. https://doi.org/10.1111/j.1475-6765.2008.00784.x

Scheidegger, R., & Staerklé, C. (2011). Political trust and distrust in Switzerland: A normative analysis. *Swiss Political Science Review*, 17(2), 164–187. https://doi.org/10.1111/j.1662-6370.2011.02010.x

Schlager, E., & Blomquist, W. (1998). Resolving common pool resource dilemmas and heterogeneities among resource users. Paper presented at the *7th Biennial Conference of the International Association for the Study of Common Property*, Vancouver, BC, June 10–14.

Searle, J. (1969). *Speech acts*. Cambridge University Press.

Stephany, F. (2017). Who are your Joneses? Socio-specific income inequality and trust. *Social Indicators Research*, 134(3), 877–898. https://doi.org/10.1007/s11205-016-1460-9

Stevens, D., Alger, D., Allen, B., & Sullivan, J. L. (2006). Local news coverage in a social capital capital: Election 2000 on Minnesota's local news stations. *Political Communication*, 23(1), 61–83. https://doi.org.10.1080/10584600500477062

Stevens, D., Sullivan, J., Allen, B., & Alger, D. (2008). What's good for the goose is bad for the gander: Negative political advertising, partisanship, and turnout. *Journal of Politics*, 70(2), 527–541.

Sudulich, L., Wall, M., & Baccini, L. (2015). Wired voters: The effects of internet use on voters' electoral uncertainty. *British Journal of Political Science*, 45, 853–881. https://doi .org/1017/S0007123413000513

Savills News. (2023, September 25). *Total global value of real estate estimated at $379.7 trillion – almost four times the value of global GDP*. Savills News. https://savills.com/ insight-and-opinion/savills-news/352068/total-global-value-of-real-estate-estimated-at-$379 .7-trillion—almost-four-times-the-value-of-global-gdp

Tversky, A., & Kahneman, D. (1981). The framing of decisions and the psychology of choice. *Science*, 211(4481), 453–458.

(1986). Rational choice and the framing of decisions. *Journal of Business*, 59(4), S251–S278.

Uslaner, E. M. (Ed.). (2018). *Oxford handbook of social and political trust*. Oxford University Press. https://doi.org/10.1093/oxfordhb/9780190274801.001.0001

Vasilopoulou, S., & Talving, L. (2023). Euroscepticism as a syndrome of stagnation? Regional inequality and trust in the EU. *Journal of European Public Policy*, 31(6), 1494–1515. https://doi.org/10.1080/13501763.2023.2264891

Wardle, C., & Derakhshan, H. (2017). *Information disorder: Toward an interdisciplinary framework for research and policy making*. Report for The Council of Europe. https:// rm.coe.int/information-disorder-toward-an-interdisciplinary-framework-for-researc/ 168076277c

Wilkinson, R. G., & Pickett, K. E. (2009). Income inequality and social dysfunction. *Annual Review of Sociology*, 35(1), 493–511. https://doi.org/10.1146/annurev-soc-070308-115926

Zimmermann, F., & Kohring, M. (2020). Mistrust, disinforming news, and vote choice: A panel survey on the origins and consequences of believing disinformation in the 2017 German Parliamentary Election. *Political Communication*, 37(2), 215–237. https:// doi.org/10.1080/10584609.2019/1686095

15

Getting a Grip on Disinformation

From Distrust to Trust within Learning Communities

Deike Schulz, Joyce Kerstens, and Dustin Sajoe

This chapter examines how citizens – individually and as part of their community – can be empowered to fight disinformation from the ground up. An experimental pilot project was carried out with three separate regional learning communities in the northern part of the Netherlands (hereafter the Frisian Area) between September 2022 and September 2023 and comprised citizens from different backgrounds and age groups who jointly engaged in investigating and exposing disinformation. These three communities operated as independent entities, with the participants developing their own rules and roles of investigation and information sharing.

The goal of the project, called "De Pit," was to experiment with methodology to empower communities to recognize and fight disinformation. Our main hypothesis for this experiment was that there is no "silver bullet" or panacea (a common lament from Elinor Ostrom). By comparing the three communities we have learned that citizens will develop their own and different kinds of solutions. Following this approach, the central question of our research was how participants of learning communities develop their own ground rules, roles, and agreements to critically collect, analyze, understand, and report on the information surrounding them in online and offline spaces.

To answer this question, we present a multiple (experimental) case study to discuss and compare the aforementioned aspects of the three different learning communities. Our aim was to provide as much autonomy as possible to these communities so that they could create their own solutions. Considering the different backgrounds, level of education, ages, and geographical locations enabled us to learn if people create similar or different solutions to fight disinformation.

Additionally, Ostrom's Institutional Analysis and Development (IAD) framework (2005) has supported us in understanding these learning communities and how the participants have developed a research approach enabling them to interpret the facts behind information circulating in the public sphere. More importantly, key aspects are identified and discussed on the basis of monitoring and mutual comparison of how the three learning communities develop, interact, and collaborate.

Finally, as part of this chapter, we present a "roadmap" with conditions and recommendations to implement a successful learning community to inspire and support others in setting up similar initiatives.

The chapter is structured as follows. First, we briefly introduce the project context in connection with recent theoretical developments in disinformation and citizen science studies. Second, we present Ostrom's IAD framework that supported us as a lens to investigate the three learning communities. Third, we present our methodological approach. A multiple (experimental) case study supported us in collecting and analyzing data from (participants of) the three learning communities. Fourth, we discuss the results of our multiple case study through the lens of Ostrom's IAD framework to identify and compare key aspects of the three learning communities. Finally, and based on the identified key aspects, we present a "roadmap" with conditions and recommendations to build a successful community to support future citizen-driven initiatives in unmasking disinformation on their own level.

DISINFORMATION AS A DRIVER FOR LEARNING COMMUNITIES AND DIGITAL CITIZENSHIP

Digitization gives us easy access to an (over)abundance of information that we increasingly seem to distrust. In the social-political discourse on the role of information in society, concerns about the negative effects of fake news, filter bubbles, and troll armies would appear to predominate. Information (sharing) plays a crucial role in our society. However, information is not something that "just" happens to us: The role and responsibility of citizens who send and receive information through various media channels is pivotal. Citizens, for example, can unintentionally spread disinformation which in turn can become misinformation.

Based on Benkler, Faris, and Roberts (2018, p. 6), we define disinformation as "'the intentional manipulation of beliefs' and misinformation as 'the unintentional spread of false beliefs.'" According to the Dutch National Coordinator for Counterterrorism and Security (NCTV) (2023), disinformation can be used to disrupt democratic processes such as elections or to question the political and administrative integrity of parliament and the judiciary. In addition, disinformation can be used to pursue an economic agenda and to spread messages that can lead to unrest. In general, literature on disinformation mainly focuses on the analysis of the threat (e.g., Bastos, Mercea, & Goveia, 2021; Benkler, Faris, & Roberts, 2018) or response to the threat (e.g., Chan et al., 2017; Stieglitz et al., 2022) of dis- and misinformation. Very few academics (Hassain, 2022; Heinrich, 2019) focus on how to empower citizens through communities to become more resilient to disinformation. In our project we have focused on disinformation, keeping in mind that misinformation of citizens may develop through false information circulated online and offline. Our intent is therefore to support citizens in learning how to identify and investigate disinformation and become more resilient to its threat. As a result, the aim of the Pit project is also to "equip" participants to prevent misinformation. With these developments in mind, we set up three learning communities aiming to encourage and equip citizens to investigate the facts behind (local, regional, or international) news and information circulation in the public, online, and offline domains. Participants in these learning communities work together as citizen journalists to strengthen digital citizenship as part of an applied research community. In that sense, digital citizenship relates to a person who uses the internet regularly and effectively (Mossberger, Tolbert, & McNeal, 2007). However, looking at recent developments such as online polarization and the massive growth either in the spread of dis- and misinformation in online (e.g., online communities on Facebook or Reddit) or offline spaces (e.g., through face-to-face conversations), this definition seems inadequate to cover the whole spectrum of the problem. Hintz, Dencik, and Wahl-Jorgensen (2017, p. 731) discuss digital citizenship as something that is "... *typically defined through people's actions, rather than by their formal status of belonging to a nation-state and the rights and responsibilities that come with it. It denotes citizens creating and performing their role in society.*" Citizen journalism, according to Bowman and Willis (2003), is based on citizens taking an active role in the process of collecting, reporting, analyzing, and disseminating news and information. According to Papacharissi (2015), citizen journalism can be seen as an alternative to news organizations that dominate the circulation of information. This means that citizen journalism can be a powerful approach to enhance digital citizenship and critical thinking of citizens in an innovative way. According to Koulolias et al. (2018, p. 22), "... governments need to take collaborative action with stakeholders and invest in innovative ways to deal with misinformation." The authors suggest that citizens should be empowered to fight misinformation by "... creating a trusted environment for citizens with the adequate educational instruments." The main aim of our experimental project was to enable participants to navigate and understand "complex information landscapes" based on problem-solving approaches as part of a central community (Glassman & Kang, 2012). Moreover, they act as qualitative researchers of their personal experiences, analyzing identities, events, and cultural phenomena (Markham, 2019). Based on these insights, we decided to work in three learning communities, based on trustful relationships and with the possibility of using tools that empower participants to unmask or fight disinformation.

OSTROM'S IAD FRAMEWORK AS A LENS TO IDENTIFY KEY ASPECTS OF LEARNING COMMUNITIES

Through our experimental research, we aim to disseminate firsthand experiences from three projects to inspire others to establish similar initiatives within the

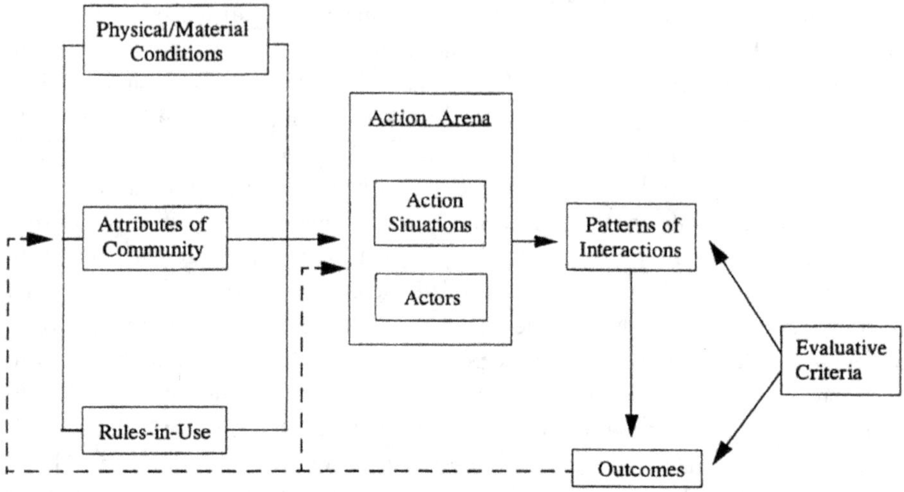

FIGURE 15.1 A framework for institutional analysis. *Source*: Adapted from E. Ostrom, Gardner, and Walker (1994, p. 37).

Netherlands and beyond. Additionally, we will provide a comprehensive roadmap of necessary conditions and recommendations to facilitate the establishment of successful learning communities. These communities will serve to empower citizens in their efforts to combat disinformation while enabling them to develop the necessary skills to investigate and effectively interpret information. The results of our research can serve as a valuable guideline or implementation plan, offering easily achievable requirements and conditions for citizens to collaboratively address disinformation within their local communities.

To achieve this goal, we use the IAD framework to identify how the participants in the three learning communities work together, communicate, carry out research, and jointly come up with community rules and roles. In line with Ostrom et al. (2014, p. 68), we research how "… individuals may legally self-organize in voluntary associations and craft their own rules of interaction." Figure 15.1 presents the IAD framework as presented by Ostrom, Gardner, and Walker (1994).

This research looked into "face-to-face discussions" related to the "rules-in-use" area of the IAD framework, as well as the "Action Arena" of each project investigating the various "Action Situations" in order to explain "regularities in human actions and results" by applying a common set of seven variables of Action Situations to understand of each of the learning communities: (1) the set of participants; (2) the specific positions to be filled by participants; (3) the set of allowable actions and their linkage to outcomes; (4) the potential outcomes that are linked to individual sequences of actions; (5) the level of control each

TABLE 15.1 *Additional conceptual questions for analyzing the Action Arenas of the three communities*

Action Situations	Conceptual question(s) based on Ostrom (2007, pp. 29–30)
1. The set of participants	Who are the participants (e.g., demographics, background, motivation to participate)?
2. The positions	What positions (or roles) exist or how are these appointed as part of the group process (e.g., which roles are developed and how are these roles appointed by the participants)?
3. The set of allowable actions and their linkage to outcomes	Which types of research technologies and tools are used? What topics are important for the participants (e.g., are they using online research tools, or offline approaches; what kind of training is used or needed; how do participants make sure that they are safe while researching online or offline information; and what topics are chosen by the participants)?
4. The potential outcomes	How do participants collect and share the outcomes of their research? What is the important learning for sharing outcomes?
5. The level of control over choice	Do participants share their outcomes, how and with whom? What agreements are made within and outside of the community (e.g., before starting research, choosing a topic, conducting research, are there internal or external threads in choosing a topic)?
6. The information available	How do participants use, engage with, and collect informational resources (e.g., how a research topic is chosen by the group, how data is collected, how do participants bring their results together)?
7. The costs and benefits of actions and outcomes	What are important elements for participants to participate? (e.g., what is the added value for the participants to join, be part of the community, how often do the participants meet, what are concerns in researching online and offline information, what did the participants learn)?

participant has over choice; (6) the information available to participants about the structure of the action situation; and (7) the costs and benefits – which serve as incentives and deterrents – assigned to actions and outcomes (Ostrom, 2007, pp. 29–30).

Based on our specific "Pit Action Situations," we added additional conceptual questions (see Table 15.1) to support us in analyzing and understanding each community, inspired by those of Ostrom (2007, pp. 29–30) in the context of over-harvesting from a common-pool resource situation.

METHODOLOGY

The Digital Citizenship Lab at NHL Stenden University of Applied Sciences is conducting research by monitoring this project. This Digital Citizenship Lab is the fruitful result of a crossover partnership between two professorships at NHL Stenden University of Applied Sciences: Organisations and Social Media and Cybersafety.

Following replication logic, we based our research design on multiple cases (Yin, 2009), allowing us to observe different approaches in the development of the three research communities in order to understand "*… values, norms, rules and structures that constrain and enable behavior of human actors*" (Groenewegen, 2011, p. 16). For this multiple (experimental) case study, we have chosen to conduct research in different areas (local library, higher and vocational education) and with participants from different backgrounds and age groups. Three projects were set up to gain insights into the development of each community based on different rules, roles, and actions. These three learning communities were situated in different parts of the Frisian Area: The Library of Drachten (located in the city of Drachten in the Smallingerland region); Firda School for Vocational Education (located in the city of Drachten); and NHL Stenden University of Applied Sciences (located in the city of Leeuwarden). More detailed information about the three organizations and an additional supporting organization can be found in Appendix 1.

Figure 15.2 illustrates the start of each community, the number of participants, their ages and backgrounds, who supported them during the project, and who was part of the research project group.

Our data collection was based on various data sources such as information shared by and between participants (e.g., emails, announcements, meeting minutes, and presentation sheets). Additionally, we conducted individual semi-structured interviews in May 2023 with five lecturers/experts (these are marked as *C1–C5*) who coordinated or supported the communities of the project and three separate focus group sessions in June and July 2023 with participants (n = 14, these are marked as *P1–P14*) and three coordinators (*C1*, *C2*, *C4*) of each community to gain insight into how they developed, implemented, and evaluated each project. Although two research communities were organized at NHL Stenden, the decision was made to organize one combined focus group with students who had previously participated in the first and/or second semester due to participant dropout.

Throughout the project, at least one coordinator (lecturer/or expert on digital citizenship) from each community joined the research project group meetings to exchange thoughts on the progress of each community and also to ensure clear communication concerning the project aim or practical issues, such as data collection. Two researchers from NHL Stenden coordinated the project, supported by student assistants. Additionally, the coordinators and researchers received support

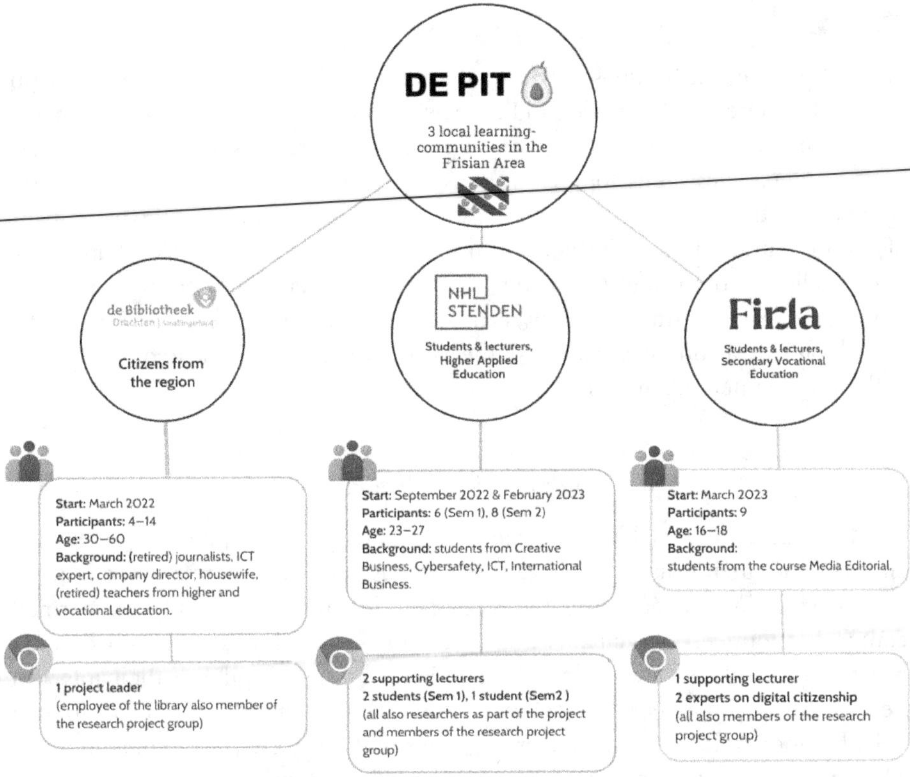

FIGURE 15.2 Overview of the three learning communities

and advice from local experts in the area of digital citizenship (from "Fers," see Appendix 1).

Participants from each learning community carried out research by collecting information through surveys, interviews, and evaluations with internal and external stakeholders. Because of the experimental nature of this project, we used the focus group meetings and individual interviews with coordinators to identify how research was carried out in practice and how the participants experienced the process of community building, data collection, analysis, and sharing.

In July 2023, we also organized a mini-conference, inviting participants from the three communities to exchange thoughts and experiences. As a part of the program, the participants briefly presented their Pit project and shared the essential learning gained.

All participants received research consent forms via the group coordinators related to data collection and assurance of anonymity. Finally, all collected data were stored in a central and secured digital research environment at NHL Stenden University of Applied Sciences, accessible only by the authors.

FINDINGS

We will present our findings regarding the three Pit learning communities, beginning with a general introduction to this experimental project and the three separate learning community cases. Next, we will present the three cases by describing their Action Arena, research topics, working approach, communication, research approach, and experiences along with a set of learning outcomes of the participants of each community. To illustrate the three cases, we utilize the IAD framework. Specifically, we delve into the participants' "Action Arena" and examine the "patterns of interaction," such as the roles and agreements that evolved over time. Lastly, we will provide a concise summary of the collective key insights shared by attendees at the mini-conference held in July 2023.

Introduction to 'De Pit'

In March 2022, a local library in the Frisian Area started a pilot project to help citizens find their way in a society where dis- and misinformation circulates. Following a limited recruitment campaign, a learning community was formed, comprising fourteen participants from the same regional area, but with different backgrounds and educational levels. Essentially, during this pilot, participants were free to decide on which subject they wanted to investigate, be it gossip in a neighborhood watch WhatsApp group, conspiracy theories, or (regional) news. This first learning community was called the "Pit," a local information evaluation initiative; in Dutch, "*Plaatselijke Informatie Toetsing.*"

Following this pilot project, two additional Pit projects were set up in September 2022 by engaging with students, lecturers, and researchers from secondary vocational education and higher professional education. Each group was able to investigate one or more self-chosen research topic(s), based on different research approaches. For example, students from NHL Stenden University of Applied Sciences applied hands-on tools (such as reverse image search) within various online channels and platforms to analyze and validate online information, additionally building a Discord community to evaluate their findings. The participants of the secondary vocational Pit at the Firda School chose applied field research, such as interviews with internal and external stakeholders, to gain an understanding of topics closely related to their daily life.

Case 1: *The Pit at the Local Library in Drachten*

The Action Arena of the Library Drachten Pit

The Pit in the Library of Drachten was set up in March 2022 as a pilot initiative with the aim of developing a larger project with different communities in the Frisian

FIGURE 15.3 Announcement for the first meeting of the Pit in March 2022 (translated from Dutch).

Area. This citizen initiative was started by C1, an expert in innovation in information science at this very library. Participants were recruited by placing an announcement in the local newspaper inviting interested parties to the very first Pit meeting on March 16, 2022 (see Figure 15.3).

Fourteen citizens (seven women and seven men) from various backgrounds (e.g., a retired journalist, teachers with various expertise, a housewife, a company director, and an ICT specialist), aged between thirty and sixty, responded to this call. All participants live in the city of Drachten and exhibit a deep sense of engagement with their immediate living environment. The number of individuals involved varied between four and twelve, with a core group of four participants maintaining regular contact.

The Drachten Pit can be characterized as a local research community with a focus not only on gaining insights into digital disinformation but also in promoting more social cohesion in the neighborhood by discussing quality of life, social well-being, and social and physical safety with local residents. The working language is Dutch.

Participants Roles

Participants find it difficult to define their role within the group. *"There is no clear division of roles."* Participants see themselves primarily as (field) "researchers," while *C1* is mainly the driving force and project leader (see Figure 15.2). According to the focus group participants, one member has the role of a digital researcher specifically to double-check information or cross-reference information gathered from the neighborhood and share these insights with the group.

Research Topics

According to *C1*, the first project was based on a local rumor about young men causing problems by recklessly driving motorboats on a village canal system. Participants had heard different versions of the story and decided to investigate by gathering information through online research, interviews, and by visiting the neighborhood. They discovered that there had only been one incident involving two young men, whereas the rumors circulating in the neighborhood and media had blown it out of proportion. They decided to inform the people in the direct neighborhood and not the press to eliminate polarization and rumors.

The choice of research topics is primarily based on the interests of the participants, often around a specific topic or situation in their direct environment with the aim of discovering what is precisely going on and to what extent the resident(s) in question are causing a nuisance. One example related to a local resident's messy front garden full of clutter and waste in the neighborhood where *P2* lives. *P2* decided to conduct a small neighborhood survey. This resulted in determining that clutter is a subjective concept and that those living in the direct vicinity do not experience any nuisance. Although a man with mental health issues lives in the house in question, residents accept him as he is. *P2* indicated that her research was "not unbiased." However, by testing her own ideas and thoughts, she adjusted her initial impression of a resident who she thought had been intentionally causing problems in her neighborhood.

Another approach in choosing research themes is by going into the neighborhood and asking passersby what they think of their living environment, what they are concerned about, and what they would like to change. One topic that recently emerged is loneliness among residents of a recently renovated apartment building. In this complex, the communal meeting space has been removed to make way for new residential units. This means there is no longer an opportunity for apartment residents to meet each other easily and undertake activities together. The Pit staff are now investigating how an alternative communal meeting space can be created. They have also decided to keep in touch with residents on a regular basis.

Interaction Approach

The Pit meets approximately once every four weeks in the Drachten library. Participation is on a voluntary basis. Although participants repeatedly indicate that their working method is "still work in progress," it usually goes as follows:

1. Go into the neighborhood to collect data and make a report – in writing or not.
2. Discuss feedback of findings during Pit meetings.
3. Discuss with other Pit participants whether and how the findings can be followed up. Can we do anything with this? Is further (online) research necessary? Has adversarial hearing been applied?
4. In-depth/nuance of the current research or start of new research.

Communication

Communication is mainly analogue among the participants. During the physical meetings, the participants discuss their current and future investigations. A recurring point of discussion is whether to publish research findings. Publishing could be a way to bring certain neighborhood problems to the attention of a broader audience. Publishing could also ensure that the problems are placed on the agenda of policy-makers or other relevant actors. Nonetheless, the decision not to publish is made again and again. The reason given is that it could potentially damage the bond of trust with residents who have acted as a source of information. However, there is an explicit desire to share the results of the neighborhood research and additional fact-checking through online research with local residents, particularly those who raised the questions. According to the focus group, residents who have participated can then decide for themselves what they wish to do with the findings. More importantly, this allows them to control the way in which the problems they experience are tackled. Finally, the decision not to publish did lead to the departure of two participants: They did not agree with this decision and considered participation in the Pit no longer relevant.

Outside the meetings, there is incidental contact between participants (telephone, email). This usually concerns contact between an individual participant and the coordinator of the community (*C1*). During the Pit meetings, *C1* clearly has a leading role. He also has the final say when it comes to decisions, such as removing a participant from the group (should a participant push topics that would only be for personal benefit and not for the local community). He also decides on the themes being investigated or whether to participate or to publish. From the focus group meeting, we therefore learned that participants rely strongly on *Cl* to make final decisions.

Research Approach

Almost all research activities are analogue. Participants go out alone or sometimes in couples. There is no clear research strategy: "*we go into the neighborhood looking for information.*" The motto is an open, listening attitude to "*find out the truth.*" A training course on effective interview skills was initially planned; however, participants feel that this is no longer necessary. They have noticed – sometimes to their own surprise – that people respond openly to their questions. They had also expected to encounter opposition or aggression, but so far this has not happened. The explanation they give for this is that they may not be seen as "officials" (pastor, social worker, or local police officer); they are "just" involved fellow citizens who are genuinely interested in people's stories. *P1* pointed out: "*We don't have a cap (in Dutch 'pet'), we have the Pit.*"

Little to no information is recorded (and certainly not systematically) about findings gained from street interviews and door-to-door investigations. However, participants point out that their experience and impressions are always discussed during a following Pit meeting.

The idea of enriching the street interviews with other research, for example, by also asking questions to people from the municipality, police or welfare work, has not really gotten off the ground yet. The idea of feeding a "completed" study back to the stakeholders, in this case the problem holder(s), has yet to be implemented.

Participants' Experiences

Participants find it fun and educational to be part of the Pit. They feel they are contributing to enhancing connections between people in the neighborhood. People's openness is mentioned as a positive experience. The participants pointed out that residents like to be able to tell their story, and they enjoy being able to offer a listening ear and thus get a more nuanced picture of what is going on and what people are concerned about.

Participants' Learnings

- The PIT community is local, open, independent, and socially relevant.
- Equality among participants is crucial; everyone must contribute and engage critically.
- Exploration beyond the secure environment of the Pit is encouraged.
- The common goal is fostering connectivity within the neighborhood.

Case 2: *The Pit at NHL Stenden*

The Action Arena of the NHL Stenden Pit

At NHL Stenden, the Pit project was organized twice. Students were recruited via an online intranet announcement and through short guest lectures at various courses to promote the project. The first community was carried out between September 2022 and December 2022 with six students. The second learning community was organized between February 2023 and July 2023 with eight students. On both occasions, the students were supported by student assistants. Both groups were provided with hands-on training sessions in different areas, such as the use of Open Source Intelligence Tools (OSINT). Students also received an OSINT toolbox (developed by the student assistants), with links and examples. According to C2, participants got to know each other via an initial online research exercise by "looking up" one of the team members on the internet and finding as much information about that person as possible. Later, based on the collected information, they introduced the chosen participant to the group without mentioning a name. Besides being an informal introduction, the exercise served as an eye-opener to show participants what kind of information is circulating about them in the public domain. The participants of the first group decided to investigate disinformation in the Russian–Ukrainian war and anti-Western propaganda. Additionally, they developed ground rules for the group based on a group discussion that was held at the beginning of the project (Vissia, 2022):

- The group's cooperation is key. The results of the research and working with OSINT come second.
- To maintain momentum, a fixed pattern in meetings is important. We meet once a week for 1.5 to 2 hours.
- Respecting each other's opinions is important in good collaboration.
- A negative atmosphere and undesirable behavior are the two most important indicators of an unsuccessful research group.
- Designating roles is not desirable but will be gradual within the collaboration. There is a democratic system in decision-making.
- The group is autonomous and makes decisions together, but there is an umbrella organization that they can fall back on if necessary.
- Contact with each other is via Microsoft Teams and WhatsApp.

Based on these ground rules and the observations of the participants during the first semester, six important outcomes were brought forward by one of our student assistants (van der Hooft, 2022):

1. **Working together:** Create a pleasant ambience between participants. Openness and respect for each other's opinions and ideas is key.
2. **Leadership:** There is an overarching organization that the group can fall back on. The group is autonomous and makes mutual decisions.

3. **(How to) research:** Directly address issues brought up by the group members. Choose subjects that can be researched with OSINT tools.
4. **Motivation:** Be aware of the influence of intrinsic versus extrinsic motivation to join the project because some students get credits, others do not but join voluntarily.
5. **Apply a structured approach:** A permanent structure is important for motivation and continuity. Divide research into phases to keep it structured.
6. **Knowledge:** Sufficient knowledge about the research methods and the dynamics of the group is a must. Every group is different! Therefore, ask for feedback per meeting.

Based on these outcomes, we set up another learning community in the second semester. The Pit in the second semester started in February 2023 and closed at the end of the study year in July 2023. Since this Pit community mainly consisted of students who had volunteered, this community has unfortunately not continued into the new study year 2023/2024 due to study-related time constraints, in spite of the enthusiasm felt by the students.

All participants were bachelor students and between twenty-three and twenty-seven years old. During the project they focused on the war in Ukraine and aimed to investigate how and by whom war information (or war propaganda) is shared and to what extent this information is reliable.

From the focus group meeting, we learned that participants had a shared interest that gave direction to their research. In addition, participants pointed to the "diversity" of their community, as it consisted of students from different higher education courses (see Figure 15.1) and with different cultural backgrounds (Indo-Chinese, German, Costa Rican, Dutch, Surinamese Javanese). The working language was English.

Roles of Participants

During the focus group meeting, participants reflected on their role during the project. One participant (*P5*) called himself an "investigator" but noted his experience acting as a project manager – a role he had never held up to that point, but one which he would like to adopt later. Other participants (*P6* and *P4*) characterized their role as "participant." Both felt they had done little research up to that point as "the Pit is still in its early stages." This is also due to other activities at the university. However, the participants indicated a desire to continue with the Pit in the future. One participant (*P4*) believed that the allocation of roles should be determined democratically if a new setup was to come in September 2023. A student assistant (*C2*) took on the role of "supervisor" and "expert" to coach and support the community.

Research Topics

To share initial ideas and democratically choose a research topic, the participants used the interactive online tool Mural, a digital whiteboard for brainstorming.

Participants were unanimous in their preference for a research topic: the Russian–Ukrainian war. Subsequently, subthemes were introduced: (1) *Force on Force* – military activities and developments at the front and (2) *Humanitarian Impact* – consequences of the war for the civilian population. One participant preferred to work individually and focused on disinformation and war propaganda.

Another participant *(P5)* said he followed international news closely. The invasion of Russia and the subsequent developments had his full attention. He stated the war was a major problem: "*this is a mess and this is going to last a long time.*" According to this participant, the Pit's role was to maintain attention on the war and its impact on civilians. "*I see that the news about the war is disappearing from the front page and shifting to pages 2, 3, 4 . . ., but I want to continue following it even if it gets obscured.*"

Participant *P4* was particularly interested in the Russians' use of Western technology, such as, the participation of Dutch companies in the construction of the controversial Russian bridge between Russia and Crimea. *P5* indicated his personal interest in "*modern warfare*": "It raises a lot of questions – and for unanswered questions there is a *deep dive* needed."

Finally, *P4* recognized the war as a significant conflict. He saw the advantage of this current topic and the many sources available. According to him, this made it relatively easy to conduct research. *P5* agreed: "*it is world news!*"

Interaction Approach

The NHL Stenden Pit met approximately every week. Apart from some physical meetings, the meetings were online. Discord, an online community platform, was chosen as a meeting space to communicate and share information with each other. Given the activities (study, work) of the participants, two meetings took place every Friday. Participants were able to decide which timeslot they would like to join to discuss their research, questions, and findings.

Our student assistant and supervisor (C2) started each meeting with a workshop or mini-lecture on, among other things, conducting safe online research, the use of OSINT and legal and ethical frameworks. *P5* indicated that he appreciated this very much: "*I am not an IVK student (= safety science student) nor IT professional. So, I needed extra help. For example, when installing and working with a TOR browser. I have also learned to handle it carefully: don't do it alone.*" Through the workshops, *P4* learned more about security, the use of Proton Mail, VPN, TOR, and virtual machines. He said: "*there are enough hackers.*" Furthermore, the participants indicated that they also needed help using OSINT. There was therefore a clear need for guidance and explanation in doing online research and C2 provided this with lectures and an OSINT toolbox.

Communication

Initially, Microsoft Teams was chosen to communicate with each other as well as Discord among participants. Occasionally, email was used, for example, to share central announcements or reminders about upcoming meetings. Informal contact took place via the app Signal. One *participant also* indicated that physical meetings were essential for the community – "*that works better*" (*P4*).

Research Approach

Participants indicated that little research had been conducted. Except for *C2*, participants had little to no experience of doing online research. They indicated that it was important to first have a basis: about dos and don'ts, OSINT usages, and safety issues regarding online investigations. This learning process progressed over several months, with participants noting during the focus group meeting that: "*They now feel they know more and want to get started.*"

P5 indicated that he saw many parallels between the current war and the situation in 1917. According to him, Russia is unstable. He therefore aimed to find out how citizens talk about the war and what sentiments are at play to get a better picture of the (in)stability in Russia. *P5* started studying online comments on VKontakte (VK), the largest Russian social media platform – comparable to Twitter (now X). He used a translation tool to analyze the comments on VK.

No agreements were made about when a study was completed or when certain findings would be suitable for publication. One participant explicitly indicated that he wanted to publish.

Participants Experiences

Participants explained they are intrinsically motivated. This ensures involvement and bonding. The participants also wanted to continue with the Pit. *P4* indicated that they learned to work together in a group – not because they happened to be in the same class, but on a voluntary basis. *P4* went on to mention that "*working with others and making new contacts*" was an important experience. Because the Pit is not part of the curriculum, collaboration was more difficult to organize as everyone had their own agenda, which meant that not everyone could always be there at the same time.

Everyone indicated that it was fun to work together on a subject that really interested them. In addition, learning to work with OSINT was a plus for everyone. Participants indicated that a lot of information about the war could be found online, but that it was not always clear what had been posted by whom and to what extent so-called *troll farms* were active. A Pit experience was to learn to look more critically at a "news fact" by consulting multiple sources (Dutch News NOS, Al Jazeera, etc.) and to search more actively for different perspectives on news. Finally, *C2* – a student himself – mentioned supervising a group of students as a learning experience.

Participants' Learnings

- Facilitate strong foundation with comprehensive knowledge and advanced skills in online research, security, ethics, and OSINT.
- Exhibit decisive leadership, provide clear guidance to the group.

- Establish focused research themes early.
- Foster genuine interest and motivation.
- Promote collegiality and familiarity.
- Maintain consistent communication through scheduled meetings.
- Encourage collaboration and proactive initiative.
- Optimal participant number.
- Set goals and interim deadlines.

Case 3: *The Pit at Firda School*

The Action Arena of the Firda School Pit

All participants were vocational education students aged between sixteen and eighteen years old who were very interested in what was going on at their school and motivated to investigate which topics were important to fellow students and teachers.

The Firda Pit was started with twelve participants consisting of first-year editorial media students and a coordinator/teacher. Ultimately there were nine active participants, four boys and five girls. The working language was Dutch. Due to time constraints, the Pit was integrated into the regular curriculum with limited contact hours.

The project began in March 2023 with an interactive session in the social sciences program for Firda students hosted by a youth organization. During this session, the topics the students would choose for their Pit project were determined through interaction. Additionally, according to C5, an expert on digital citizenship and project leader on the topic at Firda School and Fers, the students also took part in an awareness workshop about "online filter bubbles" and "online group polarization" provided by an external expert.

Participants' Roles

A characteristic of the Firda Pit was that participants had a clear shared interest in which they adopted multiple roles and had "*respect for each other*."

P9 called herself a "*researcher*" and conducted research on the theme of poverty. To this end, she created questions for interviews and a podcast. *P10* indicated that she had taken on a creative role, for example, creating posters for the podcast. *P7* chose an editorial function, for example, contacting guests for the podcast, but also working creatively, recording an intro for the podcast. *P9 and P12* both indicated contributing to the theme "*discrimination and prejudice*" and worked together on the podcast. Regarding the topic, *P13* specifically studied a case on a Dutch food brand that developed an anti-poverty campaign by examining various websites and blogs on this case. *P11* also chose a dual role as a researcher and creative participant. *P14* took on the role of project leader because her fellow students elected her and she was also motivated to take on this job.

Research Topics

To choose a research topic, the aforementioned session was held with an external agency that has experience in brainstorming with young people. Step-by-step and through a joint voting process, the students ultimately chose a main topic, namely, inequality of opportunity. There were three subthemes linked to this: poverty, social prejudice, and discrimination. Poverty was ultimately the most important topic for the students. This was partly because students in the group had personal experience of poverty. *P12*: "*. . . because I was talking about the influences of what poverty does to children and then you know what. Yes, it wasn't really poverty for us, but we were tight on cash.*" This topic was then divided into specific subthemes: menstrual poverty, money, and life. The students eventually conducted interviews with experts and professionals at school and processed these topics into a podcast with the aim of putting these issues on the school's policy agenda.

Interaction Approach

The participants worked on the project in close consultation with each other. There were four to five physical meetings during the project.

The coordinator/teacher (C4) supported the students where necessary and, as a coach, also offered space to work on the project. He also helped the group make decisions at crucial moments, for example, creating the podcasts to bring attention to the issues. During the interview, C4 claimed that working together intensively for a short period and keeping the flow going had several advantages over working over a longer period irregularly with occasional contact. The Pit at Firda was partially integrated into regular education and therefore the participants could work on Pit activities without distractions. This resulted in high productivity with concrete output, that is, a podcast and special cabinets for sanitary towels at school. Furthermore, there was an intensive collaboration that fostered effective communication among the participants. Every participant was actively engaged and dedicated to completing their mission within the limited time frame.

Communication

The students communicated via WhatsApp, Microsoft Teams, and Snapchat. The students had different types of app-groups, study-oriented, project related, or more fun and leisure related. They also met during class and individually contacted C4 for advice. In the context of communication, the students also indicated how important it was to create ground rules with each other and to stick to these.

Research Approach

The students opted for interviews with experts and professionals. They had prior knowledge of research skills, and specifically interviewing, due to previously completed assignments in this area with provided literature. In addition, the students also engaged in desk research using search engines such as Google. Examples of keywords they used related to the research themes were "poverty," as well as the name of the retail brand linked to promoting school breakfasts for underprivileged children to fight hunger. Websites and blogs were also consulted. All students claimed to have "double-checked" information during the research. *P13*: "Check if something is reported differently somewhere else. Double check. Just look it up separately and then see where the source comes from and whether it is reliable." The students indicated they are taught this at school and are also reminded by teachers to check their sources. The students also took notes of their collected sources, for example, website URLs.

The information collected by the students was shared directly during the podcast conversations. The students had agreed on this. The aim was that sharing the information would have a surprising effect as *P9* states: "*... we did it this way, because we had all agreed not to share information for the podcast, because then it would be a surprise and then you can really see the reactions to it.*"

Agreements were made to complete the research before the end of the academic year and to share the results via the podcast in the autumn of 2023. It is not yet clear who the podcasts were shared with internally/externally. The students themselves felt that the results/podcast should be made public.

Experiences

Participants were intrinsically motivated, which ensured involvement and bonding. Some of the participants were also experts through their personal experience with poverty and indicated that the research had not specifically generated new knowledge but had helped to make the topic of poverty more visible at their school.

They indicated that it was fun to work together on a subject that really interested everyone. Another advantage was that as first-year editorial media students, they could learn and apply skills related to their studies, such as making a podcast and developing other creative media products such as posters. Besides this, they were also trained in fact-checking.

The participants were less satisfied with the communication at the beginning of the project and would have liked more clarity about the goals of the project. Ultimately, a topic was chosen that was not directly related to disinformation. This was partly due to the lack of clear communication about the project at the outset and about the expectations toward the students.

The students were very proud that their research, particularly the conversations with experts, such as the location manager of Firda, ensured that the topic of menstrual poverty was put on the map and that menstrual products are now available free of charge on every floor of their school building. *P13* says about this result: "*But I actually think that is the best result. It really had a purpose, so I think that's what we achieved with it.*" They were also proud of the way they worked together and how, as first-year students, they supported each other to just try things out, even though it seemed difficult to them at first, for example, organizing and conducting interviews and making podcasts. The coordinator/teacher C2 also emphasized the importance of a close-knit team, in which members trust each other and work toward a common goal. In this case, although the participants had known each other for quite some time, additional investments in team building were made at the start of the project.

Finally, the students were happy to have worked on a project related to their future work with room for everyone's opinion and open discussions, as P12 states: "*It is also part of our profession, what we will do later, if we join this profession, we also have to experience it. So, I just thought it was nice to see as a class that we quickly agree with each other. And if we didn't, that we could tell both sides, well different sides, stories and then make a choice.*"

Participants' Learnings

- Start sessions with comprehensive information about online research and disinformation.
- Foster a professional atmosphere for meetings. Establish communication agreements.
- Encourage mutual respect and diverse perspectives.
- Foster an inclusive environment.
- Encourage teamwork and problem-solving.
- Define shared objectives.
- Promote willingness to explore new approaches.
- Prioritize thorough research and seek assistance when needed.

Joint Learning from the Three Learning Communities

As described earlier, in July 2023 we organized a mini-conference inviting the coordinators and participants from all three learning communities to get to know each other and share their experiences. During interdisciplinary sessions, we asked the participants to share important joint learning gained for future Pit projects. Figure 15.4 provides an overview of these essential learnings of the participants.

Identifying the Similarities and Differences in the Three Learning Communities

Following the presentation of the three experimental cases and essential outcomes from the coordinators and participants, we present the similarities and differences in the three learning communities based on our additional conceptual questions (see Table 15.1). Figure 15.5 provides a visual overview of the key aspects we have identified in each case. These key aspects and the joint essential outcomes from participants (see Figure 15.4) will also provide the basis for our "roadmap" for future community projects and initiatives to fight disinformation.

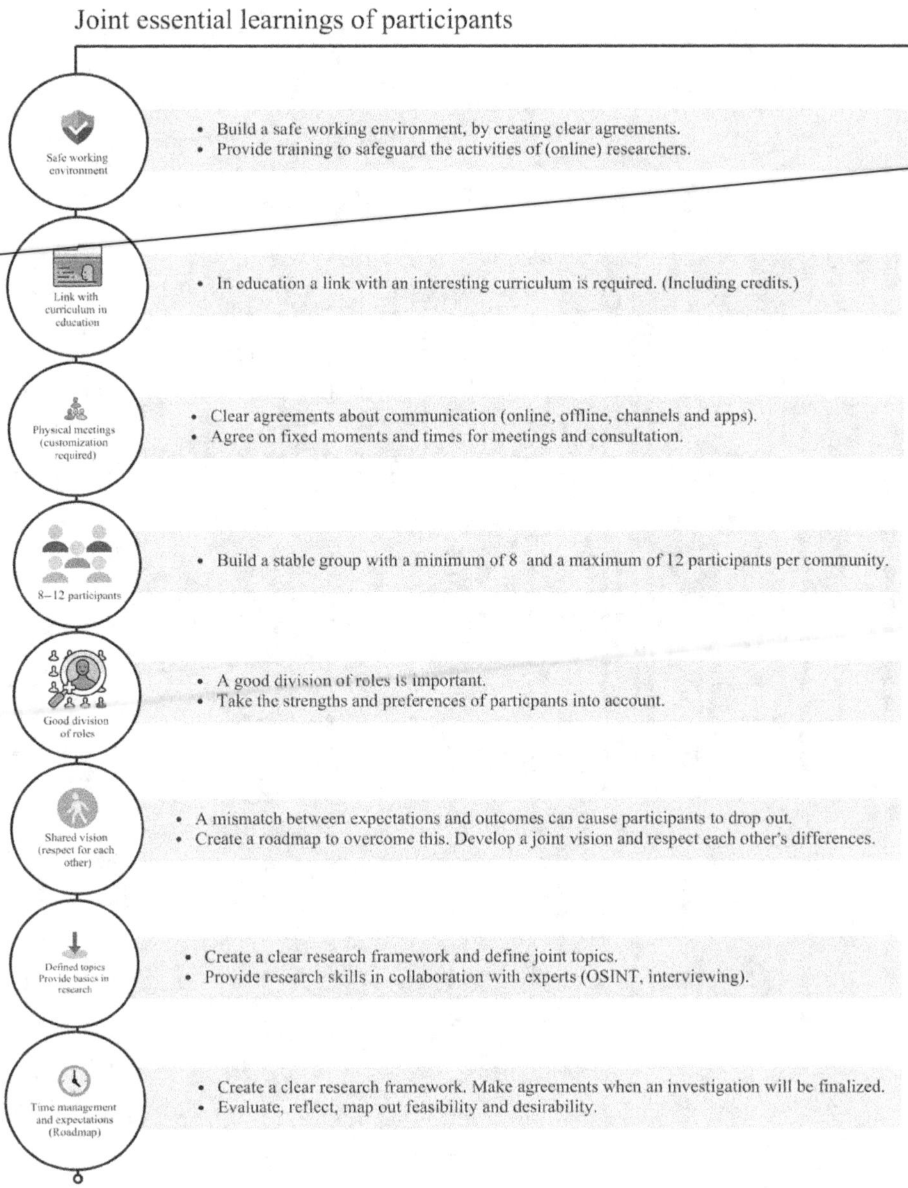

FIGURE 15.4 Important joint learnings for future Pit projects.

The participants in this study represented diverse age groups. Participants primarily identified themselves as researchers. However, they were also capable of assuming multiple roles and responsibilities within the community. The participants were free to select their preferred role, while a project leader was appointed to provide guidance and direction. The techniques utilized for investigation may vary, with

	Case 1 (de Bibliotheek)	Case 2 (NHL Stenden)	Case 3 (Firda)
1 The set of participants	Age 30–60, various educational levels, different professions, retired and working, investigated local neighborhood topics.	Age 23–27, BA students, investigating international topics.	Age 16–18, media editorial students,vocational level, are investigating school topics.
2 The positions	(Digital) researcher, participant, driving force, (project leader) Self-choice (except for project leader).	Investigator, participant, supervisor, moderator, expert (project leader) Self-choice, switching roles is possible.	Researcher, creative, project leader, coach Self-choice, combining roles is possible.
3 The set of actions	Neighborhood survey and street-door-to-door interviews. Open, listening attitude to "find out the truth". Interview skills. No training provided. Meso theme: Addressing local themes and promoting cohesion among residents. Themes include impoverishment, street lighting, unsafe traffic, and lonely elderly people.	Online research workshops on conducting secure research, using Open Source Intelligence Tools (OSINT), and understanding legal and ethical frameworks. Support from teachers and researchers. Training on research safety using safe browsers. Macro theme: Research on the Russian-Ukrainian war, with sub-themes on military activities, humanitarian impact, and war propaganda.	Experts interviews and desk research. Learn to double-check information from online sources. Support from an external expert and teacher. Research skills in curriculum. Workshop on filter bubbles and group polarization. Microtheme: What's going on at our school? Translate results into media products (podcasts) and solutions. Main theme: social inequality. Subthemes: poverty, prejudice, and discrimination. Solution for period poverty at school.
4 The potential outcomes	Data is collected offline from the direct neighborhood. Findings are reported and discussed in group sessions. Outcomes are shared among participants during meetings.	Data is collected via various online channels, communities, and platforms. Findings are reported and discussed in group sessions. Outcomes are shared among participants during meetings.	Data is collected via interviews with stakeholders and via online desk research. Findings are reported and discussed during podcasts (surprise effect). Outcomes are shared among participants and translated into media products (podcasts) to share with fellow students and stakeholders at school.
5 The level of control over choice	Options closed to share findings with media. Open to share with citizens who were interviewed or brought up investigation topics. Different opinions in the group, project leader decides.	Option open how to share findings. Different opinions, sharing or not sharing have to be discussed.	Option open how to share findings. Different opinions, sharing or not sharing have to be discussed.
6 The information available	Topic choice via investigating sentiment and questions in the neighborhood, discussing the topics, or by testing own viewpoints. Participants are free to choose a topic individually or as teams. Stepwise process.	Topic choice via a collaborative interactive process using Mural. Stepwise process. Funneling ideas and voting for final topics.	Topic choice via co-session with professional youth communication organization and with the support of the coach of the the group. Stepwise process. Funneling ideas and voting for final topics.
7 The costs and benefits of actions and outcomes.	Monthly library meetings in the evening + email. Voluntary participation. Choose a role that matches interests and skills. Time constraints for researching topics. (Start/end) Learn how to engage with local residents and collect or solve problems. or revisit standpoints. Try new research approaches with group support.	Weekly school meetings on Discord, with two time slots. Voluntary participation for credit. Choose a role based on interests and skills. Limited time due to course obligations. Students like meeting others from different courses/faculties. Learn OSINT tools safely.	Flexible meetings based on planned lessons with the coach at school and contact via WhatsApp and email. Mandatory participation. Choosing and combining a role that matches interests and skills. Learning to work closely in a group with respect. Trying new approaches supported by the group in a safe environment.

FIGURE 15.5 Comparing the three learning communities; visual overview of the key aspects identified in each case.

global subjects being addressed through online data investigation and local subjects through direct inquiry of stakeholders. Nevertheless, an array of interview techniques was utilized throughout the research process by all groups. Extensive discussions were held on research topics and dissemination of findings. Furthermore, the selection of research topics was a collaborative process, with both online and offline approaches being employed to facilitate the decision-making process. Meetings were scheduled regularly, either on a weekly or monthly basis, or in a flexible manner to accommodate the availability of all participants.

Participation was voluntary but could be connected to earning credits or fulfilling course requirements. The participants enjoyed working as a research and learning community, as it allowed for the exchange of ideas and sharing of findings. Acquiring new skills through experts or learning by doing is experienced positively. Mutual encouragement is fostered among the participants, inspiring them to explore novel avenues, while also promoting respectful engagement with all members involved in the community.

A Roadmap for (Future) Learning Communities

After conducting a comprehensive analysis of the three learning communities, we have developed a roadmap (see Figure 15.6) encompassing multiple factors and providing recommendations to establish a highly effective learning community. This roadmap will serve as a valuable resource, for both new and existing projects that seek to empower individuals within their respective (local) communities to fight disinformation at their own level.

CONCLUSION AND DISCUSSION

In this case study, we have analyzed three experimental learning communities each of which has a central purpose: to become more resilient to the threat of disinformation by jointly exploring information within an offline citizen-driven learning community.

Through this experimental approach, we learned that not every group focused directly on the analysis of disinformation in online environments but also on offline field research and topics close to their hearts. The decision-making process was open for each group, with no interference from the authors on the choice of topic. This made it very interesting to observe how the group process influenced the way participants decided to collect, analyze, and discuss their findings in each of the learning communities.

Throughout, all community participants were engaged in informed discussions on whether they should share their findings internally and/or externally, and what risk this could entail in creating online and offline polarization, endangering participants, or leading to a loss of trust in their community as they collected and

FIGURE 15.6 A roadmap for (future) learning communities to fight disinformation at their own level.

analyzed information circulating in the public sphere. Additionally, participants from one learning community were also trained in using OSINT tools, and another was trained in fact-checking all information collected via desk research. One community succeeded in connecting with local citizens by openly communicating as "fellow citizens" with their neighbors despite no prior interview training. A central motivation for each community was their choice in shared subjects of concern under the guidance of a project leader or teacher.

Interestingly, each group chose to share their findings differently with others, either by sharing results internally with other students and teachers or with citizens whom they had previously interviewed during the research. Additionally, students from Firda School shared their findings with internal stakeholders by developing a podcast on the topic of inclusivity. Negative friction in group dynamics was noticeable in all communities in the later stages of their investigation, caused by considerations of whether or not to share findings. A conclusion that can be drawn from this is that future communities should discuss and decide on these issues at the outset of a project.

Even if the three communities had different backgrounds, topics, and approaches, we identified key aspects important to empower citizens to engage in learning communities to fight disinformation on various levels, for example, at a local level supporting their direct neighborhood, at school to improve their direct surroundings, or to understand the larger coherence in a global setting. In these learning communities, critical thinking, learning skills, and tools are essential. However, we noticed that it is even more important that the participants develop a deeper understanding of the impact of information sharing on online and offline spaces. By investigating topics that are close to their heart, they also learn to reflect on their viewpoints and behavior. This supports them to engage with ethical considerations, promoting more conscious and mindful participation in a world where online and offline communication are closely intertwined. It also helps them to become more resilient to disinformation, stops them from drawing premature conclusions, and motivates them to respectfully challenge and question perspectives, identifying biases and assumptions.

We also learned the importance of building communities in an open setting with clear agreements on the organization of space and time and supported by a coordinator (preferably chosen by the participants). For digital investigation team participants, it is of utmost importance to provide a joint training module on online investigation and safety.

Finally, most of the participants indicated that building and becoming a community is not something that comes naturally. Participants should take time to get to know each other, set clear goals for research (under the guidance of a coordinator), democratically decide on the choice of topic, and if and how their findings will be shared. Creating a trusted environment is key for each learning community as with trust comes resilience and empowerment to engage in meaningful online and offline investigations benefiting both individuals and society.

Current policy developments by the European Commission have established ambitious goals for ensuring that 80 percent of the population acquires fundamental digital competencies by the year 2030 (European Commission, 2023). This means more innovative approaches are needed to support local governments and citizens to develop the ability to form and articulate well-informed opinions and actively participate in societal discourse through open dialogue. Our research demonstrates that learning communities, supported by local public institutions such as libraries, (vocational) schools, and universities, can serve as a reliable and safe space for acquiring and practicing these skills in a real-life setting. Ultimately, this can contribute to both online and offline depolarization efforts, effectively engaging individuals from diverse backgrounds and educational levels. Our findings also show that learning communities are not about "sending information" or teaching about disinformation in front of a class or group of citizens. Its success is rooted in providing a secure environment, where individuals can govern themselves with experts' guidance. In closing, as our experimental research shows, defending democracy may start at the heart of offline communities contributing to an open debate about local as well as global issues we are facing right now.

REFERENCES

Bastos, M., Mercea, D., & Goveia, F. (2021). Guy next door and implausibly attractive young women: The visual frames of social media propaganda. *New Media & Society*, 25(8). https://doi.org/10.1177/14614448211026580

Benkler, Y., Faris, R., & Roberts, H. (2018). *Network propaganda: Manipulation, disinformation, and radicalization in American politics*. Oxford University Press. https://doi.org/10.1093/oso/9780190923624.001.0001

Bowman, S., & Willis, C. (2003). *We Media: How audiences are shaping the future of news and information*. The Media Center at The American Press Institute. https://ict4peace.org/wp-content/uploads/2007/05/we_media.pdf

Chan, M. S., Jones, C. R., Jamieson, K. H., & Albarracín, D. (2017). Debunking: A meta-analysis of the psychological efficacy of messages countering misinformation. *Psychological Science*, 28(11), 1531–1546. https://doi.org/10.1177/0956797617714579

European Commission. (2023, December 14). Europe's Digital Decade: digital targets for 2030. https://commission.europa.eu/strategy-and-policy/priorities-2019-2024/europe-fit-digital-age/europes-digital-decade-digital-targets-2030_en

Glassman, M., & Kang, M. J. (2012). Intelligence in the internet age: The emergence and evolution of Open Source Intelligence (OSINT). *Computers in Human Behavior*, 28(2), 673–682. https://doi.org/10.1016/j.chb.2011.11.014

Groenewegen, J. (2011). The Bloomington School and American Institutionalism. *The Good Society*, 20(1), 15–36. https://doi.org/10.5325/goodsociety.20.1.0015

Hassain, J. (2022). *Disinformation in democracies: Improving societal resilience to disinformation*. NATO Strategic Communications Centre of Excellence. https://stratcomcoe.org/publications/disinformation-in-democracies-improving-societal-resilience-to-disinformation/241

Heinrich, A. (2019). How to build resilient news infrastructures? Reflections on information provision in times of "fake news." In I. Linkov, L. Roslycky, & B. D. Trump (Eds.), *Resilience and hybrid threats: Security and integrity for the digital world* (pp. 174–187). IOS Press. https://doi.org/10.3233/NICSP190031

Hintz, A., Dencik, L., & Wahl-Jorgensen, K. (2017). Digital citizenship and surveillance society: Introduction. *International Journal of Communication (IJOC), 11*, 731–739. https://ijoc.org/index.php/ijoc/article/view/5521/1929

Koulolias, V., Jonathan, G. M., Fernandez, M., & Sotirchos, D. (2018). *Combating misinformation: An ecosystem in co-creation*. Organization for Economic Co-operation and Development (OECD).

Markham, A. N. (2019). Critical pedagogy as a response to datafication. *Qualitative Inquiry*, 25 (8), 754–760. https://doi.org/10.1177/1077800418809470

Mossberger, K., Tolbert, C. J., & McNeal, R. S. (2007). *Digital citizenship: The internet, society, and participation*. The MIT Press. https://doi.org/10.7551/mitpress/7428.001.0001

Nationaal Coördinator Terrorismebestrijding en Veiligheid (NCTV). (2023, February 14). Desinformatie. https://nctv.nl/onderwerpen/desinformatie

Ostrom, E. (2005). *Understanding institutional diversity*. Princeton University Press.

(2007). Institutional rational choice: An Assessment of the Institutional Analysis and Development Framework. In *Theories of the Policy Process*, Second Edition (2de dr.). Routledge.

Ostrom, E., Gardner, R., & Walker, J. (1994). *Rules, games, and common-pool resources*. University of Michigan Press. https://doi.org/10.3998/mpub.9739

Ostrom, E., Gibson, C., Shivakumar, S., & Andersson, K. (2014). An institutional analysis of development cooperation. In S. Barrett, K.-G. Mäler, & E. S. Maskin (Red.), *Environment and development economics* (pp. 117–141). Oxford University Press. https://doi.org/10.1093/acprof:oso/9780199677856.003.0004

Papacharissi, Z. (2015). *Affective publics: Sentiment, technology, and politics*. Oxford University Press.

Stieglitz, S., Hofeditz, L., Brünker, F., Ehnis, C., Mirbabaie, M., & Ross, B. (2022). Design principles for conversational agents to support Emergency Management Agencies. *International Journal of Information Management*, 63, 1–11. https://doi.org/10.1016/j.ijinfomgt.2021.102469

van der Hooft, K. (2022). *Framework PIT-Project for students*. NHL Stenden University of Applied Sciences.

Vissia, J. (2022). *Kaders gesteld door de leden van de onderzoeksgroep de Pit, semester 1*. NHL Stenden University of Applied Sciences.

Yin, R. K. (2009). *Case study research: Design and methods* (L. Bickman & D. J. Rog, Red.; vol. 5). Sage. https://doi.org/10.1097/FCH.0b013e31822dda9e

Appendices

APPENDIX 1 OVERVIEW OF THE PARTICIPATING AND SUPPORTING ORGANIZATION(S)

Firda School for Vocational Education	The library of Drachten	NHL Stenden University
Firda School for Vocational Education offers comprehensive education and training programs for approximately 15,000 students. They also provide customized training programs for companies and institutions.	The library of Drachten has 12,000+ members and 25 employees. They also organize workshops and meetings on educational support, energy, health, sustainability, digital literacy, critical thinking, communication, collaboration, and creativity.	NHL Stenden University (n.d.) is a regional institution of higher education with a strong international emphasis. NHL Stenden is a multicampus university with a student body of 24,000, a staff of 2,250, and students from 90+ nationalities.
Supporting organizations: FERS		
Next to these three organizations, regional experts from the public organization "FERS" led this project to support the three learning communities in project management and knowledge support. Since digital skills are becoming increasingly popular, FERS (2023) aims to stimulate the digital citizenship of the Frisian population by supporting all Frisian libraries in the field of digital citizenship and media literacy.		

APPENDIX 2 FUNDING

This project was funded by a joint call, "Getting a Grip on Disinformation," in 2021 and 2022, by the Dutch Domain Registration Fonds (SIDN) and the Limelight Foundation. By supporting disinformation initiatives, SIDN Fund (2023) wants to contribute to a better understanding of disinformation in the Dutch context, what its impact is and how we can better equip our society to deal with it. In doing so, SIDN Fund focuses on tools that provide a grip on disinformation (or help citizens to become more resilient), and research into the mechanisms behind disinformation and awareness projects.

REFERENCES

FERS (2023, May 15). FERS: Samen naar de allerbeste versie van Fryslân. https://fers.nl/

SIDN Fonds (2023, May 15). We stand for a strong internet for all | SIDN fonds. https://sidnfonds.nl/excerpt

Index